REHABILITATION SERVICES:

An Introduction for the Human Services Professional

Third Edition

Edited by

Jason D. Andrew, PhD CRC/R NCC/R
Owner, Aspen Professional Services

Clayton W. Faubion, PhD CRC
University of Maryland Eastern Shore

Published By

Aspen Professional Services
63 Duffers Drive
Linn Creek, MO 65052

2014

Rehabilitation services: an introduction for the human services professional
[edited by] Jason D. Andrew and Clayton W. Faubion

Includes bibliographical references
ISBN 978-0-9853389-0-9

To Secure Additional Copies · Contact

Aspen Professional Services
63 Duffers Drive
Linn Creek, MO 65052
jandrew@socket.net
573.317.0907
573.286.0418 Cellular
aspenprofessionalservices.com

TABLE OF CONTENTS

TABLE OF CONTENTS (CONT'D.)

EDITORS AND CONTRIBUTORS

EDITORS

JASON D. ANDREW, PHD CRC/R, NCC/R was an Associate Professor, Graduate Program Coordinator, and Head of the Department of Rehabilitation Education and Research at the University of Arkansas. Prior to that, he was the Associate Commissioner of Education and state Director of Rehabilitation for the state of Nebraska. Currently, he is the owner of Aspen Professional Services, a company that publishes textbooks in the field of rehabilitation. He received his PhD from the University of Iowa in 1970.

CLAYTON W. FAUBION, PHD CRC is an Associate Professor, Department of Rehabilitation Services, at the University of Maryland Eastern Shore. He received his PhD from the University of Arkansas in 1998.

CONTRIBUTORS

QUINTIN BOSTON, PHD, LPC, CRC is an Assistant Professor and Program Coordinator of the Mental Health-Rehabilitation Counseling program at North Carolinas A & T State University. He completed his Doctorate in Rehabilitation from Southern Illinois University-Carbondale.

MARTIN G. BRODWIN, PHD, CRC is Professor and Coordinator of the Rehabilitation Counseling Program, Charter College of Education, California State University, Los Angeles. He is also a vocational expert for the Office of Disability Adjudication and Review of the Social Security Administration.

LORI A. BRUCH, EDD is an Associate Professor and Graduate Program Director at the University of Scranton. She received her EdD from George Washington University in 1997.

STEVEN DIAMOND, MED is a Vocational Rehabilitation Counselor for the Massachusetts Rehabilitation Commission. He received a Bachelor of Science in Biblical Studies from Lancaster Bible College and Master's degree in Rehabilitation Counseling from Springfield College. His research interests include Ethics, Asperger's Syndrome, and Work Readiness. He is the father of seven children.

J. CHAD DUNCAN, PHD, CRC, CPO, LPO is an Associate Professor at Alabama State University, serves as Chair of the Department of Prosthetics and Orthotics and is past program coordinator for Rehabilitation Services. While program coordinator, Dr. Duncan guided the Rehabilitation Services in 2012 in becoming one of six inaugural undergraduate programs to receive accreditation through CORE. Dr. Duncan went to Auburn University for his PhD in Rehabilitation and Northwestern University for Prosthetics and Orthotics. He is a certified Rehabilitation Counselor (CRC), ABC Certified Prosthetist & Orthotist (CPO), and is licensed as a Prosthetist and Orthotist in Alabama (LPO).

ALO DUTTA, PHD is an Assistant Professor in the Department of Rehabilitation and Disability Studies at Southern University, Baton Rouge. She is also the Principal Investigator of the NIDRR funded Rehabilitation Research Institute for Underrepresented Populations. She received her PhD from the University of Illinois at Urbana-Champaign in 2001.

DOTHEL W. EDWARDS, JR. is a professor and chair of the Department of Rehabilitation Studies in the College of Health Sciences at Alabama State University (Montgomery AL). In addition to his full-time faculty and administrative responsibilities at ASU, he provides vocational expert witness testimony for the Social Security Administration Office of Disabilities Adjudication and Review (ODAR); he is a registered Rehabilitation Supplier under the Georgia State Board of Workers' Compensation, and has certifications as a Rehabilitation Counselor (CRC) and Life Care Planner (CLCP). His research interests are quality of life issues among persons with developmental disabilities, multicultural counseling, professional ethics in vocational rehabilitation, life care planning, and forensic rehabilitation. Dr. Edwards has authored and co-authored several articles in peer-reviewed journals, and he has conducted many presentations and workshops relating to the above-mentioned topics.

YOLANDA V. EDWARDS, PHD is chair of Department of Educational Leadership, Counseling and Professional Studies and Program Coordinator and Professor of Rehabilitation Counseling Program at Winston Salem State University since 2007. She has authored several articles and books chapters dealing with disability issues including mental health issues for African Americans and employment issues for youth with disabilities. Dr. Edwards has held several leadership positions in state and national professional organization including past president of American Rehabilitation Counseling Association (ARCA) as well principal investigator for numerous of RSA training grants.

TOM EVENSON, PHD is the Dean of the College of Public Affairs and Community Service at the University of North Texas. He currently serves as the President of the Council on Rehabilitation Education and is on the Editorial Board of the Journal of Rehabilitation. He was instrumental in developing the Commission on Undergraduate Education that ultimately led to the Accreditation of Undergraduate Programs in Rehabilitation and Disability Studies.

LAKEISHA L. HARRIS, PHD, CRC is an Assistant Professor and Graduate Program Coordinator, Department of Rehabilitation at the University of Maryland Eastern Shore. She received her Ph.D. from the University of Iowa in 2007.

DEANNA HENDERSON, PHD is a tenured track Assistant Professor in the Rehabilitation Counseling Program at Alabama State University. She was previously employed at The Ohio State University as a Disability Program Manager. She has held many senior leadership positions. Prior to becoming an academician, she served as the Chief Operations Officer of The Neighborhood House, Inc., and Director of the Residential Treatment Center at Ohio Hospital for Psychiatry. DeAnna Henderson is a Licensed Professional Counselor and a Certified Rehabilitation Counselor. She holds a PhD in Counselor Education and Supervision from Ohio University, a Master of Arts Degree in Rehabilitation Services from The Ohio State University, and a Bachelor of Arts degree in Sociology from Kentucky State University.

JENNIFER HERTZFELD is the Workers' Compensation Claims Manager for Motorists Insurance Group. She is responsible for overseeing all workers' compensation operations for five companies within the group that span 37 jurisdictions.

Ms. Hertzfeld has over 16 years of experience in the field of disability. She has authored many articles on universal design, assistive technology, and accommodations. She earned an MA in Rehabilitation Counseling. She is a certified rehabilitation counselor (CRC) and a qualified rehabilitation provider (QRP) in the state of Ohio.

LINDA HOLLOWAY, PHD is a Professor and Chair of the Department of Disability and Addiction Rehabilitation at the University of North Texas. She currently serves as the Chair of the Commission on Rehabilitation Counselor Certification and the Editorial Board for the Journal of Rehabilitation. She previously coordinated the undergraduate rehabilitation program at UNT and has worked in many community rehabilitation settings.

STANLEY M. IRZINSKI, EDD is the retired Administrator of United Rehabilitation Services, a comprehensive community rehabilitation program in Northeastern Pennsylvania. He received his EdD in counselor education from Pensylvania State University in 1968.

KATHERINE KLINE, PHD, CRC, LPC is an Assistant Professor of Maryville University's Rehabilitation Counseling and Services programs. She holds a B.A. degree in Psychology, an M.A. in Rehabilitation Counseling and a Ph.D. in Rehabilitation Counselor Education. Katherine has worked in both the public and private sectors, assisting persons with disabilities. Much of her background consists of working with individuals with traumatic brain injuries, and youth with disabilities. Katherine's primary interests include case and caseload management, as well as transition counseling. Katherine teaches graduate and undergraduate courses in vocational rehabilitation, supported employment, practicum case management, job placement, and career development. In addition to teaching, Katherine continues to work in private practice, providing counseling and adjustment services to persons with disabilities.

ANNA M. KOCH, PHD, NCC, CRC, LPC-S works as a Licensed Professional Mental Health Counselor with the Veteran Administration counseling Veterans with substance use disorder and serious mental illness. Dr. Koch has published in the areas of substance use disorder, distance counselor supervision, Veterans, and traumatic brain injury. Dr. Koch is a graduate of The University of Iowa Rehabilitation Counselor Education program where she earned her PhD.

D. SHANE KOCH RH.D , CRC, CAADC is a Professor at the Rehabilitation Institute, Southern Illinois University Carbondale and serves as the Associate Dean at the College of Education and Human Services. Dr. Koch's main area of research is in rehabilitation of persons who experience coexisting disabilities.

MADAN M. KUNDU, PHD is the Chair and Professor of the Department of Rehabilitation and Disability Studies at Southern University, Baton Rouge, LA. He serves as the Project Director of three grants from the Rehabilitation Services Administration and one grant from the National Institute on Disability and Rehabilitation Research. He received his M.A. and Ph.D. degrees in Rehabilitation Counseling from Michigan State University

VIVIAN M. LARKIN, PHD is a retired faculty member from Auburn University with more than 35 years of experience as an educator, administrator, researcher, and advocate for social justice. Her primary research focused on the utility and credibility of vocational assessment instruments. Her work includes publications that address reliability and validity of both computer-supported and pencil and paper assessment tools and increasing service access and integration of under-represented/underserved populations. Similarly, her research has also focused on changing trends and best practices in vocational assessment and rehabilitation services. She served as Journal Editor for Vocational Evaluation and Career Assessment Professionals (VECAP) and Visiting Editor for Rehabilitation Engineering & Assistive Technology Society of North America (RESNA) Journal.

MICHAEL LEAHY, PHD, is a professor of rehabilitation counseling and director of the Office of Rehabilitation and Disability Studies. He has a doctorate in Rehabilitation Psychology from the University of Wisconsin-Madison, and over 35 years of experience in rehabilitation as a counselor, administrator, researcher, and educator. Dr. Leahy is a Licensed Professional Counselor (LPC), and a Certified Rehabilitation Counselor (CRC). His continuing research interests include professional competency development and education, professionalization, regulation of practice, vocational assessment, disability and rehabilitation policy, case management practices, outcomes, evidenced-based practices in rehabilitation counseling, and services for individuals with intellectual disability and autism.

PAUL LEUNG, PHD is Professor and Chair, Department of Rehabilitation, Social Work and Addictions at the College of Public Affairs and Community Service, University of North Texas. He has held academic and administrative appointments at the University of Arizona, Tucson, the University of North Carolina at Chapel Hill, the University of Illinois/Urbana-Champaign and Deakin University, Melbourne, Victoria, Australia. He received his PhD from Arizona State University in 1970.

RUTH TORKELSON LYNCH, PHD is a retired Professor in the Department of Rehabilitation Psychology and Special Education at the University of Wisconsin-Madison. She was a staff rehabilitation counselor and the director of vocational services at the University of Wisconsin Hospital and Clinics Rehabilitation Center from 1982-1990. She has held an affiliate faculty position in the UW-Madison Department of Orthopedics and Rehabilitation since 1982. She received her PhD from the University of Wisconsin-Madison in 1982.

ESTHER MENDEZ, BA has six years of direct service provision in community based Mental Health Counseling, including Psycho-Social Rehabilitation. She will graduate with an M.S. in Rehabilitation Counseling, a certification in Rehabilitation Counseling and Behavioral Addictions, and a focus on Trauma Informed Care. She has worked for NC A&T University Counseling department as both as a Research Assistant and at the NC A&T Center for Behavioral Health and Wellness as a Senior Graduate Assistant, providing trauma informed Hispanic victim advocacy for the Greensboro Child Response Initiative as well as providing therapeutic Spanish-language interpretation.

LEO M. ORANGE, M.S. is Coordinator of the Disabled Student Programs and Services, Oxnard College in Oxnard, California. He publishes and presents at professional conferences, and serves as an ADA consultant providing reasonable accommodation to business and industry.

GINA OSWALD, PHD, CRC, PC is an Assistant Professor at Wright State University, as well as the Program Director for both the undergraduate in Rehabilitation Services program and the postgraduate Transition To Work Endorsement program. Prior to working at WSU, she was an assistant professor at Maryville University of St. Louis for four years. Dr. Oswald's rehabilitation experience spans county developmental disabilities services, state vocational rehabilitation, and the coordination of a special education graduate student training program that provided career exploration and experiential employment for youth with disabilities at Kent State University.

BRUCE J. REED, PHD is a Professor and Interim Chair in the Department of Rehabilitation at the University of Texas-Pan American; he has previously served as chair and Dean at the College of Health Sciences & Human Services. He received his PhD from the University of Northern Colorado in 1993. Professional interests include grant writing, assistive technology, drug & alcohol abuse, administration, mentoring, and leadership.

MONA ROBINSON, PHD, PCC-S, LSW, CRC is an Associate Professor and Program Coordinator in Counselor Education at Ohio University. Dr. Robinson's areas of expertise include rehabilitation counselor education, psychiatric rehabilitation, multicultural counseling, dual diagnosis, clinical supervision, and advocacy issues with an emphasis on multicultural concerns for vulnerable populations. Dr. Robinson has held leadership positions in several counseling organizations and currently serves as a Vocational Expert for the Social Security Administration Office of Disability Adjudication and Review.

CARL W. SABO, PHD, CRC is an Assistant Professor and the Director of the Graduate Degree Programs in Rehabilitation Counseling at Wright State University. Dr. Sabo has an extensive background in Rehabilitation Counseling. Prior to becoming a fulltime academician, he worked as a vocational rehabilitation counselor for 21 years, and 4 years as a vocational rehabilitation manager directing several statewide vocational rehabilitation support programs. Both of these positions were held at the Ohio Rehabilitation Services Commission. Dr. Sabo was the 2002 Ohio Rehabilitation Services Commission Counselor of the Year/Dream Team recipient. He was the 2005 Ohio State University Doctoral Student of the Year. Dr. Sabo was the 2007 Ohio Rehabilitation Counseling Association's

Ohio Rehabilitation Professional of the Year. He is the 2013 President of the Ohio Rehabilitation Association.

SHAWN P. SALADIN, PHD, CRC, CPM is an Associate Professor in Rehabilitation and the Associate Dean for the College of Health Sciences and Human Services at the University of Texas-Pan American. He received his PhD from The University of Texas in 2004. Professional interests include Deafness, leadership, assistive technology, and administration.

AMOS SALES, ED.D., CRC, Professor Emeritus, Rehabilitation Counseling, University of Arizona and Arizona Licensed Psychologist formally retired at the end of summer of 2011 but continues to work with doctoral students. He completed his B.S degree in Secondary Education in 1965 and his M.S. degree in Rehabilitation in 1966 from the University of Arizona and his doctorate degree in Counselor Education in 1971 from the University of Florida. Dr. Sales held academic and administrative appointments at Kansas State Teachers College prior to being recruited to the Rehabilitation faculty of the University of Arizona in 1973 where he became Department Head of Rehabilitation in 1977. He has spent just under half a century dedicated to developing more positively impactful rehabilitation services, providing advocacy and leadership to this end through involvements in state, regional and national rehabilitation associations, and facilitating learning of empowering counseling concepts and practices. He generate over 28 million dollars in grant support of these efforts and his contributions have been recognized by over 40 national awards to include NRA's highest awards at state, regional and national levels for professional contributions to the field, NCRE's "Distinguished Career Award," ACA's "Berdie Memorial Research Award," National "RSA Commissioner's Award for Distinction in Training" and, in 2009, the RCEA "Living Legend Meritorious Award." Dr. Sales has delivered over 200 national and international presentations, has published over 80 articles, and has authored and/or edited 6 texts, the one most reflective of his teaching, research and service career is his 2007 text, "Rehabilitation Counseling: An Empowering Perspective."

FRANCES W. SIU, PHD, CRC is Assistant Professor and Undergraduate Program Coordinator of the Rehabilitation Counselor Education Program at California State University, Los Angeles (Cal State L.A). She received her Ph.D. in Special Education and Counseling, option in Rehabilitation Counselor Education, from the University of Texas at Austin. Her M.S. in

Rehabilitation Counseling and her B.A. in Psychology are from Cal State L.A. Research interests of Dr. Siu include psychosocial aspects of disability and violence against people with disabilities. Dr. Frances Siu is the recipient of the 2011 New Career in Rehabilitation Education Award, honored by the National Council on Rehabilitation Education. She is also a recipient of the 2013 Distinguished Women Award from Cal State L.A.

RONALD J. SPITZNAGEL, EDD is a retired Associate Professor in the Department of Rehabilitation Counseling and Coordinator of the Vocational Consultation Service in the department. He received his EdD from Auburn University in 1988 in Vocational Evaluation and Rehabilitation administration.

JOSEPH F. STANO, PHD is a professor of rehabilitation counseling at Springfield College. He received his PhD from the University of Connecticut in1982.

KATHERINE E. STANO, BS, MS is a graduate of Smith College and Springfield College. She is currently a doctoral candidate in Higher Education Administration at Argosy University.

KEITH B. WILSON, PHD, CRC, LPC, NCC, ABDA (Diplomate) is The Dean of the College of Education and Human Services (COEHS) and Professor in the Rehabilitation Institute at Southern Illinois University Carbondale. He was employed at Penn State University for 15 years as a Professor and an Administrator before becoming Dean of COEHS. He received his B.A., M.Ed., and Ph.D. degrees from Wilberforce University (1984), Kent State University (1985), and The Ohio State University (1997), respectively. In addition, he completed his post-doctoral studies at Harvard University in June 2007 in the Management Development Program. Dr. Wilson was the owner and Director of Counseling, Consultation and Psychotherapy, and Services (CCPS) in State College PA from approximately 2004-2012. Dr. Wilson's research interests are primarily centered around three areas: (1) Cross-cultural/multicultural issues among persons with disabilities in the state-federal vocational rehabilitation system and (3) privilege based hue/color skin color in the vocational rehabilitation system and in the United States (i.e., Black and White Hispanics). Dr. Wilson has been honored with several service (e.g., Multicultural Resource Center, Diversity Recognition) and research awards (e.g., Outstanding Researcher Award, Presented by the Pennsylvania Counseling Association).

Finally, Dr. Wilson is very active in the Upward Bound, Summer Opportunity Research Program (SORP), and McNair programs contributing as a workshop presenter, social, and research mentor. These programs are in place to facilitate college and/or graduate school success for students from underrepresented populations in the United States.

LISA X. ZHENG, PHD is an Assistant Professor, Department of Rehabilitation at University of Maryland at Eastern Shore. She received her PhD from the University of Wisconsin-Madison in 2011.

HISTORY OF REHABILITATION MOVEMENT: PATERNALISM TO EMPOWERMENT

AMOS SALES
UNIVERSITY OF ARIZONA

CHAPTER TOPICS

- Introduction
- Pre-1900s
- 1900 – 1920s
- 1930s – 1950s
- 1960s – 1970s
- 1980 – To Date
- Summary

INTRODUCTION

Rehabilitation can be defined as a philosophy, a concept, a discipline, or a service delivery system. However defined, it refers to a process of restoring an individual to the fullest levels of functioning possible. Vocational rehabilitation refers to a comprehensive sequence of services designed to maximize employment or independence of individuals with disabilities. Rehabilitation, for the purposes of this chapter, is very broadly defined as a societal response, as reflected in public and private service efforts, to individuals with a disability. The United States population of individuals with disabilities who could benefit from rehabilitation services is estimated at one in five (over fifty million) persons.

The political, social, economic, and/or vocational form of rehabilitation and its emphasis reflects society's beliefs about, and perceptions of, individuals with disability at any given time. A review of rehabilitation as a formal response to disability reflects evolving improvement in social attitudes toward disability within our society. This response has evolved from providing a right to simple survival, dependency, and custodial care to a right to independence and full inclusion. In the United States, the historical evolution of rehabilitation has been from "paternalism" to "empowerment." This evolution is a consequence of changing social movements, individual leadership, changing public attitudes and beliefs regarding individuals with disabilities, and increasing advocacy for and by consumer groups.

Rehabilitation, as it exists in the United States today, is a result of dozens of interrelated historical movements, events, organizations, academic disciplines, and professional fields. For example, advocacy groups in support of various disability groups have highlighted recognition and concern for rehabilitation services since the nineteenth century.

Medically based rehabilitation began in the early twentieth century primarily as a response to veterans who were disabled in wars. Vocational rehabilitation for citizens in the United States followed as a logical consequence of providing such services to World War I disabled veterans.

Rehabilitation reflects the value our society places on work. A core belief is that everyone should work, if possible. In our capitalist society, work is a right, and rehabilitation services have become an established right for individuals with disability in the United States. Our entire way of life is based on the assumption, as guaranteed within our Constitution, that every individual has the right to life, liberty, and the pursuit of happiness. These rights impose a corresponding obligation upon the United States government to provide the necessary services to insure equal access of its citizenry to these rights. Therein lays the rationale for the existence of the federally legislated state/federal program of vocational rehabilitation. For those individuals in our society who, because of disability, do not have equal access to employment, the federal government has the obligation to insure this right. Other rationales have been identified as justification for the formal federal rehabilitation response. These range from awareness of intrinsic dignity of man to cost-effectiveness of the service. None, however, provides as valid a rationale as that of the federal government's obligation to provide the services needed to insure equal access.

The rehabilitation movement in this country is much broader than the story of the development of the federal legislation establishing a state/federal partnership. It has evolved from the basic values of our society. Its roots are in the ideals, customs, and traditions of the United States citizenry. The rehabilitation service system, as it has evolved, encompasses services provided through the federally legislated state/federal program, the not-for-profit community rehabilitation programs, and the private for profit businesses. These areas of rehabilitation and rehabilitation service have grown and evolved as an expression of public support of and services for individuals with disabilities.

This chapter will attempt to highlight the history of rehabilitation in the United States by identifying the cultural context, rehabilitation-related developments, and resulting federal rehabilitation legislation in the following time frames: pre-1900s, 1900-1920s, 1930-1950s, 1960-1970s, and 1980 to date. Much of what is shared in this chapter has been written before from different perspectives. Much of it is a digest of the following works, the authors of which need to be fully credited: C. Esco Obermann's 1965 History of Vocational Rehabilitation in America;[9] N. Groce's 1992, The U.S. Role in International Disability Activities: A History and Look Towards Future;[3] G.W. Wright's 1980 Total Rehabilitation;[14] A. P. Sales' 1986 History of the National Rehabilitation Association "Journal of Rehabilitation,"[12] and the 1999 Institute on Rehabilitation Issues.[6]

The reader is encouraged to review these reference sources for further detail and information that is more specific. The history of rehabilitation in the United States is, in reality, a history of the impact of its leadership. This chapter will be able to identify only a select few of that leadership.

PRE-1900s

CULTURAL CONTEXT

In order to provide a context in which to place historical events in rehabilitation, the following historical highlights are provided. The North American colonies were populated by a mass immigration of religious dissenters and poor people during the seventeenth and eighteenth centuries. Immigrants primarily from the British Isles, Germany, and the Netherlands came to farm or support farmers. Three million non-natives had arrived by the 1770s and the small Native American population was greatly reduced by European diseases and by wars with the various colonies.

The colonists held a high regard for alcoholic beverages and considered them an important part of their diet. Drinking was pervasive because alcohol was regarded not as an intoxicant, but primarily as a health substance with preventive and curative powers. Alcohol played an essential role in daily rituals and in collective activity, such as barn raising. While drunkenness was condemned and punished, it was viewed only as an abuse of a God-given gift.

Cocaine and opium were legal during the nineteenth century and were favored drugs among the middle and upper classes. Opium and morphine were common ingredients in various potions. Until 1903, cocaine was an ingredient of Coca Cola. Heroin, which was isolated in 1868, was hailed as a non-addicting treatment for morphine addiction and alcoholism. By the end of the nineteenth century, concern had grown over the indiscriminate use of these drugs, especially the addicting patent medicines. Cocaine was ruled illegal after it became viewed as predominantly used by African Americans following Reconstruction. Opium was first restricted in California in 1875 when it became associated with Chinese immigrant workers.

During the 1770s, the British attempted to control colonial trade by taxing colonists to pay for British colonial administration. This clashed with colonial traditions of self-government and eventually resulted in rebellion and the successful American Revolution. The U.S. experienced increased immigration, and the exploitation of great natural resources fueled economic growth into the nineteenth century. The developing support of public education and antislavery sentiment reflected a widespread democratic ethic.

In the early 1800s, the first temperance movement began in response to dramatic increases in production and consumption of alcoholic beverages. Agitation against ardent spirits and the public disorder they spawned gradually increased during the 1820s. The belief that alcohol was addicting and capable of corrupting the mind and body took hold among the general population. The American Society of Temperance, created in 1826 by clergymen, spread the anti-drinking gospel. By 1835, out of a total population of 13 million citizens, 1.5 million had taken the pledge to refrain from distilled spirits. This wave of temperance resulted in dramatic reductions in the consumption of distilled spirits, although beer drinking increased sharply after 1850. A second wave of the temperance movement occurred in the late 1800s with the Women's Christian Temperance Movement embracing the concept of prohibition. Carey Nation, Kansas' anti-saloon crusader, began raiding saloons with a hatchet. Recruitment of women into the movement was major and the crusades to close down saloons were prevalent.

The War of 1812 with Britain had, as one result, the British burning the Capitol and the White House before a treaty was signed in 1814. The Mexican War (1846-1848) occurred in relation to annexing of Texas and, by the U.S. winning, Texas, California, and other territories were annexed. The Gadsden Purchase in April 1854, included territory now part of Arizona and Mexico. In

February 1861, seven southern states set up the Confederate States of America. The Civil War began in April 1881 when confederates fired upon and captured Fort Sumter in Charleston, South Carolina. By May, eleven states had seceded from the Union. President Lincoln issued the Emancipation Proclamation in January 1863, freeing all slaves in areas still rebelling. In April 1865, the confederates surrendered. President Lincoln was assassinated prior to the conclusion of the war. In 1867, Alaska was sold to the United States by Russia for $7.2 million.

The English industrial revolution spread to the United States in the mid nineteenth century and caused an explosion of industrial demand for raw materials and new markets. Inventors provided the means for larger-scale production. Transportation and communication enhanced this growth. Railroads were first introduced in the United States in the 1820s, with the first continental railroad completed in 1869. Morse perfected the telegraph in 1844, and the first telephone exchange went into operation in 1878. A new class of industrial workers was needed, lacked job security, and suffered from dangerously overcrowded conditions at work and at home. This need resulted in a population shift in the late nineteenth century. By 1890, as many industrial wage earners existed as did farm laborers, tenants, and farm owners.

REHABILITATION RELATED DEVELOPMENTS

The history of rehabilitation-related developments in the United States long predates the turn of the twentieth century. American ideas and attitudes toward individuals with disabilities were brought from England, home to many of the early colonists. One colonial perception was that disability was the result of God's punishment. Colonial response to disability was custodial, with care provided by the family, church, or community. These early ideas, perceptions, attitudes, and practices provided a base on which America's subsequent rehabilitation efforts would rest. One influence on these ideas and attitudes was the Poor Relief Act of 1601, passed in England shortly before major immigration to America began. This Act was considered a milestone in the history of social legislation. It represented, for the first time, a national government acknowledging public responsibility for "disabled in need." One negative of the Act was that it made a clear distinction between those deemed "worthy" of assistance and those who were not. Another negative was that the Act did not encourage restoration of disadvantaged persons to productive lives.

The Poor Relief Act was American law for the first 150 years of the colonies existence. After the Revolution, it would remain the model for future legislation. The Act's distinction between "worthy" and "unworthy," and resulting rights granted by society, would influence society for centuries. The first almshouse for "worthy poor" vagrants, mentally ill, and disabled was founded in Boston in 1662. The first hospital for mentally ill patients was established in 1773 in Virginia. Fifty years would pass before the next similar institution, the Eastern Lunatic Asylum, was established in Lexington, Kentucky. In 1742, the Quakers, with the help of Benjamin Franklin of the Pennsylvania Provincial Assembly, established the first general hospital of the colonies, the Pennsylvania Hospital near Philadelphia, which accepted all kinds of illnesses, including mental illness. A second general hospital, the New York Hospital, was founded in 1791. Hospitals proved important in the evolution of rehabilitation as human conditions other than medical began to be recognized.

The eighteenth century era of Enlightenment, with its emphasis on systematic analyses of bodies of knowledge, encouraged the scientific study of disability as a human condition. In the United States, examples of such studies were treatises on whether individuals who were profoundly deaf could reason and, if not, how could they know of the existence of God. Many of these inquiries addressed whether individuals with disabilities could be "trained." This led to the discovery that individuals with disabilities, when provided the same educational and social advantages as non-disabled, often demonstrated greater promise and potential than expected. It also resulted in a gradual change in perception among the public as it became apparent that people with disabilities could do more. Scholars, by trial and error, began to develop educational schemes and techniques, which, by the late eighteenth century, resulted in the beginnings of schools and institutions for children and adults with disabilities.

The 1880s saw an increase in public interest in disability and special programs in facilities. The first few decades of the nineteenth century saw the development of schools, benefit societies, and advocacy groups dedicated specifically to one particular type of disability, such as blindness or deafness. This development represented a positive shift from earlier eras' perceptions of all individuals with disabilities as "the infirm" or "the cripples." This emphasis on differences between various disabilities, rather than on common concerns, became a legacy for at least a century and a half. A "favored pecking order" related to the various disability groups arose among the public. Blindness, followed by deafness, was of primary concern to the public, whereas mental retardation was not.

Interest in establishing special programs for children with disabilities began to grow in the first quarter of the nineteenth century. The first United States educational institution for disabled children, a private school for deaf children, was founded in Baltimore in 1812. In 1815, Abbe Sicard, of the National Institute of Deaf Mutes in Paris, sent one of his teachers, Laurent Clerc, with Thomas Galludet, to Hartford, Connecticut, to help establish the first public school for individuals who were deaf. The school remains in operation today and is known as the American School for the Deaf. European experts in other disability areas came to the U.S. to establish schools, institutions, and associations. All of these efforts were greatly aided by the mid nineteenth century growth in organized charities. The mid to late nineteenth century saw the United States continuing to develop services based on contributions from Europe.

In the early 1800s, the forerunners of the federal vocational rehabilitation program were rehabilitation facilities and the vocational services they provided. In 1837, the first workshop-type program began at the Perkins Institute for the Blind near Boston. One major United States development in 1864 was the establishment of Galludet, a college for deaf education. This college is now Galludet University, and continues to be the only liberal arts institution of higher education specifically designed for persons who are deaf.

A large number of service societies were established between 1840 and 1890, but were criticized as being opposed to the concept of "rugged individualism" prevalent at that time. One example is the Red Cross, formed in 1881, although it dated back to the Civil War when Clara Barton delivered volunteer services.

Interestingly, the historical development and treatment of individuals with physical disabilities differed significantly from other disability groups. Service for such individuals occurred several decades after other disability groups. Physical disabilities were linked directly or indirectly to medical treatment in hospitals. During the mid to late nineteenth century, numerous hospitals, schools, and institutions were established for those with physical disabilities.

American surgeons who provided Civil War medical services were the first to explore what would come to be known as "rehabilitation," a term not in regular use until after World War I. These efforts to improve or restore some functioning to an individual with a physical impairment were by no means comprehensive. Once medical care or surgery and prostheses were provided, most children and adults with physical disabilities were still in need of care and supervision by their family or a state-run "poor farm."

Individuals with mental retardation were housed in lunatic asylums, poorhouses, almshouses, or local jails throughout most of the nineteenth century. Some attempts to meet their special needs began in the middle of the century. An experimental school, first funded by the Massachusetts legislature in 1848 to train "pauper idiots," was successful and incorporated in 1851 as the Massachusetts School for Idiotic and Feeble-Minded Youths. It later was renamed the Walter E. Fernald State School. Other examples include the Pennsylvania Training Program for Feeble-Minded Children in 1853, The Ohio State Asylum for Education of Idiotic and Imbecile Youth in 1857, the Connecticut School for Imbeciles in 1857, and the Kentucky Institute for the Education of Feeble Minded Children and Idiots in 1860.

Positive learning related to rehabilitation and special education came from these schools. Individuals with mental retardation were found to be teachable, and many could learn to function in the community. In 1863, the Hospital for the Ruptured and Crippled opened in New York, and addressed vocational needs of children with disabilities. A renewed interest in training children with orthopedic problems resulted in legislation establishing facilities for the care, treatment, and education of crippled children. The first such facility opened, in Minnesota in 1897 followed by Wisconsin, Indiana, Iowa, New York, North Carolina, Nebraska, and Massachusetts.

The first school to train children to earn a living, The Industrial School for Crippled and Deformed Children, was opened in Boston in 1893. Classes for handicapped children in public schools began in the latter part of the nineteenth century. An example is special classes for children with mental retardation instituted in Springfield, Massachusetts in 1896. Special education as a distinct profession, however, was slow to develop.

In the late nineteenth century, Dorothea Dix's concern for a more humane treatment of people with mental illness led to a movement to build hospitals for them in the United States. The number of such hospitals rose to 123 in 1890, of which 75 were state owned. Dorothea Dix founded 32 of these 75. At the height of industrialization in the late nineteenth century, religion was dedicated to individualism and the government's doctrine of laissez faire. Henry Ward Beecher, a prominent Protestant minister, preached the theory of Social Darwinism—survival of the fittest in the economic world. Despite this, many new social programs emerged from the Protestant faith. Examples include the Salvation Army, which came to the United States by way of Britain in 1879, and the start of Goodwill Industries in 1902 by a Methodist minister, the Reverend Edgar Helms.

In the 1890s, there was tremendous growth and interest in the field of psychology. William James, the United States' first prominent psychologist, stressed the application of psychology in the classroom with an emphasis on the individual rather than the social goals of education. C. Stanley Hall, the first president of Clark University, established the American Journal of Psychology and, in 1892, helped found the American Psychological Association. Hall emphasized the uniqueness of the individual in his studies of children and adolescents. Jane Addams created the first organized secular program of social welfare, called Hull House, in Chicago in 1889. Addams also helped bring about the first 8-hour day work laws for women, the first child labor laws, and the first juvenile court. She was a strong supporter of reform in education.

FEDERAL REHABILITATION LEGISLATION

The first federal rehabilitation legislation in the 1700s in the United States was indeed paternalistic. It was based on a perceived need to take care of and to provide services to veterans as payback for becoming disabled in the Revolutionary War of 1776 and as Merchant Marines in 1789. This first national pension law, passed on August 26, 1776, provided veteran benefits and compensation for service-connected disability. Loss of limb or disabled to the degree one could not work, resulted in half of their service pay for life.

The need for additional federal legislation in this area did not surface for eighty-six years. The large number of veterans with disabilities resulting from the Civil War, required additional national legislation by Congress in 1862. The General Law, as it was called, applied to service members of the Civil War and all subsequent wars. It remained unchanged during the war with Spain and was still in effect at the start of World War I. The Law required that to receive compensation, an individual must have become ill or wounded from their military service. It added new benefits for widows, children, and dependent relatives of deceased service men. For the first time, veterans' preference was provided in federal Civil Service. Preference was also given to those applying for homesteading, with time in service counted toward the residency requirement for asserting a claim.

1900s – 1920's

Cultural Context

From the 1900s to 1920, societal and demographic changes were significant in the United States. The population doubled, from 50 million to 102 million, with the majority of this increase coming from immigration. This rapid growth coincided with a dramatic increase in the number of people living in cities, from a ratio of rural to urban population of 50-50 in 1890 to 30-70 in 1920. Increasing urbanization brought greater access to education, newspapers and magazines, and a loss of the closely-knit family unit and community support base.

The Industrial Revolution resulted in marked changes in the nature of work and roles of workers, who had to acquire specialized skills and function within a supervised hierarchy. For the first time in the United States, social status was affected by what one did for a living rather than bloodline or land holdings. New technology and inventions, such as Thomas Edison's practical light bulb, electric generating system, sound recording device, and movie projector, helped shape the future. In 1908 Henry Ford introduced the practical, low-cost Model T, nicknamed the "Tin Lizzie," which put the common person in the driver's seat and ushered in the age of mass automobile travel. By 1927, fifteen million Model Ts had been produced.

With major increases in city populations and industrialization, the urban boss, who dealt in public privileges and commanded public support, became a very powerful and influential person. Growing out of the abuses of the urban boss, the Populist-Progressive Movement began in the 1890s, and continued until the start of World War I in April 1917. This movement pressed for reform of graft in politics and government, and was significant in that it was the first political movement to insist that the federal government had some responsibility for the commonwealth. The Progressive Movement spanned the presidencies of Theodore Roosevelt, Taft, and Wilson, and stressed the need for assuring most Americans some fairness in a society in which power and wealth were in the hands of a few. In 1913, an amendment to the Constitution authorized the collection of a federal income tax that made possible federally supported rehabilitation programs. The Progressive Movement, generated for women's suffrage and led by Susan B. Anthony to enfranchise the women's vote, resulted in a bill that was presented to the Senate in 1886. Twenty-three years later, the bill received a majority vote, President Wilson signed the bill in 1919, and it was ratified by an adequate number of states in 1920 as Amendment XIX to the Constitution.

The passage of this amendment was the culmination of the Women's Christian Temperance Movement, a response to the heavy drinking practices of the major influx of European immigrants in the late nineteenth century, who became the new lower class. The Liquor Prohibition Amendment prohibited the manufacture, sale, and transportation of alcoholic beverages in the United States. This resulted in police destroying barrels of beer during the 1920s era of bootleggers, speakeasies, indulgence, corruption, and crime; typified by infamous Chicago gangster Al Capone.

Economic prosperity increased following World War I with an increase in women workers, women's suffrage (1920), and a drastic change in fashion (flappers, mannish bobbed haircuts for women, and clean-shaven men).

Two ineffectual presidents characterized the 1920s. Harding, inaugurated in 1921, was viewed as totally inept, more interested in playing cards than serving as president. His successor, Coolidge, believed that the less done as president the better. Hoover began his term in 1929 with Black Thursday, October 24, of that year bringing the Great Depression. Hoover's philosophy of rugged individualism did not help resolve the depression.

Rehabilitation Related Developments

Several social concerns at the turn of the century set the stage for the federal government to become increasingly involved in disability issues. An awareness and concern was present to assist those who had work-related disabilities. Work-related disabilities were increasing because of new dangers from more complex manufacturing and processing technologies in mines, in factories, and on farms. Once an injury occurred, workers who had moved from small cities to big cities lacked family and community support networks.

The concept of employer responsibility for workers disabled on the job was in its infancy. Worker injuries were considered a personal misfortune. Injured workers, or their families, were responsible for care. Injury to the primary wage earner often brought poverty to an entire family, and a life dependent on what little charity was available. The only exception to this was the long established practice of providing small pensions to those severely injured in warfare.

In 1883, President, Benjamin Harrison, urged Congress to adopt a program similar to that adopted in Germany. At the close of the nineteenth century, common law stated that the master or employer was responsible for the injury or death of employees when the employer was negligent. With industrial expansion, the number of accidents increased as did lawsuits citing negligence. Many states, between 1900 and 1910, by judicial act, exempted employers from responsibility for disabilities resulting from work. The first Worker's Compensation legislation was passed in New York in 1910 followed by forty-five states and territories by 1921. Initial laws did not include rehabilitation. With this legislation, employees were compensated for occupational injuries, but no longer had the right to sue their employers.

At the turn of the twentieth century, a variety of groups, both religious and secular, began establishing workshops. Goodwill Industries, St. Vincent de Paul, Volunteers of America, and the Salvation Army began salvage programs that employed individuals with a disability or alcoholism. These types of facilities spread across the United States. During the first decades of the twentieth century, a number of hospitals and institutions for "cripples" existed outside the mainstream of the general medical community. No rehabilitation was provided. Medical care and supervision was the emphasis. Children born with major physical disabilities might spend the first six to ten years of their lives in facilities for "crippled" children, often never returning to, or seeing their parents. Improved surgical techniques and better prosthetics and orthotics permitted greater quality of life for some, but little was done to try to integrate individuals with disabilities into the broader society.

A great system of free public education developed in the United States starting in the mid 1800s. By 1900, 33 states had passed compulsory attendance laws and, by 1920, all states had these laws. John Dewey, a psychologist, stands out as the education leader in the early 1900s. His research interest, and emphasis in a child-centered school system, was based on freedom of the child to investigate and experiment in an individually supportive environment. Dewey was very supportive of vocational education, which was consistent with his belief in learning by doing. Only isolated vocational education programs existed in public schools in the early part of the twentieth century. They were confined to industrial schools for poor and delinquent children. Through federal support, at the turn of the century, vocational education became part of most curricula in the public schools. This experience was fundamental to the development of vocational rehabilitation. During this time, there was a continuing growth and interest in psychology. Hall brought Sigmund Freud to Clark University for a series of lectures in 1909. Considerable interest also developed in the French psychologist, Alfred Binet, whose objective measurement studies of children's intelligence led to the development of the first intelligence scale, the Binet-Simon IQ Test. Louis Terman, in his work at Stanford University, revised the Binet scales in 1916, resulting in the development of the well-known Stanford-Binet test for intelligence.

Medical advances during this time increased the population of individuals with disabilities. The first public health hospitals were established at the turn of the century. Medical advances and increased sanitation resulted in people living longer and living with disability after an injury or illness. World War I resulted in a large population of men with disabilities. Societal response to this was, as in the past, to implement pay back programs of vocational education and training through federal education and rehabilitation legislation in the early 1900s.

In the United States, World War I (1914 - 1918), with its massive casualties and forced refinement of surgical and post surgical care, might be considered a watershed for the field of rehabilitation. For the severely injured, survival rates were not significantly better than they had been in the nineteenth century. Of 400 American service men that became quadriplegic during World War I, half died at the battlefront and 8 of 10 who survived died within 90 days of returning home.[2] For those with less severe injuries, medical and surgical techniques had experienced some improvement, but comprehensive services were yet to be provided. Medical care, in even the best of civilian hospitals, was no better. Henry Kessler, as quoted in Groce,[5] recalls that during his orthopedic surgeon residency days in New Jersey, paraplegic patients "....were allowed to lie in a bed of sawdust, treated almost like animals. The theory was that if their bowel and bladder could not be controlled, at least the bed could be kept clean by removing the sawdust."[pp. 20-21]

An exception in this era was the work of Fred Albee in New Jersey. Albee, an orthopedic surgeon who had gained international fame for adapting techniques devised for tree grafting to grafting of human bones, believed the restoration needs of war injured veterans could be supported by "three legs of a tripod," physical restoration services, vocational guidance, and placement. This idea was revolutionary, yet supported by the United States Surgeon General through the construction, in Colonial, New Jersey, of one of three comprehensive rehabilitation hospital facilities Albee proposed. The hospital remained unique in delivering the tripod services proposed by Albee until it was closed at the end of World War II. One of Albee's students, Henry Kessler, carried forth these early ideas of rehabilitation medicine.

In the years following World War I, new volunteer groups in support of individuals with physical disabilities, began to flourish. The creation of facilities that would come to be called rehabilitation centers was one of the first national efforts to focus specifically on vocational rehabilitation for the physically disabled. The establishment, in 1889, of the Cleveland Rehabilitation Center began the expansion in the early twentieth century. In New York, in 1917, the Red Cross Institute for the Crippled and Disabled—now the International Center for the Disabled (ICD)—was established.

Supported by a philanthropic donor as an experimental school for war injured veterans, the Institute quickly expanded to include the civilian population, and served as a national clearinghouse for sharing the latest information on rehabilitation and disabilities. In 1917, the Red Cross also set up retraining programs for the disabled at Walter Reed and other Army hospitals. The Red Cross took on Braille transcription as a volunteer service in 1921. Goodwill Industries, first founded in 1902 with a welfare emphasis, began to expand vocational efforts in their facilities. A great number of other private voluntary organizations, specifically devoted to physical disability issues, were soon established at local, regional, and national levels. The majority of these organizations supported disability specific populations, and concentrated on research and improved services.

These organizations added to the numerous advocacy groups and societies supporting specific disabilities such as deaf or blind. Most of these organizations grew out of a sense of civic duty. They were supported by religious denominations or were linked to hospitals or institutions. Following World War I, these organizations filled a vacuum, and no significant, coordinated, federal government umbrella structure for providing service to adults and children with disabilities was available.

One of the unique characteristics of our American democracy is the volunteer organization. Through these organizations, people with common interests and goals may freely come together and organize to carry out their purposes. The National Rehabilitation Association (NRA) epitomizes the influence that voluntary associations have had in the development of our society and its institutions. NRA has been one of the primary leaders in the development of rehabilitation in this country as it relates to legislation, programs, and attitudes. NRA is, unquestionably, one of the oldest and strongest advocates for persons with disabilities.

Organizations usually have their beginnings in attempts by groups to meet their needs or to solve their problems. If some difficulties are presented that cannot be resolved by individuals acting as individuals, group action is typically taken. The forming of the NRA was no exception to this general rule. In the second decade of the twentieth century, the new service of "vocational rehabilitation" was emerging as a formal attack on one of the most pressing problems stemming from disability—unemployment. While the medical profession, the workmen's compensation movement, and voluntary organizations contributed to the beginnings of this new service, the education profession produced the combinations of interests and capabilities that most nearly met the vocational requirements of people with disabilities. The men and women who took up this work generally came from the field of education, and the programs that were started in the several states were generally in state departments of education and were a special function of divisions of vocational education.

The United States' reliance on voluntary organizations versus a more unified federal role continues to influence how society approaches disability issues. Some beliefs and practices continue today that negatively impact public opinion. For example "helping the disabled," continues to be defined as a good deed or a charitable act. Thus, it is one's "civic duty" or requirement, to contribute to the many non-profit, tax-deductible organizations. This results in individuals with disabilities being perceived as needing continuing support from charity rather than being perceived as competent citizens and taxpayers. Dependence on voluntary contributions of funds results in fierce competition for monies between various disability groups. This has tended to limit a free exchange of ideas and collaboration across disability groups. One result of this competition has been the need, on the part of those soliciting funds, to portray a particular disease or disability in the most pathetic terms in order to be the most deserving of contributions. National telethons and the "poster child" exemplify this. This competitive soliciting contributes to much of society's confusion regarding the roles and responsibilities of state and federal governments and the rights and responsibilities of individuals with disabilities.

Early vocational guidance programs greatly influenced the developing process of vocational rehabilitation. Frank Parsons, a social worker, established the first vocational guidance programs in the United States, in Boston, in 1908. Parsons' program emphasized understanding oneself, understanding the requirements and conditions for success, and reasoning in relation to these two. As Parsons' concepts spread, advocates in education, social work, business, and government joined together in founding, in 1913, the National Vocational Guidance Association, the forerunner of the American Counseling Association. World War I brought an increased need to choose the right man for the right job, as stressed in Parsons' theory. Selective tests were devised. The first group of intelligence tests, the Army Alpha and the Army Beta, were used respectively for literate and illiterate recruits. Following World War I, these testing techniques extended to all areas of vocational guidance, including vocational rehabilitation.

At the 1923 meeting of the National Society for Vocational Education, in Buffalo, the specialists in vocational rehabilitation held a sectional administrative meeting where these issues and the possibility of a separate organization were discussed. At a later business session on December 8, 1923, a new group was formed titled the National Civilian Rehabilitation Conference. The new National Civilian Rehabilitation Conference met in Indianapolis in 1924 in conjunction with the National Society for Vocation Education. During the meeting, a formal vote was passed to establish the conference as an independent association. At the meeting in Memphis in March 1927, the Conference changed its name to the National Rehabilitation Association.

FEDERAL REHABILITATION LEGISLATION

In 1917, the federal government passed the Smith-Hughes Act that served as a model for future state-federal legislation and authorized grant-in-aid support to states for vocational education. The Act provided federal monies for vocational education to states that matched some percentage of these funds and met certain requirements as listed in their State Plans. This precedent for human service programming was administered under a new Federal Board for Vocational Education. In 1918, for the first time, the United States House and Senate unanimously approved federal legislation on disability and rehabilitation. The Act, which essentially established the field of rehabilitation, was referred to as the Soldiers' Rehabilitation Act. It was designed as a program for veterans to meet what was perceived as a governmental payback obligation for military service and injury. Because of the retraining emphasis of the Act, the Federal Board of Vocational Education was authorized to oversee the Act's program services provided to disabled veterans. This legislation provided an opening for similar legislation related to the civilian population, and Congress was soon debating whether such a program should be available to civilians. Industry leaders who viewed such programs as dangerously "socialistic" raised strong opposition. In 1920, Congress passed the Smith-Fess Act, (Civilian Vocational Rehabilitation Act). Like the 1918 legislation, it only provided for training to workers who had become disabled on the job and was funded on a temporary basis. The Act remains significant as the first federal action in the US to provide vocational rehabilitation services for citizens with disabilities, and the first to reflect a social obligation to insure access to employment for individuals with disability.

The Smith-Fess Act of 1920, as a grant-in-aid program, provided federal funding as an incentive for states to develop plans and deliver rehabilitation services. Today, state programs in all fifty states, the District of Columbia, and the Commonwealth of Puerto Rico, make up what is referred to as the state/federal vocational rehabilitation program. Within this program, counselors are responsible for locating consumers, determining eligibility and rehabilitation potential, providing counseling and related services necessary to attain a vocational objective, and arranging directly or indirectly for placement. From the earliest days until quite recently, the delivery of vocational rehabilitation services followed the medical model. Eligibility for state-federal vocational services required a medically definable disability that presented a handicap or barrier to employment or independence, and a determination by the counselor of a successful outcome that was reasonably obtainable. The Act targeted occupationally injured populations and called for cooperative agreements to be established with existing workers' compensation boards and commissions. It also established an ongoing office within the federal government dedicated to disability issues. This office provided a focal point to bring together concerned individuals to share ideas and concepts of national importance. This federal legislation, in response to the needs of citizens with disabilities, was tenuous in that it had to be reauthorized each year. From 1920-1930, only 45,000 individuals had been rehabilitated and slightly over $12 million in federal dollars had been spent. Other federal and state efforts on behalf of individuals with disabilities were less visible in the early twentieth century. During this time, there was a tremendous growth, on a state-by-state basis, in the area of special education.

1930s -1950s

CULTURAL CONTEXT

The impact of voluntary organizations was significantly reduced as the Great Depression, resulting from the stock market crash in October 1929, grew in the early 1930s. Unemployment reached more than 12 million, many of whom became homeless and stood in long lines for free food and baths. In radio "fireside chats," President Franklin Delano Roosevelt broadcast hope for recovery under his "New Deal." Although some new legislation such as the Social Security Act evolved, the Great Depression reduced the national tax base and voluntary contributions from the public. State rehabilitation-related programs were hit hard. Special education programs funded through local taxes were cut. Hospitals and training centers also eliminated rehabilitation services.

Nevertheless, this period represents one of growth in public awareness of disability. The public debate about eugenics and, by extension, disability, had been growing since the turn of the century and increased after the rise of the Nazi party in Germany. Franklin Delano Roosevelt easily gained the presidency because of a platform of government responsibility for the state of the economy and the relief of starving and homeless individuals suffering under the depression. President Roosevelt concentrated on trying to overcome massive societal problems such as inadequate food, housing, and employment. Even though he himself was disabled, the needs of individuals with disabilities were not addressed.

When Adolph Hitler declared war on Poland in September 1939, Britain and France declared war on Germany. After two years of trying to avoid involvement, the United States entered the war after Japan bombed Pearl Harbor on December 7, 1941. World War II involved sixty-one countries and resulted in the deaths of an estimated fifty-five million soldiers and civilians. In addition, Hitler's Nazi party killed some five to six million Jews in the Holocaust. Germany surrendered to the Allied Forces in May 1945. Japan surrendered shortly after Harry Truman, who succeeded Roosevelt as President in 1945, approved the dropping of atomic bombs on Hiroshima and Nagasaki in August 1945.

The post-war baby boom increased the number of infants born with impairments and the polio epidemic of the late 1940s and early to mid 1950s further added to this population. Demographic changes began to have a direct impact on disability and related programs. In the years following World War II, families began to move away from rural areas or small towns and their traditional support networks. Growing numbers of people spent the workday in offices, stores, or factories. The need for new support systems was evident and people looked to the government for help.

At that time, the medical profession and the public were much more aware of "rehabilitation" as a process. Returning veterans, and the advocacy groups they formed at the close of the war, were particularly effective at articulating the needs of Americans with disabilities. The 1950s reflected tremendous economic growth and technological advances and the Korean War, 1950-1953, brought increased public awareness of disability and the need for rehabilitation services. The philosophical concepts underlying rehabilitation were very compatible with President Eisenhower's philosophy of dynamic conservation.

The post-war military activities of the Soviet Union in the late 1940s led to United States' fear of further Soviet advances. This fear resulted in the formation in 1949 of the North Atlantic Treaty Organization, a military coalition, and the start of the "Cold War." Economic growth changed life patterns for middle and working classes, with suburban "tract" housing becoming the norm. President Dwight D. Eisenhower served two terms, from 1953 through 1960. His philosophy of dynamic conservatism and his war experiences resulted in his strong support of federal rehabilitation programs. The administrations of Eisenhower, Kennedy, and Johnson, 1953-1969, saw a federal expansion in rehabilitation services that has been referred to as the Golden Era of Rehabilitation.

Rehabilitation Related Developments

Franklin Delano Roosevelt, who dominated most of the 1930s and 40s as the United States' President, was disabled because of polio. He downplayed this fact and, except in indirect ways, did not advocate for disability organizations. Eleanor Roosevelt, on the other hand, exhibited great interest in disability issues from the 1920s until after World War II.

In the late 1940s and early 1950s, major rehabilitation centers were developed as models of medical care and professional and vocational training. These included the Institute for the Crippled and Disabled in New York, the Cleveland Clinic (later the Cleveland Rehabilitation Center), the Sister Kenney Institute in Minneapolis emphasizing care for children and adults with polio, Rusk's Institute of Physical Medicine and Rehabilitation in New York, the Kessler Institute for Rehabilitation in New York, and Henri Viscardi's Abilities, Inc., in Long Island. By 1946, state rehabilitation agencies were involved in funding the development of comprehensive rehabilitation centers. In 1954, the Hill Burton Act provided some support for their development. In 1965, federal rehabilitation legislation provided considerable funding for rehabilitation centers and staff.

These non-profit rehabilitation centers and community workshops provided, in addition to the federal rehabilitation programs and private for profit rehabilitation programs, the third major emphasis in rehabilitation service. In the late forties and the fifties, the efforts of these centers led to the American mass media—movies, newspapers, magazine, and radio—addressing disability issues with growing frequency and candor. Numerous movies depicting the return to civilian life of veterans had powerful impressions on audiences. Helen Keller gained media notoriety and the Readers' Digest regularly carried "true life" stories about individuals "facing" and, almost invariably, "overcoming" a disability. Although inspirational, these stories presented detailed facts about people and families coping with disabilities. Media attention began to focus on "gifted" individuals with disabilities.

Inspirational stories became the vogue. It would be decades before descriptions of an individual with a disability would no longer contain words such as "noble," "inspirational," and "courageous." Not all disabling conditions received this attention. It was only after World War II that public discussions of mental retardation began and not until the 1970s that similar discussions occurred related to mental illness.

In the early years of World War II, service members who were permanently disabled remained in the Army hospitals, such as the Walter Reed Hospital, until medicine could do no more for them. They were then discharged to civilian life with services to be provided by the Veterans Administration that had no comprehensive programs. This lack of services became more pronounced as new antibiotics controlled infections and resulted in more service members surviving serious injuries. As the enormity and complexity of the needs of newly disabled service members became clear, the United States military responded with innovative programs.

Rehabilitation, as a part of physical medicine and war-related injuries, was an idea whose time had come. Two physicians who played key roles in its development, during and after the war, were Henry Kessler and Howard Rusk. Kessler, a member of the Naval Reserves was called to service as a Lieutenant Commander and had been involved in physical medicine and rehabilitation for two decades. He performed front line surgery in the South Pacific. In 1943, he was transferred back to the United States to build a new amputation center, the Mare Island Naval Hospital in California, which became a leading military rehabilitation facility. Kessler was known for ensuring comprehensive state-of-the-art services that encouraged patients to become informed consumers. He touched the lives of not only thousands of individuals with disabilities, but also hundreds of medical professionals who studied with him.

Howard Rusk, an Internist from St. Louis, enlisted in the Army Air Force in 1942 and served as Head of Medical Services at the Jefferson Barracks in

Missouri. With no training in rehabilitation or disability, he noted the simple fact that his patients made better progress when they were intellectually and physically challenged. He developed programs to accomplish this, and gradually formulated the idea that rehabilitation should be a specialty within general Internal Medicine and not exclusively the domain of surgeons. Rusk emphasized the "rehabilitation of the individual," not the injury. Soon he was in charge of initiating rehabilitation programs, titled Convalescent Training Programs, in Army Air Force hospitals, and developed twelve such programs where hundreds of medical personnel were introduced to his rehabilitation concepts.

World War II was a stimulus for improved medicines and medical technologies that permitted longer and healthier lives for individuals with disabilities. Of equal importance were advances in prostheses and orthotics that began during the war and progressed rapidly in the next few decades. Dr. George Deaver, one of Rusk's assistants, was the first to prove that individuals with paraplegia could walk if properly braced.

Henri Viscardi, an advocate with a disability, spent the World War II years as an American Red Cross volunteer at the Walter Reed Hospital. He and two other individuals with amputations confronted Rusk in his office over the practice of providing veterans with shoddy wooden prostheses. Within weeks, and with the support of the hospital's commanding officer, the army instituted an ongoing research project funded by Congress that developed improved and innovative prostheses over the next decade. By 1945, U.S. researchers had pioneered the use of new, lightweight materials such as plastics to replace heavier and more cumbersome steel and wood.[9]

The close of World War II marked a new era for rehabilitation in the United States. Federal and private non-profit rehabilitation programs had to be rebuilt, and expansion of rehabilitation facilities was a natural consequence. Programs were comprehensive, but maintained a strong physical restoration component. Special education programs had all but disappeared, and there continued to be few alliances across the various disability specific groups. At the close of the war, government and civilian agencies initiated studies to determine how best to serve returning disabled veterans. It was soon evident that veterans were being fairly well served, but the needs of the disabled civilian population were great and largely unmet. One study estimated that 23 million were disabled in some way and the numbers were growing because of advancements in medicine, surgery, and antibiotics. Only 10% of paraplegic veterans in World War I survived the first year, whereas, 80% of World War II paraplegic veterans were alive and active a decade later. Survival rates in this time frame were equally dramatic in the civilian population.[9]

In some ways, the mid 1950s through the 1960s were the heyday of United States based rehabilitation and expertise. Medical and technological advances, improved professional training, research, and comprehensive legislation on disability made the United States preeminent. One example is Rusk establishing in 1950 what is now titled the Howard A. Rusk Institute of Rehabilitation Medicine at the New York University Medical Center. Training programs flourished in fields such as physical therapy, occupational therapy, rehabilitation counseling, social work, special education, speech pathology, and rehabilitation medicine. Students of these different disciplines shared ideas and literature. However, communication between these fields frequently lagged behind communication within them. The division among academics reflected the past divisions found within private organizations and specific groups of individuals with disabilities. Scarce funding and minimal public attention often drove professional groups to compete rather than collaborate. While there were a few exceptions, the emphasis for most in rehabilitation was on how the individual with a disability could adapt to society, and the sociological concept of "stigma" associated with a disability dominated the era.

The early 1950s through the late 1960s saw the development of two social action movements of great significance; the Parents' Movement and the Disability Rights Movement of Persons with Disabilities. These two movements would eventually overlap and begin to unite with rehabilitation. The Parents' Movement was on behalf of children with mental retardation and in support of special education. While individuals who were severely retarded had been institutionalized, special programs and classes for mildly and moderately retarded children had evolved since the mid nineteenth century, but were the exception in most American school districts. Most educators in the early 1900s felt that little could be done for "retarded children" and that the public school system was not necessarily responsible for their education. It is not surprising that the first academic programs to be eliminated under the impact of the Great Depression were special education programs. "Higher functioning" retarded children were abandoned to the back of the regular classroom and the more severely impaired were simply sent home or institutionalized. The impact is seen in New Jersey where there were more children in public school special education classes in 1918 than in 1950.

Within the general public, retardation was still considered to be a shameful condition, a reflection of "weak" or "poor" genes, and a punishment or "cross to bear" by God. Parents often sent such children to a private institution for the mentally retarded. The late 1940s and early 1950s saw the beginning of a consumer driven parents' movement that sought to obtain services for developmentally disabled children and adolescents. From modest beginnings evolved the National Association for Retarded Children (NARC), which served as a catalyst for parent advocates nationally. In 1950, this association held its first nationwide convention. By 1956, it had well over 50,000 members with branches in every state, dealing with legislation and parent education. Dr. Salvatore De Michael was the first Executive Director of NARC. He came to the organization with expertise in legislation from Switzer's Office of

Vocational Rehabilitation in Washington. De Michael's successor, in 1957, was Gunnar Dybwad, whose background as a lawyer helped frame consumer entitlement issues in legal terms. Parents involved with NARC became aware that medical and educational professionals often knew little about mental retardation beyond their ability to identify and name certain conditions. As a result, the parents supported education and research programs. In 1957, the Office of Education and Switzer's Office of Vocational Rehabilitation (OVR) began to support teacher training programs and research in special education. While early advocates of mainstreaming argued that special education should be part of the public school curriculum, most of the energy was in trying to convince public educators that they had a responsibility to these children.

The parents' movement not only addressed educational issues but, as their children grew older, the focus broadened to issues of preparing the mentally retarded child and young adults for a "normal" life. The concept of normalization, as discussed by Bengt Nirje of Sweden and Wolf Wolfensberger, was essentially mainstreaming and was related to providing age-appropriate activities for individuals with mental retardation in an environment approximating that of nondisabled peers.[13]

The Disability Rights Movement had its beginnings in the early origins of Independent Living, a byproduct of the polio epidemic of the 1950s. By returning post-polio persons to their home, significant savings occurred. As a result, individuals with disabilities and their families gained experience in various aspects of independence. Because they represented large numbers, special summer camps, youth groups, and education programs were made available to them. This provided opportunities to meet and learn from others with similar experiences. Other influences included deinstitutionalization, normalization, and mainstreaming. As early as 1956, the National Rehabilitation Association passed a resolution in support of legislation in this area. In 1957, and later in 1961, legislation failed.

Beginning with its inception, the National Rehabilitation Association assumed a leadership role in national legislation. In 1930, the Association took major responsibility for the renewal legislation for the State-Federal Vocational Rehabilitation program. It drafted its own bill and succeeded in getting it introduced in Congress. When it became apparent that close watch would have to be kept on this legislation, the Association made a special appeal to its members for funds to finance sending representatives to Washington as needed to lobby for passage of the bill. A fund of $3,449.00 was raised by this special appeal. This was a phenomenal amount, since the normal budget of the Association was less than $200.00 a year.

With legislative activities taking so much time of the Association, in 1930 it was decided to establish a headquarters in Washington, DC. With the depression, plans to hire an Executive Director had to be abandoned. Instead, the Association placed major energies behind successfully implementing the

1936 and 1940 rehabilitation legislation. Growth within the Association saw the development of sub-units and regions. E. B. Whitten was employed as Executive Director in 1948.

State chapters were authorized in 1950 and professional divisions in 1957 with the start of the National Rehabilitation Counselor Association. The Association's national political support was very strong and the Rehabilitation Act of 1954 resulted in expansion of services and programs and in construction of facilities through the 1965 Amendments.

FEDERAL REHABILITATION LEGISLATION

The 1933 Amendments to the Rehabilitation Act reflected the government's effort under President Roosevelt's "New Deal" to combat the Depression. Vocational Rehabilitation was still considered charitable work. The professional rehabilitation worker was titled "agent." The continuing emphasis in service delivery was on what needed to be done to the individual with disability rather than involving them in their own rehabilitation. In 1935, the Rehabilitation Act, virtually unchanged, was made a permanent program. This resulted from lobbying for an amendment to the Social Security Act of 1935 by representatives of the National Rehabilitation Association. The Randolph Sheppard Act (1936) allocated funds for the development and expansion of facilities for people who are blind and gave them exclusive rights for vending machines in federal buildings. The Wagner-O'Day Act (1938) made it mandatory for the federal government to purchase products from blind individuals. In 1939, Amendments to the Social Security Act increased annual grants and appropriations for rehabilitation.

Between 1920 and 1943, the Rehabilitation Act provided services only to the physically disabled. The growth of disability advocacy groups and organizations was slowed by the Depression and the start of World War II, as disability issues became a lower priority. In contrast, federal involvement with disability groups and programs increased for two reasons—the need to utilize all available workers on the home front, and the need to rehabilitate injured veterans. Immediately after the U.S. involvement in World War II, President Roosevelt asked the Federal Security Administration to study what would constitute an adequate vocational rehabilitation program during and after the war. Recommendations resulted in great expansion of the Rehabilitation Act and generated interest, still discussed today, in the state-federal vocational rehabilitation program being a part of the Department of Labor. World War II directly influenced the first major expansion of the Rehabilitation Act and of eligibility for services within it. The goals of the 1943 Disabled Veterans Rehabilitation Act, Public Law 78-16, signed by President Roosevelt, were clear. They were to direct "disabled manpower" into war production and provide comprehensive services necessary for employment of disabled veterans in peacetime pursuits. For the first time, the Act received strong support from government and business. It provided more liberal funding, extended services to the mentally handicapped and the mentally ill, provided for the option of a separate state/federal vocational rehabilitation program for persons who are blind, and established the Office of Vocational Rehabilitation (OVR) within the Federal Security Agency. More importantly, the Act expanded the provision of services from job training to medical, surgical, mental health, and physical rehabilitation services. Surveys funded under this law found that the civilian population of people with disabilities was much larger and received fewer services than previously believed.

Enormously high unemployment rates and poverty subsistence levels were universal among all disability groups at the end of the War. Large numbers of newly disabled veterans who wanted to return to the work force became increasingly vocal about these problems. From the mid 1940s, employment became the prominent issue for disabled individuals and groups. In 1944, the Serviceman's Readjustment Act, called the "GI Bill of Rights," was passed. It provided extensive support for readjustment and rehabilitation. In 1945, Congress enacted Public Law 79-176 to establish the National Employ the Physically Handicapped Week and paved the way for President Truman's organizing The President's Committee on Employment of the Physically Handicapped. As a non-government agency, the Committee served in a national advocacy role on behalf of employment for disabled individuals. The Committee's work resulted in an increase in numbers employed and a growing public awareness of the problems confronted by people with disabilities. The Committee's employment activities led to questions regarding transportation, accessibility, workers' compensation, legal protection, independent living, social equality, and ultimately, civil rights.

In 1957, President Eisenhower established the Department of Health, Education, and Welfare (HEW), the new home of the Office of Vocational Rehabilitation (OVR). Mary Switzer was appointed the first Director. Her long-standing interest in rehabilitation and her personal and professional contacts with rehabilitation leaders, such as Howard Rusk, provided entree to the OVR position. She was noted for her innovative ideas, her genius for bringing individuals and programs together to reach a workable consensus, and her respect for and ability to lobby Congress. These activities inspired increased expansion and funding of the federal rehabilitation program during the 17 years of her administration. In her tenure, funding for the program increased forty-fold. By using the example of restoring individuals with disabilities to "taxpayers," with a return of $10 for every dollar expended on their rehabilitation, Switzer argued that the program was an example of a productive public program that could justify its expenditures.

Switzer lobbied Congress to pass the 1954 Rehabilitation Act Amendments. This legislation launched what has been referred to as the Golden Era of Rehabilitation. The Amendments were based on the government's search for ways to address mounting welfare and dependency needs. They broadened state federal programs and provided for the establishment of public and non-profit rehabilitation facilities. Evaluation and work adjustment services for state agency consumers were approved and the utilization of rehabilitation facilities was increased. In addition to service, research, and demonstration areas, funds for training grants were approved. Switzer was now empowered to fund whatever she chose in the field of rehabilitation. Her emphasis on training was at the graduate level.

Rehabilitation counseling had the unique distinction of being the only profession established by an Act of Congress. Those employed in the field were labeled rehabilitation workers, agents, or advisors. The establishment of graduate level training programs in 1954 identified the competencies necessary to serve as a rehabilitation counselor. However, the requirement that all "counselors" in the state/federal program have the Masters degree in rehabilitation was not mandated for another 44 years, in 1998. Research on a wide range of psychological, social, educational, and behavioral aspects of disabling conditions was funded. For the first time, information on disability was to be systematically studied and integrated into training, policy, and service programs.

The effective funding of a wide range of rehabilitation programs from the 1950s through the 1970s is directly attributable to Mary Switzer's vision. She funded some of the first movements toward independent living and disability rights. Other funding interests included Playwrights, the National Theatre for the Deaf, and film captioning. Her Office of Vocational Rehabilitation (OVR) provided a central focus for rehabilitation issues throughout the government.

1960s -1970s

CULTURAL CONTEXT

Political and social strife and reform movements characterized the 1960s. Non-violent demonstrations of Afro-Americans resulted in the Civil Rights Act of 1964, but violent riots occurred within urban ghettos, Watts and Detroit, in the mid 1960s. New concern for the poor led to President Johnson's Great Society Programs, the Medicare Act, the Higher Education Act, and the Water Quality Act. Feminism became a national cultural and political movement, and the National Organization for Women was founded in 1966. Nineteen Sixty-Four saw the beginning of the Vietnam War. In 1965, United States' troops were deployed, and their numbers reached a high of 543,900 in 1969. Opposition to the United States' involvement in Vietnam became increasingly more violent, particularly by college students in 1969, the same year that astronauts Neil Armstrong and Buzz Aldrin became the first humans to set foot on the moon. A cease-fire agreement was signed in Vietnam in 1973.

Increases in alcohol consumption as well as illegal drugs during the 1960s raised public concern. LSD, legal in the 1950s, became illegal in 1965 when it became associated with the counter-culture. The use of cocaine reappeared about 1970. At first, its use was viewed as a harmless tonic, but as the street price fell, the acute and long-term effects began to alarm the public. In 1970, Jerry Rubins claimed that marijuana makes each man God. Timothy O'Leary's recommendations to turn on, tune in, and drop out characterized the prominent drug use of the time. Alcohol and drug use was synonymous with the large counter-culture, symbolized by Woodstock, a music festival held in Bethol, New York that drew almost one-half million people.

In late 1963, a stunned nation came to a standstill as it reacted to the assassination of President Kennedy. Ten years later, the American constitutional system faced its worst challenge since the Civil War. From April 1973 through August 1974, the nation tensely watched the resignation of the Vice President and the unfolding developments of Watergate that eventually, under threat of impeachment, led to the resignation of the President of the United States, Richard Nixon, on August 8, 1974. The Watergate revelations and scandal not only led to a loss of faith in government, but also galvanized Congress. It led to a new emphasis on congressional oversight, of not only implementing laws but also evaluating their effects.

The economic boom of the 1960s began to falter in the 1970s and resulted in a severe recession in 1974—1975. Protectionist trade practices, the decline of the dollar, and monetary instability resulted in inflation. The impact of the energy crisis was devastating in terms of general inflation and unemployment. Attempts to curb inflation drove the prime interest rate to over 20% by 1980, thus greatly reducing automobile and housing sales. High inflation destroyed retirement programs and individuals spent rather than saved because commodities would cost more the next year. The energy crisis caused a re-evaluation of government priorities. Many programs such as vocational rehabilitation were told, "...to do more with less," and there was increased accountability on the part of federal programs. Within this sluggish economy developed a growing distrust of big government and a weakening support for new social policies, i.e. school busing and racial quotas were opposed in court.

REHABILITATION RELATED DEVELOPMENTS

The parents' movement had progressed so quickly that when the initial civil rights legislation began redefining rules for African-American children, it became apparent to several people in the parents' movement that these rules were also pertinent to retarded children. By the early 1960s, increasing numbers of retarded children were being served with the more severely retarded beginning to receive attention, but progress was very slow. In 1960, no more than 1 in 4 eligible mentally retarded children had been enrolled in special public school classes. Interest in mental retardation was helped enormously when President Kennedy initiated the President's Panel on Mental Retardation in 1961. It was furthered by the public admission by Eunice Kennedy Shriver, President Kennedy's sister, of their sister Rosemary's mental impairment. Suddenly, politicians were willing to take issues of mental retardation seriously.

The 1960s and 1970s were turbulent years of great social strife and change in the United States with many minority groups, through protest, civil disobedience, and consumer voter power, demanding changes in the status quo. Social unrest sparked action in the disabled community as well. During the civil rights movement of the 1960s, culminating in the Civil rights Act of 1964, many of the activists were individuals with disabilities. Under a civil rights commitment, individuals with disabilities began to argue that their shared problems and concerns outweighed their differences. Many Americans with disabilities began to realize they were dealing with issues similar to those of other minority groups. They began to see that their disability was not an issue of specific medical diagnosis, but a minority status, and that they deserved the same rights and protections granted other minority groups. With this came a new activism. By the mid-1970s, numerous organizations administered for and by people who were disabled, were founded to address political, economic, and social concerns. These organizations worked closely with one another, and their actions represented a social movement that came to be known as the Disability Rights Movement or the Independent Living Movement

Independent living rehabilitation represents an expansion of support into life areas other than work. The Independent Living movement is based upon other social movements in the 1960s and early 1970s, including civil rights, consumerism, decentralization, self-help, and deinstitutionalization. In 1972, the first Center for Independent Living was incorporated in Berkeley, California. Individuals with disabilities staffed it as peer counselors and advocates. Other centers developed at the Universities of Texas, Ohio, and Michigan. By 1985, a directory listed 298 independent living programs in the United States with at least one program in each state. Centers for Independent Living (CIL) were created to be community-based, non-residential, private not-for-profit, consumer-controlled organizations. Consumer controlled meant that the majority of employees and the Boards of Directors were to be people with disabilities. CILs now exist under federal rehabilitation funding in all states. Their primary goals are to serve as advocates for eliminating environmental, economic, human rights, and communication barriers that are detrimental to people with disabilities; provide public awareness and education to dispel myths about disability and people with disabilities; and offer direct services to individuals with disabilities.

While CIL operations will vary from location to location, all have a core of four direct services:

- Information and referral wherein information is provided to help consumers self-assess their problems and situation;

- Peer counseling composed of one-on-one or group supportive and non-therapeutic interactions with other people with disabilities are used for self-exploration and help with self-advocacy;
- Skill training in which acquisition of specific skills or competencies is attained in such areas as health maintenance, application and management of financial benefits, job development skills, household management, personal/interpersonal communication skills, and self-care in activities of daily living (e.g., bathing, dressing, transportation); and,
- Advocacy and information services designed to help consumers act on their own behalf to maintain or improve independent living skills.

The Golden Era of rehabilitation began to wane in the late 1960s. Switzer retired in 1970, and the rehabilitation orientation in the social and rehabilitation services reverted to a social welfare persuasion. A struggle for priority and attention in the federal program increased between individuals with severe disabilities and individuals who were disadvantaged and had been brought into the system by President Johnson's War on Poverty. The 1970s also saw states rights issues having a major impact on rehabilitation. Large state umbrella service agencies began absorbing state rehabilitation programs, which were traditionally independent and unique human services systems. In the early 1970s, an active militancy on the part of individuals with severe disabilities resulted in scrutiny of the program by Congress. The Rehabilitation Act experienced its first veto by President Nixon in 1973. Nixon did not support the Act's funding of public offenders and opposed proposed independent living provisions. Congress deleted Independent Living provisions and Nixon signed the Act that year. Ford similarly opposed rehabilitation appropriation. President Reagan's targeted destruction of the Act in the early 1980s through a Block Grant approach and reduction-in-funding proposals highlighted just how fragile and at risk were rehabilitation legislative gains. NRA, through its Legislative Network, is credited with insuring the survival of the Rehabilitation Act, as well as insuring increases over presidential budget proposals for funding the State/Federal Vocational Rehabilitation Program.

As the Rehabilitation Act and its amendments from the 1920s to the 1970s targeted specific disability populations, the occupationally disabled population no longer was the sole focus of the state/federal rehabilitation program. Private-for-profit rehabilitation had its greatest growth after the 1975 California legislation that mandated the addition of vocational rehabilitation services to the medical services provided through state Workers' Compensation Law. The private for profit emphasis is on case management necessary to return an injured worker to gainful employment versus the public sectors' emphasis on maximizing potential. Many states followed with "mandatory" vocational rehabilitation legislation causing a tremendous growth in employment in the private sector that exceeded the growth in other federal programs. Recent studies show that almost forty percent of qualified rehabilitation counselors are employed in private-for-profit rehabilitation firms, about thirty percent in the state federal rehabilitation program, about ten percent in private nonprofit rehabilitation facilities, and almost ten percent work in private practice.

The National Rehabilitation Association began to see a loss in its national legislative leadership role in the mid-to-late 1970s when it began to experience a significant loss in membership. This loss resulted, in part, from a major change in the organizational administrative structures within state agencies providing vocational rehabilitation services. From 1973 to 1978, the number of state agencies administratively housed in "umbrella" state social service agencies had increased from only a few to over thirty. Within these states, NRA membership dropped dramatically as state vocational rehabilitation administrators lost their autonomy and their ability to provide administrative support for state agency employees' participation in NRA chapter programming and activities. In addition, within these states, many new state directors were appointed with no background in rehabilitation and without an appreciation for the benefits accrued to the agency by supporting employees in a strong and active state NRA chapter.

Directors of State/Federal Vocational Rehabilitation agencies had provided the primary leadership within NRA since 1923. In 1974, the Council of State Administrators for Vocational Rehabilitation, an affiliate within NRA, severed their administrative linkage with NRA to become a separate and independent association. Their exit resulted in loss of support for employee membership. In 1975, NRA successfully intervened through the court system in the well-known "Florida test case" over compliance issues related to service delivery within that state. In some states, membership was discouraged because of NRA's position, and significant losses in NRA membership were experienced that year. NRA's reduction in national political impact has been proportional to its loss in chapter membership.

During the early 1970's, the following developmental milestones in relation to rehabilitation counselor education occurred:

- The Council on Rehabilitation Education (CORE) was formed in June of 1971 in order to accredit Rehabilitation Counselor Education (RCE) programs through the continuing review and improvement of master's degree level RCE Programs. CORE described the Rehabilitation Counselor as "a counselor who possesses the specialized knowledge, skills, and attitudes needed to collaborate in a professional relationship with people who have disabilities to achieve their personal, social, psychological, and vocational goals" (CORE, 1996).[4] The purpose of accreditation is to both promote excellence in education and to protect the customers receiving services (CORPA, 1995).

- In 1974, the Commission on Rehabilitation Counselor Certification (CRCC) was incorporated as an independent, not-for-profit organization to certify Rehabilitation counselors. Since then, more than 35,000 counselors have fulfilled the certification requirements. As this document is written, the Certified Rehabilitation Counselor (CRC) designation is generally recognized as the standard for determining that VR counselors have achieved a certain level of competence. Application for the CRC certification requires that the individual is of good moral character; holds a minimum of a master's degree in rehabilitation counseling or a counseling discipline; completes a supervised work experience; and passes a certification exam (CRCC, 2005).[3]

Federal Rehabilitation Legislation

President Lyndon Johnson's War on Poverty resulted in the Rehabilitation Act Amendments (1965) literally doubling the federal government's financial support and increased the federal financial share contributed to states from 60% to 75%. Congress broadened the definition of disability to include those who had "behavior disorders," as diagnosed by a psychologist or psychiatrist. This expanded definition meant that services were provided through the state/federal program to people with alcoholism and drug addiction and those with antisocial personality and sociopathic diagnoses. The amendments also strengthened the growth of rehabilitation facilities by authorizing new construction of vocational rehabilitation facilities and sheltered workshops. The 1965 Amendments and the preceding 1954 legislation stimulated phenomenal growth in the number of new facilities.

The Amendments of 1968 increased the federal funding share to 80% and provided a further response to social need; the "socially disadvantaged," were identified as eligible for service. The amendments also broadened consumer eligibility to include deaf, blind, and migratory worker populations. During this time, reorganization in Health, Education, and Welfare resulted in the development of Social and Rehabilitation Services with OVR becoming the Rehabilitation Services Administration under this unit.

The legislation that has had the broadest impact on the field of rehabilitation was the Rehabilitation Act of 1973. Its sweeping impact was due, in large measure, to consumer advocacy that influenced its civil rights orientation. These amendments reflect a philosophical shift in legislation wherein the traditional "medical model" of public vocational rehabilitation was diminished by championing a partnership between the counselor and consumer.

The Act consisted of four sections.

- The civil rights portion of Section 501 mandated nondiscrimination by the federal government in its own hiring practices in the hope that the federal government would prove to be a role model for private sector employers.

- Section 502 addressed concerns about accessibility, especially architectural barriers and their handicapping effect on people with disabilities, and established the Architectural and Transportation Compliance Board to enforce accessibility standards.
- Section 503 prohibited discrimination in employment on the basis of physical or mental disability and required affirmative action on the part of all federal contract recipients and their subcontractors who received more than $2500 in federal funds.
- Section 504 prohibited exclusion based on disability of an otherwise qualified person with a disability from participation in any federal or federally sponsored program or activity, such as attending school (elementary, secondary, and post secondary), or day-care centers, and access to hospitals and public welfare offices. This section emphasized accessibility of buildings and programs. A person with a disability could not be found unqualified without considering whether a reasonable accommodation would render the individual qualified.

In addition to Sections 501-504, the Rehabilitation Act of 1973 provided for rehabilitation research by establishing the National Institute of Handicapped Research (NIHR), now the National Institute on Disability and Rehabilitation Research (NIDRR). NIDRR is responsible for disseminating information on ways to increase the quality of life for people with disabilities, educating the public about ways of providing rehabilitation to people with disabilities, conducting conferences on rehabilitation research and engineering, and producing and disseminating statistics on employment, health, and income of people with disabilities.

The Rehabilitation Act of 1973 also regulated the daily practice of rehabilitation counseling in the state/federal system. It gave rehabilitation service priority to those people with the most severe disabilities and emphasized "consumer involvement." Consumer involvement meant that people with disabilities (i.e., the consumers of rehabilitation services) shared an equal role with the rehabilitation counselor in the development of rehabilitation plans. The Act mandated the use of an Individualized Written Rehabilitation Program (IWRP) that must specify vocational objectives and services provided, as well as how progress toward the objectives is to be evaluated. Mandates for consumers to serve on state agency policy development boards were provided.

The Rehabilitation Act of 1973 also broadened the definition of disability. Disability could now be documented by the existence of a physical or mental impairment that substantially limits one or more of the major life activities. These include having a record of such an impairment (such as recovering alcoholics or drug addicts, people with a history of mental illness, people with epilepsy who have been seizure free), or being regarded as having such an impairment, (such as having a disfigurement), or obesity. The 1973 Rehabilitation Act also authorized a study of the needs of severely handicapped people.

The Rehabilitation Act of 1973 was amended in 1974 to provide transfer of the Rehabilitation Services Administration to the Department of Health, Education, and Welfare, to convene the first White House Conference on Handicapped Individuals (now called the National Council on Disability), and to establish Regional Rehabilitation Continuing Education Programs (RRCEP's) to provide in-service training to staff on a regional basis. The Rehabilitation Extension Act of 1976 continued the act for two years with no changes. While not specifically rehabilitation legislation, the landmark special education legislation of 1975, Individuals with Disabilities Education Act (IDEA), should be noted because of its impact on rehabilitation because of transition needs of students. This legislation increased the numbers of students with disabilities served and graduating from the public schools. One indirect outcome of this legislation was increased parental awareness of the resource limitations of the state/federal vocational rehabilitation program in meeting their offspring's needs.

Another act having a major impact was the Developmental Disabilities Assistance and Bill of Rights Act of 1976. Its purpose was to ensure that persons with developmental disabilities received the services necessary to achieve their maximum potential. The Act required that each state have a network of protection and advocacy organizations independent of the agencies that provide service. These networks provided support for the developing Parents Movement.

The 1978 rehabilitation legislation, signed by President Carter, was titled the Rehabilitation Comprehensive Services and Developmental Disabilities Amendments. These amendments provided significant funding for a whole new dimension of rehabilitation services for independent living. The amendments authorized funds for Centers for Independent Living and agency independent living services to people with severe disabilities who may not have any vocational objectives. The intent of independent living services was to assist people with disabilities to gain maximum control over their lives and to minimize reliance on others for self-maintenance. Services include prevention of dependency, early intervention activities designed to reduce or postpone dependency (e.g. teaching people with spinal cord injuries to prevent pressure sores or decubitus ulcers), rehabilitation for independence, special training for daily living skills (e.g. bathing, grooming, dressing, cooking, cleaning), and maintenance of independence services designed to avoid relapses, some of which, like attendant care, may be needed for a lifetime.

The 1978 amendments also expanded the program by establishing the

American Indian Vocational Rehabilitation Program Tribal 130 project(s) (now known as Section 121 Programs), and authorizing the National Institute of Handicapped Research, later renamed the National Institute on Disability and Rehabilitation Research (NIDRR) as a funding agency for individual research grants and Rehabilitation Research and Training Centers. Another funded program established was the Helen Keller Center for the Deaf/Blind.

The 1979 Rehabilitation Act Amendments provided that individuals with disabilities be guaranteed substantial involvement in policies governing their rehabilitation. The Office of Special Education and Rehabilitation Services (OSERS), with the Rehabilitation Services Administration as one unit, was created within the newly established cabinet-level Department of Education in 1979. This was seen as an important move for two reasons. It established the position of Commissioner for Rehabilitation Services Administration (RSA) as a presidential appointment approved by the Senate. It also reduced the levels of government between the Commissioner of Rehabilitation and his/her supervisor by having the Commissioner answer directly to the Assistant Secretary of Education.

1980 TO DATE

Cultural Context

The last two decades of the twentieth century and the first decade of the 21st century saw the computer and wireless internet access transform society and industry. The personal computer, with software and Internet connection, became a fundamental tool in offices, homes, and schools. The Reagan Years, 1981-1988, brought one of the largest eras of economic prosperity to the United States economy. This was the result of increased defense spending, budget and tax cuts, and deregulation that led to the largest federal budget and trade deficits in United States history. These, in turn, led to a stock market crash in 1987.

The 1980s began with Ronald Reagan becoming President. His political philosophy identified a limited role for government in meeting the needs of disadvantaged persons or persons with disability. He cut state medical benefits to disability groups when he was governor of California. When President Reagan took office, disability benefits under Social Security Disability Insurance (SSDI) and Supplemental Security Income (SSI) programs for needy aged, blind, and disabled persons were being paid to about seven million disabled citizens. The Social Security Administration began a review two months after Reagan took office of 30,000 SSDI and SSI cases a month. Approximately forty percent of the cases reviewed (75,000 people receiving benefits) were cut off in what was considered a purge of the disability roles. During the Reagan years, a forceful anti-communist foreign policy ran parallel with major social change and eventual reform of the Soviet Union. These two factors contributed to the end of the "Cold War" near the end of the decade.

The 1980s brought increased demands for zero tolerance of drug use and punishment for casual users. Crack cocaine use in the lower socioeconomic levels of society was one influencing factor. The Omnibus Drug Bill of 1986 provided for punishment and prison. The failed War on Drugs has been ongoing since the middle 1980s.

In 1988, George Bush was elected President. In August 1990, Iraq's Sadam Hussein invaded and conquered Kuwait. George Bush organized a United Nations approved international force that began bombing Iraq in January 1991 and a ground attack in February 1991 to stop the invasion. A cease-fire was accepted in April 1991 with sanctions imposed on Iraq.

In the 1992 presidential election, Democrat Bill Clinton defeated President Bush. In 1994, Republicans gained control of both houses of Congress. President Clinton won reelection in 1996, but a Republican controlled Congress who pursued President Clinton for perceived and real scandals plagued his administration. Major Congressional investigating energies resulted in limited activity on legislation. Congress did pass legislation in which federal protection for welfare recipients ended, and programming funds were turned over to the states. Clinton was impeached but served the rest of his term with George W. Bush elected in a close and controversial election as President in 2001.

President G. W. Bush inherited from the Clinton administration a booming economy, and the highest federal budget surpluses ever. However, tax cuts, a recession, and the "War on Terror", targeting Osama Bin-Laden, the "mastermind" behind the September 11, 2001 terrorist "kamikaze type" commercial airplane attacks destroying the World Trade Center Towers and damaging the Pentagon, soon eliminated this federal surplus in the first year of the Bush term. During the first few months of the War on Terror, military expenditures were estimated at over one billion dollars monthly when Bush ordered the invasion of Pakistan in search of Osama Bin-Laden with U.S. and "international" coalition of military troops. This monthly military expenditure was projected to have doubled when President Bush, in 2003, led an invasion of Iraq with the resulting military occupation of that country.

President Bush was reelected in 2004 and his domestic policies and his "staying the course" commitment to the Afghanistan and Iraq wars resulted in the largest U.S. budget deficit ever. For example, as opposed to the conservative yearly estimate in 2002 of $12 billion a year being spent in Afghanistan and Iraq, recent yearly expenditures related to the wars are now over 140 billion yearly. By comparison, the state federal vocational rehabilitation program, under the Rehabilitation Act, is funded at two billion dollars yearly. From 2002-2006, a Republican dominated Congress did little to oppose war expenditures or address a variety of pressing social issues. Because of the public's growing concern regarding this and escalating violence in the war in Iraq, Democrats were elected in control of both House and Senate in

2006.

The U. S. economy entered its longest post World War II recession in December 2007, resulting in the Bush administration taking more control of the economy by proposing and enacting multiple economic programs intended to preserve the economy's financial system.

Barack Obama, the first African American to hold the office, was elected in 2008 and inaugurated as president on January 20, 2009. He inherited an economic depression that included a major drop in housing prices caused by bankers, unsecured house mortgages, and "bundled" debt from mortgages sold on the stock exchange. Banks, major corporations, and the automobile industry were all at risk with unemployment rising steadily. President Obama signed the $787 billion economic stimulus legislation—already proposed by Bush—into law in the form of the American Recovery and Reinvestment Act in February 2009. The following month, he intervened in the troubled automotive industry by providing loans and setting terms for bankruptcy and reorganization of General Motors Corporation, which gave the U.S. government a temporary 60% equity stake in the company.

In 2010, he signed into the law the Tax Relief, Unemployment Insurance Reauthorization and Job Creation act of 2010. This legislation kept the U. S. economy from collapsing but did not greatly improve it. In 2011, national unemployment rates are at 9.6% with the housing market reflecting continuing foreclosures in housing and drops in the value of homes.

One of Obama's campaign pledges was to end the war and bring troops home from Iraq. He indicated that he would withdraw troops from Iraq in 18 months but, to the dismay of his supporters, he increased troop levels in Afghanistan. In 2011, troop levels in Afghanistan were at 100,000 and in Iraq 50,000 with an estimated similar level of "contract" forces equaling these levels in each country. On May 11, 2011, Obama announced that a small team of American Navy Seal forces, acting on his direct order had killed All-Qaeda leader Osama Bin-Laden in Pakistan. Additional war costs were incurred when Obama led and contributed to the United Nation's military intervention of Libya in 2011. As a result of the recession and efforts to resolve it, the War on Terror, and continuing costs on three war fronts, the U. S. national debt as of 2011 was at a record high $12.9 trillion dollars and obviously in need of reduction. With a Congress split politically on how to resolve this, little hope for early resolution of this problem existed.

REHABILITATION RELATED DEVELOPMENTS

Under the continuing Disability Rights Movement, individuals with disabilities began to oppose the role of passive recipient of care. They advocated for independent roles in society and for input into the established organizations that made decisions on their behalf. They began to challenge society's paternalistic attitude toward them, and many rehabilitation professionals and organizations changed their advocacy emphasis. Individuals with disabilities believe they are fully equipped to direct and control their own lives and asked service providers to shift from roles of decision makers to technical advisors. Many organizations and agencies changed along with consumers while others paid only lip service. Some even ignored the new activism and carried on as usual. This new activism among individuals with disabilities in the United States is reflected in changes in national legislation, in restructuring of some organizations to enable increased input from consumers, and in a better-educated public on disabilities issues.

The progress of the disability movement is a reflection of broader social and demographic considerations. The majority of consumer leaders, as well as individuals with disabilities, were born during or influenced by, the post-war baby boom generation. In the 1950s and 1960s, these leaders saw special education and rehabilitation as avenues of early support. In the 1970s and 1980s, they began to be concerned with employment issues for people with disabilities. Social and economic equality assumed a more prominent role, as they demanded the right to equal treatment and economic self-sufficiency. In the period from the 1980s to-date, issues for individuals with disabilities expanded to retirement and geriatric services. Their political advocacy has reflected their interests over this time.

A backdrop of the disability rights and the independent living movements has been an increase in public understanding of disability issues. The public is also increasingly aware of the cost of individuals with disabilities if they remain outside mainstream employment. This understanding, and the support of advocacy and consumer groups, has resulted in federal legislation through the 1980s intended to improve participation and quality of life for individuals with disabilities. It also resulted in several national initiatives to increase the employment of individuals with disabilities. Likewise, it provided the context for the 1992 Amendments to implement ADA concepts and the 1998 Amendments to the Rehabilitation Act to re-emphasize employment. The 1998 Amendments were incorporated into a broad Workforce Investment Act that transferred administration for workforce training and development to local communities.

As opposed to rehabilitation programs designed in the 1970s to insure equal access because of perceived handicap and to address needs of what society perceived as a vulnerable citizenry, the 1990s legislation began to question the relevance of this perspective. Given improvements in economic opportunities, greater public and consumer understanding of disability, significant advances in medical, social, and rehabilitation technology, and the disability rights movement, special programs or protections for people with disabilities are viewed with skepticism by individuals with disability and by legislators. Prior legislation deemed specialized services, entitlements, cash payments, and social subsidies as appropriate. Current legislative pressures relate to consolidation and integration of services, and to utilizing technology. Political discussions have begun to focus on what should comprise publicly appropriate resources to meet a person's needs.

The interrelatedness of consumer advocacy and increased awareness of disability issues by the public resulted in a consensus that consumers have the right to determine to what end their rehabilitation should be directed. The solutions proposed in legislation throughout the 1990s reflect this consensus as can be seen in requirements of "informed choice" and "empowerment" in the 1992 Rehabilitation Act Amendments. This right is also institutionalized in the 1998 amendments to the Rehabilitation Act that gave a consumer-controlled entity–the State Rehabilitation Council (SRC)–the authority and responsibility to participate in the development, review, and implementation of state plans within the state federal rehabilitation program. SRCs have continued the legislative shift toward more consumer control and empowerment.[1]

As public policy supporting their access to employment broadened, individuals with disabilities were confronted with an ever-changing work environment. The Protestant work ethic at the turn of the century has become a minority position in our society. Additionally, work itself has changed dramatically. With global competition and downsizing, employers view workers as expendable. The commitment by a company to an employee is linked specifically to the company's need for employees' skills and their ability to produce. Careers within organizations are no longer the mode. Now organizations provide avenues through which individuals pursue personal goals. In this new economy, key worker requirements are autonomy, self-direction, flexibility, and continuous learning. This new economy presents a far more challenging labor market for individuals with disabilities.

To ensure its leadership in advocacy position, the National Rehabilitation Association finalized reorganization efforts at the turn of the 21st Century. From its beginnings in the early 1920s, the National Rehabilitation Association has proven to be the driving force behind every major rehabilitation initiative since the implementation of national rehabilitation legislative efforts at the turn of the twentieth century. The history of the Association's successes is a distinguished history of effective leadership and impact. Its failures are similarly linked to leadership. The Association must benefit not only from its successes, but also from its failures as its membership works together for a better future. NRA's newly developed professional identity proposes a commitment to proactive initiatives and broader issues. To maintain a leadership role, the Association must pursue its purpose collaboratively with related associations, consumer advocacy groups, and consumer groups. What future federal rehabilitation legislation may bring depends on the Association's and related professional and consumer partners' impact and leadership.

FEDERAL REHABILITATION LEGISLATION

Throughout the 1980s, federal rehabilitation legislation continued with emphasis on trying to ensure adequate funding levels necessary to provide individuals with disabilities the possibility of inclusion. During this time, legislation was greatly influenced by public endorsement of the Disability Rights Movement. In 1980, a continuing resolution reauthorized the Act. Again, in 1982 and 1984, it was reauthorized with no major changes. In 1984, because of consumer advocacy, the word "qualified" was inserted before the word personnel. In 1986, reauthorization endorsed the concept of supported employment, offering support strategies to provide needed assistance to individuals who are severely disabled to work in competitive environments. Services to help consumers transition from high school to work were also emphasized, but minimal funding was provided in supported employment and transition. The legislation also added support for individual consumer rights and revised the IWRP format to include consumer statements of their own rehabilitation goals.

The Technology-Related Assistance for Individuals with Disabilities Act of 1988 established a national information and program referral network and developed a state-level consumer-responsive program of technology-related assistance. It also developed training and funded demonstration and innovative projects designed to increase public awareness.

Perhaps the most widely recognized rehabilitation related legislation is the Americans with Disabilities Act (ADA) of 1990. Like the Rehabilitation Act of 1973, the ADA is a very significant piece of civil rights legislation. This legislation is regarded as landmark civil rights legislation that prohibits discrimination against people with disabilities in virtually every aspect of society. It provides enforceable standards against disability-based discrimination and a role for the federal government in enforcing those standards.

The ADA defined disability using Section 504 of the 1973 Rehabilitation Act, and added a category of disability for those with contagious diseases. The substantial number of people with Acquired Immune Deficiency Syndrome (AIDS) was nonexistent in 1973 when Section 504 was written, and this population was given protection against discrimination. The ADA also explicitly excludes certain groups who might otherwise be considered disabled, including individuals who use illegal drugs, transvestitism, exhibitionism, homosexuality, compulsive gambling, kleptomania, and pyromania.

The ADA is organized into five sections or Titles. Title I, the Employment Provision, prohibits discrimination because of disability in hiring, job training, promotion, and firing. Essentially, it requires employers with 15 or more workers to make reasonable accommodations for qualified job applicants with disabilities, if accommodation is not an undue hardship. Reasonable accommodations relate to a variety of changes such as physical modification of the workplace, part-time or modified work schedules, provision of amplification devices or computer equipment, modifying the job application process such as giving a job application exam orally, and providing readers or interpreters. The two disability categories of alcoholism and drug addiction were specifically excluded from Title I.

Title II, the Public Service Provision, is an extension of Section 504 of the 1973 Rehabilitation Act. It prohibits discrimination against individuals with disabilities in state and local government programs and activities, such as public housing or use of a library, and requires that individuals with disabilities have equal access to the services and benefits of public entities, including access to buildings, telephones, and bathrooms where services are provided. This Title also requires access to public transportation. All newly built buses used for public transportation, on fixed routes, must have wheel chair lifts. If accessible buses are not available, the city/state must offer an alternative. In addition, rail systems/subways must have at least one car per train that is accessible.

Title III, the Public Accommodation Provision, prohibits discrimination on the basis of disability in public establishments such as hotels, restaurants, theaters, lawyers' offices, auditoriums, laundromats, insurance offices, museums, parks, zoos, private schools, gymnasiums, day-care centers, banks, and health care centers. All structural barriers must be removed, and reasonable accommodations must be made. Examples of Title III accommodations are adding grab bars to bath tubs, lowering telephone booths and drinking fountains, adding raised letter and Braille markings on elevator controls, having Braille bank loan application forms, and using flashing alarm lights.

Title IV, the Telecommunications Provision, requires that access to telephone and radio communications must be provided at a reasonable cost to those with hearing or speech impairments. One option, a Telecommunication Device for the Deaf (TDD), is a device that uses a keyboard to transmit written messages over the telephone. Dual Party Telephone Relay Services that provide operator assistance must be available for use in relaying communications to third parties who use a conventional telephone. Telecommunication services must be comparable to the services that everyone else receives. For example, it should be available 24 hours a day with no limits on length or location of calls. ADA's Title V addresses procedural guidelines, litigation, and technical assistance for people with disabilities who wish to use the ADA to combat discrimination.

Because of numerous court cases seeking clarification of wording, the American Disability Act was amended in 2008. The amendments revised the definition of "disability" to more broadly encompass impairments that substantially limit a major life activity, specified that assistive devices, auxiliary aids, accommodations, medical therapies and supplies have no bearing in determining whether a disability qualifies under the law.

The 1992 Amendments to the Rehabilitation Act (PL 103-73) incorporated the values and philosophy of ADA. The amendments were perceived as an instrument to further the goals of ADA. The Amendments were crafted around the principles of consumer empowerment and involvement in the rehabilitation process. They stress respect for individual disability, personal responsibility, self-determination, and pursuit of meaningful careers, all within the context of informed choice. They reflect consumer concerns about the potential for power, disparity between counselor and consumer, and provide for demonstration projects that will increase consumer choice, including the possibility of consumers selecting their own providers of vocational rehabilitation service. The Act emphasizes the need for counselors to be partners with individuals with disabilities in encouraging their self-determination and full participation.

The 1992 Amendments increased consumer control and participation in determining policies and procedures of the delivery system. They established Rehabilitation and Independent Living Advisory Councils, consisting of a majority of people with disabilities who may address topics such as eligibility determination, prioritizing the consumers who are served first, and program evaluation. In response to Disability Movement concerns, the 1992 Amendments also modified the eligibility criteria for services by eliminating "feasibility." Feasibility had been the third requirement of the eligibility triad. For many years, eligibility was based upon the presence of the disability, a handicap to employment, and a reasonable expectation of being able to benefit from services, i.e., feasibility. It is obvious that the removal of the feasibility requirement was a significant change.

The 1992 Amendments also changed the term "handicapped" to the more acceptable term "disabled" throughout the Rehabilitation Act, and determined that all IPE plans were to be reviewed annually with involvement by consumers and/or their guardians. The 1992 Amendments also expanded support for the programs of transition from school to work services, on-the-job training, supported employment services, and continued support of research and development for rural areas, severe disability, personal care assistance, and underserved/minority groups.

The late 1990s exhibited somewhat conflicting concerns regarding the growing costs of disability and the need to enhance independence and employment outcomes for individuals with disabilities. These conflicting concerns, along with political pressures regarding high disability costs, provided the backdrop for the reauthorization of the Rehabilitation Act in 1998. In an effort to contain cost, or at least contain growth in public costs, federal legislators reauthorized the Act, not as separate legislation, but as a part of a larger piece of workforce reform legislation to consolidate and devolve multiple workforce and training programs to the states. Since its inception in 1920, the vocational rehabilitation legislation had been a separate and distinct law dedicated to service for people with disabilities.

For the first time in its history, the authorization of the Rehabilitation Act linked rehabilitation services with other "labor" programs in the Workforce Investment Act in the 1998 Amendments. The preamble to the 1998 Rehabilitation Act Amendments states that one purpose of the Act is "to empower individuals with disabilities to maximize employment, economic self-sufficiency, independence, and inclusion and integration into society." While rehabilitation maintained its employment intent, this language made a clear statement that the purpose of the state federal program is not just to assist with employment but also to have broader goals related to consumer self-sufficiency. The Amendments required state vocational rehabilitation agencies to collaboratively develop employment programs in "one-stop centers," in cooperation with the Department of Labor. The Amendments also changed the Individual Written Rehabilitation Plan (IWRP) to the Individual Plan of Employment (IPE). They also allow the counselor to expand informed choice by permitting the consumer to write his/her own plan, and self-employment and small business opportunities were added as vocational goals for consumers. A major reauthorization of the Rehabilitation Act has been deferred by Congress since 1998.

From 1998 to-date, the state federal vocational rehabilitation program has been addressing two major challenges. One of these is internal and related to the federal mandate to implement a Comprehensive System of Personnel Development (CSPD) and the other is external, the need to obtain employment opportunities for individuals with disabilities during one of the worst recessions of this last century.

In an effort to improve rehabilitation outcomes, the 1992 Rehabilitation Amendments provide an outline and the 1998 Amendments require the implementation of a Comprehensive System of Personnel Development (CSPD). CSPD requires that all staff be hired at or trained to the highest level of professional certification at the state or national level. It was written into the legislation as a consumer protection to insure that qualified rehabilitation specialists provide services to individuals with disabilities. In its implementation, CSPD first targeted rehabilitation counselors employed and hired within the state/federal vocational rehabilitation agency, with the standard for counselors predominantly being national certification as a Certified Rehabilitation Counselor (CRC). In 1998, 43% of the rehabilitation counselors employed within the state/federal vocational rehabilitation program did not meet this standard. Following major efforts initiated to provide rehabilitation counseling master's degree options to counselors, in 2002, 37% did not meet this CSPD standard.[10] Over the past nine years, some increases in the numbers of practicing master's level counselors within the state-federal vocational program have been reflected nationally; however, some state rehabilitation agencies opt out of using the CRC as a standard, and others use it but do not hire at this level of experience. The national challenge of CSPD provides hope for ensuring quality service to consumers and improved consumer outcomes are attained. The success of CSPD, however, will be measured in the future.

In April 2009, as part of the American Reinvestment and Recovery Act, Congress appropriated $540 million of new funding to the state federal vocational rehabilitation program. This one-time over twenty-five percent increase in funding was viewed as an unprecedented opportunity to improve employment outcomes to consumers. Utilizing these funds, states were able to activate numerous individuals off of the "wait" lists and initiate services. Most of these consumers are still in early stages of the vocational rehabilitation process with actual results of this increase in funding not determined.[8]

SUMMARY

As the debate continues over what constitutes appropriate public policy in terms of fiscal and social responsibility, rehabilitation legislation and programs will increasingly be pressured to demonstrate impact in terms of increases in the number of persons gainfully employed and decreases in the number relying on public subsidies due to disability. This pressure on the state/federal vocational rehabilitation program would appear to indicate that the program would not be supported with significant additional resources. Since its inception in 1920, the state federal vocational rehabilitation program has been funded at a level where only a small fraction, 1/20th, or fewer, of those needing the service could access it. The state federal vocational rehabilitation program currently serves just over a million individuals a year in a partnership with American Indian vocational rehabilitation programs. Employment outcomes are obtained for approximately half of these. This program now includes 80 agencies with vocational service programs in every state, the trust territories, and the District of Columbia.

The review of the history of rehabilitation in this chapter has described its evolution in our society from paternalism to empowerment. The field of disability and rehabilitation, as it exists in the United States today, has its roots in dozens of historical movements, events, organizations, academic disciplines, and professional fields. For example, advocacy groups in support of various disability groups existed from the nineteenth century. Rehabilitation, a term rarely used prior to World War I, evolved as a medically-based discipline in the early twentieth century primarily as a response to veterans who were disabled in wars. Federal vocational rehabilitation legislation for citizens in the United States followed as a logical consequence of providing such services to disabled World War I veterans. This early legislation was indeed paternalistic but has changed in recent decades to legislation supporting empowerment of individuals with disability.

The United States vocational rehabilitation effort represents a countrywide, consistent industry of service delivery. Collaborating with it are facilities within the private not-for-profit area. These facilities have developed a unique partnership with the state/federal program that has brought strength and stability to both facilities' and state agencies' efforts. The public, the private not-for-profit, and private rehabilitation programs have evolved and is reflected in the changing attitudes toward individuals with disabilities in our society. One obvious change in society's perception of individuals with disability can be documented in the language used to identify them. The late twentieth century references were to the "crippled," "idiotic," and "feebleminded." References in the early twentieth century continued to be specific to the disability, the "blind," the "deaf," the "mentally retarded," et cetera. Just after the mid twentieth century, references emphasized first the individual and then the disability, such as individuals with visual impairments. Late twentieth century popular references by society to the "physically challenged" underscore a greater public awareness and understanding of disability. Disability advocates will continue to influence how people describe and refer to people with disabilities. The recent disability movement's value of, and identity with, disability, will influence and determine new preferred references for individuals with disabilities.

Advocacy by people with disabilities began in the early nineteenth century, but its effectiveness was sporadic. Because of social, economic, and conceptual issues, self-advocacy groups of individuals with disabilities rarely worked cooperatively with one another. They often found themselves in open competition for scarce funding sources and public attention. What unity individuals with disabilities had was being defined socially and legally as "objects of charity" and, in a later period, as potential beneficiaries of medical and rehabilitation initiatives. Recent awareness and advocacy efforts among individuals with disabilities relate to a developing recognition that they have a right to participate openly and fairly in society. Advocates of the Disability Rights and the Independent Living Movements have fostered collaborative efforts in demanding civil rights as citizens rather than as recipients of charity, or patients, or consumers within medical or vocational treatment programs.

Significant legislative advantages such as the 1990 Americans with Disabilities Act, and the 1992 and 1998 Rehabilitation Act Amendments are evidence of these efforts. With emphasis on respect for individual dignity, personal responsibility, self-determination, informed choice, and inclusion, this legislation is truly empowering. The preamble to the Rehabilitation Act Amendments of 1998 states the one purpose of the Act is "to empower individuals with disabilities to maximize employment, economic self sufficiency, independence, and inclusion and integration into society."[4] This purpose, unfortunately, is not guaranteed in practice. Many older, disability related, national societies and professions have had to alter their perceptions to be in tune with this new thinking. Many of the thoughts behind empowerment are not new. What is new is the unity with which individuals with disabilities now expect equal treatment under the law, fair employment practices, equal access, and the right to accessible housing and transportation. This unity has resulted in individuals with disability having an impact on how rehabilitation services designed for them, must now be designed with them.

Service providers and consumers recognize the needs of the individual with a disability that must guide rehabilitation services in the state/federal program and in the private sector. What the future brings in relation to rehabilitation and rehabilitation counseling will be dependent, as was noted in the first paragraph of this chapter, on society's evolving perception and response to individuals with disabilities.

REFERENCES

[1]Buckland, K., McDaniel, A., Hughes, J., (2010). The struggle for independent living rights, pp.31-34, American Rehabilitation, Washington D.C.: Rehabilitation Services Administration.

[2]Commission on Recognition of Postsecondary Education (CORPA, (1995). The CORPA Handbook, Washington, DC: Author.

[3]Commission on Rehabilitation Counselor Certification, (2005). The Certified Rehabilitation Counselor (CRCC) Certification. Retrived January 11, 2005 from http://www.crcccertification.com.

[4]Council on Rehabilitation Education (CORE) (1996). Accreditation manual for rehabilitation education programs. Rolling Meadows, IL : Author.

[5]Groce, N. (1992). *The U.S. Role in International Disability Activities: A history and a look towards the future*. New York, NY: Rehabilitation International.

[6]Institute on Rehabilitation Issues. (1999). *Achieving Employment Outcomes Through VR Counselors Who Meet the Comprehensive System of Personnel Development Requirements.* Fayetteville, AR: University of Arkansas, Department of Rehabilitation, Human Resources and Communication Disorders, Region 6 Rehabilitation Continuing Education Center.

[7]Institute on Rehabilitation Issues. (2003). *Promoting Consumer Empowerment Through Professional Rehabilitation Counseling.* Report from the Study Group, 29th IRI, Hot Springs, AR: Region VI Rehabilitation Continuing Education Program.

[8]Martin, R., West-Evans, Connelly, J., (2010) Vocational Rehabilitation: Celebrating 90 years of careers and independence, pp.15-18, American Rehabilitation, Washington D.C.: Rehabilitation Services Administration.

[9]Obermann, C. E. (1965). A History of Vocational Rehabilitation in America. Minneapolis, MN: T. S. Denison.

[10]Rehabilitation Services Administration (RSA). (April, 2005). Employing the talents of Americans with disabilities: Results from business-vocational rehabilitation partnerships. Washington, D.C.: Author.
[11]Rusk, H. A. (1977) *A World to Care For.* New York: Random House.
[12]Sales, A. P. (1986). History of National Rehabilitation Association, Special Issue, *Journal of Rehabilitation*, July, August, September.
[13]Wolfensberger, W. (1972). The principle of normalization in human services. Toronto: National Institute of Mental Retardation.
[14]Wright, G. W. (1980). *Total Rehabilitation,* Boston: Little, Brown and Company.

PHILOSOPHY, SOCIAL POLICY, AND REHABILITATION

Paul Leung
University of North Texas

Chapter Topics

- Introduction
- Origins of our Philosophy
- American Rehabilitation: Current Context
- Philosophy and the Rehabilitation Process
- What About My Own Philosophy?
- Philosophy and Ethics
- Future Challenges of Philosophy

INTRODUCTION

Some of you may question why this book contains a chapter on philosophy when you just want to work with people who have disabilities. Maybe you chose rehabilitation so you did not have to take subjects such as philosophy. You may believe philosophy to be a bit esoteric and even boring for an active practical person such as yourself. You are not alone in your thinking.

For many who practice, or want to practice rehabilitation as a career, our first thoughts about philosophy are associated with Greek names such as Aristotle and Socrates, or with hard to pronounce names such as Sartre or Kierkegaard. These famous philosophers are far removed from those of us who are interested in the rehabilitation process. Indeed, philosophy seems to be about questions such as what is reality or how do we know what is real? Writings by Sartre are a bit esoteric. The answers to these questions are the stuff of philosophy and the subject matter for philosophy majors. There is, however, another side to philosophy and that is philosophy's influence and application in everyday life. We must understand this side of philosophy if we are to work effectively with people. Be aware that a bit of license is used in this chapter because strict definitions of philosophical terms have not been adhered to in the writing.

We all have a philosophy even though we may not always be able to articulate it completely. Self-help books, the media, and even our worship services confront us about our existing philosophies of life or about what our philosophies of life ought to be. Even when we may not be totally aware of what our philosophy is, it remains important because it has an influence on our day-to-day behavior. More accurately, our everyday actions reflect our philosophy. It is not a matter of whether a philosophy is right or wrong, but the more important question is whether a particular philosophy is appropriate for you and what you want to do. You may have chosen to study rehabilitation because you want to do something related to people with disabilities. If this is true, a philosophical viewpoint, or perspective, has brought you to where you are now. How we act, and what we want to do, is an indication of our philosophy. An awareness of our personal philosophy and its impact on our behavior is important if we want to be effective in what we do. Sometimes we may need to understand the philosophy (often unspoken or not articulated) of those we work with if we are to understand their perspective.

We can look at philosophy in several ways. We can view it from a personal perspective as well as from a broader societal perspective. The broader perspective is important because it has specific implications for how our society relates to its citizens. The broader view leads directly to our society's social policy, i.e. policies adopted by society and reinforced by legislation and regulations. Policy also determines the programs our government may or may not fund.

The second part in the title of this chapter relates to social policy because government drives many programs for persons with disabilities, such as the vocational rehabilitation program or the Social Security program. These programs reflect policies that are deemed important or significant by society. Social policy is the implementation of particular philosophical beliefs of a society in the same way that our behavior is often dependent on what we value or believe as individuals.

Personal philosophy consists of, among other things, what we believe and what we value. In turn, these determine how each of us behaves, and they may have an influence on what we choose to do. For example, we may have chosen to study rehabilitation because of what we believe and value. Personal philosophies are important in that they are the foundation of our daily activities as rehabilitation professionals.

This chapter will look at philosophy as it relates to rehabilitation from both a personal perspective as well as a programmatic or social policy perspective. It is important to note that as individuals, we are also influenced by the broader community's underlying philosophy. In other words, while the philosophical foundation of rehabilitation is not necessarily difficult to understand, the combination of factors related to a philosophy of rehabilitation is sometimes complex, convoluted, and even contradictory. Our philosophy as individuals can only be seen within a context. In addition, we may find that our individual philosophical beliefs are in conflict with those of the broader society or with the individuals with disabilities with whom we work. As rehabilitation professionals, we must understand what our own philosophies are and work through possible philosophical conflicts. Such conflicts may interfere with our clients achieving positive outcomes.

ORIGINS OF OUR PHILOSOPHY

Both personal and societal philosophies stem from origins that range from the mundane to the quixotic. These subtle influences on our philosophical perspectives may be difficult to discover. We are not always aware of the things that have influenced our particular philosophical outlook. Our parents and families are certainly a primary source for our philosophy. Race, gender, cultural background, religion, and the society in which we live are other influences that have shaped our thinking. Our educational experiences have helped mold our philosophies, as have personal experiences in our development to adulthood. Personal experiences, what we read, and who we interact with bring more factors into the equation. These influences may not be immediately apparent. It may take some time, reflection, and considerable thought to discover what they are and how important an influence they have been. It is not that this is a difficult process but it is a time consuming one.

Our collective societal philosophy has its probable beginnings in history with writers that we now call philosophers. These individuals were able to conceptualize and record how they and their communities struggled to identify who they were as human beings and what issues influenced them and their behavior. Many of their struggles mirror what we still go through as individuals and as communities. We can learn by reading and reflecting on the writings of those who lived before us. For those who profess to be Christian, the Bible may be a source book of their philosophy in the same way that the Koran is for Muslims or Buddhist writings are for those who are Buddhist. All of these may be considered religious writings, but they form the basis of philosophical beliefs and exert a considerable influence on what we do. For example, the Golden Rule, which suggests that we treat others as we wish to be treated, has its source in religious writing.

Individuals who do not consider themselves to be religious, or who do not believe in a God, hold equally valid perspectives that have philosophical roots. Some individuals who reject a more supernatural belief can still have profound faith in humankind. The relationship holds for philosophies even more removed from religion, such as those related to human services work and rehabilitation.

Philosophy is relevant for those of us interested in human beings, counseling, disability, and rehabilitation because it influences behavior. It is important to note that psychology has its origins in philosophy for the very reasons suggested in the previous paragraph. The Webster's dictionary[10] definition of philosophy is "a theory underlying or regarding a sphere of activity or thought," and theory is defined as the "general or abstract principles of a body of fact, a science, or art." Using these definitions, philosophy can be described as the *a priori* assumptions and beliefs about life, human beings, and the nature of human existence. Philosophy can thus be defined as how we view our relationships to others and ourselves.

It would be impossible in the space of a chapter to reiterate all of the different forms of philosophy. Philosophers divide their discipline into many different spheres such as moral philosophy or the philosophy of science. These various spheres of philosophy do have some relevance to rehabilitation although some have more than others do. Rather than attempt a comprehensive review of philosophical thought, this chapter will look at those aspects of philosophy that seem to have a direct bearing on rehabilitation, social policy, and the rehabilitation practitioner.

It is helpful and time efficient to look at some of the background and history that influence contemporary rehabilitation practice. Emener[3] traced the history of changes in philosophical thinking that have influenced rehabilitation in the United States. The following borrows and paraphrases a summary described by Rubin & Roessler.[6] Early Greek philosophers considered issues that have current relevance for rehabilitation. For example, the relationship between mind, body, and spirit has probably been an issue since the beginning of time. Rehabilitation's adoption of this holistic approach reflects the philosophical position that humans cannot be artificially divided into categories. Other philosophical beliefs influence how societies define disability. In earlier periods of history, persons who exhibited behavior different from that of the standards of the majority were accused of being possessed by demons. This is an example of a philosophy that has been rejected by the rehabilitation community in western society.

The Renaissance and Reformation eras ushered in a more humanistic and secularist philosophy where human beings were given a central place in the total scheme of things. This led to the belief in the 1800s that humans can change things for the better, but there was a dark side to this thinking. Eugenics was an attempt to improve society following the Darwinian notion that survival of the fittest bettered humankind. Any disability was considered a negative indicator and, therefore, persons with disabilities could be sacrificed for the greater good. Rehabilitation has accepted the idea that human beings can change things but has not accepted the notion that people with disabilities should be isolated or discarded. An important conclusion of this historical overview is that changing philosophical viewpoints affect how people with disabilities were treated over the centuries. Those who practice rehabilitation today have accepted some of these historical notions and have rejected others. One must remember that the philosophical ideas discussed in this paragraph are perspectives prevalent in western society and come from a generally European background. We can similarly trace philosophy and its effect on the societies of Africa or Asia. Eastern philosophical traditions occur within a context quite different, with an emphasis more in line with maintaining balance and harmony with natural forces rather than eliminating or "fixing" what appears to need correction.

AMERICAN REHABILITATION: CURRENT CONTEXT

American society has flourished and become a world power by using a market economy with a political structure composed of two primary political parties. These parties represent the extremes of a continuum of underlying philosophical differences between conservatism and liberalism.[4] The former espouses smaller government and less governmental intrusion in the lives of its citizens, and the latter promotes programs and interventions of government that attempt to equalize the playing field for those who are more vulnerable due to economic circumstance, race, and disability.

Market economies rest upon the fundamental principle of individual freedom that is a major philosophical principle held collectively in American society, as well as personally by many of us. As consumers, we are free to choose among competing products and services. As producers, we are free to start or expand a business and share its risks and rewards. If we are workers, we are free to join a labor union or change employers.

The current debate on whether rehabilitation consumers have the freedom to choose a rehabilitation provider is more directly related to rehabilitation. A prime example is Social Security disability reform and the "ticket to work" program where consumers ostensibly can use their "ticket" to purchase rehabilitation services.[8] While this is a concrete example of what is happening today, the debate itself reflects two philosophical perspectives.

Even in a market driven economy there is recognition that some people may not have the skills or the resources to earn a living. Most governments, including the United States, engage in programs or policies that attempt to redistribute income more fairly within the population. American tax policy reflects this attempt, as do our welfare programs. Yet, what is considered a fair distribution is dependent on one's philosophy.

Proponents of extensive redistribution argue that the role of government is to limit the concentration of wealth. They believe in a wider diffusion of economic power among more households. Just as antitrust laws are designed to maintain competition and provide a wider diffusion of power and resources among producers, proponents of redistribution believe there is a need for policies that provide a better distribution to those with greater barriers to their participation. On the other hand, opponents of redistribution income programs counter that additional taxes on high-income families decrease the incentives of these groups to work, save, and invest, to the detriment of the overall economy and eventually to all citizens. This has been called a "trickle down" philosophy.

Rehabilitation policy and the government's response to disability are a bit more complex. These opposing philosophical viewpoints and the attempt to create a policy consensus have created some very real difficulties in implementing programs. The reality is often a system in conflict with itself that results in some government programs providing cash and others providing services.[1] Though there has been some change, the United States has put into place a system in which "income maintenance continues to predominate over rehabilitation in disability policy."[1, p.163]

In spite of this, Berkowitz concludes that for all of its dilemmas and missed opportunities; the public vocational rehabilitation program "still stands as the major 'corrective' American disability program."[p.183] It is important to note that the philosophy of the public vocational rehabilitation program is also the foundation of private sector rehabilitation programs. The differences between the programs are not in the rehabilitation process, but in who is responsible for providing rehabilitation. While rehabilitation programs in general, and vocational rehabilitation in particular, are arguably not income redistribution programs, rehabilitation is an attempt to "even the playing field" by allowing persons with disabilities to be able to compete with their non-disabled peers.[6, p.172] The hoped for outcomes of public vocational rehabilitation policies are self-sufficiency and the regained capacity to contribute to society. This last sentence is grounded in mainstream American philosophical belief and has been used to justify the rehabilitation process.

PHILOSOPHY AND THE REHABILITATION PROCESS

Rehabilitation philosophy includes general principles that make up what we know as rehabilitation and the rehabilitation process. In reality, rehabilitation philosophy is more complex than is superficially apparent. One reason is that rehabilitation involves so many different disciplines, arenas, or domains. For example, rehabilitation has its roots in the medical professions because disability is often the result of injury, disease, or faulty developmental processes. Physicians who specialize in rehabilitation medicine, known as physiatrists, are a subset of the broader practice of medicine.

There are rehabilitation professionals in allied health professions, such as occupational therapists or physical therapists, who also subscribe to the medical model. Rehabilitation counseling has roots in counseling and psychology. Finally, the process of rehabilitation is often seen as an educational function where an individual is taught to cope and adapt to disability. Each of these disciplines has a philosophical orientation that determines what is considered important for that domain. Each orientation has an influence on what is done as part of the rehabilitation process. The programs that are offered in vocational rehabilitation, such as counseling or evaluation, are based in part on these assumptions or philosophies. The philosophical underpinning may be as general as the idea that human beings can learn and have abilities, or the idea that work is good. Other philosophical beliefs are more specific in that every individual, whether or not they have a disability, should be able to choose what they want to accomplish rather than having their goals dictated to them.

Beneath these specific philosophical ideas are some general principles accepted as significant by a majority of Americans. Some examples are independence, self-sufficiency, work, physical beauty, and certain types of valued behaviors.[7] The work ethic and self-sufficiency are particularly important, and it is reflected in subtle ways. Americans often work longer hours and have fewer vacations than the people of many other nations in the world. Because Americans value work so highly, rehabilitation within a vocational context is the cornerstone of our rehabilitation social policy. Still other philosophical beliefs relate to cultural values such as independence, which is the ability of individuals to define what they want.

In addition to these primary philosophical principles, rehabilitation in the United States has evolved through efforts of persons who have disabilities. Many disabled persons advocated for a philosophy that includes and integrates people regardless of disabling conditions. The roots of this philosophical idea of the integration of persons with disabilities into all levels of society are found in the minority model borrowed from the American civil rights movement. This model was developed by persons of African American descent in their fight against discrimination.

Rehabilitation has essentially adopted the philosophy that whenever possible, persons with disabilities will be integrated into the least restrictive environments. In other words, an individual with a disability is assumed to have the capacity to function, and rehabilitation is seen as a process that identifies the environment of best fit. Inherent in this philosophy is a commitment to equalize opportunities so persons with disabilities are able to participate with all the rights and privileges available to all citizens. Accommodations provide equal access to opportunity. There is a corollary commitment to support persons with disabilities in advocacy activities in order to enable them to achieve full status and thus empower themselves. This philosophical base, translated into practice, has become the process of rehabilitation.

American government policy is driven by an "ideologically determined view of the public good."[4, p.12] Rehabilitation philosophy in the United States reflects that ideology along with tensions inherent with the American work ethic and our notion of justice. For nearly a century, Congress has continuously funded the vocational rehabilitation program. This commitment reflects the philosophy that persons with disabilities need not be dependent but can be contributing members of society. Employment figures indicate high unemployment rates among persons with disabilities, which suggest that these persons may not be able to perform work as well as their non-disabled counterparts.

In 1970, Bitter[2] summarized three primary principles that provide a philosophical base for rehabilitation. They were equality of opportunity, the holistic nature of the person, and the uniqueness of every individual. Equality of opportunity is defined as the justice component, which recognizes that all persons, regardless of their gender, race, sexual preference, or disability, have the same rights as do all other citizens in a democratic society. Legislation guarantees these non-discrimination rights and forms the basis for the rehabilitation process. Rehabilitation is a means to allow persons with disabilities to participate in the larger community.

Bitter's second principle relates to the perspective that human beings must be viewed holistically. The artificial divisions of mind and body are a disservice to and distract from the rehabilitation process. Rehabilitation must attend to the whole person to be effective. Veterans Administration physician Dr. Herbert Talbot expressed this perspective in 1961. He wrote that rehabilitation is "a state of being to which one aspires" and "a way of life."[9, p.358] Even vocational rehabilitation, which emphasizes employment, suggests the need to attend to full integration and participation in a community.

The third principle identified by Bitter has been interpreted in different ways in the literature. The principle is that each individual is unique. Beatrice Wright, a pioneer in rehabilitation psychology has spent a career reiterating a set of "value laden" principles that have applicability to persons with disability. These principles reflect this individualistic approach within rehabilitation.

Wright[11] presented 20 principles in a revision of her classic 1960 book, *Physical Disability-A Psychological Approach.* Five are reprinted here as illustrative of this individualistic approach.

- Every individual needs respect and encouragement; the presence of a disability, no matter how severe, does not alter these fundamental rights.
- The assets of the person must receive considerable attention in the rehabilitation effort.
- The significance of a disability is affected by the person's feelings about the self and his or her situation.
- The active participation of the client in the planning and execution of the rehabilitation program is to be sought as fully as possible.
- Because each person has unique characteristics and each situation its own properties, variability is required in rehabilitation plans.

What do these five principles say to a rehabilitation practitioner aside from the need to pay attention to the person first and foremost? The following discussion is an attempt to place rehabilitation's time-honored ideas within a philosophical context. You may or may not agree with the analysis but the important point is to explore fundamental issues underlying ways to approach clients or consumers. It is possible to put a practical matter into words that have a philosophical definition.

In a philosophical sense, Wright's five principles are grounded in phenomenology and existentialism. Phenomenology has been called the description and study of appearances. The term has come to be associated with emphasizing human experience. Phenomenology recognizes the problem of accessing the external world through our perceptions. The five principles also reflect a philosophical stance known more formally as existentialism. In simple terms, existentialism is concerned with the "here and now," (i.e. the present). It does not mean that history is meaningless or that it has no effect on an individual. Existentialism emphasizes what is happening right now. Therefore, every individual has the means to choose what happens and in so doing, discovers what is beneficial for self.

Kierkegaard was one of the first persons to call himself an existentialist. He challenged the universal concept of "good" which Plato suggested is the same for everyone and substituted the concept that one had to discover a personal definition of good. Kierkegaard said that "the most tremendous thing which has been granted to man is: the choice, freedom." The French philosopher Sartre carried this notion to the next step. He wrote that existence precedes essence, therefore, people are responsible for who they are. Awareness of self implies that the responsibility of existence is up to the individual. Emener[3] wrote that while Kierkegaard suggested the individual has the responsibility for defining both self-identity and personal potential, Sartre stated that the ultimate responsibility for doing this rests with the individual. In this philosophical context, the role of the counselor in rehabilitation settings is to assist the client in finding self across all of the domains of the rehabilitation process.

Another philosophical idea that bears some discussion is logical positivism as the foundation for how we obtain knowledge. This concept serves as the basis of the scientific method. The two sources of knowledge recognized within logical positivism are logical reasoning and empirical experience. A thorough description of logical positivism is beyond the scope of this chapter, but it is important to remember that these two sources of knowledge form the cornerstone of the majority of scientific research, including that done in rehabilitation. Logical positivism is the underlying philosophical perspective on which we base our actions and interventions as rehabilitation practitioners.

We digressed from the discussion of Bitter's primary principles to introduce some formal philosophical perspectives to describe how philosophy may be used within rehabilitation. There are different ways to explore the rehabilitation process. Martin and Gandy[5] interpreted Bitter's third principle in a slightly different way. They interpret this principle to reflect the American value of succeeding against hardship and adversity, commonly referred to as "rugged individualism." Putting this interpretation into practice can be problematic. Too often rehabilitation practitioners who have experienced adverse situations believe that rehabilitation clients must also go through difficulty to be able to learn and to cope with reality. While there is no research that suggests this to be true, being overly protective, and not allowing a client to fail may be detrimental. What you decide to do when faced with such a situation reflects your philosophical stance. Because this point of view is inherently an American philosophical view, it is important that we realize we may carry this bias and may inadvertently impose it in our practice.

Persons with disabilities have had a major influence on rehabilitation philosophy. Contemporary rehabilitation philosophy has gone through several paradigm shifts during the past half century. These shifts reflect changes in society's beliefs about disabling conditions, and about persons with disabilities. For example, rehabilitation has moved from a purely individual problem-solving approach to an ecological approach. The emphasis is no longer on changing only the individual, but now also includes removing environmental barriers. The medical model, with its emphasis on illness and pathology, is no longer the only focus of our profession. We now incorporate the movement toward integrated community-supported living and independent living models in rehabilitation. This new stance of rehabilitation advocates for consumer choice and empowerment, and full consideration must be given to the individual's right to fail as one potential outcome involved with choice, growth, and risk. The current philosophy of rehabilitation embraces a person's right to choose his or her relationships and goals, both personal and vocational.

These contemporary philosophical foundations have their roots in a changing society. Rehabilitation in the United States has evolved from a variety of perspectives,[7, 3] and will continue to do so. From an isolationist and separation stance, to social Darwinism, rehabilitation in America has moved toward an integrated and inclusive approach. Rehabilitation has generally adopted a philosophical perspective reflecting the societal context in which rehabilitation occurs. Whether this is positive or negative is open to discussion. The last section of this chapter will take a brief look at changes that may take place in the near future. In preparation for this, let us explore where we are as individuals.

WHAT ABOUT MY OWN PHILOSOPHY?

Crucial to the practice of rehabilitation on the personal operational level is an examination of our own philosophies and beliefs. If one of our beliefs is that work is healthy and to be encouraged, we are more likely to be optimistic and enthusiastic in working with disabled persons who seek employment. If our philosophy of rehabilitation is holistic rather than involved only with developing physical capacities, we may encourage utilization of a variety of approaches involving a diversity of activities. Our philosophy is a determining factor in what we set out to do.

Current rehabilitation philosophy, with its emphasis on individualism, is a reflection on the existential philosophy perspective that came to fruition during the late nineteenth and early twentieth century. This philosophy permeates American life. This position may be present, consciously or unconsciously, and can have a great influence on the clinical practice of rehabilitation practitioners. Some have argued that the inordinate influence of the clinical model may be outdated. Many of us have been trained and educated in this model of rehabilitation. It has been dominant in both the public and private sectors, and has served rehabilitation and persons with disabilities well.

Vocational rehabilitation policy has accepted that employment, or what one economically contributes to society, is important. This is further reinforced by the western societal perspective that our identity is closely tied to what we do for a living. The driving assumption of this philosophy can be seen in the traditional arguments of the importance of a vocational rehabilitation program in the United States. Vocational rehabilitation enables persons who have disabilities to become contributing members of society. They become citizens who pay taxes in excess of the costs of their rehabilitation, and they no longer draw welfare.

There is a need to understand the political philosophical ramification of our rehabilitation practice in addition to one's personal perspective. We do not practice in a vacuum, and both practitioner and clients are affected and influenced by what is happening in society. For individuals who practice or plan to practice rehabilitation, our philosophy comes from both our own experience and our understanding of the broader collective societal philosophy.

An excellent example of changing philosophical perspective in rehabilitation is the evolution of the independent living movement. The notion of independence is a particularly Western notion. Persons from an Eastern or Asian tradition may interpret independence differently. These differences may become barriers to participation by clients who have differing philosophical or cultural perspectives. The philosophy of the independent living movement is the belief that each person with a disability is unique and has the same civil rights as persons who do not have a disability. Independent living advocates have articulated their philosophy in the following statements:

- People with disabilities should be able to live, work, shop and play where they choose within the community.
- In order for people with disabilities to live in the community instead of a hospital environment, the community has a responsibility to be accessible.
- Expecting equal access to social, economic, and political opportunities for people with disabilities can be compared to expecting equal access for ethnic minorities.
- People with disabilities are not sick. A person with a disability may become ill, but disability is not always an illness.
- People with disabilities should not be in a hospital environment, unless they are sick and in need of acute medical care.
- People with disabilities have the same aspirations as people who do not have disabilities.
- People with disabilities do not wish to be described as "very brave" when they are successful, nor do they seek pity in the manner of the "poster child" image.
- People with disabilities know best what their barriers to independence are, what they need in order to live independently, and should have a say in what happens in their community that affects them.

PHILOSOPHY AND ETHICS

While ethics and rehabilitation are covered elsewhere in another chapter, it is helpful to remind ourselves that ethics are a part of the philosophical inquiry or moral philosophy as it is traditionally called. The judging of whether something is considered "right" behavior or "wrong" behavior comes from the values important to an individual or group and so, is inherent to philosophy as a field of study.

Ethics have often been categorized as metaethics, normative, and applied. Normative ethics as implied by the term involves the setting of standards. Metaethics is an attempt to explore the larger picture and the nature of ethical theory. Applied ethics involves the application of ethics to practical issues. Rehabilitation counseling and other human service ethical codes would be considered under the rubric of applied ethics.

FUTURE CHALLENGES OF PHILOSOPHY

It is hoped that you are considering the importance of philosophy as you finish reading this chapter. You may have begun to reflect and to think about your philosophy as a rehabilitation services practitioner. Perhaps you have gained a sense of the philosophy behind rehabilitation, and the impact it has had in framing what is an acceptable result of the rehabilitation process.

As we look ahead, there will continue to be philosophical issues that will impact each one of us, and our society. Questions are continually raised regarding the responsibilities and roles of rehabilitation and rehabilitation practitioners in a world where national boundaries are less restrictive. What will be our role as the world becomes effectively smaller and smaller? It is already as easy to communicate with someone in another continent as it is to someone across town. Economic barriers are decreasing, and nations are becoming increasingly connected. What occurs overseas impacts us immediately. There are new issues related to who will drive the philosophical assumptions inherent to rehabilitation practice. Will insurance carriers, health maintenance organizations, legislators, or persons with disabilities dictate what interventions are acceptable and what will be our philosophical base?

The answers to these questions will raise further questions. Perhaps the philosophy that has brought us to this point may not be sufficient to carry us further into the future. Will we need new ways of thinking about what we do? Will we need new philosophical perspectives? Will we go back to history and past traditions? As individuals, and as part of a global society, we may need to rethink and explore anew what philosophies will drive the profession. Yes, it is a challenge, but it is also an exciting possibility that awaits your input.

REFERENCES

[1]Berkowitz, E. D. (1989). *Disabled Policy.* Cambridge: Cambridge University Press.

[2]Bitter, J. A. (1970). *Introduction to Rehabilitation.* St. Louis: C. V. Mosby.

[3]Emener, W. G. (1997). Paradigms of practice: theory and philosophies in Maki, D. & Riggar, T. F. (Eds.), (1977). *Rehabilitation Counseling.* New York: Springer.

[4]Karger, H. J. & Stoesz, D. (2002). *American Social Welfare Policy: A Pluralistic Approach.* Boston: Allyn & Bacon.

[5]Martin, E. D. & Gandy, G. L. "Philosophical and educational considerations of the rehabilitation process" in G. L. Gandy, E. D. Martin, R. E. Hardy, & J. G. Cull (Eds.), (1987). *Rehabilitation Counseling and Services.* Springfield, IL: C. C. Thomas.

[6]Rubin, S. & Roessler, R. T. (2001). *Foundations of the Vocational Rehabilitation Process* (*4th* ed.). Austin, TX: Pro-Ed.

[7]Rubin, S. & Roessler, R. T. (2001). *Foundations of the Vocational Rehabilitation Process* (5th ed.). Austin, TX: Pro-Ed.

[8]Social Security Administration (2011). Social Security Online. Retrieved from http://www.socialsecurity.gov/work/aboutticket.html

[9]Talbot, H. S. (1961). "A Concept of Rehabilitation" *Rehabilitation Literature 22*(12) 358-364.

[10]*Websters New Collegiate Dictionary* (1975). Springfield, IL: G. & C. Merriam Co.

[11]Wright, B. A. (1983). *Physical Disabili – A Psychosocial Approach* (2nd ed.) New York: Harper and Row.

STATE/FEDERAL VOCATIONAL REHABILITATION PROGRAM

RONALD J. SPITZNAGEL

UNIVERSITY OF FLORIDA

CHAPTER TOPICS

- Introduction
- State/Federal Program Defined
- Programs
- The Vocational Rehabilitation Process
- Goals and Objectives of State/Federal Rehabilitation Program
- State Vocational Rehabilitation Agencies
- Summary
- Suggested Readings

INTRODUCTION

Stretching back into past millennia, individuals who experienced physical, mental, and/or emotional problems have always been a part of society. There is ample evidence from literature and history to document the presence of people with disabilities across a diversity of cultures. The manner in which these persons were helped or discriminated against has varied over the centuries and in the areas of the world in which they lived. The picture certainly is not a pretty one. At one time or another, in every part of the planet, discrimination has existed against persons with disabilities.

Persons with obvious physical problems were sometimes placed in segregated areas away from the general population, e.g., lepers, as far back as the time of Christ. Babies born with abnormalities were carted off to the garbage heap outside the city and left to die in the city-state of Sparta. Wealthy individuals who incurred a disability were given much better treatment. Nonetheless, as documented in Roman history, they were treated as pariahs rather than as persons who needed assistance. Church groups in the Middle Ages opened hospitals catering to people with physical disabilities. Limited funds, the mentality of the times, and inexact knowledge of handicapping conditions created a sparse and frugal atmosphere for the dispensing of proper treatment and care. Mental institutions were places to leave unwanted or hard-to-care-for relatives and friends to live out their lives in squalid lock-up. Institutions designed for specific handicaps, such as deafness, blindness, and mental retardation, were operated well into the latter part of the twentieth century.

Approximately eighty years ago, a somewhat novel concept was considered. The legislative body of the United States discussed several pieces of legislation that would ultimately change the manner in which persons with disabilities would be assisted in their pursuit of independent living. The first of a number of bills to be deliberated by Congress was passed and subsequently signed into law on June 20, 1921. The Smith-Fess Act can be directly linked to the legislation from which the State/Federal Vocational Rehabilitation Program was ultimately developed. From these small beginnings, a vast complex arose that has become a beacon of hope in all fifty states and territories that comprise the United States of America. This program has become a rallying point for all persons with disabilities as a place where services are offered to assist the individual with a disability to obtain a more ordered life, whether it is for independent living or competitive employment.

STATE/FEDERAL PROGRAM DEFINED

This program has evolved over the past eighty years as one that authorizes the allocation of federal funds on the basis of a specific formula for the administration and operation of a vocational rehabilitation program to assist individuals with disabilities in preparing for, and engaging in, gainful employment. The U.S. Congress has established the Rehabilitation Services Administration as the principal federal agency authorized to carry out the various acts and other legislation that Congress enacts and which the President signs into law. The current State/Federal program is authorized under the Rehabilitation Act of 1973 and subsequent amendments to that act. In addition, the State/Federal program is also impacted by other legislation including the Randolph-Sheppard Act and its amendments and the Helen Keller National Center for the Deaf-Blind Youth and Adults Act. The Rehabilitation Services Administration (RSA) is currently housed in the Office of Special Education and Rehabilitative Services in the Department of Education. A Commissioner appointed by the President of the United States is the primary authority and oversees the RSA in all its aspects. This individual reports to the Assistant Secretary for the Office of Special Education and Rehabilitative Services (OSERS). The Rehabilitation Services Administration (RSA) is comprised of two divisions: State Monitoring and Program Improvement Division (SMPID) and Training and Service Programs Division (TSPD). In addition, the office of the commissioner provides leadership and direction to one staff office: Program Support Staff (PSS).

The State Monitoring and Program Improvement Division that has supplanted the Regional Offices, carries out major activities related to the following programs:

- Basic Vocational Rehabilitation State Grants
- Supported Employment State Grants
- Independent Living State Grants
- Centers for Independent Living (CIL) Discretionary Program
- Independent Living Services for Older Individuals Who Are Blind
- Client Assistance Program (CAP)
- Protection and Advocacy of Individual Rights (PAIR)
- Protection and Advocacy for Assistive Technology Program (PAAT)
- Program Improvement
- Evaluation

The SMPID conducts state plan reviews for approval. It also monitors RSA formula grant programs to establish adherence with federal requirements. The administration of three advocacy programs is housed in this division: the Client Assistance Program, the Protection and Advocacy of Individual Rights Program, and the Protection and Advocacy for Assistive Technology Program. The division also includes one discretionary grant program, the Centers for Independent Living Discretionary Program. The SMPID is divided into functional units and state teams. Each person in the division participates on both. The functional units carry out activities that enable the state teams to monitor and assist states to improve their programs. For more information about functional units and state teams, please go to the following web site: http://www.ed.gov/about/offices/list/osers/rsa/smpid.html.

RSA provides leadership, administration, and coordination of the state programs, formula grant programs, various service projects, and a number of rehabilitation training discretionary grant programs. These programs have been developed to implement the comprehensive programs of vocational rehabilitation, including supported employment and independent living for persons with disabilities. This takes place through a coordinated system of services, training programs, research, and economic opportunities designed to maximize the potential of people with disabilities in becoming employed, independent, and fully integrated into the community and the workplace.

RSA oversees the Vocational Rehabilitation (VR) program that currently has more than 1.2 million individuals eligible for services. Of these, over 80% have a significant disability. These persons would be classed as "severely disabled." According to the most recent amendments to the Rehabilitation Act, priority for services is given to these individuals. In order to be eligible for VR services, a person must have a physical, mental, and/or emotional impairment that is deemed a substantial impediment to employment, be able to benefit from VR services in terms of employment, and require VR services to prepare for, enter into, or retain employment. The State VR agencies assist persons with disabilities to locate employment by developing and maintaining close relationships with employers and a broad range of service providers. Persons who benefit from this program become tax-paying citizens and, ultimately, reduce or eliminate their reliance on other entitlement programs in the governmental system.

For all of the above to take place, the State VR agency has to provide rehabilitation services that are comprehensive in scope and expand upon those found in general training efforts. Some of these comprehensive services include vocational evaluation, assistive technology assessment (accommodations and modifications at the work site), career counseling services, and a wide variety of medical and therapeutic services. With these services and others, nine million persons with disabilities have been assisted in obtaining employment since the inception of the VR program in 1921. In 2012, more than 180,000 persons with disabilities (91% with significant disabilities) have entered or returned to the competitive labor market. Approximately 74% of those who obtain employment each year indicate that their income is the primary source of support for them and their families. The cost of the VR basic state grants program was $3,231,000,000 for fiscal year (FY) 2013. The President's budget request for fiscal year 2014 was slightly higher at $3,302,100,000. In addition to these funds for the basic state programs, there are many other funds for specific programs like the Client Assistance Program ($12,200,000), Training ($30,200,000), or institutions such as Gallaudet University ($207,400,000).

BASIS FOR THE SYSTEM

The RSA Commissioner has organized an efficient and effective manner in which to administer the funds and oversee that the mandates of the laws are being followed. In place are planning, policies, and evaluation staff, as well as the financial management and information systems staff needed to fulfill these responsibilities. Two distinct units fall under this latter staff grouping, i.e., budget and financial operations, and data management. To direct specific elements of the program, several divisions have been established. These divisions are Program Administration, Blind and Visually Impaired, Resource Development, and Special Projects. At the state level, each state has developed its own organizational chart.

The Office of the Commissioner has been designed to provide the executive leadership to the Rehabilitation Services Administration. The Commissioner is to establish realistic goals and objectives for assisting persons with disabilities. Part of this effort would be to develop proper standards, criteria, guidelines, policies, and regulations to provide direction in the administration of the variety of programs offered through RSA. This office is a conduit to the Office of Special Education and Rehabilitative Services' Assistant Secretary regarding problems affecting the eligibility of individuals for the program and advocating for the rights and needs of those eligible for services through the program at the state level. Reports and analyses of outcomes are normal activities for the office, as well as program oversight and development activities. Publications such as *American Rehabilitation* are produced periodically to educate and inform the general population about the program in general and specific disabilities in particular.

A special function of the Office of the Commissioner is to work closely with the National Council on Disabilities on issues directly related to Section 400 of the Rehabilitation Act of 1973. The office also is advised to coordinate with the Equal Employment Opportunity Commission on compliance with Section 501 of the same Act, with the Architectural and Transportation Barriers Compliance Board on Section 502, with the Department of Labor on Section 503, with both the Civil Rights Division and the Department of Justice on Section 504, with the Interagency Coordinating Council on Section 507, and with the General Services Administration on Section 508 – all of the same Act. Besides the office coordination efforts, the Office of the Commissioner will respond to various inquiries and problems that ordinarily arise in such a large national undertaking; will maintain relations with numerous organizations that represent persons with disabilities; will continue to evaluate and consider suggestions regarding RSA programs, projects and so on; and most definitely will be cognizant of the current situation and recognize the need for new and additional programs to upgrade the services offered to persons with disabilities through the state programs.

The focus of this chapter is the state/federal program of vocational rehabilitation. The division in the RSA that most closely identifies with that is the Program Administration Division (PAD). According to the organizational chart, the PAD administers the State Vocational Rehabilitation Program, Client Assistance Program, Protection and Advocacy of Individual Rights Program, American Indian Vocational Rehabilitation Service Projects, and the State Supported Employment Program. In addition to oversight of the above programs, this division is also committed to developing policies that affect Community Rehabilitation Programs, implementing initiatives regarding deafness and communicative disorders, providing guidance regarding RSA formula grants monitoring systems, handling audit management functions, acting as liaison to such institutes and agencies as the Social Security Administration, Institute on Rehabilitation Issues, National Occupational Information Coordinating Committee, the Council of State Administrators of Vocational Rehabilitation, and the Department of Labor. Two units have been designated to provide leadership, one to the states and the other to the deafness and communicative disorders community.

STATE PLAN

In order for a State to participate in the State Vocational Rehabilitation Services Program authorized under Title I of the Rehabilitation Act of 1973 and its subsequent amendments, it must have an approved Title I State Plan and a Title VI, part B supplement to the Title I plan.

The Title I State Plan and its companion supplement reflect the state's commitment to administer these two formula grant programs in compliance with the provisions of the plan and its supplement, including the Federal statutory, regulatory, and policy requirements. This plan outlines and describes in detail the state's activities on various administrative and operational levels connected with these programs. This plan is the chief tool employed by RSA to monitor a State's use of the allotted Federal funds. The procedures for writing the State plan are complex and will not be dealt with here. Imbedded in the plan are assurances that the state will follow all rules and regulations not only encased in the laws, but also the rules and regulations of the Rehabilitation Services Administration, the Office of Special Education and Rehabilitative Services, and the Department of Education.

An integral part of writing the State Plan is to conduct public meetings throughout the state with adequate notice of these meetings. These meeting are designed to provide ample opportunity for the public in general, and for persons with disabilities in particular, to provide input into the writing of the plan. Other entities may need to be consulted, such as Native American tribal organizations, and Native Hawaiian organizations.

A draft State Plan is submitted to RSA for its review. Potential problems can be resolved at this level before the actual submission of the official State Plan and its associated materials. Some states require that a state oversight committee review the draft. In this case, this step should be taken prior to the draft being sent to RSA. Submission dates are established and must be strictly adhered to, in order to ensure the flow of money to the states from one year to the next. A complication with the process is the fact that the Workforce Investment Act (WIA) also requires states to prepare and submit a plan. A state can develop a unified State Plan with the VR Services and WIA combined, or the state can write two separate plans. In any case, both plans are due at the same time. Provisions are made for sending electronic copies. However, an original hardcopy is necessary.

During the course of the plan's timeline, amendments can be made due to circumstances that arise in state policy or in federal law. States can amend the plan if a significant and relevant change will occur, such as a change in the administration or operation of the plan, change in assurances, and/or change in the organization, policies, or operations of the state agency that receives funds under the plan and/or supplement.

SELECTED COMPONENTS OF THE PLAN

The Rehabilitation Act Amendments of 1998 significantly modified the designated state agency provision or stipulation. Previous to this, the regulations were rather strict and confining. Now the State has the flexibility to locate the designated State Vocational Rehabilitation agency wherever it chooses within the state's organizational chart. If the state's structure places the agency in an entity that is not vocational rehabilitation oriented, the state must still have a designated vocational rehabilitation bureau, division, or other named organization unit that is primarily devoted to the provision of vocational rehabilitation services to persons with disabilities. This entity or unit is responsible for administering the program as described in the State Plan. It must have a full-time state director with appropriate staff to coordinate the allocation of funds and the provision of services. If this unit is within another agency or unit, the organizational make-up should be comparable to the other parts of the agency or unit.

It is strongly suggested that each state have State Rehabilitation Councils. Their purpose is to provide input to the agency. The Council provides recommendations to the state on such topics as analysis of consumer satisfaction, review of various reports, and so on. There is a mechanism in place for providing reasons why the recommendations of the Council are not followed.

Local administration is addressed specifically and in some detail in the rules and regulations of RSA. In general, the state can designate local agencies to administer the provisions of the State Plan for a designated area with the state. There is a requirement that if local agencies are used, these agencies are subject to the supervision of the state unit. This means that the state unit is responsible for the actions taken by the local agencies. However, the rules and regulations do not require day-to-day supervision.

In general, the State Plan is to be in effect in all political subdivisions of the state. However, this provision can be relaxed. A state can increase or expand the scope of services that are available in one or more political subdivisions if

- non-federal share of the cost of the services is met from funds provided by a local public agency, including funds contributed to a local public agency by a private agency, organization, or individual,
- services are likely to promote vocational rehabilitation of substantially larger numbers of individuals with disabilities or of individuals with disabilities with particular impairments, and
- the state includes in its State Plan, and the Secretary approves, a request for a waiver of the statewide requirement. If a state does request this waiver, the State Plan must
  1. identify the types of services to be provided,
  2. contain a written assurance from the local public agency that it will make available to the state unit the non-federal share of funds,
  3. contain written assurance that state unit approval will be obtained for each proposed service before it is put into effect, and
  4. contain a written assurance that all other State Plan requirements, including a state's order of selection, will apply to all services provided under the waiver.

RSA authorizes joint programs in which the designated State Vocational Rehabilitation agency shares its programmatic and fiscal responsibilities and control with another agency. The focus of a joint program should be on better coordination of existing services through the mechanism of shared funding and administration, rather than the expansion of services or introduction of new approaches. If the state chooses this option of joint program, it must meet the following requirements:

- describe the nature and scope of the joint program,
- enumerate the services to be provided,
- detail the respective roles of each participating agency in the provision of services and in their administration, and
- indicate the share of the costs to be assumed by each agency.

Third-party cooperative agreements are recognized by RSA as a potential need and, therefore, appropriate for inclusion in the State Plan. The state unit can enter into agreements with another agency to provide or administer vocational rehabilitation services. These agencies could furnish part or the entire federal match. In signing agreements of this type, the state unit must retain administrative responsibility for third party agreements. The state must make the following final assurances before any third-party agreement can take effect:

- Services provided by the cooperating agency are not customary or typical services provided by that agency but are new services that have a vocational rehabilitation focus or are existing services that have been modified, adapted, expanded, or reconfigured to have a vocational rehabilitation focus.
- Services provided by the cooperating agency are only available to applicants for, or eligible recipients of, services from the designated state vocational rehabilitation unit.
- Program expenditures and staff providing services under the cooperative arrangement are under the administrative supervision of the designated state vocational rehabilitation unit.
- All State Plan requirements, including a state's order of selection, apply to all services provided under the cooperative program.

The State Plan must include that the designated state vocational rehabilitation agency has cooperative agreements with other entities that are components of the statewide workforce investment system. These also need to be replicated at the local level between individual offices of the designated state unit. These mechanisms are to be in place to ensure effective communication, collaboration, coordination, and cooperation between the vocational rehabilitation program and its partners in the statewide workforce investment system.

A comprehensive system of personnel development (CSPD) is also required as an integral part of the State Plan. This is to ensure an adequate supply of qualified rehabilitation professionals and paraprofessionals to provide consistent services to persons with disabilities. The particulars of the CSPD requirements are to be found in the Code of Federal Regulations. The agency's personnel standards must be based on the highest requirements in the state applicable to a particular profession. Training, retraining, and hiring of competent personnel is of the highest priority. For the State Plan to fulfill this part of the requirement it must:

- establish personnel standards on the highest requirement in the state for vocational rehabilitation counselors,
- analyze the needs of its staff with respect to how many either meet or do not meet these standards,
- examine factors, such as pay, that may adversely affect its ability to hire qualified staff and develop a strategy to address such barriers,
- identify the number of personnel who do not meet the standards and develop a plan to assist such personnel to meet the required standards in a reasonable timely manner,
- commit funds for the implementation of a retraining plan to meet the highest standards, and

- evaluate results of its planned recruitment efforts to ensure that all personnel, particularly counselors, meet the standards. An annual update on this section is required to be submitted.

The Rehabilitation Act Amendments of 1998 require an annual estimate of the number of individuals with disabilities who will be declared eligible for services, the cost of these services, goals and priorities, strategies, and reports of progress. Innovation and expansion of service opportunities are required to be incorporated in the State Plan. The Act now requires that a portion of its allocation sent to the state be set aside for the development and implementation of innovative approaches to expand and improve the various vocational rehabilitation services. Attachments to the State Plan will describe in detail how the state will utilize the funds for this effort and how funds for this effort were used in the preceding year.

Mediation and impartial due process are both highlighted in the regulations and must be part of the State Plan. If a state does not have a fair hearing board, then an attachment must identify the state unit's mediation process in sufficient detail to allow service seekers to understand what recourse they might have if they disagree with any decisions during the vocational rehabilitation process.

The State Plan must contain language that indicates that it is able to provide a full range of rehabilitation service to all eligible individuals. The state must fulfill the Code of Federal Regulations (CFR) requirements in this regard and describe how it will:

- continue to provide services to all individuals currently receiving services,
- provide assessment services to all individuals expected to apply for services in the next fiscal year,
- provide services to all individuals who are expected to be determined eligible for services in the next fiscal year, and
- meet all program requirements. If the state unit makes a determination it cannot provide the full range of vocational rehabilitation services to all eligible individual, an attachment must contain:
    1. the order to be followed in selecting eligible individuals to be provided such services,
    2. a justification of that order, and
    3. the service and outcome goals and the time within which these goals may be achieved for individuals in each priority category within the order.

State Plans can be reviewed by making a request to the state director in each state. A certain number of State Plans are currently available for review via the Internet. The address for this site can be obtained by querying under the Department of Education, Office of Special Education and Rehabilitative Services, Rehabilitation Services Administration.

PROGRAMS

The programs described below are those that are contained in the RSA program of services to the states. Most, if not all, are offered on the state level. For a complete enumeration of services contained in the State Plan, contact the VR state director or the local VR administrator. A copy of the plan should be made available. The following information on the programs was taken from the RSA web page.

BASIC VOCATIONAL REHABILITATION SERVICES

The scope and purpose of this basic program is to allocate federal funds on a formula basis (78.7% federal, 21.3% state matching – unless otherwise determined) for the administration and operation of a vocational rehabilitation program. The VR program is to provide a wide range of services to persons with disabilities to assist in preparing for and engaging in competitive, gainful employment. Priority is given to those with the most significant disabilities. A person must have a physical, mental, and/or emotional impairment that is a substantial barrier to employment and/or independent living to be eligible for services. These services are comprehensive in nature and include assessments across many disciplines, work evaluation, assistive technology for determining modifications and accommodations, career counseling and placement, many types of therapy, job training, education, and other services that may be needed to assist the person with a disability to live independently and/or obtain substantial gainful employment.

REHABILITATION TRAINING PROGRAMS

The purpose of this program is to ensure that skilled personnel are always available to serve the rehabilitation needs of persons with disabilities. This program supports training and related activities designed to increase the number of qualified personnel providing rehabilitation services. Grants and contracts are awarded to states, public, and nonprofit agencies to pay all or part of the cost of conducting training programs. In addition to these long-term training opportunities, there are awards given for continuing education, short-term training, experimental and innovative training, training interpreters for persons who are deaf or hard of hearing, and training for persons who are deaf-blind. The content, methodology, and type of trainee vary from program to program. It should be noted that the long-term training program supports academic training grants, with 75 percent of funds received by the institution of higher learning being directed to trainee scholarships. The law requires that students who receive assistance through this grant program work for a period of time in public or non-profit rehabilitation agencies or related agencies, or they have to pay back the assistance they have received.

The VR state agency and recipients of long-term training grants should work together to build closer relationships. Together, they need to promote careers in public vocational rehabilitation programs, identify potential employers who would meet the requirements for student payback, and assure that employment data on students receiving assistance are accurate. Specifically mentioned in the RSA policies is the need to set aside 15 percent of training funds for in-service training programs. This is to assist the state VR program in the training of agency staff to meet the basic requirements for both professionals and paraprofessionals and to meet the arising needs of training for the new technologies and systems for provision of services to persons with disabilities. The Comprehensive System of Personnel Development (CSPD) mentioned earlier is critical in meeting the highest requirements for personnel standards within the state. The President's budget for FY 2014 is $30,200,000.

CLIENT ASSISTANCE PROGRAM

The scope and purpose of this program is to set in place an advocacy system that informs and advises all applicants for, and recipients of, services funded under the Rehabilitation Act of 1973, as amended, of the benefits available under the Act. It also requires that this program provide assistance to and advocate for applicants and recipients of services funded under the Act in their relationships with projects, programs, and services provided under the Act. This advocacy includes assistance in pursuing legal, administrative, and other appropriate remedies to ensure the individual's rights are protected. In addition, the program is to inform individuals with disabilities of the availability of services and benefits under Title I of the Americans with Disabilities Act of 1990 (ADA) and to provide assistance and advocacy directly related to facilitating employment and services under Title I of the ADA. The funding request for FY 2014 is $12,000,000.

DEMONSTRATION AND TRAINING PROGRAMS

This category of programs provides competitive grants to, or contracts with, eligible entities to expand and improve the provision of rehabilitation and other services authorized under the Act. Specifically, the program supports activities that increase the provision, extent, availability, scope, and quality of rehabilitation services under the Act, including related research and evaluation activities. Demonstrating methods of service delivery, technical assistance, systems change, special studies, evaluation, dissemination, and utilization of findings from previously funded projects are all examples of what could be funded under this program. Expanding and improving rehabilitation and other services is the basis for awarding a grant under this program. One element that is emphasized under this program structure is increased client choice through new and better program of services.

PROTECTION AND ADVOCACY OF INDIVIDUAL RIGHTS

The scope and purpose of this program is to support the protection and advocacy system in each state that is designed to protect the legal and human rights of persons with disabilities. To be eligible under this program, a person with a disability must:

- be ineligible for the protection and advocacy of developmental disabilities program, or
- be ineligible for the protection and advocacy for individuals with mental illness, and
- need services that are beyond the scope of services authorized by the client assistance program.

The Rehabilitation Act requires that each protection and advocacy of individual rights (PAIR) program set annual priorities and objectives to meet the needs of persons with disabilities in its own state. Most PAIR programs deal with accessible and affordable housing, communication and transportation barriers, and participation in community life. Persons with severe disabilities are to be involved in the development and implementation of this system. The funding request for FY 2014 is $18,000,000.

INDEPENDENT LIVING STATE GRANTS PROGRAM

Independent living programs have been developed to maximize leadership, empowerment, independence, and productivity of persons with disabilities and to integrate these individuals into the mainstream of American society. This program provides financial assistance to aid, expand, and improve independent living services. The entire program is to provide support statewide through a network of independent living centers. This program highly encourages and strongly endorses coordination between the various independent living centers and the state rehabilitation program, Statewide Independent Living Councils (SILC), and other relevant federal and non-federal programs.

For a state to be eligible for funds under the independent living state grants or centers for independent living programs, a state must establish a SILC. Each state that wishes to receive this funding must also submit a State Plan for Independent Living that is jointly developed and signed by the director of the designated state Vocational Rehabilitation unit and the chairperson of the SILC.

Funds are based on the most recent population data reported by the Census Bureau. States may use these funds to support the operation of the SILC and for one or more of the following purposes:

- to demonstrate ways to expand and improve independent living services,
- to provide independent living services,
- to support the operation of the centers,
- to increase the capacity of public and non-profit agencies and organizations to develop comprehensive approaches or systems for providing independent living services,
- to conduct studies and analyses, gather information, develop model policies and procedures, and present information, findings, and

recommendations to federal, state, and local policy makers,
- to provide training on IL philosophy, and
- to provide outreach to populations who are un-served or underserved.

Funding for this program in the budget request for FY 2014 is $23,400,000.

CENTERS FOR INDEPENDENT LIVING

This program is similar to the independent living program, but important differences do exist. The centers for independent living (CIL) program provides grants for consumer-controlled, community-based, cross-disability, non-residential, private nonprofit agencies that are designed and operated within a local community by persons with disabilities and provide an array of independent living services. At a minimum, centers are required to provide the core services of information and referral, independent living skills training, peer counseling, and individual and systems advocacy. Most centers are actively involved in one or more of the following activities: community planning and decision-making; school-based peer counseling, role modeling, skills training; working with local governments and employers to open and facilitate employment opportunities; interacting with local, state, and federal legislatures; and staging recreational events that integrate persons with disabilities with their non-disabled peers.

A population-based formula determines the amount available for discretionary grants to centers in each state. If state funding exceeds the federal funding level in a fiscal year, the state unit may request authority to award grants in the following fiscal year. Only three states are eligible, and they have elected to manage their own centers program. Up to two percent of the funds in this program are to be used by the centers for evaluation, planning, development, and administration. Annual performance reviews are necessary and must outline the needs for training and technical assistance for both the centers and the SILCs.

The Act establishes a set of standards and assurances that must be met by each center. Compliance in the following areas is especially important: philosophy, including consumer control and equal access; provision of services on a cross-disability basis; support for the development and achievement of the independent living goals chosen by the consumers; advocacy to increase the quality of community options for independent living; provision of independent living core services; resource development; and community capacity-building activities. Each year, the department must conduct compliance reviews of at least 15 percent of the centers and one-third of the designated state units funded under this program. The budget request for FY 2014 is $80,000,000.

INDEPENDENT LIVING SERVICES FOR OLDER INDIVIDUALS WHO ARE BLIND

This program is essentially the same as the preceding two programs discussed, with the exception that this program supports services to assist individuals aged 55 or older whose recent severe visual impairment makes competitive employment extremely difficult to obtain, but for whom independent living goals are feasible. Funds are used to provide independent living services, conduct activities that will improve or expand services for these individuals, and conduct activities to improve public understanding of the problems of these individuals. Services are designed to help persons served under this program to adjust to their blindness by increasing their ability to care for their individual needs.

Prior to FY 2000, grants were awarded on a competitive basis. Now that appropriations have exceeded $13 million, awards are being made to states according to a formula based on the population of individuals who are 55 years of age or older. The budget request for FY 2006 is $34,000,000.

PROGRAM IMPROVEMENT

This program is authorized to provide technical assistance and consultative services to public and nonprofit private agencies and organizations, including assistance to enable agencies and organizations to facilitate meaningful and effective participation by individuals with disabilities in workforce investment activities under the Workforce Investment Act of 1998. The funds for this program may also be used to provide short-term and technical assistance, conduct special demonstrations, develop and disseminate educational or informational materials, and carry out monitoring and conduct evaluations.

EVALUATION

The scope and purpose of this program is to evaluate all programs authorized by the Act, their effectiveness in relation to their cost, their impact on related programs, and their structure and mechanisms for delivery of services, using appropriate methodology and evaluative research design. It requires that standards be established and used for evaluations, and that persons who are not immediately involved in the administration of the program or project evaluated conduct the evaluations.

HELEN KELLER NATIONAL CENTER PROGRAM

Briefly, the Helen Keller National Center for Deaf-Blind Youth and Adults was created by Congress in 1969, and operates under the auspices of Helen Keller Services for the Blind, Inc. The center provides services on a national basis to individuals who are deaf-blind, their families, and service providers through three component programs. These is a national headquarters center with residential training and a rehabilitation facility where deaf-blind individuals receive intensive specialized services; a network of ten regional field offices that provide referral and counseling assistance to deaf-blind individuals and technical assistance to service providers; and an affiliate program that provides incentive grants to public and private agencies that serve individuals with deaf-blindness. The center is current-funded and receives an award on a non-competitive basis.

The purpose of this program is to provide direct service for persons with deaf-blindness in order to enhance their potential for employment and to live independently in their home communities. The objectives of the program are to provide clients with meaningful contact with the environment, effective means of communication, constructive participation in the home and community, increased employability, and other services pertinent to their rehabilitation.

Ten federal regions are under the authority of the national center. Headed by regional representatives, these offices provide a variety of services including training for service agency staff, general technical assistance, and help in developing direct service plans for the deaf-blind clients for state Vocational Rehabilitation counselors, mental health workers, and special education programs.

The national center also operates a number of special projects related to this specific disability. These include a service project for elderly deaf-blind persons and a national parent and family services project. An international internship program is also run by the center. The budget request for FY 2014 is $9,100,000.

RANDOLPH-SHEPPARD PROGRAM

Under the Randolph-Sheppard program, state rehabilitation agencies recruit, train, license, and place individuals who are blind as operators of vending facilities located on federal and other properties. Current data regarding number of persons served, number of sites, income of operators, etc. is not available on the U.S. Department of Education website.

MIGRANT AND SEASONAL FARM WORKERS PROGRAM

The migrant and seasonal farm workers program makes comprehensive vocational rehabilitation services available to migrant or seasonal farm workers with disabilities. Projects also develop innovative methods for reaching and serving this population. The goal of this program is to increase employment opportunities for the segment of the population who have disabilities. Persons with disabilities in this group, and their family members, are eligible to receive services when such services will contribute to the rehabilitation of the worker with a disability.

This program is administered in coordination with other programs serving the same population. The other programs may include the Elementary and Secondary Act of 1965, Public Health Service Act, Migrant and Seasonal Agricultural Worker Protection Act, and the Workforce Investment Act of 1998. Funding requests for this program are subsumed under the General VR program.

PROJECTS WITH INDUSTRY PROGRAM

Projects with industry (PWI) create and expand job and career opportunities for persons with disabilities in the competitive labor market by engaging the participation of business and industry in the rehabilitation process. Business advisory councils identify jobs and careers available in the community. This group also provides advice on appropriate skills and training needed for persons with disabilities to be able to be considered for these jobs.

Job development, job placement, and job training are all components of this program. These services are available to persons with disabilities so that they may obtain or advance in employment in the competitive labor market.
PWI grants are made to a variety of agencies and organizations, including business and industrial corporations, community rehabilitation programs, labor organizations, trade associations, and foundations. Grants are awarded to projects in geographic areas that are considered un-served or underserved.
PWI grantees must provide to the Office of the Commissioner, an annual evaluation of project operations with established program standards and compliance indicators. Included in the report would be the number of persons with disabilities served and the number who achieved a competitive employment outcome; the improvement of participants' employment status and earning power following services; and information on employment retention. Continuation awards are possible with the filing of particular data. Funding for this program is included under the basic VR program.

SUPPORTED EMPLOYMENT STATE GRANTS PROGRAM

The purpose of this program is to assist the states in developing collaborative programs with appropriate public and private non-profit organizations to provide supported employment services for individuals with the most significant disabilities. Achievement of employment outcomes is the primary objective of this program. For the purposes of this program, the term "supported employment" includes both individuals in competitive work and individuals in an integrated setting working toward competitive work. Persons in competitive work must earn at least minimum wage.

Supported employment placements are achieved by augmenting short-term vocational rehabilitation services with ongoing support provided by other public and private non-profit agencies. State VR agencies provide time-limited services for a period not to exceed 18 months, unless a longer period to achieve job stabilization has been previously established in the rehabilitation plan for the person with a disability. Funding for this program is now included under the basic VR program.

The above overview of the programs administered by the Rehabilitation Services Administration (taken from the RSA web page) was presented to give the reader an indication of the variety of programs available to each state to assist persons with disabilities in their quest for gainful employment and/or to live independently.

THE VOCATIONAL REHABILITATION PROCESS

While the programs authorized by the Act and developed and implemented by each state according to the State Plan, are important, the backbone of rehabilitation, as witnessed in the State Plan's daily activities, is the process itself. This process is elemental in working with the person with a disability so that the Vocational Rehabilitation counselor can assist that person to achieve gainful employment and/or independent living.

The manner in which a person with a disability can become eligible for services and continue to remain eligible for services, is highly structured. The person must navigate a series of "statuses" before a definitive outcome is achieved. These statuses can be roughly divided into four areas: referral, service planning, service provision, and closure. For a better understanding of the process in general, and the statuses in particular, each status will be reviewed.

STATUS 00: REFERRAL

Every individual must go through this status. It is likened to the entry point of any process. A person can be referred by anyone, preferably a person who knows of the current status of the individual. Many times this is a professional in the medical field or a closely related field. Individuals can, however, refer themselves to the VR agency. Basic demographic information (usually contact information) is required at this initial step in the process. A client file is begun at this time. The person is contacted and an initial appointment is scheduled between the person and a counselor.

STATUS 02: APPLICANT

In many instances, the referral and the applicant status take place at the same time. However, applicant status is where the person achieves some degree of identity in the process. At this time, the client (customer or consumer is preferred in some agencies) begins to interact with staff and, possibly, a vocational rehabilitation counselor. This is the point where the client comes to the office and officially signs a document indicating a willingness to participate in the rehabilitation process. The application requires the person with a disability to give some very important demographic information. In addition to that information, clients will also be asked to document the problems (barriers to employment) that keep them from working or leading independent lives. Clients are also requested to list in detail their work history, training, and education level. According to the Rehabilitation Act, as amended, the counselor is required to make an "eligible for services" decision within sixty (60) days. If this cannot be accomplished and there are legitimate reasons, the counselor can extend this period briefly. The main purpose of placing an individual in applicant status is to allow the counselor time to acquire the information needed through past records or through current evaluation reports to make the eligibility decision.

STATUS 06: EXTENDED EVALUATION

Counselors place an individual in this status when they are unable to make an eligibility decision within sixty (60) days or a slightly longer period. The basic reason for placing an individual in this status is to allow for more time, up to 18 months, for collecting the information needed to make a fair eligibility decision. Individuals with severe disabilities are usually placed in extended evaluation because the counselor is not entirely certain that the client will benefit from any services that may be offered. Extended evaluation calls for a specific plan to be written that is developed jointly by the client and counselor. When the extended evaluation period concludes, the counselors should be able to determine if the client is eligible and then place the person in status 10. If the client cannot substantially benefit from services, the case is closed in status 08. In either case, the counselor must have documentation to support the rationale behind the decision. Vocational Rehabilitation counselors are trained to use this status only with very good reason. Clients may be underserved when placed in this status if the VR counselor does not effectively manage the caseload.

STATUS 08: CLOSED FROM REFERRAL, APPLICANT, OR EXTENDED EVALUATION

This is a general status that identifies all those individuals who have come in contact with VR in any way and who were closed as not eligible for services. Reasons for closure may be singular or multiple and include (a) unable to locate, (b) refused services, (c) died, (d) helped by another more appropriate agency, (e) institutionalized in prison or other facility, (f) failure to cooperate, (g) no vocational handicap or disability, (h) handicap/disability too severe, (i) did not meet order of selection policy, and (j) all other reasons. Whenever a counselor uses any of the above reasons, specific documentation must be contained in the file. The client must be notified by letter of such a decision if their file is closed on the basis of having too severe a handicap or disability or no vocational handicap or disability.

STATUS 10: ELIGIBILITY AND INDIVIDUALIZED PLAN FOR EMPLOYMENT

This is the status where the client becomes eligible for services offered by the VR agency. The client and counselor are obliged to sit down together and develop a program of services that will meet the needs of the individual with the ultimate outcome being employment. A certificate of eligibility is placed in the case folder. From this status, all following services are derived. The Individual Plan for Employment (IPE), developed at this time, is a working document and can be changed only with the input of the client and counselor. Both parties sign the plan. If revisions are made to the plan, both parties must agree and sign the revised plan. Copies are given to the client, sent to the state office, and placed in the case folder.

STATUS 12: INDIVIDUAL PLAN FOR EMPLOYMENT

The client is placed in this status once the IPE has been completed and the client is waiting for services to begin. Generally, this is a holding status until one service has been started. At that time, the client is placed into another status, dependent upon the service offered.

STATUS 14: COUNSELING AND GUIDANCE

While this status is seldom used since most clients have multiple services in their IPE, it is still necessary, because there are some clients who only need counseling and guidance services. This particular service is given to every client who has been declared eligible. It is a most basic component of the process. A client may be placed in another status (16, 18, 20) and then placed in status 14 because additional counseling and guidance has been shown to be necessary.

STATUS 16: PHYSICAL AND MENTAL RESTORATION

This status is one that is used predominantly by counselors for restoration services that are necessary so that the person with a disability can be restored to the fullest possible potential, with the ultimate outcome of obtaining and maintaining substantial gainful employment. Medical restoration services, such as surgery and other corrective measures, can be accomplished in this status. Other services included in this status would be various types of therapy. Physical and occupational therapy, and psychiatric and psychological treatment are examples of the more traditional forms of restoration offered. Complimentary or alternative therapies, such as chiropractic care, message therapy, and hypnotherapy are increasingly being considered. If a client is in need of a prosthetic or an orthotic device, this is the status in which the client would receive this service, plus the training to use the device. It would be appropriate during this status for the VR counselor to review the various reports collected to this point and determine if any accommodations or modifications would be need for the client, either during training and/or at the start of employment. The client remains in this status until the full regimen of therapeutic services has been completed or until the client has no more need for the services. A licensed professional or one who holds a certificate specific to the service requested can provide services in this category. The person, agency, or institution has to be on the VR services' provider list, as do all providers when VR is purchasing services for clients.

STATUS 18: TRAINING

This particular status is used to provide training that prepares the client to enter and maintain competitive employment. Some of the types of training that are included in this status would be academic training, vocational training, and business courses. A special type of training, work adjustment, is recommended for those individuals who may have a difficult time in maintaining employment. This type of training is one that is very necessary especially, for those individuals who have been out of the labor force for at least a year or more. Another type of training, on-the-job, is suggested for those who need some additional training for a specific job. On-the-job training is frequently used when the client only needs to refresh previously held skills or when the training is not available from formal training providers. Any individual or group that is in good standing and on the current vendor list for VR services' providers can provide this training.

STATUS 20: READY FOR EMPLOYMENT

This status means what is says–the client has been provided all the needed services and is ready for competitive employment. It is at this time that the client, along with the assistance of the VR counselor, will begin the initial job search. It is suggested that the client and counselor jointly develop a Placement Plan. This plan will outline the responsibilities of the client as well as what the counselor is expected to do. While the client is in this status, job interviews and counseling, as needed, will take place. If job accommodations or modifications to the work site are needed, it is during this status that the prospective employer is notified.

STATUS 22: IN EMPLOYMENT

The client has begun employment. This is the final stage of the client's vocational rehabilitation process and the most critical phase. It requires that a client remain in this status and be continuously employed for at least 90 days. It is during these three months that clients will meet their greatest obstacles. Careful observation of the client, usually through the eyes of the employer, is absolutely necessary. While the client is in this status, the VR counselor and employer will have to maintain close contact. The counselor must visit the client on the job on a periodic basis. However, the employer will give notice to the counselor if more-frequent visits are appropriate.

STATUS 24: SERVICE INTERRUPTED

At any time during the rehabilitation process after the client's IPE has been approved, and for whatever reason, service may be interrupted. The cause for such interruption could be serious illness, accident, injury, or other problems that may arise. The client is held in this status until the causes of the service interruption have been resolved. At that time, the client continues the rehabilitation process in the status most appropriate to the client's situation.

STATUS 26: CASE CLOSED – REHABILITATED

Once the client has been on the job for ninety (90) consecutive days and has completed all the services as outlined on the IPE, the client's case can be closed as rehabilitated. Closure signifies that the client has proceeded through the entire VR process and is considered successfully employed. Prior to closure, the counselor and client will discuss the closure and the possible need for post-employment services. The employer should also be notified that the counselor would no longer be following the client. It is important to note that 90 days is the minimum time that the client must be employed before the case can be closed. In actual practice, the counselor may hold the client in status 22 (employment) for as long as necessary until the client and counselor agree that case closure is the appropriate action to take at that time.

STATUS 28: CLOSED OTHER THAN EMPLOYED AFTER CLIENT'S IPE WAS WRITTEN AND SERVICES WERE STARTED.

A person who was anywhere in the process from the point where the IPE was signed through status 24 can be closed for a variety of reasons. The reasons for closure are generally the same as were presented for Status 08, with the exception that a person cannot be closed in this status for having no disability or vocational handicap or for not meeting the order of selection criteria.

STATUS 30: CLOSED BEFORE IPE WAS DEVELOPED

An individual closed in this status is one who was declared eligible (accepted) for services but for whom no plan of services (IPE) was developed and signed by the client and counselor. The reasons for closure are identical to the reasons that are used in 28 Status.

STATUS 32: POST-EMPLOYMENT SERVICES

Only those individuals who were closed in 26 Status can be opened in status 32. Post-employment services are offered to the client for simple, short-term services that will enable the client to remain on the job. While these services have no set time limit, they are necessarily short lived. If the client needs longer-term services, then that client would need to again apply for VR services, since significant services are needed in order to allow the person to obtain and maintain full time competitive employment.

STATUS 34: CLOSED FROM POST-EMPLOYMENT SERVICES

When the services provided in post-employment are completed, this status is used. In general, the above statuses are used in all the states in fulfillment of the State Plan for providing rehabilitation services to those individuals who apply for services in compliance with the Rehabilitation Act of 1973, as amended. Some states may prefer not to use all statuses. This system is a valuable coding system for keeping accurate account of the progression of each client through the VR process. It allows administrators a quick view of where each client is in particular and where the caseload is in general. It should help counselors in the day-to-day management of their caseload. Each counselor will be able to see at a glance what files need to be worked on at any specific time. It is also a legitimate system for determining program outcomes. The status system has been the major source of data used to demonstrate the value of the VR system to Congress and other interested parties.

GOALS AND OBJECTIVES OF STATE/FEDERAL REHABILITATION PROGRAM

The mission of the State/Federal Vocational Rehabilitation program can only come to fruition through the development of goals and objectives. These goals and objectives are generally consistent over the years, with varying strategies being put into place to ensure that the goals and objectives are met. With the changing technologies and make-up of the market place, some goals and objectives do change as appropriate. Selected goals and objectives currently in place are listed below. These are consistent with the RSA programs enumerated earlier in the chapter. Each state, in developing their State Plan, will reflect the goals, objectives, and strategies listed below. These three factors will reflect current conditions in a specific state.

The information given below was taken from the US Department of Education Annual Plan for FY 1999, Rehabilitation Services, Disability Research, and Special Institutions as found on the USDOE web page.

GOALS AND OBJECTIVES

1) GOAL: INDIVIDUALS WITH DISABILITIES SERVED BY THE VOCATIONAL REHABILITATION STATE GRANT PROGRAM WILL ACHIEVE HIGH QUALITY EMPLOYMENT.

Objective: Ensure that individuals with disabilities who are served by the Vocational Rehabilitation State Grant Program achieve employment consistent with their unique strengths, resources, abilities, capabilities, and interests.

Strategies: 1. Develop a state improvement plan jointly with state agencies that are performing below standards. 2. Develop coordinated approaches among federal agencies that affect employment of individuals with disabilities. 3. Identify and disseminate information regarding best practices for assisting individuals with disabilities to achieve appropriate employment outcomes. 4. Develop a monitoring and technical assistance plan for states. 5. Award grants for system change to encourage coordination between state VR agencies and state-level job training programs.

Objective: State VR agencies will operate a comprehensive, effective, efficient, and accountable program of vocational rehabilitation.

Strategies: 1. Identify low-performing agencies and assist states to identify problems and develop plans to improve services. 2. Strategies will address how funding for direct services to consumers significantly affects outcomes. 3. Encourage all state agencies to implement streamlining plans through training.

Objective: RSA will help states improve services and outcomes for consumers.

Strategies: 1. Ensure that staffs are trained and able to effectively use RSA's monitoring and technical assistance guide. 2. Award a technical assistance contract to procure expertise in identified problem areas. 3. Sponsor national conferences, training, and implementation activities in response to program needs. 4. Provide targeted training to state VR agencies through regional continuing education programs. 5. Distribute evaluation results on promising practices through publications targeted to the VR community.

Objective: Increase the number of individuals with the most severe disabilities receiving supported employment services who achieve high quality supported employment outcomes.

Strategies: 1. Identify poor performance and provide targeted technical assistance.

2) GOAL: TO IMPROVE EMPLOYMENT OUTCOMES OF NATIVE INDIANS WITH DISABILITIES WHO LIVE ON RESERVATIONS BY PROVIDING EFFECTIVE TRIBAL VOCATIONAL REHABILITATION (VR) SERVICES.

Objective: Ensure that eligible Native Indians with disabilities receive vocational rehabilitation services and achieve employment outcomes consistent with their unique strengths, resources, abilities, capabilities, and interests.

Strategies: 1. Provide linkage with National Institute on Disability and Rehabilitation Research (NIDRR) capacity-building project to improve the number and quality of applications. 2. Through monitoring and technical assistance, provide guidance to projects to increase the scope of their outreach activities; to improve their networking with other tribal and non-tribal agencies; and to provide interagency training to improve appropriateness of referrals. 3. Conduct an evaluation study that examines the consumer characteristics, services provided, and management of the program.

3) GOAL: TO PROVIDE ASSISTANCE AND INFORMATION TO HELP INDIVIDUALS WITH DISABILITIES SECURE THE BENEFITS AVAILABLE UNDER THE VOCATIONAL REHABILITATION STATE GRANTS PROGRAM AND OTHER PROGRAMS FUNDED UNDER THE REHABILITATION ACT OF 1973, AS AMENDED.

Objective: Provide appropriate information and adequate services to resolve the concerns of individuals.

Strategies: 1. Provide technical assistance on new data collection reporting elements. 2. Provide technical assistance on how CAPs should approach each case in a comprehensive manner.

Objective: Resolve cases at lowest possible level.

Strategies: 1. Develop a model "alternative dispute resolution" policy for the CAPs. 2. Provide technical assistance on how CAPs can use alternative dispute resolution effectively.

Objective: Meet expectations of individuals served regarding their satisfaction with CAP services.

Strategies: 1. Develop a model client satisfaction survey for CAPs to use.

Objective: Accurately identify problem areas requiring systemic change and engage in systemic activity to improve services under the Rehabilitation Act.

Strategies: 1. Compile and assess CAP narrative regarding systemic activities.

4) GOAL: TO PROVIDE THE PUBLIC VOCATIONAL REHABILITATION (VR) SECTOR WITH WELL-TRAINED STAFF AND TO MAINTAIN AND UPGRADE THE SKILLS OF CURRENT STAFF.

Objective: Produce graduates to work within the VR system to help individuals with disabilities achieve their goals.

Strategies: 1. Develop revised reporting forms to capture more accurate information. 2. Provide grantees with clearer guidance on the purpose of ED program and ways to respond better to program goals

Objective: Maintain and upgrade the knowledge and skills of personnel currently employed in the public vocational rehabilitation system.

Strategies: 1. Special study of Regional Continuing Education Programs and In-Service Training programs scheduled for FY 2002.

Objective: Increase and enhance the skill of manual, tactile, oral, and cued speech interpreters so as to be better able to provide communication access for individuals who are deaf or individuals who are deaf-blind in a greater variety of situation.

Strategies: 1. Improve guidance on performance report to collect baseline and change data. 2. Build a special evaluation component for this program into the next grant competition for the national projects to assess the quality of training provided by the regional training programs. 3. Increase the number of workshops or training sessions that offer continuing education unit credits.

5) GOAL: TO EXPAND AND IMPROVE THE PROVISION OF REHABILITATION SERVICES TO INDIVIDUALS WITH DISABILITIES.

Objective: Demonstrate innovative and experimental approaches to the provision of vocational rehabilitation (VR) services.

Strategies: 1. The Rehabilitation Services Administration (RSA) will implement an annual plan to reflect need for baseline data, specify outcomes for next performance period, and disseminate clearer guidance to grantees for reporting data. 2) RSA will provide technical assistance to grantees in order to promote successful outcomes.

Objective: Disseminate information about successful new types or patterns of services or devices for individuals with disabilities.

Strategies: 1. RSA will identify and disseminate information to other grantees and state VR agencies regarding best practices.

Objective: Improve the provision of supported employment services.

Strategies: 1. RSA will monitor project performance via monthly teleconference and review annual performance reports to determine progress in meeting project goals and objectives. 2. RSA will review evaluation in relation to level of reported satisfaction of providers receiving technical assistance.

6) GOAL: TO INCREASE EMPLOYMENT OPPORTUNITIES FOR MIGRATORY AGRICULTURAL WORKERS OR SEASONAL FARM-WORKERS WHO HAVE DISABILITIES.

Objectives: 1. Ensure that eligible migratory agricultural workers or seasonal farm-workers with disabilities receive vocational rehabilitation services and achieve employment outcomes. 2. Improve accuracy and consistency of data reported on the number of agricultural workers or seasonal farm-workers with disabilities served by the state vocational rehabilitation agencies and these projects.

Strategies: 1. Grantees provided with clearer guidance on the purpose of ED program and ways to respond better to program goals. 2. RSA works to coordinate activities with the State Vocational Rehabilitation agency. 3. RSA will conduct telephone monitoring twice a year to all continuing projects to assess program activities and provide technical assistance. 4. RSA will conduct an internal review of performance reports to determine effectiveness of the program in terms of meeting its stated objectives.

7) GOAL: TO FACILITATE THE ESTABLISHMENT OF PARTNERSHIPS BETWEEN REHABILITATION SERVICE PROVIDERS AND BUSINESS AND INDUSTRY IN ORDER TO CREATE AND EXPAND EMPLOYMENT AND CAREER ADVANCEMENT OPPORTUNITIES FOR INDIVIDUALS WITH DISABILITIES.

Objective: Ensure that Projects with Industry (PWI) services through partnerships result in competitive employment, increased wages, and job retention for individuals with disabilities.

Strategies: 1. Monitor placement rates by conducting off-site monitoring with grantees. 2. Provide technical assistance on building strong partnerships with industry. 3. Provide technical assistance to grantees that demonstrate difficulty or non-compliance with the wage standard defined in PWI regulations. 4. Design and pilot a data collection instrument to measure job retention rates.

Objective: Ensure that PWI services are available for individuals with the most need.

Strategies: 1. Provide technical assistance to grantees that demonstrate poor performance.

8) Goal: Individuals with significant disabilities served by Title VII, Chapter 1 programs achieve consumer-determined independent living goals; and independent living services will be provided and activities will be conducted to improve or expand services to older individuals who are blind.

Objective: Increase the number of individuals with significant disabilities who are served by and benefiting from Title VII, chapter 1 programs.

Strategies: 1. Develop technical assistance action plans that will assist grantees that are performing below standards and indicators of compliance. 2. Identify and disseminate information regarding best practices for assisting individuals with disabilities to achieve appropriate independent living centers.

Objective: Increase the satisfaction of consumers who receive these services (IL).

Strategies: 1. Identify and assist low-performing service providers. 2. Revise the reporting requirements for the SPIL and 704 to include consumer satisfaction data.

Objective: Improve access to personal assistance services (PAS), housing, transportation, and community-based living through increased advocacy efforts.

Strategies: 1.With training and technical assistance providers, provide coordinated assistance to CILs on advocacy techniques and strategies. 2. Present information at national meetings of CIL directors on the importance of facilitating community change.

Objective: Increase the amount of funds in addition to Title VII funds that support Chapter I grantees.

Strategies: 1. Identify and publish potential funds availability, increase grantees' capacity to obtain grants, and identify and share replicable model local and state resource development techniques and strategies. 2. Identify significant outcomes of the Chapter 1 program and disseminate results to grantees and other potential funding sources.

Objective: Increase the coordination, cooperation, and communication between the Chapter 1 programs and other entities serving individuals with significant disabilities in states.

Strategies: 1. Develop coordinated approaches among federal agencies that affect independent living goals of individuals with disabilities. 2. Work jointly with other agencies and other ED programs to ensure that students with disabilities receive appropriate transition services. 3. Encourage increased collaborative efforts with non-Rehabilitation Act providers assisting individuals with significant disabilities.

9) GOAL: TO SUPPORT THE CONDUCT AND DISSEMINATION OF HIGH QUALITY RESEARCH THAT CONTRIBUTES TO IMPROVEMENT IN THE QUALITY OF LIFE OF PERSONS WITH DISABILITIES.

Objective: NIDRR grantees will conduct high-quality research that leads to high-quality research products.

Strategies: 1. Provide training for prospective peer review panels. 2. Use various systems of review and evaluation to assess quality, productivity, and relevance of NIDRR research. 3. Contract an impact study to assess productivity, relevance, and quality of research. 4. Involve broad constituency in planning, priority setting, and program reviews.

Objective: Disseminate and promote use of information on research findings, in accessible formats, to improve rehabilitation services and outcomes.

Strategies: 1. Survey consumer and provider needs. 2. Develop targeted Dissemination and Utilization (D&Y) projects. 3. Publish and distribute accessibility guidelines for publications, meetings, and web sites, and provide a model of accessibility in NIDRR's own products, communications, and meetings.

Objective: Expand system capacity for conduct of high-quality rehabilitation research and services by ensuring availability of qualified researchers and practitioners, including persons with disabilities and other underserved groups

Strategies: 1. Develop pre-college awareness programs that target persons with disabilities and individuals from underserved groups. 2. Expand "new scholars" undergraduate program. 3. Develop cooperative training activities between RSA and state VR. 4. Emphasize the training of graduate researchers in all centers, and encourage grantees to target persons with disabilities and individuals from underserved groups. 5. Improve the clarity of goals of Research Training Grant (RTG) program.

10) GOAL: TO INCREASE AVAILABILITY OF FUNDING FOR, ACCESS TO, AND PROVISION OF ASSISTIVE TECHNOLOGY DEVICES AND ASSISTIVE TECHNOLOGY SERVICES.

Objective: Through systemic activity, improve access to and availability of assistive technology (AT) for individuals with disabilities who require assistive technology.

Strategies: 1. Provide technical assistance to states on accessibility issues. 2. Attend meetings of professional organizations for special education and vocational rehabilitation, and provide technical assistance; disseminate information about successful activities developed between education programs for children with disabilities and Tech Act projects. 3. Increase collaboration with state VR agencies. 4. Monitor Tech Act reports for indications of reduction in number of barriers to accessing assistive technology by underrepresented populations and rural populations.

Objective: Through systemic activity, increase funding for assistive technology devices and services.

Strategies: 1. Provide technical assistance and disseminate information to AT grantees regarding funding of AT services and devices.

STATE VR AGENCIES

Information about the state vocational rehabilitation agency can be obtained by contacting the state director of the agency. In some states, this agency may be a department within the state government structure, a division within a department, or some other designation suitable to the state agency structure. Information can be obtained more immediately from the local VR agency offices. Offices can be found in most major cities and in outlying areas in all the states. Brochures, booklets, and pamphlets are published by the state VR agency to provide the reader with basic information about the VR system and process. One example is the pamphlet/booklet published by the State of Florida's Occupational Opportunity Access Commission (OAOC) of Vocational Rehabilitation Services.

STATE OF FLORIDA: HANDBOOK OF SERVICES

This pamphlet is basically for the person with a disability who is referred to or comes to the agency for help. The purpose of the agency is clearly outlined followed immediately by eligibility criteria. These criteria and purposes are not singular to the state, but reflect the Rehabilitation Act of 1973, as amended. The topic of informed choice is explained briefly, indicating to persons seeking services that they will be able to choose who the counselor will be, what services one will receive, who will provide those services, and what job one wishes to attain. Some of these may be singular to the State of Florida, for example, choice of counselor. In some states, the choice of counselor is on a rotating basis or may be governed by the ethnic or cultural identity of the person seeking services. Part of the informed choice section includes shared responsibility with the counselor for identifying options and exploring the various aspects of each of the options.

The steps to rehabilitation are clearly outlined and include: applying for services, evaluation, rehabilitation planning, receipt of services, job placement, and closure. A short paragraph explaining each step is contained in the pamphlet. Other services are identified, such as transportation and vehicle modification; books, occupational tools, equipment, and other training materials; occupational licenses; assistive technology to help in each step of the process; maintenance to cover cost of living during the rehabilitation process, if needed; interpreter services; and referral to agencies as necessary.

The remainder of the pamphlet outlines the client's responsibilities as well as the person's rights during the process. Included in the rights are policies regarding confidentiality and non-discrimination in provision of services while in status. The notion of an ombudsman is presented and the right to appeal and the steps involved if the client does not agree with any decision made during the process. Finally, the client assistance program is briefly presented.

The pamphlet concludes with a notation that satisfaction is important to Vocational Rehabilitation Services. Clients are requested to sign the booklet to acknowledge that they received it and it was reviewed with the VR counselor. This signature is kept in the client's file.

INTERNET ACCESS

Many states have information pertaining to the State Plan and provision of services outlined on the Internet. Information contained on these web pages from selected states follows.

Connecticut: The Bureau of Rehabilitation Services (BRS) is housed within the Connecticut Department of Social Services. The web page provides an overview of BRS followed by a brief description of the organization and the various services provided by the BRS. A very complete accessibility link is given and has been updated most recently.

Kentucky: The home page for the Kentucky Department of Rehabilitation Services has all the links one would need to assess the viability of the program and the process that one would use in working through the program to the desired goal of the individual with a disability. The Home Page has as its first link a "consumer guide" that essentially gives the viewer a total glance at the entire program within the State of Kentucky. A current directory of all offices within the state is presented. It should be noted that the web site had been updated within a month of this writing and it is accessible according to 508 accessibility guidelines.

Ohio: The Rehabilitation Services Commission (RSC) is the designated agency in the State of Ohio for the provisions of services to persons with disabilities. The Home Page for this state commission outlines what can be located within the site. There are links to: frequently asked questions, VR services, services for employers, consumer advisory, careers at RSC, hot news, ADA, field office listings, publications and videos, recognition (awards), and even a fun page for the kids. The web site is available in Spanish at the click of the mouse or in other languages of one's choice. This web site had been updated as recently as two months prior to this writing.

Arkansas: This web site contains a welcome, what we are (leadership, recognition, directory), what we do (employment services, employer services, training, rules and regulations), news (newsletters, press releases, calendar, publications), and contact. This particular state web site contains the *Client Services Handbook* that can be easily downloaded. It contains much the same information as in the Florida handbook but with more detail.

New York: Services for persons with disabilities is coordinated through the Office of Vocational and Educational Services for Individuals with Disabilities (VESID) maintained in the New York State Department of Education. The Home Page for the VESID contains basically the same information as seen in the previous selected states, with some format changes and certain services introduced. A Pocketbook of Goals and Results for Individuals with Disabilities is a special feature of this web site. It outlines in detail the goals and the results for the VESID over the past four years.

California: The California Department of Rehabilitation (DOR) has its Home Page filled with ten basic categories that link to pages within the site. These ten include direct services to persons with disabilities, ADA, employment opportunities at DOR, assistance for current consumers, IL information, information about DOR, grants, assistance for service providers, employment resources, and FYI. Each provides complete information through its links for an individual who wishes to receive services.

SUMMARY

The State/Federal Vocational Rehabilitation Services program has been in existence for over eighty years. The program is currently authorized and funded through the Rehabilitation Act of 1973, as amended. It originated in 1920 in the Smith-Fess Act. The Rehabilitation Services Administration is the federal government entity that oversees the rules and regulations stipulated in the Act, and allocate the funds enacted by Congress to the states. Federal funds are matched according to the present formula of 78.7% federal contribution and 21.3% state match.

The states are required to develop and submit a State Plan each year to the RSA, matching the plan with the goals and objectives of the RSA. The programs reflect both the general and specific needs of persons with disabilities and a variety of populations including minorities, underserved, and underrepresented groups. In general, states are consistent with the services they provide during the rehabilitation process. They are guided by the code of statuses to monitor where any person is at any time in the rehabilitation process. Some states have special programs for specific populations, e.g., migrant farm workers with disabilities.

Goals and objectives for ten programs within the RSA umbrella were presented to provide the reader more appreciation for the intricate approach needed to serve the population of persons with disabilities. Other programs not noted were those that served populations of hearing impaired and visually impaired.

Information concerning state VR programs is critically important for the person with a disability. It is also important for other groups. The Internet can be a chief source of this information, especially since it is readily available to the public in libraries and government buildings at the local, state, and national level. For a more personal review of the program, a visit to the local VR office would be helpful. States were selected at random across the country to provide a brief overview of their web sites. The reader is encouraged to visit one or more of these web sites to gain additional information.

Outcomes in the form of data allow the agency and other entities, including Congress, to review the effectiveness of the program in terms of the number of individuals who are served by the program. Data such as given in this chapter do not begin to tell the entire story. These data are just part of the entire story. For complete details, one is encouraged to contact the local VR agency and/or the state office to obtain more information.

REFERENCES & SUGGESTED READINGS

[1]Brolin, D. E. (1976). *Vocational rehabilitation of retarded citizens.* Columbus, OH: Charles E. Merrill Publishing Company. (See: c. 4)

[2]Malikin, D., & Rusalem, H. (1969). *Vocational rehabilitation of the disabled: An overview.* New York: New York University Press. (See: c.1 and c.3)

[3]Parker, R. M., & Szymanski, E. M. (1998). *Rehabilitation counseling: Basics and beyond* (3rd ed). Austin, TX: pro-ed. (See: c. 6)

[4]Rehabilitation Act of 1973, 87 Stat. 355, 29 USC # 701 *et seq.* Rehabilitation Services Administration. (221.31).

[5]Rehabilitation services administration home page.
www.ed.gov/about/offices/list/osers/rsa/index.html
www.ed.gov/about/overview/budget/budget07/summary/edlite-section26.html
www.ed.gov/about/offices/list/om/fs_po/osers_orgchart.html

[6]Rubin, S. E., & Roessler, R. T. (1983). *Foundations of the rehabilitation process.* (2nd ed.). Baltimore: University Park Press. (See: c. 1 and c. 3)

[7]Szymanski, E. M., & Parker, R. M. (1996). *Work and disability: Issues and strategies in career development and placement.* Austin, TX: pro-ed. (See: c. 3)

[8]United States Department of Education (1998). *Annual Plan: Rehabilitation Services, Disability, Research, and Special Institutions.* Washington, D.C: www.ed.gov/pubs/AnnualPlan/RSDRSI.html.

[9]Wright, G. N. (1980). *Total rehabilitation.* Boston, MA: Little, Brown and Company. (See: ch. 6, 6.7; ch. 7; and ch. 12, 12.2)

OVERVIEW OF DISABILITIES

RUTH TORKELSON LYNCH
University of Wisconsin, Madison

LISA ZHENG
CLAYTON W. FAUBION
UNIVERSITY OF MARYLAND EASTERN SHORE

CHAPTER TOPICS

- Living With A Disability
- Categories of Disability
- Utilizing Disability Information for Rehabilitation Planning

Rehabilitation professionals need a basic understanding of a variety of disabilities in order to coordinate effective plans. The ultimate goal of the counselor-client partnership is to achieve life goals by coordinating resources, improving health, and enhancing functioning. What constitutes a disability? The Americans with Disabilities Act of 1990 (ADA) includes a legal definition of disability, which in part defines a person with a disability as one who has

a physical or mental impairment that substantially limits one or more major life activities.

However, there is more to the concept of disability than the presence of a disease or injury condition. Disability is more accurately viewed as the outcome of the interaction between a health condition (e.g., disease, injury) and contextual factors (i.e., environmental and personal factors).[30] Social attitudes, architectural features, and terrain are examples of environmental factors while age, gender, coping factors, social background, character, and personality are examples of personal factors that influence how disability is actually experienced by an individual. The exact same "diagnosis" (e.g., spinal cord injury, epilepsy, schizophrenia) may be experienced differently depending on personal and environmental context. This chapter, however, will focus on an overview of the most common underlying diseases and injuries (i.e., the health conditions) rather than focusing on the contextual factors since those are covered elsewhere in the text.

There is a real need for services, support, and information related to disability. In 2002, 51.2 million people (18% of the population) in the U.S. had some level of disability and 32.5 million (11.5% of the population) had a severe disability. Older people were more likely to report having a disability with the disability rate successively higher for each age group (e.g., people 65-69 years old are twice as likely to have a disability compared to those 45-54).[27] More than 10 million people ages 6 and over need personal assistance for activities of daily living (ADLs including getting around inside the home, getting in or out of bed or chair) or instrumental activities of daily living (IADLs such as keeping track of money and bills, taking prescription medications at the right amount at the right time, preparing meals). Disability clearly has an impact on the lives of many Americans–especially for individuals who have a disability themselves and those who assist a family member with a disability.

Rehabilitation professionals can be increasingly effective if we address both functional improvement and healthy living. The medical and rehabilitation systems traditionally tend to be illness management systems rather than health promotion systems. For example, individuals with adult onset physical disabilities often do not receive guidance in how to modify their exercise and diet as their lifestyle becomes more sedentary. It is not uncommon in many residential settings for individuals with disabilities to be offered primarily high calorie, high fat food options with minimal exercise (e.g., pizza and a movie rather than fruit and vegetables with scheduled daily walks).[19]

Medical science breakthroughs, technology innovations, and healthcare interventions are constantly evolving. Prevention of health problems and promotion of healthy living have become increasingly emphasized in our healthcare system. This emphasis on health promotion and prevention has been slower to take hold in serving people with disabilities but is now a national priority. *Healthy People 2010*, formulated by the Office of Disease Prevention and Health Promotion within the U.S. Department of Health and Human Services, is a national 10-year plan intended to encourage and guide federal, state, and local community health promotion and wellness activities and policies to improve the health of Americans.

The importance of health promotion and disease prevention in the lives of people with disabilities are recognized throughout *Healthy People 2010*. Two major goals related to people with disabilities are to increase the quality and years of healthy life and to eliminate disparities in health. Compared with people without disabilities, people with disabilities have less participation in health promotion and preventative health activities including:

- less preventive use of the health-care system (e.g., oral health exams, mammography),
- higher rates of chronic conditions (e.g., elevated blood pressure, depression, obesity),
- lower rates of social participation (e.g., high school completion, employment), and
- lower rates of recommended health behaviors (e.g., stopping smoking, cardiovascular activity, leisure-time physical activity).

People with disabilities are experiencing many more health-related problems that are often unrelated, or only secondarily related to their underlying disability:

- preventable secondary conditions (e.g., pressure sores, fractures),
- high rates of emergency room visits and hospital stays, and
- early deaths from co-morbidities (e.g., diabetes-related cardiovascular disease associated with obesity, poor nutrition, and lack of exercise).[21]

Helping individuals to optimize function, utilize resources, and eliminate environmental and attitudinal barriers are among the most crucial contributions of rehabilitation professionals. Rehabilitation professionals are now strongly urged to add health promotion and prevention to their job descriptions. In order to help prepare professionals for this array of tasks, this chapter will address several key themes including the key categories of disabilities and trends in health promotion and prevention.

LIVING WITH A DISABILITY

Long-lasting, chronic illnesses and disabilities are often not so severe that they are life threatening, but they may have a lifelong presence. During the past 100 years, there has been a shift from acute illnesses (e.g. pneumonia, influenza) being the leading causes of illness and death in the United States to chronic illnesses (e.g. heart disease and cancer) as the leading causes of illness and death. This shift toward chronic conditions has resulted in individuals living for long periods with varying levels of activity limitation rather than the past pattern of either recovery or relatively quick progression to death.

Physical health, psychological health, social health, and spiritual health are all components of health and wellness that apply to everyone including persons with disabilities.[20] Physical health gets the most attention because we tend to think of health in terms such as body mass index and physical energy/vitality. Psychological health (e.g., life satisfaction, perceived well-being, emotional stability), social health (e.g., social connectedness, social integration), and spiritual health (e.g., meaning or purpose in life, optimism) are important components of health and wellness.

People with chronic health conditions may feel reasonably well at times and more restricted in activities at other times. Some people with disabilities have relatively good overall health and practice healthy living (e.g., physical exercise, nutrition). Steinmetz[27] reported from U.S. Census Data that 33.4% of persons with a non-severe disability and 12.7 of persons with a severe disability perceived their health status as very good or excellent. Even though these figures are substantially below the 72.5% of persons with no disability who perceive their health status as very good or excellent, it still may be surprising to many readers that anyone who has a disability feels "healthy." This is likely due to a common misperception that living with a disability equals illness or lack of health. People with chronic illnesses and conditions (e.g., diabetes, multiple sclerosis, spinal cord injury, epilepsy) often have to make lifestyle and life management changes for the long term and many of those changes (e.g., modifying drinking or smoking, changing diet) can actually benefit overall health. In addition to adopting health-promoting behaviors that benefit anyone (e.g., stopping smoking, eating healthy foods), individuals with disabilities can also improve their health outcomes through prevention of secondary conditions and maintenance of assistive devices.

A person's life does not have to be defined by the disability. The individual may change perceptions of self, may face financial and life activity challenges, and experience changing relationships with family and friends. People cannot tolerate a crisis state for very long, however. Thus, in coping with a chronic condition or disability, the individual resorts either to healthy adaptation or unhealthy adjustment and psychological deterioration. The problems faced are different than those that individuals with an acute illness must manage. Chronic illnesses and disabilities differ in their impact–not in terms of severity, but in how much they disrupt lives. Even serious illnesses and conditions can be assimilated into the daily life of an individual. Individuals with chronic disability can live their life without constant "definition of self" in terms of the diagnosed condition and it is still possible to attain a satisfying level of emotional, spiritual, social, and physical health.

CATEGORIES OF DISABILITY

Although there may be an impact on more than one aspect of functioning, most chronic medical conditions have a primary impact on either physical, sensory, cognitive, or emotional/psychosocial functioning. This chapter will present an overview of disabilities by grouping conditions according to the primary aspect of functioning that is affected. Always keep in mind that some health conditions (e.g., multiple sclerosis, HIV/AIDS, traumatic brain injury) may impact multiple aspects of functioning.

Functioning is of interest for effective rehabilitation planning. You could have two individuals with the same diagnosis and their functional situation may not be alike at all. Each person may be experiencing a unique level of disease severity or progression; have different complicating illness features (e.g., obesity, poor cardiovascular health); and may receive different types of medical care and therapy. Each person also has differences in psychosocial circumstances (e.g., family, social support, finances, living situation), personal resources (e.g., resilience, coping skills) as well as differing education, vocational skills, and occupational history. In all cases, the rehabilitation professional or case manager must be prepared to analyze the individual's situation thoroughly. Considering the importance of understanding the functional impact of disability, the next section is organized by function rather than disease or diagnostic terms.

PHYSICAL FUNCTIONING: PROBLEMS AND SOLUTIONS

Chronic difficulties in physical functioning stem most frequently from (a) injuries or (b) diseases and disorders of the musculoskeletal (i.e., bones, skeletal muscles), connective tissue (i.e., ligaments, tendons, cartilage), and neuromuscular systems. Injuries that result in permanent difficulties in physical functioning may be of traumatic onset or due to repetitive motion injuries (also referred to as cumulative trauma disorders or overuse syndromes).

Spinal cord injury resulting in paralysis and loss of motor and sensory functioning usually has a sudden onset due to major trauma from a motor vehicle accident or diving in shallow water. A spinal cord injury is the result of a major flexing (extension), bruising, or actual severing of the spinal cord that results in paralysis with partial or complete loss of function in both motor function and sensation. Since the spinal cord is the principal transport mechanism for messages to and from the brain, both kinds of messages stop when the cord is injured.

Motor vehicle accidents, falls, acts of violence, and sports are the major causes of spinal cord injuries. The higher the cord is traumatized from injury (e.g., closer to the head), the more pervasive are the effects on physical functioning. Lower-level spinal cord injury (i.e., paraplegia) principally affects the hips, abdominal muscles, legs, feet, as well as bowel and bladder functioning. High-level spinal cord injury (i.e., quadriplegia or tetraplegia) produces paralysis and loss of sensation not only in the lower body and bowel/bladder, but also in the torso, arms, hands, and fingers, along with varying degrees of compromised respiratory function.

The point in the spinal cord where damage has occurred determines the functioning that an individual has after a spinal cord injury. The level of injury and the severity of the damage to the spinal cord have major ramifications for rehabilitation intervention, for levels of independence in activities of daily living, and for the type of wheelchair used (usually manual for paraplegia and motorized for quadriplegia level injuries).

While permanent paralysis and loss of sensation are, by no means, a minor matter, individuals with spinal cord injuries are able to use assistive technology and adapted equipment to enhance their physical functioning. The impact of the initial injury is not the only concern for an individual who sustains a spinal cord injury. It is critically important for individuals with spinal cord injury (and their rehabilitation professionals, families, friends, and employers) to take preventative health seriously. Complications that could seriously impact their life functioning, quality of life, and even long-term survival can then be minimized or avoided.

The most common aspects of health and prevention that individuals with spinal cord injury need to attend to include

- bowel and bladder management (e.g., careful monitoring of foods and liquids, following a regular voiding regimen to avoid infections),
- skin care (e.g., periodically relieve sitting pressure by shifting positions in the chair; responding immediately with bed rest if there is discoloration or the beginning of a pressure sore),
- spasticity management (e.g., monitor and treat if these reflexes disturb sleep, cause public embarrassment, or create a safety risk),
- monitor conditions of pounding headache, dizziness, and sweating with shooting blood pressure because these can be symptoms of potentially life-threatening autonomic dysreflexia,
- maintain movement of joints and stretch muscles daily to avoid contractures (to avoid permanently flexed joints),
- promote breathing and cough function through environmental modifications (avoiding smoke and irritants) especially in individuals with quadriplegia level injuries,
- manage neuropathic pain (e.g., through medication, physical movement, relaxation training).[4]

DISEASES OR DISORDERS

A disease or disorder that impacts physical functioning is exemplified by arthritis (rheumatoid and osteoarthritis). Chronic back pain and amputations are examples of disorders that reduce physical functioning and may occur from either injury or disease.

Arthritis refers to inflammation of a joint and the term includes a variety of autoimmune (i.e., the body fighting itself) conditions that affect joints, cartilage, and bones. Pain and stiffness are the functional result that leads to everyday physical tasks, such as climbing stairs or opening a jar, being difficult to do.

Rheumatoid arthritis is an autoimmune disease in which the normal immune response is directed against an individual's own tissue, including the joints, tendons, and bones. The most commonly affected joints are the fingers, hands, and wrists. Among the larger joints, knees are most commonly involved followed by shoulders and hips. The treatment goals are to control pain and inflammation with medication, to retard the progression of joint destruction, and to provide assistive tools and training in joint protection (e.g., minimize stress with proper posture, avoid joint overuse during acute pain episodes, and avoid prolonged periods in the same position).[11]

Osteoarthritis is a degenerative joint disease characterized by progressive loss of cartilage and the physical impact is mainly to the weight-bearing joints such as the knees, hips, and lumbosacral spine. Significant functional disability in osteoarthritis occurs in the form of fractures, bone deformity, and pain. Exercise is a clear benefit to improve range of motion, muscle endurance, aerobic capacity, proper walking gait, and balance, and for overall reduction of pain.

Chronic back pain may be an extension of symptoms due to injury, or it may be due to degenerative diseases such as osteoporosis or a narrowing (stenosis) of the spinal canal. Pain is always a subjective experience, and the term has three important components:

(1) a sensory component indicating biological underpinnings;
(2) an emotional component (e.g., learned), and
(3) a component as it is defined by the individual.[25]

Another perspective on the pain experience describes pain in three dimensions:

(1) a sensory-discriminative dimension (the physical, sensory component),
(2) a cognitive-evaluative dimension (an ongoing perception and appraisal of the meaning of the sensation), and
(3) the affective-motivational dimension (the mood dimension). Therefore, there is no laboratory or imaging study (e.g., X-ray) that can "show pain."

How does pain result in reduced physical functioning? Respondent behaviors may be seen in acute pain as a spontaneous reaction to the stimuli, such as shaking your finger after you touch a hot burner. Volitional behaviors, such as walking slowly or using a cane, emerge in an attempt to decrease pain. Some physical functioning behavior becomes operant pain behavior if the individual has been encouraged and reinforced. This type of behavior (e.g., limping, moving slowly) may eventually control and limit the individual's mobility and physical functioning unnecessarily. The lack of movement and exercise in turn leads to a reduction in physical conditioning that perpetuates the pain and limits activity, many times to an unnecessarily restricted degree.

Early intervention for pain is crucial to prevent acute pain from becoming chronic pain and to minimize the functional impact of chronic pain, if it occurs. There are numerous interventions that are used to manage pain including various modalities (e.g., traction, ultrasound, massage, acupuncture), medication therapy, surgery, exercise, and complementary approaches (e.g., cognitive-behavioral therapy, relaxation training).[16]

Carpal tunnel syndrome is a disorder that is caused by pressure on the median nerve that runs down the forearm to the thumb, index finger, the middle finger, and half the ring finger of the hand. The median nerve passes through a passage in the wrist called the carpal tunnel. Irritation to the carpal tunnel tissue causes inflammation that presses on the median nerve. Symptoms of carpel tunnel syndrome can range from a tingling sensation, to numbness, to severe pain. Carpal tunnel syndrome is most often associated with injury due to repetitive motion such as typing for hours at a time, or repeatedly carrying heavy dishes in a restaurant. Individuals who work in industries that deal with repeated, heavy lifting and vibration are also susceptible to carpal tunnel syndrome. While these types of repetitive, heavy duty activities are commonly associated with carpal tunnel syndrome, other factors put individuals at risk as well. Obesity, smoking, diabetes, and rheumatoid arthritis have also been associated with carpal tunnel syndrome. While repetitive motion and diseases are associated with carpal tunnel syndrome, congenital predisposition is likely for many individuals–they are just born with a smaller carpal tunnel.[12]

Carpal tunnel syndrome can be treated in a number of ways. For some individuals, relief can be obtained by stretching and exercises that strengthen the affected areas. Passive splinting and cold packs are other relatively simple interventions that are effective for some people. Drug interventions that may be effective include over the counter anti-inflammatory medications, as well as diuretics or corticosteroids. Prescription medication interventions should, of course, only be taken under a physician's supervision. For some individuals, surgery may be required to obtain symptom reduction. Surgery is a much more invasive approach and generally considered a "last resort." If symptoms are severe and aren't being successfully impacted by the less invasive approaches, surgery may be warranted. The goal of carpal tunnel surgery is to enlarge the carpal tunnel area so that pressure on the median nerve is reduced. Endoscopic surgery may be an option for some individuals, which can result in a quicker recovery time. Even with surgery, complete recovery from carpal tunnel syndrome may not occur.

While these interventions can bring relief to individuals who have carpel tunnel syndrome, the best approach is, of course, prevention. Whenever possible, redesigning work processes so that repetitive motion injuries do not occur should be the first intervention. Particular attention should be paid to the positioning of the wrist in the work process. Ensuring that the wrist stays in a natural position, as well as taking frequent breaks and wearing gloves to keep the hand warm may also help.[13]

Fibromyalgia (FM) is a syndrome that affects the muscles and soft tissues of the body and can have a wide range of possible symptoms. Chronic pain, multiple tender spots, fatigue, and sleep disturbance are common. The chronic and widespread nature of the symptoms of fibromyalgia can negatively affect virtually all aspects of a person's life, including psychological health. Many health care practitioners are not well acquainted with fibromyalgia, and patients can go years before being accurately diagnosed. Because fibromyalgia is a syndrome that has a wide range of possible symptoms and because diagnosis comes largely from patient self-report, symptoms can be confused with other disorders. No concrete diagnostic measure, such as a blood test, exists for fibromyalgia. Diagnosis is based on at least 11 of 18 specific points of the body being tender or in pain with a duration of at least three months.[13]

No specific causes of fibromyalgia have yet been discovered. It is theorized that individuals with FM have an increased sensitivity to pain due to a neurotransmitter or neuroendocrine malfunction. Stress and injuries have also been linked to FM. Treatment for FM includes medication for pain management, emotional support for dealing with the stress of a chronic illness, and ensuring that the patient has good sleep habits such as avoiding caffeine and other stimulants in the evening hours. Some individuals with FM may also find alternative treatments helpful such as yoga and acupuncture.[15]

Amputations are another condition that impacts physical functioning and the underlying reason for the amputation can stem from either an injury, a disease process (most frequently diabetes or cancer), or from a congenital limb anomaly present at birth. An amputation is the surgical removal of all or part of a limb. The greatest cause of limb loss in the United States is peripheral vascular disease (65% of all amputations) that is often associated with diabetes and occurs most frequently in individuals 60-75 years of age.[7] Peripheral vascular disease interferes with blood and oxygen flow to the lower extremities. When this occurs together with peripheral sensory neuropathy (losing feeling in the extremities), then foot ulcerations (sores) and gangrene can occur requiring amputation to save the person's life. Amputations of at least a portion of both legs are rather common, with amputation of the second leg occurring within five years of the first amputation in nearly half the cases of amputation due to diabetes.

Physical functioning after amputation has a great deal to do with age and overall health. Older individuals, usually with underlying vascular disease due to diabetes and other coexisting health problems, use more energy during walking than their younger counterparts who usually lost their limb due to trauma but may otherwise be healthy and fit. Chronologic age alone should not, however, determine whether an individual with an amputation is a candidate for a prosthesis. Effective use of a prosthesis or artificial replacement limb depends more on the condition of the skin, because sores, swelling in the residual limb (stump), scar tissue, nerve pain, or phantom limb pain can compromise effective application of a prosthesis. Physical functioning is dependent on proper fit, skin care, and physical conditioning since it takes considerably higher energy (estimates between 40-100% more energy) to accomplish a task with a prosthesis.[2] The sensation of the missing portion of the limb is very common (80-100%), but unless the sensation is also painful (i.e., phantom pain) there is usually no functional impact.

SENSORY FUNCTIONING: PROBLEMS AND SOLUTIONS

The five senses are sight, hearing, touch, taste, and smell. Although all five senses are valued and serve a function in quality of life, problems with sight and hearing tend to create more challenges to functioning in a sight and hearing-oriented world.

Vision problems referred to in this section are those that affect functioning because they cannot be corrected with the common accommodation of eyeglasses or contact lenses. Vision impairment varies from individual to individual, and blindness to the extent of not even seeing light is actually very rare. The term legal blindness in fact does not refer to the absence of light perception. The most common definition for legal blindness is that the best-corrected visual acuity is either 20/200 or worse in the better eye (with standard lenses or contacts), or the peripheral visual field is restricted to 20 degrees or less.

The main impairments affecting visual function are reduced visual acuity, visual field loss, poor contrast sensitivity, and lighting and glare problems. An individual with reduced visual acuity is unable to resolve detail. When glasses cannot resolve acuity difficulties, then some form of magnification may be used. Magnification is accomplished by either making the object larger (e.g., large print books, clocks), by moving the object closer (e.g., sitting at the front of the room, moving closer to the television), or using an optical device to make the object look bigger (e.g., telescope magnifier). Visual field loss has a primary impact on mobility because it is important to be able to detect objects around us not only directly in front of us.

A loss of vision in an area is referred to as a scotoma, and scotomas in the visual field can vary in size and shape. Difficulties with contrast are noted more in real-life situation than from the visual acuity charts used in standard eye exams (with very black letters on light background). Contrast difficulties are usually related to lighting and glare, and can be modified with visors, special lighting, or use of special filters.

Vision problems increase with age, due primarily to eye diseases such as cataracts and macular degeneration that are more common in older adults. The development of cataracts is actually a normal part of aging and the greater the progression, the greater the visual impairment due to glare, loss of contrast, and decreased visual acuity. Surgical removal and replacement of the cataract with an intraocular lens is very common and surgery is indicated when visual function is impaired to a degree that it has started to affect normal daily activities such as reading and independent travel.

Macular degeneration results from degenerative changes to the part of the eye that function like the film in a camera. The effect on vision is distortion, a decrease in visual acuity, a decrease in color recognition, a loss of contrast, or loss of vision in a part of the field of vision.

Another group of individuals who are at higher risk for functional vision deficits (25 times higher) are individuals with diabetes. Diabetic retinopathy may start with small hemorrhages in the eye. Functionally, individuals with this condition can experience problems due to glare, reduced contrast sensitivity, problems with visual field loss, and/or double vision.

When considering rehabilitation for an individual with a visual impairment, attention should be focused on enhancing the ability to perform tasks functionally. Rehabilitation efforts focus on providing the best possible residual vision (vision enhancement) and assisting the individual to develop non-visual skills that can substitute for lost visual function (vision substitution).[22] Vision enhancement includes the use of magnifiers, telescopic aids, colored filters, and computer or video magnification screens. Non-visual means of increasing functioning (visual substitution) includes the use of Braille, talking clocks and books, orientation and mobility training, and activities of daily living training.

Hearing involves the detection, transmission, analysis, and integration of sound into meaningful symbols. Similar to vision impairment, significant hearing impairments that have an impact on functioning are not limited to "total" loss of the ability to hear sound. Hearing loss is classified as conductive (involving the outer and middle ear), sensorineural (middle ear), and mixed (a combination of conductive and sensorineural). Hearing aids are useful for conductive loss, because with this type of loss, the volume of sound is affected rather than the clarity of sound. Sensorineural losses can result in distortion or blockage of both loudness and pitch. Hearing aids may amplify sound but do not improve clarity. Cochlear implants (a surgical intervention) can improve detection of sound, but in some cases, lip reading is still required for recognition of words.

Individuals with profound hearing loss who cannot understand conversational speech through the ear with or without a hearing aid are considered deaf, and individuals who have difficulty understanding speech alone, with or without a hearing aid, are referred to as hard-of-hearing. People who are deaf communicate in different ways depending on the age of onset, the type of deafness, their lip-reading skills, their knowledge of sign language, and a variety of other factors.

Deafness, or other severe hearing impairment at a young age, has an impact on the development of language and speech and has significant socialization effects because of interference in child-to-child communication.[2] The most commonly used form of sign in the U.S. is American Sign Language (ASL) that has its own grammar and syntax and is very different from signed English that uses English word order.

Technology for enhancing communication includes the telecommunication device for the deaf (TDD) that is utilized to enhance communication via the phone lines. The Americans with Disabilities Act (ADA) requires all telephone companies that offer services to the public to have 24-hour telephone relay services available to individuals who have hearing limitations so they can access essential communication. Workplace accommodations might include the use of qualified interpreters, signaling devices, amplified telephones, communication aids, flashing lights and alarms, vibrating pages, modified acoustics, or workstations that limit outside noises.[10]

COGNITIVE FUNCTIONING: PROBLEMS AND SOLUTIONS

Cognitive functioning encompasses a wide array of information processing and decision making skills that utilize attention, verbal and nonverbal memory, short and long-term memory, perceptual abilities, planning, task initiation, and problem-solving. Modern western society is highly verbal and fast-paced, with high value placed on independence and personal decision-making. Therefore, deficits in cognitive functioning, especially quick and complex cognitive functioning, pose a challenge and concern for independence.

Mental retardation: The American Association of Mental Retardation's (AAMR) definition of mental retardation includes the following phrases:

> *substantial limitations in present functioning; sub-average intellectual functioning; and concurrent related limitations in two or more of the following adaptive skills areas: communication, self-care, home living, social skills, community use, self-direction, health and safety, functional academics, leisure, or work.*

Mental retardation manifests before age 18, but the degree of developmental delay or mental retardation ranges from mild to moderate and from severe to profound. These very different levels of cognitive functioning correspond to a range of assistance, support, and supervision needs. In fact, the current AAMR categorization system refers to the intensity of supports needed: intermittent, limited, extensive, and pervasive.

There are known causes of mental retardation, but many cases have no known etiology. The major categories of causes include metabolic disorders (e.g., Tay-sachs disease), brain malformation, chromosomal abnormalities (e.g., Down Syndrome), prenatal infection (e.g., German Measles), maternal use of drugs and alcohol (e.g., Fetal Alcohol Syndrome), fetal malnutrition, prematurity, birth trauma, and lack of oxygen. Phenylketonuria (PKU), a deficiency in the production of an enzyme necessary for metabolism, is another cause of mental retardation.

The most critical functional difficulties that correspond to mental retardation are slower rates of learning than typical peers and difficulty generalizing or transferring information learned in one situation to another.[8] This does not mean that learning cannot occur, but it does infer that people with mental retardation need to be taught specific skills in environments where they would naturally perform those skills. The practice of supported employment stems from this recognition of learning in the actual environment. Supported employment describes the provision of employment in community job settings with support or assistance to do the job.

General health management is critical to case management for persons with mental retardation because other secondary health problems often compromise functioning. Many persons with mental retardation lead relatively sedentary lives with resulting obesity, nutritional, and cardiovascular concerns, but these secondary conditions can be improved significantly with targeted physical conditioning and health promotion programs.[25]

Traumatic Brain Injury: While the cognitive limitations of mental retardation often are present from birth, the cognitive limitations from traumatic brain injuries frequently occur in young adults (the highest rate of injury is to males between the ages 15-24). The changes to cognition, personality, and sometimes physical functioning may be so dramatic that the person seems to be a different person compared to what they were pre-injury. Traumatic brain injuries result from a variety of causes including motor vehicle accidents (45-50%), falls (20%), assaults, sports accidents, and gunshot wounds. There are factors that contribute to the occurrence of traumatic brain injuries (e.g., alcohol use, risk taking activities, impaired cognition or reaction time due to legal or illegal drugs) as well as factors that are critical to prevention of traumatic brain injuries (e.g., use of seat belts and motorcycle helmets, vehicle airbags, not drinking and driving).

Closed head injury refers to injuries in which the brain sustains damage from rapid acceleration and deceleration from a motor vehicle accident or fall. Closed head injuries result in damage to diffuse areas of the brain because of the brain moving and hitting the skull during the initial trauma and from swelling and bleeding after the initial traumatic event. The initial medical concerns are to prevent swelling and infection and to stabilize any other injuries (e.g., skeletal trauma, limb fractures). Since damage can be diffuse throughout the brain, and since the brain is the central control for all functioning, the functional implications after a traumatic brain injury are unique for each individual. Numerous diffuse limitations may result from a closed head injury, and these limitations may be physical or sensory (e.g., balance, fatigue, uneven gait, decreased motor speed, seizure disorders, double vision); emotional/psychological (e.g., emotional lability, flat affect, impulsivity, disinhibition, depression); and/or cognitive (e.g., impairment in attention/concentration, memory, perceptual processing, verbal reasoning, critical thinking, initiation, problem-solving).[26]

Open head injury refers to injuries such as by stabbing or gunshot where the actual brain matter has been penetrated. With an open head injury, there is a greater risk of infection complications to develop, but the damage is more likely to be localized to a specific site in the brain.

Traumatic brain injury produces a wide continuum of outcomes ranging from death to normal function, with varying degrees of limitation in functioning for most survivors. The depth or level of unconsciousness after the initial injury, the duration of coma, the duration of Post-Traumatic-Amnesia (PTA), and radiological findings regarding sites and severity of damage to the brain are all early measures of severity and subtle predictors of later outcome. The age of the individual is also a factor with people under 20 generally doing much better than those over 60 who have the same kind of injury.[14]

Much of the recovery occurs in the first six months after injury, and the early stages may include relatively rapid improvement in basic attention, day-to-day memory, and performance of physical (e.g., walking) and self-care skills. The re-acquisition of complex cognitive and interpersonal skills are a much longer-term process, and these thinking, communication, and personality aspects of functioning usually cause the greatest frustration to friends and family.

A significant proportion of individuals evidence clear cognitive and behavioral/personality change and yet report that they have nothing wrong with them. This quandary can be one of the most challenging aspects of working with individuals who have sustained a traumatic brain injury. The capacity for self-awareness is believed to be a primary function of the frontal lobes of the brain and since individuals with traumatic brain injury often sustained damage to the frontal portion of the brain, they are vulnerable to problems with awareness. Not all unawareness is neurologically based, however. Psychological denial may appear as a form of self-protection in the face of such dramatic changes in pre-injury to post-injury functioning. Unawareness or refusal to recognize limitations can make rehabilitation efforts challenging, because the individual is less likely to participate in new skill development or the use of accommodations.

The wide variation in functional limitations and needs requires rehabilitation to be a team process for traumatic brain injury. Interventions tend to vary somewhat depending on the stage of service:

- acute rehabilitation services focus on physical support to prevent problems related to coma and inactivity (e.g., contractures, pressure sores) and to provide sensory stimulations and nutrition management,

- sub-acute care programs focus on increasing basic physical and cognitive/behavior functioning and training in activities of daily living, and
- post-acute rehabilitation services focus on transition from hospital and intense rehabilitation to the community with day rehabilitation programs, transitional living programs, home health services, family intervention, alcohol and substance abuse treatment, and vocational rehabilitation.[5]

Some individuals benefit from learning compensatory strategies and then can resume at least a modified version of their former routines (work, school, independent living). Other individuals benefit from intense physical skill intervention from occupational and physical therapists, which may range from re-learning to walk to learning to button a shirt with one hand due to paralysis on one side of the body (hemiplegia). Speech therapy may be involved for a range of tasks from swallowing to forming sounds and re-learning to speak. Cognitive therapy or cognitive remediation/retraining may be incorporated into all of the rehabilitation activities and is designed to use areas of cognitive strength to compensate for areas of weakness. For example, an individual with memory difficulties may learn to use a beeping wristwatch, a date book, or a handheld computer for memory cues throughout the day. Depending on the nature and scope of functional limitations, rehabilitation interventions for independent living and return-to-work may range from long-term supported employment and job coaching to remediation and modification of specific work tasks.

EMOTIONAL/PSYCHIATRIC FUNCTIONING: PROBLEMS AND SOLUTIONS

Severe emotional or psychiatric disabilities can significantly impair one's ability to take part in major life activities for extended periods of time. Psychiatric disabilities can make it very challenging for one to reach important life developmental goals, such as obtaining independent living, providing sufficient self-care, securing satisfactory employment, having intimate relationships, and enjoying life through recreational and spiritual activities.[3] Schizophrenia and mood disorders (major depressive disorder and bipolar conditions) are diagnoses commonly associated with psychiatric disabilities that can have significant functional limitations on the emotional realm as well as various psychosocial aspects of life.

Schizophrenia. Schizophrenic disorders are a complicated set of psychotic conditions that may vary in course, severity, and outcome, but share similar symptoms and dysfunctions and are best conceptualized as a spectrum disorder. These disorders result in substantial disruption of thinking, perception, emotions, judgment, motivation, and behavior (especially social interaction).

Schizophrenic disorders usually become evident during late adolescent and early adulthood (usually before age 25). Persons who have an initial acute episode may have a full recovery (20-25%), may have mild residual effects (20-30%), or have long-term moderate to severe lifelong effects (40-60%).[1]

Research into the etiology of schizophrenia has not produced any major breakthroughs, but evidence indicates that genetic and prenatal factors increase an individual's vulnerability to schizophrenia. Both genetic and prenatal factors interact with environmental factors, such as exposure to stressful events especially during adolescence, which can trigger the behavioral expression of this vulnerability.[29]

Cognitively, individuals with schizophrenia often experience hallucinations and delusions. The most commonly reported type of auditory hallucinations are voices. The content of voices varies greatly. Voices may comment on the person's behavior as "very loud thoughts" that are distinct from one's own thoughts. Often, two voices may argue with one another about the person. Other times, voices can tell the person what to do. This command type of auditory hallucination can be soft and suggestive or it can be as irresistible and compelling as "it must be obeyed."

Delusions are fixed, erroneous beliefs that the individual is not willing to change despite indisputable evidence available to the contrary. Delusions of persecution, grandiosity, and reference are common. The individual may feel there is conspiracy against them. They think that someone from much higher social rank, for example the President of United States, has sought their guidance and advice. Random occurrences in life are no longer random. All manner of things may refer and pertain to the individual with special personal references, codes, or messages. In addition to hallucinations and delusions, individuals may experience thought broadcasting, thought insertion, thought blocking, or racing thoughts. Thoughts do not belong to the individual but are influenced by outside forces. "Disorganized speech" is another indication of cognitive impairment. The patient's speech becomes illogical; ideas seem to have no coherent connections, thus making it difficult for others to "make sense of" or follow. A diminution of thoughts is also reflected in poverty of speech (Alogia).

Emotionally inappropriate affect may appear. The natural connection between thought and affect seems to be lost. There is an inconsistent emotional response to a particular situation–for example, no signs of grief at the loss of a loved one. Flat affect is most common among persons with schizophrenia, where a person would respond to normally emotional situations with few signs of appropriate verbal or nonverbal expression. Most of the time, the range of emotional expressiveness is diminished, with little eye contact or body language. Another noticeable inappropriate affect is seen when an individual, for no apparent reason, may break into uncontrollable laughter that does not seem to correspond to how the persons feels at that moment.

Disorganized or catatonic behavior is found in some persons with psychotic disorders. Grossly disorganized behavior manifests in difficulties in performing daily living activities such as maintaining basic hygiene. The individual may appear with childlike silliness or unpredictable agitation such as shouting or swearing with unidentifiable motivation. Markedly unkempt appearance and/or inappropriate dress in terms of weather or setting may be observed. Catatonic motor behaviors include motoric immobility (maintaining a rigid posture) and excessive, purposeless motor activity.

People with schizophrenia are characterized by an inability to embark on and persist in goal-direct activities (avolition). They often show much difficulty in interpersonal functioning such as showing little motivation or interest in engaging in any aspect of social interactions. Lack of a natural desire to interact with other human beings as well as a lack of skill in forming those social relationships, present substantial barriers for these individuals to achieve important life goals.

The clinical features of schizophrenic disorders are usually divided into two categories referred to as (a) positive symptoms and (b) negative symptoms. Positive symptoms are overtly out-of-the-ordinary reactions and behaviors, including hallucinations, delusions, disorganized thinking, catatonic and grossly disorganized behaviors. Negative symptoms, on the other hand, include decreased or missing reactions and expressions compared to what would be expected, and these symptoms persist during the chronic or recurring stages (i.e., are present when the person is not actively demonstrating psychotic symptoms.) The negative symptoms account for a substantial degree of the dysfunction associated with the disorder, which may appear as apathy, low energy, lack of motivation, poverty of speech, and social withdrawal.

Mood Disorders (major depressive disorders and bipolar disorders). Mood disorders are among the most common type of psychiatric disorders. Approximately 20.9 million American adults, or about 9.5 percent of the U.S. population age 18 and older, have a mood disorder.[29,17] Many people, however, do not suffer long-term disabilities due to the illness. They may experience relatively mild to moderate symptoms that do not have a significant negative impact on their everyday functioning. The most debilitating mood disorders are recurrent, episodic, and cause significant functional deficits in social, educational, occupational, or other important areas of life. Three types of episodes are associated with mood disorders; depressive episode, mania episode, and mixed episode. If individuals experience more than one instance of two out of the three types of episodes, they may meet the criteria for bipolar disorder.

Depressive episodes are characterized by consistently depressed mood or a loss of interest or pleasure in daily activities throughout most of the day and for at least a two week period. The sad mood must represent a change from the person's normal mood. Major depression includes vegetative symptoms such as either persistent insomnia or sleeping significantly more hours than usual and increased or decreased food consumption leading to weight gain or loss. Individuals may also experience daily fatigue, loss of energy, feelings of worthlessness, and unreasonable guilt; impairment in the ability to think, concentrate, and make decisions; feelings of hopelessness and emptiness; suicidal ideation and/or behavior.

The symptoms of manic episodes are almost the opposite of those of a depressive episode. They are marked by an unusually "high" or happy mood and sometimes feeling irritable or "jumpy" for at least one week. Individuals may feel unrealistically confident and important, energetic, and creative. Manic episode are also characterized by the person being more active than usual; having decreased need for rest or sleep; pressured speech; and jumping from one topic to another in order to catch up their racing thoughts. They tend to engage in excessive pleasure seeking activities. Their impulsive and often destructive behaviors, like spending too much money, having unprotected sex, or driving recklessly can cause serious consequences for themselves and their families.

A person with mixed episode meets the criteria for both types of depressive and manic episodes, experiencing both mood extremes simultaneously or in rapid sequence. For example, it is possible that the individual may feel full of energy, but at the same time feel blue and hopeless. During severe episodes of mood disorders, psychotic symptoms like hallucinations and delusions can also occur.

The goals of psychiatric rehabilitation are to assist the person with severe and persistent mental illness to achieve meaningful recovery, maximum community integration, and the highest possible quality of life.[24] The new concept of recovery represents hope and opportunities while individuals learn to positively adapt to the lasting mental illness and its symptoms; embark on the new journey of incorporating one's mental illness as part of one's reality; explore the way to recovery which is unique for each individual; and be open to possible failure because relapse is a part of the non-linear journey to recovery.[6] Psychiatric rehabilitation helps the person develop necessary illness self-management skills, as well as the social, emotional and intellectual skills that are needed to live independently in the community, interact with the real life environment ,and use community resources and supports. Regardless of the phases and severity of the person's mental illness, achieving reasonable quality of life is always important via meeting needs for shelter, food, social support, employment, and recreation.

Medication is considered a cornerstone of effective treatment for acute episodes of severe mental illness. Even when symptoms have subsided, it is believed that medication continues to play a vital role in relapse prevention and minimizes the risk of future psychotic episodes. However, since medications can cause serious and unpleasant side effects, people with schizophrenia or mood disorders may be reluctant to take them consistently. Following a medication management plan in collaboration with doctors and families becomes vital for the individual to avoid taking antipsychotic drugs on an irregular basis or to stop taking them altogether.

After the most debilitating symptoms from acute episodes are controlled through medication intervention, psychosocial treatments, (nonmedical approaches) start to play a very important role in the recovery process. Many communities have programs for people with severe mental illness. Services include housing, jobs, self-help groups, and dealing with crises. These psychiatric rehabilitation services help the person develop the necessary self-management skills as well as social, emotional, and intellectual skills that are needed to live independently in the community, interact with the real life environment, and use community resources and supports. Effective psychosocial treatments include various forms of psychotherapy (i.e., individual, group, and family therapy), social skill training, vocational counseling, and on-site job training. All of these interventions help provide individuals the necessary skills to lead productive lives.

UTILIZING DISABILITY INFORMATION FOR REHABILITATION PLANNING

It is not possible to cover every disease, disorder, or injury in one chapter. This chapter has attempted to provide a functional structure (i.e., physical, sensory, cognitive, emotional/psychosocial) for understanding the impact of diseases, disorders, or injuries for purposes of designing rehabilitation interventions. Each individual is unique and his or her experience of disability is unique. Many diseases or injuries have an impact on more than one of those functional categories, but for purposes of this chapter, diseases were presented in the category where the impact is the greatest in most cases. If a rehabilitation professional converts medical diagnostic and disability information about an individual into functional categories–physical, sensory, cognitive, emotional/psychosocial–it will be much easier to effectively design rehabilitation interventions that actually address what each person needs to enhance functioning.

It is an important skill for rehabilitation professionals to be able to translate medical information into how an individual's life is affected by disability. Rehabilitation professionals need to understand what to look for and how to interpret what is in medical records; be familiar with some of the key recommendations (e.g., new treatments, medication updates, how to prevent complications, how to promote health) for various disabilities, be able to participate in verbal discussions with other health care professionals; and be able to interpret this information into rehabilitation planning discussions with clients and their families. It is important to interpret medical information accurately, to ask for clarification when meanings are unclear, and to avoid the use of technical terms with clients, families, and other persons (e.g., teachers, third party payers) unless the meanings are clearly understood.

When we first work with an individual with a disability, it is a good idea to clarify whether the condition appears to be temporary or permanent and if the situation is expected to improve, remain the same, or deteriorate. The presence of a disease or injury, in and of itself, does not automatically correspond to life functioning limitations. Rehabilitation professionals need to develop an understanding not only of the medical concepts of disease and injury but also an understanding of how health behavior, other personal characteristics, and the environment influence life functioning. Secondary health complications (e.g., reduced lung capacity from smoking, fatigue and mobility difficulties from gaining excess weight) are major barriers to functioning for individuals with an underlying chronic illness or disability.[19] These secondary complications can be reduced or eliminated by incorporating a health and wellness promotion perspective into rehabilitation planning. It can be extremely rewarding to assist individuals with disabilities to enhance all aspects of their functioning including promoting health behaviors and defeating health-limiting behaviors.

REFERENCES

[1]Andrew, J. & Andrew, M. J. (2012). *The disability handbook.* Linn Creek, MO: Aspen Professional Services

[2]Bowe, F. (2000). *Physical, sensory, and health disabilities: An introduction.* Upper Saddle River, NJ: Merrill.

[3]Corrigan, P. W., Rao, D., & Lam, C. (2005). Psychiatric rehabilitation. In F. Chan, M. Leahy, & J. Saunders (Eds.) *Case management for rehabilitation health professionals (2nd ed): Volume 2* (pp. 132-163). Osage Beach, MO: Aspen Professional Services.

[4]Crewe, N. (2005). Spinal cord injury. In F. Chan, M. Leahy, & J. Saunders (Eds.) *Case management for rehabilitation health professionals (2nd ed): Volume 2* (pp. 164-185). Osage Beach, MO: Aspen Professional Services.

[5]Cunningham, J. M., Chan, F., Jones, J., Kamnetz, B., & Stoll, J., (2005). Traumatic brain injury rehabilitation. In F. Chan, M. Leahy, & J. Saunders (Eds.) *Case management for rehabilitation health professionals (2nd ed): Volume 2* (pp. 91-131). Osage Beach, MO: Aspen Professional Services.

[6]Deegan, P. E. (1988). Recovery: The lived experience of rehabilitation. *Psychosocial Rehabilitation Journal, 11),* 11-19.

[7]Eftekhari, N. (2002). Amputation rehabilitation. In B. O'Young, M. Young, & S. Stiens (Eds.), *Physical medicine and rehabilitation secrets* (2nd ed.) (pp. 553-561). Philadelphia: Hanley & Belfus.

[8]Falvey, M. A., Bishop, K. D., & Gage, S. T. (2002). Mental retardation. In M. G. Brodwin, F. A. Tellez, & S. K. Brodwin (Eds.), *Medical, psychosocial, and vocational aspects of disability* (pp. 119-128). Athens, GA: Elliott & Fitzpatrick.

[9]Harmon, R. L. & Horn, L. J. (2002). Traumatic brain injury. . In B. O'Young, M. Young, & S. Stiens (Eds.), *Physical medicine and rehabilitation secrets* (2nd ed.) (pp. 194-202). Philadelphia: Hanley & Belfus.

[10]Harvey, E. (2002). Hearing disabilities. In M. G. Brodwin, F. A. Tellez, & S. K. Brodwin (Eds.), *Medical, psychosocial, and vocational aspects of disability* (pp. 143-155). Athens, GA: Elliott & Fitzpatrick.

[11]Hicks, J. E., Goe, G. O., & Shah, J. P. (2002). Rehabilitative management of rheumatic diseases. In B. O'Young, M. Young, & S. Stiens (Eds.), *Physical medicine and rehabilitation secrets* (2nd ed.) (pp. 337-351). Philadelphia: Hanley & Belfus.

[12]http://www.ninds.nih.gov/disorders/carpal_tunnel/detail_carpal_tunnel.htm

[13]http://www.webmd.com/pain-management/carpal-tunnel/carpal-tunnel-syndrome-topic-overview

[14]http://fmaware.org/PageServerda3b.html?pagename=fibromyalgia_diagnosed

[15]http://www.webmd.com/fibromyalgia/guide/fibromyalgia-treatment-care

[16]Johnson, K. L. (2005). Chronic disabling pain: A biosocial disability. In F. Chan, M. Leahy, & J. Saunders (Eds.) *Case management for rehabilitation health professionals (2nd ed): Volume 2* (pp. 210-227). Osage Beach, MO: Aspen Professional Services.

[17]Kessler, R. C., Chiu, W. T., Demler O, Walters, E. E. (2005). Prevalence, severity, and comorbidity of twelve-month DSM-IV disorders in the National Comorbidity Survey Replication (NCS-R). *Archives of General Psychiatry*, 62, 617-627.

[18]Lynch, R. T. (2005). Promotion of health and enhanced life functioning for individuals with traumatic injuries and chronic health conditions. In F. Chan, M. Leahy, & J. Saunders (Eds.) *Case management for rehabilitation health professionals (2nd ed): Volume 2* (pp. 44-63). Osage Beach, MO: Aspen Professional Services.

[19]Lynch, R. T. (2006). Health promotion to enhance functioning: lessons for rehabilitation counselors. *Minnesota Rehabilitation Counseling Association Newsletter*, May, 1-3.

[20]Nosek, M. A. (2005). Wellness in the context of disability. In J. E. Myers & T. J. Sweeney (Eds.), *Counseling for wellness: Theory, research, and practice* (pp. 139-150). Alexandria, VA: American Counseling Association.

[21]Office of Disease Prevention and Health Promotion. (2000). *Healthy People 2010: Understanding and improving health (2nd ed.).* Washington, D.C.: U.S. Department of Health and Human Services.

[22]Panek, W. C. (2002). Visual disabilities. In M. G. Brodwin, F. A. Tellez, & S. K. Brodwin (Eds.), *Medical, psychosocial, and vocational aspects of disability* (2nd ed.) (pp. 157-169). Athens, GA: Elliott & Fitzpatrick.

[23]Patil, J. J., Guarino, A., & Staats, P. (2002). Pain management. In B. O'Young, M. Young, & S. Stiens (Eds.), *Physical medicine and rehabilitation secrets* (2nd ed.) (pp. 363-369). Philadelphia: Hanley & Belfus.

[24]Pratt,C.W., Gill, K. J., Barrett, N. M. & Roberts, M. M. (2007). *Psychiatric Rehabilitation.* (2nd ed.). Burlington, MA: Elsevier Science & Technology.

[25]Rimmer, J. H. & Hiss, S. B. (2005). Physical activity and fitness. In W. M. Nehring (Ed.), *Health promotion for persons with intellectual and developmental disabilities* (pp. 87-128). Washington, D.C.: American Association on Mental Retardation.

[26]Schwartz, S. H. (2002). Traumatic brain injury. In M. G. Brodwin, F. A. Tellez, & S. K. Brodwin (Eds.), *Medical, psychosocial, and vocational aspects of disability* (pp. 363-373). Athens, GA: Elliott & Fitzpatrick.

[27]Steinmetz E. (2006). *Americans with Disabilities:2002. Current Populations Reports, P70-107.* Washington, D.C.: U.S. Census Bureau.

[28]U.S. Census Bureau Population Estimates by Demographic Characteristics. Table 2: Annual Estimates of the Population by Selected Age Groups and Sex for the United States: April 1, 2000 to July 1, 2004 (NC-EST2004-02) Source: Population Division, U.S. Census Bureau Release Date: June 9, 2005. http://www.census.gov/popest/national/asrh/

[29]Walker, E., Kestler, L., Bollini, A. & Hochman, K. M. (2004). Schizophrenia: etiology and course. *Annual Review Psychology, 55,*

[30]World Health Organization. (2002). *Towards a common language for functioning, disability, and health.* Geneva, Switzerland: World Health Organization.

5

ADDICTIVE DISORDERS AND DISABILITY

D. SHANE KOCH

SOUTHERN ILLINOIS UNIVERSITY-CARBONDALE

ANNA M. KOCH

MARION VA MEDICAL CENTER

CHAPTER TOPICS

- Introduction
- Attitudes Towards and Beliefs about AD Disorders
- Cultural Beliefs about Psychotic Substance Use: To use or not to use?
- Outside Looking In
- Cultural Attitudes Toward Substance Use Disorders
- Professional Beliefs About Substance Use Disorders
- Personal Experience
- Family History of Substance Use Disorders
- The Extent of the Problem
- Defining AD Disorders
- The Effects of Psychoactive Substances
- Substance Disorders Defined
- The Continuum of Substance Use Disorders
- Case Studies
- Ad As A Coexisting Disability
- Role of the Rehabilitation Professional
- Self Help and AD Treatment
- Summary

INTRODUCTION

Addictive Disorders (AD) as both primary and coexisting disabilities significantly impact the rehabilitation process and present considerable challenges for both the persons experiencing these disorders and the rehabilitation professionals who serve them. Whether one experiences pre-existing AD or onset of AD after disability, extremely negative medical, vocational, social, and psychological consequences will directly result from the substance abuse as well as from the interaction of the substance abuse with physiological and psychological aspects of the individual's other disabilities.[18,6] Research regarding prevalence of AD among persons with disabilities varies, but a review of epidemiological research reported by West, Graham, & Cifu[23] would support the fact that AD rates among persons with disabilities are likely the same or greater than those within the general population. The presence of coexisting AD complicates the rehabilitation process, negatively influences rehabilitation outcomes, necessitates collaboration with other agencies, and in many cases, requires direct involvement of outside AD specialists.

Although AD counseling is often perceived as a sub-specialty of rehabilitation or as a separate professional group entirely, rehabilitation professionals are obligated to be aware of the impact of these disorders across the population of persons with disabilities and to be able to provide appropriate, effective, individualized service to these consumers so that they may have a fair opportunity to benefit from rehabilitative services. Despite these obligations, rehabilitation professionals are often unprepared to meet the challenge of serving this population. Historically, research has shown that rehabilitation counselors providing vocational rehabilitation services indicate an immediate need for training in this area.[9,10,15,19,18]

As a consequence of the complexity of the issues arising when persons experience AD disorders, a thorough review of the various aspects of these disabilities will be helpful for rehabilitation professionals who are involved in general practice, even if they never serve in positions where their primary responsibility is to serve clients with these disabilities. While many professionals have had informal experiences (direct or indirect) with these disabilities, this experience is seldom sufficient to prepare counselors to serve this population. The goal of this chapter will be to identify and review:

- the impact of individual and cultural attitudes, beliefs and values on this disability population,
- factors that influence drug effects,
- models of AD disability and the diagnostic criterion for substance use disorders,
- coexisting disabilities,
- treatment alternatives available for this population, and
- case management strategies for rehabilitation professionals working with this population.

ATTITUDES TOWARD AND BELIEFS ABOUT AD DISORDERS

The counseling relationship does not occur in a vacuum and as the field of rehabilitation has long recognized, it is often the interaction of persons with disability with the able-bodied population that may create the most substantial barriers for persons with disabilities. In this sense, AD disabilities represent one of the most significant challenges due to the multiple contradictory messages about substance use and abuse that arise within both the popular and professional cultures. These cultural messages influence the beliefs and behaviors of both counselors and consumers. If rehabilitation professionals are to be successful in intervening with this population, they must become aware of some of the dangerous misconceptions surrounding these disabilities and avoid them in their practice.

While it is beyond the scope of this section to explore all of the socio-cultural forces impacting alcohol and other drug use in American society, we will briefly examine the issue of attitudes toward AD disorders and their impact on the rehabilitation process. To accomplish this goal, this section will explore:

- underlying forces within the culture influencing both AD consumers and the professionals who serve them,
- professional attitudes, beliefs and values affecting the counseling relationship, and
- personal factors that can significantly affect services for this population.

CULTURAL BELIEFS ABOUT PSYCHOACTIVE SUBSTANCE USE: To use or not to use?

Central to understanding the cultural issues underlying all work with this population is the reality of our society's inability to come to consensus about the appropriate use of psychoactive substances. Any discussion about alcohol or other drug use, abuse, and dependency is likely to evoke powerful positive and negative responses as a consequence of America's ambivalence about substance use.

Today, in America, it can be exceptionally difficult to determine if substance use is helpful or hurtful. Our nation has historically maintained a "love-hate" relationship with psychoactive substances ever since colonial days when Dr. Benjamin Rush first sought to distinguish between good and bad alcoholic beverages.[8] This conflict has continued throughout American history with our public institutions variously seeking to monitor and control all forms of substance use, while at the same time individual citizens have continued to experiment with and to use an ever-expanding menu of substances. Despite significant attempts by health care professionals, community leaders, and politicians to control, regulate, and/or prevent the use of psychoactive substances, Americans' psychoactive substance use, misuse, and abuse has escalated to epidemic proportions, causing a severe national health problem.

Although, our public and private institutions have sought to regulate substance use through legislation and value formation, other communications within the popular culture have often encouraged the use of substances. For example, it would be surprising to view a weekend sports event on television without its accompanying advertisements informing us of the wonderful benefits of consuming alcoholic beverages. Viewers typically witness ordinary individuals involved in ordinary social activities who, upon consumption of the substance in question, experience wonderful transformations (often involving the opposite sex) greatly enhancing the quality of their lives due to the use of the beverage. One might come to believe that the use of alcohol will result in users becoming more attractive, confident, and self-assured, at the very least!

It is not unusual, however, to find these advertisements interspersed with public service announcements informing us of the dangers of using psychoactive substances. These messages delivered by the media and reinforced by our law enforcement agencies; community, state and federal prevention programs; churches; and in some cases, our families, just as earnestly warn us that psychoactive substances may lead us to our ruin. Those who would caution against substance use may even remind us that the misuse of alcoholic beverages, the only legal recreational substance at this time, results in more deaths than all illegal substance use combined. Consequently, that wonderful substance advertised during the half-time break and reputed to be safe and beneficial, may not be safe at all!

In summary, it can be very difficult to figure out whether psychoactive substance use is a blessing or a curse given these messages that constantly bombard the general public with quite contradictory information. If Shakespeare were writing today, perhaps he would have described this situation with a variation on his famous quote, "To use or not to use, that is the question."

OUTSIDE LOOKING IN

Given this environment, it can be exceptionally difficult for able-bodied individuals to determine whether or not they should use substances, but the question of substance use can be even more complex for persons with disabilities. For these individuals, the choice to use may be associated with many other factors (loss of freedom, reduced social interaction, increased stigma) that rehabilitation professionals should be aware of when addressing substance use by persons with disabilities.

While it has long been recognized that young people may begin to use alcohol and drugs to "fit in" or to relieve social discomfort, and that this type of using behavior may lead to other problematic use of substances, professionals are not always aware that this same impulse to use alcohol and drugs as a means to reduce social barriers may be magnified for persons with disabilities. Persons with disabilities may find themselves on "the outside looking in" throughout much of their lives due to a variety of handicaps as well as social discrimination. Making a choice not to use substances as a social or recreational outlet can be just one more way in which they perceive themselves to be isolated from "normal" activities.

Additionally, individuals who do not understand the capabilities of persons with disabilities may assume that these individuals have "nothing better to do than to stay drunk or high all of the time." When peers or family members believe that a person with disabilities is unable to fulfill the role of an independent, productive member of the community, they may even contribute to helping persons with disabilities use alcohol or drugs (enabling) irresponsibly, believing that they are somehow "helping" the person to cope with the disability. In this way, harmful use may be sponsored by the very people who care the most for the person who is at risk of experiencing negative consequences.

CULTURAL ATTITUDES TOWARD SUBSTANCE USE DISORDERS

Despite the fact that cultural messages may be indefinite regarding whether it is okay to use substances or not, our society is firm in its beliefs about drug abusers. The best illustration of our cultural beliefs about substance abusers has been articulated in a seminal article by James Statman, who found that, in our culture, our beliefs and attitudes toward drug abusers closely resemble our attitudes toward "the enemy during wartime."[21] His research would indicate that many in our society would judge persons with AD disorders to be beneath contempt and undeserving of public support.

If Statman is right, persons experiencing alcohol and other drug abuse are subject to this same extreme viewpoint. The "war on drugs" has become a "war on people," where persons with alcohol and other drug abuse (AD) disorders may be perceived as anti-social deviants or dangerous villains. In wartime, the enemy is to be destroyed rather than rehabilitated and programs that seek to serve this population are not valued or desired.

At the very least, it is certain that the American public views substance abuse as an extremely negative phenomenon and drug abusers as dangerous persons. Even the judicial system has failed to afford persons with AD disabilities equal protection under the law. Koch[9] reviewed cases where persons with AD disabilities sought employment protections under the Americans with Disabilities Act, and in case after case, found that persons with AD disabilities rarely received legal protection due to the fact that they were often perceived as being "dangerous" in the workplace. If a person's disability makes them dangerous to others, they can be legally discriminated against under the Rehabilitation Act or the ADA.

These attitudes toward and beliefs about AD disorders have been prevalent throughout history and have often been encompassed in what has been labeled the "moral model" of addiction. This model would suggest that persons with substance use disabilities are to blame for their own problems, and that the consequences of these disabilities are "just punishment" for bad judgment and behavior. According to the moral model, if individuals "reformed" by exercising their willpower and adopting correct attitudes, beliefs, and values, the AD disorders would be cured and perhaps these individuals could then "use responsibly." Despite decades of research conducted by numerous reputable researchers that has thoroughly discredited this conceptual model of addiction, it is still pervasive among both the general population and professional counselors.

PROFESSIONAL BELIEFS ABOUT SUBSTANCE USE DISORDERS

One might expect that professional helpers would be immune to negative opinions about AD disorders due to their education, experience, and insights. Professional preparation ought to prepare individuals to be unbiased and to suspend their own moral beliefs when serving clients. Contradicting these expectations, H.R.1789, the Health Professionals Substance Abuse Education Act[5] documents that fewer than ten percent of physicians believe that treatment works despite the accumulated evidence from decades of research demonstrating that treatment is effective.

Rehabilitation professionals are not immune from inaccurate and often negative beliefs held within the broader culture. Koch, Sneed, Davis, and Benshoff[13] found that many rehabilitation professionals misunderstood the basic concepts necessary for managing consumers with AD disorders and that they often failed to perceive that substance dependence was a medical disorder and not deviant behavior. Finally, one of the few surveys of rehabilitation counselors working in the state-federal vocational rehabilitation system regarding attitudes about AD, counselors reported very negative beliefs toward persons with substance abuse problems and felt that they may not benefit from rehabilitation services and would fail to achieve positive rehabilitation outcomes.[24] Davis, Sneed, & Koch[4] identified similar challenges amongst counselor trainees. These findings constitute a serious problem since rehabilitation professionals subscribing to these beliefs and holding these values may be much more likely to discriminate against consumers with these disorders and/or mismanage their cases.

A final factor influencing attitudes, beliefs, and values about AD disorders occurs as a consequence of the formal education, training, and clinical practice of our professional groups. The human service disciplines have developed multiple models for disease and disorder and numerous interventions for addressing human distress resulting from physical and psychological disabilities. Each discipline seeks to formally prepare professionals to perform roles and functions commensurate with the focus of the profession. Despite the fact that these professionals may be fully prepared to competently serve a wide variety of consumer needs, they must recognize that their general preparation to practice in their field may be insufficient for practice with this unique disability group. Excellent counselors may be misled by their general competence and their specific skills with other consumers into the belief that they possess the necessary skills and training to address the special problems arising during case management and counseling for this population, without pursuing specific training in this area.

PERSONAL EXPERIENCE

Our own personal experience may influence our attitudes toward AD disorders to an even greater extent than our professional cultures and the broader popular culture. When considering our response to these disabilities we might want to consider whether our own use or non-use affects how we view the substance use of our client. Although there are many circumstances that might influence an individual's perception of these disorders, there is a few that merit specific exploration before we conclude the topic of attitudes and AD.

The first situation is one in which a person has either limited experience with substance use or has experimented with substances and has not found them at all interesting. For this person, it may be difficult to understand why a consumer might choose to use substances and especially how an individual could lose control of their substance use. Fortunately, this challenge is easily overcome if the counselor has an open mind and is willing to seek the knowledge necessary to comprehend the addiction process.

A more difficult hurdle to overcome for these professionals may be their sense that they have nothing to offer these clients due to their lack of experience. When consumers raise this issue, it can be very daunting for rehabilitation professionals. In this situation, it is important to recognize that professionals do not have to have direct experience with substance use or abuse to be helpful to their clients. Willingness to gain knowledge about these disorders and to acquire the specific skills necessary to manage these cases can easily be obtained and utilized effectively even if the counselors have never had substance use disorders themselves. While consumers may assert that "you can't understand me if you haven't done what I have done," years of research on working with AD clients has shown that this is simply not the case.

When professionals have had direct experience with substance use themselves or have been closely involved with a friend or family member who has been using or abusing substances, they face an entirely different set of challenges. Counselors who are in recovery from substance dependence or who have overcome substance misuse problems themselves are often too quick to assume that the experiences of consumers they serve will be very much like their own. Helpers who fall into this trap may make premature judgments about the behavior of others or begin to give advice from their own experience when that advice is not wanted. In the worst cases, counselors may spend so much time discussing their own history that they do not allow clients to explore their own issues. For this reason, persons who are in recovery or who have had direct experience with substance use disorders may want to explore these issues with their supervisor before beginning to utilize self-disclosure with their clients.

FAMILY HISTORY OF SUBSTANCE USE DISORDERS

Another frequently unidentified factor that significantly impacts professionals' attitudes toward and interactions with persons with AD disorders is their own family of origin. AD disabilities negatively affect the lives of all persons who are involved with the person experiencing these disorders. Professional helpers who have grown up in families where there is substance abuse, or who have been involved with significant others who have had substance use disorders, may be susceptible to falling into many unhelpful behavior patterns as a result of their interactions with these individuals. If these issues remain unidentified, they can influence the counseling relationship in unexpected and unhelpful ways.

Professionals may find themselves emotionally affected or involved with clients in ways that are not desirable and that do not enhance the therapeutic relationship. Supervision may be helpful in this case, as well as professional counseling when necessary to resolve clinical issues originating in the professional's family of origin or personal history that may affect their role as rehabilitation professionals. While it may be tempting to avoid or deny our past in this regard, many counselors have grown through confronting these issues in themselves and have become able to effectively work with consumers who have AD disorders. Whenever rehabilitation professionals feel discomfort with this population, it may be a signal to examine their own history in regard to AD disorders.

It is important to recognize the impact of all of these forces on consumers themselves. When individuals experience a severely stigmatizing disorder that results in their experiencing unpleasant social sanctions and direct discrimination, it is likely that they will have deep reluctance about discussing the disorder as well as suffer from profound emotional conflicts due to the shame and guilt associated with substance misuse. Professionals who recognize these issues as part of the disorder rather than seeing client behavior as resistance or non-compliance can better succeed in serving this population.

THE EXTENT OF THE PROBLEM

There is considerable evidence suggesting that individuals from most disability groups are at the same or higher risk for substance dependence than the general population.[15,17,18,23] Increased risk factors for persons with disabilities are thought to be related to causal factors such as treatment failure and limited or partial rehabilitation as well as coping styles developed by persons who seek to ameliorate the effects of their disability through the use of alcohol and other drugs.[16,18,10]

As a result of the overall prevalence of AD disorders, it has been reported that rehabilitation professionals are increasingly providing services for persons with these disorders as both primary and secondary disabilities.[2,15,20] While the majority of rehabilitation professionals choose to work in non-AD specific treatment settings, they will, nonetheless, need to possess specific knowledge and skills pertaining to this population as well as be aware of their own attitudes and beliefs about this disability group. The next section presents specific information needed by professionals to both understand and identify AD disorders.

DEFINING AD DISORDERS

In this section, the factors contributing to and influencing the effects of psychoactive substance will be identified, the continuum of substance use will be reviewed, and diagnostic criteria will be examined. The goals of this section will be to facilitate an understanding of the formal definition of these disorders through review of the historical models from whence the formal diagnostic criteria were derived. Thorough understanding of this material will enhance rehabilitation professionals' ability to:

- identify AD disorders and assess their impact on the lives of consumers,
- provide insight into the formal diagnostic labels utilized by AD professionals, and
- communicate accurately and effectively about their consumers ' AD problems, facilitating effective and appropriate case management for persons with these disabilities.

THE EFFECTS OF PSYCHOACTIVE SUBSTANCES

There are four primary factors that influence the effect that psychoactive substances produce when used by any individual. These factors include the type of substance used, the route by which the substance is administered, the biopsychosocial set of the individual who is using the substance, and the setting in which the substance is used. Each of these factors contributes in varying degrees to the experience of the person who uses the substance. For these reasons, two persons using the same drug under the same circumstances may have significantly different experiences, and the effects of the substance may be dissimilar in the extreme.

TYPES OF SUBSTANCE

Since psychoactive substances tend to produce discrete psychological and physical changes that can be identified by their effect, psychoactive substances are often grouped according to these properties. Consequently, drugs of abuse are often organized into four major classes: stimulants, depressants, psychedelics, and inhalants. Stimulants include drugs such as methamphetamine, cocaine, caffeine, and nicotine. Depressants include alcohol, barbiturates, opiates, and opioids. The psychedelic classification includes lysergic acid diathalmide (LSD), peyote, marijuana, and psilocybin. Inhalants include many types of solvents, glues, and anesthetics such as nitrous oxide.

The psychoactive substances directly stimulate the central nervous system causing the physical effects of increased energy, increased heart rate, decreased appetite, and hypertension. Stimulant users may experience a variety of physiological complications including circulatory problems, seizure, and/or extreme cardiovascular stress that may result in death. The typical psychological effects of these substances include increase in self-confidence, increase of motivation, and euphoria. Over time and with increased dosages, individuals may experience extremely negative psychological effects including anxiety, delirium, and paranoia.

The physiological effects of central nervous system depressants are slowed cardiopulmonary function, relaxation, reduced energy, or lethargy, and impaired sensory functioning. Many of these drugs cause an inability to perform sexually as well as produce constipation and nausea. Death can result due to overdose of these substances. Individuals who are dependent on these substances typically require medically supervised detoxification when they discontinue use, due to the high risk of serious medical complications arising during withdrawal. Psychologically, these substances may produce euphoria and well-being, but they also tend to lower inhibitions, reduce the individual's reaction/response times to external stimuli, and produce mental confusion and disorganization with larger doses.

Psychedelics create a wide variety of psychological and physiological effects that are often quite unpredictable and which vary greatly according to which substance is used. Marijuana users often report increased appetite, but psylocibin users may experience nausea or vomiting. LSD and ecstasy may cause physiological effects similar to those produced by stimulants, while PCP may produce anesthetic effects. The psychological effects of psychedelics may include mental confusion, sensory overload, illusions, hallucinations, and in some cases psychotic symptoms.

Inhalant use typically results in the physical effects of dizziness, ataxia, difficulty organizing speech, and disorientation. Users often faint due to the cardiopulmonary effects of these substances, and in some cases, these fainting spells can be lethal when the substance continues to be inhaled after consciousness is lost. Since many of these substances cause very serious physiological complications, including damage to brain and lung tissues as well as liver and kidney damage, even infrequent or experimental use can result in very serious, long-term, physical, and psychological impairment.

While it is not unusual for individuals to experiment with many different substances, persons with AD disorders may prefer one particular substance to others. When this occurs, it can be said that they have identified a drug of choice. Individuals may prefer a particular substance or class of substances solely due to their effect. Their choices may also be influenced by the cost and availability of substances in their geographical area. It should be recognized that many persons use multiple substances so that they have secondary and/or tertiary substances that may be used along with their primary choice.

ROUTE

A second factor that influences drug effects is the route of administration. Psychoactive substances can generally be inhaled directly, inhaled through smoke, administered intravenously, and/or ingested orally. How a drug is delivered to the bloodstream and thereby to the brain will determine, to a great degree, how quickly the drug will take effect as well as the type of effect that may be expected. The route of administration will also affect the types of negative consequences that may be associated with psychoactive substance abuse.

The secondary consequences of substance abuse are particularly troubling for persons with disabilities. In many cases, new physiological or psychological conditions may develop, and frequently existing conditions are exacerbated. Each route of delivery poses its own set of unique problems and dangers. Any introduction of non-medically monitored psychoactive substances can lead to potentially hazardous (even fatal) consequences for someone with pre-existing conditions.

The intravenous route of administration can result in many serious complications for persons with disabilities due to failure to ensure sterilization or the presence of a variety of adulterants. While it is widely known that individuals who are using drugs intravenously are at risk for contracting the HIV virus, there are many other serious complications that can occur including abscesses due to bacterial infection, inflammation and scarring at the injection site, and endocarditis, as well as a variety of pulmonary complications. In cases where an individual's health is already compromised, intravenous administration of drugs is exceptionally dangerous.

While initially appearing less threatening, inhalation and oral consumption also pose specific health risks. Repeated inhalation of psychoactive substances can cause extreme irritation and inflammation of the nasal passages and the substances that are inhaled (solvents glue, nitrites, and other household chemicals) can cause asphyxiation, renal and liver damage, cardiac arrhythmia, and immune system suppression. When smoke from substances such as tobacco, marijuana, or hashish is inhaled, tissues become irritated. Users may be at risk for cancers of the mouth, throat, and lungs as well as at risk for a variety of other cardio-pulmonary related problems. Oral consumption, most commonly associated with alcoholic beverages and the ingestion of pharmaceutical tablets, may be the least risky of all the routes of administration. However, long-term use of alcohol contributes to health related problems including irritation of the gastric tissues, the mouth, and esophagus, including the potential development of esophageal varices.

SET

Whenever a human being begins to use drugs or alcohol, the effect of the substance is greatly influenced by each individual's biological, psychological, and social characteristics. Therefore, the "first use" experience for a group of persons using the same drug, via the same route, and in the same setting may vary considerably. The uniqueness that each person brings to their first use of psychoactive substances is referred to as their "set."

Certain individuals may be born with genetic differences that significantly influence physiological response to psychoactive substances. Whereas one person may use a substance and exclaim, "What's the big deal?" another may react by thinking, "I want to do this as much as I can!" While the earliest researchers sought to explain this phenomenon as an allergic reaction to specific substances, today's researchers have sought to examine each individual's neurochemical responses to substances in an attempt to determine if individual neurotransmitters may play a role in determining how an individual may respond to a given psychoactive substance.[22] As we learn more about these characteristics, researchers may be able to predict which individuals develop problematic psychoactive substance use, based on these neuropsychological characteristics.

Many other factors influence the individual's "set" during first use including mood, the presence/absence of other psychological or physiological disorders, and even the individual's expectations regarding the substance's potential effect.

The high co-morbidity of substance abuse with other mental disorders has long been recognized as indicative of individual attempts to "self-medicate" negative emotional states such as depression or anxiety. If an individual's first use results in alleviation of social stress, psychological stress or other emotional discomfort, it is easy to understand how that individual may experience a much more favorable reaction to their experiment with substance use. Even the expectation that one is going to have a positive or negative experience can sometimes influence psychoactive effects.

Other factors influencing "set" include gender, age, health status, and culture of origin. While it is somewhat unconventional, one might also include current prescribed medications as a part of an individual's "set". This is an important consideration for many persons with disabilities who may be using one or more medications on a more or less permanent basis. For these persons, experimentation with alcohol and drugs can be particularly dangerous, due to the fact that drug interactions may often lead to unexpected and sometimes paradoxical effects.

SETTING

The final factor that can influence the effect of psychoactive substances is the setting in which those substances are used. Individuals may have first use experiences in a variety of different social and environmental settings, and these surroundings may influence the individual's experience in both positive and negative ways. Depending on the type of stimuli that are present in the environment, continued use may be reinforced or deterred by these factors.

For example, if an individual's first use occurs in a social environment where there is danger to themselves or others, or where there may be great risk of negative consequences, individual use may be discouraged. Many persons cease their substance use after limited experimentation due to just this sort of negative environmental pressure. When an individual's environment is stimulating, exciting, and safe, however, continued use may seem attractive despite unpleasant physical or psychological effects.

SUBSTANCE USE DISORDERS DEFINED

Given that each individual may experience a variety of potential effects based on the interaction of their individual characteristics, the properties of the substance, and their environment, how exactly can we determine when a person is experiencing an AD disorder? Any professional helper who wishes to be clear in communicating about the nature and extent of a consumer's involvement with alcohol and other drugs should rely on the American Psychiatric Association's (APA) *Diagnostic and Statistical Manual of Mental Disorders, 5th edition (DSM-V).*[1]

The DSM-V describes two different types of psychoactive substance use problems in the section on substance related and addictive disorders. The two types are substance use disorders (SUDS) and substance induced disorders (SIDS).

SIDS are all of the associated substance-specific effects that are "induced" by each psychoactive substance. Consequently, there sets of SID criteria for each psychoactive substance and the criteria for each of the SID diagnoses is highly individualized depending on the psychoactive properties of each individual pharmacological agent. Examples of SIDS could include substance induced intoxication and substance induced withdrawal.

A significant change in the DSM V is the movement away from two separate categories of SUDS (Abuse and Dependence) and the creation of a new categorical label: Substance Use Disorder. The DSM-V describes a continuum of substance use that comprises "substance use disorder" and utilizes a set of ten criteria to establish the severity of the diagnosis. APA (2013) in the DSM-V specifies that the categories mild (presence of 2-3 symptoms), moderate (presence of 4-5 symptoms), and severe (presence of 6 or more symptoms be specified as an indication of how the SUDS have progressed for any individual.

There are ten criteria possible within the SUD diagnostic classification system. The ten criteria utilized in making the diagnosis of substance use disorders can be described as follows:

(1) substance is often taken in larger amounts or over a longer period than was intended,
(2) there is a persistent desire or unsuccessful efforts to cut down or control substance use,
(3) a great deal of time is spent in activities necessary to obtain the substance or recover from its effects,
(4) craving or a strong desire or urge to use the substance,
(5) recurrent substance use resulting in a failure to fulfill major role obligations; continued substance use despite having persistent or recurrent social or interpersonal problems caused by or exacerbated by the substance,
(6) continued substance use despite having persistent or recurrent social or interpersonal problems caused or exacerbated by the effects of the substance,
(7) important social, occupational, or recreational activities are given up or reduced because of substance use,
(8) recurrent use of substances in situations where it is physically hazardous,
(9) substance use is continued despite knowledge of having a persistent or recurrent physical or psychological problem that is likely to have been caused or exacerbated by the substance, and

(10) tolerance as defined by the need for markedly increased amounts of the substance to achieve intoxication or the same effect and or a markedly diminished effect with continued use of the same amount of the substance.[1]

While rehabilitation counselors typically will not be called upon to diagnose consumers, it will be important for them to be familiar with the criteria used to identify AD disabilities so that they can communicate effectively and coordinate services among interdisciplinary teams that likely will be involved in serving consumers with coexisting disabilities. If professionals cannot specifically identify the disorders with which they are working and are unfamiliar with the diagnostic labels utilized for these interdisciplinary communications, case management activities will likely be ineffective.

Familiarity with the DSM-V diagnostic criteria may support rehabilitation counselors in the:

- determination of consumer eligibility for receiving rehabilitation services,
- completion of individual screening and assessment, and
- establishment of this particular class of consumers as a legitimate disability group.

THE CONTINUUM OF SUBSTANCE USE DISORDERS

Any person's substance use may be described as a point on a continuum from non-use to severe substance use disorders. There is great variation among substance users as well as among those who develop substance use disorders. It is important, however, for rehabilitation professionals to be able to recognize when an individual's substance use begins to progress from appropriate use to problematic substance use disorders.

SUBSTANCE USE

A substance user could be described as a person who uses substances but who does not experience any negative effects from this use. In this category it would be expected that social, vocational, and interpersonal relationships would be totally unaffected by their use, and that use will have resulted in no other negative physiological, psychological, or social consequences. This person would either abstain from use or use moderately in most situations and would rarely, if ever, become fully intoxicated.

CASE STUDY

JOE

Joe is a twenty-five year old college student who was injured in a car accident when another driver lost control on an icy road striking Joe's vehicle in a head-on collision. Although Joe survived the accident, his injuries were severe. When the paramedics arrived at the accident site, they quickly determined that Joe had sustained a C-4 fracture as well as potential traumatic brain injuries.

Prior to the accident, Joe had occasionally used alcohol with his friends on the weekends consuming several beers, but he only became intoxicated on two occasions; once on his twenty-first birthday and another time when, as a teenager, he consumed too much hard liquor while playing a drinking game with his friends. Joe had no history of driving while drinking. His alcohol consumption had never interfered with his relationships, work, education, or physical health. When Joe's doctor suggested, during consultation while in physical rehabilitation, that he abstain from drinking alcohol so as to minimize possible complications of his recovery, Joe agreed to abstain and did not take another drink. Joe, in this case, would most probably be considered to have been a substance user.

MILD TO MODERATE SUBSTANCE USE DISORDERS

When a person progresses into problematic substance use disorders, their substance use has begun to interfere with their lives in a significant way. When interviewing the substance abuser you may find that this individual is using alcohol and/or drugs when driving or in other situations in which they may be harmed. This person may be experiencing familial, educational, or vocational problems due to their drinking. For example, they may be missing work, getting into arguments with significant others over when and where they might be drinking, or they may have been charged with driving while intoxicated or public intoxication. When asked about their drinking behavior, they may suggest that their problems are due to their employer, spouse, or the "government." Again, mild SUDS are described as the presence of 2-3 of the ten symptoms and moderate severity is described as the presence of 4-5 symptoms.

SUDS can be distinguished from substance use based on the presence of these problems or other similar difficulties. For the person with substance use disorders, alcohol and drugs are causing significant problems in their lives on multiple occasions. While some persons may be able to resolve their substance use problems on their own, many rehabilitation consumers who meet the criteria for substance use disorders will need formal intervention by skilled AD treatment providers if they are to benefit from rehabilitation services.

CASE STUDY

ERIN

Erin is a twenty-eight year old female who is seeking vocational rehabilitation services as a result of a back injury that occurred six months ago. She had been employed for two years as a secretary at the local bank, and she had held seven other jobs since the age of seventeen, prior to her banking job. Erin attended two semesters at the local university but left after being placed on academic suspension. Although she states that she had planned to go back to college, she says she has "never gotten around to it." Erin was on time for her first appointment but has shown up late for other appointments.

During your interview with Erin, you question her about her job history and find out that she has a history of losing jobs due to her absenteeism and poor work habits (showing up late). You also find out that she has been convicted of two charges of driving while intoxicated in the past year and that she was on probation at work due to her repeatedly missing Monday mornings. Erin explains that her boyfriend and she often go away on the weekends to the local lake to "party" with their friends, and that it is hard for them to get back on time. When questioned about her educational history, she admits that she was "partying a lot" since her classes were so boring. Erin explains that her professors never really gave her a chance and that she never seems to find an employer who will be fair to her. Finally, she says that she has tried to cut down her use of alcohol in the past but she has never been successful. Due to her repeated problems with alcohol, Erin would likely meet the criteria for substance use disorders and may be described as having a substance use disorder based on the behavior she has described.

SEVERE SUBSTANCE USE DISORDERS

In the case of severe substance use disorders, individuals often appear to have totally lost control of their drinking or drug use behavior. Once use has progressed to this point, individuals in this class will rarely be able to control or to discontinue their substance use on their own. In most cases, some formal AD treatment intervention will be required in order to enable them to participate successfully in the rehabilitation process, and these persons may have been treated previously for their substance use problems.

Although the person who has progressed into a severe SUD may recognize that they have a problem, they may not see any alternative to their current behaviors, and they may be very unwilling to acknowledge that their substance use is the root cause for many of their problems. These individuals will often fail to benefit from the rehabilitation process unless they receive treatment. In fact, in many cases they will not be able to complete the most basic objectives and will have been terminated from rehabilitation services or closed as "non-compliant."[11] In these cases, rehabilitation professionals may not recognize that these consumers are unable to meet basic objectives, and may believe these consumers to be unwilling to fulfill their individual rehabilitation plans.

CASE STUDY

BOBBY

Bobby is a thirty-two year old person who is blind due to complications arising from type I diabetes. He has been legally blind since the age of sixteen and has been a consumer of rehabilitation services for most of his adult life. As a young adult, Bobby was twice sent to the state's residential training program to assist him in improving his orientation and mobility skills, as well as to provide him with the training to perform all of the activities of daily living necessary for him to live independently. Both times Bobby left the center before completing his program. Bobby has never held a full-time job and continues to live with his aunt, who provides him with housing and some meals.

After interviewing Bobby's aunt, other rehabilitation professionals who have worked with Bobby in the past, and Bobby himself, you learn that Bobby has been smoking marijuana since the age of twelve and that he has been a daily smoker since the age of sixteen. His aunt reports that he is "high" all day every day, that he has given up all of his social activities and that he only spends time with his "druggie friends." She explains that these friends give Bobby rides to the bar and to social events almost every day, but that they rarely come into her home.

Review of medical records indicates that Bobby has had many accidents and injuries since becoming visually impaired. His previous counselor explains that he is constantly having accidents because of his drug use, and even though he repeatedly promised to "chill out" and stop smoking long enough to complete his rehabilitation plan, he was never able to do it. In fact, the counselor indicated that Bobby stated he left the residential program because his "bag ran out."

As a result of Bobby's inability to complete assignments and to fulfill his obligations, his counselor had referred him to outpatient AD counseling. Despite making repeated promises to go and to quit using altogether, he never attended any of the scheduled sessions. When you interview Bobby, he discloses to you that he has been trying to smoke only one joint in the evenings, but that he often smokes first thing in the morning and then continues all day, even though he only intends to do a "few hits." He explains that there is just nothing else for him to do and that "you would stay high all of the time too, if you were blind."

Finally, Bobby reports that his physician has recommended that he stop smoking due the effects that his chronic marijuana use have produced on his cardiovascular system. Bobby reports feeling very anxious and depressed most of the time and he indicates that while the marijuana used to alleviate his mood problems, it doesn't seem to work for him anymore. Bobby says he has significant urges to smoke in the morning and other times throughout the day even though the "pot isn't working for him" like it used to.

In this case, Bobby would likely be described as having progressed into a severe cannabis use disorder. In a case such as this, Bobby may need residential treatment in an AD treatment facility in order to help him break free of the cycle of addiction, and he will probably not benefit from receiving rehabilitation services until his substance use disorder is in remission.

AD AS A COEXISTING DISABILITY

Providing effective case management and coordinating effective rehabilitation services for a person with a single disability is a rigorous challenge, but providing appropriate services for an individual with multiple disabilities is significantly more difficult. In most cases, rehabilitation professionals will find themselves working with consumers who are not struggling with AD as a disability by itself but with AD as coexisting disabilities occurring along with other serious disabling conditions. When AD co-occurs with other disability, it often becomes necessary to coordinate services that will address both disabilities concurrently.[15,20]

A common mistake of rehabilitation professionals and/or AD treatment providers is to direct a person with coexisting disabilities to address one disability before seeking services for the other. For example, an AD treatment provider may suggest that a person who is hearing impaired must complete the rehabilitation process and gain necessary communication skills before attending AD treatment. Similarly, rehabilitation professionals might require a period of abstinence prior to providing necessary rehabilitation training that can improve communication. Consumers with disabilities may be caught in a trap whereby they can never meet the criterion necessary to receive the services they need. In order to successfully serve consumers with coexisting AD disorders, rehabilitation professionals must have specific knowledge about the impact of the coexisting disabilities as well as make a commitment to utilize an interdisciplinary and often multi-systemic approach to providing services.

AD PRECEDES ANOTHER DISABILITY

In many cases, consumers with disabilities may experience substance use disorders prior to acquiring other disabilities and the AD may have caused or contributed to the coexisting disability. Several factors that are often present for a person with an AD disorder may lead to further disability including:

- increased risk-taking or other impulsive behaviors,
- either failure to develop or loss of skills for self-care,
- negative physiological and psychological effects of substances, and
- poor access to health care services.

In nearly every case where a person experiences AD disabilities, they will be vulnerable to additional health problems; injury due to accidents or violence; and/or lack of social, educational, and financial resources.

The Substance Abuse and Mental Health Services Administration (SAMHSA)[20] and Moore[15] state that it is important for rehabilitation professionals to recognize that the AD disabilities will significantly impact the consumer with other disabilities and will negatively influence their ability to benefit from rehabilitation services. While each individual may experience negative consequences in varying degrees, it is likely that they will be experiencing significant psychological, social, and vocational challenges that may need to be remediated so that the individual can adjust/adapt to their current life situation. The negative consequences of substance abuse are often extreme, and if unidentified, they may be a sort of "time bomb" waiting to sabotage the best-laid plans of rehabilitation professionals.

Long-term substance use disorders typically result in either a delay in development of emotional coping skills or loss of existing skills so that these individuals are at a distinct disadvantage when they must overcome limitations arising from another disabling condition. Long-term, persons who experience substance use disorders may also have very limited social skills and social supports. Their families may have abandoned them or they may have abandoned their families. They may have a very limited work and educational history. Finally, they may have legal problems that both stigmatizes them in general society and complicates the job placement process due to employer biases and stereotypes.

Bobby from case three represents the issues that must be confronted when working with an individual whose substance abuse preceded his identified disability. His lack of work history, lack of positive social supports, and loss of control of his substance use, probable emotional problems, and coping skills deficits will be significant hurdles that must be overcome if he is to become an independent, productive member of society. In order for Bobby to move forward, he may need to receive AD treatment concurrent with his residential rehabilitation program so that all of his presenting problems may be addressed.

AD Co-Occurs with Another Disability

In other cases, AD co-occurs with another disability, and it can be difficult to determine how to proceed with providing services due to the interaction of both disabilities. There are many examples of co-occurring onset of disabilities, but rehabilitation professionals will most probably encounter this phenomenon when working with persons who are experiencing mental health disabilities. Persons experiencing co-occurring disorders may be among the most challenging populations that are served by rehabilitation service providers.

Persons with mental health disorders are at a high risk for developing substance use disorders and persons with substance use disorders are at a high risk for developing mental illness. In the first case, individuals may use psychoactive substances for the purpose of "self-medication" and in so doing may find that their "cure" has both exacerbated their existing problems and led to the formation of entirely new ones. On the other hand, persons who may have no prior history of mental health problems may begin to experience psychological consequences as a result of their substance misuse. For both types of consumers, AD disorders and mental health disorders become intertwined with such complexity that it can be difficult to determine exactly what is taking place.

AD treatment providers refer to this class of disabilities as "dual diagnosis" and describe their clients as persons who are "dually diagnosed." Rehabilitation professionals serving this population must consult with AD counselors to identify specialized programs and services that are targeted toward the needs of this specific population. If providers do not subscribe to the current treatment philosophy that these issues must be treated concurrently, consumers may not receive appropriate services. As stated previously, providers may insist that either of the disabilities be addressed before the other. In fact, it is unlikely that one of the co-occurring disorders can be successfully treated without treating both disabilities simultaneously.

AD Occurs After Another Disability

For consumers in this category, substance use disorders may occur either directly or indirectly in response to primary disabilities but may not fully develop until years after the onset of their primary disability. There is tremendous variation among the population of persons with coexisting disabilities due to differences in individual adjustment to the primary disability and to functional limitations. When working with this population, it can be critical to determine whether the substance use is a direct attempt to respond to the primary disability (self-medication) or if the substance disorder has developed due to other factors.

In either case, individuals' residual capacity and functional limitations will determine the extent to which they may experience difficulties when referred for AD treatment. Accordingly, rehabilitation professionals working with persons in this group can be of great assistance during the referral process as well as during the provision of AD services. Consumers have the best chance of success when rehabilitation professionals participate throughout the treatment process (assessment, treatment planning, and service delivery) as full members of the interdisciplinary treatment team. When AD counselors and treatment professionals are provided with the history of the case and a functional capacity assessment of the consumer, they are in a much stronger position to provide treatment and to accurately identify the critical issues to be addressed in the AD treatment plan.

ROLE OF THE REHABILITATION PROFESSIONAL

While rehabilitation professionals must possess the skills to be able to coordinate services for persons with AD disabilities, they are not required to have the skills to provide AD treatment services directly to this consumer group. Consequently, there are several roles entailing specific functions that rehabilitation professionals will be expected to fill in order that consumers may successfully complete the rehabilitation process. This section reviews those roles and functions, the AD service delivery model, and community self-help resources.

SCREENING AND IDENTIFICATION

Within the role of rehabilitation case management or as a direct service provider, the ability to recognize when an individual is experiencing complications due to alcohol and other drug abuse disorders is an essential skill. As described earlier in the chapter, familiarity with the DSM V criteria and knowledge about the continuum of substance use disorders are a good foundation upon which to develop the ability to screen for and identify AD disorders, but there are a few other simple tools that may be easily used to enhance rehabilitation professionals' ability to correctly identify when there is a problem.

Perhaps the simplest AD screening tool utilized today is the CAGE questionnaire. The CAGE asks four simple questions. Those questions are:

- Have you ever tried to **C**ut down your use of alcohol?
- Do you become **A**nnoyed when persons complain about your drinking?

- Do you ever feel **G**uilty about your drinking?
- Do you ever drink an **E**ye-opener in the morning to relieve the shakes?

Whenever two or more questions are answered affirmatively, the CAGE has been found to accurately determine when individuals may be experiencing substance use.[2]

Chestnut Health Systems have created new instruments for AD screening and assessment that are also very useful for rehabilitation professionals. The Global Assessment of Need (GAIN)-Quick is a 15 page (15-20 minute) version for a basic assessment of a targeted population that is designed to identify the eligibility and need for referral to specialty health, mental health, and/or substance use systems, and/or to support motivational interviewing related to substance use.[3] The GAIN family of instruments has been shown to be reliable and valid across very diverse populations including some groups of persons with specific disabilities (HIV and Deafness). In addition to the GAIN-Quick, there are instruments that are more comprehensive available to professionals who wish to perform comprehensive AD assessments.

Identification of potential problems using screening instruments is just that: identification of potential problems. Although there is some correlation between the results of screening instruments and formal diagnoses, these instruments should not be used for diagnostic labeling. Rehabilitation professionals must receive specialized training, and in most states become licensed or certified as professional counselors or psychologists, before they are qualified to determine diagnoses. Screening instruments are utilized to determine whether there is a need to refer consumers to specialists with these credentials for further testing and evaluation.

CASE MANAGEMENT AND REFERRAL

Once an individual has been identified as potentially having an AD disorder, further assessment and specific AD treatment services must be provided to the client. In most cases, the rehabilitation agency will not provide these services directly (unless they have a qualified specialist on their staff) but will refer consumers to outside agencies to provide the necessary services. This section provides some specific details about "levels of care" and the types of AD services that may be provided for the rehabilitation consumer with coexisting disabilities.

LEVELS OF CARE

Although many AD treatment providers may be unfamiliar with the concept "least restrictive environment" as used in rehabilitation, professionals working in AD treatment have developed a continuum of treatment or "levels of care" to ensure that consumers receive appropriate care given the severity of their substance use disorder. This continuum of care ranges from the least restrictive types of interventions that occur in outpatient settings to the most restrictive settings usually involving twenty-four hour medically managed services. In most cases, when an individual has completed the AD assessment process, recommendations will be made specifying the level of care that will be most effective in meeting the consumer's individual needs.

Outpatient counseling is the least restrictive level of care provided for person with AD disorders. A person receiving outpatient services would, typically, see a counselor individually at least once a week in addition to participating in a group intervention. Group work in this level of care would often tend to be didactic in nature. Outpatient services (and all other levels of care) are provided by public or private service providers depending on the organizational structure and service delivery system utilized by the state in which the consumer lives. In order to be eligible for this level of care, consumers must satisfy most or all of the following conditions:

- a limited history of prior AD treatment/intervention,
- high levels of motivation,
- good social and familial supports,
- very low risk of biomedical complications due to withdrawal from substance use,
- low potential for relapse, and
- minimal emotional or psychological problems.

The next level of care that is widely available for persons with AD disorders is typically intensive outpatient counseling (IOP). Like other outpatient services, IOP typically requires a combination of individual counseling sessions and group work, but intensive programs typically require the participant to attend from nine to twenty hours of group intervention per week. These groups tend to be both didactic and experiential in their focus but often lean heavily on psycho-educational models. In order to be eligible for this level of care, consumers must satisfy most or all of the following conditions:

- past history of AD treatment,
- somewhat resistant to participating in treatment,
- lack of positive social supports,
- very low risk of biomedical complications due to withdrawal from substance use,
- moderate risk for relapse, and
- moderate or minimal emotional and/or psychological problems that require little psychiatric intervention and formal mental health care services.

Residential treatment is typically the next level of care that is provided for AD disabilities. At this level of care, consumers are required to be "in residence" twenty-four hours a day for the duration of the treatment program.

Historically, many programs were "twenty-eight" day programs, although residential programs may extend to several months or more than a year. Due to changes in funding and the move toward managed care, residential program lengths have been decreasing during the past decade.

Residential treatment typically requires six or more hours of group participation per day as well as multiple individual counseling sessions during the week. In addition to individual and group work focusing on AD problems, residential programs typically offer a wide range of programming intended to strengthen social, recreational, and coping skills. Some programs even offer vocational skills training and educational services, but this is rather rare. Finally, residential programs tend to be monitored by medical personnel with medical services available as needed. Consumers who are eligible for this level of care would typically meet most or all of the following criteria:

- past AD treatment,
- quite resistant to participating in treatment,
- significant lack of positive social supports and a negative recovery environment,
- low risk of biomedical complications due to withdrawal from substance use,
- high risk for relapse, and
- moderate or severe emotional and/or psychological problems that require some medical/ psychiatric intervention and formal mental health care services.

The most restrictive level of care is medically managed or hospital based residential treatment. These programs are staffed by medical personnel twenty-four hours a day and the program structure closely resembles the structure of residential programs. They are typically designed to intervene with clients who are experiencing "dual diagnosis" issues, and they most often have a very strong mental health emphasis. Frequently, these programs are "secure" and a client's movement is restricted by secured doors and windows as well as through the supervision of medical personnel. Consumers who are eligible for this level of care may present with:

- a varied history of AD treatment,
- potentially high resistance to participating in treatment,
- significant lack of positive social supports and a negative recovery environment,
- high risk of biomedical complications due to withdrawal from substance use and/or severe emotional and/or psychological problems that require continual medical/ psychiatric intervention and formal mental health care services,
- high danger to self or others due to relapse or suicidal ideation or lethal intention.

COORDINATION OF SERVICES

There are several important factors that can significantly assist rehabilitation professionals in making effective referrals to AD treatment providers. These factors include awareness of federal confidentiality requirements specific to AD, knowledge of available resources within the community and region, strong personal relationship with treatment providers, and knowledge of other community supports including self-help groups.[20] Given adequate preparation in each of these areas, professionals can achieve better rehabilitation outcomes resulting from appropriate case coordination and referral.

Although rehabilitation professionals are often prepared to respect client confidentiality, they may be unprepared for the stringent federal guidelines governing release of information for consumers involved in AD treatment. Federal law was established to protect individuals receiving AD services from the stigma and discrimination that are often associated with substance abuse, and consequently, consents to release information for these consumers are quite specific and restrictive in nature. In order to assure that proper communication exists between all members of the team, the person who is referring the consumer for services should carefully review the consent to release information form utilized by the treatment provider so that all parties fully understand what information may be exchanged. If the consent to release information is not specific, or if necessary consents are not given, it can be remarkably difficult for professionals outside the treatment facility to engage in the treatment process. Given what has been said about concurrent treatment for coexisting disabilities, these consumers are always best served when interdisciplinary teams, representing expertise in each of the disabilities, participate to provide services addressing all of the consumers' needs.

Knowledge about community resources and strong personal relationships cannot be over-emphasized when providing effective case management services for this population. Koch and Nelipovich[11] found that professionals involved in serving persons with coexisting disabilities felt that familiarity with service delivery agencies, their specific agency cultures, and their individual personnel were not only desirable but were necessary to ensure proper delivery of services. Given that rehabilitation professionals and AD counselors come from very different professional cultures with extremely diverse external contingencies and two unique perspectives on service delivery, the odds are against effective cooperation even in the best of circumstances. However, when treatment providers have established relationships with one another as well as knowledge of one another's systemic quirks and requirements, case coordination can be greatly simplified.

Finally, rehabilitation professionals involved with serving persons with coexisting disabilities must be familiar with local twelve step groups and resources. When working with this population, involvement with self-help groups such as Alcoholics Anonymous (AA) and Narcotics Anonymous (NA) is inevitable. In order to be fully prepared to effectively utilize these community-based supports, rehabilitation professionals must gain knowledge about the recovery community in their own region, cultivate relationships with leaders in that community, and gain some specific knowledge about how these programs work. Significant problems may arise when self-help is utilized without proper preparation.

SELF-HELP AND AD TREATMENT

Substance abuse treatment professionals have a long relationship with self-help groups and they rely extensively on peer support groups, the twelve steps, and literature of these programs for supporting the treatment process. Koch and Rubin[12] and Koch and Benshoff[10] have suggested that in the U.S., the AD treatment community has relied on the AA community for staff recruitment and that there rehabilitation professionals need to be both aware of and wary about the impact of the "recovery culture" on substance abuse treatment. Recovering persons have worked in specialized AD treatment facilities providing services at the professional and paraprofessional level, creating a unique treatment environment existing only in the U.S. This intimate relationship between self-help and AD treatment has resulted in the creation of a corresponding treatment "culture" saturated with twelve step beliefs, values, and techniques.

This traditional model of substance abuse treatment was first described as the "AA Model of Treatment" over twenty years ago.[14] A basic assumption of this model is that the primary source of support for recovering persons is the twelve step fellowships, and that participation in these programs is highly beneficial for anyone experiencing substance abuse disorders. It should be recognized that the dominance of this culture within the substance abuse treatment community could be so entrenched as to discourage alternative treatment approaches. The consequences of this cultural pressure are that rehabilitation professionals are faced with a treatment community that has been characterized as a "one size fits all" treatment tradition.[12]

GAINING A WORKING KNOWLEDGE OF SELF-HELP

The phenomenon known as "self-help" began in 1935 with the establishment of what has become the oldest 12 step based self-help group, Alcoholics Anonymous (AA). AA began when two persons, describing themselves as alcoholics, determined that they could remain sober by employing a simple program of action based on a contemporary spiritual group's program for self-change combined with purposeful work with alcoholics. The groups co-founder, Bill Wilson, along with other group members, composed the basic text of AA. This text contains Bill's story, an exploration of alcohol abuse and dependence, discussion of a program of action suggested by those who were in recovery and a number of individual stories of recovery. The first one hundred sixty-four pages of the basic text, *Alcoholics Anonymous*, have remained unchanged since its first publication in the 1930s, but later editions have updated the story section to more closely reflect current changes in group membership. For the rehabilitation professional, thorough understanding of twelve step programs may begin with a reading of this text combined with exploration of the recovering community in their city or region. Reading the basic text of AA (or texts for other self-help groups) is a great start toward understanding the dynamics of the recovery community. It is insufficient, however, for gaining the sort of familiarity necessary to provide effective referral and case management for this population.[10]

Rehabilitation professionals might be understandably hesitant to appear at recovery group meetings, but attending meetings within the community and developing relationships with leaders in the recovery community can go a long way toward enhancing a professional's ability to utilize self-help as a treatment adjunct. Meetings are typically easy to find and readily available in most communities. Finding a meeting is often a matter of finding the telephone number or web page of the local "intergroup." Meeting lists can be obtained detailing not only the time and place of meetings but explaining what structure is utilized at a particular meeting as well as indicating whether non-alcoholics are welcome. It is important to call first or to review the meeting list since self-help meetings may be either "open" to the public or "closed" for recovering persons only. Professional anguish may be greatly increased if one shows up at a closed meeting!

Many individuals have a stereotypical view of AA as a person standing in front of the room telling his or her story. This type of meeting, speaker or "lead" meeting, does exist, but it is only one type of meeting that is available. There are many other types of meetings in most communities including open discussion meetings, step studies, text studies, and other specialized meetings focusing on a particular topic or issue. Groups may be incredibly diverse due to the establishment of groups for special populations (dual diagnosis, gender specific, et cetera) as well as a result of the individual flavor of the community. Different groups within the same community, surprisingly, may represent very divergent classes, beliefs, and values.

EFFECTIVE UTILIZATION OF SELF-HELP

How does a rehabilitation professional make effective use of self-help groups? There is an ethical obligation to ensure that organizations to which consumers are referred must be both appropriate and accessible. Obtaining firsthand knowledge about the available groups, including where they meet (accessiblity), characteristics of group members, and other factors differentiating the group (meeting content, topics, et cetera) can assist the professional in facilitating an effective match between consumers needs and group characteristics. If referral is treated very formally, including obtaining consent to release from the consumer and formal contact with group leaders, it is entirely possible that the group will be ready, open, and willing to support the consumer with special needs.[10]

Ineffective use of self-help occurs when persons who do not understand self-help groups and have no real connection with these resources indiscriminately refer their consumers without investigating what may be occurring in those groups. This often occurs where professionals "mandate" a number of meetings per week but spend little time or effort determining whether there is any benefit obtained when the consumer attends those meetings. In the very worst case, consumers may be sent to meetings that are socially and/or environmentally inaccessible to them and they experience significant frustration and embarrassment as a result.

OTHER BARRIERS TO EFFECTIVE CASE COORDINATION

A person with coexisting disabilities exist in a sort of "in-between" environment where they do not truly fit into a single service delivery system. AD counselors who are unfamiliar with disabilities may lack the specific knowledge and skills to provide services to persons who are blind or visually impaired resulting in a systemic/professional rejection of the consumers. There also is strong evidence that non-AD counselors may resist serving persons who experience substance abuse problems. Lack of cross-training and formal education about each disability and the effects of coexisting disabilities may result in consumers failing to benefit from interaction with either system.

Due to complex agency regulations and procedures, it may be extremely difficult for professionals to understand eligibility requirements and successfully complete referral to other agencies. Given that both private and public agencies typically have unique documentation and procedural requirements in addition to policy oversight from disparate entities, case managers and counselors can find themselves engaged in a confusing quagmire of paperwork and artificial barriers. This lack of integration of services may present a significant barrier to providing effective services. Given that consumers may be wary about seeking services in the first place, it is not surprising that they may fail to comply with the tedious process necessary to engage multi-agency providers to access services.

Further complicating the process is the frequently difficult challenge of identifying a primary case manager. It may be difficult for individuals in separate agencies, operating under different exigencies for providing services, to agree on what interventions may be appropriate. Koch and Nelipovich[11] have suggested that without clear memorandums of understanding, specific protocols for providing services, and a well defined case management process, a "who's on first" sort of confusion can develop among agencies, significantly impeding the rehabilitation process. This is not, unfortunately, solely a problem of interagency politics but instead may lie deep in the context of the debate over AD etiology.

AD PROGRAM ACCESSIBILITY

Even in cases where counselors and case managers collaborate and manage to access and coordinate referrals to AD treatment services, there is a final challenge to overcome. Substance abuse treatment programs may rely on educational materials that must be altered in order to accommodate the needs of persons who are blind or visually impaired. Despite the need for reasonable accommodations, NAADD[17] and Moore[15] identified that AD treatment providers are seldom prepared to provide accessible services for persons with disabilities. Consumers with coexisting disabilities cannot be expected to succeed in treatment unless their individual needs are accommodated by providing literature and treatment opportunities that are accessible.

SUMMARY

Rehabilitation professionals are increasingly recognizing the need to identify effective strategies for working with persons with disabilities who are experiencing coexisting AD disorders. These consumers present an extremely complex set of challenges requiring those who would serve them to examine both their own beliefs and attitudes toward this disability group as well as traditional models of service provision. In order to enhance rehabilitation outcomes and provide effective, appropriate rehabilitation services for this population, case managers, counselors, and other rehabilitation professionals must receive specific training increasing their awareness about AD disorders and their impact as a coexisting disability.

Finally, rehabilitation professionals must reach out to their colleagues who provide AD treatment services, as well as the recovering community, to build effective linkages that may ease the tensions created during coordination of services for this population. The intersection of these two professional cultures with the recovery culture presents a unique opportunity for creating a supportive, empowering, individualized, therapeutic environment where interdisciplinary collaboration and cooperation with persons with disabilities can lead to improved outcomes for this population.

REFERENCES

[1]American Psychiatric Association (APA) (2013). *Desk reference to the diagnostic criteria from DSM-5.* Washington, D.C.: APA.

[2]Benshoff, J. J., & Janikowski, T. P. (2000). *The rehabilitation model of substance abuse counseling.* Stamford, CT: Brooks/Cole.

[3]Chestnut Health Systems (2007). *Global assessment of individual need (GAIN).* Retrieved from http://www.chestnut.org/LI/gain/index.html. January, 3, 2007.

[4]Davis, S. J., Sneed, Z. B., & Koch, D. S. (2010). Counselor trainee attitudes toward Alcohol and other drug abuse. *Rehabilitation Education, 24*, 35-42.

[5]*H.R. 1789 Health Professionals Substance Abuse Education Act.* 109th Congress, Session One (2005).

[6]Hollar, D. (2008). The relationship between substance use disorders and unsuccessful case closures in vocational rehabilitaiotn agencies. *Journal of Applied Rehabilitation Counseling, 39*(2), 25-27.

[7]Humphreys, K. (1997). Clinicians' referral and matching of substance abuse patients to self-help groups after treatment. *Psychiatric Services*, *48*(11), 1445-9.

[8]Inaba, D. S., & Cohen, W. E. (2004) *Uppers, downers, all arounders: Physical and mental effects of psychoactive drugs* (4th ed). Ashland, OR: CNS Publications.

[9]Koch, D. S., (1999). Protections in federal rehabilitation legislation for persons with alcohol & other drug abuse disabilities. *Journal of Applied Rehabilitation Counseling, 30*(3), 1-5.

[10]Koch, D. S. & Benshoff, J. J. (2002). Rehabilitation Professionals' familiarity with and utilization of alcoholics anonymous. *Journal of Applied Rehabilitation Counseling,33*(3), 35-40.

[11]Koch, D. S., & Nelipovich, M. (1999). *Project for the most severely disabled: Needs assessment data: Focus groups & existing record review.* Tallahassee, Fl.: Florida Division of Blind Services.

[12]Koch, D. S., & Rubin, S. E. (1997). Challenges faced by rehabilitation counselors working with alcohol and other drug abuse in a "one size fits all" treatment tradition. *Journal of Applied Rehabilitation Counseling, 28*(1), 31-35.

[13]Koch, D. S., Sneed, Z., Davis, S. J., & Benshoff, J. J. (2006). A pilot study of the relationship between counselor trainees' characteristics and attitudes towards substance abuse. *Journal of Teaching in the Addictions, 5*(2), 97-111.

[14]Miller, N. S., & Mahler, J. C. (1991). Alcoholics anonymous and the "AA" model for treatment. *Alcoholism Treatment Quarterly, 8*(1), 39-51.

[15]Moore, D. (2005) *Substance use disorder treatment for people with physical and cognitive disabilities (TIP 29).* Rockville, MD: U.S. Dept. of Health and Human Services, Public Health Service, Substance Abuse and Mental Health Administration, Center for Substance Abuse Treatment.

[16]Moore, D., Greer, B. G., & Li, L. (1994). Alcohol and other substance use/abuse among people with disabilities. *Psychosocial Perspectives on Disability, 9*, 369-382.

[17]National Association on Alcohol, Drugs and Disability (NAADD) (1999). *Access limited: Substance abuse services for people with disabilities: A national perspective.* San Mateo, CA: Author.

[18]Rehabilitation Research and Training Center (RRTC) on Drugs and Disability (2002). *Proceedings of the second national conference on substance abuse and coexisting disabilities: Facilitating employment for a hidden population.* Dayton, OH: Author.

[19]Robertson, S. L., Davis, S. J., Sneed, Z., Koch, D. S., & Boston, Q. (2009). Substance abuse counselors: Treatment issues and competency concerns when working with coexisting disabilities. *Alcoholism Treatment Quarterly, 27, 265-279.*

[20]Substance Abuse and Mental Health Services Administration (SAMHSA) (2000). *Integrating substance abuse treatment and vocational services.* Rockville MD: Author.

[21]Statman, J. M. (1993). The enemy at home: Images of addiction in American society. *Journal of Adolescent Chemical Dependency, 2*, 19-29.

[22]Thombs, D. L. (2006). *Introduction to addictive behaviors (3rd ed).* New York: Guildford Press.

[23]West, S. L., Graham, C. W., & Cifu, D. X. (2009). Rates of persons with disabilities in alcohol/other drug treatment in Canada. *Alcoholism Treatment Quarterly, 27*, 253-264.

[24]West, S. L., & Miller, J. H. (1999) Comparisons of vocational rehabilitation counselors' attitudes toward substance abusers. *Journal of Applied Rehabilitation Counseling, 30*(4), 33-37.

ABUSE AND NEGLECT OF PEOPLE WITH DISABILITIES

FRANCES W. SIU

MARTIN G. BRODWIN

CALIFORNIA STATE UNIVERSITY, LOS ANGELES

CHAPTER TOPICS

- Understanding Abuse
- Issues Related to Abuse and Neglect
- Recommendations for Rehabilitation Services Providers
- Conclusion

Abuse of people with disabilities takes many forms. It is often caused by the abuser asserting power over the victim's mind and body. Neglect is the most common form of abuse found among individuals with disabilities and people of old age. Studies have shown alarming rates of abuse: 67% of women with disabilities reported abuse, and 65% of men with disabilities experienced abuse.[15] From the holistic viewpoint appropriate for rehabilitation professionals, the traumatic experiences of abuse and neglect have significant impact on the devastated individuals, functionally, psychosocially, spiritually, educationally, and vocationally. Securing financial resources through employment is likely to be the most significant motivation for abused individuals to leave their harmful relationships and pursue a better quality of life.

Rehabilitation professionals have crucial roles in helping abused survivors because they are trained and dedicated to enhance the independence and promote equality of opportunity for individuals with disabilities. Rehabilitation professionals may be the first line of defense in detecting abuse, which may require specialized knowledge and a referral network not commonly available in a rehabilitation setting.

This chapter presents an overview of abuse and neglect issues among people with disabilities, and aims to increase the preparedness of rehabilitation practitioners to help clients confront abuse issues. Besides providing basic characteristics of abuse and neglect among people with disabilities, this chapter addresses abuse- and neglect-related issues, discusses intervention and prevention, and offers recommendations for rehabilitation professionals.

The crime of abuse and neglect against people with disabilities cuts across cultures and penetrates through all socio-economic levels affecting people of all religions, ethnicities, economic levels, and educational backgrounds, as well as of varying ages, physical abilities, mental capacities, and lifestyles.

According to the 2007 National Crime Victimization Survey (NCVS), US Department of Justice [USDOJ],[22] violent crimes against people with disabilities was 150% higher than the rate for people without disabilities, while rape and other sexual assaults was twice the rate for people without disabilities. Individuals, especially women with cognitive disabilities (31.3%), experienced a much higher rate of violent crime when compared with those with sensory (9.8%) and physical (12.2%) disabilities. Over 50% of violent crimes against people with disabilities were targeted toward those with multiple disabilities. Violent crimes against women with disabilities doubled that of females without disabilities.[22] In another national survey of 200 women and 275 men with physical and cognitive disabilities, 65% of men and 67% of women reported experiences of abuse. These individuals usually experienced multiple acts of violence.[18,24] Research data have historically been collected mainly on violence against women with disabilities. As a result, a majority of the information presented in this chapter is based on studies of women with disabilities who have experiences of abuse and neglect.

UNDERSTANDING ABUSE

The phenomenon of violence against people with disabilities is a complex health, social, criminal justice, and human rights problem occurring in this country and throughout the world.[9,15] The most common context of violent abuse of women is between intimate partners, a crime commonly referred to as domestic violence, intimate partner violence, spousal abuse, or wife abuse. Females constitute the vast majority of victims, while males comprise the majority of perpetrators.[5,15,20]

Each year, approximately 4.8 million incidents of intimate partner violence occur in the United States. In 2010, the percentage of female victims of intimate partner violence was four times that of male victims. The highest rate of domestic violence occurs among young women between 16 and 24 years of age. Intimate partner violence costs this country $8.3 billion in medical and mental health service expenses, and the loss of worker productivity each year.[17]

Cycle of Abuse

The cause of intimate partner violence occurs when the abuser exerts power to take control of the abused person.[1,19] As identified by many domestic abuse survivors, the cycle of abuse is a vicious cycle that proceeds in three stages: tension building, explosion, and honeymoon period.[13] Tension building is when the abuser appears to be edgy, moody, unpredictable, easily agitated, and there is an air of heightened anxiety causing the intended victim emotional distress. Explosion is when the abuser becomes intensely emotional, angry, violent, and abusive in physical and/or sexual assaults. The honeymoon period is when the abuser acts regretful, apologizes for violent actions, and returns to being a loving individual. When compared with people without disabilities, those with disabilities endure the malicious cycles for longer periods while the honeymoon stage disappears after the first cycle or two. Victims experience many feelings, from anger to love to confusion, with fear being a constant emotion.

Types of Abuse

Physical, sexual, and emotional abuses, as well as financial exploitation are common forms of abuse, and often occur concurrently. In general, physical abuse is a violent act that causes bodily pain, such as slapping, punching, pinching, hitting, shoving, kicking, burning, chocking with bare hands, or assaulting with an object or weapon that may cause permanent injuries. Persons with disabilities experience abuse unique to their disabilities, which persists for significantly longer periods of time.[15,19] These include coercion, control/restraint such as removing the battery from a power wheelchair, stealing money and property, arbitrary deprivation of liberties, withholding of food and liquids, concealment of medication, restriction of mobility, and the threat of such acts. Not only do these individuals experience intimate partner abuse, they also experience institutional abuse, because people with disabilities and individuals of older age are more likely to be institutionalized and encounter abusive service providers.[24] While abuse and violence are seriously underreported, the NCVS documented nearly 590,000 incidents of physical assaults or aggravated assaults against individuals with disabilities in 2007. In the same year, 48,000 incidents of sexual assaults against people with disabilities in the United States were reported.[22]

Sexual violence refers to a completed or attempted sexual activity without the willful consent of the victimized individual or involving a victim who is unable to consent or refuse due to age, disability, unconsciousness, or being under the influence of drugs or alcohol.[5] Common forms of sexual abuse include rape, molestation, fondling, unwanted kissing, unwanted touching, and coercion to perform sex acts or watch pornography. Due to their vulnerability, predators prey on individuals with disabilities, especially those with cognitive disabilities since most are unable to report the crime. Those individuals who report are less likely to be considered creditable reporters–they are not believed and not heard. Sexual violence is a significant problem in society that is impacting many victims' physical health and emotional well-being.

Emotional abuse is a collective act of behaviors to diminish the spirits of a person. The effects of emotional abuse negate a person's existence and are as damaging as physical and sexual abuse, if not worse.[5] A pattern of emotional abuse is likely to undermine a person's perceptions of self and reality. For many physically battered individuals, emotional abuse is an ongoing backdrop against which physical abuse occurs. As a result, any posttraumatic stress symptoms may reflect the anxiety of dealing with repetitive name calling, humiliation, demeaning remarks, threats, and segregation from other family members and society.[1,2]

Financial exploitation and financial control are additional forms of abuse unique to people with disabilities; these include stealing of income and robbery of assets. Many of these individuals are recipients of governmental benefits, such as Supplemental Security Income (SSI), Social Security Disability Insurance (SSDI), pension, retirement funds, and private contributions from family members. The fund recipients may be financially exploited by caregivers whether they are family members or hired service providers.[9]

NEGLECT AND ISOLATION

Due to the limitations of individuals with disabilities, especially those with mobility and cognitive disabilities, neglect is a common form of abuse. There are three categories of neglect:

- active neglect,
- passive neglect, and
- self-neglect.[3]

Situations such as leaving an individual with spinal cord injury nude, cold, and wet in the bathtub after a bath, locking up or keeping medications, food, and drinks out of reach, are willful failures to provide care, known as active neglect.

A caregiver without proper knowledge and ability to care for an adolescent with diabetes mellitus, who needs special dietary regiments resulting in non-willful failure to provide care, is considered passive neglect.

The failure to monitor an elderly person or the ability of a person with disability to self-care, such as leaving an elderly parent with Alzheimer's disease alone without supervision constitutes self-neglect.

Using isolation to cover-up abuse and/or to control a victim's actions, communications, and any outside involvement, and justifying the actions in the name of jealousy, is a typical tactic of abusers. Confiscating hearing aids or telecommunication devices from a deaf person and removing a cane from a blind person are deprivation of liberty unique to their disabilities. These and similar actions result in isolation of these individuals.

INSTITUTIONAL ABUSE

All forms of abuse mentioned above can be found in both domestic and institutional settings. While domestic refers to the home environment, institutional refers to hospitals, group homes, and residential settings. Other institutional settings where abuse occurs are educational institutes, healthcare providers, vocational and rehabilitation facilities, and other places where these individuals receive services.[9,15]

HATE CRIME

Similar to racially and religiously motivated offenses, certain people in society have biases against individuals with disabilities merely because they may not look or act like other persons. According to the NCVS, the disability-related hate crime rate in 2007 increased nearly 80% from 2003.[22] Behaviors motivated by hatred towards people with disabilities takes many forms, ranging from slurs, graffiti, humiliation, bullying, and often involve physical assault, sexual violence, property damage, and even murder.[3] Disability-related hate crimes are underreported due to shamefulness, fear of disbelief, worry about retaliation, and terror of increasingly severe "punishments." Impacts of bias against people with disabilities often include inequities in education, employment, housing, and public accommodations.

ISSUES RELATED TO ABUSE AND NEGLECT

The dynamics of abuse and neglect are multifaceted. Frequently, people with disabilities are abused repeatedly and habitually by the same abusers; their risk becomes even greater with multiple victimizations over prolonged periods of time.[9,20] The effects of abuse for these individuals are likely to be severe.

This section addresses the physical impact of abuse, beginning with abuse-induced behaviors, followed by psychological effects and emotional effects. Also discussed are abuse-related substance use and effects on families and friends.

ABUSE-INDUCED BEHAVIORS

Abuse is often difficult to detect because of the absence of obvious signs and symptoms. Behavioral signs may be the initial indicators of abuse, including abnormalities such as noncompliance, aggressive behaviors, withdrawal, fearfulness of others, atypical attachment, eating disorders, sleep disturbances, learning disabilities, distrust, and self-harm.[15] A number of abused women react to violence with shame, guilt, anger, and sadness. Other behavioral changes may simulate behavioral characteristics found in individuals with neurological, developmental, mental, and mobility disorders. A common outcome of abuse is disconnection from one's sense of safety, self, and self-in-relation to others; efforts at self-regulation of intimacy and anger may be impacted by media stereotypes, interactions with family and friends, and lack of comprehensive diagnostic constructs.[9]

A history of being victimized physically or sexually is correlated to the increasing likelihood of becoming a perpetrator of abuse on others. Abuse-reactive models stress specific behaviors as a response to particular features of the original victimization.[13] Severe self-injury and aggressive behaviors have been common among young women with intellectual disabilities who were abused during childhood. Sexual violence during childhood is associated with adult intimate partner abuse, and is more strongly connected to sex trade, attempted suicide, and other self-endangering behaviors.[7]

Abuse trauma may cause an inability to associate or talk about an abusive episode or feelings about being victimized. Traumatic experiences may linger for long periods with symptoms like irrational fears, sleep disturbance, nightmares, and resistance to revisit or even go near the "crime scenes" of a woman's hostile encounters. Individuals with speech-impairment-related disabilities that hinder them from properly articulating their experience of abuse often find their creditability discounted.[11] Self-reporting of abuse, especially of sexual abuse, is one of the most humiliating experiences one may encounter; it becomes more devastating when such reports are met with disbelief. Such situations are often exacerbated when the expertise of service workers at limited-access abused women shelters and rape-crisis centers leads workers to respond to abused women with disabilities by turning them away and/or disbelieving their claims.[18]

An abused survivor's behaviors during interactions with a rehabilitation service provider may appear to be manipulative. Without knowledge that manipulation is often developed as a survival skill, rehabilitation personnel may have difficulty developing rapport with and may become resentful towards these individuals.[11] Similarly, rehabilitation personnel may not be aware that abusive experiences can cause a survivor to fluctuate in the desire for distance or closeness in a relationship. To avoid remembering their abusive experiences, women may choose to take the avenue of withdrawal from the rest of the world.[11] Yet, these women yearn for support from and connection with others to diminish their terror, eradicate feelings of desertion, and fulfill their constant need for attention.

ABUSE-INDUCED PHYSICAL HEALTH PROBLEMS

According to the Centers for Disease Control and Prevention,[5] violence is a serious public health problem. It is the number one health problem facing women in the United States. Evidence suggests that violence and abuse pose significant health risks for women with disabilities. Violence and abuse have been proven to endanger women's physical and mental health and impair their ability to function.[9,13] They harm women's capacities to manage their primary disabilities, often leading to the onset of secondary debilitating conditions. Abuse may cause symptoms such as amnesia, hypertension, eating disorders, disturbed sleep patterns, musculoskeletal disorders, skin disturbance, respiratory illness, gastrointestinal distress, and gynecological problems.

Women with disabilities are often challenged by uncertainty related to health problems even as they endure constant, long-term abuse because of their health limitations; poor physical fitness due to mobility limitations, pain, and illness; inadequate nutrition; environmental barriers in health care facilities; and poverty because of low income.[20,24]

Staggs, et al.,[21] studied the effects of intimate partner violence on low-income women's health and employment, finding that increased severity of violence was positively correlated with increased health problems. They reported three specific findings of importance:

- women who were living in an abusive relationship experienced worse health outcomes than did those without a history of abuse;
- abuse produced a stronger negative impact on health than did poverty; and
- health problems subsided after the abuse had ended. Up to 63% of women respondents mentioned having abuse-related health problems, including cardiovascular disorders, musculoskeletal injuries, vision difficulties, and gastrointestinal distress.

In addition to chronic illnesses and physical injuries, sexually transmitted diseases are highly associated with sexual violence. Childhood sexual abuse is related to higher rates of women testing HIV positive, and it is responsible for an increased prevalence of HIV infection, alcohol abuse, and heroin addiction. Abused victims with HIV and AIDS are at an increased risk for additional abuse from their intimate partners. Disclosing HIV-positive status can result in battering. A simple request for a partner to use a condom can provoke violence.[7] In addition, the abuser may believe that the abused individual's HIV status is the result of sexual activity with another partner.

Prescribed medications may cause an abused woman to become desensitized to the effects of abuse and to the dangers surrounding her, mimicking the results of self-medication by means of using drugs and the excessive intake of alcohol. As a result, enhanced sedation can raise the physical risks faced by a woman and her child(ren), due to decreased cognitive ability and delayed response time. Furthermore, abused women are often suicidal; medication that is readily available may increase the risk by providing the means to carry out self-harmful behaviors.[24] Studies reviewed in the next section address important mental health issues that arise because of violence in the lives of people with disabilities.

ABUSE-INDUCED MENTAL HEALTH ISSUES

Depending upon the degree of violence and other circumstances, survivors of abuse have been found to suffer an increased risk of developing Posttraumatic Stress Disorder (PTSD), depression, and anxiety disorders.[5] Individuals with abuse-related PTSD are likely to experience memory loss, dissociation, and related psychological effects resulting from the severe abuse. Abused women often report excessive vigilance, insomnia, irritability, poor concentration, and restlessness.[9,19] Other symptoms are likely to be observed, such as increased startle response and avoidance of activities, conversations, feelings, people, places, or thoughts reminiscent of the trauma. PTSD symptoms are common among abused women, especially those who have experiences of rape. Following sexual violence, PTSD symptoms—such as sleep disorders, nightmares, anxiety, diminished sexual desire, and pleasure—are among other disorders found in survivors. Others report disturbing flashbacks, panic attacks, high anxiety, and hyper-vigilance. PTSD is usually co-morbid with depression.[9,8]

In circumstances in which a woman remains in an abusive relationship, some service providers would label her as mentally ill. A woman admitted to emergency care with injuries from abuse or attempted suicide is usually treated initially with sympathy. As these admissions become frequent, the woman is often regarded as exhibiting a mental disorder or a borderline personality disorder. Intimate partner violence has a direct negative impact on a person's mental well-being.[8] Society's judgmental responses, skepticism about reported experiences of abuse, and inflexible response services perpetuate a response paradigm that stigmatizes abuse victims.[19]

Abused women with children fear that the abuser and service providers will use her mental health situation as an excuse to remove children from her custody "for the sake of the children's safety." Trying desperate measures without medical intervention, women may inadvertently cause themselves harm and worsen their disabilities.[24] A woman who needs prescriptions for mental health conditions, such as anxiety and panic attacks, may refuse to take these medications because of the stigma and the possibility of treatment being used against her, as in a custody battle for her children. The woman with mental health issues who refuses medication may exacerbate her psychiatric condition.

Upon departure from abusive relationships, many abuse survivors recover from their mental health problems; those who undergo them for longer periods are likely experiencing depression and PTSD—risk factors for long-term mental problems—simultaneously.[8] Ethnic minority women were significantly more likely to endure substantial problems, both emotionally and physically, beyond the six-month mark after separation, presumably for similar reasons. Compared to the recovery progress of women who have not been sexually assaulted, the recovery of survivors of sexual assault is a more difficult process and the woman takes longer to heal.[7]

Mental illnesses resulting from abuse have devastating impacts on work performance and employment retention.[21] Symptomatic behaviors, such as intensified negative emotions and inappropriate social behaviors interfere with the survivor's interactions with others and with work performance.

Abuse-induced poor physical and mental health affects other aspects of abused women's lives. Staggs et al.,[21] reported four important findings about such effects:

- Poor physical and mental health results in reduced employment opportunities and dims prospects for employment retention, resulting in lower income.
- Both abuse and poor health are markers for welfare dependency.
- The negative impact of abuse may be greater among women living in lower socioeconomic levels than among the general population.
- Necessary components associated with stable employment include social support, education, work skills, and employment experience.

Coutler[6] examined the relationship between experiencing domestic violence and employment patterns, using physical and mental health problems and service use as mediating variables, finding that employment success was highly correlated with physical health. Many women reported struggling with keeping jobs, due to their own health limitations or to the health problems of other family members, often a child. In the case of women with disabilities who were still in abusive relationships, they felt that good health, technical training, and job skills helped earn support from employers.

ABUSE-INDUCED VOCATIONAL PROBLEMS

Violence against women is a significant barrier to employment, affecting the search for meaningful employment and the prospects for job retention, due to increased mental and physical health hazards.[6] Difficulties in job attainment and retention are compounded for women with disabilities who are survivors of abuse, who may experience further social, emotional, and psychological problems, including poverty, homelessness, and the loss of role identities related to work.[21]

Abusers frequently interfere with the victims' efforts to acquire employment, job skills, and education. Some abusers physically prevent victims from going to work or threaten them with harm if they continue to work. A batterer may beat a woman to the point that she is too injured or embarrassed to go to work, or the abuser may stalk or harass her at the workplace. As a result, women may develop diminished vocational and general self-concept, which in turn may lead to decreased attendance at work.[6]

Women with disabilities often experience distinctive types of abuse, such as deliberate sabotage of assistive devices, which may further impact their ability to maintain a job or receive promotions. Some abuse may be intended specifically to prevent a woman from obtaining the employment or education that would allow her to become economically self-sufficient. Many perpetrators deliberately aim to maintain control over their "victims" through financial dependency and social isolation.[2]

In a study of the relationship between domestic violence and employment, researchers found that the effects of abuse by perpetrators on their victims' jobs were complicated and difficult to comprehend.[14] Even though employment provides income, abusers are usually not in favor of their victims working; batterers use interfering tactics before, during, and after work. Before work, abusers' tactics include physically restraining women, beating them to the point that they could not or would not go to work because of bruises or scars in the facial area, depriving them of sleep, destroying or ruining their work clothes, and purposely not bringing home shared vehicles.[6] During work, abusers' tactics include stalking, telephone harassment, physical appearances at work, verbal abuse, harassment of the victims' coworkers and supervisors, requests for victims to leave their job immediately, and beating at the workplace. After work, tactics include stalking or assaulting in response to disapproval of regular work-related actions the victims took during the day, such as speaking to male customers.

Such tactics often cause women to lose their jobs because of abuse-related tardiness, absenteeism, poor job performance induced by the heightened stress level, lack of concentration—all consequences of violent episodes and harassment. Many reasons for missing work are indirectly associated with emotional distress. Abused women call in sick or simply fail to show up for work, with most of them eventually resigning or being terminated.[18]

Helfrich, et al.,[14] investigated the development of worker role identity in abused women with disabilities, finding that women obtained fulfillment in exploring and building upon the roles of mother, family member, church member, and community member, but not in building on the role of worker. In the United States, nearly 80% of people with disabilities are unemployed,[23] while a common predictor of the likelihood of a return to work is the presence of a strong work identity, which is usually absent among abused women with disabilities.

Abused women with disabilities were able to communicate the occupation or profession of interest; yet, they all fell short on their education, experiences, and abilities to perform the identified jobs.[14] Although some women in the study identified more attainable jobs as their interim positions, nobody had any idea for or commitment to a job that was substantial or long-term. Perhaps due to their low self-esteem, abused women with disabilities often described what they were "incapable of" instead of describing their abilities when asked to define their work experiences. Consequently, they created their own barriers to employment and self-sufficiency.

Barriers to the employment of abused women with disabilities include lack of education, training, skills, and accommodations. Women often report that they are also limited by lack of childcare and transportation. Because of their difficulties with employment, women may turn to welfare or return to their abusive relationships for financial support.[21]

PSYCHOLOGICAL EFFECTS

The nature, severity, and circumstances of abuse and neglect, along with individual personalities, can effectively disconnect women from their perceptions of safety, self, and self in relation to other people in their lives.[3,19] Female survivors show stronger reactions to abuse, including both distress and self-blame at the time of the incident, as well as greater reliance on maladaptive coping strategies. Along with maladaptive coping and negative social reactions, longer delays in disclosing are associated with greater severity of psychological symptoms.[3]

Several symptoms of the psychological effects of or dysfunction resulting from violence against women can be discerned: panic, anxiety, posttraumatic stress disorder, dissociation, depression, denial, suicide, grief, sexual maladjustment, sexual dysfunction, and feelings of isolation and stigmatization.[8,9] Important psychological effects have been found among survivors, including overwhelming fear for their lives and that of their children's, difficulty in trusting others, and low self-esteem. Women who have experienced sexual abuse are reportedly more depressed than those who give accounts of physical assaults only.[24]

Society may impose on women with disabilities the role of a victim of illness because they are perceived as unfit to participate in traditional nurturing, care giving, and sexual roles.[20,15] Hence, such women often feel a lack of efficacy in being able to perform. In this way, the implications of traditional role expectations for women as wives and mothers, along with social discrimination towards women, affect how women with disabilities experience abuse.[12] Prejudice and discrimination against women with disabilities diminish the victims' emotional defenses and lower their self-esteem, imparting a stigma and isolation from society, which reduce these women's worthiness in the minds of the abusers and themselves.[13] These pressures likely contribute to abused women's hopelessness and helplessness, causing them to stay or to return to abusive relationships.

Physical and psychological abuses produce similar effects in a victim's emotional development. Victims of abuse who have disabilities experience effects similar to those experienced by victims without disabilities. It is crucial that rehabilitation practitioners understand the total impact of abuse to address its psychological and behavioral effects.[20]

EMOTIONAL EFFECTS

Abuse and neglect are directly associated with a victim's severe emotional distress. When asked if abuse has affected health, 47% of urban women and 88% of rural women with individual abuse histories reported being stressed and increasingly depressed because of the abuse.[9,24]

Women with physical disabilities, especially those who are limited by pain, recent abuse, neglect, and isolation, reported high levels of stress. They are likely to experience life stress related not only to violence but also to social isolation, poverty, and other forms of victimization and chronic health problems.[9]

The increased stress level induced by an incident of violence can cause physiological and psychological changes in women's bodies. Instead of stress, anxiety, and depression, some women complain about somatic problems such as migraine headaches, back pain, fatigue, insomnia, and restlessness.[3,15] Moreover, assault-induced stress can lead to functional impairment of body defense systems, such as the immune and endocrine systems. As a result, a victim becomes more susceptible to infectious disease.

SUBSTANCE USE

Many women turn to alcohol and other drugs to cover up traumatic feelings of emotional distress. To cope with violence, abused women may consume alcohol almost daily, and sometimes to the point of extreme intoxication during the period of an explosion of violence. Constant and prolonged alcohol consumption negatively affects their health and impairs judgment.[11] Violence is significantly correlated with alcohol and other drug abuse for people with disabilities.[10] Equally important, childhood sexual abuse has been found to be responsible for many health-risk behaviors, such as misuse of alcohol, drug use and overdose, and addiction. Abuse survivors are more likely to abuse alcohol and other drugs than are those who have not experienced abuse.

James, et al.,[16] found correlations among the presence of a social network, domestic violence, poverty, and drug use. The lack of social networks is a characteristic of severe drug users living in violence. Among a group of 35 female participants receiving Temporary Assistance for Needy Families benefits and with histories of drug and alcohol use, 71% reported that they had minimal social networks (0 to 2 persons) and relied heavily on family members, especially their mothers, for support. Approximately 46% of participants in the study reported that they lived in a context of current intimate partner violence, and some admitted that their initial use of drugs occurred as a means of coping with abuse by their intimate partners. Others reported that they stayed with their abusers and endured the violence because of easy access to drugs.

Interactions between social networks at the low socioeconomic level and substance abuse are likely to be aggravating factors in the behavior of abused women with addiction. Abused women are challenged by the reality of limited resources, including financial, physical, and emotional supports—limitations that are increasingly severe for women living at lower socioeconomic levels, particularly within minority groups. Many abused, drug-addicted, impoverished women adopt roles as drug dealers, sex slaves, partners, and mothers simultaneously in the hostile environment of American street culture.[16]

EFFECTS ON FAMILY AND FRIENDS

Violence not only distresses "victimized" individuals but also those around them, such as family members, friends, and acquaintances at home, school, or work.[3] The effects on surrounding people may range from concerns as the result of knowing about the abuse, to actual threats, harm, and damages caused directly and indirectly by domestic violence. Children who have witnessed domestic abuse often isolate themselves from others, are overwhelmed with guilt and self-blame; other symptoms including headaches, sleeplessness, depression, loneliness, and dislike by others. Some children feel worthless and others regard life as not worth living. Children (more likely boys) witnessing violence at home have been found to be more likely to abuse their own partners and children when they grow up. In environments outside the home, witnesses may be confronted with emotional challenges, while some have to deal with physical threats. For example, acts or threats of violence at the workplace may affect a woman's co-workers; employers may suffer losses of productivity and damage to property.[21]

The family of a victim and others involved, such as friends and relatives, may need counseling after abuse occurs, with decisions required to determine whether they should be counseled together or separately, by the same or different therapists. Because conflicts not easily resolved may surface when the abuse survivor is counseled together with her caregivers, either party or perhaps both may lose trust in the counselors because of the conflicts.[20]

RECOMMENDATIONS FOR REHABILITATION SERVICES PROVIDERS

With the prevalence rate of violence against people with disabilities, counselors need to be prepared with knowledge and skills to help survivors of violence and abuse. There is no universal method to treat or help these individuals. Like any counseling cases, every case has unique characteristics of its own.

COOPERATION AND COLLABORATION

Cooperative efforts across disciplines, organizations, and individuals are essential to producing positive influences among people dealing with abuse issues in their lives.[20] To reduce violence against people with disabilities in a meaningful way, greater collaboration among professionals is needed, for three principal reasons. First, most abuse-related programs are developed without consideration of addressing limited accessibility and making reasonable accommodation to meet the needs of people with disabilities. Second, most helping professionals deny responsibility for providing special care unique to people with disabilities. Third, multiple-discipline support team members need to incorporate a focus on violence and abuse prevention as part of their operations.

INTERVENTION AND PREVENTION

The number one goal when structuring abuse intervention and prevention teams should be to prioritize representation by all relevant disciplines to produce effective interdisciplinary teamwork that inspires reputable working relationships and sensible communication among all team members.[9,20] Due to the unique needs pertinent to people with disabilities, abuse intervention and prevention team members must be able to discuss cases with experienced consultants within the service systems. Psychologists, social workers, therapists, and counselors have primary responsibility for designing and implementing programs to help victims of abuse overcome the negative effects of their experiences. Rehabilitation professionals can assist other team members to work together and promote the recovery of any individual who lives with a disability.[20] Rehabilitation professionals, especially rehabilitation counselors, must consider casting themselves as prominent representatives, striving to provide a better quality of life for abused individuals by providing rehabilitation services with sensitivity and cultural understanding.[11]

Consistent with the objectives of developing rehabilitation plans "with," not "for," consumers and of respecting their autonomy, Glover-Graf and Reed[11] suggested that people with disabilities should be included in meaningful ways in every aspect of violence and abuse prevention, the extent and nature of their involvement based on a woman's unique situation. Rehabilitation professionals must understand that safety is the most essential and valuable need, not only for the victim at risk but also for everyone in her family. Direct service providers need to take an active role in prevention and intervention. The most effective approach is to assemble a violence prevention support task force made up of disability specialists, medical experts, and other helping professionals, who can share experiences and information, support each other's rights to be free of harassment if there is a report of abuse,[20] and integrate a meticulous safety plan into the abused consumer's rehabilitation plan.

CONCLUSION

Abuse and neglect are complex issues in the community of people with disabilities whom rehabilitation professionals serve. Because of abuse, many people who have disabilities acquire additional disabilities, not only contributing to the growth of the population of people with disabilities but also causing a paradigm shift concerning the dynamics of the rehabilitation client-base, and creating needs for knowledge, skills, and services that are not in the traditional rehabilitation arena.

It is apparent, therefore, that the effects of abuse are powerful and experienced in many forms in any location, victimizing individuals physically, mentally, vocationally, and socially. As a result, many individuals with limitations live in poor health or are in jail in hostile environments for long periods. Some abuse victims consume drugs and alcohol, contract sexually transmitted diseases, and engage in illegal activities. Abuse-induced effects produce particularly harmful outcomes for people with disabilities, bearing on their mind and body, disrupting their harmony, and invading their safety, while creating negative implications for the society.

Rehabilitation professionals can begin to assist people with issues of abuse by routinely asking about abuse and addressing issues of safety and control during rehabilitation planning. We can provide valuable information, resources, and support that may help prevent abuse from occurring and assist individuals for whom abuse has occurred. While information pertinent to this area is being disseminated, a network of resources within the community helpful to all parties involved in abusive relationships is needed.

Because of the vulnerability and highly dependent nature of women with disabilities, they rarely complain or voice anger and humiliation. Advocating for these clients who have abuse issues is a significant part of the rehabilitation professional's job responsibilities. Professional referral to psychologists, social workers, and vocational training centers provides holistic support to clients. Working collaboratively with other helping professionals to secure the safety of victims is important and needs to be a top priority.

The recovery process for abused persons with disabilities has two essential goals: (a) establishing safety and (b) restoring self-control over the survivors' lives. Establishing safety often begins by focusing on control of the body and then moving outward toward control of the environment. Body control focuses on regulating functions consisting of eating, sleeping, and managing symptoms such as anxiety, depression, flashbacks, and states of dissociation. Rehabilitation service providers, especially rehabilitation counselors, can assist survivors in establishing safety and control over their lives by several means: fostering them in a self-image as income-generating workers; providing information about and assisting in connecting with agencies and resources; supporting them as they establish those connections; empathizing with their frustrations, fears, and stresses during the process; and acknowledging their successes. As a result, efforts to aid recovery from abuse have implications for rehabilitation in the areas of health care, transportation services, attendant care, and vocational or career counseling.

REFERENCES

[1]Alhabib, S., Nur, U., & Jones, R. (2010). Domestic violence against women: Systematic review of prevalence studies. *Journal of Family Violence, 25*(4), 369-382.

[2]Brodwin, M. G., & Siu, F. W. (2007). Domestic violence against women who have disabilities: What educators need to know. *Education, 127*(4), 548-551.

[3]Brown, S. L. (2007). *Counseling victims of violence: A handbook for helping professionals*. Alameda, CA: Hunter House.

[4]Centers for Disease Control and Prevention (CDC; 2009). Sexual violence surveillance: Uniform definitions and recommended data elements. Retrieved on June 1, 2012 from http://www.cdc.gov/ViolencePrevention/pdf/SV_Surveillance_Definitionsl-2009-a.pdf

[5]Centers for Disease Control and Prevention (CDC; 2012). Injury center: Violence prevention. Retrieved on June 1, 2012 from http://www.cdc.gov/ViolencePrevention/index.html

[6]Coulter, M. (2004). *The impact of domestic violence on the employment of women on welfare* (Award Number: 1998-WT-VX-0020. Document No.: 205294). Retrieved January 11, 2012, from https://www.ncjrs.gov/pdffiles1/nij/grants/205294.pdf

[7]De Garmo, M. J. (2011). Review of 'violence against women: Vulnerable populations'. *Victims & Offenders, 6*(2), 232-235.

[8]Focht-New, G., Clements, P. T., Barol, B., Faulkner, M. J., & Service, K. P. (2008). Persons with developmental disabilities exposed to interpersonal violence and crime: Strategies and guidance for assessment. *Perspectives in Psychiatric Care, 44*(1), 3-13.

[9]Fitzsimons, N. M. (2009). *Combating violence & abuse of people with disabilities: A call to action*. Baltimore: Brookes.

[10]Gilbert, L., El-Bassel, N., Chang, M., Wu, E., & Roy, L. (2012). Substance use and partner violence among urban women seeking emergency care. *Psychology of Addictive Behaviors, 26*(2), 226-235.

[11]Glover-Graf, N., & Reed, B. J. (2006). Abuse against women with disabilities. *Rehabilitation Education, 20*(1), 43-56.

[12]Hassouneh-Phillips, D., & Curry, M. A. (2002). Abuse of women with disabilities: State of the science. *Rehabilitation Counseling Bulletin, 45*(2), 96-104.

[13]Hassouneh-Phillips, D., McNeff, E., Powers, L., & Curry, M. A. (2005). Invalidation: A central process underlying maltreatment of women with disabilities. *Journal of Women & Health, 41*(1), 33-50.

[14]Helfrich, C. A., Badiani, C., & Simpson, E. K. (2006). Worker role identity development of women with disabilities who experience domestic violence. *Work, 27,* 319-328.

[15]Hughes, R. B., Lund, E. M., Gabrielli, J., Powers, L. E., & Curry, M. A. (2011). Prevalence of interpersonal violence against community-living adults with disabilities: A literature review. *Rehabilitation Psychology, 56*(4), 302-319.

[16]James, S. E., Johnson, J., & Raghavan, C. (2004). "I couldn't go anywhere" - Contextualizing violence and drug abuse: A social network study. *Violence Against Women, 10*(9), 991-1014.

[17]National Center for Victims of Crime (2011). Resource center: Domestic/partner intimate violence. Retrieved on June 1, 2012 from http://www.ncvc.org/ncvc/main.aspx?db Name=DocumentViewer&DocumentID=38711

[18]Powers, L. E., & Oschwald, M. (2005). *Violence and abuse against people with disabilities: Experiences, barriers and prevention strategies.* Retrieved August 1, 2011 from Oregon Health & Science University, Oregon Institute on Disability and Development, Center on Self-Determination Web site: http://www.directcareclearinghouse.org/download/ AbuseandViolenceBrief%203-7-04.pdf

[19]Siu, F. W., & Brodwin, M. G. (2011). Domestic violence and women with disabilities. In E. M. Wolf, J. B. Allen, & L. Vande Creek (Eds.), *Innovations in clinical practice: A 21st Century sourcebook – Vol 2* (pp. 215-225). Sarasota, FL: Professional Resource Press.

[20]Sobsey, D. (1994). *Violence and abuse in the lives of people with disabilities.* Baltimore: Brookes.

[21]Staggs, S. L., Long, S. M., Mason, G. E., Krishnan, S., & Riger, S. (2007). Intimate partner violence, social support, and employment in the post-welfare reform era. *Journal of Interpersonal Violence*, 22, 345-367.

[22]U.S. Department of Justice. (2009). *National crime victimization survey: Crime against people with disabilities, 2007.* (USDOJ Publication NO. NCJ 227814). Washington, DC: U.S. Government Printing Office. Retrieved from http://bjs.ojp.usdoj.gov/content/pub/pdf/ capd07.pdf

[23]U.S. Department of Labor (USDOL; 2012). *Office of Disability Employment Policy: Current disability employment statistics*. Retrieved on June 30, 2012 from http://www.dol.gov/odep/

[24]Yoshida, K. K., Odette, F., Hardie, S., Willis, H., & Bunch, M. (2009). Women living with disabilities and their experiences and issues related to the context and complexities of leaving abusive situations. *Disability and Rehabilitation: An International, Multidisciplinary Journal, 31*(22), 1843-1852.

7

ATTITUDES TOWARD DISABILITY

MARTIN G. BRODWIN

CALIFORNIA STATE UNIVERSITY, LOS ANGELES

LEO M. ORANGE

OXNARD COLLEGE, CALIFORNIA

CHAPTER TOPICS

- Historical Perspective
- The Americans With Disabilities Act
- Attitudes, Beliefs, Values, and Behaviors
- Attitudes of Society Towards Disability
- Reactions to Disability by People With Disabilities
- Minority-Group Model: Disability as a Socio-Political Issue
- Disability, Attitudes, and Ethnic Minorities
- Interaction and Communication
- Language about People with Disabilities
- Disability and Sexuality
- Family Issues
- Suggestions for Rehabilitation Service Providers
- Conclusions

An infinite variety of flowers grow in this world – all different, all beautiful, all with the same rights to sunshine, rain, and nutrients from the earth. Some just need a little more nurturing. Everyone deserves an equal opportunity to bloom.

Deborah Lee, *PersonalCommunication*, December, 1991

Attitudes toward people with disabilities are complex and multifaceted; a rehabilitation professional's attitude toward disability directly affects the quality of services they provide their clients. Understanding attitudes is a central concern in rehabilitation. A top priority of rehabilitation counseling educators is to teach positive attitudes to their students. Service providers must understand their own attitudes and actions when offering services to clients with disabilities. Today, the influence of negative attitudes toward individuals with disabilities and their families is profound. Attitudes toward disability can be effectively changed through education, contact, and positive interaction.

Over 50 million people in the United States have disabilities; one in eleven Americans of working age identify themselves as having a disability. These figures exclude individuals with non-visible disabilities and those who choose not to identify themselves as having a disability. Non-visible disabilities, those that cannot be perceived without disclosure or a medical examination, include substance abuse, AIDS, psychiatric disabilities, diabetes, pulmonary conditions, epilepsy, and chronic pain syndromes,

Through interventions involving rehabilitation services, persons with disabilities are able to participate more fully in society–pursuing an appropriate education, career, and taking an active part in social and recreational activities and functions. The term rehabilitation, as used in this chapter, is based on the definition by Banja:

> *A holistic and integrated program of medical, physical, psychosocial, and vocational interventions that empowers a disabled person to achieve a personally fulfilling, socially meaningful, and functionally effective interaction with the world.*[3, p. 615]

Family members and service providers are active members of the team providing rehabilitation interventions. They help people with disabilities to overcome obstacles and achieve positive adjustments in medical, emotional, social, academic, and vocational aspects of life. Yet, negative attitudes that currently exist within society prevent full participation and achievement of persons who have disabilities. Rehabilitation team members need to attend to significant issues such as assisting clients in dealing with social isolation and alienation; working through and adapting to a new self-image; and focusing on abilities related to education, employment, social integration, and one's right to be involved in society.

HISTORICAL PERSPECTIVE

Negative attitudes and behaviors toward people who have disabilities and chronic illnesses have existed in all cultures since early times. People with disabilities have always been viewed as different from that which society dictates to be normal. These attitudes and behaviors promoted by society throughout time have been displayed as the rule, rather than the exception. In some cultures, however, adults with disabilities have been protected and assigned specialized tasks, although with little latitude or public support and isolated from normal everyday interaction and the established social network of the society. When isolated in this way, people with disabilities have had problems with social adaptation, in addition to the difficulties they face adjusting and adapting to disability. This situation leaves little latitude for living independently or achieving maximum potential, singling them out of the mainstream and assigning them to their own "minority" group status.[1]

These negative views crosscut boundaries of culture and suggest that discrimination emanates from human nature itself. In most cultures, people with disabilities tend to be set apart, treated as different, and devalued by the society. As a result, quality of life, opportunities, and extent to which they can reach their potential are profoundly impacted.

In the past, the history of attitudes and rehabilitation of people with disabilities has focused on treatment of these individuals as socially deviant in at least one of the following areas–physical appearance, physical functioning, intellectual functioning, emotional balance, and behavior. Many cultures have equated physical imperfection with moral and intellectual deficiencies. Acceptance or rejection of persons with disabilities also varies according to the type of disability, with medical conditions involving physical limitations receiving more positive acceptance. Least negatively viewed disabilities are those that are less identifiable. The least accepted disabilities are those regarded by others as self-imposed (e.g., substance abuse), and have the most negative attitudes directed toward them. People are most accepting of disabilities where there is no perceived fault by the person with the disability.

Prior to current times, social isolation inhibited persons with disabilities from achieving their educational, vocational, and social maximum potential. Beyond this, persons with disabilities have been classified as deviant from the majority. They are forced into an inferior social position with the negative evaluations that are typically placed on ethnic minority groups.[23] Society determines whether a group of people will be regarded as different through selection of certain facets of their being and by attaching to these facets positive or negative labels and identifications. Persons with disabilities have typically been given negative labels. Recently, there has been an attempt to use labels that emphasize the person over the particular disability (e.g., "person with a disability" rather than "disabled person").

During the 1800s, the population of persons with disabilities was systematically discriminated against as a group and deprived of the pursuit of basic rights, such as competitive employment, education, and participation in political, social, and economic areas of society. By the end of the 19th century, there was a significant political movement that began to emphasize the government's responsibility to care for problems occurring within the society, including the various areas within rehabilitation.

The first federal program in which the government assumed responsibility for rehabilitation came in the form of providing vocational rehabilitation services to persons who had served in the military. The Soldiers' Rehabilitation Act, passed in 1918, offered vocational rehabilitation benefits and programs for veterans of World War I who had disabilities because of the war. This was followed in 1920 by the Smith-Fess Act (the Civilian Vocational Rehabilitation Act) that addressed the needs of the civilian population. During World War II, women and persons with disabilities were called on to replace the labor force that had been inducted into military service. At the conclusion of the war, returning veterans resumed their prior employment. Though only temporarily, people with disabilities had proven their ability in employment. Once again, however, people with disabilities returned to their status as being an invisible and powerless group.

Additional rehabilitation laws enacted since World War II have focused on specific populations of persons with disabilities.[14] Even with these legislative attempts, discrimination and negative attitudes toward persons with disabilities continue to exist in our society, especially within the area of employment. The government, recognizing the prevalence of these attitudes, attempted to resolve ensuing problems with passage of the Rehabilitation Act of 1973. This legislation reflected a congressional commitment to persons with disabilities and emphasized the provision of rehabilitation services to persons with severe physical and emotional disabilities. The stated goal of the Rehabilitation Act of 1973, to enhance the civil rights of persons with disabilities, could not be effectively enforced. Discriminatory practices continued to occur.

THE AMERICANS WITH DISABILITIES ACT

The Americans with Disabilities Act (ADA) passed in 1990, attempted to remedy discriminatory practices by including elements of the Civil Rights Act of 1964 for "coverage and enforcement," and "terms and concepts" from Section 504 of the Rehabilitation Act of 1973 in its definition of discrimination. This legislation guaranteed the civil rights of Americans with disabilities and chronic, medical conditions. The intent of the ADA was that society and employers, in particular, change their thinking and behavior. People with disabilities were to be treated fairly, with equality and without discrimination in areas of employment, public services, accessibility, transportation, and telecommunications. The ADA provides persons with disabilities visibility, social consideration, a little more power, and increasing acknowledgment of rights to equal opportunities. Although laws do not ensure that society improves attitudes toward people with disabilities, as interaction increases, social attitudes become more open and, hence, more positive.

The ADA definition of a person with a disability was specified as follows:

- The person must have a physical or mental impairment which substantially limits one or more major life functions;
- The person must have a record (history) of such an impairment; (or)
- The person must be regarded as having such impairment.

A major purpose of the ADA was to enhance participation of persons with disabilities in all aspects of American life, especially employment. The law is based on the presumption that people with disabilities have not been active participants in the labor market in part because:

- employers continue to discriminate and
- there is a lack of adequate access to buildings and public transportation, preventing many individuals from getting to work.

Enforcing the ADA, in part, falls within the role and function of rehabilitation service providers. Supplying services for their clients, providers need an awareness of how the ADA defines disability, how this definition impacts persons with disabilities as a minority group, and how the intent of this Act helps in overcoming discrimination.

The 1990s involved continuing economic growth, resulting in higher income and employment rates for all income groups, except people with disabilities. This disparity can be traced to negative employer attitudes toward people with disabilities.

Title I of the ADA (employment) pertains to discrimination in employment practices, and has a provision that current and prospective employees provide reasonable accommodation, whenever possible. Employers who have hired people with disabilities have positive attitudes about the work capacities of these individuals, dispelling many negative stereotypes. Yuker[25] noted that a good, productive experience with a person with a disability is directly related to a positive attitude. Employers who hire employees with disabilities value the employees' job skills, social skills, and dependability, and the disability is less of a focus. When an employee with a disability demonstrates these traits, the employer's attitude and experience tends to be more favorable.

Perceptions of persons with disabilities change slowly, unless practices reflective of enlightened professionals become institutionalized.[1] Service providers, both in the private and public sectors, need to be advocates for people with disabilities. The ADA regulations allow persons with disabilities to take active and productive roles in our society. It is part of the responsibility of the rehabilitation provider to stimulate various aspects of our society to address the anti-discrimination regulations of the ADA. This can be accomplished through a conscious effort to educate family members and the professional community and to take an active role in changing current practices toward people who have disabilities.[20] An attempt to educate the professional community is occurring through educational programs, publications, professional seminars, and workshops. It is only through open communication that understanding and positive social interaction can occur and bring about a positive change in attitudes and behavior.

ATTITUDES, BELIEFS, VALUES, AND BEHAVIORS

Attitudes are often compared with such concepts as beliefs, opinions, and values and related to behaviors. *Beliefs* are traditionally conceived of as the cognitive component of attitude. They are viewed as statements indicating the probability that an attitude object possesses a particular characteristic, quality, or attribute. Beliefs are associated with the amount of information an individual has about a particular object. This informational base leads to the formation of a certain attitude toward the object, eventually directing the person to behave in a particular manner (positive or negative) toward that object.

Values are broad, abstract attributes used to characterize various related attitudes. A certain degree of worth is ascribed by the individual to the referent. When specific attitudes, both positive and negative, are organized into a hierarchical structure, they create a value system. The more central the role of an attitude in an individual's value system, the more closely related to the person's self-concept and the more difficult it is to change.

Attitudes are neither a necessary nor a sufficient cause of behaviors; they are a contributing factor. They exert both a directive and dynamic influence on behavior, thus mediating between environmental stimuli and the individual's response act.[18] Attitudes are acquired through experience; therefore, they represent the socialization process and the contribution of direct past events. Controversy surrounding the relative importance of heredity and environment in determining one's behavior may also be generated by attitudes. Attitudes may be conceived of as bridging elements, formed by the interplay of genetic factors and learning, which influences the individual's behavior.

Behaviors may be predicted from a person's attitudes. A person's attitudes toward a given object, individual, group of people, or event, in conjunction with knowledge of various situational and other personality variables, aid researchers to better understand, explain, and ultimately predict behavior. Ability to identify the mechanisms underlying the development and structure of attitudes may assist researchers to alter people's reactions to various human interactions, such as those encountered in education, counseling, and therapy. Knowledge of the structure and development of attitudes toward people with disabilities is considered to be necessary for changing attitudes, and thereby behaviors, potentially increasing the integration of people with disabilities into mainstream society.

Opinions toward people with disabilities may be conceived as operating in three distinct and interacting social circles. The innermost circle comprises attitudes exhibited by family, friends, and peers of people with disabilities. Attitudes of these groups influence not only the development of the individual's self-concept, but also socialization of the person into typical community activities.

The next attitudinal circle encompasses the relationships of people who have disabilities with the professionals with whom they come into contact. This group includes practitioners such as physicians, nurses, psychologists, counselors, social workers, teachers, and clergy. In these roles, rehabilitation providers and educators present information, services, and reinforce client stability. Their attitudes have a strong impact on the medical and psychosocial process of an individual's adjustment to disability. Attitudes of these professionals also may influence attitudes of the members of the first social circle and that of society.

The third and outermost circle is composed of public attitudes. Negative attitudes of society toward people with disabilities create obstacles to the fulfillment of their roles and the attainment of life goals.[16] These attitudes are apparent in employment practices. People with disabilities as a group have a higher rate of unemployment and underemployment. Unfavorable attitudes of employers toward people with disabilities often impede vocational possibilities and result in reduced opportunities for securing on-the-job training, educational opportunities, vocational training, and gainful employment. When hired, people with disabilities frequently are offered inferior positions, lower wages, and have fewer opportunities for advancement.[2]

A person's social roles are related to how he or she is regarded by others. The occupancy of a social role that is valued by others is likely to engender positive attitudes toward the occupant, even if that same person also possesses social characteristics that, on their own, are poorly regarded (e.g., person with a criminal record). For an individual cast in the role of person with a disability (a devalued role), access to valued social roles will tend to offset the typical negative attitudinal response in favor of a more positive attitude.

The feeling and reality of having a disability is either imposed by:

- human-made parts of the physical environment, or
- social customs, values, attitudes, and expectations.

As a society, our expressed values toward people with disabilities traditionally tend to be positive. Feelings and behaviors, more realistic of a person's actual attitudes are typically negative.[4] What a person publicly states as a belief toward a particular group can be very different from how the person actually feels and acts toward that group. People require knowledge about the experience of being denied access to full participation in our society based on disability to comprehend what this means.[22] They need to realize the goal is not preferential treatment, but rather equal opportunity to participate in all aspects of life.

Cultural proficiency in rehabilitation is a necessary skill for practitioners to be effective in interacting with individuals with disabilities who are from diverse ethnic and cultural groups. It is also necessary to understand their beliefs, preferences, and values.[2] As enumerated by Crabtree, et al.:

> *At best, the potential lack of agreement on basic values, beliefs, or attitudes complicates the issues to be addressed for successful outcomes and confounds the rehabilitation practitioner's efforts to provide competent and effective services. At worst, conflict between ethnic and cultural beliefs, values, and attitudes undermine the best intentions of rehabilitation practitioners and the efforts of consumers to lead lives that for them are consistent with their own ethnic and cultural beliefs and values.*[8, p. 4]

ATTITUDES OF SOCIETY TOWARDS DISABILITY

Western civilization has historically defined its standard of beauty and health by the image of an impeccable and physically fit body. The obsession with a tall, slim, and beautiful appearance is exemplified by adoration of mythical characters such as Apollo and Venus. All cultures typically perceive persons with disabilities as weak, unattractive, and undesirable. Among Americans, social stigma attached to disability partially depends on whether or not the person with a disability is perceived as being responsible for his or her own state of limitation. The inner beauty of people with physical disabilities is often overshadowed by a less attractive outer appearance.

Studies have demonstrated that women with disabilities are more likely than men to be stigmatized. A study conducted by an Australian university asked undergraduate students their opinions about social issues related to sexuality and disability.[6] There was significant non-acceptance of the sexuality of women with disabilities as compared to non-disabled women and men both with and without disabilities. Women with disabilities have been devalued and marginalized in American culture, often being neglected, mistreated, harassed, and abused. A woman of minority ethnicity with a disability endures three times the discrimination–she is devalued by the stereotypes associated with her gender, minority status, and disability. Denial of a woman's sexuality is denial of her humanness and negatively affects her view of herself as well as her place in the world.[4]

Persons with disabilities tend to develop negative feelings about their own and other types of disabilities and limitations. When a physical disability is acquired, there is considerable resistance to the sudden change of body image that may damage and debase one's self-esteem. Denial of the alteration of body image is a common defense mechanism used by people with recently acquired disabilities to deflect the devaluation imposed on them. Other defensive reactions include over dependency, withdrawal, aggression, depression, and secondary gain through manipulation. Although a person with a disability may find the courage and energy to handle physical or mental limitations, there are times when coping is emotionally difficult. Even Franklin Delano Roosevelt went to great lengths to shield his disability from the American public. Of the hundreds of official pictures taken while he was in office as the 32nd president, only a few showed him using a wheelchair. It is not known why President Roosevelt hid his disability; possible reasons that have been postulated include perceived concerns about national security, feelings of personal maladjustment, or living in an unsympathetic social climate that devalues people who have disabilities.[5]

It takes time for people with disabilities to come to terms with newly acquired limitations. Despite having to learn to use wheelchairs, become knowledgeable about assistive equipment, or have personal attendants to compensate for impairments, persons with disabilities felt adjusting to societal attitudes was the most challenging. Vash and Crewe,[24] in discussions of the psychology of disability and psychospiritual aspects of rehabilitation, noted that some individuals embrace their disabilities for various reasons, such as God's intervention or fate. Depending on the locus of control by which persons with disabilities operate, some will forever be depressed and unable to overcome disability, blaming the world and people around them for their perceived suffering. Others will internalize the ideal of becoming a "complete" person by taking responsibility for ensuring better outcomes for their own lives.

When people with disabilities have positive attitudes toward their disabilities (self-acceptance, disability acknowledgment, adjustment, and disclosure), this often has a favorable effect on the attitudes and actions of those around them. Effective social skills also affect positive evaluations. When others perceive interaction with persons with disabilities as personal, rewarding, and characterized by cooperation, intimacy, and equal status, enhanced attitudes and behaviors result.

MINORITY-GROUP MODEL: DISABILITY AS A SOCIO-POLITICAL ISSUE

The largest minority group in the United States is people with disabilities. Until recently, they have been unable to make progress in obtaining equal rights and benefits that has occurred for other minority groups. The minority-group model of disability accepts Dworkin and Dworkin's[11] definition of a minority group and applies it to individuals with disabilities. Criteria for this definition include "identifiably, differential power, differential and pejorative treatment, and group awareness."[p. viii] People with disabilities clearly fit this definition.

Throughout history, individuals with disabilities have been viewed as different. They have been forced into an inferior social position with the devalued evaluations and attitudes given ethnic minorities. Limitations people with disabilities have, according to this model, are not their functional impairments, but the social and psychological reactions of society and the socio-political structure. With a changed socio-political structure and positive social attitudes, one could perceive an entirely different view of disability: How disabling would paraplegia be if all cities were barrier-free? How disabling would deafness be if everyone learned sign language in school?

People with disabilities have historically been treated differently and have been afforded a minority status; they have been barred from society, confined to their homes or put in institutions, and often pitied. Although individuals with disabilities were considered "worthy poor," the assistance they received from society generally perpetuated segregation and stigma, and was not initiated with the purpose of integration or equal access.

Disability has frequently been considered synonymous with helplessness, dependency, and passivity. The tendency has been to consider people with disabilities as:

- Victimized by the disability condition and limitations, and
- needing treatment, not rights.

People with disabilities were not considered equal citizens and efforts were not made to allow their full participation in society; they were perceived as "dependent children," with all the condescending connotations identified with this term.

The socio-political approach views disability as a product of interaction between the individual and the environment and attitudes of people within those surroundings. Disability limitations are seen as located in the environment people encounter rather than limitations within particular individuals. A "disabling environment" is viewed as causing functional limitations, such as the myriad of architectural barriers encountered by people using wheelchairs for mobility.[14] To change all this, one must change both public policy and attitudes.

DISABILITY, ATTITUDES, AND ETHNIC MINORITIES

In 1835, Alexis De Tocqueville saw great injustices permeating the social structure of America when he addressed the conditions of the three races inhabiting the nation at that time:

> *The first who attracts the eye, the first in enlightenment, in power and in happiness, is the white man, the European, man par excellence: below him appear the Negro and the Indian. These two unfortunate races have neither birth, nor face, nor language, nor mores in common; only their misfortunes look alike. Both occupy an equally inferior position in the country that they inhabit; both experience the effects of tyranny; and if their miseries are different, they can accuse the same author for them.*[10]

The ADA is an important step toward recognizing the needs and rights of persons with disabilities. Human service professionals, however, need to take a further step in recognizing the additional issues specific to ethnic minorities. To the extent that society discriminates and creates social barriers, ethnic minorities with disabilities are minorities within minorities, facing multiple barriers to education, full employment, financial resources, and integration.

Disabilities, in the context of interpersonal relationships and society, require dealing with all the social ills that affect ethnic minorities. Rehabilitation service providers need sensitivity to the feelings of the individuals and their families in interacting with their own ethnic groups, as well as with the mainstream group. Despite civil rights and equal opportunity legislation, barriers to ethnic minorities in education and employment are common occurrences. Attitudinal biases, beyond the scope of legislation, are difficult to change.[19]

Earlier in this chapter, we discussed the conceptualization of people with disabilities as a minority group. Human service professionals should take one further step in leading the field to recognize additional issues particular to ethnic minorities. In examining issues faced by ethnic minorities with disabilities, there are two major questions to address:

- How is that particular disability viewed by the mainstream culture and the minority culture?
- How does the mainstream group view a particular ethnic group?

The first question pertains to the ways different cultures perceive various types of disabilities. For example, surveys of mainstream American respondents have generally found that persons with mental retardation are rated more favorably than persons with psychiatric disabilities or substance abuse problems. In addressing the issue of discrimination toward persons with disabilities, one must examine the mainstream culture and the particular minority culture, instead of assuming that the presence or absence of social barriers or stigma in mainstream society holds true for every group. In working with ethnic minorities with disabilities, rehabilitation service providers must be sensitive to the needs and feelings of individuals and their families in dealing with their own ethnic group as well as with the mainstream group.

The second question pertains to the status of ethnic minorities in American society.[16] Barriers to ethnic minorities in education and employment are common occurrences. Human service professionals need an awareness of the obstacles faced by ethnic minority clients. To what extent is the family genuinely willing to support the client's goals? To what extent is an employer willing to hire an ethnic minority person? To what extent will fellow employees befriend employees with disabilities and relate to them as equals? To what extent are rehabilitation, counseling, job placement, and other services available to minorities living in the inner cities or ethnic enclaves? Can institutions provide culturally sensitive services to these populations? Are bilingual services available to those who have not acquired sufficient English proficiency? Counselors and other service providers must be careful not to let the client's disability obscure the ethnic or racial issues as separate subject areas. They can adequately serve the client only be addressing both concerns.[2]

INTERACTION AND COMMUNICATION

Persons with disabilities are frequently referred to as "handicapped." This label has many negative connotations and portrays people as weak, ineffective, and powerless. Historically, the term "handicapped" originated when society believed that people with disabilities were incapable of working to earn their livelihood. They were relegated to begging for money. In doing this, some individuals took off their "caps" and held them in their hands to receive donated money; hence, the word handicapped (cap in hand) arose. "Disabled person" was the term that replaced handicapped; it was believed that this term would be viewed more favorably. More recently, recommended terminology has changed from referring to people as disabled ("not able") to identifying them as "people with disabilities." In this manner, emphasis is on the individual, rather than the disability or limitations. The person is seen as an individual with various characteristics (many of them positive), rather than simply a disabled person. "A person with mental retardation" is preferred terminology over mentally retarded"; "a person with an amputation" is preferred over "amputee."

Misunderstandings between people who are not disabled and people with disabilities often occur in social interactions. Rehabilitation service providers need to be aware of possible misunderstandings occurring between their clients and themselves. Persons with disabilities and people who do not have disabilities differ significantly in their perceptions of what is considered to be the most positive attitude.

In a research study assessing attitudes of people who are not disabled toward people with disabilities, respondents with disabilities felt that positive attitudes involved either totally dispensing with the category of disability or in promoting the rights of persons with disabilities. Respondents without disabilities felt that positive attitudes involved a desire to be nice, helpful, and ultimately to place the person with a disability in a "needy" situation. Although respondents without disabilities believed they were doing their best to be helpful, persons with disabilities often took their actions and attitudes as offensive. Two examples cited by Makas[15, pp. 49-50] are illustrative.

CASE #1

Doris goes to her friend's house for a game of Trivial Pursuit. Much to Doris' surprise, she finds that one member of the group, Suzanne, is blind. Determined to show Suzanne that she is not prejudiced against people with disabilities, when Suzanne mistakenly names Portland as the capital of Maine, Doris insists that Suzanne be given another chance. Suzanne responds angrily that she can do well in the game without Doris' help and that Doris should mind her own business. Doris decides that she will never again try to be polite to people who have disabilities.

CASE #2

Mike learns that Rick, the new employee hired by his company, has a physical disability. He stops by Rick's office to welcome him. He tells Rick that he is looking forward to getting to know him, since he has always considered people with disabilities to be easy-going and very courageous. Rick tells Mike to get out of his office and slams the door behind him. Mike decides that people who have disabilities are not so nice after all.

Learning occurs through communication. Interactions between people often become distorted. As in the examples just cited, a person may be attempting to communicate a particular feeling, but the recipient perceives the communication in a different way, based upon certain needs, feelings, past history, and opinions about the other person. There are possibilities for misperceptions at any point. The person wants to be seen as friendly, open, and caring, but is instead perceived as unfriendly, hostile, and aggressive. Attitudes and perceptions play significant roles in these interactions.

Makas[15] suggested that people without disabilities should be educated about areas in which their behaviors offend persons with disabilities. Persons with disabilities also need to work with people who do not have disabilities in correcting, but not overreacting to those statements and accompanying attitudes and actions. Overall, persons with disabilities want equality through civil rights, not special treatment afforded because of disability. Society must be educated about the experience of being denied equal access and full participation in society.

LANGUAGE ABOUT PEOPLE WITH DISABILITIES

The definitions below are helpful in clarifying attitudes and terminology that can be confusing.

- *Impairment* - Describes an abnormality or loss of a physiological structure or bodily function.
- *Disability* - Refers to the consequence of impairment – a restriction or lack of ability to perform some activity that is considered appropriate.
- *Handicap* - The means of social disadvantage that results from an impairment or disability.

Impairment does not necessarily produce a disability; a disability need not be a handicap. Disability and handicap are both socially defined terms, and thus influenced by attitudes, while impairment is not. Poor vision, corrected by glasses, is not a handicap. Old age is a handicap in our culture, but not in cultures that revere the elderly as leaders and allow them to serve as a source of knowledge and experience. The word "handicapped," however, should never be used when referring to a person.

Hadley and Brodwin[12] noted that language portrays persons with disabilities in imprecise, stereotypical, and devalued ways. Language should follow four simple principles:

- *Precision* - Language should convey a person's intended meaning. For example, a person is not "wheelchair-bound," or "confined," but uses a wheelchair for mobility.
- *Objectivity* - Language that expresses unwanted, surplus meanings or treats opinions as fact should be avoided. Objective language does not carry biases.
- *Perspective* - Emphasis should be on the person, not the disability. For example, the term "paraplegic" emphasizes the disability; a "person with paraplegia" places emphasis on the person.
- *Portrayal* - Persons with disabilities should be portrayed as actively going about the business of living as others do, not as passive victims, tragic heroes, or super-heroes.

Rehabilitation practitioners need to use "nondisabling language" when referring to people with disabilities. More than two decades of rehabilitation literature has called attention to the use of imprecise, stereotypical, and devaluing language when discussing people with disabilities and disabling conditions. Language should be precise and convey a person's intended meaning in an exact and unambiguous manner. The use of imprecise language can give one the feeling of decreased capability and diminished power.

Words such as "victim" and "sufferer" should not be used because of the negative innuendoes and passive connotations of these and similar words. Although it is true that the issue of terminology is partially the choice of the client, the practitioner is the professional. This person can set the tone of the working relationship by the language used in addressing the client. Although the exact relationship between language terminology and attitudes is still unclear, the ADA of 1990 strongly encouraged the use of language that places the person first, the disability second.

DISABILITY AND SEXUALITY

As stated, interactions between people who have disabilities and individuals without disabilities are severely tested by attitudinal and architectural barriers.[4] Many common social and recreational patterns that occur during dating involve physical skills or activities that are beyond the capacity of people with major disabilities. Both the person with a disability and the person without a disability may face intense resentment from others, including parents and friends who may regard the relationship as inappropriate or inadvisable. As a result, dating relationships between people with disabilities and individuals without disabilities are subjected to unique and constant stressors. Those who are able to overcome the effect of adverse attitudes and taboos against physical contact between persons with disabilities and those without disabilities must still confront the obstacles resulting from ambiguous social values and dating norms. Social customs, perhaps more than physical differences, are powerful deterrents to these relationships.[19]

Despite the progress achieved in today's society, the continued lack of recognition of sexuality as part of the lives of people with disabilities continues. Assuming that people with disabilities do not need to express themselves as sexual beings denies them opportunities to develop healthy identities in relation to intimacy and sexuality. The cultural stereotype "beauty and strength are good" pervades American culture and is admired by society. At the interpersonal level, physically attractive people are evaluated on the basis of their sexuality in the normative sense. A physical disability, on the other hand, may be used as a cue to categorize a person as abnormal, not worthy, or deviant. When used to discredit an individual in this stereotypical manner, it becomes a source of stigmatization.

One of the most challenging accomplishments in life is being courageous enough to take chances with love, especially as it requires loving oneself and another person. It takes self-esteem for people with disabilities to think in positive ways. Anxiety due to disability may cause an individual to withdraw and, as a result, lead to depression, withdrawal, and loneliness. This loneliness or depression is often a symptom of frustration. Increased loneliness, anxiety, and depression make it problematic for people with disabilities to assimilate in society.

Sexuality goes beyond physical and physiological functioning to the psychological feelings associated with gender identity, self-worth, and social attitudes.[19] Service providers and family members need an understanding of the interrelatedness and interaction of disability with issues of intimacy and sexuality. Negative societal attitudes often inhibit individuals from accepting and acknowledging their sexuality and considering themselves sexually functioning people. Defined in its narrowest sense, sexuality is the expression of our physical urges; yet, it is much more than that. Sexuality is how we feel about ourselves, how we present ourselves to others, and how we fulfill our roles in society.

Rehabilitation service providers need an awareness of the myths and negative attitudes associated with disability and sexuality. Some of these myths and misconceptions are listed below:

- Disabled people are asexual.
- Disabled people are over-sexed and have uncontrollable urges.
- Disabled people are dependent and child-like and, thus, need to be protected.
- Disability breeds disability.
- Disabled people should stay with and marry their own kind.
- If a disabled person has a sexual problem, it is usually the result of the disability.
- If a person who is not disabled has a sexual relationship with an individual who has a disability, it is because they cannot attract anyone else.[7, pp. 2-4]

Lim-Kee[13] and Brodwin and Frederick[4] noted that when it comes to marriage, people with disabilities have as much right as anyone else to be autonomous in making marital choices. When two persons decide to live together and share their lives, whether through marriage or as partners, the underlying need is the sense of belonging with a mate. Isolation and loneliness, often a consequence of living alone, can be two of the most stressful aspects of living with a disability.

Researchers in the fields of counseling and disability issues have conducted studies to dispel the myth that people with disabilities have no interest in having intimate relationships with the opposite sex. Cromer, et al.[9] administered a self-image questionnaire for adolescents to teenagers with chronic disabilities to assess their knowledge, attitudes, and behavior related to sexuality and marriage. Results showed that 88% of the respondents expressed a desire to marry. Individuals with less severe disabilities appeared to have more knowledge about sexuality than their counterparts with more limited body functions.

Miller, et al.[17] studied the willingness of college students without disabilities to engage in personal relationships with students with disabilities. Students without disabilities were significantly more willing to have friends and acquaintances that have mild to moderate disabilities and persons with sensory, health, and physical impairments. They were least willing to consider dating, marrying, or having intimate partnerships with people with disabilities.

While the public is more accepting of persons with disabilities as colleagues or casual friends, people are hesitant to perceive individuals with disabilities as potential dating or marriage partners. Myths, prejudice, and misunderstanding of disabling conditions continue to have a negative effect on the interaction of people with disabilities and those without disabilities. The most difficult challenge in a relationship where one partner has a disability and the other does not is the constant negative experiences they encounter in society.

Discouragement is a common deterrence to the development of a potential relationship. Partially due to negative societal attitudes, the mere presence of a disability can have a "desexing" effect on an individual.

FAMILY ISSUES

Family has been defined as the most important institution within society.[21] This is particularly apparent for people who have disabilities as the patterns of development, self-identity, and ability are often influenced by the family environment. Family concerns are crucial because families, like individuals, have different coping capabilities. Many families can maintain a state of positive adjustment and equilibrium with the support and understanding of skilled professionals to help them cope with the difficulties associated with disability status. The family helps determine the outcome of rehabilitation efforts, as well as the reaction and eventual adjustment of the family member with a disability.

Quality of the interpersonal relationships within the family unit can be as crucial as the disability itself. If a family communicates positive attitudes of worth to the family member with a disability, an affirmative self-concept is reinforced. This enhances the likelihood that the individual will be willing to participate in life activities, including the rehabilitation process. If rehabilitation efforts fail for no apparent reason, it is suggested that dynamics within the family be thoroughly examined.

Research[16] has been conducted on the wives of men with spinal cord injuries regarding the process of coping with their husbands' disabilities and limitations. Information provided from this research identified recurrent themes indicative of the process of coping and adapting. Initially, there was fear, primarily involving images of the husband's potential death, During the early months after onset, interpersonal support from family and friends was crucial to these women. It was during this time that the wives believed they had to be controlled and emotionally strong when interacting with their husbands who were involved with their own emotional coping processes; this was often encouraged by hospital personnel. Yet, these women were denied their own emotional needs, illustrating the importance of involving family members in the counseling process. When addressing the issues of disability with the client, rehabilitation service providers may want to ensure that family members who need help in coping are not neglected.

Onset of a disability imposes a series of lifestyle adjustments on the family. One of these adjustments involves the pace of life. The person with a disability, especially a physical one, will require more time to perform many of the basic activities of life; this is a potential source of frustration to other members of the family. A tendency to assist the person "just to get ready faster" can ultimately add to the disability by undermining the individual's attempts at and progress toward living more independently.

Another impact of disability is allocation of income. Living with a disability imposes a financial burden on the individual and the family. Further, the family often experiences a decline in social and leisure-time activities. After the onset of disability, friends have a tendency to drift away because they themselves cannot cope with the person's disability and subsequent limitations. Consequently, the individual, couple, and other family members may find themselves eliminated from their former social circle due to the reactions of others to the disability, and perhaps by the reactions of the individual who has the disability.[21]

Living with a disability assaults one's personal identity and the lives of family members who are providing support and encouragement.[4,19] The individual with a disability and family members need to feel they can direct and control their lives. A process toward coping with a disability involves adaptation to one's disability. A most important family function in the rehabilitation process is supporting the social adjustment of the person with a disability in dealing with all aspects of life, including avocational and leisure activities. The family can help the individual learn to use leisure time more productively. Having hobbies or returning to social activities helps in the adjustment and return to a normal life.

SUGGESTIONS FOR REHABILITATION SERVICE PROVIDERS

- Use non-disabling language when referring to people with disabilities, whether the discussion is with someone who has a disability or with others.
- Negative attitudes pose one of the most significant barriers for people who have disabilities. A service provider's positive attitudes and actions serve as a model for other professionals and for society.

- Although initial attitudes toward persons with disabilities are often influenced by disability-related characteristics, after some interaction, the disability becomes less a focus and personal characteristics become more central.
- When counseling a person with a disability, if the disability is unrelated to the subject matter, it need not be discussed, unless the service provider needs clarification of the condition to provide appropriate services to the client.
- An individual who has a disability usually feels comfortable discussing the disability and interrelated issues. If a question related to the disability arises, a service provider should use professional judgment in making sure the client is comfortable addressing these issues.
- Focus on what the client can do, not on what cannot be done. One needs to emphasize an individual's knowledge, capabilities, and skills, not limitations.
- Make sure the offices you use are fully accessible to persons with all types of disabilities. If not, attempt to have physical (architectural) barriers modified or removed. The ADA requires that accommodations be provided, including removal of architectural barriers, so that people who have disabilities can participate fully in all phases of society and life.
- Employers value employees with disabilities who have job skills, social skills, and dependability. Those who have had experiences with employees with disabilities usually have positive attitudes, particularly toward the disabilities with which they are familiar.
- If unsure about a particular disability condition, consult someone with knowledge and expertise in that area. The person with a disability frequently has the most extensive information.
- Become familiar with Section 504 of the 1973 Rehabilitation Act and the ADA. There are classes, workshops, and published resources available on various topics.
- Be sensitive to attitudinal barriers. These barriers will be observed in the manner in which the public interacts with people who have disabilities. Attitudinal barriers often occur when meeting with an employer to return a person with a disability to work. The provider can offer flexible and innovative services addressing attitudinal and architectural barriers.
- Develop cultural awareness, essential for all rehabilitation professionals.
- Many cultures are hesitant about revealing personal information to people outside their families. Proceed slowly and cautiously when exploring sensitive issues.

CONCLUSION

Once established, people have always been resistant to changing their beliefs and attitudes. Anxiety and fear induced by unfamiliarity with a group of a different background is one main reason that society resists new concepts and ideas. Yet, stereotypes may gradually be corrected once positive contact is initiated and developed. Geographic proximity, with its reinforcement, provides insight into the process of interaction between persons without disabilities and those with disabilities.[25] Frequent contact enables people to create new perceptions of one another, based on knowledge derived from positive interactions. When misconceptions are clarified and greater understanding is achieved, psychological barriers diminish between persons with disabilities and those without disabilities.

Determinants of unfavorable societal responses toward people who have disabilities include perceived cause of the disability, perceived threat of the disability, perceived responsibility for the disability, prevailing economic conditions, and sociocultural values. Positive attitudes toward people with disabilities usually result in positive behavior and increased interaction. Negative attitudes result in bias and discriminatory behavior. Discriminatory attitudes and practices create barriers that prevent persons with disabilities from full participation in society.

To conclude this chapter on attitudes toward disability, we cite the insightful words of Maya Angelou:

> *It is hoped that we can have the compassion to see through complexion and impairment to our common humanity, the respect to value our differences, and the courage to create a more just society.* [2, p. 390]

REFERENCES

[1]Arokiasamy, C. M. V., Rubin, S. E., & Roessler, R. T. (2008). Sociological aspects of disability. In S. E. Rubin & R. T. Roessler, *Foundations of the vocational rehabilitation process* (6th ed., pp. 167-195). Austin, TX: Pro-ed.

[2]Balcazar, F. E., Suarez-Balcazar, Y., Taylor-Ritzler, T., & Keys, C. B. (2010). *Race, culture, and disability: Rehabilitation service and practice.* Sudbury, MA: Jones and Bartlett.

[3]Banja, J. D. (1990). Rehabilitation and empowerment. *Archives of Physical Medicine and Rehabilitation, 71*, 614-615.

[4]Brodwin, M. G., & Frederick, P. C. (2010). Sexuality and societal beliefs regarding persons living with disabilities. *Journal of Rehabilitation, 76*(4), 37-41.

[5]Brodwin, M. G., Orange, L. M., & Chen, R. K. (2004). Societal attitudes toward the sexuality of people with disabilities. *Directions in Rehabilitation Counseling, 15,* 45-52.

[6]Chandani, A., McKenna, K., & Maas, F. (1989). Attitudes of university students toward physically disabled people. *British Journal of Occupational Therapy, 52*(6), 233-236.

[7]Cornelius, D. A., Chipouras, S., Makas, E., & Daniels, S. M. ((1982). *Who cares? A handbook on sex education and counseling services for disabled people* (2nd ed.). Baltimore: University Park Press.

[8]Crabtree, J. L., Royeen, M., & Benton, J. (2006). Cultural proficiency in rehabilitation: An introduction. In M. Royeen & J. L. Crabtree, *Culture in rehabilitation: From competency to proficiency.* Upper Saddle River, NJ: Pearson Prentice Hall.

[9]Cromer, A., Enrile, B., McCoy, K., & Gerchardstein, M. J. (1990). Knowledge, attitudes, and behavior related to sexuality in adolescents with chronic disability. *Developmental Medicine and Child Neurology, 32*(7), 602-610.

[10]De Tocqueville, A. (1835). *Democracy in America.* Retrieved October 12, 2008, from http://xroads.virginia.edu~HYPER/DETOC/1_ch18.htm

[11]Dworkin, A., & Dworkin, R. (1976). *The minority report.* New York: Praeger.

[12]Hadley, R. G., & Brodwin, M. G. (1988). Language about people with disabilities. *Journal of Counseling and Development, 67,* 147-149.

[13]Lim-Kee, J. Y. (1994). Sexuality, marriage, and disability. *International Journal of Adolescent Medicine and Health, 7*(3), 199-202.

[14]Livneh, H., & Cook, D. (2005). Psychosocial impact of disability. In R. M. Parker, E. M. Szymanski, & J. B. Patterson (Eds.), *Rehabilitation counseling: Basics and beyond* (4th ed., pp. 187-224). Austin, TX: Pro-ed.

[15]Makas, E. (1988). Positive attitudes toward disabled people: Disabled and non-disabled persons' perspectives. *Journal of Social Issues, 44,* 49-61.

[16]Marini, I., & Graf, N. M. (2011). Spirituality and spinal cord injury: Attitudes, beliefs, and practices. *Rehabilitation Counseling Bulletin, 54*(2), 82-92.

[17]Miller, E., Chen, R., Glover-Graf, N. M., & Kranz, P. (2009). Willingness to engage in relationships with people with disabilities. *Rehabilitation Counseling Bulletin, 52*(4), 211-224.

[18]Moore, C. L., & Feist-Price, S. (1999). Societal attitudes and the civil rights of persons with disabilities. *Journal of Applied Rehabilitation Counseling, 30*(2), 19-24.

[19]Orange, L. M. (2009). Sexuality and disability. In M. G. Brodwin, F. W. Siu, J. Howard, & E. R. Brodwin (Eds.), *Medical, psychosocial, and vocational aspects of disability* (3rd ed., pp. 263-272). Athens, GA: Elliott and Fitzpatrick.

[20]Riggar, T. F., Maki, D. R. (Eds.) (2004). *The handbook of rehabilitation counseling.* New York: Springer.

[21]Roland, J. S. (2005). Chronic illness and the family life cycle. In B. Carter & M. McGoldrick (Eds.), *The expanded family life cycle: Individual, family, and social perspectives* (3rd ed., pp. 492-511). Boston: Allyn and Bacon.

[22]Smart, J. (2008). *Disability, society, and the indivi*dual (2nd ed.). Austin, TX: Pro-ed.

[23]Stone, J. S. (Ed.). (2005). Culture and disability: Providing culturally competent services. Thousand Oaks, CA: Sage.

[24]Vash, C. L., & Crewe, N. M. (2003). *Psychology of disability* (2nd ed.). New York: Springer.

[25]Yuker, H. E. (1992). Attitudes toward disabled persons: Conclusions from the data. *Rehabilitation Psychology News, 19,* 17-18.

8

PSYCHOSOCIAL ADAPTATION TO DISABILITY AND CHRONIC ILLNESS

LaKeisha L. Harris

Lisa Zheng

University of Maryland Eastern Shore

Chapter Topics

- Psychological Adaptation to Disability and Chronic Illness
- Models of Adaptation
- Adjustment to Specific Disability
- Summary

Chronic health problems and disability are common experiences in the lives of many individuals. In 2005, almost one out of every two adults, 133 million Americans, had at least one chronic illness. About one-fourth of the people with chronic conditions have one or more daily activity limitations.[5] These chronic illnesses and disabilities profoundly interfere with the physical, psychological, social, vocational, and economic functions of those affected.[19] Psychosocial adaptation and issues with adjustment among people with disabilities and chronic health problems present significant barriers to successful rehabilitation outcomes. These barriers often create overwhelming burdens to the individuals and their families in terms of long-term care and community integration.

This chapter will discuss the adjustment process by describing several adjustment models and the affect on individuals with disability at different phases. This chapter will also look at several categories of disabilities and their characteristics that may affect adjustment. The adaptation process among individuals with acquired disabilities is the focus versus congenital disabilities because people with congenital disabilities are likely to go through the same developmental stages as their nondisabled peers.[2]

Adjustment to disability has been a popular subject that has been studied and debated among rehabilitation counselors, researchers, and educators over the past 50 years.[18] Many researchers are intrigued with the complex phenomenon of adaptation to chronic illness and disability. Accordingly, several models are developed to address questions such as:

- How do people view and cope with their acquired disabilities and chronic health issues, e.g., traumatic brain injuries (TBI) or spinal cord injuries (SCI)?
- What psychological reactions do people typically show?
- Do these reactions constitute a process of adaptation to the disabilities?
- If so, can this process be ordered both temporally and hierarchically?
- What kind of disability-related factors contribute to successful adjustment?

These questions, along with an overview of the predominant models of adaptation to disabilities, as well as outcome studies for adjustment to TBI, SCI and Multiple Sclerosis are addressed in this chapter.

The concepts of psychosocial *adjustment* and psychosocial *adaptation* are quite similar and often are indistinguishable in the literature in coping with adverse life crisis or disability issues.[19] At a fundamental level, adaptation may be conceived as a *process* of responding to the functional, psychological, and social changes that occur with the onset and experience of living with a disability or chronic illness. This process has been characterized in terms of movement toward adjustment outcome.[2] Adaptation is an evolving, dynamic, and general process. Adjustment, on the other hand, is the clinically hypothesized *final state*, where the person reaches the goal of achieving an optimal level of harmony between the renewed sense of worth and the external world, demonstrating competency to manage one's environment and integration with communities.

MODELS OF ADAPTATION

The following section will describe and discuss four theoretical frameworks of psychosocial adaptation to disability and chronic illness that are usually found in the rehabilitation literature. The models are interactive, linear stage, pendular, and ecological.

INTERACTIVE MODELS

Interactive models of psychosocial adaptation, also called somatopsychological model, were built on Kurt Lewin's field theory.[21,22] Lewin stated that adaptive behaviors were the function of two sets of interactive variables that are internal and external aspects of the individual with disabilities. The internal aspects are associated with physical elements (e.g., type and severity of the disability) and psychological aspects, (e.g., self-concept, stress management skills). The external environmental factors include social, vocational, and physical environment barriers. An individual's level of adaptation reflects the bi-dimensional, conjoint effects of internal characteristics and the external forces.

Based on the principles of the somatopsychology, Wright[31,32] developed a model of adjustment to disability emphasizing disability acceptance. The major changes indicative of the acceptance of the disability includes the individual being able to recognize that significant meaning remains in his or her life, rather than focusing on what has been lost because of the disabling condition. The person begins to embrace meaning in alternative abilities, activities, and life goals.

As the scope of what the person *values* broadens, the relative importance placed on society's biased view of physical attractiveness and completeness decreases. Instead, other intrinsic characteristics, such as intelligence, determination, wisdom, persistence, and quality relationships gain more and more importance. The individual begins to moderate how negatively the disability will impact life and the initial perception of devastation begins to reside. They gain the capacity to see objectively the true impact of the disability without generalizing it to other domains of life. Wright distinguished the differences between assets values and comparative values. Assets values are intrinsic, which allow for evaluation based purely on the qualities of the person, whereas comparative values are evaluations based on a standard of "normal." When a person uses a wheelchair, the wheelchair is perceived for its usefulness as a means of mobility for the user, rather than to the comparative value as if it is inferior to walking. Wright stated disability could be regarded as either a surmountable challenge and something that could be coped with or something to succumb to and tragic. Personal choice on how to adapt to one's disability makes a substantial difference in the outlook the individual has about life.

LINEAR STAGE MODELS

Early models of psychosocial adaptation emphasizing the sequential nature of the adaptation process are called linear stage models.[20,10,28] Focusing on the psychological impact the individual experiences once the permanent, irreversible damage done to the physical body is understood, with the corresponding functional limitations, these theoretical models imply the linear progression of stages would be automatically activated. The person would then go through the emotional phases of shock, denial, anxiety, anger, acceptance, and to the final stage of "adjustment."[20,18] The arrival of the more advanced stages depends on the successful completion of each previous stage, indicating that one has to "work through" all the stages to reach the final stage of adjustment.[30]

After conducting an extensive literature review, Livneh[16] synthesized more than 40 stage models to create a unified model of adaptation to physical disability. These partially overlapping psychosocial reactions were later grouped into three main categories:

- earlier reactions (e.g., shock, anxiety, denial);
- intermediate reactions (e.g., depression, anger), and
- later reactions (e.g., acknowledgement, behavioral adaptation, disability integration).[17,18]

According to Livneh,[16] one may initially experience *shock*, resulting from the impact of an overwhelming experience, such as the sudden onset of severe physical injury (e.g., spinal cord injury) or learning about a diagnosis of a terminal disease (e.g., liver cancer). Shock is evidenced by little emotional reaction, psychic numbness, and depersonalization with reduced mobility and speech. These emotional responses appear to serve as a psychological anesthesia to push away a vaguely sensed seriousness of the present condition.

Anxiety follows the short-lived shock reaction as one starts to sense the possible consequences and severity of the traumatic event. Different from anxiety as a personality trait, anxiety after an acquired severe disability is associated with learning about the medical aspects of the disability, waiting for test results, and worrying about the possible complications and recurrence of symptoms of a chronic condition. Hysteria-like reactions are characteristic at this stage.[29] Anxiety is indicated by panic features, such as confused thinking, purposeless over-activity, and physiological symptoms (e.g., hyperventilation, rapid pulse rate). Individuals may start to sense the enormity of the traumatic event along with possible major life changes that will likely need to occur. At this stage, the individual lacks the ability to think logically and plan strategically.

Regarded as an early, protective psychosocial reaction, *denial* is viewed as an attempt to ward off unmanageable levels of emotional pain caused by the overwhelming realization of the future implications of the chronic illness and disability. Denial may include an unrealistic expectancy of condition improvement or even a full and speedy recovery. The person in denial may appear to be aloof and indifferent to the actual environment while selectively attentive to the information that appears to support this wishful version of reality. The presentation of impractical hopefulness sometimes may be referred to as "pseudo-optimism." Some argue that only after denial diminishes can the individual start the journey toward optimal recovery. This is because the individual in denial is not even in touch with reality. With a somewhat impaired perception of reality, individuals in denial may have less motivation to learn new adaptive skills that accommodate the acquired limitations. It is likely they would say to themselves, "Why bother? I will soon be fully recovered." On the other hand, others may argue denial helps to maintain a cohesive sense of self and is an important facilitative mechanism for hope. It provides much-needed strength to help the individual confront and face the reality of the sudden, overwhelming loss. Denial, in fact, serves important psychological functions. By minimizing or totally avoiding an unpleasant reality, denial purposefully redefines the implications of a critical condition and protects the self from being emotionally shattered. Denial may significantly mitigate the pain associated with the psychological awakening state of anxiety. However, in the long term, denial is often deemed unproductive and maladaptive, especially when it interferes with processing important therapeutic recommendations, resulting in self-harming behaviors.

Depression is the most researched and observed experience following the onset of acquired disability. It is considered a normal reaction of grieving after realizing imposed limitations and required modifications in important domains of life, such as, family, work, and socialization. Instead of mourning for a specific loss, people with chronic illness and disability may sink into depression of a more general and diffuse nature as well as one of a longer duration. Feelings of helplessness, hopelessness and despair, self-deprecation, as well as social withdrawal and general psychomotor retardation are often reported.

The reaction of *anger* has two expressions: internalized anger and externalized hostility.[19] Upon realizing the chronic and irreversible condition of the impairment, some individuals may attribute the onset of the condition as being their own fault. Internalized anger manifests as self-directed resentment and bitterness. Feelings of guilt or self-hate may be expressed. Suicidal ideation as well as other self-destructive acts may follow as ways to be self-punitive. However, externalized hostility is directed toward others and aspects of the environment that are associated with the onset of disability or difficulties encountered during the rehabilitation process. A defense mechanism called displacement is assumed to operate at the stage of externalized hostility when hostility is aimed at less emotionally invested subjects such as medical staff, an inconvenient physical environment, rather than targeting family members.[16] Very low tolerance of frustration, acting impatiently, being provocative, being verbally or physically abusive, as well as passive-aggressive behaviors may be observed.

The later reactions of adaptation include the sub stages of *acknowledgement and adjustment.* Acknowledgement is the first sign that an individual has reached a state of cognitive reconstruction of how the self is viewed, the ability to cope with the challenges imposed by the external environment, and finally reconciling the permanence of the condition and its future implications. As the final phase of the adaptation process, adjustment is a theoretical concept that is envisioned as "ideal" because once the final phase of adjustment is reached, a continuation of a harmonious state is expected for the long term. The person would internalize functional limitations into the self-concept, assimilate new meanings in life, realize remaining valuable potential by actively pursuing personally and socially meaningful goals, as well as demonstrating self-approval and mastery in tackling obstacles in daily activities.[19,18]

Criticism of Stage Theory. Stage theory gives us a useful theoretical framework to understand common experiences people with chronic illness or acquired disability might experience. However, imposing the expectations that an individual must go through these stages in linear fashion, one after another, could result in unintended harm. Clinically, people do not progress through these stages in a linear fashion—it does not match with the experience of many people with acquired disabilities and chronic illness. For many of them, psychological recovery does not follow an orderly, predictable sequence of reaction phases. Neither are these psychological reactions mutually exclusive. It is possible for an individual with acquired disabilities to experience several stages simultaneously, or an individual might skip different stages, or cycle through various stages rapidly when confronting environmental or attitudinal barriers. Criticisms to the linear models also include the underlying assumptions that depression is necessary for successful adjustment.[30] Those who do not manifest depression following the traumatic loss may be accused of being in denial of their loss or too weak to initiate the grieving process. According to Wortman and Silver,[30] the "requirement of mourning" is not supported by research. However, research has also indicated that individuals who are most distressed soon after disability onset are more likely to be depressed one to two years later. Another myth about the adaptation process is that the final state of adjustment will be attained because of "working through" each developmental stage of the adaptation process. In reality, not all individuals who become disabled reach the theoretical end of the adaptation process—the final adjustment. Many will be 'stuck' at a certain phase along the adaptation continuum, characterized by increased dependency, continued inconsolable anger and hostility, prolonged depression and self-destructive behaviors, particularly when disability onset is sudden or unexpected. In addition, linear stage models are criticized for their lack of consideration of the importance of the impact of social and environmental factors on the individual's psychosocial adaptation to acquired disabilities journey.[20]

PENDULAR RECURRENT MODELS

While linear stage models depict the general progression trend towards adjustment, pendular models in which adaptation is viewed as an ongoing cycle, seem to capture the recurrent, unpredictable, and complex nature of the psychosocial adaptation process.

Following a sudden traumatic onset of acquired disabilities, the former "automatic"/"natural" ways of understanding or dealing with the everyday life and the world is likely to be challenged. Having to cope with permanent, irreversible effects done to the physical body with the imposed functional and activity restrictions, the adaptation process may involve prolonged crises when one has to "expand" oneself to a degree never imagined before. The process of adaptation tends to occur in a dual directional pendular trajectory that swings back and forth between the former nondisabled self to the current disabled self.[6,7] The individual would be repeatedly "reminded" of the loss by various aspects of the environment and the need to face challenges and accommodate accordingly. Tremendous effort must be put forth to gain a sense of mastery and control over one's physical environment and to manage the disabling condition. The individual will likely search for meaning in the disability as well as protect and further enhance the self and the post-disability identity.[1,14] Initially, one can be overwhelmed by the tasks of making sense of the disability and acquiring new abilities to master the suddenly changed reality. As time passes, new information and skills of handling the new environment are learned and a more positive attitude towards life may be achieved.

Yoshida[33] conceptualized the identity reconstruction following traumatic spinal cord injury as a pendulum that swings back and forth between the former nondisabled self at one extreme, and the totally disabled self at the other extreme. When the individuals compare their current limitations to their former nondisabled status, the swings tend to bring much disappointment and pain by idealizing the pre-disability identity and defining themselves only in relation to being disabled and focusing on the presumed loss. These kinds of big swings often lead to diminished self-worth, isolation, and depression. The pendulum trajectory also travels across three other identities: the supernormal identity, the middle self-identity, and the disabled identity as an aspect of the total self. The supernormal identity is characterized when the individual swings back towards the former nondisabled self in an over-compensating form, such as refusing any assistance from others, attempting to engage in extraordinary activities in an attempt to fight against "negative identifying images" associated with disability and further prove that they are just like other people. The supernormal identity is often referred to as denial.[14] As the need to prove oneself becomes less important, the pendulum oscillates back towards the acceptance of the disability aspects of self, and eventually the middle self is reached when the pendulum reaches its temporary balance. The middle self is defined as a clear understanding and realistic acceptance of limitations associated with the disability, along with social awareness and consideration of other individuals with disabilities. Clearly, the self has been expanded to incorporate a wider social concern for other persons with disabilities and include other segments of society. The pendular model captures the dynamic, shifting nature of identity transformation after the onset of chronic illness and acquired disability. The dual-directional process implies no limit to the number of times this pendulum process can occur nor the frequency of each process. The movement between different identities, evolving from moment to moment and across situations may continue over a long period.

ECOLOGICAL MODELS

Recent conceptualizations of psychosocial adaptation represent a more complex and comprehensive approach known as the ecological model. Livneh[17] categorized four primary classes of variables inherent in the adaptation process, and further grouped them into two groups, the internally and externally associated factors. The internally associated factors are composed of three classes of variables, (i.e., disability-related, general sociodemographic, and personality characteristics; while the external factors refer to one class of variables), (i.e., physical environment, community-based environment, and social environment). Disability-related variables include severity of symptoms and extent and effect of functional limitations; whether the course of the disability is progressive or stable; whether the disability is associated with pain; and how the disability impacts personal appearance. Sociodemographic variables include age, sex, ethnicity, religion, education, marital status, and employment status. Personality characteristics include self-concept, self-efficacy, perceived sense of control or mastery of one's disability, cognitive competency, body image, optimism, and coping styles. The external environmental variables include degree of social isolation, restricted mobility, environmental inaccessibility, attitudinal barriers, available social support system, and financial resources. The first three classes of internally associated variables interact with the fourth class of external variables to determine the degree and speed of psychosocial adaptation process. These variables are conceptually dynamic and interactive in nature and more congruent with the clinical observation that psychosocial adaptation is a multidimensional, complex and a highly individualized process.[2,17] However, because ecological models are descriptive rather than predictive, it is hard to utilize the knowledge to promote the wellbeing of individuals via rehabilitation counseling practice.[2]

Another recent ecological model is proposed by Bishop[2,3] as a disability centrality model, which is based on the synthesis of several theories and models of adaptation as well as from the quality of life literature to provide a comprehensive framework that may capture the complex, multidimensional, and highly individualized nature of the adaptation process.

According to Bishop[2,3] the concept of quality of life or subjective quality of life is being assessed as physical health, psychological health, social support, employment, and financial well-being. The term of "centrality" is used to imply the hierarchical organization of the domains of quality of life as each of these domains would have different value to different people. In addition, each domain may vary in its importance by the same person over the course of adaptation. It implies that satisfaction in more valued domains of life will have more weight in the overall consideration of well-being than those areas of lesser importance. The quality of life based model has several advantages in assessing and understanding the impact of acquired disability in terms of clinical interventions. The format of the assessment offers a means of prioritizing the interventions needed for the most "central" domains of the individual's quality of life to promote healthy adaptation. The shift of the importance placed upon different domains of life could provide a wealth of information to understand the adaptation process, either positive or negative. It helps to address the criticism of previous measures that only focus on assessing the negative aspects of disability experience.

ADJUSTMENT TO SPECIFIC DISABILITY

In the following section, several categories of disability and the distinctive traits that may have an impact on successful adjustment will be described. While it is impossible to cover every type of disability, the three major categories that have been extensively covered in the rehabilitation literature will be reviewed. These are:

- traumatic brain injury,
- spinal cord injury, and
- multiple sclerosis.

TRAUMATIC BRAIN INJURY

According to Faul, et al.,[11] there are approximately 17 million people in the United States who have acquired a traumatic brain injury (TBI). A person with a TBI has experienced a severe head trauma generally caused by an accident, fall, stroke, or some other type of serious injury to the brain.[19] Common among younger people, a TBI can range in levels of severity and may cause major disruption in a person's life physically, socially, cognitively, and behaviorally.[15] Many researchers have investigated the psychosocial effects of having a TBI and many have found the cognitive and social effects to be among the most detrimental to a person attempting to adjust. The type and severity of the person's injury will have a major impact on those cognitive and social deficits and will play a major role in how individuals perceive themselves post-injury.

Traumatic brain injuries often tend to limited critical thinking and decision-making skills of affected individuals. A person with a TBI may experience feelings of depression, anxiety, anger, and frustration at not being able to perform at pre-injury skill levels.[19] Depression can be especially acute during the adjustment phase as a person comes to the realization that their injury is permanent and will not likely be reversed. Often, this awareness of limitations can also lead to episodes of anger.

In addition to medical interventions that occur after acquiring a TBI, rehabilitation may also include counseling and social skills training. Individuals with traumatic brain injuries must re-learn basic communication skills that are important for appropriate functioning in society. Family support and caregiver support is especially crucial during the rehabilitation phase as a person adjusts to their new level of functioning. Former relationships may be disrupted, as the person with a TBI has to cope with severe cognitive difficulties.[15] In a study of family members of persons with acquired brain injuries, Braine[4] found that families' experiences centered on the complexity of behaviors displayed by their affected loved one.

Complete adjustment to a TBI is dependent upon the treatment interventions utilized, the severity of injury that the person has incurred, and the amount of support the individual has during the coping process. In a study of psychosocial outcomes in individuals with brain injuries 10 years after the initial injury, it was found that while many functions improved, depression and anxiety tended to be among those issues that need consistent support.[9] Successful adjustment would include the person with the TBI being able to reside and work independently within their limitations[19] and maintain their independence by using appropriate coping skills.

SPINAL CORD INJURY

According to the National Institute of Neurological Disorders and Stroke,[25] spinal cord injuries (SCI) occur approximately 12,000 times per year in the United States, with over half of the cases being individuals between the ages of 16 and 30 years of age. A spinal cord injury occurs when there is severe damage to the spine resulting in either paraplegia or quadriplegia. Spinal cord injuries are often caused by motor vehicle accidents, falls, gunshot wounds, and stabbings with the majority of patients being young men. Depending on the severity of the injury, SCI can negatively impact many aspects of the individual's life; including having mobility restrictions, losing sensation, and possibly resulting in chronic pain.[24] These challenges may lead to vocational limitations, as well as limitations in other major life domains.

Early focus on the person with SCI tends to center around acceptance and adjustment. Research has shown that in the early stages of injury, the person who acquires SCI will have an intensive amount of motivation, as they believe that their injury is only temporary and they will eventually be able to walk again or regain other lost functions. As realization becomes apparent that the SCI is permanent and there is little chance of reversal, individuals may progress through the grief process as they mourn the loss of their pre-injury self. There is some disagreement among researchers about the trajectory of this process.[19] Evidence to shows that as time progresses, many individuals are able to adjust successfully as they learn to cope with their limitations.[19]

Depression is one of the major reactions to SCI as the individual is faced with chronic pain and major functional limitations.[8] Rehabilitation programs tend to combine physical therapy with counseling and motivation-building exercises to increase the individual's participation in their own recovery. Depression also follows the realization that interpersonal relationships will change because of the injury. Many may feel that they are a burden to their family and friends and they will notice when others treat them differently because of their condition.

An increasing measure of adjustment among persons with a spinal cord injury involves a review of the individuals' quality of life and their ability to function independently.[12] There is a consensus that successful adjustment to a spinal cord injury will occur if the person is constantly motivated and feels encouraged about their ability to manage and control their lives in spite of their disability-related limitations. Factors that play a role are levels of mobility, levels of social support, perceptions of independence, and vocational ability.[12]

MULTIPLE SCLEROSIS

Multiple sclerosis (MS) is a neurological disorder affecting over 400,000 people in the United States.[27] Onset of MS tends to occur most frequently among individuals aged 20 to 40 with no known etiology or prevention methods available.[19,26] Multiple sclerosis is an autoimmune disorder that affects the brain and central nervous system. MS affects the ability of nerve cells in the brain and spinal cord to communicate with each other effectively. MS can be particularly destructive because the body's immune system is eating away at the nerves that support this communication. Upon onset, MS typically progresses rapidly and unpredictably through the body and can result in disruption to a number of functions. Some of the symptoms commonly associated with MS include problems with mobility and motor functioning, paralysis, and issues with excessive fatigue that often lead to side effects that are more serious. There is currently no cure for MS, but there are medications that help to slow the attacks to the immune system.

As found in many other categories of acquired disability, MS often results in bouts of depression, as the individual has to cope with declining functions and abilities. Depression results as the person with MS must rely more on family and friends in order to perform even the basic daily functions which can often cause stress in those close relationships.[13,26] Having to rely on others and the feeling of having no control over one's life, further leads to decreased satisfaction and feelings of anxiety about the future.

Another unique aspect of MS is that person's with the disease may encounter periods of remission, meaning the disease is not actively progressing through the body. These periods of remission may result in feelings of hope, which may soon diminish if the person has a relapse.[19] Successful adjustment to MS for an individual with the disease will include interventions that will raise the person's self-concept and accurate awareness of their functional limitations as well as their new abilities. In addition, the person must have support from family and rehabilitation professionals as they seek more independence in their lives.

SUMMARY

Despite the specific types of chronic illness or disability any one individual or groups of individuals may incur, psychosocial adaptation is always a dynamic and complex process through which individuals move as they work to reach a maximum state of functioning and strive to achieve the optimal state of adjustment. Many models have been developed to explain this process and they offer valuable insight for rehabilitation professionals to devise effective interventions that assist clients to achieve the desired level of adaptation and harmonious interaction between the individuals and the environments in which they live and work.

REFERENCES

[1]Barnard , D. (1990). Healing the damaged self: Identity, intimacy, and meaning in the lives of the chronic illness. *Perspectives in Biology and Medicine, 33*, 535-546.

[2]Bishop, M. (2005). Quality of life and psychosocial adaptation to chronic illness and acquired disability: A conceptual and theoretical synthesis. *Rehabilitation Counseling Bulletin, 48,* 219-231.

[3]Bishop, M., Shepard, L., & Stenhoff, D.M. (2007). Psychosocial adaptation and quality of life in multiple sclerosis: Assessment of the disability centrality model. *Journal of Rehabilitation, 1*, 3-12.

[4]Braine, M. E. (2011). The experience of living with a family member with challenging behavior post acquired brain injury. *Journal of Neuroscience Nursing, 43*(3), 156-164.

[5]Centers for Diseases Control and Prevention. (2012). Chronic Disease Prevention and Health Promotion. Retrieved from http://www.cdc.gov/chronicdisease/overview/index.htm

[6]Charmaz, K. (1983). Loss of self: A fundamental form of suffering in the chronically ill. *Sociology of Health & Illness, 5*, 168–195.

[7]Charmaz, K. (1995). The body, identity, and self: Adapting to impairment. *The Sociological Quarterly, 36*, 657–680.

[8]Craig, A., Tran, Y., and Middleton, J. (2009). Psychological morbidity and spinal cord injury: A systematic review. *Spinal Cord, 47*, 108-114.

[9]Draper, K., Ponsford, J., & Schonberger, M. (2007). Psychosocial and emotional outcomes 10 years following traumatic brain injury. *Journal of Head Trauma Rehabilitation, 22*(5), 278-287.

[10]Dunn, M. E. (1975). Psychological intervention in a spinal cord injury center: An introduction. *Rehabilitation Psychology 4*, 165-178.

[11]Faul, M., Xu, L., Wald, M. M., & Coronado V. G. (2010). Traumatic brain injury in the United States: Emergency department visits, hospitalizations and deaths 2002-2006. Atlanta, GA: Centers for Disease Control and Prevention.

[12]Heinemann, A. W., & Rawal, P. H. (2005). Spinal cord injury. In Zaretsky, H. H., Richter, E. F. & Eisenberg, M. G. (Eds.), *Medical aspects of disability* (pp.611-647). New York: Springer Publishing Company.

[13]Irvine, H., Davidson, C., Hoy, K., & Lowe-Strong, A. (2009). Psychosocial adjustment to multiple sclerosis: exploration of identity redefinition. *Disability and Rehabilitation, 31*(8), 599-606.

[14]Kendall, E., & Buys, N. (1998). An integrated model of psychosocial adjustment following acquired disability. *Journal of Rehabilitation, 2*, 16–20.

[15]Khan, F., Baguley, I. J., & Cameron, I. D. (2003). Rehabilitation after traumatic brain injury. *The Medical Journal of Australia, 178*, 290-295.

[16]Livneh, H. (1991). A unified approach to existing models of adaptation to disability: a model of adaptation. In R.P.Marinelli & A.E.Dell Orto (Eds.), *The Psychological & social impact of disability (3rd Ed.)* (pp. 111-138).New York: Springer Publishing Company.

[17]Livneh, H. (2001). Psychosocial adaptation to chronic illness and disability: A conceptual framework. *Rehabilitation Counseling Bulletin, 3*, 151-160.

[18]Livneh, H., & Antonak, R.F. (2005). Psychosocial aspects of chronic illness and disability: A primer for counselors. *Journal of Counseling and Development, 83*, 12-20.

[19]Livneh, H., & Antonak, R.F. (1997). *Psychosocial aspects of chronic illness and disability (1st ed.)*. Gaithersburg, MD: Aspen Publishers, Inc.

[20]Livneh, H., & Parker, R.M. (2005). Psychological adaptation to disability: Perspective from chaos and complexity theory. *Rehabilitation Counseling Bulletin, 1*, 17-28.

[21]Lewin, K. (1935). *A dynamic theory of personality.* New York: McGraw-Hill.

[22]Lewin, K. (1936). *Principles of topological psychology.* New York: McGraw-Hill.

[23]Lussier, A. (1980). The physical handicap and the body ego. International Journal of Psychoanalysis, 39, 265-272.

[24]Molton, I. R., Stoelb, B. L., Jensen, M. P., Ehde, D. M., Raichle, K. A., & Cardenas, D. D. (2009). Psychosocial factors and adjustment to chronic pain in spinal cord injury: Replication and cross-validation. *Journal of Rehabilitation Research and Development, 46*(1), 31-42.

[25]National Institute of Neurological Disorders and Stroke, National Institutes of Health. (2012). *Spinal cord injury: Hope through research* (NIH Publication No. 03-160). Retrieved from http://www.ninds.nih.gov/disorders/sci/detail_sci.htm?css=print

[26]Pakenham, K. I. (2005). The positive impact of multiple sclerosis (MS) on carers: Associations between carer benefit finding and positive and negative adjustment domains. *Disability and Rehabilitation, 27*(17), 985-997.

[27]Shepard, L. (2007). Psychosocial adaptation and quality of life in multiple sclerosis: Assessment of the disability centrality model. *The Journal of Rehabilitation, 73*(1), 3-12.

[28]Shontz, F.C. (1965). Reactions to crisis. The Volta Review, 5, 364-370.

[29]Well, D.J., & Miller, P.M. (1977). Emotional reactions of patient, family and staff in acute-care period of spinal cord injury: Part I. *Social Work in Health Care, 4*, 369-377.

[30]Wortman, C.B., & Silver, R.C. (1989). The myths of coping with loss. *Journal of Consulting and Clinical Psychology, 3*, 349-357.

[31]Wright, B.A. (1960). *Physical disability: A psychological approach.* New York: Harper & Row.

[32]Wright, B.A. (1983). *Physical disability: A psychological approach* (2nd ed.). New York: Harper & Row.

[33]Yoshida, K.K. (1993). Reshaping of self: a pendular reconstruction of self and identity among adults with traumatic spinal cord injury. *Sociology of Health & Illness, 2*, 217-245.

9

ASSISTIVE TECHNOLOGY

BRUCE J. REED

SHAWN P. SALADIN

UNIVERSITY OF TEXAS-PAN AMERICAN

CHAPTER TOPICS

- BACKGROUND
- KEY ENTITIES
- PRINCIPLES
- AT DEVICES
- THE ASSISTIVE TECHNOLOGY MATCH
- TECHNOLOGY ABANDONMENT
- AT TEAMS
- ASSISTIVE TECHNOLOGY SETTINGS
- FUNDING
- RESOURCES
- CURRENT TRENDS

By some estimates, today's typical American will learn and use over 20,000 tools or devices in their lifetime. Everyday examples include a comb, doorknob, car keys, and a remote control. The impact of technology in our lives is so enmeshed in everyday activities that its use is taken for granted. Technological developments are also having a profound impact on the lives of people with disabilities. Simple independent living devices such as a grabber (allowing a person to reach items otherwise not reachable) can decrease, or possibly eliminate, the need for home assistance. Sophisticated electronic equipment, such as a laptop computer with voice output, as a classroom aid may allow a student with a visual impairment to participate and succeed academically. Communication devices, from simple to complex, can allow a person to talk with others, perhaps being able to order food independently at a restaurant for the first time. A person with mobility impairment can still actively participate in all aspects of life with the use of a wheelchair.

Assistive technology, or AT, was defined by The Technology-Related Assistance for Individuals with Disabilities Act of 1988 (P.L. 100-407, now reauthorized under H.R. 4278) as "any item, piece of equipment, or product system, whether acquired commercially, off-the-shelf, modified, customized, that is used to increase, maintain or improve the functional capabilities of individuals with disabilities". Using a slightly broader approach, AT has been additionally defined as "the applications of science, engineering, and other disciplines that results in processes, methods, or inventions that support people with disabilities."[5, p. 2] Both definitions support the idea that assistive technology is designed to help people with disability eliminate functional barriers and increase participation in activities of daily life, in work, and in social settings through its use.

For some individuals, the use of technology is a required necessity to function; kidney dialysis equipment, for example, is life saving. For others, it is a quality of life issue. For all, the appropriate application of AT devices and services can greatly increase one's independence and choices. As many authors have noted[6, 43] isolation can be the most damaging aspect of disabling conditions. The ability to be involved in society, be it in the area of recreation, work, education, or social activities, has powerful effects. AT can assist people in becoming full, participating members of society. The use of technology gives an individual with a disability many more choices and options; it is an empowering tool. Marcia Scherer, a well-known author on the impact of technology upon the lives of people with disabilities, believes that AT is about quality of life issues.[40]

This chapter will provide a general background on this field as well as discuss AT principles, matching of AT to the user, technology abandonment, funding, types of devices and services, common settings that AT is used in, and current trends. Where to find more information on AT will also be shared.

BACKGROUND

Assistive technology is an important tool in the rehabilitation process. Yet, it is only one tool, not a "cure all." Seldom is it as simple as finding the right piece of equipment that will solve the individual's functional and environmental limitations. Other variables that can enter into the picture include adjustment to disabilities issues, environmental match (the device may work well in one setting, such as the rehabilitation hospital, but not in other settings such as in the community), poor product design, lack of support from the person's family and other key support groups, and user motivation. One needs to avoid the faulty thinking that technology alone will remove the barriers, physical as well as attitudinal, for people with disabilities.

HISTORICAL PERSPECTIVE

Although recent events in American rehabilitation have pushed AT to the forefront, assistive technology is not a new concept.[31, 25] Early uses of crutches fashioned from tree branches can be considered assistive technology. Artificial limbs and wheelchairs are further examples of AT that have been around for a number of years. Federal legislation, new and improved technologies such as microcomputer chips, and increased consumer empowerment have all converged to greatly increase the role of AT in people with disabilities' lives.

FEDERAL LEGISLATION

Although assistive technology is not directly addressed in legislation prior to 1986, legislative roots can be traced to earlier laws.

Rehabilitation Act of 1973(Public Law [P.L.] 93-112).[35] One section of this law mandated giving a service priority to people with severe disabilities (defined as a disability that requires multiple services over an extended period). The use of AT devices and services can minimize, or may eliminate the functional limitations of people with severe disabilities. Therefore, although P.L. 93-112 did not directly address assistive technology, the fact that individuals with severe disabilities became a service priority created more of a need for AT devices and services. This federal legislation also created the Rehabilitation Engineering Centers system. The centers, each specializing in one main facet of AT, have often led the way in assistive technology research, development, and service provisions.

R*ehabilitation Act Amendments of 1978 (P.L. 95-602).*[33] With this legislation, services related to increasing or maintaining the independent functioning of a rehabilitation client became possible. For the first time, vocational rehabilitation services were not directly tied to a vocational outcome. As in the 1973 Rehabilitation Act, P.L. 95-602 did not directly mention rehabilitation technology, but the delivery of independent living services to people with severe disabilities is often dependent upon assistive technology techniques.

Rehabilitation Act Amendments of 1986 (P.L. 99-506).[34] With this legislation, reauthorizing the Rehabilitation Act of 1973, assistive technology was addressed for the first time. Rehabilitation engineering was defined and the provision of technology services was added to the list of available supports to people with disabilities by state agencies (Institute on Rehabilitation Issues [IRI], 1986). The act mandated that technology related services, when appropriate, be included on a person's Individually Written Rehabilitation Program (IWRP). Of particular importance to vocational evaluators was mention of the need to consider assistive technology when assessing an individual's ability to perform in a vocational environment.

Section 508 of the act dealt with accessibility to electronic equipment such as copiers, electronic typewriters, and computers, stating that all employees of government agencies or companies leasing electronic equipment from the government must have equal access to all electronic devices. In other words, a person could not be denied employment, promotions, or transfers solely on the basis of a lack of electronic accessibility. As the federal government is one of the largest purchasers of electronic devices, this component of the law encouraged many manufacturers to address keyboard and other types of equipment accessibility. Through enactment of P.L. 99-506, Congress was recognizing the growing role of AT in the lives of people with disabilities. Soon to follow was the first federal legislation focused specifically on AT.

Technology-Related Assistance for Individuals with Disabilities Act of 1988 (P.L. 100-407).[42] Having seen the value of AT, federal legislation sought to greatly expand the role and availability of assistive technology. Congress stated that assistive technology devices and services allowed some people with disabilities to:

- have greater control over their lives;
- participate in and contribute more fully to activities in their homes, school, and work environment and in the community;
- interact to a greater extent with non-disabled individuals; and
- otherwise benefit from opportunities that are taken for granted by individuals who do not have a disability.[p.1044]

Also known as the "Tech Act," the purpose of the law was to encourage the development and implementation of AT service delivery systems by awarding grant monies to individual states. State projects were called upon to become active in "spreading the word" about the potential power of rehabilitation technology. Although each state submitted its own grant proposal for funding, and therefore, have differing methods of accomplishing the Tech Act mission, some common services were offered. For example, most of the Tech projects offered technical assistance, outreach services, and information referral networks. Direct AT services to users were not the primary focus, but rather encouraging further use and integration of AT from a broad perspective. By

1992, 42 states had received demonstration grants with each receiving a minimum of $500,000 in funding. Today, all 50 states plus six territories have AT centers.[25]

Americans with Disabilities Act (ADA) of 1990 (P.L. 101-336).[1] By passing this landmark legislation, Congress sought to extend non-discrimination protection into broader public sectors as well as the private sector. In a sense, this enactment said that individuals with a disability must have equal access to participation in American society including transportation, work, communications, public events, and facilities, both public and private.

The use of assistive technology is one key tool in turning much of this law into practice. For example, in employment, if worksite modifications are needed, the modifications may very well have a technological component. Employers are required to provide "reasonable accommodations," ones that do not impose an undue financial hardship, if requested. Assistive technology also has a potential role in fulfilling the accessibility mandates of the ADA. When considering access to public transportation systems, public establishments, and telecommunications, all key facets of this bill, AT can often provide a viable solution. For example, a public sporting event may be required to provide FM hearing systems for customers with hearing impairments that would allow them to hear the public announcements.

Assistive Technology Act of 1998 (P.L. 105-394).[2] Also called the AT Act, this piece of legislation continued the work and focus of the Tech Act of 1988. Continuation monies were allocated to the existing 56 AT projects.[25] Many of the capacity building services were continued with the renewed financial supports including community outreach, public awareness, advocacy, and overall technical assistance. Additionally, the Act initiated an AT loan program that was utilized in six states.

Assistive Technology Act of 2004 (P.L. 108-364).[3] The Assistive Technology Act of 2004 is an amendment to the Assistive Technology Act of 1998. This Act, along with the former Technology-Related Assistance for Individuals with Disabilities Act of 1988, were set up in part to provide states and service providers of AT with the infrastructure to establish systems of delivering AT to people who could benefit from such services. The Assistive Technology Act of 2004 was written to strengthen the ability of people who benefit from AT by mandating easier access and a larger portion of the state grant funds be applied to direct client services. These services include direct aid, device loan, reutilization, demonstration, and alternative financing programs. In addition to providing direct services, accountability for the programs was increased and more detail in new grant applications is required. Recipients of the grants must be able to document measurable goals and demonstrate a system of continuous program evaluation in order to qualify for the funding.[25]

KEY ENTITIES

There are several key entities that have contributed significantly to the field of AT. Particularly in the areas of technological advancement, rehabilitation engineering, and rehabilitation research related to AT, the Veterans Administration, Rehabilitation Engineering Centers/Rehabilitation Engineering Research Centers, and the National Institute on Disability and Rehabilitation Research, along with other federal agencies, have been pivotal in advancing the field. Professional organizations, such as the Rehabilitation Engineering & Assistive Technology Society of North America have also made invaluable contributions to AT in rehabilitation.

Veterans Administration (VA). The VA has long been a key player in the advancement of AT. Historically, beginning as early as the Civil War, technological developments occurred as injured veterans required services.[29] As services and equipment used to assist injured veterans was found useful, the technology would later become available to the general population. The development of prosthetics (artificial limbs) is a good example of this trend.

Following both World War I and World War II, the VA system led the way in disability related research.[29,31] In 1945, the National Academy of Science collaborated with the Surgeon General of the United States Armed Forces in research designed to determine the feasibility of providing artificial limbs to returning soldiers. The collaboration established that research and development regarding prosthetics were not sufficient given the injured soldiers' needs. A program was designed to integrate both engineering and medical approaches; from this, the first biomedical teams emerged.[18]

Rehabilitation Engineering Centers (RECs)/Rehabilitation Engineering Research Centers (RERCs). Rehabilitation engineering is "the application of engineering to improve the quality of life of disabled persons through a term approach to rehabilitation combining medicine, engineering, psychology, counseling, and other rehabilitation disciplines."[18, p.10] Beginning in the early 1970's, the Rehabilitation Services Administration (RSA) began providing federal funds for the specific development of Rehabilitation Engineering Centers. In 1972, the first five centers were created. By mandate, each center had a major area of research focus such as aids for the blind. Each center was required to be affiliated with an established medical and engineering university and to provide direct patient rehabilitation technology services. An emphasis was placed on developing interdisciplinary teams involving researchers, rehabilitation professionals, physicians, and related health professionals.

In 2006, there were 22 RERCs throughout the United States, each with an area of specialty. The focus remains on applying engineering as well as scientific and psychological principles to help solve rehabilitation problems and remove or minimize existing barriers. An additional emphasis has been placed on access to the information and services by people with disabilities. Each project works in a collaborative environment involving users of technology, scientists, business, product developers, policy makers, and many other key players to help improve the lives of people with disabilities.

Table I

REHABILITATION ENGINEERING RESEARCH CENTERS

Accessible Medical Instrumentation
Communication Enhancement
Ergonomic Solutions for Employment
Hearing Enhancement
Information Technology Access
Improved Technology Access for Land Mine Survivors
Mobile Wireless Technologies for Persons with Disabilities
Prosthetics and Orthotics
Recreational Technologies and Exercise Physiology Benefiting Persons with Disabilities
Rehabilitation Robotics and Telemanipulation: Machines Assisting Recovery form Stroke
Technologies for Children with Orthopedic Disabilities
Spinal Cord Injury: Technologies to Enhance Mobility and Function for Individuals with SCI
Technology for Successful Aging
Technology Transfer
Telerehabilitation
Universal Design and the Built Environment (Buffalo)
Universal Design and the Built Environment (North Carolina)
Universal Telecommunications Access
Wheelchair Transportation Safety
Wheeled Mobility
Workplace Accommodations
Smith-Kettlewell Eye Research

National Institute on Disability and Rehabilitation Research (NIDRR). The National Institute on Disability and Rehabilitation Research (NIDRR; formerly known as the National Institute of Handicapped Research) was created in 1978 and charged with establishing and coordinating a comprehensive rehabilitation research network.[29] The institute was expected to effectively disseminate information to rehabilitation professionals and people with disabilities related to AT, and to coordinate the efforts of the RECs as well as the Rehabilitation Research and Training Centers, a network of over 20 sites. More recently, the President's 2012 budget set aside $120 million for NIDRR with a focus on support of internet based cloud computing technology that uses internet infrastructure to improve on-demand technologies and increase accessibility.[28] NIDRR currently remains the leading agency for coordinating the federal efforts of research and promotion of assistive technology.

Other Federal Agencies. The National Aeronautical and Space Administration (NASA) and the National Science Foundation (NSF) have had key involvement in the development of assistive technology.[31] In 1979, the federal legislation that created NSF designated $2 million specifically for disability related research.[29] Projects focused on hardware development such as computer adaptations to assist users with visual impairments. NASA has contributed to the field of assistive technology through bioengineering research and the use of technology transfer. In the late 1970's, Congress mandated that NASA use its unique engineering expertise to help people with disabilities. However, little funding was made available to carry out this charge. Nonetheless, some transfer of technology gained through NASA investigations did positively impact people with disabilities such as the development of rechargeable cardiac pacemakers.

Rehabilitation Engineering & Assistive Technology Society of North America (RESNA).[36] Founded in 1980, RESNA has been a professional organization comprised of multiple disciplines, all related to AT. Originally conceived as the Rehabilitation Engineering Society of North America, the organization was multi-disciplinary in scope. At the onset, RESNA was mostly a technical organization, dominated by research, development, and engineering. More recently, however, the association has incorporated the delivery of assistive technology services as a key component in its overall agenda. Today, rehabilitation engineers, physical therapists, occupational therapists, rehabilitation counselors, and school-based technologists (such as those in special education) are just some of the occupations represented. Accordingly, the group has changed its name to reflect the importance of AT by becoming the Rehabilitation Engineering and Assistive Technology Society of North America, although the original acronym has been retained. RESNA continues to be a leader in disseminating state of the art information and materials key to the utilization of AT.

PRINCIPLES

Several critical principles can guide the planning, development, purchasing, and utilization of AT. User involvement and information access are important starting points. The recognition of the need for consideration of a continuum of AT solution complexity, changing AT needs, an individualized process, and a holistic approach that involves professional services and natural supports are also vital AT principles.

INVOLVE THE USER

The user (person with the disability) should always be the first source of information when considering technology. When this is not possible (because of cognitive or speech limitations, for example), people closest to the user such as family members need to be involved. This may sound like a simple concept and it is, yet it is sometimes forgotten. Who knows better than the person with the disability does, what problems or barriers are being encountered? What the user does not typically know are the technological possibilities to overcome the problems and barriers. That is where the professionals come in—to evaluate, recommend, help select, acquire, and possibly train the person on AT equipment.

By involving the user early and throughout the process, commitment and follow through is greatly increased. Learning to use a new device may not always be a pleasant task; it may involve frustration, fatigue, or uncertainties. Wanting to quit and return to the previous way can be a common desire. For example, if learning to use a manual wheelchair post-injury for the first time, the person might long for the times when someone else was always there to push and assist with transfers in and out of the chair. Internal motivation, a strong desire for self-determination, and commitment will be important factors in successfully making the transition to greater independence. We all, disability or not, tend to stay with a decision longer if it was our idea rather than someone else telling us what we have to do it ("Well, it wasn't my idea anyway—it was the occupational therapist who told me I have to do it").

ACCESS TO INFORMATION

Access to information is the key. Technology changes so rapidly that it is very difficult to remain current. Even experts tend to have somewhat narrow areas of expertise. For example, one technologist may be well versed in computer software, but know little or nothing about wheelchairs. As a professional or technology user, you need not know everything. You need a general idea of the available technology how to find information about the technology. Fortunately, the advent of the Internet and the proliferation of information readily available have simplified this task.

THE KISS (KEEP IT SIMPLE, STUPID)! PRINCIPLE

Whenever possible, take the simplest path; do not overcomplicate a situation. In the field of AT, there can be a tendency to think of the higher technology solutions first when in fact homemade, low technology solutions might be the most effective.

Maria is a young woman with cerebral palsy. She uses a power wheelchair. On her first day on a job in light assembly, it is seen that her chair will not fit under the workstation. What can be done? One solution would be to buy or build a new workstation, possibly one that has adjustable height settings. Another solution (the KISS principle) would be to raise the height of the table by safely using blocks of wood.

In many cases, the simpler solutions not only represent significant cost savings, but also have other advantages including adaptability and normalization. Adaptability refers to the flexibility of the assistive technology. Simpler, more adaptable solutions tend to allow others, not just the user, to more fully utilize the area, be it at the workplace, school, or at home. For example, another worker can use Maria's workstation raised with blocks of wood, by simply sitting in a taller chair. Normalization refers to how "normal" or similar the device is to others around the technology user. For some people, especially those still psychologically adjusting to a disability, the desire to look like their peers without a disability can be strong. If the AT device does not stand out as being noticeably different, it will be valued and used more. In the case of Maria, her work area would be a bit higher than others would but not different in any other way.

AT Needs are Fluid

Needs change; technology changes. Each year, new and often highly specialized AT devices aimed at particular disability groups become available, and the individual's needs can be highly fluid as well.[5] There are many reasons that a persons' needs change. Changes in the functioning of the user and changes in the users' preferences (because of becoming a more informed consumer, for example) are just a few possibilities. What might be the best technological solution today may not be in the future. For many technology users, the need to change technology may be an ongoing process. Such changeability should not be seen as a failure of the technology or the technology match, but rather, as a normal part of the process.

Individualized Process

Approach people as unique individuals. Each individual's needs and preferences are different. As with all service deliveries within human services, as professionals we need to approach each person individually. The selection of a wheelchair is a good example. You may be assisting two clients with similar functioning. The first client wants a motorized chair to be able to get around. The other client prefers a manual chair, which will require more assistance (on ramps, for example) but allow the person to maintain upper body strength by pushing the chair as much as possible. The first client also wants a chair that stands out with neon green flags and decals, whereas the second client wants the standard chrome and black vinyl model. As with all consumer product-buying decisions, people have differing tastes. The more we can respect these tastes, the more successful the technology match will be.

Focus on Functional Limitations not Disability Type

It is important to focus on the individuals' functioning as opposed to the diagnosed condition. In the field of rehabilitation, we tend to assess the functional limitations of our clients and design treatment strategies to help minimize these limitations. Functional limitations are defined as restrictions in the physical or mental functioning that limit a person's ability to perform activities of daily living.[12] It is faulty logic to assume that people with the same diagnosis will have the same needs. Ten different people with moderate mental retardation, for example, may have ten different sets of needs. Some of these people may be heavy technology users while others may function well without any AT.

Holistic Approach

When considering technology needs and strategies, it is important to take a holistic approach; that is, to take into account all areas of the individual's life. What may work fine in one setting (the rehabilitation hospital, for example), may not work at all in another setting (such as the workplace or the home). Service providers are also well aware that for the technology to be used to its fullest capacity it must be embraced by more than just the user—the family and other important peer groups of the individual must also support the use.

AT DEVICES

Assistive technology devices are devices that are used to maintain or increase the functional capabilities of individuals with disabilities in the home, in employment and educational settings, and for recreation purposes, among others. AT devices can be placed in various categories depending upon the purpose of the device, such as whether the device is used for environmental control, for communication, for mobility, or for instruction.[5] However, there is no one agreed upon classification system in the field.

Most broadly, AT devices can be categorized on a continuum of complexity, since AT may range from the very simple, such as a pencil to push the keys on a keyboard, to the very complex and exotic such as robotics. Accordingly, AT devices are frequently referred to as low-tech (non-electronic, simply made) and high- tech (electronic, professionally made). Of course, many devices do not fit neatly into these two categories.

Low-tech

Low-tech devices are most commonly basic, cheap, readily available devices, and equipment. Fundamental problem solving strategies often lead to these low-tech solutions. For example, a piece of Velcro to attach a calculator to a desktop is a simple solution for preventing the calculator from moving when used with a mouth stick. Attaching foam or tape to a pen can allow a person with a gripping limitation to use the pen.

As stated with the KISS principle, low-tech solutions have obvious advantages over high tech ones. Not only do they provide the cheapest option, but they also are more easily replaced, require little or no training to use, replacement costs are low, and often do not stand out as being different from peers without disabilities, an issue for some people with disabilities.

HIGH- TECH

By contrast, high-tech devices are typically ones that are electrical or electronic and can be expensive. Depending upon many variables (user's knowledge, funding sources policies, adjustment to disability, etc.), a technology evaluation may be warranted prior to purchase. Sometimes high-tech devices can be purchased "off the shelf" (meaning in common retail stores such as Wal-Mart or Radio Shack), from specialized AT vendors, or are custom-made. Training, maintenance, repairs, and replacement costs can all be ongoing factors with high-tech devices.

Examples of these devices are numerous. They include talking calculators, which say what figures have been inputted. Computers can have output formats other than print including speech and Braille. A refreshable Braille computer in which a strip of Braille print moves along the keyboard as the user inputs material allows the person to read in Braille format. Sophisticated electrical wheelchairs that include seating and positioning technology, mobility control devices, and environmental control devices can greatly empower the user.

Table II

CATEGORIES OF ASSISTIVE TECHNOLOGY DEVICES

Communication Aids – devices that assist in communication for those with speech limitations. Examples: communication boards (both electronic and non-electronic) and speech synthesizers.

Computer – a variety of computer applications involving hardware, software, and input and output devices that enhance computer accessibility and functioning. Examples: Braille printers, voice activated systems, text enlarger software, and alternative keyboards.

Controls – devices used for activation of an electrical or electronic device. Examples: joystick, sip-and-puff switch, and remote control.

Mobility Aids – devices that increase an individual's mobility. Examples: wheelchairs (manual and powered), walkers, and scooters.

Prosthetics and Orthotics – devices used to replace or augment missing or limited parts of the body. Examples: artificial limbs, splints, and inserts.

Recreation – devices that increase a persons' ability to participate in recreational activities. Examples: beeping soccer ball, adapted skis, and arm powered cycle.

Seating & Positioning – devices and techniques used to provide proper seating and positioning of the body to increase stability, healthy posture, and a reduction of pressure sores. Examples: cushions, head supports, and lumbar supports.

Sensory Aids – devices designed to increase sensory functioning especially as related to vision and hearing. Examples: magnifiers, text enlargers, Braille and speech output devices, telety
pe devices for the deaf (TDD), hearing aids, and flashing alarms.

Transportation Aids – devices that increase transportation accessibility and options. Examples: wheelchair lifts, vehicle hand or feet controls, and other adapted driving aids.

Vocational – devices and strategies that increase vocational options and productivity. Examples: modified workstation, scooter with a basket for transporting materials, and accessible bathrooms.

AT SERVICES

Services related to assistive technology are an important part of the field. AT services are defined as those services that assist a person with a disability in selecting, obtaining, and using AT devices. For some, in particular the person with little AT knowledge, these services can be critical in obtaining a positive technology match. For any of us, with or without a disability, we become better consumers of a given type of product through trial and error. When our knowledge base is low, we need more assistance from others. AT services can include evaluations, assistance related to purchasing or leasing, training, repairs, and customizing.

ASSESSMENT AND EVALUATION

Technology evaluations are often an early crucial step in determining needs. Conducted by a trained professional, a technology evaluation will provide the potential user and the rehabilitation counselor (or case manager) specific, objective information. Depending upon the type of evaluation, the professional involved might be a physical therapist (PT), occupational therapist (OT), computer specialists, speech therapist (ST), or rehabilitation engineer. Evaluations can be as varied as the types of devices. The evaluation might center on the person's ability to use computers, augmented communication boards, environmental control units, seating and positioning needs, or modified driving controls. Frequently, both cognitive and physical functioning is assessed.

TECHNICAL ASSISTANCE AND MAINTENANCE

A person may need technical assistance in understanding purchasing or leasing options (although these opportunities are few). This service may be provided by an informed counselor or case manager, a technology specialist, therapist (PT, OT, ST), or a vendor (realizing the potential for conflict of interest). Repairs and routine maintenance of devices is another area of service. Many devices will not require these services, such as most low-tech ones. Other devices will most commonly be replaced rather than repaired. For some high-tech devices such as wheelchairs, lifts, and augmented communication boards, repairs and maintenance is a normal part of the process. Mechanics, specialized vendors, agency personnel, or the company from which the purchase occurred might provide these services.

Unfortunately, problems exist for many technology users related to repairs. There are often few qualified vendors to do this work, especially for users not living in major metropolitan areas. Some repairs that involve warranty coverage are shipped to the vendor. In some cases, the vendor then ships the damaged parts or unit to the manufacturer. This process can take weeks or even months. As many of these devices are the more expensive types (an electric, customized wheelchair system can cost $12,000—$20,000), many users cannot afford a back-up system.

If one is dependent upon technology to live an active lifestyle, when the technology is not available, the impact is very real. Imagine needing your wheelchair to get to work or attend school and being told that the repairs would take 1—2 months. Ask almost everyone who uses a lift to get their wheelchair into a van and you will hear stories of being stuck either in the van or even on the lift when it has malfunctioned for hours at a time. It is common that heavy technology users themselves, or a family member, become adept at problem solving and repairing their equipment. As the old saying goes, "necessity is the mother of invention!"

CUSTOMIZATION

Customizing services are needed either to modify an existing device or to create one. Perhaps hand controls on an electric wheelchair need to be moved from one side to the other. Perhaps a customized workstation needs to be designed and fabricated. Typically, a technology specialist or rehabilitation engineer will perform such services.

THE ASSISTIVE TECHNOLOGY MATCH

To ensure increased functioning and independence (the ultimate goals of using assistive technology), the right match must occur. If not, the likelihood of continued use of the technology is minimized. Although the need to make the technology match is often prevalent, the more time that can go into assessing, analyzing, and planning prior to the financial commitment, the better. There are assessment instruments such as the Human Activity Assistive Technology Model (HAAT),[8] Matching Person and Technology Model (MPT),[39] and the Psychosocial Impact of Assistive Devices Scale (PIADS),[10] to name a few, to help in the selection of AT.

Most of us as consumers can think of times that a hasty purchase of some new device or gadget turned out to be a poor decision. If we had spent more time studying the situation including our own needs and preferences as well as available products, our money would have been spent more wisely. In addition to identifying the increase in function a person receives from using a device and the control they are able to exert on their environment to complete needed activities, careful consideration of the psychosocial variables competence, adaptability, and self-esteem are strong predictors of adoption of AT.[38]

Matching the device to the user can occur in various ways. It is preferable, utilizing the KISS Principle, to use the most basic modality possible. These options are presented from simplest to complex:

- Change the way the task is performed so that the functional limitations are eliminated.
  Example: A secretary cannot fasten paper clips to a stack of documents but can operate a stapler.
- Use a readily available device that was designed for another purpose.
  Example: A person with limitation of arm and hand strength uses the eraser end of a pencil to activate computer keys.
- Modify an existing device.
  Example: The wheelchair joystick control is moved from the left side of the chair to the right to take advantage of better functioning.
- Purchase a device.

Example: A vibrating alarm clock that fits under the pillow of a person who is deaf wakes him up.

- Design and fabricate a device.
  Example: When attempts to modify a workstation prove unsuccessful, a customized one is built.

The Institute on Rehabilitation Issues[18] discussed characteristics that the user and the professional should look for when considering a technology match.

THE TECHNOLOGY

- type
- capabilities
- functional limitations that it helps overcome

PERFORMANCE

- ease of use
- training needs
- safety concerns
- reliability of equipment (does it work consistently?)
- comfort

DURABILITY

- length of functioning ("shelf-life")
- ability to use and abuse
- ongoing maintenance needs
- likelihood of repairs.

AVAILABILITY

- ease of purchase ("off-the shelf", specialized vendor, customized?)
- training
- repairs

COST

- device cost
- training costs
- maintenance costs
- repair costs
- modification costs

AESTHETICS

- acceptability by the user
- wear–will it continued to be aesthetic even normal use?

ENVIRONMENT

- holistic–needs to work effectively in all environments of the user
- transportation of the device
- power–if powered, reliable sources and backups needed.

FUNDING

- source of funding
- future funding needs–maintenance, repairs, replacement costs

In a similar breakdown of key categories of information to consider, Lueck, et al.[23] postulate that at least seven key categories exist: *accessibility* (will the device allow the individual access that functional limitations are preventing? In other words, will it work?), *affordability, availability, compatibility* (does it work with other needed devices), *portability, usability,* and *trainability.* The authors reinforce the idea that selecting the right AT for a user is best done when all assessment of functional limitations needs and preferences have been completed.

TECHNOLOGY ABANDONMENT

Research suggests that despite the functionality of a device, people are not likely to adopt and use AT if they do not feel it will improve their quality of life, their psychological well-being, independence, self-esteem, or sense of control and empowerment.[10,11, 38] Technology abandonment occurs when technology is no longer used. Abandonment can occur for a wide variety of reasons, some more positive than others. Positively, assistive technology is discontinued because the condition that resulted in the need for it has improved.[9] Some abandonment decisions are simply developmental; that is, the user over time has changing needs or preferences that necessitate different technology. More negatively, some AT is not used due to a poor initial match between the person and product. AT devices may not be used because they produce unwanted attention from peers or the public. Devices that require more energy or greater effort to use are also less likely to be adopted than less demanding alternatives.[10, 11, 38]

Abandonment (also called "non-use") of AT is a common occurrence. The National Survey on Abandonment of Technology conducted at the National Rehabilitation Hospital concluded that 29% off all devices in its sample were abandoned.[27] Other studies show discontinuance rates of AT up to 75%, most of which occurs within the first three months of attempted use.[4, 10,14, 41] It has been suggested that non-use occurs at a much higher rate for those with a recently acquired disability. This happens because, over time, a person tends to develop better insights as to needs, personal preferences, and an expanded knowledge base as to what devices work and which ones do not work. AT that has positive psychosocial impact for the user helping them feel able, confident, and motivated to explore possible uses, is more likely to be adopted and retained.[20, 38]

Use or non-use of a device is influenced from three separate domains—the environment, the user, and the device itself.[40] Environmental factors might include acceptance and encouragement (or a lack thereof) from family, peers, and other key support groups; physical accessibility of the various environments the user operates in; and the need for external supports such as technical assistance. Issues related to the user that influence non-use include motivation, a change in functioning, acceptance of the need, self-esteem, anger, depression, and a lack of skills required to utilize the device. Device related factors might include difficulty of use, lack of quality and quick maintenance/repair options, use of the device does not deliver the anticipated effect, and other better solutions or devices have become available.

Research in this emerging field of study has indicated that understanding abandonment issues is a complicated process. Preliminary research results do indicate that the effectiveness of the device and level of consumer involvement in the decision making process are two key elements.[37] The variable of consumer involvement is yet another reminder to rehabilitation professionals that maximum consumer involvement in the rehabilitation process is not only the right thing to do, but it also will yield better outcomes.[32]

When abandonment happens without replacement, that is, when a more effective one does not replace the device, losses occur. There is a loss in functioning and independence by the individual.[40] The impact of this loss can be magnified as it may impact the family, who now needs to provide more assistance, and the person's ability to be involved in work, recreation, and community life. Losses also occur from a fiscal perspective. All funding sources, state-federal rehabilitation system, Medicaid/Medicare, public schools, and private insurance operate with restricted budgets. Purchasing decisions must be made very critically; spending to support one client may prevent helping another one. Therefore, minimizing abandonment and the accompanying losses is important.

It is also important to remember that some non-use is developmental in nature. When technology such as leg braces or seating and positioning systems, for example, is used for a child, it is known that replacements will be needed; this is a cost of doing business. Likewise, someone using adapted computer equipment for the first time may gradually master easier software or input devices before being able to "graduate" to more complicated but more efficient technology. A person with a newly acquired disability will simply not have the knowledge base of device options and personal preferences that will be developed over time. Therefore, the user will most likely listen more to others rather than being as involved in the decision-making process. This can lead to choices that are not effective. None of these cases should be seen as a failure of the match of technology to the user but, rather, a naturally occurring process. This is an important concept for funding sources as well as the user to consider.

AT TEAMS

The use of interdisciplinary teams in rehabilitation is well-established practice. Given the nature of the field, this makes sense. We are often called upon to consider medical, psychological, environmental, and personal perspectives to most fully assist a person with a disability. Within the field of AT, many professionals, in addition to the user, may provide key information.

The user of technology, in other words the person with the disability, should always be the first source of information. He or she knows firsthand what limitations are present and what solutions may or may not work. If the user cannot provide thorough information (e.g., severe cognitive impairment or communication limitations), key family members or other support networks can provide input.

There typically is the need to have one coordinator of the process. This role will likely fall upon the rehabilitation counselor, case manager, social worker, or other professional depending upon the situation. The more technology foundation this person has, the better. However, the primary role of this professional is to coordinate services. This may include completing the necessary paperwork, justifying the request, ordering, providing quality control to the process, and ultimately holding all the other team members accountable.

Other key team members will include those with medical expertise such as a physician or nurse. Physical therapists, occupational therapists, and speech therapists are all potentially involved in technology evaluations, product reviews and recommendations, training, modifications, repairs, and routine maintenance. In educational settings, special education staff including technology specialists may be part of the team. At postsecondary settings, a campus office that provides supports to students with disabilities is an important part of the team.

Professionals directly involved with AT include technology specialists and rehabilitation engineers. Technology specialists may or may not have received formal training in AT. Frequently, they have acquired their knowledge and skills from direct experiences not training. They tend to be "handy" people with general problem-solving and mechanical skills. Technology specialists are well versed in tools and materials and have an understanding of mechanical, electrical, and electronic systems. A healthy dose of creativity is also helpful. Rehabilitation engineers, by contrast, have had formal training in both engineering principles and disabilities, especially anatomy and physiology. It is common that rehabilitation engineering academic training programs are housed in biomedical teaching facilities associated with large rehabilitation hospitals. In addition to being involved with directly assisting clients with technology needs, rehabilitation engineers are also typically engaged in research and development of new products or techniques.

ASSISTIVE TECHNOLOGY SETTINGS

Assistive technology is used in every setting possible; it is an integral part of the users' life. In some cases, such as a ventilator, it is literally always at the users' side. In other situations, the device is used in only one distinct setting such as on the job site. Four separate settings (home, work, education, and recreation) in which technology is used will be discussed.

HOME

Disability or not, we all have the need to eat, sleep, cook, bath, clean, wash clothes and dishes, and relax. A disabling condition, however, may change the way some of these activities of daily living are accomplished. Our home is much more than just the physical structure we live in; it is part of us.[17] For all of us, especially those with disabilities, a house must be accessible in order to be a home. Accessibility can cover many facets including getting into and around the home, activation of appliances and devices, and use of the kitchen, bathroom, and laundry facilities.[30]

The need exists for a thorough and accurate evaluation that is ideally conducted at the home site, but a simulation and in-depth interviews by an evaluator may suffice. Important variables to be assessed are:

- The person's level of functioning (stamina, strength, grasping, cognitive abilities, and awareness, for example).
- The physical characteristics of the house, for example, stairs, door width, types of cabinet handles, and flooring.
- The expectations and goals of the individual. The expectations may focus on the level of independence that the person is hoping to obtain.

Following an analysis of the individual and the home environment, modifications to the existing structure and/or the installation of new devices will probably be needed. Other factors will enter into the picture such as how much money is available for modifications.[30] Physical restrictions such the house size or the fact that the structure is on a steep hill may also influence accessibility options.

For those with mobility limitations, especially users of wheelchairs, scooters, or walkers, the physical layout of the house is important. Doorways must be wide enough (ideally at least 32 inches) to accommodate the device. There must also be sufficient space to turn around and maneuver. Stairs present an obvious barrier. Other potential problems relate to being able to reach high enough to get items in storage such as in the kitchen or storage cabinets. The traditional round door handles and facets can be difficult to use if strength and grasping limitation exist. All of these potential barriers can be overcome with the proper application of AT.

Although some barriers such as stairs require home modifications or high-tech solutions, many times "off-the-shelf," low-tech devices can be used very effectively. Loops of material on a drawer can provide an alternative that works for opening the drawer. Fastening home items such as a toothbrush or comb to a Velcro strip on the wall by the sink will help someone who has a hard time picking up small objects on the counter. Organizing small items in the kitchen, sewing area, or workbench in revolving bins called "lazy Susans" that efficiently use and organize space can remove the need for higher storage.

People with sensory limitations have different needs at home. Those with hearing impairments can be helped by substituting visual for auditory signals. Telephones, alarm clocks, smoke alarms, and doorbells can all be purchased or modified so that they emit a bright flashing light rather than signal through sound. Television and video with closed captioning is readily available. In some cases, for people with some residual hearing, sound amplifications may be sufficient. For people with visual impairments, one of the most important factors is a having unobstructed pathways.[17] For those with some sight left, proper lighting and magnifying devices can increase independence. Sensory aids such as the intentional texturing of walls or floors to provide environmental cues is an option.

EDUCATION

Federal legislation has clearly mandated that individuals with disabilities be allowed to have the same educational opportunities as everyone else. Technology can help make this possible. In public school settings, students with disabilities are entitled to a "free and appropriate" education in the "least restrictive environment." In other words, students are to be mainstreamed (included) in classrooms and school activities with students without disabilities as much as possible. The amount of inclusion for students with disabilities varies greatly from state to state and from school district to school district.

Assistive technology and related services are a core part of special education programs. Most districts have technology teams comprised of a special education teacher, technologists with specialized knowledge in computers for example, and therapists (OT, PT, and ST). As needed, other expertise's can be contracted for and utilized. In most cases, the AT devices purchased by the school district remain the property of the school district. Cases can be made and won that the technology must accompany the student home <u>if</u> the technology is essential in completing homework assignments.

The technology needs of the students should be assessed at least yearly and be included in the Individual Education Plan (IEP). The IEP is, in essence, a contract between the school district and the students (and legal guardians) that states what services will be provided. If the technology needs of the student are listed on the IEP and both parties sign the agreement, the district is obligated to provide the devices and/or services. By federal law, a school district not having sufficient funds to provide the required services is still obligated to provide the services; in other words, a lack of funds is not a legal excuse. In some cases, students and their guardians argue the need for AT on the IEP while the school district argues that the need is not present. Parent advocacy groups exist that will mentor and train parents and guardians in how to maneuver successfully through the complicated and sometimes intimidating process.

For students who enter postsecondary academic settings, federal laws such as Section 504 of the 1973 Rehabilitation Act provide mandated supports. For any postsecondary institution that receives even $1 of federal support including financial aid grants, it must not discriminate against students (and potential students) with disabilities. There must a central office or at least a person who is designated as the disability support office. Common services for the eligible students with disabilities include note takers, interpreters, peer counseling, library assistance, extended test time, and advocacy. Depending upon the institution, such services as transportation on campus, wheelchair maintenance and repairs, modified housing, and personal care attendant services may be available. Campus accessibility is usually coordinated through such a support office for students with disabilities.

The provision of many of the support services requires the use of assistive technology. For example, for the library to be truly accessible to students who are visually impaired there will need to be text enlargers that allow the student to place printed copy on a tray, slide it into the magnifying device, and see the enlarged text on a TV monitor. Computer systems at the student computer lab will need to have speech synthesis as an output device as well as Braille printers.

Technology plays a very powerful role in making education a possibility for students with disabilities. It is through education, be it to learn a marketable trade or obtain a college degree, that people with disabilities, especially severe ones, can become competitive in the job market.

WORK

The work we do in American society is a core identifier for many of us. How many times have you met someone new and the first question is, "So what do you do"? Fair or not, identity and self-worth are often tied to "what do you do?" Unemployment rates in the past 5 years for the nation as a whole have ranged from 4—6%. For people with disabilities the unemployment rate is 67—70% and about 40% for college graduates with disabilities![15] The rate is even higher for those categorized as having a severe disability. The discrepancy is remarkable and totally unacceptable. Many services and service providers such as rehabilitation counselors exist to assist people with disabilities to become employed.

Recognizing that people with disabilities have the same rights to employment as others, federal legislation such as the Americans with Disabilities Act have been enacted. Employers with at least 15 employees are required to hire the most qualified applicant while not discriminating based upon disability. Employers are also required to provide "reasonable accommodations" when requested by the person with a disability. Reasonable accommodations are ..."modifications or adjustments to the job, the work environment, or the way that things are usually done that enables an individual with a disability to do his or her job effectively or more effectively."[21, p. 29] If the accommodations impose significant financial expenses in relation to the size and profitability of the company, called "undue hardship", the accommodations do not have to be provided. Examples of reasonable accommodations include alternative formats (e.g., Braille, large type, and tape recording), modified work schedules, job restructuring, work site modifications, and assistive technology.

Employers typically provide reasonable accommodations at the worksite only. Items that will benefit the user outside the work environment, such as a lap top computer, are not their responsibility. As with other areas involving the match of the user to the technology, the first step should be an in-depth evaluation. The goal is to understand the functioning and functional limitation of the worker with a disability as compared to the environmental and job related demands. Job accommodations are, in essence, alternative means to accomplishing the same goal—to complete the job in a manner satisfactory to both the employer and the employee.

The use of job analyses (analyzing and recording all facets of a job) and task analyses (the individual steps or tasks of a job) are key tools in assessing workplace needs. Both of these processes involve a systematic, detailed analysis of how the job is accomplished by a worker. It is common that the employer is very knowledgeable about the work demands but uninformed about accommodation possibilities. This is where the experience and, often times, the creativity of the rehabilitation specialist is needed.

Curtis, who has been blind since birth, has worked successfully for 8 years at a computer assembling plant. His light assembly job involves building hard drive components. Curtis is well liked and valued on the job. However, problems have arisen as the entire units' job duties have been recently changed. Curtis has not learned the new procedures to the satisfaction of the line supervisor.

The area vocational rehabilitation service was called for assistance. An accommodation specialist was sent to the plant. After completing the assessment (which included interviews with Curtis and the line supervisor as well as job and task analyses), simple modifications were made to Curtis' work area. Bins holding small components were arranged in sequential order that matched assembly steps, bins holding supplies were marked with Braille, and power tools were hung above him to clear more room on the assembly table. Coworkers, who were either refilling the parts bins or borrowing tools, were educated about putting items in their proper place. Additionally, some limited orientation and mobility services were provided that helped Curtis learn the new configuration of the work area.

These reasonable accommodations were inexpensive—really only involving the salary of the specialist. Curtis was able to save a job he liked and the employer saved a valued employee.

Technology at the worksite can be the kind that makes the environment more accessible such as ramps, elevators, wider bathroom stalls, and grab bars. Technology applications can also be more specific to the individual worker. The use of talking calculators, sign language interpreters, voice activated computer systems, and a modified work area are examples of individualized applications. Of course, the use of AT in the workplace is not always easy or inexpensive. Employees with severe disabilities may require multiple modifications and technology. Yet, in most cases, the financial investment pays off. Researches confirms the fact that people with a disability, in general, miss less work and remain on the job longer than employees without a disability.

RECREATION

Recreation is an important part of most everyone's life. Recreational activities can range from very physically active, such as mountain climbing or hang gliding, to sedentary, such as playing cards or going to the theater. The common thread is that they all lead to enjoyment and a healthy escape for the participant. Recreational activities frequently also include socialization and community involvement. Numerous writers in the field of rehabilitation have stated that social isolation is the most damaging aspect of having a disability. Finding ways to develop or maintain ones' leisure activities can greatly assist the person in staying socially connected and being an active, full participant in society.

CHILDREN

For children born with a disability or having acquired it at an early age, being able to participate with peers in recreational activities is vital. No one likes being left out of social interactions; this is especially true at early developmental periods. Participation, even if it is limited or conducted in modified ways, has a powerful impact. Participating children are more likely to be accepted into peer groups and judged for their own talents and personality. That differences in physical or mental functioning are present will become less and less important over time.

Adaptive techniques can be something as simple as using an old egg carton, turned upside, to hold playing cards so that the child with grasping limitations can play. This also works well for children with small hands. Battery operated toys and devices usually come with very small switches that are impossible to activate for some. Simple modifications that cost little can transform the activation device from the small switch to a much larger one are easily done. In addition, specialized toys can be purchased from adaptive toy vendors. The opportunities are somewhat numerous. Chirping soccer balls or baseballs that emit a sound allow visually impaired children to play.

David was an 8-year-old boy with limited movement and strength in his legs due to cerebral palsy. In every other way, however, he was a typical, active 8 year old. He, of course, wanted to play in the neighborhood like his sister and friends. When the other kids would take off on their bikes, David was left behind. That is, until David's parents learned about arm-controlled bicycles. With these bikes, the gears that power the device are mounted at arm level. Instead of turning the pedals with legs, arms and hands are used. Before long, David was zipping down the street with all the others.

ADULTS

Adults have the same need for recreational activities as children do. In fact, it was through the efforts of adults who wanted to regain an active lifestyle after injury that led to much of the development of therapeutic recreation.[22] Such individuals, typically with a spinal cord injury, help develop wheelchair athletics and modified skiing programs, both on snow and water. Also influencing this expanding specialty area has been technological developments such as lighter, stronger materials for wheelchair construction and more positive attitudes in a society that is receptive to inclusion of people with disabilities. Athletic movements and events such as the Paralympics and Special Olympics for developmentally disabled adults are evidence of this growth and support.

Devices and equipment can be either modified or purchased as specialty products. Equipment exists in every imaginable recreational area including fishing, dancing, camping, gardening, sports, travel, music, and crafts. Active participation is a reality when the spirit of trying, acceptance and encouragement from others, and adaptive recreational devices are all present.

FUNDING

Along with inadequate information on assistive technology, the lack of funding is the single largest barrier to acquiring needed AT devices and services.[16] There simply is not enough money available to meet all of the needs. Therefore, one must work hard at learning about all potential funding sources. The most successful at finding sufficient funding are those that are good at using networks and that are persistent and tenacious. Being the "squeaky wheel" is often necessary.

One of the challenges in acquiring funds is the complicated, often changing world of funding possibilities, policies, and procedures. Ask almost anyone who has navigated through the bureaucratic process of Medicaid, for example, to purchase an AT device, and you will likely hear that, even for informed consumers and professionals, it is a confusing process. Having a funding strategy can help.

FUNDING STRATEGY

A strategy consists of an articulated plan to accomplish a goal. Developing a funding strategy will help to give structure to the process. Although the application and appeals process will differ by the funding source, the process remains generally the same. One needs to be able to clearly define the problem, justify why the requested devices are the solution, demonstrate why cheaper options are not viable, and be able to state what the positive outcome will be.

Mendelsohn[24] states that a funding strategy should:

- Define the problem – functional limitations and needs; specific devices needed; costs; timelines.
- Identify possible funding sources – personal finances; eligibility for funding sources.
- Prepare the request – varying depending upon funding source; detailed, articulate justifications for all requests.
- Initiate the appeal process – knowledge of the appeal process; reason for denial.

FUNDING TIPS

Meaningful funding strategies can address many AT funding challenges. An attention to detail, good organization, persistency, and an advocacy approach are among several additional considerations. There are several important tips to follow that can further increase success.

Be informed and organized. Information is power. As the technology user or his/her advocate, you absolutely must know the details of funding sources' rules and regulations. They are typically confusing, complicated, and seemingly ever changing. Nevertheless, to successful negotiate through these systems, accurate and current information is needed. The funding process (including applications and appeals) can be drawn out. It can also involve working with various individuals within an agency. Document all of your interactions. For example, it always much better to be able to state that *on this date, at this time, you talked to this person* about your issue. In your documentation, record relevant quotes so that these can then be used in future discussions. Develop your own system (using a calendar, log entries, computer program, etc.) for recording when future action is needed. Review your work on a regular basis.

Be persistent. Do not give up easily. Be polite and professional, yet firm. Show the person that you will not easily go away. Ask for an explanation when you are told of a negative outcome. As needed, ask to speak to the persons' supervisor.

Network. Do not become locked in on one source of funding. Develop as many possibilities as you can. Ask questions of other technology users, professionals, and advocates. Learn from their experiences. Use their network, if possible.

Advocate. Especially if new to seeking funding, find an advocate, someone who is knowledgeable and will assist you.[16] This person will already know the "ins and outs" of working with funding sources. Advocates may be found at the area independent living center, disability support organizations, parent support groups, rehabilitation agencies, and advocacy groups. Know your rights as mandated by laws.

Funding Sources. In general, there are three types of funding sources: individual, credit, and third party payers. In some cases, purchases use a combination of these sources. A clear option is for the technology user or their family to pay for the devices and services directly. In some cases, this is an ideal option depending upon the cost and the family resources. Most often this is not financially possible. Either the initial cost or the continuing nature of anticipated expenses precludes many individuals or families from purchasing directly.

Funding AT through credit is another potential funding source. This might be arranged through a conventional loan program. Sometimes, a vendor may be connected with a credit program. For example, automobile manufacturers and dealers can assist a buyer in obtaining credit for both the purchase of the vehicle as well as required modifications. Currently, there are six states AT loan programs funded by the 1998 Tech Act as a polite project. Credit options, however, remain limited in nature. The vast majority of funding options come in the form of third-party payers. Examples of these funding sources include Medicaid, state-federal vocational rehabilitation, public education, and the Muscular Dystrophy Association.

Table III

Potential Funding Sources

Source – Public	Eligibility	Coverage
Medicaid Varies by state	To cover the basic health care needs of "categorically needy." Includes those eligible for Aid to Families with Dependent Children or Supplemental Security	May cover home medical equipment, prosthetics, orthotics, and augmentative communication services.

	Income programs. Must be a "medical necessity."	
Medicare Varies by state	Persons over 65 years or disabled sufficiently as to be eligible for SSDI for at least 24 months.	Limited. Durable medical equipment that typically has repeated use.
State-federal vocational rehabilitation services	Individual with a disability that interferes with the ability to work; must benefit from services.	Purchases are tied to vocational goals or to increase independent functioning.
Special Education	Children with disabilities from birth to age 21.	Devices are tied to educational goals. Usually equipment remains the property of the school.
Veterans Administration	Veteran with a service or non-service connected injury. Different categories of eligibility based upon veterans income.	Equipment tied to medical or rehabilitation goals. May include mobility transportation, prosthetics, orthotics, and visual & auditory aids. Dependent upon category of eligibility.
Workers' Compensation*	Injured workers. Dictated by state law and the employer's compensation policies.	Medical and sometimes vocational rehabilitation services including devices. Goal is to return the injured worker to work.

Source – Private	Eligibility	Coverage
Private lenders (individual loan sometimes arranged by AT vendor)	Varies according to the lender's policies and procedures.	Varies according to the lender's policies and procedures.

Source – Other	Eligibility	Coverage
Civic groups (e.g., Lions Club, Telephone Pioneers of America, Kiwanis Club)	Varies.	Varies.
Church groups	Varies – may need to be of that particular faith.	Varies.
Disability organizations (e.g., Muscular Dystrophy Association, National Federation for the Blind)	A person with that particular disability.	Varies.

RESOURCES

Access to information is vital. Where to turn to find the answers to questions or to find a vendor of the latest products requires developing and maintaining an information network. Virtually every person involved in AT will have a different network. There may be significant overlap, yet also contain differences. There are a number of quality resource books and manuals such as the *Workplace Workbook* by Mueller[25] or the *Assistive Technology Sourcebook* by Enders and Hall[13] on the market but these tend to become outdated soon after publication. The advent of the Internet and World Wide Web has changed and streamlined the information gathering process. Now, a few clicks on the Web and resources are readily available, although cautions about the validity of the source are always wise.

One of the problems with developing and disseminating a resource guides or lists is that just as soon as it is published, it is outdated. Contacts, telephone numbers, and especially electronic addresses, change. In general, government supported clearinghouse type sites tend to be stable. These make a logical foundation when developing and using resources.

Table IV

Assistive Technology

Information Centers and Resources

ABLEDATA http://www.abledata.com	800-227-0216 301-608-8912 (TTY)	Information on over 29,000 assistive technology products useful to individuals with disabilities.
Center for Assistive Technology http://cat.buffalo.edu	800-628-2281	
Center for Assistive Technology & Environmental Access http://www.catea.org	404-894-4960	Design, develop, and evaluate assistive technology and accessible environments.
Centers for Universal Design http://www.design.ncsu.edu/cud	919-515-3082	National research, information, and technical assistance center promoting universal design.
Closing the Gap http://closingthegap.com	507-248-3294	Organization that focuses on computer technology for people with disabilities. Publishes a newspaper and Resource Directory that highlight recent product developments.
HEATH Resource Center http://www.heath.gwv.edu	800-544-3284	Provides information on technology particularly relevant in a Special Education setting.

Infinitec http://www.infinitec.org	312-464-1608	Project of United Cerebral Palsy to help people with disabilities and their families access technology.
Job Accommodation Network (JAN) http://jan.wvu.edu	800-526-7234 877-781-9403 (TTY)	Information available on job accommodations and the employability of people with disabilities including the use of assistive technology to modify the work environment.
Rehabilitation Engineering & Assistive Technology Society of North America (RESNA) http://www.resna.org	703-524-6686 703-524-6639 (TTY)	Prof. organization dedicated to the research, development, and dissemination of assistive technology.
RESNA Technical Assistance Project http://www.resna.org/taproject	703-524-6686 703-524-6639 (TTY)	Administers the 56 state and territory assistive technology programs as authorized by the AT Act of 1998.
Trace Research & Development Center http://www.trace.wisc.edu	608-262-6966 608-263-5408 (TTY)	Research and development since 1971. Specializes in computer access, augmentative communications and telecommunications systems and accessibility.

CURRENT TRENDS

The future of assistive technology and its impact upon the lives of people with disabilities is very exciting. Some future technological trends are predictable. We can safely say that computers and computer chips will continue to become faster, more powerful, smaller, and cheaper.[7] Continued advancements in high-tech applications such as improved internet infrastructure, robotics, materials, and nanotechnology (the manufacturing of devices at the atomic and molecular level), just to mention a few examples, all will lead to improved applications. "Smart" homes and appliances that require less physical activation by the user are beginning to hit the marketplace. Virtual reality applications already in use that allows a wheelchair user to "move" through a home to examine accessibility will become more commonplace. The continued growth of universal design (the designing of commercial products with properties that allow use by all people, not just those without a disability) will eventually decrease the need for accessibility modifications. It is also predictable that input devices for computer-based technologies such as voice activation will continue to be improved. In the not too distant future, keyboards as the standard computer input device will be obsolete. Yet to be invented technologies will contribute in ways we cannot even imagine; that is the nature of technology.

RECOMMENDATIONS

- Remember the AT principles discussed in this chapter—the user as the first source of information, access to information, the KISS principle, and making decisions in a systematic way from simplest to complex.
- Access is the key to information. The field is too broad and rapidly changing for anyone to be an authority in many areas. Therefore, it is important to know where to find current product and service information.
- When purchasing a device, especially high-tech, remember to consider *all* potential costs, not just the purchase price. Be aware of the potential costs of training, routine maintenance, repairs, "shelf life" (how long will the product last), and replacement costs. Although we can never plan for all possibilities, we can minimize mistakes by realistically projecting potential costs to see if the purchase is feasible.
- Provide options. When recommending technology, always try to present choices. Being involved in the decision making process is essential for consumer empowerment. People who make the decision for themselves, rather than being told, tend to stick with it longer.
- Remember that some technology abandonment is normal and not a failure of the match. In some cases, technology replacement occurs in which a more effective device is substituted for the original one. In other cases,

abandonment is developmental and the user may have experienced changing needs or preferences.

CASE STUDY

Jessica is a 33-year old, single parent who has multiple sclerosis. She is gradually losing functioning and having more difficulty with stamina, balance, and coordination. Her goal is to be able to continue to take care of her 3-year-old daughter at home. She is very concerned that the Department of Human Services will decide she is unable to properly care for her child and take her daughter away. A technology specialist has been contracted to assess her situation and provide recommendations.

The technology specialist began by spending time with Jessica in her home. Her dwelling is a two bedroom, one bath mobile home. Times were scheduled at various periods throughout the day so that a realistic picture of Jessica's functioning could be determined. The evaluation consisted of observation and discussion.

Upon completion of the assessment, the following limitations or concerns were noted:

- *Due to fatigue, Jessica had difficulty providing care in the afternoon.*
- *Except for the kitchen and bathroom, the floor covering was thick, shag carpeting. Throw rugs were in the kitchen and bathroom. This presented a possible safety hazard.*
- *Storage in the home (kitchen, bathroom, closet, and laundry area) included shelves above Jessica's head, which were difficult for her to reach. This also presented possible safety concerns.*
- *Jessica appeared to have some difficulty accepting the fact that she is losing functioning. She voices resistance to using assistive devices that "stand out" such as a walker (She stated, "That's what old people use – I'm not old!").*

The following recommendations were made to minimize the impact of the concerns:

Help Jessica realize and accept that she would get tired each afternoon. Plan accordingly.

- Prepare snacks and drinks for the child to be used in the afternoon. Place them on a low shelf of the refrigerator that the child could get.
- Be sure to take a nap each afternoon, ideally with the child. If the child is not napping, close off the napping area. This might include the use of child safety gates that can be put up temporarily.

- Have Jessica become more self-aware of things she can do to conserve her energy. This should include trying to get her to accept the fact that a walker will both provide safety and conserve her strength.

Remove the throw rugs. Remove the carpet in favor of linoleum. If this is not feasible, put plastic or rubber runways (also called "runners") over the most used pathways.

Redesign her storage areas. By making the space efficient, items need not be placed on shelves above her head. Use "lazy Susans" on the kitchen counter to store smaller items. Organize storage so that items needed by the child are within her reach. For example, cups and juice boxes should be stored on low shelves. If needed, purchase a "grabber" for Jessica that will allow her to reach and grab items above her head.

CONCLUSION

Assistive technology is a powerful tool that can greatly enhance independence, quality of life, and choices for a person with a disability. With its proper use, barriers such as physical accessibility and social isolation can be minimized or even eliminated.

REFERENCES

[1]Americans with Disabilities ACT of 1990, Pub. L. No. 101-336, 2, 104 Stat. 328 (1991).

[2]Assistive Technology Act of 1998, Pub. L. No. 105-394, 112 Stat. 3627 (1998).

[3]Assistive Technology Act of 2004, Pub. L. No. 108-364U.S. 118 Stat. 1707 (2004).

[4]Bat-Chava, Y., Deignan, E., & Martin, D. (2002). Rehabilitation counselor's knowledge of hearing loss and assistive technology. *Journal of Rehabilitation, 68*(1), 33-44.

[5]Bryant, D. P. & Bryant, B. R. (2003). *Assistive Technology for people with disabilities*. New York: Pearson Education, Inc.

[6]Buscalgia, L. (Ed.). (1994). *The disabled and their parents: a counseling challenge 3rd edition* Thorofare, NJ: C. B. Slack.

[7]Cook, A. M. (2002). Future directions in assistive technology. In M. J. Scherer (Ed.), *Assistive technology: matching device and consumer for successful rehabilitation* (pp. 269 - 280). Washington, DC: American Psychological Association.

[8]Cook, A. M., & Polgar, J. M. (2007). *Cook and Hussey's assistive technologies: Principles and practice 3rd edition.* St. Louis, MI: Mosby Elsevier.

[9]Cushman, L., & Scherer, M. (1996). Measuring the relationship of assistive technology use, functional status over time, and consumer-therapist perceptions of AT. *Assistive Technology, 8*(2), 103-109.

[10]Day, H., & Jutai, J. (1996). Measuring the psychosocial impact of assistive devices; the PIADS. *Canadian Journal of Rehabilitation, 9*, 159-168.

[11]Day, H., Jutai, J., & Campbell, K. A. (2002). Development of a scale to measure the psychosocial impact of assistive devices: lessons learned from the road ahead. *Disability & Rehabilitation, 24*(24), 31-37.

[12]Dowd, L. R. (Ed.). (1993). *Glossary of terminology for vocational assessment, evaluation, and work adjustment.* Menomonie, WI: Materials Development Center.

[13]Enders, A., & Hall. M. (Eds.). (1990). Assistive *technology sourcebook.* Washington D.C.: RESNA Press.

[14]Galvin, J. C., & Scherer, M. J. (Eds.). (1996). *Evaluating, selecting, and using appropriate assistive technology.* Gaithersburg, MD: Aspen Publishers, Inc.

[15]Hughes, D. (2006). Advocates work to boost employment of disabled. *The Atlanta Journal-Constitution.* Retrieved from http://jobnews.ajcjobs.com/news/content/careercenter/articles/2006_0507_diverse1.html

[16]Infinite Potential Through Assistive Technology. (n.d.). *Finding the money.* Retrieved from http://www.infinitec.org/learn/money/findingthemoney.htm.

[17]Informed Consumer's Guide to Accessible Housing. (1995). *Introduction.* Retrieved from http://www.abledata.com/abledata_docs/icg-hous.htm.

[18]Institute on Rehabilitation Issues. (1979). *Rehabilitation engineering – a counselor's guide.* Menomonie, WI: Research and Training Center.

[19]Institute on Rehabilitation Issues. (1986). *Rehabilitation technologies.* Menomonie, WI: Research and Training Center.

[20]Jutai, J. (1999). Quality of life impact of assistive technology. *Rehabilitation Engineering.* 14, 2-7.

[21]Langton, A. J., & Ramseur, H. 2001). Enhancing employment outcomes through job accommodation and assistive technology resources and services. *Journal of Vocational Rehabilitation, 16*, 27 – 37.

[22]Longmuir, P. E., & Axelson, P. (1996). Assistive technology for recreation. In Galvin, J. G., & Scherer, M. J. (Eds.), *Evaluating, selecting, and using appropriate assistive technology* (pp.162–197). Gaithersburg, MD: Aspen.

[23]Lueck, A. H., Dote-Kwan, J., Senge, J. C., & Clark, L. (2001). Selecting assistive technology for greater independence. *Review, 33,* 13- 21. Retrieved from the Psychology & Behavioral Sciences Collection database.

[24]Mendelsohn, S. (1996). Funding assistive technology. In Galvin, J. G., & Scherer, M. J. (Eds.), *Evaluating, selecting, and using appropriate assistive technology* (pp.345 – 359). Gaithersburg, MD: Aspen.

[25]Mendelsohn, S., & Fox, H. R. (2002). Evolving legislation and public policy related to disability and assistive technology. In M. J. Scherer (Ed.), *Assistive technology: matching device and consumer for successful rehabilitation* (pp. 17-28). Washington, DC: American Psychological Association.

[26]Mueller, J. L. (1995). *The workplace workbook 2.0: An illustrated guide to workplace accommodation and technology.* Amherst, MA: Human Resource Development Press.

[27]National Rehabilitation Information Center. (n.d.). *NARIC Quarterly, 3*, (2, 3). Silver Springs, MD: National Rehabilitation Information Center.

[28]Office of Management and Budget. (2011). *Winning the future of people with disabilities*: The federal budget fiscal year 2012. Washington, D.C.: Author. Retrieved from http://www.whitehouse.gov/search/site/NIDRR?filters=im_og_gid:10275

[29]Office of Technology Assessment (1982). *Technology and handicapped people* (Library of Congress Card Number 82-600546). Washington, D.C.: Government Printing Office.

[30]Peterson, W. A., & Perr, A. (1996). Home and worksite accommodations. In J. C. Galvin & M. J. Scherer (Eds.), *Evaluating, selecting, and using appropriate assistive technology* (215-236). Gaithersburg, MD: Aspen Publishers, Inc.

[31]Reed, B. J. (1993). Historical overview of assistive technology. *Vocational Evaluation and Work Adjustment Bulletin, 26* (1), 7-11.

[32]Reed, B. J., Fried, J. H., & Rhoades, B. J. (1995). Empowerment and assistive technology: the local resource team model. *The Journal of Rehabilitation, 61*(2), 30-35.

[33]Rehabilitation Act Amendments of 1978, Pub. L. No. 95-602, 92 Stat. 2992 (1978).

[34]Rehabilitation Act Amendments of 1986, Pub. L. No. 99-506, 100 Stat. 1807 (1986).

[35]Rehabilitation Act of 1973, Pub. L. No. 93-112, 87 Stat. 355 (1973).

[36]Rehabilitation Engineering & Assistive Technology Society of North America. (n.d.). Rehabilitation Engineering Research Centers (RERC). Retrieved from http://web.resna.org/resources/rerc-publications.dot.

[37]Riemer-Reiss, M. L., & Wacker, R. R. (2000). Factors associated with assistive technology discontinuance among individuals with disabilities. *Journal of Rehabilitation, 66*(3), 44-50.

[38]Saladin, S. P. (2004). Psychosocial variables in the adoption of assistive technology among deaf and hard of hearing adults. *Dissertation Abstracts International, 65-10A*. (UMI No. 3150722)

[39]Scherer, M. J. (1991). *The Scherer MPT model: matching people with technologies*. Webster, NY: Scherer and Associates.

[40]Scherer, M. J. (2004). *Living in the state of stuck: How assistive technology impacts the lives of people with disabilities.* Cambridge, MA: Brookline Books.

[41]Scherer, M. J. (1996). Outcomes of assistive technology use on quality of life. *Disability and Rehabilitation, 18*, 439-448.

[42]Technology-Related Assistance for Individuals with Disabilities Act of 1988, Pub. L. No. 100-407, 102 Stat. 1044 (1988).

[43]Vash, C. L. & Crewe, N. (2004). *The Psychology of disability.* New York: Springer Publishing Company.

PROFESSIONALISM

THOMAS L. EVENSON

LINDA L. HOLLOWAY
UNIVERSITY OF NORTH TEXAS

Chapter Topics

- What is Professionalism?
- Professionals
- Professions
- Professionalism
- Characteristics of a Professional
- Individual Professionalism
- Relevance to Undergraduate Rehabilitation Students
- Professional Ethics
- Professionalism is About You
- What Can You Do?
- Work Habits
- Interpersonal Skills
- Rehabilitation Philosophy
- Professional Development

WHAT IS PROFESSIONALISM?

Workers trained in rehabilitation and disability studies bring an important dimension to rehabilitation services and to the rehabilitation profession. With fewer than 60 undergraduate rehabilitation programs and fewer than 90 graduate rehabilitation programs in the United States, there are far too few qualified personnel to meet the needs of people with disabilities in public and community rehabilitation programs. Evenson & Holloway[14] found that only 25% of the workers employed by community rehabilitation programs hold baccalaureate degrees. Of this 25%, only 7% held bachelor's degrees in rehabilitation studies. In other words, of every 100 workers providing rehabilitation services in this group, fewer than two had degrees directly in rehabilitation.

The real losers in this shortage of qualified rehabilitation workers are people with disabilities. Programs in rehabilitation studies are typically designed to develop specialized knowledge, skills, and attitudes that prepare students to assume unique roles and responsibilities that allow them to collaborate with people with disabilities to live independent, productive, and self-fulfilling lives. Specialized knowledge includes such areas as rehabilitation philosophy and processes, public and private rehabilitation systems, disability management, etiology, progression and treatment of major disabling conditions, career information, job development and placement, transferable skills, job modification, school-to-work transition, rehabilitation legislation, program evaluation, and many other areas. Specific skills include behavioral change techniques, communication, case management, assessment techniques, report writing, job analyses, job placement, individual program planning, group work, teaching, and a multitude of interpersonal and community organization skills.

Finally, rehabilitation students are challenged to refine and develop attitudes that place a premium on autonomy, respect, equality, empowerment, being non-judgmental, open-mindedness, confidentiality, and a genuine belief in the consumer's ability to accomplish personal, social, and vocational goals. Specialized training of rehabilitation personnel is important because of the level of responsibility that practitioners assume in virtually every employment setting that provides services to people with disabilities. Employers expect that applicants from undergraduate and graduate programs in rehabilitation will come equipped with a foundation of knowledge about an array of topics relevant to work with individuals, families, social systems, and communities. Equally important is the expectation that graduates of credible academic programs will come equipped with the skills necessary for effective intervention and collaboration with these constituencies.

In addition to rehabilitation skills, employers also seek qualities such as honesty, responsibility, trustworthiness, personal appearance, enthusiasm, commitment, a strong work ethic, and personal integrity. In other words, employers want workers who behave in a "professional" way. This is true not only in rehabilitation settings—96% of employers who participated in a national survey related to professionalism among young workers, stated that this played a role in their decision to hire an individual.[52] They noted that one's attitude or demeanor as well as the ability to communicate indicated the level of professionalism.

PROFESSIONALS

For some, status as a "professional" is reserved for those who have earned graduate degrees, Still, rehabilitation workers with bachelors' degrees are expected to have specialized knowledge, maintain high levels of work performance, be able to work autonomously, adhere to ethical standards, place the interests of their clients as their highest duty, and commit to collaborative interpersonal relationships. While they may not be officially classified as professionals, employers of these workers expect them to behave and perform like professionals.

Despite the official definitions of a "professional," rehabilitation workers are increasingly asserting their rights to be perceived as professionals. They are not doing this through loud protestations and demands or by staging sit-ins. They are doing it through the way they approach their responsibilities in the world of rehabilitation. On the basis of the qualities that characterize their commitment to rehabilitation work, they demonstrate that "professional" is the only appropriate word to describe them. Rather than arguing about who or what constitutes a "professional," baccalaureate-level workers use their educational preparation as the foundation for developing a level of professionalism for which they earn the respect of both consumers and colleagues.

Rehabilitation and human service educators who have made a conscious effort to incorporate individual professionalism as a central theme within the human service academic program can enhance their students' self-perception, self confidence and, ultimately, the quality of services delivered to the individuals they serve.[24] Rehabilitation alumni occupy a wide range of jobs within the human service sector. Studies conducted of undergraduate rehabilitation alumni find a broad range of job tiles and activities.[16,22] Regardless of job titles, it was clear that these alumni perform professional tasks with a high level of autonomy. Reinders[43] also found that human service professionals are "driven by a sincere desire to help others"[p. 570] that at times means advocating for their clients over the goals of the organization.

PROFESSIONS

The root word for both professional and professionalism is profession. The word "profession" comes from the Latin term "profiteri," which means to declare or avow something out loud or publicly. Originally, the avowal was related to entering the religious life. By the 16th century, it had evolved to include declaring the entrance to an occupation that is devoted to saving lives or souls...or the kind of work carried out by priests, doctors, and attorneys. By the 19th century, the term was informally broadened to include any legitimate occupation by which an individual made money. The 20th century saw special application of the term to distinguish athletes and entertainers who were paid for their play, from amateurs who played for fun.

Does one have to be a member of a recognized profession to be a "professional?" If so, there are probably a limited number of professionals. There are a small group of established occupations, such as law, medicine, dentistry, and the clergy, that appear to meet the kinds of standards normally required of professions. Others, like engineering and architecture, meet most of these standards.[3] Some disciplines, such as psychology, counseling, social work, and teaching, strive to reach the status of profession, but are not fully recognized as such despite the arguments of their respective advocates.

The connection between the terms profession and professionalism is more relevant to rehabilitation education than whether the discipline of rehabilitation meets the specific criteria for eligibility as a "profession." The real question is whether rehabilitation workers with bachelor's degrees are considered professionals even if rehabilitation services are not officially deemed a profession. According to Van Zandt,[53] the answer is yes. He claimed that it is possible to be "professional" without necessarily being a member of a recognized profession. Hughes[26] suggested that the "culture and technique, the etiquette and skill of the profession, appear in the individual as personal traits..."[p. 36]

PROFESSIONALISM

The concept of professionalism is described in terms of attitudes, behaviors, or a combination of the two. Weiss[54] believes that professionalism extends beyond knowledge and skills. It reflects people's commitment as professionals and their socialization into the role of a professional. Peterson and Nisenholz[39] do not see professionalism as something that is accomplished but as a process that extends throughout one's lifetime. Pascarella[38] describes professionalism as a quest for excellence. Maister[32] suggests that the opposite of professionalism is not "unprofessional" but "technician." Technicians are specialists in the competencies that they develop through special training. The core of professionalism is attitude rather than a set of competencies. He defines a real professional as a "technician who cares."[p.16] Hoyle[25] used the term professionalism "to describe enhancement of the quality of service."[p.146] According to Boyt,[7] "professionalism consists of the attitudes and behavior one possesses towards one's profession."[p. 322] A concise explanation of professionalism was provided by a business manager cited by Maister[32] who said: "Professional is not a label you give yourself—it's a description you hope others will apply to you. You do the best you can as a matter of self-respect. Having self-respect is the key to earning respect and trust from others."[p. 17]

CHARACTERISTICS OF A PROFESSIONAL

Maister[32] presented professionalism within a context that clearly extends beyond the established professions when he identified characteristics that distinguished a great secretary from a good secretary:

> *They take pride in their work; they are committed to quality; they seek out responsibility; they take initiative; they anticipate what needs to be done; they go beyond their assigned role but know what their limits are; they act in ways that streamline the loads of others; they make a point of learning and understanding the business/company/agency; they genuinely listen to the people they work for and with; they can represent the people they serve because they have made a point of understanding and thinking like them; while they appreciate themselves, they are not self-absorbed; they are team players; they can be trusted to keep confidences; they are willing to learn, accepting of feedback and open to change; and they are consistently honest, trustworthy, and loyal.*[p. 15]

Hoch[23] believes that it is not so much what people do, but how they do it that determines professionalism. Among the characteristics that go into the practice of professionalism, according to Hoch, are courtesy, trust, ethics and integrity, personal appearance, communication, enthusiasm, positive attitude, ability to relate well to others, involvement with professional organizations, program involvement, service as a mentor, fairness, and personal improvement.[pp. 10-11]

Maister's[32] and Hoch's[23] lists of professional qualities are generic and are, therefore, probably relevant to workers in any occupation. Corey[10] identifies the characteristics that describe effective counselors. Corey submits that effective counselors:

- have an identity
- respect and appreciate themselves
- recognize and accept their own power
- are open to change
- are making choices that shape their lives
- feel alive, and their choices are life-oriented
- are authentic, sincere, and honest
- have a sense of humor

- make mistakes and are willing to admit them
- generally live in the present
- appreciate the influence of culture
- have a sincere interest in the welfare of others
- become deeply involved in their work and derive meaning from it
- are able to maintain healthy boundaries.[pp.18-19]

While there is no agreement on exactly how to define professionalism, the commonalities among the Maister,[32] Hoch[23] and Corey[11] lists suggest that there is a general understanding of what constitutes professional behavior. People with an approach to work as described by Maister[32] are likely to be characterized as more than "very good" secretaries. People would likely use the term "professional" to describe them. Coaches and teammates working with an athlete who exhibits the characteristics listed by Hoch[23] may use the term professional to describe that player. Corey[11] acknowledges that his counselor characteristics are really ideals to which the counselor strives. Still, they represent the kinds of qualities that would help a person be successful in any occupation. In short, we know a professional when we see one—and the development of graduates who qualify as professionals is a goal of rehabilitation education.

INDIVIDUAL PROFESSIONALISM

According to Ritzer[44] professionalism consists of two important realms. One is occupational professionalism, which is concerned with whether or not a particular occupation meets the criteria for recognition as a profession. The other is individual professionalism, which has to do with whether or not a particular worker behaves in a professional manner. Formal recognition of rehabilitation services as a profession is not under the exclusive control of rehabilitation service workers. You have considerably more control over whether or not you are recognized as a "professional." You can take personal responsibility for reaching that goal.

Professionalism is something that need not depend on level of education, number or type of credentials, years of experience, or even the occupation one is in. Students graduating from undergraduate and graduate programs in rehabilitation services are as capable of being as professional as the most dedicated doctors, lawyers, or architects. At a minimum, students graduating from rehabilitation service programs can begin their careers as professionals by understanding and subscribing to the meaning and principle of the Latin root word for profession, *profiteri*.... to declare or avow something out loud or publicly. The foundation for their development as rehabilitation professionals will be their pride in and commitment to the kind of work they intend to do.

You might ask if you see yourself as a technician or as a professional among rehabilitation service workers. Similarly, how do you expect to see yourself after five years in this business? It is important not to underestimate the value of being a technician. A technician is competent in terms of knowledge and skills related to the occupation. Whether you aspire to be a technician or a professional, you must master the knowledge and skill areas as well as develop core attitudes that are required as a rehabilitation worker. What distinguishes the professional from the technician is in the "how" rather than the "what" of rehabilitation practice. Most of this difference can be traced directly to the individual as a person. A technician can be developed through an educational program. Professionals have to bring the basic ingredients with them into the program. Education will help to accentuate those qualities and facilitate their further development. The real test is how individuals assume responsibility for perpetual refinement throughout their career.

Use the lists of qualities identified by Maister,[32] Hoch,[23] and Corey[10] as guides for self-reflection. Do not use them as checklists of qualities that can be mastered one at a time and, once all are covered, you turn into a "professional." Instead, use them as a means of thinking about your personal strengths and weaknesses in these areas. Find ways to solidify the strengths that you are bringing with you into your rehabilitation career. Develop strategies for addressing the weakest areas. Perfection should not be the goal. Professionalism is a journey, not a destination. You will maintain a steady path on this journey through a genuine commitment to doing the best work you can with consumers and continually striving to know, understand, and accept yourself as an individual.

RELEVANCE TO REHABILITATION STUDENTS

You are entering the rehabilitation profession at a most interesting time. The nature of the role of the "helping" professional has experienced a progressive and profound change over the last 25 years. This change has had a particularly important impact on rehabilitation workers because rehabilitation consumers have assumed such an active leadership role in meeting the rights and needs of people with disabilities. No longer are professionals viewed as the "sole experts" who have a responsibility for "helping" or "changing" the consumer. Rehabilitation professionals are expected to work as collaborators with consumers in applying their distinct areas of expertise in getting consumers to where they want to be, but they are not "in charge." They work *with* the consumer. Effective professionals understand this and encourage the consumer to assume personal responsibility for change. They avoid getting in that person's way with their personal preferences, priorities, and needs.

PROFESSIONAL ETHICS

One important thing that separates a professional worker from a nonprofessional worker is the professional's commitment to ethical practice. An established code of ethics is a requisite for any occupation that aspires to become a recognized profession. Similarly, individual professionalism calls for a personal commitment to a standard of practice that is consistent with the most commonly used ethical principles.

The topic of professional ethics is expansive and complex. A simple but accurate way of referring to ethical practice is that it entails the engagement of "right and proper" behavior. While this is accurate, it is not a very specific description. The perennial question with ethical issues is "Just exactly what is 'right and proper' behavior in a particular situation?" Ethical challenges are inherently ambiguous. While various legal requirements, codes of ethics, and standards of practice all provide guidance, ultimately, most decisions as to what is "right and proper" come down to the individual worker. It is for this reason that rehabilitation professionals must know, understand, and accept themselves.

Perhaps the most important point to make in discussing professional ethics is that *you* are the "bottom line." You must use principles of ethics, codes of ethics, and standards of practice to guide you. You will access supervisors, colleagues, and experts to advise you. The decision, ultimately, on what to do when faced with an ethical dilemma is yours. You have earned the right to this responsibility precisely because you are a professional. By virtue of this status, you are entrusted with the right to make the difficult calls, because you are the one with the knowledge and expertise necessary to deal with the case situation that confronts you.

Our purpose is not to cover professional ethics "from A to Z." Ethics is covered in detail elsewhere in this book. However, because ethical behavior is such a critical component of individual professionalism, we want to present you with the five fundamental principles[30] that underlie the ethical conduct within the counseling profession. Each of the principles is derived from fundamental values subscribed to by professionals. The five ethical principles are:

- *Beneficence* is based on the value of *doing something of benefit* to the consumer. This value motivates most of us to pursue a career in rehabilitation in the first place.
- *Nonmaleficence* relates to the value of *avoiding doing harm* to the consumer. It is sometimes referred to as the "first among equals" among the five ethical principles.
- *Autonomy* is based on the values of *independence and individual choice*. It is a principle that not only relates to the ultimate rehabilitation goal but one that guides the entire rehabilitation process.
- *Justice* is based on the value of fairness. It promotes the equal treatment of all consumers regardless of their personal values, beliefs, goals, or personal characteristics.
- *Fidelity* is based on the value of *loyalty* and calls on the professional to remain committed to the consumer, the profession, and the workplace.

The Commission on Rehabilitation Counselor Certification added *Veracity* to its code in 2010. Veracity is based on the value of *honesty*. It requires you to be accurate and careful in your plan of action. These ethical principles and the values that underlie them form a foundation for "right and proper" behavior on the part of the rehabilitation professional.

Undergraduate education is in the process of being approved for accreditation by the Commission on Higher Education Accreditation. As a part of this, an ethical code specific to undergraduate rehabilitation and disability studies will be adopted.

PROFESSIONALISM IS ABOUT YOU

By this time, you should be able to recognize that there is an opportunity for professionalism within the career area you have chosen. It should also be apparent that becoming a professional is pretty much up to you. Your effectiveness as a rehabilitation worker depends upon your knowledge about people, disabilities, employment, communities, multiculturalism, and a variety of related areas. It further depends on the level of your skills in organization, planning, communication, interpersonal interactions, behavioral change techniques, and case management, among other skills. As vital as your knowledge and skills will be for your success in rehabilitation, they will only be a part of it. What is more, they are the easy part of your work. You already have a number of skills that you can immediately use and develop further. The same is true of your knowledge base. You already know something about working with people, and further development of that knowledge is the purpose of your formal and continuing education. Knowledge and skills development have the additional benefit of being fairly concrete and measurable.

The extent to which you are able to understand and use yourself as an "instrument" in the rehabilitation process will ultimately determine your level of professionalism. This is a more abstract responsibility than developing knowledge and skills. It is personal and entails dealing with issues and experiences that have been a part of you for a long time. Your own personhood will be your most important tool. It is challenging because it requires a level of effort that makes developing knowledge and skills, or even earning a college degree, seem easy. You must not only get "in touch" with who, what, and why you are, but continually stay in touch with yourself. This must be a challenging goal because so many people seem to avoid trying to accomplish it. This avoidance is not a luxury that a professional who is responsible for working with other people can afford.

SELF-HONESTY

If there is a single most important quality in developing your professionalism, it is that you are honest with yourself. Rehabilitation professionals must consider "who" we are because our real selves are what provide the cornerstones for our professionalism. In preparing for a rehabilitation career, students are challenged to look at themselves in ways that they may have never before seriously considered. Self-analysis requires an inventory of one's strengths, limitations, needs, fears, values, beliefs, doubts, assumptions, aspirations, and prejudices with complete self-honesty.

Self-honesty may sound easy on the surface, but most of us find it difficult to do. It can be a little risky to take a close and honest look at who we are. Despite our numerous strengths, there are parts of us that we tend to conceal from others. There are even parts that we might want to conceal from ourselves. Still, these qualities, thoughts, values, attitudes, and beliefs are all a very real part of us. If we are not very proud of some of them, we probably want to try to make some changes, but it is impossible to change things that we do not recognize or do not acknowledge. The same point applies to some of our strengths. People in the helping professions are frequently modest. Many even underestimate themselves in the name of modesty. The price we eventually pay is unawareness of whom we are and what we really have to offer.

For example, in our business, we need to practice being nonjudgmental of other people. You can practice being nonjudgmental by considering yourself. We do not have to "like" what we recognize in ourselves, but that does not mean we need to reject or run from our faults. By acknowledging them, we are in a position to understand them and see where they fit. When we understand their purpose and their effect on others, and us, we are in a position to decide whether we want to make some changes. If we decide to make changes, we can proceed with a more complete understanding of what really needs to change. In other words, we retain control over ourselves. When we deny something about ourselves, we are really abdicating control.

WHY YOU?

A good place to start an investigation of yourself and your potential for professionalism is to examine what it is about you that you think is "right" for the important work of rehabilitation services. Regardless of the majors that college students select, they do themselves a great favor by exploring two areas. One relates to the question "What do I hope to get out of a career in this area?" The second question should be "What do I plan to bring to this career area that will allow me to contribute something to it?"

These can be complicated questions, but they are not worth asking unless you are willing to invest some time and energy in honestly answering them. The questions do not have any "right or wrong" answers. In responding to them, consider questions like:

- How did I get interested in this area?
- What is it about me that will make me good at it?

- How am I different from other people so that I am probably more suited to this kind of work than others might be?
- How does this particular career area "fit" my personality?
- What motivations do I have for working with people?
- How is my value system similar to those of people who are already in this field?
- How do I seem different from people who are already in the field?
- What life experiences do I bring with me that influence my beliefs about people with disabilities?

Before considering these questions, commit yourself to self-honesty in answering them. It is equally important that you avoid judging your responses to the questions. Do not stop with just answering the questions. Reflect on your responses. Think of other questions that you might ask to help clarify why you chose this career. Ask some of the questions of someone who knows you well. Get their perspective. You can move a long way toward knowing yourself better if you can engage in this kind of introspection. It will also help you decide whether a career in rehabilitation is right for you.

NEEDS

Another avenue of self-exploration is to build on the question of what you hope to get out of a career in this area. The question is "What's in this career for me?" What do you want? What do you need?

There may be as many reasons for pursuing a rehabilitation career as there are rehabilitation professionals. Needs, values, and beliefs are individual and personal. They can be traced to experiences that we have had, lessons we have learned from significant people in our lives, and our personal interpretation of all of these events. A few examples of common needs of human service workers include the need for approval, self-respect, security, to do for others what someone has done for you, recognition, success, to be needed, to return a favor for help received, and many others. All of these are legitimate needs. They have influenced most of us, at one time or another, in our rehabilitation careers.

It is important to note that there is no such thing as a "good" need or a "bad" need. These are judgmental terms and judgment will only inhibit our willingness and ability to look at what we really need and want out of our careers. The behavior that we engage in to fulfill these needs can be beneficial, neutral, or even harmful to our consumers. Some workers may be completely unaware that what they are doing within a rehabilitation relationship is really better designed to meet their own needs than it is to be of real help to the consumer. It is not a matter of being "evil" or of trying to harm the consumer. Either we do not recognize our more self-centered motivations, or we deny them by covering them up with other motives that are more altruistic. The point is that personal needs and wants of the worker can influence the process, so it is important that we are aware of the ones we bring with us.

We cannot possibly discuss all of the needs and motivations that rehabilitation workers might have in relation to this kind of work. The following are four common need areas that might be helpful to use as examples as you look more closely at your own needs. One area relates to the need to be wanted, valued, or needed. Feeling needed or valued may be a good example of something that we would like to have but do not "require" in order to be effective rehabilitation workers. If it is something that we simply prefer and comes as a "bonus." It is not likely to have a negative effect on your work. If it is a personal need, it could shift your focus from the consumer to yourself. For example, some consumers are not going to need or value you. Would you treat them differently than you would treat those who are clearly appreciative? How will you react to consumers who not only do not need you but also make it clear that they do not even want you in their lives? Closely related to this is the "need" to be liked. Most of us would not see "being liked" as a need, but many of us have experienced times when we would go to almost any length to avoid being disliked. Wanting to be liked is not a bad thing. On the contrary, the value that we place on being accepted by others is probably accompanied by our ability to be sensitive to, and empathize with, other people. The desire to be valued and liked can prompt behaviors that help us to be effective in our work. We want to be careful when this desire or preference is really a need, because unrecognized needs tend to move to the top of our priority lists.

The needs for respect, prestige, or status are also common among rehabilitation and other human service workers. Consider how important these things are to you. Then think about how much you "have to have" them in order to be okay. The value of placing a priority on respect and prestige is that you are more likely to understand the importance your consumers place on these needs. Many of them will have direct and extensive experience with being unfairly scrutinized and treated with disrespect. Your appreciation of the importance of human respect can have a positive influence on how your consumers perceive you. There will be times when some people will devalue both you and your consumers. You are in a position to help consumers understand that the most important kind of respect is self-respect. Status and prestige determined by external entities can be powerful reinforcers for both rehabilitation professionals and for consumers. If we are depending on (needing) this external validation, we could be disappointed. You can establish your own criteria for success and progress that is based on an honest self-assessment. You can help your consumers do the same thing. That way, external endorsement will be nice but serves only as a bonus that supplements your assessment of your own efforts and accomplishments.

A third area for you to consider involves the need for control, power, and influence. At first glance, you might wonder how someone could imply that you might be looking for ways to obtain power and control in this business. If you stop and think about it, there are few occupations where you have as much opportunity to influence the lives of other people as you do in human services. You will be in a position to work with people who not only feel vulnerable but who are vulnerable. They may have been taken advantage of and dehumanized to a point where they may not even know whether someone new is harming them. Your role is to provide support and expertise to consumers in their effort to gain control and power in their lives and not to serve as a replacement for some other "power broker" in their world.

It is unlikely that you would deliberately abuse consumers with any of the power that comes with your role and position. More likely, you will use opportunities to "influence" your consumers to do what you think is best. You are using your position to determine what is best for the consumer. Your commitment to your consumer makes you want to ensure that it is done "right." We may think we know what "should" happen, but we must be sure that the consumer wants the same thing. Some consumers may want the worker to decide what is best. Exploring possibilities, considering alternatives, making plans, and coming up with strategies are areas that require that we collaborate with consumers. Then, the consumer decides. While it may be more "convenient" for both the consumer and the worker if the worker makes the decision, the rehabilitation process works best if it is a collaborative decision. Sometimes this means that the consumer will choose something different from what we recommend or prefer. Ultimately, our job is to ensure that the choices are based on the best and most complete information and resources available.

The fourth need/want that we address may seem a little surprising. Sometimes people will joke that rehabilitation workers are just in it "for the money." This statement is amusing because large salaries are rarely part of most rehabilitation positions. We mention it because salary is a very common concern for most people, regardless of their occupations. Rehabilitation workers have as much right as anyone else to a decent standard of living and we should not be embarrassed to identify it as a legitimate want. We are not in this business as volunteers. We have expertise of value to people with disabilities and to society in general, and the idea of subpar financial remuneration is demeaning to professionals who are highly skilled, knowledgeable, and able to deliver quality services. Few rehabilitation and other human service workers embark on their careers for monetary reasons, but that does not mean that securing a respectable income is not of importance. If workers receive inadequate salaries, they are likely to get discouraged, burn out, and eventually leave the profession for something that is more financially rewarding, even if they would prefer to continue in this business. Being underpaid can cause some good workers to resent their work and distract them from focusing on the needs of their consumers. Eventually, they become no different from workers in other occupations whose sole motive for working is related to financial needs.

These four needs are simply four legitimate and frequently seen needs. None of them may even apply to you. Meeting these needs can contribute to the effectiveness of the rehabilitation professional. Examine your own needs and anticipate how they might be met through rehabilitation work. Do not look for clear-cut, easy answers, because our needs are not always conspicuous or simple. The clearer you are about them, the better chance you have of meeting them. More importantly, you will be better positioned to control any unwanted influences they might have on your consumers and on your work as rehabilitation professionals.

VALUES

One of the cornerstones of your approach to working with people within rehabilitation, or any other kind of human service setting, is your personal value system. Because values are personal, they are not very objective. They represent the way that we would like our world to be and the way that we believe things should be if they are going to be "right." Cultural background, family members, religions, education, and our varied experiences all influence our values. Rehabilitation professionals are challenged with the responsibility of examining, clarifying, and understanding their personal value systems, because they play a key role in working with other people.

Our values are an inherent part of us and play a critical role in determining what we believe, what we think, what we learn, how we behave—and how we interact with other people. They pertain to what is "of value" to us as individuals. Think for a minute. What do you consider to be of greatest value to you in your world? It may be your parents, your mate, your children, your home, your job, your education, your freedom, your health.... any of a multitude of possibilities. Who is to say that one of the values that you identify for yourself is not "valuable?" Let us take it to a less dramatic level. What if one of your identified values is your car, your music collection, your flower garden, your horse or cat...or something equally personal to you? Who has a right to suggest that what is valuable to you is not as valuable as something else might be to another person? There really is no room for judgment when it comes to values. Still, many of us have experienced some level of judgment directed at something we value. Rehabilitation professionals must avoid doing that to their consumers and their consumers' value systems.

You should consider several things in relation to personal values.

- What are they?
- Where did they come from?
- Who influenced them?
- How have they changed?
- Are they temporary or permanent values?
- How do they influence us...our thinking, our choices, our behavior?

Make a list of the ten things that you value most in your world. Do it without a lot of thought and write down quickly what comes to mind. After you have made the list, think about how much time/energy you devote to "attending" to each item on the list. This assessment will tell you a good deal about how important these values are to you.

For example, a father says that his children are first on his list of values. Yet, upon honest self-reflection, he acknowledges that he really does not have much time to spend with them. He spends his time on the job, at school, playing golf, doing home repairs, et cetera. What does he really value? The point is that a good barometer of what we value can be determined by the amount and quality of time we spend on it. What do you spend your time doing? What do you think you will spend your time doing five years from now? What can these time investments tell you about your personal value system?

Considering how you spend your time can also give you insight into what some of your deeper values might be. For example, the father could say that he works so much in order to provide his children with the financial security that he never had. Thus, security for his children (and possibly for himself) is one of his primary values. That seems reasonable. There is no judgment about his value list. His children may eventually challenge him about which has more value, them or the importance that he places on their security as he defines it. Understanding his response to such a challenge can help him be clear about what his motives are, the reason for his motives, and where and how he can channel his energy in the ways that are most important to him.

Take the next few weeks to consider what you value most in your life and in this world. As you go through this process, consider the individuals (parents, family members, teachers, and friends) that have had an impact on shaping what is valuable to you. Think about how your cultural background and environment have influenced your current value system. Identify special events or experiences in your life that have affected your value system. Reflect on ways that your values have evolved and changed over the years.

Rehabilitation professionals have a responsibility to support clients in reaching the goals they establish. We have neither the right nor the responsibility to set goals for our clients or to determine what is "right" for them. A client's personal value system, not the professionals, should be the guiding principle in determining their goals. Some workers, directly or indirectly, "persuade" their clients to see things as the worker does and to adopt values that are similar to the worker's values. The ones who do it deliberately are usually so overt that they are not tolerated for long. More common are workers who are unable to recognize when they are trying to change others to "fit" the way they think things should be. They are subtle and consequently more difficult to detect. They have trouble understanding why their consumers are resistant. They do not recognize that they may be doing more harm than good to their consumers.

Our job is to help clients clarify their own value systems. Our challenge is to help clients identify those parts of their value systems that prevent them from getting where they want to be. We do not substitute our values for values that are truly a part of the client's own system. Understandably, you cannot be expected to leave your values at home or to be completely "value neutral" in your work with people. Your values are a part of you, and denying or ignoring the fact that you have certain values is impossible. For that reason, it is important that you be aware of and understand your values so that you are in a position to ensure that you do not impose them on your clients.

Because you have your own values, you will inevitably encounter value conflicts in your work. You will be confronted with conflicts that your clients have with themselves, with others, and with you. In addition, you can expect to experience value conflicts of your own when dealing with the diverse clients that you will have in your work. You cannot expect to be effective in assisting your clients or in managing your own conflicts unless you are grounded within your personal value system.

Consider this scenario. You are working with a young client with a disability who is capable and qualified for a number of jobs, but she is unwilling to put forth the effort to seek and obtain employment. She has the potential to be successful in college, but clearly states that she has no interest in going back to school. She tells you that she believes it is "the government's responsibility" to take care of her because she has a disability. Your strong work ethic and value for education puts you in direct conflict with her position. What kinds of thoughts, emotions, and actions do you think would be a part of your response to her?

Another example might be your work with a married mother with a disability who is seeking rehabilitation services so she can find a job and move out on her own. She has three children ranging in ages from five to 15 and feels as though her life is slipping away from her. She dropped out of school when she was seventeen and pregnant. She is married, never worked, and is very bored with her life. She wants a job so she can escape from her family and live on her own. She said she loves her children but cannot take living with them or with her husband anymore. What kinds of thoughts, emotions, and actions do you think will be a part of your response to her?

Other examples of client value issues that commonly confront rehabilitation and other human service workers include abortion, religious differences, racial prejudice, divorce, pre-marital or extramarital affairs, the use of illegal drugs, and gay or lesbian lifestyles. Because these behaviors tend to be perceived as moral issues, many people are inclined to believe that there is a "right" and a "wrong" approach to them. The rehabilitation professional must be careful about drawing such conclusions and attempting to steer the client to a certain way of thinking. The ethical, albeit more challenging, responsibility is helping clients determine what is "right" and best for them.

BELIEFS AND ASSUMPTIONS

Closely related to our value system are the assumptions and beliefs that we have developed. Beliefs are just what the term implies. They are what we believe to be true about certain issues and they frequently evolve into assumptions about people. Beliefs significantly influence the thinking, behavior, and emotions that we apply in our interactions with our clients. Like values, we develop beliefs through our experiences in life and from what we have been told by people we trust. We treat beliefs as if they were facts rather than products of our personal perceptions and unique experiences. We incorporate them into our way of life and frequently never reconsider them.

Your beliefs are important as they pertain to human behavior and behavior change. Human service professionals hold different beliefs on these topics. In fact, these differences are the reason that we have such a variety of counseling theories. Some believe that the most effective way of helping people reach their goals is by focusing on behavior change. Others are convinced that real change will not take place unless primary emphasis is placed on having clients develop insight into their feelings and emotions. Still others believe that the focus should be on helping clients modify their thinking and self-talk, and that will result in behavior and emotional changes. You may have beliefs that coincide with one of these general lines of thought. If not, you will develop or formulate your own counseling theory or philosophy.

It is important that you consider the beliefs about human nature that you have brought with you as you prepare for a career in rehabilitation. In an effort to prime the pump for this process, consider the following questions and the extent to which your own beliefs coincide with these statements using this simple 1-5 scale: 5 = Strongly believe 4 = Believe 3 = Somewhat believe 2 = Disbelieve 1 = Completely disbelieve.

Be completely honest in your ratings. You do not have to share them with anyone else, so you do not have to worry about others' judgment. Just remember not to judge yourself either. You are simply trying to get some insight into beliefs that may affect your approach to rehabilitation work.

To what extent do you believe:

- people are basically good?
- people are inclined to growth and personal development?
- people are basically in control of their lives?
- people are basically happy?
- people genuinely want to find a meaning and purpose in life?
- peoples' lives are pretty much determined by their genes and environment?
- people cannot really understand themselves unless they understand their past?
- people are basically capable of understanding and acting on their problems?
- the most important thing a helper can give to a client is good advice?
- most of the problems that people have are connected to ineffective relationships?

- most of the problems that people have are connected to money?
- most of the problems that people have are related to what happened to them in childhood?
- what is more important than reality is the client's perception of reality?
- the most important roles of the helper are to serve as instructor, advisor, and problem solver for the client?
- i is more difficult for older people to change than for younger people to change.
- the best counselor for a person with a disability is someone who also has a disability.
- adolescents are generally resistant to change.
- people with mental retardation are usually happier than other people.
- people will make real change only if they are pushed into it.
- women make more motivated clients than men.
- people learn best by learning from their mistakes.
- effort does not count for anything unless the goal is achieved.
- some people do not want to change.
- people will only work with a counselor that they trust.
- rewards are more effective than punishment in getting people to change.

We already know something about the beliefs of professional helpers. Corey[11] suggests that truly effective helpers have a positive view of people and of life in general. The most effective workers believe in what they are doing because their work is grounded in their basic value and belief systems. They are confident and secure enough in themselves to be able to get into the worlds of others with genuine care and compassion. They respect others as people without necessarily condoning all of their behavior. They are open to change and personal growth, including a willingness to reassess their personal thinking, values, and beliefs.

BELIEFS RELATED TO PEOPLE WITH DISABILITIES

There is one specific area where beliefs are of particular importance to rehabilitation professionals. It is essential that people who embark on careers in this area carefully consider their beliefs, assumptions, and possible biases in relation to individuals with disabilities. All of us enter this career with noble intentions. We want to act on our belief that all people should have equal opportunities to realize their goals. We want to do something to equalize those opportunities. Some of us have direct experience with our own disabilities or with family members who have a disability. Others have not had these experiences. Yet, they believe they have something to contribute to this field. Regardless of our backgrounds, it is essential that we honestly and carefully assess what we believe and what we assume about people with disabilities.

It is no secret that the biggest handicaps faced by most people with disabilities are the attitudes of society. Our good intentions negate neither those experiences nor the effects that societal attitudes have had on our own thinking, beliefs, and perceptions. Therefore, before we get too deeply into a rehabilitation career, we have a responsibility to check out some of our beliefs about people with disabilities. We may have some hidden beliefs, but they will surely "seep" through unless we become aware of them.

Begin by taking about five minutes to brainstorm all of the adjectives that pop into your mind when you think about people with disabilities. Write the adjectives down. After you have finished, look at the words on your list and examine the values and attitudes that might be associated with these adjectives. Identify the words that you think may be a product of stereotypes about people with disabilities. Identify the words that most accurately depict what you think and how you feel about people with disabilities. Follow two rules to ensure that you will get something useful out of this little exercise. First, be honest with yourself; second, do not judge yourself.

Now, let us consider blindness as one example of a disability. Remember, these questions are also applicable to people with any kind of disability (deafness, mental retardation, spinal cord injury, cerebral palsy, stroke, head injury, mental illness, et cetera).

- Do I *really* believe that people who are blind can obtain and hold a job?
- What do I believe would be the most difficult obstacle for a person who is blind in getting a job?
- What do I think would probably interfere with a person who is blind getting a job that would not be an issue for a sighted person?
- What limitations do I believe people who are blind face in their social life?
- What kinds of problems do I believe a young person who is blind might experience in terms of dating?
- What kinds of problems do I believe a mother who is blind might have in raising her children?
- What kinds of problems do I believe that a worker who is blind would have working as a rehabilitation professional?
- Consider someone that you know who is blind, and then think of someone who is sighted but otherwise similar to the first person (age, gender, educational level, et cetera). What are some ways that I have responded differently to the person who is blind versus the other person? What different thoughts, feelings, and behaviors (even the most subtle) might there have been?

Consider other questions as you investigate your beliefs about people with disabilities and think about them as you examine the beliefs you bring to your career. It is important that you apply these kinds of questions to people with other kinds of disabilities including developmental disabilities, mental illnesses, substance abuse, HIV-AIDS, and others. Many rehabilitation professionals with disabilities have been affected by prejudice and adverse attitudes. Nevertheless, they may display similar attitudes toward people with disabilities that are different from their own. No one is immune to mistaken beliefs, but we cannot eliminate the ones we have unless we make an effort to become aware of what they are.

The purpose of these questions is not to get you to catch yourself or to find beliefs that are "wrong." Rehabilitation professionals have a higher responsibility to examine our beliefs, challenge some of them, and reestablish the validity of others. We are all products of experiences, observations, and lessons from our past. What might have seemed reasonable or unreasonable to you at an earlier time might change if subjected to scrutiny as you prepare yourself for a career in rehabilitation. The fact is that no one is perfect. We bring baggage with us into our careers just as we bring valuable strengths.

WHAT CAN YOU DO?

You will have many challenges as you embark upon your career in rehabilitation. One of the most important is that you rise to a level of individual professionalism that allows you to maximize the contributions that you are capable of making in your work with individuals with disabilities. Much of the work you have to do in developing your professionalism might be referred to as "inner work." You need to get to know yourself better by carefully examining your needs and motives for wanting to do this kind of work. You need to identify and clarify your personal values, beliefs, and assumptions as they relate to other human beings. Of particular importance is the need to understand and examine your attitudes and beliefs about people with disabilities. All of this will take time and should accompany your efforts in acquiring the knowledge and skills that are required to be an effective rehabilitation worker.

We have identified three general responsibility areas that are of particular importance to serious professionals. They include work habits, interpersonal habits, and professional development. As you review these areas, consider how you "fit" in terms of these three areas. You already have evidence on how you assume responsibilities by the way that you have approached your education and how you have handled yourself on various jobs, even if they were not in the field of rehabilitation.

We have already mentioned ethics, which is one of the most important realms of responsibility for a professional person. Ethics involves integrity and honesty. Without discussing it with anyone else, assess your own integrity as a student. To what extent have you done your own work? To what extent have you "cut corners" in terms of assignments and meeting course requirements? How frequently do you cut class because you can get away with it? Have you ever cheated on an assignment or an exam? These questions are not designed to embarrass you. They are private and their purpose is to provide examples of some of the ways that you can assess how well you carry out professional responsibilities.

It is very easy to look at a list of ethical qualities and say, "Yes, I can meet those," but things may change when it is time for action, and past behavior is the best predictor of future behavior. You have the power to change certain behaviors if they do not measure up to the standards that you want to set for yourself as a professional.

WORK HABITS

The first area of responsibility relates to "work habits." Professionals work both harder and smarter than workers who are simply doing their jobs. They are singled out and advance in their careers. This is because of the kind of work habits that they bring to and maintain on the job. One of the advantages of effective work habits is that they can be acquired and are not dependent on unique opportunities, inherent talents, intelligence level, physical strength, or external factors. They are under your control. Punctuality, communication skills, appearance, and initiative are four areas in which you can demonstrate work habits that support your level of professionalism.

PUNCTUALITY

Punctuality may seem like a message from your parents, or teacher, or spouse, but think about how frequently it is violated by people. Few things people value as much as their time. For most people, even money seems to take second place to time. Consideration of other peoples' time is a matter of courtesy. Being on time for work conveys the priority that you place on the job and the organization. With a little more organization and planning, you can acquire a reputation for being on time for appointments and meetings—a habit that gets favorable attention. Make a similar commitment to be sensitive to responding to telephone calls, electronic mail, and regular mail in a timely manner. The same principle applies to maintaining records, submitting reports, and meeting deadlines promptly and consistently. Be prepared for appointments, meetings, reports, and other responsibilities. The extent to which you have prepared yourself—even if others are not as conscientious—will reinforce your image as someone who places a priority on others' time and needs. People, from the boss, to the colleague, to the consumer, to the unknown inquirer, interpret it as an interest in them as individuals. That is precisely the message that a rehabilitation professional should convey.

COMMUNICATION

Another area on which you can build while you pursue your education is written and verbal communication. Rehabilitation workers are frequently more skilled in verbal communication than in written communication. Many of us are drawn to the human services field because others have recognized our effectiveness as listeners and communicators. Verbal interaction is usually one of our strengths. Written communication skills are frequently more challenging because most of us do not have as much "practice" with them. Regardless of your perceived strengths in terms of communication skills, there is always room to expand.

Reflect on the qualities that you personally consider a good communicator to have. Identify people (friends, relatives, work colleagues, teachers) that you consider to have exceptionally effective communication skills. What is it that they do that makes them so effective? What do they avoid doing that cause other people to be less effective in their communication skills? Find a model that you can quietly emulate in terms of verbal communication. Almost certainly, one of the strengths of that model will be the ability, and the willingness, to listen with understanding in any situation.

It is important to improve your writing skills. You will probably be responsible for extensive paperwork no matter what rehabilitation position you take. You will be expected to write clearly, concisely, and thoroughly. Two things are necessary for effective development of these skills. One is practice. Use every written assignment as an opportunity to practice your writing skills. Ask for feedback on your writing and for suggestions on ways you can improve it. Ask colleagues to review your work and give you suggestions on ways that it might be improved. Writing is a very personal activity and another person will always be more objective than you are when looking for ways to improve what you have written.

As previously mentioned, "the ability to communicate factored as the top method of evaluating professionalism."[52, A18] The study, conducted by the Polk-Lepson Research Group, included a relatively new area, internet etiquette, as one that many young workers are lacking. They mentioned things such as "texting, survey the internet, or responding to calls at inappropriate times"[A18] as problems in the workplace. This has the potential to be even more problematic in the rehabilitation field where good attending and listening skills are especially important.

APPEARANCE

While it may vary depending on the work setting, professionals have a certain amount of freedom about how they look and the appearance of their offices or work areas. The challenge is to balance that freedom with responsibility and good judgment. It is important that you pay attention to your appearance. One's appearance influences other people's perceptions and people draw conclusions based on our appearance. We have control over how we look, and we can use it to communicate our strengths. We can quietly reveal our good judgment, respect for others, awareness of propriety, and confidence in ourselves through the way that we present ourselves to others. Our personal grooming, hygiene, posture, body language, and dress can all be combined to demonstrate a level of professionalism that can gain the respect of other people. Do not confuse expensive clothing with a professional look. While expensive clothes may be of some help in making us look good, they can also run the risk of sending a message of poor judgment. It is as inappropriate to wear extravagant clothing to a homeless shelter, as it is to wear old jeans to an awards banquet. It boils down to personal judgment. When you are not sure about what is right, you are wise to check it out with colleagues or a supervisor.

Appearance also pertains to how you present your work area to consumers, colleagues, and others. Control over your immediate work environment is a privilege that comes with the status of your position. You want to balance that privilege with judgment and a level of responsibility that is consistent with your position. The setting in which you work tells a lot about you. It conveys something about your interests, your values, your work habits, and your consideration of others. You may not be able to control some things such as office size, quality of the furniture, carpeting, et cetera. What is important is how you take advantage of what is under your control. In some ways, your work area is an extension of your personality, and you have a right to set it up in a way that is pleasing to you. At the same time, your work involves other people and you will want to make a point of ensuring that your area is comfortable for consumers and colleagues. Distractions interfere with communication, and it is easy for an office or work area to have distractions. A messy and disorganized office is usually distracting for anyone who is interested in getting something done.

INITIATIVE

One of the things employers value most in an employee is the ability to see things that need to be done and then to act on that perception. Employees with initiative do not have to be "told" what to do; they anticipate what needs to be done and then they do something about it. Initiative is frequently a strong indicator of both professionalism and potential. Employers have plenty of workers who know how to do their jobs but never go beyond them. It does not occur to these employees to think outside the routine of their job even when they have some down time. These workers will do the work, but they need to be told to do it. In contrast, the person who takes initiative looks for opportunities to improve things. People with initiative are willing to go out of their way to contribute. Their motive is not to get special recognition or advancement—they simply take an approach to work that reflects their seriousness about it and their enjoyment of the challenge.

INTERPERSONAL SKILLS

A second area of development that can coincide with your educational preparation pertains to interpersonal skills. These skills are not "automatic" just because one has an interest in working with people. Like all skills, they must be developed and refined. Even if you work well with consumers, professional interactions are not limited to your work with consumers. You will also be engaged with colleagues, supervisors, administrators, parents, families, employers, and public officials, to name just a few. You need to be effective in all of all of these interactions.

Application of Rogers'[45] three core conditions for an effective helping relationship can take you a long way in any kind of relationship that you have as part of your job. First, you must be real. Take advantage of the work you have been doing to understand yourself as a person by becoming more authentic. People not only appreciate genuineness, they trust it. The pretentious person is easy to spot in our profession.

Second, make an effort to respect everyone. You do not have to like them, approve of their behavior, or agree with their thinking. Respect them simply because they are human beings. You try to do that with your consumers, but it can be applied in all types of relationships. You have to allow yourself to separate behavior and ideas from the person. It is not always easy, but a genuine respect for another person will break down communication barriers that others encounter simply because they do not allow themselves to see the basic worth that exists in everyone.

Finally, try to see things from the perspective of the other person. You do not have to agree with that person or change your own perspective. You will simply have a greater command of the issue or situation if you can empathize with others and open yourself to their views. The greater your understanding of the matter, the better your chances of getting your objectives met. Rogers believed these three core conditions were essential within a helping relationship, and we believe that incorporating them into any relationship, personal or professional, will result in a stronger and more productive relationship.[45]

You will probably be working with people with a variety of disabilities. The cardinal rule in your interactions with them is to relate to them in the same way that you would with anyone else. You will know enough about different disabilities to know what you should do (e.g., offer your arm rather than taking the arm of a person who is blind, position yourself to maintain eye contact with someone in a wheelchair, talk directly to a person with an intellectual disability rather than through another person). You will also know what to avoid (e.g., finishing sentences for someone with verbal aphasia, amplifying your voice for a person who is blind, covering your mouth when speaking around someone who lip-reads). Rehabilitation professionals have a responsibility to understand and practice basic etiquette around people with different disabilities. Other people will rely on you for cues on the proper way to behave. The most important lesson you can provide to them is that someone with a disability deserves and expects to be treated in the same way and with the same level of respect that you would provide to anyone else. The best way to deliver that message is to practice it.

In addition to the points that have been made about effective relationships, there are some suggestions that will distinguish you from those who take a less professional approach to their interactions with colleagues and supervisors. Remember that rehabilitation work is not "solo work" and that you will usually be a part of a staff or team. Collaboration is a critical responsibility, so put your ego aside because you are not competing with other team members. Be the one who always places the interests of the consumer as the team's top priority. Be willing to ask questions of others and be open to their feedback. At the same time, be willing to provide feedback to them, but do it with genuineness and respect if it is to have any constructive impact. Carry your share of the load and follow through on your assignments. Respect confidentiality, but always share information that other professionals need to do their jobs effectively. Make a point of learning agency policies and procedures. They sometimes make for boring reading, but you cannot follow them unless you know what they are. Understanding policies and procedures may not only streamline your work effort, but they can save you from potentially harmful mistakes. Avoid gossiping, bad-mouthing, or criticizing your agency or coworkers. It is very easy to fall into this habit regardless of your work setting, but negativity is destructive. Others may engage in it, but you can challenge yourself to stay away from it. It is not only inherently disrespectful of people; it is beneath the standards of professionalism.

REHABILITATION PHILOSOPHY

One of the definitions of the term "philosophy" is that it represents "the most general beliefs, concepts, and attitudes of an individual or group."[36] Rehabilitation professionals develop personal philosophies of rehabilitation through their work and personal experiences, but these personal philosophies are significantly influenced by the values, beliefs, attitudes, and priorities of the field as a whole. One of the attractions of rehabilitation as a career field is that it is dynamic in its reflection of the values and beliefs of society toward people with disabilities. Changes that have substantial effects on rehabilitation workers and the people they serve are happening constantly. As a professional, you have a responsibility to be aware of how your own philosophy of rehabilitation is evolving. Among the most critical current issues to the disability and rehabilitation communities are choice, language, integration, advocacy, and employment. Remember that it is not the issues but the values that underlie them that are relevant to the development of your personal rehabilitation philosophy.

Relinquishing "control" has been a difficult process for some rehabilitation workers. Many human service workers outside of rehabilitation continue to struggle with the idea of exchanging control for collaboration. They want to "help" people—but they want it to be on their terms. New professionals will be instrumental in transforming rehabilitation philosophy to one of "collaboration." Consumers cannot empower themselves unless they can make choices. They cannot make choices unless they have access to information about those choices. Rehabilitation professionals will ensure that their consumers are informed and in a position to make their own best decisions. They will then support consumers in following through on those decisions.

The language that rehabilitation personnel use reflects change. People with disabilities are no longer referred to as "handicapped." A handicap is viewed as a barrier that society imposes on people with disabilities, such as stairs or inaccessible buildings. Another change is the use of "people first" language. To reinforce the fact that the individual is more relevant than the disability, it is considered preferable to refer to a "person with a disability" or "individuals/persons with disabilities" rather than to "disabled person/people." Similarly, rather than "wheelchair bound" we talk about a person who is a wheelchair user and rather than a "CP" or "MR" we talk about a person who has cerebral palsy or a person with mental retardation. Individuals with disabilities generally endorse people first language, but there are exceptions to its general rule. For example, some people who are deaf or blind prefer to use these terms first ("deaf person" or "blind person") rather than "people who are deaf" or "people who are blind." It is important that you take note of how people with disabilities refer to themselves and then model your language after them. If in doubt, use people first language.

Integration is another fundamental philosophical concept within the field of rehabilitation. The deinstitutionalization of people with mental illness began in the 60's and soon began to focus on programs serving people with developmental disabilities. The movement was based on the conviction that people would be better served within their own communities in smaller, homelike settings, rather than in large institutions. While this trend has continued over the past 40 years, it has not included everyone. The fight against segregation of people with disabilities won a major battle in 1999 when the U.S. Supreme Court handed down what is known as the Olmstead[40] decision. This decision essentially ruled that people with disabilities had a right to live in the least restrictive environment possible.

Olmstead[40] was a court decision in which two women living in a state hospital sued the state for the right to live in the community. The physician treating the women agreed that they would be better served in the community, but the state kept them institutionalized because it was more "cost effective." The Supreme Court ruled in favor of the women. The Olmstead[40] decision is expected to have a major impact on the delivery of vocational rehabilitation services, because it is applicable to all settings in which an individual receives rehabilitation services.

While not the exclusive domain of rehabilitation workers, advocacy is one more major responsibility of professionals in this field. With societal attitudes and behaviors constituting the most restrictive barriers to freedom for people with a disability, rehabilitation personnel must constantly work with consumers to advocate change of these practices. Together, they must educate the public about the rights of people with disabilities as well as the contributions that they make to society. One example of disability advocacy is compelling businesses to make their buildings accessible to people with disabilities. In an effort to level the employment playing field for individuals with disabilities, educating employers about non-discriminatory hiring practices is a primary advocacy focus for rehabilitation professionals. Using people first language and politely correcting others who use derogatory language are other ways of advocating for people with disabilities. Contacting the media when they stereotype people with disabilities lends support to the rights of people with disabilities.

A major arena for advocacy of people with disabilities is in legislation and public policy. The whole field of rehabilitation has been shaped, in large part, by legislation at the federal level. Rehabilitation professionals have a responsibility to be alert to the constant evolution of issues affecting disabilities and rehabilitation. This can be fascinating because changes can sometimes be profound. For example, the Workforce Investment Act (WIA), the Ticket to Work and Work Incentives Improvement Act (TWWIIA),[51] and the Rehabilitation Services Administration's (RSA) Regulations have all been implemented within the last decade. Each of these initiatives has had major implications for employment opportunities of individuals with disabilities.

Policy, and the legislation that institutes it, will happen with or without you. As a rehabilitation professional, you will have opportunities to influence legislation at both the state and federal levels through advocacy activities. You will have an obligation to stay informed, not only of rehabilitation-related legislation, but also on a wide range of legislative issues that have direct and indirect effects on your consumers. Far from boring or mundane, being in command of public policy and pending legislation can be among the most powerful tools that you have as a practicing professional.

Unemployment among people with disabilities is approximately 70% and is a central issue for many rehabilitation programs. In addition to being a means of self-support and independence, employment in this country plays a key role in one's self-concept. Employment is one area in which people with disabilities have clearly been left behind.

The U.S. Department of Education's Rehabilitation Services Administration, the federal agency that oversees the implementation of the Rehabilitation Act, recently developed regulations to change the definition of "employment." In the past, extended or sheltered employment was considered acceptable vocational outcomes. The public vocational rehabilitation (VR) program's top priority is promoting access to competitive employment for people with severe disabilities. With this priority in mind, extended employment and sheltered employment are no longer considered viable vocational goals. This means that people who received services from a state VR system must receive services leading to jobs in the community that include people without disabilities. Make-work programs and jobs that pay sub-minimum wages may be personal options for some people with disabilities, but they are no longer supported by VR. The public program believes that people with severe disabilities have the ability to be competitively employed, if they are given the opportunity. It is to this end that the state VR agencies are investing their resources.

PROFESSIONAL DEVELOPMENT

The third area for which you can begin laying a foundation for the remainder of your rehabilitation career is to take care of yourself professionally and personally. Like most career areas in the 21st century, rehabilitation is constantly changing and the changes happen fast. Graduation is only the beginning. Your rehabilitation education will never really end. As a professional, you simply take over primary responsibility for it. Evans[13] defined professional development as "a process whereby people's professionality and/or professionalism may be considered to be enhanced."[p. 35] Evans states our role is to advocate for policy and practices that improve service provision. This includes advocating for legislation and policy that will support the independence and inclusion of people with disabilities in their communities. Recently, there has been much discussion about the use of evidence-based practice in rehabilitation. At a minimum, we owe it to our consumers to keep abreast of the literature and new developments in the field. Gray & McDonald[19] discuss the need to consider all aspects of an issue, including potential consequences, so that we can make better decisions. McLaughlin, et al.[35] advocate for using evidence-based research in our practice as well as using one's own experience and self-reflection. At any rate, practitioners demonstrate their professionalism and, thereby, their commitment to their consumers by staying abreast of current research.

CREDENTIALS

One way of ensuring that you keep up to date with your profession is to attain credentials related to it. You are in the process of earning one essential credential by completing your degree program. A degree in rehabilitation, or a closely related field, will qualify you for higher-level positions that are more challenging and better paying than those are that do not require a degree. Your degree may also qualify you for certification or licensure in specialty areas related to rehabilitation and human services.

While many licensure and certification credentials are restricted to individuals with master's and advanced level degrees, people with bachelor's degrees can qualify for a number of them. Examples of some of the certifications that may be available to undergraduate rehabilitation majors include Certified Disability Management Specialist (CDMS), Certified Biofeedback Therapist, Certified Psychiatric Rehabilitation Practitioner (CPRP), and Certified Case Manager (CCM). Most certifications require that you demonstrate knowledge and competencies in a specialized area. Certification is usually administered by a national organization and passing a standardized exam is typically required. It also requires having supervised experience, providing letters of reference, preparing a professional portfolio, or a combination of these.

Licensure is administered by individual states and the requirements are usually similar. Licensure tends to carry more weight than certification, because it has a legal base and restricts practice of the specialty to those who have earned licenses. States vary in the types of licenses they offer and their requirements so you will need to check on what kinds of licenses are available in your own state. Information on both licensure and certification should be available through your academic department. In many states, the licensed chemical dependency counselor (LCDC) only requires a bachelor's degree.

A credential demonstrates that you have met certain preparatory requirements and holding one can put you at an advantage over applicants and workers who do not have one. Possessing a credential suggests to your employer that you will be updating your knowledge and skills through continuing education activities. Virtually all credentials require that you engage in a specific number of continuing education contact hours each year relevant to your specialization. Most have specific requirements for training in professional ethics as part of the certification renewal process. Continuing education is an example of the kind of responsibility that you assume as a professional in your occupation. While your employer may not "require" it, you can continue your training through workshops, seminars, and conferences because of your personal commitment to quality performance as a rehabilitation professional.

PROFESSIONAL ORGANIZATIONS

Another valuable resource to help you keep your rehabilitation knowledge and skills current is the professional organization. These organizations are designed to provide a collective voice for professionals and to give members opportunities to interact on issues of relevance to their profession. Most organizations sponsor annual or biannual conferences at which practitioners, researchers, and experts exchange information on new and innovative practices in the field. Additionally, the organization usually publishes a journal with articles that are of direct interest and relevance to its membership. The journals are one of the most convenient and practical means you have for keeping your information, ideas, and practices up to date. While new information is usually a product of research, most rehabilitation journals are geared to the practitioner and the research is presented in a way that can be understood and used by people who are providing rehabilitation services. Another advantage of involvement in professional organizations is the opportunity to become personally active in your profession.

Because professional organizations depend upon the volunteer work of members, there are opportunities to participate on committees, work groups, special projects, and hold offices within the organization. Students and new professionals oftentimes think that others would not be interested in their involvement, because they are too green. That is a false assumption. The leaders of most organizations will welcome your involvement if you are committed and willing to work. Active participation in a professional organization can be an education in itself and provide you with opportunities for new relationships and experiences that significantly broaden the scope of your rehabilitation expertise.

Here are some examples of associations related to rehabilitation that you might wish to explore:

- The National Rehabilitation Association (nationalrehab.org),
- The US Psychiatric Rehabilitation Association (uspra.org),
- The Association of Persons in Supported Employment (apse.org),
- The ARC (thearc.org),
- The Mental Health America (nmha.org), and
- The American Association of Persons with Disabilities (aapd.org).

HELPING YOURSELF

Finally, your professional development depends a great deal on how well you take care of your personal self. Working with people can be fascinating, rewarding, and fun, but it can also be demanding, stressful, and frustrating. To survive in this business, you need to make sure that you do what you can to keep yourself one-step ahead of its challenges. Too many human service workers burn out of their professions, not because the work is too much for them, but because they did not find a way to maintain their initial interest and enthusiasm. You will have experiences that will make you question whether you were really cut out for this kind of work. You will make mistakes, have conflicts with colleagues, be corrected by supervisors, and watch some of your consumers fail. You will probably come to know the frustrations that accompany working in a bureaucracy and sometimes think that no one except you really cares about the consumer. This is just part of the job, and your professionalism can be measured in part by how you handle it.

To handle these challenges, you must make sure that your life consists of more than your work. You never stop being a rehabilitation professional but you cannot focus on your work all of the time. We have all known workaholics. They stand out in the work setting because they always seem to be working so hard. The problem is that they are the ones who frequently short-change their consumers because they leave the profession early by burn out or by killing themselves with work and stress. You want to develop ways to take care of your physical, social, emotional, and spiritual self by developing balance in your life. Balance takes planning, organization, and will power. Truly effective professionals avoid the temptation to limit their energies to one thing and neglect the other areas of importance.

Another important resource in dealing with the challenges of your profession is the help that is available to you from other professionals. When things get too overwhelming in our lives, we should have the wisdom to allow ourselves to work with a counselor who can help us. Too many of us have difficulty in asking for help when we need it. We pride ourselves as specialists in giving help, but we have a poor track record of requesting it from others. That says much about our confidence in our own business. It is not easy to go to someone else for help, yet if no one did, most of us would be out of business. Just because we have a degree in one of the helping fields does not make us immune to the problems, pressures, and misfortunes that everyone experiences. Working with a counselor can help us learn how to deal with problems and live more effectively. Likewise, it usually exposes us to new ways of working more effectively with our own consumers. There are times in all of our careers when we could benefit from a counseling relationship in which we are the consumer. Use the knowledge that you have about the field of helping to take advantage of this resource in your own life.

REFERENCES AND BIBLIOGRAPHY

[1]ADA Amendments Act. (2008). *Public Law 110 – 325.*

[2]Americans with Disabilities Act. 1990. *Public Law 101-356.*

[3]Andersen, D. G. (1993). The journey toward professionalism. *National Forum 73*(1), 11-13.

[4]Barton, L. (1996). *Disability and Society: Emerging Issues and Insights.* New York: Longman Publishing.

[5]Blau, P. M. & Scott, W. R. (1962). *Formal Organizations.* San Francisco: Chandler Publishing Company.

[6]Brown, S. (2000). *Freedom of Movement: Independent Living History and Philosophy*. Houston, TX: ILRU Bookshelf Series.

[7]Boyt, T., Lusch, R., & Naylor, G. (2001). The role of professionalism in determining job satisfaction in professional services:a study of marketing researchers. *Journal of Service Research, 3*(4), 321 – 330.

[8]Cogan, M. (1955). The problem of defining a profession. *Annals of the American Academy of Political and Social Science, 297*, 105-111.

[9]Condeluci, A. (1995). *Interdependence: The Route to Community.* Winterpark, FL: GR Press Inc.

[10]Corey, G. (2005). *Theory and practice of counseling and psychotherapy* (7th ed.). Pacific Grove, CA: Brooks-Cole/Wadsworth.

[11]Corey, G. (1998). *Becoming a helper* (3rd ed.). Pacific Grove, CA: Brooks-Cole/Wadsworth.

[12]*Encyclopedia of Social Work.* 19th ed. R. L. Edwards (Ed.). (Washington, DC: National Association of Social Workers, 1994).

[13]Evans, L. (2008). Professionalism, Professionality and the Development of Educational Professionals. *British Journal of Educational Studies 50*(1), 20-38.

[14]Evenson, T. L., & Holloway, L. (2000). Competencies of baccalaureate-level rehabilitation workers in community rehabilitation programs. *Rehabilitation Education 14*, 115-132.

[15]Evenson, T. L., & Holloway, L. (2006). The state of undergraduate rehabilitation education: A Survey of undergraduate coordinators. *Rehabilitation Education 2*, 103-113.

[16]Evenson, T. L., & Holloway, L. (2007). Undergraduate rehabilitation: An essential rung on the rehabilitation career ladder. *Rehabilitation Education 21*, 73 - 86.

[17]Fine, M. & Ash, A. (1988). Disability beyond stigma: social interaction, discrimination, and activism. *Journal of Social Issues, 44,* 3 –21.

[18]Goffman, E. (1963). *Stigma.* New York: Simon & Schuster, Inc.

[19]Grey, M. & McDonald, C. (2006). Pursuing good practice: the limits of evidence-based practice. *Journal of Social Work, 6*(1), 7 – 20.

[20]Hall, R. (1968). Professionalization and bureaucratization. *American Sociological Review, 33*, 92-104.

[21]Haug, M. & Sussman, M. (1969). Professionalism and the public. *Social Problems, 17*, 153-161.

[22]Herbert, J. T., Barrett, K., Evenson, T., & Jacob, C. J. (2010). Work role and functions of undergraduate rehabilitation services alumni: a pilot study. *Rehabilitation Education, 24,* 149 – 166.

[23]Hoch, D. (2000). Professionalism. *Scholastic Coach & Athletic Director, 69* (6), 10-11.

[24]Holloway, L., & Evenson, T. (2003). Promoting professionalism in human service education. *Human Service Eduation, 23*(1), 5-24.

[25]Hoyle, E. (2001). Teachiner: prestige, status, and esteem. *Educational Management & Administration, 29*(2), 139 – 152.

[26]Hughes, E. (1958). *Men and their work.* New York: Free Press.

[27]Hughes, E. (1967). Professions. In K. S. Lynn (Ed.). *The professions in America.* (pp. 1-14). Boston: Beacon Press.

[28]Illich, I. & Zola, I. K. 1977. *Disabling professions.* London: Marion Boyars.

[29]Individuals with Disabilities Education Act. (2004). *Public Law 108 – 446.*

[30]Kitchener, K. S. (1984). Intuition, critical evaluation and ethical principles: The foundation for ethical decisions in counseling psychology. *Counseling Psychologist, 12*(3), 43-55.

[31]Loh, K. (2000). Professionalism, where are you? *ENT: Ear, Nose & Throat Journal, 79* (4), 242-245.

[32]Maister, D. H. (1997). *True professionalism.* New York: The Free Press.

[33]Mannheim, B. & Papo, E. (2000). Differences in organizational commitment and its correlates among professional and nonprofessional occupational welfare workers. *Administration in Social Work, 23* (3/4), 119 – 137.

[34]McClean, H. (1999). Never give in. *Vital Speeches of the Day, 65* (21), 663-665.

[35]McLaughlin, A., Rothery, M., Babins-Waner, R., Schleifer, B. (2010). Decision-making and evidence in direct practice. *Clinical Social Work, 38,*155-163.

[36]Miriam-Webster's On-line Dictionary—http://www.m-c.com/cgi-bin/dictionary (2002).

[37]Murphy, S. T. & Rogan, P. (1995). *Closing the shop.* Baltimore: Paul H. Brookes Publishing Co.

[38]Pascarella, P. (1997). Book Review of Maister's *True Professionalism. Management Review, 86*(9), 47-49.

[39]Peterson, J. V., & Nisenholz, B. (1987). *Orientation to counseling.* Boston: Allyn & Bacon.

[40]Olmstead V. L.C. (1999). 57 U.S. 581, 119 S.Ct. 2176.

[41]Rehabilitation Act 1992 Amendments. (1992). *Public Law 102-569.*

[42]Rehabilitation Act 1998 Amendments. (1998). *Public Law 105-220.*

[43]Reinders, H. (2009). The transformation of human services. *Journal of Intellectual Disability Research, 52*(7), 564 – 572.

[44]Ritzer, G. (1971). Professionalism and the individual. In E. Freidson (Ed.). *The professions and their prospects* (pp. 59-73). Beverly Hills: Sage Publications.

[45]Rogers, C. R. (1951). Client-centered therapy. *Boston: Houghton Mifflin.*

[46]Scott, R. A. (1991). *The making of blind men.* (2nd ed.). New Brunswick, NJ: Transaction Publishers.

[47]Shapiro, J. P. (1994). *No pity.* New York: Times Brooks.

[48]Skrtic, T. M. (1991). *Behind special education: A critical analysis of professional culture and school organization.* Denver: Love.

[49]Stubbins, J. (1988). The politics of disability. In H. E. Yuker (Ed.), *Attitudes Toward Persons with Disabilities* (pp. 22-32). New York, NY: Springer.

[50]Syzmanski, E. M. & Treuba, H. (1994). Castification of people with disabilities. *Journal of Rehabilitation, 60*(3), 12-20.

[51]Ticket to Work and Work Incentives Improvement Act. (1999). *Public Law 106 – 170.*

[52]Up Close. (2010). Young workers fail at professionalism, survey concludes. *Journal of Business, February 10, 2010,* A18.

[53]Van Zandt, C.E. (1990). Professionalism: A matter of personal initiative. *Journal of Counseling and Development, 68,* 243-245.

[54]Weiss, C. (1981). The development of professional role commitment among graduate students. *Human Relations, 34,* 12-31.

[55]Wright, B. (1983). *Physical disability: A psychosocial approach* (2nd ed.). New York: Harper & Row.

ETHICAL ISSUES IN REHABILITATION

Joseph F. Stano
Springfield College
Katherine E. Stano
Argosy University
Steven Diamond
Massachusetts Rehabilitation Commission

Chapter Topics

- Introduction
- Terminology
- Enforceable Standards of Ethical Practice
- Summary
- Case Study

INTRODUCTION

Today, both the professional and public literature is replete with articles concerning ethical issues. These ethical questions concern both the general ways that one should conduct oneself in social behavior and discourse and the ways in which various professionals must comport themselves consistent with the accepted standards of professional behavior. As the world becomes increasingly complex in a synergistic way, ethical concerns are at the forefront of many persons' thoughts. An example of the ubiquitous nature of ethics can be shown by the existence of the weekly column on ethics that appears in the Sunday New York Times Magazine. Two or three ethical issues are addressed in each column. The issues raised concern the spheres of both personal and professional behavior. The column has a wide readership and the author always bases the column upon inquiries from readers.

A logical place to begin this chapter is with a definition of the word *ethics* itself. Neulicht, et al.,[2] define ethics as "referring to character or customs, generally describes how to evaluate life through a set of standards and how to regulate behavior."

A deconstruction of this definition is now in order. One starts with the word *character*. The emphasis here can be upon the nature of one's being and how one responds to the myriad circumstances experienced on a daily basis. Another way of partially conceptualizing the term is to regard it as "a sense of right and wrong." Every day each of us has to make innumerable choices with regard to our behavior that are essentially ethical in nature even though they may initially not appear to be so. For instance, you are approaching a traffic light that begins to turn yellow. You have the choice of stopping at the light, and someone behind you honks their horn to indicate that you should have gone through so they could have, or you proceed, or speed up to get through the light. On its surface, this may not appear to be an ethical dilemma–but it is. Going through the light may be considered an ethical lapse. Traffic laws are rules of behavior and ethics are rules of behavior. There exists a considerable overlap between the two.

Our daily lives are filled with a constant stream of ethical decisions like the above. It can be argued that these instances constitute at least a partial reflection of our character. We are judged by our overt behavior(s). Our intentions cannot be judged or evaluated–thoughts cannot be measured. A logical argument can, therefore, be made that our behavior is our character. If we act consistently in an unkind, thoughtless, and hurtful manner this is an accurate reflection of who we are. This is our character. The reverse is also true; if we are thoughtful, kind, and empathic, this is who we are. Human existence and behavior is certainly more complex than this in the onrushing stream that is our daily lives, but it is a tangible place to begin the discussion.

The second component of the above definition is the word *customs*. Again, an explanation of the word is warranted. Customs cannot be understood without a context. There are actually multiple contexts involved. The first context is historical–customs change over time. As will be explored later in this chapter, the technological revolution of the last thirty years has resulted in countless changes in both social and professional behavior(s). A second context is societal. Each country or ethnic group safeguards a body of customs; members of that group are expected to adhere to these "rules of behavior." Third, customs are also familial. Individual families develop a set of customs over the course of their history. How a particular family celebrates a holiday, religious day, or a day important to that particular family, for example an anniversary or birthday, has elements of uniqueness for that family. Finally, there are individual customs or ways of behaving in routine circumstances. There is a considerable amount of overlap between these four components of customs. Certainly, different components have primacy at different times and circumstances. While this is true, it is also true that customs do have a continuing and significant effect upon our daily behavior.

The third component of the definition is concerned with "*how to evaluate life through a set of standards*." As is expected, this phrase both has to be deconstructed and it is more complex than it initially appears. The second part of this component will be addressed first–"*a set of standards*." All of us have a set of rules of behavior in our mind. These rules are concerned with both the way(s) we wish to be treated and the way(s) we wish to treat others. Even though each of us possess this internal code of behavior these "rules" may not be readily apparent to us. For one to be able to conceptualize one's own personal code of conduct an important ability is necessary. If one cannot verbalize some of the basic components of their personal code of conduct, it may not be fully formed. This person would find it difficult to act in an appropriate way when a particular circumstance presents itself. Familiarity with one's mentally formulated code of conduct, results in facility. In other words, the person acts as they ethically intended and it appears to be a seemingly "automatic" act. Our "*set of standards*" is not a natural thing–we have to devote time and mental energy to conceptualize them in our mind and be able to act seamlessly in an appropriate way.

Now the first part of the phrase, "*how to evaluate life*," will be examined. There are essentially two components to be considered here. The first is the internal frame of reference. When one evaluates one's life the internal perspective certainly is important. It is a necessary but not sufficient component of the evaluation process. Each of us constantly evaluates our behavior and its appropriateness. Was our response, both behaviorally and verbally, healthy and empathic? As mentioned above, this is predicated upon our ability to understand and evaluate, in a temporally consistent way, our behavior as it is actually occurring. While this internal frame of reference is important, it is not sufficient. One could have an unhealthy set of values, rationalize, and justify why their harmful behavior is appropriate.

The second frame of reference is, of course, the external component. One's behavior is also evaluated by others and their judgments constitute a considerable component of how we are judged in society. These judgments may be of two types: first, how the person(s) with whom we are directly interacting judge our behavior, and second, how persons who are tangentially involved in the social interaction judge our behavior. Both the internal and external perspectives are necessary components of the evaluation of behavior. If one had a skewed or pathological set of values, then one would consider that their behavior was acceptable even though others would judge the behavior as harmful. Ultimately, there has to be consistency between one's self-evaluations and the evaluations of others. If consistency is achieved, then one can reasonably assume that the behavioral response was acceptable and consistent with general societal values.

The last component of the definition will now be addressed. This is "*how to regulate behavior*." This phrase is predicated upon the fact that behavior has to be regulated. To answer the heretofore-unasked question, "yes, behavior does have to be regulated." The means and manner of behavior regulation are the crucial issues here. One can certainly make the argument that behavior can be regulated both individually and socially. Some examples of socially regulated behavior are eating and sleeping. We decide when we want to eat and what we want to eat. Likewise, we decide when we will sleep. There are economic and societal constraints on both of these behaviors. What we eat is determined by economic resources. How much we sleep may be partially determined by what responsibilities we have in our lives and how these responsibilities dictate the amount of sleep that we can obtain verses the amount of sleep we require.

Behavior is essentially regulated by reinforcement. We respond to signals or cues in our environment. Healthy interactions are positively reinforced and negative interactions are negatively reinforced. The maxim, "behavior has consequences" is certainly true. Those consequences may be positive, such as a growing sense of communication and intimacy with someone, or negative, in that we may be rejected and treated as an outcast because of our behavior. One's ability to read social cues is crucial. This is closely linked to the development of a personal code of behavior and its recognition in real time social intercourse. If there is no significant underlying psychopathology, this reinforcement system is quite effective. This does not mean that we are able to evaluate situations and ourselves accurately in every instance. We become better as time goes on if we pay attention to the feedback loop that life provides. As a simplistic example, consider how a fifteen year old would evaluate a situation as compared to a twenty-five year old.

The definition of ethics has now been thoroughly deconstructed and considered. Next, let us consider the general importance of the field of ethics and of general rules of conduct.

IMPORTANCE OF ETHICS AND CODES OF CONDUCT

The next issue has as its focus, the reason why the discussion of ethics is of crucial importance. To begin, it is important to realize that the varieties of behavior are what essentially constitute human interactions. While eighty percent or more of this behavior is verbal, physical behavior also has to be fully considered. We human beings are social creatures–we could not exist in a mentally healthy state without both human interaction and human relationships. In addition to being social creatures, we are also creatures who are governed by rules. The universe is a conglomeration of complex rules that we are only now beginning to understand. Likewise, we realize that human relationships are also governed by complex rules.

Consider the role of parents and their young children. From the perspective delineated above, a fundamental role of a parent or parents is to instill into the child that society is governed by rules and the underlying purpose of these rules. This is expanded upon when the child begins the formal education process usually around the age of five. More rules are learned, the complexities of these rules are further explored, the "on-the-job" training of applying these rules is practiced, and behavior is modified as the result of a feedback loop. Throughout the course of any individual's life, this process is repeated and the increasing complexity is an essential hallmark.

No matter what the context in life, the individual is governed by rules. Throughout history, people have espoused the concept of personal freedom. Many people draw an inaccurate and specious conclusion from these strivings. What they many times envision as "freedom" is essentially the absence of rules, or anarchy. History is replete with the case histories of groups, from families to nations, where the absence of rules was the modus operandi for varying lengths of time. The results uniformly were chaos and the surfacing of the baser nature of human instincts.

What people were yearning for in these situations was not the absence of rules, but a system of rules that were not overtly or overly repressive or restrictive. Given the above, the case has been made for both human beings and human structures, such as societies, to be rule oriented and governed. A major area of human nature is the area of the rules that govern human interactions. It must be remembered that human children are born both asocial and amoral. As hinted at above, the significant individuals in a child's life are the persons who help the child to recognize the reality of rules and to learn the consequence for either following them or not following them.

Because of the above-delineated process, each individual develops a personal code of conduct. It could be argued that life could be more manageable if each individual formalized this code of conduct by writing it down and committing it to instantaneous recall. Life is not that simple. Although much has been written about moral education, it is not directly emphasized in formal education. For most individuals, the development and use of a code of personal conduct is a process that can be characterized as "learn as you go." That is, if the individual is fortunate enough to have a variety of both individuals and experiences that result in the formulation of a code of personal conduct and its implementation as appropriate in human interactions.

What are still not addressed are the applications of general codes of conduct to specific personal and eventually professional situations. As the individual enters adolescence, with its hormone-driven components, new vistas of conduct emerge regarding both dating and mating behavior. The life of the individual becomes much more complex. Adulthood slowly begins to emerge. With this emergence, the issues of career choice, and adult and professional identity further obfuscate the landscape.

The emergence of young adulthood routinely dovetails with professional aspirations, the actual choice of a profession, the training necessary to enter the chosen profession, and entry in the profession itself. Embedded in the curriculum and professional preparation for every profession is exposure to the ethical canons and circumstances that the practitioner is likely to confront in the course of professional practice. It may be argued that a profession cannot be seen or considered a profession if there is not a code of professional conduct or ethics. Ethical canons vary from profession to profession. The ethical code of conduct of architects is different from that of professional counselors, but each code of conduct is as important to its respective profession as is the other.

For instance, if an architect ignores the laws of physics or mathematics the structure that the practitioner is designing may not be physically possible, or if constructed, may be deadly to its inhabitants. Likewise, the professional counselor is governed by a set of ethical canons. If practitioners do not follow their ethical canons, the consumers who came to them for assistance in adjusting to their life situation or for relief of pain and distress, are not adequately or ethically served. Before proceeding further, it is necessary to examine some concepts that are integral to counseling and rehabilitation practice and to contextualize these concepts.

TERMINOLOGY

TERMINOLOGY ASSOCIATED WITH ETHICAL PRACTICE

The Commission on Rehabilitation Counselor Certification (CRCC)[1] issues the "Code of Professional Ethics for Rehabilitation Counselors." The latest revision of this code of conduct was adopted in 2009. In the Glossary of Terms of this document, thirty-three terms are defined. Six of those terms are especially relevant to the present discussion. The verbatim definitions of these terms will first be provided followed by a brief discussion of the appropriateness, and relevance of each term with regard to the profession.

Autonomy. The right of clients to be self-governing within their social and cultural framework. The right of clients to make decisions on their own behalf.

Beneficence. To do good to others; to promote the well-being of clients.

Confidentiality. A promise or contract to respect the privacy of clients by not disclosing anything revealed to rehabilitation counselors except under agreed-upon conditions.

Fidelity. To be faithful; to keep promises and honor the trust placed in rehabilitation counselors.

Justice. To be fair in the treatment of all clients; to provide appropriate services to all.

Nonmaleficence. To do no harm to others.

It is perhaps appropriate to begin this discussion with the deconstruction of the term "*nonmaleficence*" since it may have the longest history of all of the terms. This term bears its ancestry directly from the ancient Greek, Hippocrates, who is generally recognized as the father of medicine. In the Hippocratic Oath, which new physicians still recite, the first rule of medicine is "to first do no harm." Our clients come to us with one overriding and preeminent expectation–that they will be helped and not harmed through our work with them.

Next to be considered is the concept of "*fidelity*." The root of this definition concerns trust. If our clients cannot trust us then we do not have a therapeutic relationship. Earning the client's trust is the initial basis of the counseling relationship. Once this standard is reached, the pragmatic of the counseling relationship can begin.

Third, is the term "*beneficence*." When one considers the ultimate role of the counseling professional, it is to promote the well-being of clients. That is why our clients come to see us. So that we can engage in a relationship of mutual respect and assist clients in working through the issues and situations that result in distress in their lives. Through the concept of beneficence, we partner with our client so that they may construct a fuller picture of self that, in turn, can be used to facilitate self-growth and problem resolution.

Fourth, "*autonomy*" involves the right of clients to make decisions on their own behalf within their social and cultural frameworks. Professional counselors have to realize that each client has the right to make all of the decisions concerning their life. The exceptions to this rule generally involve clients who are not adults and clients who have been determined by the court as incapable of making decisions that are in their best interest. Counselors must also respect the decisions that their clients make with two other exceptions; self-harm and harm to others. If these exceptions do not apply, then the counselor, within the context of their professional relationship, works with the client to evaluate possible decisions and the decision making process to result in the healthiest possible outcome. These decisions are also governed and effected by both the social and cultural frameworks in which the client is living.

Fifth, the concept of "*justice*" is also crucial to a successful counseling relationship. There are essentially two sub-components here; first, the counseling professional must be fair in the treatment of all clients and, second, the professional must provide appropriate services to all. One can argue that the first component of the definition concerns the concepts of respect and unconditional positive regard for the client. The second component involves a commitment by the professional to understand the client to meet their needs within the context of the professional relationship.

Last, the concept of "*confidentiality*" is crucial to any counseling relationship. Leston Havens, a professor at Harvard Medical School and a practicing psychiatrist entitled one of his books *A Safe Place*. His thesis was that the counseling room should be a place where clients are free to discuss the intimate details of their lives with no fear that this material will be shared with anyone else. This is essentially the concern of confidentiality. Anytime information is shared with a third party, the client must give their permission ahead of time and the client is free to deny permission and to accept the consequences of that denial.

When professional rehabilitationists enter their practice or work environment they are held to all of the canons of ethical practice as put forth by CRCC. Failure to adhere to these canons can result in various punitive measures with a subsequent devastating effect upon their career. This is the subject of the next section.

ETHICAL BREACHES AND SANCTIONS

Any ethical breach is a serious matter and the reported behavior will be investigated by a professional or governing body. A variety of sanctions may be applied to the individual. Two sources of reprimand need to be considered. If the individual practitioner holds a national certification or they are a member of a professional organization, sanctions may be imposed by either one or both of these organizations that can affect the ability to practice. Second, if the individual holds a professional license, then the state in which the license is granted will investigate the reported incident. Overriding both of the situations is the matter of legal action that could result in a civil or criminal charge being brought against the practitioner.

An ethical breach can be reported to any or all of the organizations by a client or the client's representative. Once reported, all incidents must be investigated. Sanctions are then determined by the investigating body if the practitioner is found to be in violation of one or more of the ethical canons. Because of a practitioner being found in violation, one or more actions may be taken. There are varieties of sanctions that may be implemented. The practitioner may be verbally reprimanded and additional actions may be taken. These include mandatory remediation. For instance, the practitioner exceeds their scope of practice concerning psychological testing. The mandatory remediation could include workshop participation to develop skills and supervision by a consulting practitioner to determine that the remediated practitioner has developed the requisite skills to practice in the area. Another sanction could be the suspension of a professional license for a period while the practitioner completes a remediation program. Revocation of a professional license may also be the sanction; this revocation may be for an indeterminate period or it may be permanent.

Finally, legal action may be undertaken. This could be a civil complaint resulting in a lawsuit or it may result in a criminal charge. The impetus behind any sanction is the protection of both present and potential future clients. A brief case in point will illustrate the matter. Let us assume a practitioner has the ability to bill Medicaid for third party reimbursement. The practitioner starts falsifying paperwork and bills Medicare for services that were not provided and the practitioner bills for clients not actually seen for services. The practitioner's deception is eventually discovered. The following actions then take place; each action is independent of the others. First, the practitioner is removed as a member from the requisite professional organization(s). Next, the practitioner's license to practice in any or all states is suspended and then revoked. Finally, criminal charges are brought against the practitioner. The practitioner is found guilty of the charges and the punishment will include mandatory reimbursement of the funds and a possible prison sentence. All of these actions are undertaken to protect all clients.

MULTIDIMENSIONALITY OF REHABILITATIONIST ETHICAL PRACTICE

Ethics, Codes of Ethical Practice, and Ethical Decision-Making must be considered in context. So, the question becomes, what is/are the Contexts of Ethics, Ethical Practice, and Ethical Decision-Making for Rehabilitationists? Three contexts immediately come to mind when one considers the interface of Ethics and Rehabilitation Practice. These contexts are:

- the general practice of healthcare,
- disability, impairment, and functionality within the context of medical conditions, and
- the psychological aspects of disability or the psychology of disability.

First, consider ethical practice in rehabilitation vis-à-vis the healthcare system. Since disability is ultimately seen as a diagnosable condition, whether medical or psychological, and diagnosis is the first step in medical practice, it follows that disability is a healthcare concern. Taken in this context, rehabilitationists can be seen as healthcare providers in the broad sense of the word. Rehabilitationists function within the healthcare system and/or interact within the system on a continual basis. It, therefore, follows that rehabilitationists must adhere to the ethical principles relevant to healthcare in general. These rehabilitation professionals are an integral part of the healthcare team.

Second, all chronic conditions are, by definition, disabilities. A chronic condition can be defined as one that manifests itself for at least six months duration and perhaps a lifetime. While there is no unified definition of the terms disability, impairment, and functionality, chronic health conditions are seen and described through each of these three lenses. A diagnosis of a condition that is seen as chronic is commonly seen as a disability. How the actual diagnosable chronic condition affects the individual's daily life is viewed through the prisms of both impairment and functionality. This can be considered the medical component with regard to ethics and ethical practice.

Third, regardless of the nature of the chronic health condition or disability there is a psychological component. Since chronic health conditions may lead to diminished function over time, the individual must learn to adjust or cope with both the actual condition and its progression. Adjustment is the purview of the field of Psychology of Disability. Coping and adjustment are continual processes that are never mastered. Different conditions, differing progression, and the uniqueness of the individual make for a multivariate matrix. A person with a disability must constantly call upon coping resources and continually refine and expand their coping and adjustment repertoire. This results in continual and ever-changing ethical dilemmas for the Rehabilitation practitioner. The issue then becomes the nature and scope of the actual ethical canons in Rehabilitation practice. This is the concern of the next section.

ENFORCEABLE STANDARDS OF ETHICAL PRACTICE

ETHICAL PRACTICE COMPONENTS IN REHABILITATION

CRCC has put forth twelve Enforceable Standards of Ethical Practice. Each of these standards can be considered an "area" with several components or dimensions. These areas are listed below.

- The Counseling Relationship
- Confidentiality, Privileged Communication, and Privacy
- Advocacy and Accessibility
- Professional Responsibility
- Relationships with Other Professionals
- Forensic and Indirect Services
- Evaluation, Assessment, and Interpretation
- Teaching, Supervision, and Training
- Research and Publication
- Technology and Distance Counseling
- Business Practices
- Resolving Ethical Issues

It is important to note that ethical codes of conduct are revised on a periodic basis. Any field of endeavor changes over time. Since the profession of Rehabilitation Counseling was recognized by the federal government in 1954, there have been constant and significant changes and developments in the profession. The development and growth of Private Rehabilitation, the more recent advent of Forensic Rehabilitation, the recognition of new diagnostic categories–both medical and psychological, and the explosion of technology have resulted in a continual revision process.

Codes of Professional Ethics have to be viewed as organic documents; growth and change will be a continual process. For instance, a brief consideration of technology validates this point. The current code of ethical practice addresses distance counseling. This area will be one where there will be a need for almost constant change of ethical canons. This is mitigated by the rate of change of technology itself.

Consider the technological advance of SKYPE. This service is available with any computer with Internet connectivity.

- What are the ethical issues regarding the privacy surrounding this technology?
- What about different time zones or different countries?
- What about cultural issues?
- If licensure is a state issue, what are the ethical concerns surrounding the counselor residing in one state and the client residing in another?
- In which state or states does the counselor need to be licensed?

CASE STUDY

THE CASE OF FREDERICK SOWA

Frederick Sowa is a Vocational Rehabilitation Counselor for the Montana Division of Vocational Rehabilitation. His first client on Monday morning is James Bailicki. Mr.Bailicki is a forty-three year old individual with a five year history of relapse-remitting multiple sclerosis. Until six months ago, his adult work history consisted primarily of working as a general laborer in various industries. Due to the progression of his condition, he is no longer able to do such work.

He has recently applied for Social Security Disability Benefits but no decision has yet been made. He is currently receiving Montana Transitional Assistance. He currently resides in an apartment in Bozeman with his fiancé, Brenda Larson, a twenty-year-old student at Montana State University. He is seeing Mr. Sowa and hopes to become a client eligible for services. He has applied to the university and is hoping for assistance in paying for education. He is seeking to earn a degree in agricultural economics.

Mr. Sowa begins the intake interview process so that an eventual decision can be made regarding eligibility for services. After the interview, Mr. Bailicki found several comments made by Mr. Sowa disconcerting. At one point in the interview, Mr. Sowa stated that Mr. Bailicki's fiancé was quite young. Mr.Sowa asked Mr.Bailicki why he could not find someone nearer his own age. Parenthetically, Mr. Sowa mentioned that he has a twenty-year-old daughter. Mr. Sowa also mentioned, "he was not sure, but it may be against the state rules for transitional assistance for an unmarried couple to live together." He also asked Mr.Bailicki why he did not marry Ms. Larson and "stop living in sin."

When Mr. Bailicki returned home he related his experience with Mr. Sowa to Ms. Larson; she was appalled.

SUMMARY

In this brief consideration, one sees that each profession must address ethical practices on a constant basis. We have the responsibility to be the most competent practitioner that we can be. The world and the profession are rapidly and constantly expanding and changing. Both we, as practitioners, and the profession must provide assurance that a minimum level of competency and ethical practice is present. Our clients deserve no less than that.

REFERENCES

[1]Commission on Rehabilitation counselor Certification. *Code of Professional Ethics for Rehabilitation Counselors*. Schaumburg, Illinois. http://www.crccertification.com. 2009.

[2]Neulicht, A. T., McQuade, L. J., & Chapman, C. A. (Eds.). *The CRCC Desk Reference on Professional Ethics: A Guide for Rehabilitation Counselors.* Athens, Georgia: Elliott & Fitzpatrick, 2010.

12

CAREERS AND CREDENTIALS: EMPLOYMENT SETTINGS FOR REHABILITATION PRACTITIONERS

Gina Oswald
Wright State University

Chapter Topics

- Introduction
- Rehabilitation Roles and Realities
- Characteristics and Job Titles by Sector
- Public Sector
- Private Non-Profit
- Private For-Profit
- Credentials
- Summary

INTRODUCTION

From the inception of undergraduate rehabilitation services programs, graduates have accepted employment opportunities that contribute to society in many meaningful ways, including increasing quality of life and independence for persons with disabilities, as well as providing the expertise within communities necessary for appropriate services designed to increase community inclusion. While well-rounded rehabilitation and disability educational programs have been available for decades, many programs have elected to standardize their curriculum and programmatic features. Out of the 45-60 identified undergraduate programs focused on rehabilitation and disability studies,[6,7] 27 undergraduate rehabilitation programs were listed on the Council on Rehabilitation Education (CORE)[5] registry in 2012, meeting established rehabilitation and disabilities studies curriculum and outcomes requirements. In 2012, CORE began to offer accreditation for undergraduate rehabilitation programs, initiating this process with two universities (Wright State University in Dayton, OH and the University of Wisconsin, Stout in Menomonie, WI) with six more in the process.

In order for programs to continue to strive to provide and demonstrate exemplary educational practices, program evaluations should focus on alumni employment outcomes and field-relevant curriculum. To this end, it is vital to understand that the professional paths for graduates in any of these programs are often complex and specifically centered around a preferred population or services to be delivered. With endless possibilities, students often pursue one or more career avenues based on past exposure, curriculum, and program-facilitated field experiences.

Reinforced by the breadth of career possibilities, the prescribed curriculum standards are designed to prepare students to perform requisite entry-level tasks in the most diverse employment settings typical of rehabilitation service providers. With the well-rounded nature of the curriculum, students have the opportunity to secure employment serving people with varying types of disabilities (such as developmental disabilities, mental illness, traumatic brain injury, and physical impairments) and other populations (ex-offenders, abuse/neglect, etc.). Services provided often include, but are not limited to: supported employment, independent living, community integration, educational opportunities, and service coordination. For the purposes of this chapter, positions most often requiring a bachelor's degree will be explored in further detail.

Beyond employment options for rehabilitation services bachelor-level graduates, it is important to recognize that many students go on to complete graduate degrees. One survey demonstrated that upwards of 80% of undergraduate students had completed or intended to complete a graduate degree.[6] While some jobs have flexibility on the degree requirement when coupled with years in the field, there is a clear distinction between the knowledge and scope of practice afforded by a bachelor's degree in rehabilitation services compared to a graduate degree in rehabilitation counseling or a related field. Students should be aware that often the acquisition of a master's degree would be required by certain employment settings for entry-level positions as well as promotion and management opportunities.

In analyzing the current job market for students in the rehabilitation services field, this chapter will discuss the employment opportunities and realities for undergraduate degree completers based upon typical employment trends and recent research. Compensation, benefits, common characteristics, and potential job titles will be reviewed. An overview of current national credentials related to rehabilitation work will conclude the chapter.

REHABILITATION ROLES AND REALITIES

Do to the encompassing nature of the field of rehabilitation, undergraduate rehabilitation services graduates will likely perform a multitude of roles while working with consumers in the community. Students may choose to start in an entry-level, direct care position that only requires a high school diploma and minimal onsite training. These positions often provide the most contact with consumers on a day-to-day basis. While completing a degree, students in direct care positions can gain valuable, field-related experience, beneficial for building a resume as well as paying for college. Some employers may also provide tuition assistance for employees taking courses related to the position. Titles for these entry-level positions will vary based on the type of agency and job duties. Examples include, but are not limited to, mental health technician, residential aide, community living instructor, advocate, and job coach.

While extensive work experience in the field may be substituted for an actual rehabilitation-related degree in some instances, many rehabilitation agencies are now requiring at minimum an undergraduate degree for positions requiring any type of consumer planning, program development, or supervision of direct care staff. In addition, management level positions (program managers, program directors, etc.) within non-profit agencies often expect a combination of experience in the field and an undergraduate or graduate rehabilitation-related degree. Due to newly imposed federal guidelines, all state and federal rehabilitation agencies now require at least a bachelor's degree to be a rehabilitation educator and a master's degree for all counseling personnel. Although not mandated by law, many private-for-profit agencies dealing in worker's compensation and forensic rehabilitation now prefer persons with graduate degrees or those nearing completion of a graduate degree. Beyond those specific employment settings, a bachelor's degree is often the highest degree required for entry-level employment.

Typical of any investigation into a degree and subsequent career, some of the first questions that arise during the career exploration process revolve around compensation and benefits of post graduation employment.

- *What is the typical starting salary?*
- *Are there areas or specialties that pay better?*

Unfortunately, the easiest answer is not always the most helpful. In order to provide effective information on employment opportunities, the discussion must be expanded to include internal and external determining factors. Students need to understand that compensation and other employment position characteristics must be viewed in the larger context of the whole employment experience. The opportunities and realities of employment are complicated and based on geographic location, population, work setting, task characteristics, funding source, and economic climate. Prior to delving into these factors, a review of basic contributing factors is in order.

FACTORS THAT IMPACT COMPENSATION AND WORK ENVIRONMENT CONSIDERATIONS

To begin, students should realize that the human services field is not generally considered a high wage field. With only a few rehabilitation avenues considered high paying, such as private for profit and forensic consultation work, it is also important to understand that most rehabilitation jobs provide a stable, decent income level. Many graduates choose and ultimately stay in the rehabilitation field because of the desire to help people, the challenge of a constantly evolving field, the uniqueness of each consumer and case, and the wide-ranging job duties required in any rehabilitation position. The excitement of finding a specific niche in rehabilitation that is truly self-fulfilling, in an agency that shares the same rehabilitation philosophy and values as oneself, can be all the reward a student needs to embark on a degree in rehabilitation. However, it would be unwise to ignore the realities of compensation and working conditions when contemplating a career in rehabilitation. Having a complete picture of rehabilitation as a profession and viable career path will help students make informed decisions about potential practicum/internship sites and employment opportunities.

The first contributing factor to consider is location. Depending on where your employer is located, the compensation may be lower or higher based on the economic climate and competition in the area. In addition, salary requirements should be compared to cost of living in a particular area. Does a little extra income compensate for the inflation in the area? Coupled with salary is the level and costs of benefits. Health care and retirement benefits should be a priority in the career exploration process, as counting on good health and Social Security is not something to rely upon.

Salaries are often based on educational level, certifications, and experience brought to the job. The more an applicant has of each of these the greator the possibility of negotiating for a higher salary. That being said, coming out of a program with as much accumulated experience as possible will not only improve the chances of securing employment, but also advancement. Students should be encouraged to look for rehabilitation-related jobs and volunteer experiences whenever reasonable. Not only will getting into the field early enhance resume building and interview talking points, it will also open students up for opportunities in networking/reference building, employer-provided tuition assistance programs, and augment positioning for advancement into a bachelor level job within the agency upon graduation. This can translate into a classic win-win situation for most students.

In addition to compensation, the work environment and culture can be very important to job satisfaction and longevity at an agency no matter if the job is meant to build experience, fulfill a dream, or serve as a valuable stepping-stone for a specific career ladder. Some easy questions to ask about any agency that can provide insight include:

- How long have most of the employees been at the agency?
- Why do people stay or leave?
- What are the best aspects of the job and the worst?
- Do you have the resources and support from management to be effective in your job?
- How do you balance the paperwork requirements and consumer contact?
- What is the level of supervision in this type of job?
- Are there promotion opportunities?
- Do you feel you have job security (how is the position funded-county levies, short-term grants)?
- What advice do you have for a student preparing/exploring a career in the rehabilitation field?

Questions like these can give a better understanding of how the current employees perceive working at the agency.

CHARACTERISTICS AND JOB TITLES BY SECTOR

Information on general characteristics, roles, and titles utilized in the rehabilitation field will be discussed in this section to provide a starting point for career exploration. Position types have been categorized under the most commonly associated rehabilitation sectors and are by no means meant to be exhaustive or narrowly construed. Keep in mind that as the field advances to meet the ever-changing needs of the various consumer populations, job positions and service settings will evolve to maintain the highest quality of service delivery within the framework of evidence-based practices, funding guidelines and trends. The various opportunities tempered by the realities of employment in the rehabilitation services field have been categorized across the major sectors:

- public,
- private non-profit, and
- private for-profit.

PUBLIC SECTOR

The public sector has always played a fundamental role in the employment of rehabilitation professionals. Whether county, state, or federally operated, government employment continues to provide the most consistently stable work settings in this field even during the most recent financial crises. Entry-level salaries typically range between $30,000-$35,000 a year depending on position, agency, population served, and experience. Although bonuses are not common in public sector jobs, cost of living raises and scheduled experiential/milestone raises are often built into the system. Health care benefits/costs, paid vacation and holiday time, and retirement benefits are all common reasons for seeking and retaining employment in the public sector. In addition, management opportunities and leadership roles are generally posted internally based on turnover and retirements.

In addition to the higher level of job security and comprehensive benefits packages, public sector work offers a variety of career opportunities for new professionals. Depending on the population and work, most new professionals can find an agency at one governmental level or another that offers such employment.

Below is a list of job positions/titles often located within the public sector. As you will note through the subheadings, employment can be obtained working with nearly any population from children to ex-offenders to military veterans. Many county boards providing either developmental disabilities or mental health services offer significant work opportunities with the vast majority of disability populations.

One stop centers

As funding continues to become more restricted, public and private agencies are actively looking to work collaboratively with one another to cost-share both office space as well as service delivery. Many cooperative agreements have led to an increase in one-stop designed locations where many agencies crucial to meeting a majority of the needs of a specific population can work in partnership in one centralized location. Previously, consumers might be required to visit several agencies in multiple locations to receive a variety of services in an effort to meet all of their needs. One-stop centers can offer an ease of access and coordination of services vital to a well-rounded rehabilitation plan. Whether the one stop center is a group of affiliated agencies or distinct departments in one overarching agency, the following positions are often available in these centers to better facilitate the rehabilitation process for consumers in need of numerous services.

Program Manager. Program Managers are employed to oversee all aspects of a particular community or agency program. Program managers are responsible for the development and implementation of the program's policies and services as well as recruitment, hiring, and supervision of volunteers and staff. In addition to the administrative duties, program managers often work with other community agencies and funding sources to ensure the effectiveness and sustainability of the program.

Case Manager. According to the Commission for Case Manager Certification, "Case management is a collaborative process that assesses, plans, implements, coordinates, monitors, and evaluates the options and services required to meet the client's health and human services needs. It is characterized by advocacy, communication, and resource management, and promotes quality and cost-effective interventions and outcomes."[3, p.3] Since many individuals with severe disabilities require the coordination of multiple services between and within various agencies, a case manager is often the critical facilitator as consumers attempt to navigate the complex, and frequently confusing, system of service providers. Case managers are vital in service coordination within county agencies of mental health and developmental disabilities.

Intake Specialist. Agencies with walk-in referrals are common (e.g., employment agencies, family services agencies, and private nonprofit agencies serving persons with severe mental illness and/or homelessness) generally hire intake specialists to work initially with the high volume of potential consumers. The intake specialist, as the first hurdle for entry into an agency, is expected to not only explain possible services offered by the agency, but also assess if the person is an appropriate referral to continue through the process into the agency's system. Once a consumer has been made aware of the agency's policies and its prospective beneficial services have been discussed, intake paperwork, including releases and background information as well as referrals to any appropriate service departments or coordinating agencies, would be completed by the intake specialist in order to initiate access to services. It is important to note that some public sector agencies may hire specific intake specialists depending upon demand.

Case worker. The position of caseworker can be located in many public and private sector community agencies. Persons interested in working with children may secure employment as a caseworker in the job and family services agencies and children's services agencies. Caseworkers in this arena are responsible for working with families when an incidence of abuse or neglect has been reported. The goal in this position is reunification of families unless that would not be in the best interest of the child. Whether reunification is possible or another environment must be utilized, the caseworker is responsible for developing a plan in conjunction with community resources.

In contrast, caseworkers employed in mental health agencies and psychiatric hospitals often work with people with severe mental illness. Services rendered in this setting revolve around supporting and improving quality of life through medication monitoring, crisis intervention, treatment plan development and implementation, as well as community resource teamwork.

Children's Services

Adoption Caseworker. Within children's services agencies, the adoption process is extensive in an effort to ensure the likelihood of a healthy environment placement. Adoption caseworkers prepare the children and adoptive parents for the process through home studies and interviews after a match has been determined. The caseworkers are also responsible for communication with all parties about the process and progress. Although children's services agencies are the typical employers for this position, many private, non-profit, social services agencies and private, for-profit, adoption agencies hire professionals to assist with adoptions through the court system.

Criminal Justice System

Whether you want to work with juveniles or adults, the criminal justice system has a multitude of opportunities at the city, county, state, or federal level. Often these positions require extensive paperwork and a strict adherence to predetermined guidelines and policies. Students should understand that client participation in services is often mandated with immensely high stakes for the participants that can result in elevated levels of client confrontation and work stress.

Abuse Investigator. An abuse investigator is utilized in situations where an allegation of abuse or neglect of a child has been given to a child protection agency. These investigators are in charge of analyzing the situation and validating the claim. The safety of the child must be evaluated and removal from the home may be required. In instances when familial interventions or removal of the child is warranted, an investigator often must work with a myriad of community agencies and provide documentation to all pertinent agencies.

Adult Parole Officer. There are often many concerns and challenges associated with successful reentry into society for a person recently released from prison. Parole officers are assigned to help ex-offenders assimilate to life outside of prison, providing supports and information designed to decrease the possibility of further criminal activity. Employment, housing, behaviors leading to the original offense, and other related issues are all discussed while creating a plan for release. Parole officers also work with family members and community partners to ensure the smoothest transition possible to life outside of prison. Once a plan has been developed and implemented, the parole officer is expected to follow the parolee through home and worksite visits.

Adult/Juvenile Probation Officer. Whether working with an adult population or juveniles, there is a great need for probation officers in the criminal system. Probation officers generally meet with a person arrested for various crimes in order to establish treatment options or incarceration recommendations based on the person's background and previous issues with the criminal justice system. If recommended for probation, probation officers oversee the ex-offenders in completing determined probation requirements, including drug screenings and employment/educational objectives. Some probation officers provide specific treatment programs for multiple ex-offenders throughout the course of the probationary time and complete onsite inspections of various locations (homes, worksites, schools, etc). Probation officers have the ability to re-arrest adults and juveniles violating their terms of probation. Probation officers may build specialized caseloads of ex-offender populations, such as persons with drug and alcohol issues.

Domestic Violence Coordinator (victim advocate). The criminal justice system also employs individuals directly or through various mental health centers to assist persons in the court systems resulting from domestic violence. When extended services are necessary, referral services are provided.

Guardian ad litem. A guardian ad litem is an individual appointed by the court to advocate for juveniles and protect the rights of the child throughout a trial. A guardian ad litem often must review documentation, interview anyone involved with the juvenile (including the child), discuss the case with court officials (the judge, attorneys, social workers, etc.), and provide testimony in court about the best interests of the child. As with any position within the criminal justice system, guardians are often in highly stressful situations dealing with difficult and sensitive issues on a daily basis.

INTELLECTUAL AND DEVELOPMENTAL DISABILITIES (DD)

Generally speaking, persons with both intellectual and developmental disabilities (disabilities originating prior to the age of 22) are served by specific state and county agencies through designated funding dollars. These agencies provide services to consumers in the areas of housing, employment, community integration, and much more. Below is a list of job descriptions not otherwise mentioned in other sections that are most often associated with agencies serving both the intellectual and developmentally disabled populations.

Behavioral Specialist. A behavioral specialist is a person who works within the DD system and focuses on planning and dealing with challenging behaviors. Although anyone working in this field will work on a regular basis with consumers who have challenging behaviors, the behavioral specialist is responsible for analyzing particularly challenging behavioral patterns and creating plans of action. In addition to plan development and training of staff, the specialist is also the point person for highly disruptive behavioral situations.

Contract Procurement Specialist. Many individuals with severe and multiple developmental disabilities receive either sheltered workshop services or community-based employment services on a regular basis. These opportunities are available due to the work of a procurement specialist. As the title suggests, the contract procurement specialist works with companies in the community to create or maintain contracts for work to be completed by individuals with developmental disabilities. The Department of Labor (DOL) exercises strict control over this type of work. Work such as light assembly, cleaning, and office/clerical work may be performed at a habilitation center or at the originating company. A procurement specialist must be knowledgeable not only in professional contract writing and negotiation tactics, but also in productivity level and work skill potentials of the clients served.

Individual Service Planner. Individual planners (IPs) have a wide variety of titles based on the source of employment (e.g., habilitation specialist), yet the job duties are typically the same. Planners work with individuals with intellectual and developmental disabilities in either habilitation facilities or sheltered workshops. Planners provide or oversee various assessments and interviews prior to completing an individualized plan for habilitation services. Once a plan is written, service delivery and evaluation are monitored by the planner who can make adjustments and recommendations as necessary.

Qualified Developmental Disabilities Professional (QDDP). Qualified developmental disabilities professionals oversee all service programs written for residents in facilities serving persons with intellectual and developmental disabilities. QDDPs are responsible for the development and review of training and habilitation programs for selected individuals. Facilities receiving Medicaid dollars are required to employ QDDPs.

Quality Control Specialist. A quality control specialist can be located in public sector programs at all levels. The main purpose of the quality control specialist is to determine if services are offered in accordance with established policies and effectively based on the mission of the program. A careful analysis may include case documentation review, consumer satisfaction interviews, and overall program outcomes.

Workshop Specialist. Whether consumers are working in a sheltered workshop or community placement, a workshop specialist is often employed to supervise a set group of consumers and monitor the group's level of productivity. This position is integral to plan development and daily implementation of vocational goals for each consumer. In addition to monitoring workflow and work site behavioral standards, workshop specialists must maintain documentation on individual consumers for plan evaluation as well as productivity (for accurate payment based on piece rate and hourly output for the payroll department). A workshop specialist may also be called a training and education specialist, depending upon the employer.

EDUCATIONAL/TRAINING INSTITUTIONS

Within most educational settings, there is a distinct place for rehabilitation professionals as educators and service providers. Rehabilitation professionals work in tandem with elementary and high school teachers to provide integrated educational opportunities for students of all abilities. At the postsecondary level, colleges and universities utilize rehabilitation professionals to facilitate and enhance higher education for persons with disabilities.

ABA Technician. As a result of the rising prevalence of people diagnosed along the autism spectrum and the use of applied behavioral analysis (ABA) methods, the demand for trained ABA professionals in public schools has dramatically increased in the past decade. ABA technicians (professionals/specialists) are utilized to assess individual student needs, plan ABA activities, and evaluative measures. Depending upon the school system and the current disability population within each school, ABA professionals may be either specifically responsible for providing ABA programming or may supervisor several paraprofessionals in the delivery of ABA activities.

ADA Coordinator. The ADA coordinator is in charge of compliance with the Americans with Disabilities Act (ADA) for the institution (whether an educational facility or large employer). This position often provides advice to supervisors and coworkers on accommodations for persons with disabilities, hiring/training guidelines, assimilation of all employees into a productive work environment, and any other concerns regarding the Americans with Disabilities Act.

Advising Services. Sometimes, rehabilitation specialists will provide academic advising that covers a broad range of issues pertinent to students in postsecondary institutions. An adviser may go well beyond disseminating information on college course requirements and university policy by helping students understand career paths and personal responsibility. Advisers can also work closely with students over several years, becoming the first point of contact in times of stress and frustration.

Career Services Specialist. Whether working toward a certificate or diploma, the ultimate goal for most students is education-related employment. To that end, many institutions of higher education offer career services, or services designed to help students successfully locate and transition into employment. Career services specialists help current students and recent alumni with career fairs, resume building, mock interviewing opportunities, and specific job leads provided to the office by local employers. Understanding the local labor market and employer needs is vital to assisting graduates in securing optimal field experience and employment opportunities.

Office of Disability Services. Offices responsible for handling accommodation requests by students with disabilities are often called some variation of Office of Disability Services or Student Accommodations Center. A disability services specialist is expected to determine eligibility and appropriate accommodations necessary for access to specified educational opportunities on a student-by-student basis. Typical accommodations provided by such offices include, but are not limited to, classroom selection based on architectural and physical aspects of particular buildings, testing and assignment accommodations, visual or auditory modifications of printed material, as well as mediation between student and instructor on helpful practices for full inclusion and assistive technology.

MILITARY VETERANS

Veterans Services. Within the US Department of Veterans Affairs (VA), many positions related to rehabilitation offer graduates the opportunity to work strictly with the veteran population. The VA has the capacity to provide similar employment opportunities in a wide range of service areas working with veterans, such as employment, housing, benefits determination, mental health services, and case management. It is important to note that while it is not required for a person to be a veteran to work for the VA, non-veterans have a better chance of securing employment in the VA system through a successful practicum or internship experience. Beyond Veterans Affairs, many rehabilitation facilities provide specific programs and services geared towards the veteran population.

VOCATIONAL REHABILITATION

Case Aide or Case Assistant. With the ebb and flow of state vocational rehabilitation funding and caseload requirements, some state agencies must rely on individuals with bachelor's degrees to complete job duties that assist vocational rehabilitation counselors (VRCs). Case assistants are crucial to providing high quality services to individuals with severe disabilities when caseload size and staff cutbacks require VRCs to work with an extremely high volume of consumers. Case assistants are available to complete tasks such as documentation collection, progress report meeting attendance, consumer follow up, service referral, and delivery monitoring.

Claims Adjudicator. A claims adjudicator is responsible for determining the eligibility of a person attempting to receive either Supplemental Security Income (SSI) or Social Security Disability Insurance (SSDI) benefits from the federal government. In order to make eligibility determinations, adjudicators are responsible for assessing applications and requesting verification of all physical, psychological, and intellectual impairments to employment. If necessary, the adjudicator will also refer applicants for assessments to determine the extent of impairment. Based on all documentation available at the time of review, the adjudicator would then either approve or deny eligibility of benefits.

Client Assistance Program Specialists. State vocational rehabilitation agencies are now federally mandated to provide client assistance programs for consumers within the VR system. Program specialists are available to assist consumers who feel their rights have been violated and wish to pursue filing a complaint. Aspects of this job include fact-finding, educating the consumer on the system, and remediation with state agency staff.

PRIVATE NON-PROFIT

The private non-profit sector is currently hiring the most rehabilitation professionals. While jobs in the private non-profit sector are generally easiest to locate and obtain within the majority of communities, due to the demand in services and minimal experience requirements, the compensation and benefits are commensurate with the lower expectations. An entry-level position for graduates with little or no experience ranges from $25,000 to $32,000 a year. Benefits for all private sector positions vary depending on each company, although on average, the employee's share of health care benefits cost more than comparable public sector benefits, and the holiday/paid vacation benefits are often less. It is also important to recognize that the previous stability in employment at a non-profit due to long-standing relationships and contracts with public agencies and fundraising/fee for service activities has been challenged by the national financial crisis, resulting in fewer new/refilled positions and a decrease in program sustainability. As far as advancement is concerned, experience and length with a company is highly prized at private non- profit agencies, resulting in better opportunities for internal promotion. Below, are listed several job titles and descriptions of typical positions with private non-profit agencies.

ADVOCACY

Advocacy, a cornerstone of the rehabilitation philosophy, is an essential component of any rehabilitation position regardless of the employment setting. Many professionals are called upon to act as advocates for their consumers in services within and outside of their agency. In an effort to enable people to reach optimal levels of community participation and self-determination, rehabilitation professionals must constantly strive to educate consumers how to become self-advocates, to empower them to facilitate a higher quality of life. Although necessary for any rehabilitation work, some positions are specifically designated to focus entirely on this aspect.

Advocate. An advocate is an individual who supports and educates a consumer on decision-making and service availability. When a consumer is unable or unsuccessful in self-advocating, an advocate would step in and provide supportive advocacy tactics to ensure the client's rights and proper service provision.

Guardian. A guardian is often an employee in some type of advocacy or protective services agency who is responsible for the protection and representation of a client's rights and personal preferences. Guardians are expected to attend all meetings related to the client, and when necessary, make decisions regarding the client's care and service provision. Guardians may also provide individual budgeting and purchasing support to a client depending on need.

Mental Health System

Consumers within the mental health system can develop extensive service needs based upon a chronic mental illness. Rehabilitation professionals in the mental health arena often begin working in mental health agencies, learning the intricacies of working with persons with psychiatric disabilities. Those who wish to continue providing services in this field may decide, based on scope of practice and state licensure requirements, to obtain a graduate degree in counseling (focusing in areas such as rehabilitation, clinical mental health, or school counseling).

Chemical Dependency Specialist. A chemical dependency specialist focuses on persons with addictions to alcohol, drugs, and other substances. Traditionally, persons with addiction issues receive treatment in individual and group formats. A chemical dependency specialist must be capable of working in both settings utilizing approaches designed for this population. Chemical dependency specialists are employed through the criminal justice system (sometimes referred to as "drug courts"), mental health agencies, substance abuse treatment centers, and intervention programs. Agencies working with specialized populations, such as veterans, persons with traumatic brain injury, and abuse victims, may also offer chemical dependency or dual diagnosis (comorbid mental illness) treatment.

Community Liaison. Attempting to coordinate services and reintegrate persons with mental illnesses into communities requires the support and assistance of many community partners. Understanding how to get multiple agencies to the table for collaboration as well as obtaining support from the public are persistent stumbling blocks for mental health consumers and allied agencies. A community liaison is instrumental in bringing people together and promoting the positive beliefs and attitudes necessary for continued community involvement and a seamless reentry for persons with severe mental illnesses. Speaking publicly, organizing meetings, and mediating differences or prejudices are integral skills for an effective community liaison.

Homeless Coordinator. A homeless coordinator is a person employed by an agency who specifically works with the homeless population, generally located within a mental health and/or substance abuse agency. The homeless coordinator is expected to understand the typical causes of homelessness, issues surrounding the experience of homelessness, and resources/necessary interventions to assist a person or family that has become homeless or is on the verge of being homeless.

Mental Health Technician. A mental health technician works directly with a person with a mental health issue. Often technicians or specialists are employed in a Clubhouse or on an assertive community treatment (ACT) team to provide direct programming and assistance to individuals in areas of community integration, employment, housing, and mental illness management. Depending on the model utilized and services provided, technicians or specialists may have as many as 40 consumers or as few as 10. Many programs are becoming more integrated—the specialist is assigned to a small group of consumers, but is also familiar with and available to assist any other team member's consumer.

RESIDENTIAL SERVICES

Independent Living Specialist. Within an independent living center, four core services are offered: information and referral, independent living skills training, advocacy, and peer support. Services may include resource development, specific skill development, and local to national advocacy training and activities. An independent living specialist works with individuals with any type of disability based on specific needs.

Recreational Worker. In an effort to increase the quality of life of individuals with disabilities, recreational activities are instrumental in assisting individuals to locate and participate in appropriate, interest-based activities in the community and in residential facilities. Recreational workers must understand the population's needs and general abilities, coupled with the interests of all participants, in order to develop and facilitate activities in a safe and enjoyable atmosphere. Workers in this area must have organizational skills in addition to projecting a positive, motivational approach to all consumers.

Respite Provider. Although many families gladly provide the care needed to family members with disabilities when possible, consistent care of persons with severe disabilities may be emotionally and physically draining. Respite care services provide a safe and appropriate setting for persons with disabilities on an occasional, time limited basis. These services are invaluable, allowing families to alleviate stress while freeing up a particular block of time for other activities. Respite may be scheduled from a couple of hours up to a few weeks, depending on funding and the particular needs of the family. Respite providers are generally located within disability or population specific agencies offering residential services, ensuring a good match between trained professionals and respite users.

Team Leader. Within a youth residential facility, team leaders are similar to case managers in job duties, although focus is on creating a nurturing environment and a therapeutic relationship for child growth and development. The team leader's typical partners and related issues revolve around mental health services/agencies, educational services/systems, legal/court systems, and parental involvement, when appropriate.

VOCATIONAL SERVICES

In order to help consumers reach the highest level of financial self-sufficiency and quality of life, most rehabilitation plans address the attainment of employment. Finding an appropriate job match aligned with a person's interests and abilities requires multiple layers of employment services provided by qualified employment personnel. Depending upon their level of skill and personality characteristics, students have a wide variety of employment opportunities within the vocational arena of rehabilitation.

Career Assessment Specialist (Vocational Evaluator). A person specializing in career assessment/vocational evaluation often works for a non-profit or for-profit agency on contract with either a state vocational rehabilitation agency or school system. The career assessment specialist is brought in to evaluate the employability and potential career options for a consumer or youth based on numerous factors. The assessment process can be completed through formal assessments in areas such as aptitudes, temperament, specific work-related skills and interests, as well as informal assessments through community-based situational assessments, work samples, and interviewing. Based on the results of all assessments and the information gathered, the career assessment specialist is able to develop a written report with results and recommendations for appropriate employment options.

Employment Specialist (Job Developer). An employment specialist works with a small caseload of individuals, approximately 20-40, on the attainment of appropriate employment. Employment specialists must take into account each consumer's employment interests, strengths, and abilities, as well as the local labor market and geographic/transportation limitations. Typically, an employment specialist's duties will depend on the ability level of the consumer as well as the degree of desired representation by the consumer. One consumer may require job-seeking skills training, resume development, job clubs, and specific job leads. Another consumer may require in depth contact and networking with employers, assistance with applications and interviews, as well as potentially setting up job tryouts and on-the-job training.

Job Coach. Once a job or evaluation has been obtained, many consumers may require the assistance of a job coach to learn job specific and general employability skills at a worksite. Job coaches help consumers learn the job duties and productivity levels required for a job in addition to the social and cultural climate of a new work setting. The ability to jump into ever-changing work environments, quickly solving problems, and resolving conflicts effectively while always looking for chances to fade support are all highly valued and necessary skills of any job coach.

Supported Employment Specialist. Although independent community employment is the ultimate goal for most persons in employment services, consumers with severe disabilities may require some level of support in the work environment to be successful. A supported employment specialist provides a consistent, often permanent follow along service to persons already employed in an effort to monitor issues that may arise from changes in duties, personal lives, personnel at the worksite, etc. that can have devastating effects on the employment experience for a person with a disability. These positions are often found in agencies that work with people with severe mental illnesses, traumatic brain injury, and intellectual and developmental disabilities.

Transitional Employment Specialist. Many times, persons with severe mental illness or intellectual/developmental disabilities may need supportive services similar to supported employment services on a short-term training basis. Transitional employment specialists work with individuals in community employment settings for a few weeks to a few months. During this time, the specialist is focused on teaching work and social skills to persons wishing to be transitioned into a permanent position in the community.

Work Adjustment Specialist. Being successful at any job requires a balance between productivity and soft skills for any employee. A person with minimal work experience may have difficulty understanding what is expected in relation to behavior and social interactions within the majority of work settings. Work adjustment specialists provide training in a variety of settings, including rehabilitation facilities, sheltered workshops, or the community. Their work is designed to introduce a person to the general expectations of employers. Some examples of what a work adjustment specialist would focus on are incorporating a work ethic (such as attendance and punctuality), developing appropriate work behaviors, and reinforcing appropriate ways to interact with coworkers/supervisors in an effective manner. Work adjustment is often incorporated into services occurring prior to an actual job placement.

MISCELLANEOUS REHABILITATION RELATED CAREERS

Benefits Coordinator. Consumers who currently receive social security benefits must determine if employment is the best option based on many unique personal and financial factors. A benefits coordinator will meet with a consumer to review pertinent Social Security initiatives and regulations to determine how employment wages will affect Social Security payments and other benefits. Coordinators are also available to assist consumers in creating Plans for Achieving Self Support (PASS) or Individual Work Related Expense (IRWE) Plans.

PRIVATE FOR-PROFIT

When considering salary alone, private for-profit companies offer the highest potential in pay and bonuses of the three sectors. Compensation is based on productivity and the ability to maximize billable hours of service. An entry-level private for-profit position can easily start at $32,000-$38,000 a year for individuals who manage a full caseload and meet productivity requirements. Individuals who meet high levels of productivity are often rewarded with generous bonuses. Conversely, in a private company many benefits are either nonexistent for consultants or are quite expensive compared to public sector jobs. Job security is less stable as private for-profit positions rely on client referrals, maximizing billable hours, and contracts through worker's compensation or other insurance carriers. Listed below are common positions with worker's compensation, private consultation, and private healthcare systems for rehabilitation professionals.

EMPLOYMENT SERVICES

Disability Manager/Private Rehabilitation Service Provider. There are many positions and possible titles for persons working with injured workers. Often these positions, at the bachelor-level, involve working with a company that has pre-established contracts with a worker's compensation or veteran's affairs program. These professionals complete many tasks from vocational assessments to case management and planning to job search activities. A part of disability management may also include the prevention of injury. With experience and connections, it is possible to branch out as an independent consultant, although further education will likely be required.

CONSULTANT OPPORTUNITIES

ADA Consultant. There are emerging opportunities to work with various companies and architects on ADA (Americans with Disability Act) compliance in employment practices, service delivery, and architectural accessibility. ADA consultants must be fluent in legislative language and requirements, as well as understand general and company-specific business characteristics and practices. Another developing specialization is in architectural universal design, transcending from meeting ADA requirements to fostering and developing equal access for all.

Life Care Planner. A life care planner is an individual who works with a person with a severe or multiple disabilities or a chronic illness to proactively identify and plan for all necessary medical and rehabilitation services. In addition to the development of a plan, the life care planner may be responsible for the monitoring of service delivery and coordination as well as continual re-evaluation of the plan as disability limitations and life circumstances evolve.

Forensic Rehabilitation Professional. A forensic rehabilitation professional is a person called upon during a court case to review records and provide expert testimony on the rehabilitation and disability aspects of a case. Usually, forensic rehabilitation professionals provide consultation in social security disability determination cases, although vocational rehabilitation testimony has been utilized in divorce/spousal support cases. As was stated with disability management positions, many tasks and assessments may be completed by bachelor's level professionals; however, it would be unrealistic for a person without at least a master's degree and several years of experience to be the lead forensic consultant and expert witness on a case.

Rehabilitation Technologist (Assistive Technology Provider/Trainer). Many people with disabilities benefit from commercially available and specifically fabricated assistive technologies (AT). For individuals who may benefit from AT, a referral is generally sent to a rehabilitation technologist for an assessment of the individual's abilities and technology needs. A rehabilitation technologist may specialize in employment-related technologies, computer and communication hardware and software, vehicle or home modifications, or devices for independent living. Once a thorough assessment is completed, a written report with recommendations is provided to the individual with a disability and the referral source. If equipment is purchased or fabricated, training time is often recommended and provided by the rehabilitation technologist to set up and familiarize the individual with the proper use and maintenance of the equipment.

HEATHCARE SERVICE PROVIDERS

Most people, whether living with a disability or not, will receive short or long term services from a healthcare facility at some point in their lives. Based on the circumstances, a rehabilitation professional may be employed to work with the patient and families in order to ensure proper care and support through the process.

Hospice Coordinator. Hospice coordinators working with persons who are terminally ill and their families, educate them about in-home versus facility-based services, plan for and arrange medical services, and provide support to all those involved. Grief counseling and education is provided to the family during and after the death of the individual. Hospice coordinators may be employed through hospitals, nursing homes, independent providers, and various religious organizations.

Hospital Caseworker. A hospital caseworker provides the same services as other caseworkers, only in a hospital setting. Hospital patients needing additional services within the hospital and in the community may require information and referral assistance from a caseworker. The coordination of various medical professionals and offices may be facilitated by a caseworker, resulting in a seamless and comprehensive hospital stay and transition back into the community.

MISCELLANEOUS REHABILITATION RELATED CAREERS

Human Resource Specialist. Human Resource specialists support employers with knowledge and strategies in employment legislation and practices. A firm understanding of the employment process from job description development to termination and effective strategies for navigating the process with employees will be just as important as specific company employment policies and practices. A rehabilitation professional in a human resource specialist position has employment and disability knowledge gained through a bachelor's degree that will prove invaluable in working with employees with and without disabilities.

RECENT RESEARCH IN ALUMNI OUTCOMES

After a review of potential employment opportunities, it is important to highlight new research directly related to this topic. A recent study by Herbert, et al.,[7] provides national data on employment outcomes of undergraduate rehabilitation and disabilities studies alumni. Responses from surveys completed by 179 rehabilitation services alumni demonstrated post-graduation employment experiences for students spanning the 2007/08 to 2008/09 academic years across 19 different programs. From these data, the three most common work settings after "other" (accounting for 41.9% of the sample) were community rehabilitation programs, public school systems, and community mental health agencies.[7] The top five ranked job tasks were to provide emotional support to clients, write client progress notes, advocate for client rights, identify community resources for clients, and interview clients to obtain background information. While this research illuminated the common experiences of alumni around the nation, the lack of similarity in job titles and work settings only further highlights the exponential employment opportunities available to undergraduate students.

Another study by Evenson and Holloway[6] surveyed 91 recent rehabilitation graduates. Of this group, 58.2% of respondents reported working in the rehabilitation field with the average salary being $31,197 per year. Most common positions were employment services (19.8%) and case management (15.4%). Combined, these studies clarify and highlight the realities of employment outcomes of rehabilitation alumni.

RECOMMENDATIONS FOR FURTHER CAREER EXPLORATION

It is hoped that the above information will be helpful to students in their search for meaningful employment. However, in completing a rehabilitation program, students should engage in some specific activities. Throughout the educational experience, a student should focus on two main goals (beyond learning how to be a rehabilitation professional):

- gaining insight into one's needs and interests related to work activities, and
- taking advantage of all the experiential opportunities provided through coursework.

As students learn about the different populations and practice typical job tasks, they need to start taking note of their interests and the tasks they enjoy, to further their career exploration. The options are innumerable (e.g., what segment of the disability population to work with and what services to provide).

All jobs require some balance of consumer contact and paperwork, office to fieldwork, and policy guidelines to flexibility. Most employment settings will require both, so understanding one's personal preferences will likely lead to a more enjoyable occupation in the end.

Developing a personal philosophy of rehabilitation will make it easier to connect with an agency on philosophical ideologies and work culture as reflected through the organization's mission statements, service policies, and overall delivery of services. Working in an agency that fundamentally views rehabilitation work differently can result in decreased job satisfaction while increasing tension and the potential for burnout.

Being in a rehabilitation program, students have an abundance of opportunities for networking and information gathering. Once a student begins making informed decisions about career avenues to pursue, it is important to utilize the experiences afforded through educational activities to gain valuable geographical and job specific information. Guest speakers and field trips are excellent opportunities for informational interviews and agency exploration. Ask questions about job openings and the application process, typical activities, internship opportunities, and best/worst parts of the job.

Finally, once students have narrowed the field to one or two realistic options, they can make every attempt to shape service-learning/field experience opportunities into the best possible learning experience. Following this path, students should enter the job market search with a firm understanding of their needs and the realities of whatever career path they may choose.

CREDENTIALS

Based on the various career paths students have available to them, credentials can be very helpful in obtaining or maintaining the ideal job. Some credentials are nationally recognized while others are state-specific. Students are strongly encouraged to pursue information at the regional level on employer credential preferences and expectations through informational interviews and networking opportunities. Understanding the potential impact on securing employment and advancement possibilities in applicable work settings is extremely beneficial when determining what types of credentials to pursue.

Understanding the educational and experiential requirements to obtain the credential prior to graduation can enhance the student's ability to insert additional necessary courses in one's program as electives, (as one might do for pre-requisites to a graduate program). Below is a list of national credentials that may be helpful to or required of novice rehabilitation services professionals. The information provided includes contact information and various requirements (educational, experiential, and testing), including information on continuing education units (CEUs) that will be necessary for the maintenance of said credentials. CEUs are an excellent way, whether required or not, of keeping current on rehabilitation trends and evidence-based practices. Rehabilitation professionals at any stage of practice are always encouraged to continue the learning process through additional coursework, conferences, in-service training, and professional organization activities.

CERTIFIED CASE MANAGER (CCM)

Certifying body. Commission for Case Manager Certification
15000 Commerce Parkway, Suite C, Mount Laurel, NJ 08054
856-380-6836 http://www.ccmcertification.orgccmchq@ccmcertification.org.[3]

Education requirement. In order to become a certified case manager (CCM), applicants must have completed a post-secondary degree at any level (associate through doctorate) in a field that promotes the physical, psychological, or vocational well-being of the population to be served. Applicants must also be able to legally and independently practice without the supervision of another licensed professional based on the degree obtained, and perform the following eight essential activities of case management: assessment, planning, implementation, coordination, monitoring, evaluation, outcomes, and general activities.

Work experience. Any employment within the previous 10 years prior to application may be considered, unless it was completed as part of a practicum, internship, preceptorship, or volunteer experience. Categories of employment must be verified as either 12 months of full time as an intern case manager supervised by a CCM, 24 months of full time case manager work without CCM supervision, or 12 months of full time supervisor work over people providing direct case management services. Part time work will be considered on a prorated basis. Employment experience must also include providing at least five of the following six core components (psychosocial aspects, healthcare reimbursement, rehabilitation, healthcare management and delivery, principles of practice, and case management concepts). Under each component, applicants must:

- include all eight essential activities in service delivery,
- provide a continuum of care, beyond a single episode of care that addresses the ongoing needs of the individual being served,
- be responsible for communicating with pertinent parties within the client's healthcare system,
- be primarily responsible for dealing with the client's broad spectrum of needs.

Testing information. The CCM examination is administered by Prometric testing centers. Examinations occur three times a year, allowing an applicant to schedule the exam during approximately a one-month window. All applications must be accompanied by a non-refundable application fee and a refundable examination fee, for those not accepted to sit for the exam.

Renewal requirements. CCM certification is active for five years. All certified case managers must complete 80 hours of acceptable continuing education over a five-year period in order to renew their certification without re-examination. More information may be found on the CCM Website.

Qualified Developmental Disabilities Professional (QDDP)

Certifying body. National Association of Qualified Developmental Disabilities Professionals (NAQ),2081 Calistoga Drive, Suite 1S, New Lenox, IL 60451, (815) 485-4781 http://www.qddp.org/hjanczak@qddp.org.[8]

Education requirement. In order to become a certified qualified developmental disabilities professional (QDDP), applicants must have completed a bachelor's degree and be licensed, certified, or registered to provide professional services by the state in which they practice.

Work experience. A minimum of two years work experience with individuals within the developmental disabilities population is required for QDDP certification.

Testing information. The QDDP certification is awarded to individuals who complete the application process and complete online coursework through NAQ. The application process requires the completion of an application, application essays, and a criminal background check. The applicant must provide professional references, official transcripts, and a non-refundable initial application fee. Once an application has been approved for online coursework through NAQ, applicants will be required to take seven "core" courses and three elective courses for an additional fee.

Renewal requirements. QDDP certification is active for up to five years. CEU credit requirements have not been determined at this time. More information as it develops may be found on the NAQ Website.

Certification in General Biofeedback (BCIA)

Certifying body. Biofeedback Certification Institute of America (BCIA) 10200 W 4th Avenue, Suite 310 Wheat Ridge, CO 80033 (303) 420-2902 http://www.bcia.org info@bcia.org.[2]

Education requirements. Applicants must obtain at least a Bachelor's degree from a regionally accredited academic institution in one of BCIA's approved health care fields (such as rehabilitation, psychology, social work, counseling, or recreational therapy). In addition to completion of a degree, applications must have:

- 48 hours of didactic biofeedback education,
- 20 contact hours with a BCIA approved mentor to review:
    a. 10 sessions of personal biofeedback, demonstrating self-regulation,
    b. 50 sessions of patient/client treatment (10 sessions each of Thermal, EMG, and GSR, then the remaining 20 sessions are to

include any combination of EMG, Thermal, GSR, EEG, HRV, and respiration training.)

c. 10 case conference presentations, *Sessions are a minimum of 20 minutes,*

- a comprehensive course in human anatomy, human biology, or human physiology.

Testing information. The BCIA examination is administered a few times a year at predetermined sites. Applicants may utilize any university or public library proctor for an additional fee. There is a fee for filing the application and the certification.

Renewal requirements. Initial certification is for four years. All designated holders must complete 55 accredited hours of continuing education relevant to biofeedback. Three hours must be related to ethics and professional standards.

CERTIFIED DISABILITY MANAGEMENT SPECIALIST

Certifying body. Certified Disability Management Specialist Commission
300 N. Martingale Road, Suite 460 Schaumburg, IL 60173
847.944.1335 http://www.cdms.org info@CDMS.org.[4]

Qualifications. The educational requirements for CDMS certification is a bachelor's degree in any discipline or current state licensure as a nurse. The applicant must also have "a minimum of 12 months of acceptable full-time employment providing direct disability management services to individuals with disabilities receiving benefits from a disability compensation system."[4, p.4]

Testing information. The CDMS exam is administered three times a year during an eight-day window at approximately 300 computer-based testing sites around the country.

Renewal requirements. The certification is active for five years. A total of 80 hours of documented continuing education during the five-year certification period is required for renewal without retesting.

BOARD CERTIFIED ASSISTANT BEHAVIOR ANALYST

Certifying body. Behavior Analyst Certification Board
2888 Remington Green Lane, Suite C, Tallahassee, FL 32308
850-765-0905 http://www.bacb.com applications@bacb.com.[1]

Educational Requirements. Applicants must possess a minimum of a bachelor's degree in behavior analysis or other natural science, education, human services, engineering, medicine, or a field related to behavior analysis and approved by the BACB from an accredited institution of higher education (IHE) in the United States or Canada. IHEs outside the United States or Canada must have maintained an equivalent standard of training during the period of time the applicant was enrolled.

Applicants must also complete 135 classroom hours of instruction in the following behavioral analysis content areas and for the number of hours specified:

- ethical considerations – 10 hours,
- definition & characteristics and Principles, processes & concepts – 40 hours,
- behavioral assessment and Selecting intervention outcomes & strategies - 25 hours,
- experimental evaluation of interventions, & Measurement of behavior and Displaying & interpreting behavioral data - 20 hours,
- behavioral change procedures and Systems support 40 hours.

Experience requirements. Applicants must complete 1000 hours of supervised independent fieldwork in behavior analysis. The field experience must be between 10 and 30 hours per week, at least 3 weeks out of every month until all hours are completed. Fifty hours must be directly supervised with a minimum of one supervised contact every 2 weeks.

Testing information. The BCIA examination is administered through the Pearson VUE computer-based testing centers. Examinations occur three times a year allowing an applicant to schedule the exam during approximately a one-month window. All applications must be accompanied by a non-refundable application fee and a refundable examination fee, for those not accepted to sit for the exam.

Renewal requirements. The certification is active for three years. A total of 24 hours of documented continuing education including 3 hours in ethics during the three-year period is required for renewal without retesting.

OTHER CREDENTIAL INFORMATION

As of 2008, the Commission on Certification of Work Adjustment and Vocational Evaluation Specialists (CCWAVES) discontinued the Certified Vocational Evaluator (CVE) and the Registered Community Rehabilitation Practitioner (RCRP) credentials. At this time, the Vocational Evaluation and Work Adjustment Association (VEWAA)[9] and Vocational Evaluation and Career Assessment Professionals (VECAP) are collaboratively rolling out a new credential, the Professional Vocational Evaluation (PVE) Credential. As this credential has just emerged and requires extensive field experience for bachelor-level applicants, more information can be obtained from the VEWAA website (http://www.vewaa.com/profdev/Certification/certification.htm).

SUMMARY

The field of rehabilitation services is vast and highly individual for each professional. In this chapter, general information on compensation, work settings, benefits, typical job titles with descriptions, and national credentials were reviewed. Based on the regional trends of various private and governmental agencies, the information provided is meant to be an introduction to the substantial opportunities within the field and a place to initiate further inquiry. Program instructors and guest speakers are valuable resources in an investigation into potential career paths and state-specific credentials. Students are strongly encouraged to ask questions and network whenever possible as post-graduation employment decisions may be more fluid than originally planned.

REFERENCES

[1]Behavioral Analysis Certification Board. (n.d.) Retrieved from http://www.bacb.com

[2]Biofeedback Certification International Alliance. (n.d.) Retrieved from http://www.bcia.org

[3]Certified Case Manager Certification. (n.d.) Retrieved from http://www.ccmcertification.org

[4]Certification of Disability Management Specialists Commission. (n.d.) Retrieved from http://www.cdms.org

[5]Council on Rehabilitation Education. (n.d.) Retrieved from http://www.core-rehab.org

[6]Evenson, T, & Holloway, L. (2007). Undergraduate education: an essential rung on the rehabilitation career ladder. *Rehabilitation Education, 21*(2), 73-86.

[7]Herbert, J. T., Barrett, K., Evenson, T., & Jacob, C. J. (2010). Work roles and functions of undergraduate rehabilitation services alumni: a pilot study. *Rehabilitation Education, 24*(3 & 4), 149-166.

[8]The National Association of Qualified Developmental Disability Professionals. (n.d.) Retrieved from http://www.qddp.org

[9]Vocational Evaluation and Work Adjustment Association. (n.d.) Retrieved from http://www.vewaa.com

SUPPORTED EMPLOYMENT

QUINTIN BOSTON
NORTH CAROLINA A & T STATE UNIVERSITY

DOTHEL W. EDWARDS, JR.
J. CHAD DUNCAN
ALABAMA STATE UNIVERSITY

YOLANDA V. EDWARDS
WINSTON SALEM STATE UNIVERSITY

ESTHER MENDEZ
NORTH CAROLINA A & T STATE UNIVERSITY

CHAPTER TOPICS

- Overview
- Objectives
- Key Concepts and Definitions
- Introduction
- Evolution Timeline of Supported Employment
- Legislation
- Individual Placement Models
- Employer Concerns and Attitudes
- SE Research and Best Practices
- Summary

OVERVIEW

Work is a multi-dimensional concept that takes place under multiple names such as job, position, and occupation.[22] Rothman,[17, p.5] indicates that work is defined as an "activity performed to produce goods or services of value to others." In the United States culture, work or employment is a major life activity. There have been public policies that have been established on the local, state, and federal levels that promote the idea that all citizens have the opportunity to work in an environment that is rewarding. Historically, persons with disabilities (PWD) have been disproportionately unemployed or underemployed. For example, PWD have consistently maintained an overall unemployment rate of 30% to 40%. The trend also suggests that during hard economic times and high national unemployment numbers, the percentage of PWD that are gainfully employed decreases.

The literature suggests that the majority of PWD value work. Based on the results from the 2006 General Social Survey (GSS) conducted by the National Opinion Research Center at the University of Chicago, 80% of PWD who were unemployed said they desired paid employment compared to 78% of persons who did not have disabilities.[13]

The results of the survey suggest that employment related variables such as job security, income, flexibility in the workplace, and career advancement were highly valued by the respondents. Compared to their peers without disabilities, most persons with disabilities who were unemployed did not express the same level of assurance relative to their outlook for employment.[13]

OBJECTIVES

This chapter will examine the historical and legislative beginnings of supported employment from theory to practice. Key terms will be defined, while past and present SE models, research and best practices, benefits of supported employment, and supported employment from the employer's perspective will be presented. Readers will:

- develop an understanding of key supported employment definitions concepts and terms,
- be familiar with the historical account of supported employment;
- demonstrate an understanding of policy related to supported employment,
- understand supported employment models,
- be familiar with current terminology and best practices of supported employment,
- become aware of the benefits of supported employment, and
- develop an understanding of employer concerns and attitudes.

KEY CONCEPTS AND DEFINITIONS

The following concepts and definitions are presented to provide a clearer understanding of supported employment.

- *Competitive Employment*: Employment at or above the minimum wage that constitutes part time or full-time work. The job should be readily available to all individuals with or without a disability.
- *Integrated Settings*: Involves the philosophy whereby persons with disabilities work with workers who do not have disabilities. This includes not only physical contact but also social relationships within the employment setting.
- *Natural Cues*: A natural cue involves an aspect of the work environment, job tasks, or activities that direct an employee onto the next step on the job.
- *Natural Supports*: A complex term that involves both the community and workplace or what might be called Personal Network. Personal Network would consist of inside and outside workplace supports with the unified goal of assisting individuals in maintaining competitive employment.
- *Job Carving*: Also known as job creation or job restructuring. Job carving is the process of analyzing a job and its key components in its simplest form then designating specific components or customizing components based on the individual's competencies and ability to perform the job efficiently.
- *Job Development*: The process of networking with employers, community leaders, and businesses (e.g. Chamber of Commerce) to promote employment opportunities for consumers.
- *Job Placement*: The process of identifying and placing a consumer in a job of their choice.
- *Employment Specialist/Job Coach/Consultant*: An individual who works in partnership with the consumer to a) assist in identifying strengths, provide support (personal and natural), and the facilitate vocational goals, b) provide support to activities such as on-site training, employer education, environmental modification, and workplace strategies, and c) assist in identifying natural workplace supports, resources, and strategies.
- *Extensive Support Services*: Ongoing services that assist in maintaining the consumers' competitive employment (e.g. skill training, social skills training, crisis intervention, employer education).
- *Supported Services*: These services can vary. Some examples of these services are identification and facilitation of natural supports, skills training, job-site training, and compensatory workplace strategies.

- *Supported Employment*: Employment in an integrated setting where competitive employment is performed. Under P.L.102-569, supported employment is a service provided for individuals who qualify for vocational rehabilitation and either need long- term support to obtain and maintain competitive employment or have a history of intermittent competitive employment, but have not been successful in maintaining their employment due to the nature of their severe disability.
- *APSE*: The Association of Persons in Supported Employment (APSE) is the *only* national organization with an *exclusive focus* on integrated employment and career advancement opportunities for individuals with disabilities.
- *Consumer*: A person with a significant disability seeking competitive employment.
- *Follow-along Supports*: Holistic and comprehensive network of services that are individualized within and outside the workplace that provide support to consumers to enable them to work. Examples of supports are case managers, family, various doctors, and counselors).
- *Train-Place-Train-Follow-up*: This approach involves four components: 1) determining significant employment and appropriate workplace behavior that must be learned prior to job placement, 2) training persons to obtain the necessary skills, 3) placement in competitive employment settings, and 4) if needed, follow-up training to ensure tenure on the job.

INTRODUCTION

Supported employment (SE) was highlighted by the Developmental Disabilities Assistance Bill of Rights Act of 1984, but the history of SE dates back well into the 1970's.[3] The need for supporting persons with severe developmental disabilities was not always a priority for employers or society. SE was looked upon as an alternative to other rehabilitation models that incorporated employment options for persons in the community. Because of a lack of success with these other models, SE emerged as an alternative method of serving persons with severe developmental disabilities.[27]

> *Competitive employment allows persons to earn wages and receive benefits. These factors promote increased independence and access to the community.*[11]

Little emphasis was placed on persons with severe disabilities having meaningful or competitive employment in the community. Some persons with severe developmental disabilities were confined to institutions or were not properly integrated into the community through competitive employment.[23] Because of the lack of applicable skills to manage the demands of work or a daily work schedule, a number of persons with severe disabilities had limited to no knowledge of:

- how to function successfully on a job,
- how to manage money, and
- how to navigate through an interview.

Many individuals with severe disabilities also were not aware that programs existed to help them address specific needs. Research in the area of severe disabilities indicated that persons with severe disabilities could work effectively and contribute positively to the workforce.

During the early 1970s and 80s, and even today, society evaluates people on the type of job they hold and the financial freedoms afforded to being employed. Researchers have highlighted the importance of work roles and the significance that work plays in the lives of persons with or without a disability.[23] Focusing on how to assist persons with severe disabilities obtain employment became a significant part of rehabilitation legislation. Knowing the societal impact of how PWD are viewed, it became apparent that more was needed to establish services for persons with severe disabilities.

Examining different ways in which support could be provided for persons with severe disabilities could:

- increase that person's motivation for employment,
- boost their self-esteem and morale, and
- increase the person's confidence in gaining competitive employment.

> *Historically, sheltered workshops were used to train persons with the most significant disabilities for employment. Research has shown this approach did not result in competitive employment for the majority of individuals who entered sheltered workshops. Furthermore, this approach did not take into account the customer's (i.e., PWD) wants, desires, and aspirations for employment.*

Sheltered workshops tended to be paternalistic in nature and embraced the medical model of focusing on the disability rather than providing accommodations and strategies within the environment to improve employment outcomes. Consequently, sheltered workshops did not meet the essence of the Developmental Disabilities Act of 1984 which emphasized promoting the values of independence, productivity, integration, and inclusion in the community. The National Disability Rights Network (NDRN) reported people with disabilities who work in sheltered workshops take home on average $175 a week.[15] In 2011, the Executive Director of the National Disability Rights

Network (NDRN) called for the end of the sub-minimum wage, segregated work, and sheltered employment for people with disabilities that still occurs in America in his open letter "Segregated & Exploited, A Call to Action!"

Over the past two decades, supported employment has served as a major source of employment for PWD. Supported employment began to move away from consumers having a lack of employment choice to a more autonomous model—that of a consumer-driven or consumer-centered approach for competitive employment outcomes. With the many disparities of sheltered workshops, supported employment has slowly been assisting people with disabilities in gaining employment in the competitive job market. Table 1, provided by the Dartmouth Community Mental Health Program, illustrates the evolution of SE across a 40-year period.

TABLE 1

EVOLUTION TIMELINE
OF SUPPORTED EMPLOYMENT

1960-1970	1970 -1980	1980 – 1990	1990 -2000
Sheltered workshops/adult activity centers/ state institutions for persons with disabilities	Placement into real work/ competitive employment occurs at specific entities (e.g. university centers/research based)	Federal policy and funding expanded SE services	Philosophical shift from paternalism to consumer driven SE services
Behavior analysis being implemented as a part of training	Focus on persons with mental retardation	SE expanded to all severe disabilities	International emergence of SE with the formation of the Union of Supported Employment/World Association of SE
Majority of sheltered workshops are segregated from the general workforce	The term Job Coach was introduced	National/state acceptance to provide SE services	Viability of SE being challenged by traditional philosophies of adult day centers
	Transition from institutionalization to normalization	Job coach services increased	Emphasis placed on community business and natural supports

Dartmouth Community Mental Health Program: Supported Employment Information for Policy Makers; Retrieved from http//dms.dartmouth.edu/ pre/employment

EVOLUTION TIMELINE OF SUPPORTED EMPLOYMENT

According to Wehman & Bricout,[25] the historical account of the supported employment movement began in the 1970s, whereby persons with disabilities, specifically persons with mental retardation, were placed into competitive employment settings. During this ten-year period, the term "job coach" was introduced and the philosophical transition from institutionalization to normalization became evident. The 1980s through the 1990s saw the establishment of federal policy and public and private funding to expand services to include SE services to persons with severe disabilities. Because of these policy and funding changes, SE services, such as job coaching services, increased significantly. The late 1990s through the new millennium ushered in a philosophical shift from paternalism to participant driven SE services that included the emergence of an international presence of SE with the establishment of the Union of Supported Employment/World Association of SE. Community businesses and natural supports became infused in SE services during this era.

LEGISLATION

Due to the limited employment related resources for persons with severe developmental disabilities, the federal government established legislation that helped provide a roadmap for persons with severe disabilities desiring gainful employment. The Developmental Disabilities Act of 1984 introduced and defined the concept of SE. Even though legislation was established to help persons with severe disabilities gain competitive employment, more needed to be done to ensure that people with severe disabilities were receiving appropriate services. The U.S. Congress, through the Rehabilitation Act Amendments of 1986, has assisted PWD in obtaining competitive employment through the federal/state supported employment program. Prior to the 1986 legislation, PWD were frequently viewed as:

- not being able to work competitively,
- were not seen as viable candidates for work, and
- were not capable of securing or maintaining a completive job.

Hence, the labor force was not utilizing this valuable human resource.

The 1990 Americans with Disabilities Act (ADA) provided more clarity and language to assist PWD. Some researchers have argued that this Act is one of the most significant pieces of legislation for PWD. After the ADA was passed, the idea of integrating work settings and providing jobs to people with the most severe disabilities was well received. With advancements and changes due to the ADA, the definition of SE has been revisited. The Office of

Disability Employment Policy has provided more information and expanded the definition of SE:

> *Supported employment is a program to assist people with the most significant disabilities to become and remain successfully and competitively employed in integrated work settings. Supported employment is targeted to people with the most significant disabilities for whom competitive employment has not traditionally occurred, has been interrupted or is intermittent because of the disability, or who, because of severity of their disability, need intensive or extensive services to work competitively.*[16]

Unfortunately, there remains a large number of persons with severe disabilities who are not receiving proper services to which they are entitled.[12] Continuing avenues need to be explored to expand employment options for persons with disabilities.

Individual and group placement models have been utilized for placement of persons with significant disabilities. Five models have been either modified or developed over the past 20 years. The Substance Abuse and Mental Health Services Administration and the Center for Mental Health Services (SAMHS),[24] conducted a five-year, multi-site study that identified nine model interventions in eight states across the United States. The majority of models identified combined vocational and clinical services to achieve employment goals, (See Table 2).

TABLE 2
SUPPORTED EMPLOYMENT MODELS

	Hybrid Models	Group Approach	Individual Approach	Integrated Treatment Teams	Benefits Assistance
Integrated Supported Employment (SE)			✔	✔	✔
International Center for Clubhouse Development (ICCD) Accredited Clubhouse		✔			
Individual Placement and Support (IPS)			✔	✔	
Assertive Community Treatment (ACT)			✔	✔	
ACT/IPS	✔			✔	
Family/ACT	✔			✔	
Mental Health Employers Consortium (MHEC)			✔	✔	
Employment Assistance through Reciprocity in Natural Supports (EARNS)			✔	✔	
Long-Term Employment Training and Supports (LETS)			✔	✔	✔

The Substance Abuse and Mental Health Services Administration and the Center for Mental Health Services noted there are two obstacles to successful employment of persons with psychiatric disabilities. These obstacles are stigma and discrimination. Complicating matters for persons with psychiatric disabilities is having adequate access to healthcare and appropriate support services. If an individual becomes employed, they may lose their services. This alone creates a tremendous, sometimes unanticipated, burden on the individual. The Employment Intervention Demonstration Program found the collaborative relationships between time-unlimited supports, vocational supports, and mental health treatment services were effective interventions for people with severe and persistent mental illness. The program also determined some vocational services were more effective than others were. The effective programs provided an integration of ongoing support, mental health support, vocational support, and focused on the consumer's job choice with rapid placement into the preferred job.[24]

INDIVIDUAL PLACEMENT MODELS

Individual placement models are either called Individual Placement Model or Individual Placement and Supports Model (IPS). IPS meets the essence of the Developmental Disabilities Act and is the least restrictive of any of the service delivery models. Of the models within supported employment, it has been documented that IPS is the most comprehensive approach for people with severe mental illness. Bayne[4] cites a key component of IPS, that being people who want to work are placed directly into their work preference and are supported with ongoing measures such as one-on-one assistance from an identified employment specialist. Through ongoing assistance, the person can obtain and maintain competitive employment in the setting of his or her choice. The Dartmouth Psychiatric Research Center, in their newsletter *Employment Works*,[2] identified seven key principles of IPS. These seven principles are:

- every individual who wants employment is eligible,
- services are integrated with treatment,
- competitive employment is the goal,
- personalized benefits counseling is provided,
- job search starts soon after person expresses interest in working,
- continuous follow-along supports, and
- the individual preferences are important.[2, p.4]

Another aspect of the IPS model is the assistance through education programs. The *Employment Works*[2] newsletter identified that IPS's focus is employment. The article stated that other members of the team, such as case managers, should focus on education. No supported education models have been identified as most effective. If education were a route for individuals seeking employment, IPS would only support programs that are focused on everyone, not just persons with disabilities.

Primary Service Provider Model. This model uses an employment specialist or job coach to aid persons with disabilities in obtaining and maintaining competitive employment. The employment specialist provides support in the areas of accompanying the person seeking employment, assisting with completing job applications and interview preparation, on-the-job coaching, and advocating for persons with disabilities. This model endorses physical integration and ongoing support to achieve successful employment outcomes.[11]

GROUP PLACEMENT MODELS

Group models consist of four differing models: Enclave, Mobile Work Crew, Cluster, and Entrepreneurial/Bench work model.

Enclave Model includes a group of individuals ranging from three to eight. The enclave model focuses on support from a full-time agency supervisor at a community business. Consumer's earnings within the enclave model are based upon production rate, piece rate, or sub-minimum wage.

Mobile Work Crew Model includes a group of individuals sponsored by an agency and supervised by a designated crew supervisor. The agency has contracts within the community and the work crews travel to various work sites that are under contract with the agency. Pay is similar to enclaves with respect to piece rate, and subminimum wage.

Cluster or Dispersed Group Model focuses on training consumers through an agency appointed supervisor. Cluster differs from the mobile work crew in that the business hires the consumers and they earn wages commensurate with others doing the same work. Within this model, the supported employment cluster group stays together but may perform duties in other areas at the particular business.

Entrepreneurial Model is historically known as the Bench Work Model. Botterbusch[6] described the Bench Work Model as consisting of persons with significant disabilities employed as a group (12-15 individuals) in companies more focused on assembly line type of production jobs. The entrepreneurial model focuses on the establishment of a specific for-profit company that employs larger numbers of individuals with significant disabilities to meet the needs of the local commercial companies.

EMPLOYER CONCERNS AND ATTITUDES

Employer concerns and attitudes still exist relative to hiring persons with disabilities, even though these concerns and attitudes have been refuted by research. Some of their concerns and attitudes are:

- hiring persons with disabilities will increase the risk of workplace injury, thus increasing workers' compensation insurance premiums,
- research has suggested that employers feel more negative work related issues (e.g. customers shopping elsewhere) will occur with disabled employees verses nondisabled employees, and
- employees with disabilities are more productive as compared to their nondisabled counterparts.

SUPPORTED EMPLOYMENT INCENTIVES

The expansion of SE services is heavily influenced by current and anticipated future economic changes. These changes vary from available jobs and local, regional, national, and more recently, international labor market demands. Employed persons with disabilities thus contribute to the economy as paying consumers of products and services in their communities. They also contribute to the local, state, and national economy as taxpaying citizens. According to the American Association on Intellectual & Developmental Disabilities,[1] persons with disabilities who receive supported employment services annual earnings are approximately $600 million. Likewise, they pay over $100 million annually in federal, state, and local taxes.

SE has proven to be a benefit to employers through tax incentives received when qualified persons with disabilities are hired. For the employer, job tax credits provide monetary incentives for hiring under-employed populations such as persons with disabilities. Cimera[7] mentions that employers are granted Work Opportunity Tax Credits (WOTC), equaling a portion of the wages paid to persons with disabilities. For instance, if an employer received a 40% tax credit for the first $6,000 a supported employee earns, they would save $2,400 in taxes over the first 12 months the supported employee was employed. These provisions may help ease the societal beliefs that PWD are a hiring risk. Shafer, et al.[21] found that some employers were highly motivated and receptive to the idea of hiring PWD who want to work as a means of strengthening their labor force.

DISINCENTIVES OF SUPPORTED EMPLOYMENT

The premise of supported employment includes integration and establishing professional relationships between persons with and without disabilities within a competitive work environment. Self determination is a milestone that people with disabilities, particularly people with severe disabilities, may achieve through supported employment.[19] In some cases, successful employment in an integrated work environment can be a financial disincentive. For example, Supplemental Security Income (SSI), Social Security Disability Insurance (SSDI), and Medicaid are examples of financial benefits that may be lost as a result of employment. Section 1619a and Section 1619b allow persons with disabilities to increase their income, but concerns persist.

SE RESEARCH AND BEST PRACTICES

Supported Employment has recently been documented as an evidence-based practice for the employment of people with severe mental illness.[5] In an effort to help with placement and options for PWD, the Workforce Investment Act and the Ticket to Work Incentives Improvement Act were passed to try and increase the number of resources for PWD. These two programs are examples of legislation that is working to help persons with severe disabilities obtain competitive employment. Smith and Dunn[20] analyzed the 2005 American Community Survey (ACS) and found that 37 percent of adults with disabilities are employed, while 74 percent of adults without disabilities are employed. Based on the unemployment data among adults with disabilities, it is evident that current legislation and funding are not enough. New models, methods, and SE established best practices are required to maximize employment efforts for PWDs today and in the future.

Crowther, et al.[8] conducted a comprehensive review and analysis of the literature between1982 and 1998 assessing the effects of pre-vocational rehabilitation and supportive employment. Their findings determined supported employment was a more effective means to competitive employment for individuals with severe mental illness, compared to pre-vocational training. The United States Department of Health and Human Services[24] reported that the employment rate for individuals with severe disabilities was approximately 25%. Lehman, et al.[14] performed a randomized control trial with 219 patients at a psychiatric outpatient unit and found individuals who participated in an IPS program achieved competitive employment rates 30% higher than if someone used a psychosocial approach to placement. Drake, et al.,[9] in a different randomized control trial, found that IPS was a more effective means to competitive employment.

Wehman, et al.[26] reported 10 quality measures and examples of functional indicators for a supported employment program. These measures are:

- meaningful competitive employment in integrated work settings,
- informed choice, control, and satisfaction,
- level and nature of supports,
- employment of persons with severe disabilities,
- amount of hours worked,
- number of persons from program working regularly,
- well coordinated job retention,
- employment outcome monitoring and tracking system,

- maximizing integration and community participation, and
- employer satisfaction.

The purpose for these measures is to assist in obtaining meaningful and competitive employment outcomes as well as community interaction and integration for persons with severe disabilities. Green, et al.[10] reported the best indicators for successful partnership in supported employment are sound individualized written rehabilitation plans (now known as the individual plan for employment) or similar correctly implemented plans with careful consideration of all aspects of services for persons with disabilities.

The emerging trend for evidence-based research on SE has provided sound strategies to improved employment outcomes for persons with severe disabilities. Much of the evidence-based research, however, has involved persons with mental illness. Based on this fact, much of the literature places emphasis on:

- the agency providing vocational rehabilitation services rather than "traditional" day treatment or sheltered workshop services;
- the term "rapid job search" is used to assist PWD to obtain appropriate employment instead of undergoing pre-employment assessment, training, and counseling services;
- providing employment that is based on PWD interest, strengths, and work experiences;
- consistent and prolonged follow-along supports; and
- integrating SE personnel with mental health treatment personnel.[5]

SUMMARY

Hanley-Maxwell, et al.[11] indicate that the implementation of supported employment services for persons with disabilities, particularly persons with severe disabilities, dramatically increased the number of individuals joining the competitive labor force. From the establishment of SE during the 1970s and its implementation in the 1980s, SE has proven to be a cost-efficient way to assist persons with disabilities in entering the labor force and becoming productive citizens.

SE continues to experience challenges including negative employer concerns and attitudes with regard to employing persons with disabilities. However, the benefits as established from evidence-based practices, suggest that SE provides qualified employees with disabilities on-the-job training resources, no-cost job placement services, operations analysis, post-employment follow-up, and technical assistance in workplace accommodations.

The outlook for SE services to persons with disabilities, especially persons with severe disabilities, is promising. With the increased use of assistive technology, workplace accommodation strategies, and tax incentives, employers can feel confident when they hire persons from this group.

There are important questions that relate to the future of SE:

- Does the long term cost of SE offset the long term cost for mental health and the hospitalization of persons with psychiatric disabilities, and
- What impact do SE services have on Supplemental Security Income (SSI) and Social Security Disability Insurance, medical benefits, subsidized housing, and other public services?

REFERENCES

[1]American Association on Intellectual & Developmental Disabilities (2012), http://www.aamr.org/content_196.cfm

[2]Ask your questions about IPS supported employment. (2009, Summer). Employment Works! Employment Supports for People with Mental Illness: A Newsletter for IPS Supported Employment.

[3]Babour, W. C. (1999). Supported Employment: The coming of full circle. *Journal of Vocational Rehabilitation, 13*, 165-174

[4]Bayne (2004). Supported Employment and the Individual Placement and Support model for people with severe mental illness: what is the evidence for their effectiveness? *Warwick Institute for Employment Research.* Retrieved September 16, 2011 from http://www.guidance-research.org/EG/equal-opps/EOD1/EOD3/IndexFolder.2005-02-11.5000319202/litrev

[5]Bond, G., Becker, D., Drake, R., Rapp, C., Meisler, N., Lehman, A., Bell, M., and Blyer, C. (2001). Implementing supportive employment as an evidence-based practice. Psychiatric Services. *52*(3), 313-322.

[6]Botterbusch, K. F. (1989). Supported employment models: A review of the literature. Vocational Evaluation and Work Adjustment Bulletin, *22*(3), 95-102.

[7]Cimera, R. E. (2002).*The monetary benefits and costs of hiring supported employees: A primer.* Journal of Vocational Rehabilitation. 17. Retrieve February 28, 2012 from http://www.worksupport.com/resources/printView.cfm/202

[8]Crowther, R., Marshall, M., Bond, G., Huxley, P. (2004) Vocational rehabilitation for people with severe mental illness (Cochrane Review). In: *The Cochrane Library*, Issue 3 2004. Chichester 2004, UK: John Wiley & Sons.

[9]Drake, R. E., McHugo, G. J., Bebout, R. R., Becker, D. R., Harris, M., Bond, G., Quimby, E. (1999) Randomized clinical trial of supported employment for inner- city patients with severe mental disorders. *Archives of General Psychiatry*, *56*(7), 627-633.

[10]Green, H., Brooke, V., Revell, G., West, M., & Inge, K. (1997). Quality Supported Employment Services. In Brooke,V. , Inge, K., Armstrong, A., & Wehman, P.(Eds.), *Supported Employment: A Customer-Driven Approach for Persons with Significant Disabilities.* http://sid.usal.es/idocs/F8/FDO652 8/supportedemployment.pdf

[11]Hanley-Maxwell, Owens-Johnson, & Fabian, (2003). Supported Employment. In Szymanski, B. M. & Parker, R. M. (Eds.), *Work and disability: Issues and strategies in career development and job placement (2nd ed.).* (pp. 376-406). Austin, TX: Pro Ed.

[12]Johnson, D. R. (2004). Supported employment trends: Implication for transition-age youth. *Research & Practice for Persons with Severe Disabilities, 29(4),* 243-247.

[13]Kruse, D. & Blanck, P. (September 23, 2008) People with Disabilities Want to Work, Have Similar Job Preferences as Others, Rutgers Researcher Finds Rutgers Today Retrieved July 21, 2011 from: http://news.rutgers.edu/medrel/news-releases/2008/09/people-with-disabili-20080922

[14]Lehman, A. F., Goldberg, R., Dixon, L. B., McNary, S., Postrado, L., Hackman, A., McConnell, K. (2002) Improving employment outcomes for persons with severe mental illnesses. *Archives General Psychiatry*, *59*(2), 165-172.

[15]National Disability Rights Network. (2011). *Segregated & exploited: A call to action.* Retrieved from http://www.napas.org /images/ Documents/Resources/Publications/Reports/Segregated-and-Exploited.pdf

[16]Office of Disability Employment Policy, Department of Labor (2002). Retrieved September 16, 2011 from http://www.dol.gov/odep/media/reports/ek01/support.html

[17]Rothman, R. A. (1987*). Working: Sociological perspectives*. Englewood Cliffs, NJ: Prentice Hall.

[18]Rubin, S. E., & Roessler, R. T. (2001). *Foundations of the vocational rehabilitation process* (5th edition). Austin, TX: PRO-ED.

[19]Rudrud, E. H., Ziarnik, J. P., Bernstein, G. S., & Ferrara, J. M. (1984). *Proactive vocational habilitation.* Baltimore: Paul H. Brookes.

[20]Smith, F. A., & Dunn, D. S. (2007). *Employment rates for people with disabilities and without disabilities (Data No. 10).* Boston: University of Massachusetts Boston Institute for Community Inclusion

[21]Shafer, M., Hill, J., Wehman, P., & Banks, P. D. (1988). A survey of Employers experiences with supported employment. *American Journal of Mental Deficiency.*

[22]Szymanski, B. M., & Parker, R. M. (2003) (2nd ed.). *Work and disability: Issues and strategies in career development and job placement.* Austin, TX: Pro Ed.

[23]Tyrell, W., Burns, M., & Zipple, A. (2003). Organizing supports in the workplace to sustain employment. New York, NY: Kluwer Academic/Plenum Publishers.

[24]U.S. Department of Health and Human Services, Substance Abuse and Mental Health Services Administration, center for Mental health Services. (2003). Supported employment: A guide for mental health planning + advisory councils. Retrieved from http://www.namhpac.org/PDFs/SE.pdf

[25]Wehman, P. & Bricou, J. (1999). *Supported Employment: Critical Issues and New Directions*. Retrieved February 28, 2012 from www.nytransitions.org/resources/force_download/430/article1.pdf

[26]Wehman, P., Revell, W. G., & Brooke, V. (2003).Competitive Employment Has It Become the "First Choice" Yet? *Journal of Disability Policy Studies 14*(3), 163-173

[27]Wehman, P., Gibson, K., Brooke, V, Unger, D. (1998). Transition from school to competitive employment: Illustrationsof competence for two young women with severe mental retardation. *Focus on Autism and other Developmental Disabilities, 13*(3), 130-143.

14

CASE MANAGEMENT PRACTICES IN REHABILITATION AND HUMAN SERVICES

Michael J. Leahy

MICHIGAN STATE UNIVERSITY

Katherine M. Kline

Maryville University

CHAPTER TOPICS

- Description of Case Management
- Purpose of Case Management
- Case Management Models
- Principles of Case Management
- Importance of Case Management in Rehabilitation and Human Services
- Ethical Issues in Case Management
- Working Alliance
- Technology
- Summary and Conclusions

Rehabilitation and human service workers are employed with a variety of job titles in a wide range of practice settings, and as such, must possess many skills for competent practice. Case management has been consistently recognized as one of the most important functions for effectiveness and efficiency in many of these roles.[15,11,13,14] The concept of case management is not a new one. Many rehabilitation, social services, health care, and human services professions have a long history of using various case management concepts and techniques within their specific service delivery systems. For example, for many years, social workers have coordinated the provision of services to people with mental health problems,[21] and rehabilitation counselors have historically applied case management and coordination functions in carrying out their multifaceted role.[29]

Modern case management practice has only recently become visible as an integral part of our rehabilitation, health care, and human services service delivery system.[20] With the expansion of federally supported programs in the 1960's and 1970's, the practice of case management has become prominent in the helping professions.[17] With the creation of these programs, it becomes increasingly difficult for people to understand and navigate the maze of systems that was originally established to serve them. With this, case management became a necessity.

The purpose of this chapter is to provide a description of case management that includes information on the models, principles, functions, and required knowledge that practitioners performing case management need to be aware of in providing these types of services to clients. In addition, this chapter will explore some of the central elements related to case management such as the working alliance, ethical considerations, including ethical decision making models, and the application of technology in the case management process. For more detailed information on case management, the interested reader is encouraged to explore some of the long standing comprehensive texts available in the literature, such as the comprehensive two volume set by Chan, Leahy and Saunders[4] and the textbook by Roessler and Rubin.[18]

DESCRIPTION OF CASE MANAGEMENT

The term "case management" has many different meanings in today's rehabilitation and human services delivery systems. In some instances, case management is considered a professional role, where all the associated functions and tasks serve the purpose of providing effective case management services to individuals with disabilities, within some specific service delivery setting. These types of case managers are often employed in human service settings, such as community-based rehabilitation organizations. In other situations, case management may represent one specific function and associated tasks within the overall role of the professional, as in the case of the

Rehabilitation Counselor and others (e.g., Mental Health Counselor, Social Worker). The Case Management Society of America[3] defines case management, as "a collaborative process of assessment, planning, facilitation, and advocacy for options and services to meet an individual's health needs through communication and available resources to promote quality cost-effective outcomes." According to Solomon,[22] the rehabilitation model of case management has the practitioner teaching clients necessary skills to meet their goals. This is done by providing interpersonal support until the client establishes a network of support and is the primary responsible party for coordinating care. Goering[5] demonstrates how this model has proven to be successful in increasing occupation/vocational functioning, decreasing social isolation, and creating more stabilized independent living environments (as cited in Solomon[22]). The rehabilitation practitioner is also identified as the "manager" of the case processes, and is thereby responsible for facilitating activities to be conducted at each step (e.g. intake, eligibility determination, assessment, counseling, plan development, service implementation and supervision, job placement, follow-up and post-employment services) of the rehabilitation process.[29] As such, case management should be conceptualized as a process that evolves throughout time, rather than a single event in any particular case.

PURPOSE OF CASE MANAGEMENT

Case management serves several key purposes beyond facilitation of services. One advocacy function is to increase access to services for vulnerable populations. As mentioned previously, maneuvering complex systems with limited power or background knowledge of the organizational operations may prove to be difficult for most. It is the case manager's role to open these doors for their clients and assist them in accessing services that they may deem beneficial. Another function is to increase the quality of care that client's receive under the supervision and follow-up of the case manager.[17] As services are being made available to clients, the case manager is also responsible to see that referral sources are providing timely, quality services that were agreed upon by the client.

Increasing access to services and quality of care are two steps toward the primary aim of case management—achieving a client's desired outcomes. Towards this objective are three primary factors that are central to effective case management:

- client choice,
- person-first language, and
- client/counselor mutual agreement of planned services and outcomes.

Each facet highlights the co-management process of rehabilitation, which values the "client as colleague."[18] Educating clients regarding their options when deciding upon services and encouraging them to choose makes it possible for personal motivation and strengths to be actualized. This proves to be a powerful tool towards the achievement of goals. Furthermore, avoidance of language in which the client is made to feel like just another case in a sea of cases is an important consideration. Engaging in this practice would jeopardize the co-management model (e.g."I have to do an intake on you. I have to assess you. I'll be monitoring you").[17] Instead, utilize person-first language to engage the client, like the statements that follow.

> *Please, tell me about yourself and what brings you to my office today. I feel that having more information about your academic achievement will help us determine potential college options. How do you feel about working together to gather more information about your reading, writing, and math skills? Over the next 90 days, I'll be checking in on you to see how everything is going and if I can help you in any other way.*

Finally, having mutually agreed upon and client directed goals and services are essential for the case management process. This agreement helps establish rapport, an essential piece of the relationship, while giving the client shared power and responsibility. These elements have proven to be successful in improving services to individuals with disabilities.[6]

CASE MANAGEMENT MODELS

Over the years, a variety of case management models have emerged and evolved that provide a useful framework for the case management process. While these models may differ in relation to the specific nature of the health-related or rehabilitation problems addressed, the delivery system, services provided, outcomes, and professional grounding of the individual delivering services, the process involved appears quite similar.[12] As indicated by Shaw, Leahy, and Chan,[20] the human service environment in which case management takes place, regardless of the model used to provide services, has undergone rapid change and evolution over the past decade or so. In today's environment of increased accountability and scarce resources, the case manager needs refined skills in teamwork, resource development, networking, referral, and coordination in order to identify, provide, or arrange services that address the needs of the client in an ever increasingly complex, evolving, and diverse service delivery process.[28]

The complexity encountered in understanding the various contemporary models in case management is significant. There are many definitions and models employed in practice. Yet, despite this lack of standardization, the terms case management and case management models are commonly used in the literature without any specific description of their meaning. This lack of specificity has resulted in a general inability to accurately compare models, outcomes, and effectiveness of case management services.[7] In this section of the chapter, we will describe some of these various models and their application within the rehabilitation and human service delivery process. A review of the literature suggests that one of the most basic and useful set of models has been described by Woodside and McClam,[28] who identified three fundamental case management models, whose basis is grounded in roles, organizations, and responsibilities. In their conceptualization, the three models include:

- role-based case management,
- organization-based case management, and
- responsibility-based case management.

Each of these selected models is briefly described below.

ROLE-BASED CASE MANAGEMENT

This first model focuses on the overall role the case manager performs. For example, a case manager may act exclusively as one who arranges or coordinates services, while a more discipline-based case manager may provide case management services in addition to an array of other services and functions, which taken together form their overall role. A good example of this latter model would be Rehabilitation Counselors or Mental Health Counselors. These counselors, in addition to case management, provide counseling or therapeutic services directly to the client as part of their professional role, and within the working alliance established with the consumer of services.

ORGANIZATION-BASED CASE MANAGEMENT

The second model is focused on providing a comprehensive set of services available within a particular organization or agency, such as a comprehensive rehabilitation center or a non-profit community-based rehabilitation organization. Each client served within the organization is assigned a case manager who arranges, coordinates, and monitors services provided to the individual consumer and progress toward specific rehabilitation related goals and objectives.

RESPONSIBILITY-BASED CASE MANAGEMENT

This third type of case management model provides for functions to be performed by family members, supportive personnel, volunteers, or the consumer. The focus in this type of model is on the transition of care from human service professional to non-professionals, including the consumer.

PRINCIPLES OF CASE MANAGEMENT

The guiding principles of case management, described by Woodside & McClam,[28] have direct application in the operationalization of each of the models described above, and have a particular importance in establishing a philosophical framework for the delivery of services and the relationship between the individual receiving services and the case manager. These general principles include the following:

- integration of services,
- continuity of care,
- equal access to services,
- quality care,
- advocacy,
- working with the whole person,
- consumer empowerment, and
- evaluation.

In the rehabilitation counseling literature, there are a number of additional guidelines that directly affect the delivery of case management services.[12] First, over the years there has been an effort to identify the basic principles of rehabilitation philosophy that serve to guide practice, as well as providing a useful framework for the development of ethical standards of practice to guide the provision of case management services. These principles and guidelines, known as the basic principles of rehabilitation philosophy, were first introduced by DiMichael,[2] expanded upon by Wright,[30] and modified by Parker & Szymanski.[16] The 20 principles are as follows:

- Every human being has an inalienable value and is worthy of respect for his/her own sake.
- Every person has membership in society, and rehabilitation should cultivate his/her full acceptance.
- The assets of people with disabilities should be emphasized, supported, and developed.
- Reality factors should be stressed in helping the person to cope with his/her environment.
- Comprehensive treatment involves the "whole person," because life areas are interdependent.
- Treatment should vary and be flexible to deal with the special characteristics of each person.
- Every person should assume as much initiative and participation as possible for the rehabilitation plan and its execution.
- Society should be responsible, through all possible public and private agencies, for the providing of services and opportunities to people with disabilities.

- Rehabilitation programs must be conducted with interdisciplinary and interagency integration.
- Rehabilitation is a continuous process that applies as long as help is needed.
- Psychological and personal reactions of the individual are ever present and often crucial.
- The rehabilitation process is complex and must be subject to constant reexamination – for each individual and for the program as a whole.
- The severity of handicap can be increased or decreased by environmental conditions.
- The significance of disability is affected by the person's feelings about the self and his/her situation.
- The client is seen not as an isolated individual but as part of a larger group that includes other people, often the family.
- Predictor variables, based on group outcomes in rehabilitation, should be applied with caution to the individual case.
- Self-help organizations are important allies in the rehabilitation effort.
- Provision must be made for the effective dissemination of information concerning legislation and community offerings of potential benefit to persons with disabilities.
- Basic research can profitably be guided by the question of usefulness in ameliorating problems, a vital consideration in rehabilitation fields, including psychology.
- Persons with disabilities should be called upon to serve as co-planners, co-evaluators, and consultants to others, including professional persons.

The importance of these principles, according to Leahy et al.,[12] as foundational guidelines for the practice of case management in rehabilitation and human service settings cannot be overstated. It should be noted, however, that for the Rehabilitation Counselor and other professional disciplines (e.g., Mental Health Counselors, Social Workers) who provide case management services as part of their larger role, there are specific ethical codes of conduct and practice guidelines that regulate professional practice in case management, in addition to the general guidance provided by these long-standing philosophical principles.

IMPORTANCE OF CASE MANAGEMENT IN REHABILITATION AND HUMAN SERVICES

A substantial amount of research has been conducted over the years to support the role of case management as a primary function for human service professionals. The Commission for Rehabilitation Counselor Certification (CRCC) is a leading certification organization for the rehabilitation counseling discipline[19] and includes case management as one of twelve knowledge domains incorporated into the Certified Rehabilitation Counselor Examination (CRCE). The rationale for inclusion of these knowledge domains was formed by several role, function, and knowledge validation studies of rehabilitation counselors.[11,13] For example, Leahy et al.[11] found case management was reported by rehabilitation counselors to be their most important job function. Knowledge of case management practices was also found to be highly important, second only to knowledge of medical, functional, and environmental aspects of disabilities. A follow up study found case management to be the most frequently used skill, and for knowledge in this area to be equally as important as medical, functional, and environmental aspects of disabilities, and rated as the most important knowledge for rehabilitation counselors to have.[13] A separate study conducted by Lustig and Strauser[14] indicated that State-Federal vocational rehabilitation counselors spent the most time on case management activities, citing approximately 25% of their time devoted to these tasks. Tables 1 and 2 below provide a more specific look at the case management function, associated tasks, and the required knowledge to deliver effective case management services from a rehabilitation perspective.[11,13]

TABLE 1

CASE MANAGEMENT FUNCTIONS AND TASKS
➢ Compile and interpret client information to maintain a current case record. ➢ Perform caseload management activities. ➢ Consult with medical professionals about functional capacities, prognosis, and treatment plans for clients. ➢ Obtain written reports regarding client progress. ➢ Collaborate with other providers so that services are coordinated, appropriate, and timely. ➢ Write case notes, summaries, and reports so that others can understand the case. ➢ Determine and monitor individual case management outcomes. ➢ Monitor client progress. ➢ State clearly the nature of the clients' problems for referral to service providers. ➢ Develop rapport/network with physicians and other rehabilitation professionals. ➢ Use effective conflict resolution strategies when providing case management services, ➢ Report to referral source regarding progress of cases.

- Make sound and timely financial decisions within the context of caseload management in your work setting.
- Coordinate activities of all agencies involved in a rehabilitation plan.
- Interview the client to collect and verify the accuracy of case information.
- Refer clients to appropriate specialists and/or for special services.
- Use effective time management strategies.
- Abide by ethical and legal considerations of case communication and recording (e.g., confidentiality).
- Assess the significance of the clients' disabilities in consideration of medical, psychological, educational, and social support status.

TABLE 2

KNOWLEDGE DOMAINS OF CASE MANAGEMENT

- Case management processes and tools.
- Case recording and documentation.
- Principles of caseload management.
- Professional roles, functions, and relationships with other human service providers.
- Critical problem solving and critical thinking skills.
- Negotiation and conflict resolution strategies.
- Case management process, including case finding, service coordination, referral to and use of other disciplines, and client advocacy.
- Techniques for working effectively in teams across disciplines.

Rehabilitation professionals have been working as case managers since the boom of government funded programs in the 1960s, and have worked longer on average as certified case managers than either social workers or nurses.[15] In 2006, Certified Rehabilitation Counselors (CRCs) were asked what changes they anticipated in the field within the next five years. A large number of respondents (45%) anticipated that less funding would be available and that they would be "doing more with less."[1] Additionally, counselors imagined that they will see more complex clients with multifaceted needs. Fragmented and costly services, coupled with the rise in chronic or complex conditions (i.e. ageing, PTST, co-morbid populations) is a phenomenon in the US and around the world which case management seeks to ameliorate. These emerging needs speak to the critical importance of effective and efficient case management practices.

Through the process of coordinating services, case managers can facilitate powerful practices that greatly contribute to client development. With informed consent, the client is included as an equal partner in decision-making, and educated regarding their options and opportunities. The case manager acts as an advocate for the client, supporting them in the pursuit of equitable and necessary services. Both of these activities assist to empower the client, thereby restoring control and promoting independence. Social support and independence are seen as key factors in determining an individual's quality of life,[27] and are central to effective case management.

ETHICAL ISSUES IN CASE MANAGEMENT

As indicated by Shaw,[20] case managers are no strangers to the ethical dilemmas presented by competing obligations to advocate for their clients while containing costs for the payer. Ethical dilemmas tied to dual obligation issues and confidentiality may be expected to continue to challenge case managers whenever these services are provided. Tarvydas, Peterson, & Michaelson[26] have provided a comprehensive review of ethical issues in case management and the types of conflicts that often arise in the provision of services by case managers in today's service delivery environments. The first type of conflict they discuss involves differing expectations parties may hold regarding what services will be provided or what services a case manager is capable of competently providing. There may be conflicting values regarding what services, outcomes, or relationships are worthy. In rehabilitation, this conflict may be influenced by the values of the respective service providers involving such matters as maximization of rehabilitation outcome or function, rather than restoration of the client to a minimal level of functional ability.

The second type of conflict involves concurrently owing responsibilities to differing parties in the case management process, most typically the client and the payer. As a result, differing allegiances may develop regarding goals that may conflict due to the disparate functions expected by each party to whom the case manager is obligated (i.e., advocate for the client versus compliance monitor for the payer).

The final type of conflict results from role variability, which itself results from the case manager occupying differing roles with the same party at different times (i.e., client's claims adjuster, rehabilitation counselor, or evaluator). All three types of conflicts certainly can arise periodically for all case managers. Nevertheless, the practice of case management includes all of these conflicts, at least to some degree. Uniquely well-honed skills at discerning the ethically appropriate boundary between these forces are required of the ethical case manager.[26] There is no question that continuing education is a must and case managers who relax for a moment will quickly find themselves out of date and lacking the skills necessary to practice competently and ethically.[20]

In thinking about the ethical issues and potential dilemmas, the case manager's needs to use decision models in addition to established codes of ethics to guide decisions and services. Tarvydas and Cottone[25] developed a four level model of thinking about the contexts of ethical practice that is particularly relevant to the conflicts between individual care and systems-level interests which is particularly relevant to the practice of case management. The model assists the case manager in identifying the contextual forces at each of four hierarchical levels that may impact the ethical decisions made. The four levels are:

- the clinical counseling level,
- the clinical multidisciplinary level,
- the institutional/agency level, and
- the societal resource/public policy level

These levels are interactive in that the activities or forces of one level will influence one or more of the others. Therefore, the ethically relevant threats and opportunities at each level should be recognized and addressed while attempting to understand and resolve the ethical concerns presented in the case management process.[26]

The Integrative Decision-Making Model of Ethical Behavior[24] introduces consideration of these hierarchical factors into a four-stage model. The Integrative Model focuses on the actual production of ethical behavior within a specified context, rather than prematurely terminating the process when a decision is reached about the best course of ethical action. The Integrative Model emphasizes four underlying themes or attitudes of which case managers must be mindful as they apply the specific operations detailed within the model itself. Specifically they must:

- maintain a stance of *reflection* concerning their own personal issues, values, and decision-making skills, as well as extending efforts to understand those of the other parties involved in the situation;
- maintain *balance* among various issues, persons and perspectives within the process;
- provide an appropriate level of attention to *context(s)* of the situation–specifically the hierarchical levels of counselor-client, treatment team, organizational/institutional, and societal implications and interests in the ethical situation; and
- seek to use a process of *collaboration* with all rightful parties to the decision, always being mindful of the client's ethical claim for primary consideration by the professional.[24]

WORKING ALLIANCE

The working alliance framework has evolved within the counseling field since the mid-1950's, and is recognized as being the most critical element in the case management process. The alliance is facilitated when the client and counselor make equal contributions to the relationship via three necessary components: goals, tasks, and bonds.[9] Goals are the desired and agreed upon outcomes of the counseling process (i.e. job goal, educational goal, independent living goal). Tasks are represented as the concrete actions that are taken to form the matter of the counseling process (i.e. resume development, college entrance examinations, establishing a budget, etc). Goals and tasks are built into most case management systems, however bonds are extra components. In human services, goals and tasks are often transparent and clearly defined at the beginning of the counseling relationship, and frequently reevaluated throughout the counseling process. Bonds refer to the attachment, mutual respect, understanding, trust, acceptance, and confidence that develop between the client and counselor throughout the counseling relationship.[8] While bonds between a counselor and client are not explicitly defined and explained in agency policies as goals and tasks are, they are, at a minimum, equally important to the case management process. The working alliance has been directly linked to client outcomes and is proven to be necessary for client change.[10] Effective case management provides goals and tasks— the case manager must strive to establish a bond with the client. Without an established bond, and therefore working alliance, there is a decreased likelihood of clients reaching their desired outcomes.

The utilization of various counseling techniques provided in all master's level counselor education programs are vital to the establishment of a client bond. Active listening skills are critical to making clients feel safe, heard, and understood. They require utilizing attentive body language as well as non-judgmental listening and interviewing skills.[17] Cultural competence is essential not only for establishing a bond, but also in developing a service plan with clients. It is an active, developmental, and ongoing process that effective case managers must continually strive to achieve. Competence in multiculturalism consists of three main components: the counselor's awareness of one's own assumptions, values, and biases; understanding the worldview of culturally diverse clients; and developing appropriate intervention techniques with regard to a client's worldview.[23] It is the responsibility of the case manager to seek information if they are unfamiliar with a particular culture, race, religion, or ethnicity and are not informed at a level that is necessary to understand the viewpoint of that client. As mentioned previously, person-first language is essential for rapport building and subsequent bond establishment. Always identify clients by their name and any other salient characteristics, never by their disability. By implementing these helping skills and establishing a bond, clients are more likely to connect and communicate with their case manager, which tremendously benefits the rehabilitation process.

In 2006, certified rehabilitation counselors working in the public sector anticipated an increased diversity in extenuating circumstances, disability, and requested services. This would result in caseloads becoming more complex and counselors foreseeing a trend toward having less time for counseling and fewer opportunities to develop the client-counselor relationship. These counselors also predicted that they would be serving more diverse clients (both ethnically and linguistically), which would affect the individual and family counseling process.[1] A systematic case management process that not only focusing on tasks and goals, but also on the therapeutic alliance, is key in overcoming these obstacles and fostering client change. Kierpiec, et al.[8] recommends the following counseling strategies to foster a working alliance, and specifically a client bond: in-depth exploration of client issues, being supportive, sharing client successes, helping clients share their feelings and emotions, and attending to the client's unique experiences. By establishing a working alliance, clients are more invested in the process and are more likely to participate, and therefore, benefit from services, all of which aid the case management process and positive outcomes.

TECHNOLOGY

According to Shaw et al.[20] case management is increasingly becoming a technology-driven activity. With the need for more cost-effective and efficient service comes the need to use more rapid means for information management and transmittal. There has been a significant acceleration over the years in the use of electronic case management systems by case managers. These systems provide the case manager with an electronic platform to perform work, communicate, write reports, and document case activity. Since most case managers are simultaneously working with a number of clients at the same time, caseload management is also another specific concern. These newer electronic systems are also meant to assist case managers in organizing their work relative to their overall caseload. In addition to information systems, case managers are likely to find themselves in the role of evaluating and recommending new technology, equipment, and procedures related to advances in medical science and biotechnology. Case managers have also become increasingly reliant on telephone communications with patients, providers, insurers, and others. Computer-based communication systems are increasingly replacing some phone time as more people become accustomed to communicating through e-mail and other related electronic communications.[20]

SUMMARY AND CONCLUSIONS

Case management services have evolved throughout this century to become a critical element in today's rehabilitation and health care system. Along with changes in medicine, demographics, technology, health care financing, and health care systems, case management has been and is currently undergoing rapid change. This chapter has provided an overall review of the various contemporary models of case management including role-based, organization-based, and responsibility-based models. In addition to describing the models employed in delivering case management services, eight general guiding principles and 20 principles of rehabilitation philosophy were presented to provide a useful framework for structuring the working alliance and to guide the counselor in providing case management services to the client. As an example of role-based case management, recent research on Rehabilitation Counselor competencies[11] was presented with a particular focus on the case management functions and tasks, and resulting knowledge and skill requirements for Rehabilitation Counselors providing these services. Finally, ethical issues and the increasing use of technology were explored within the context of providing effective case management services for both the Rehabilitation Counselors and other Case Managers within the rehabilitation and health related service delivery environments.

REFERENCES

[1]Barros-Bailey, M., Benshoff, J. J., & Fischer, J. (2009). Rehabilitation Counseling in the Year 2011: Perceptions of Certified Rehabilitation Counselors. *Rehabilitation Counseling Bulletin*, 107-114.

[2]DiMichael, S. G. (1969). The voluntary health agencies stake in rehabilitation. *Journal of Home Economics, 61*(6), *421.*

[3]Case Management Society of America. (2011). Retrieved June 11, 2011 from http://www.cmsa.org/

[4]Chan, F., Leahy, M. J. & Saunders, J. L. (2005). *Case Management for Rehabilitation Health Professionals*. Linn Creek, MO: Aspen Professional Services.

[5]Goering, P. Wasylenki, D., Farkas, M., Lancee, W., & Ballantyne, R. (1988). What difference does case management make? *Hospital and Community Psychiatry*, *39*, 272-76.

[6]Hein, S., Lustig, D. C., & Uruk, A. (2005). Consumers' Recommendations to Improve Satisfaction With Rehabilitation Services: A Qualitative Study. *Rehabilitation Counseling Bulletin, 49*(1), 29-39.

[7]Huber, D. L. (2002). *The diversity of case management models.* Lippincott's Case Management, 7(6), 212-220.

[8]Kierpiec, K. M., Phillips, B. N, & Kosciulek, J. F. (2010). Vocational rehabilitation caseload size and the working alliance: Implications for rehabilitation administrators. *Journal of Rehabilitation Administration, 34*(1), *5-14.*

[9]Koch, L. C. & Rumrill, P. D. (2005). Interpersonal communication skills for case managers. In Chan, F., Leahy, M. J., & Saunders, J. (Eds.), *Case Management for Rehabilitation Health Professionals* (2nd ed, 122-143). Osage Beach, MO: Aspen Professional Services.

[10]Lambert, M. J. (1992). Implications of outcomes research for psychotherapy integration. In Norcross, J. C. & Goldfried, M. R. (Eds.), *Handbook of Psychotherapy Integration.* New York, NY: Basic.

[11]Leahy, M. J., Chan, F., & Saunders, J. L. (2003). Job functions and knowledge requirements of certified rehabilitation counselors in the 21st century. *Rehabilitation Counseling Bulletin, 46*, 66-81.

[12]Leahy, M. J., Matrone, K., & Chan, F. (2005). Contemporary models principles, and competencies of case management. In F. Chan, M. Leahy, & J. Saunders (Eds.) *Case Management for Rehabilitation Health Professionals (2nd Edition). Volume I: Foundational Aspects.* Osage Beach, MO: Aspen Professional Services.

[13]Leahy, M. J., Muenzen, P., Saunders, J. L., & Strauser, D. (2009). Essential knowledge domains underlyinh effective rehabilitation counseling practice. *Rehabilitation Counseling Bulletin, 52* (2), 95-106.

[14]Lustig, D. C., & Strauser, D. R. (2009). Rehabilitation counseling graduate students' preferences for employment : Agreement between actual and perceived job tasks of state--federal vocational rehabilitation counselors. *Rehabilitation Counseling Bulletin, 52* (3), 179-188.

[15]Park, E., & Huber, D. L. (2009). Case Management Workforce in the United States. *Journal of Nursing Scholarship, 41*(2), 175-183.

[16]Parker, R. M., & Szymanski, E. M. (Eds.) (1998). *Rehabilitation Counseling: Basics and Beyond* (3rd ed.). Austin, TX: PRO-ED.

[17]Poindexter, C. C., & Valentine, D. P. (2007). Case management or service coorination. In C. C. Poindexter, & D. P. Valentine, *An Introduction to Human Services: Values, Methods and Populations Served, 2nd Edition* (pp. 115-132). Belmont, CA: Thomson Higher Education.

[18]Roessler, R. T., & Rubin, S. E. (1998). *Case Management and Rehabilitation Counseling: Procedures and Techniques, 3rd Edition.* Austin: Pro-Ed, Inc.

[19]Saunders, J. L., Barros-Bailey, M., Chapman, C., Nunez, P. (2009). Rehabilitation counselor certification: Moving forward. *Rehabilitation Counseling Bulletin, 52*, 77-84

[20]Shaw, L. R., Leahy, M .J. & Chan, F. (2005). Case management: Historical foundations and future trends. In F. Chan, M. Leahy, & J. Saunders (Eds.) *Case Management for Rehabilitation Health Professionals (2nd Edition). Volume I: Foundational Aspects.* Linn Creek, MO: Aspen Professional Services.

[21]Sledge, W. H., Astrachan, B., Thompson, K., Rakfeldt, J., & Leaf, P. (1995). Case management in psychiatry: An analysis of tasks. *The American Journal of Psychiatry, 152*(9), 1259-1265.

[22]Solomon, P. (1992). The efficacy of case management services for severely mentally disabled clients. *Community Mental Health Journal, 28* (3), 163-180.

[23]Sue, D. W. & Sue, D. (2008). *Counseling the Culturally Diverse: Theory and Practice* (5th ed, 29-51). Hoboken, NJ: John Wiley & Sons, Inc.

[24]Tarvydas, V. M. (2004). Ethics. In T. F. Riggad & D. R. Maki (Eds.) *Handbook of Rehabilitation Counseling: Issues and Methods.* pp. 108-141. New York, NY: Springer Publishing Company.

[25]Tarvydas, V. M., & Cottone, R. R. (1991). Ethical responses to legislative, organizational and economic dynamics: A four level model of ethical practice. *Journal of Applied Rehabilitation Counseling, 22*(4), 11-18.

[26]Tarvydas, V. M., Peterson, D. B., & Michaelson, S. D. (2005). Clinical decision-making and ethical issues in case management. In F. Chan, M. Leahy, & J. W. B. Saunders (Eds.), *Case Management for Rehabilitation Health Professionals* (Vol.1, 2nd ed., pp. 144–175). Linn Creek, MO: Aspen Professional Services.

[27]World Health Organization. (1997). *World Health Organization: Measuring Quality of Life.* Geneva, Switzerland.

[28]Woodside, M., & McClam, T. (2003). *Generalist Case Management: A Method of Human Service Delivery (2nd ed.).* Pacific groves, CA: Thomson/Brooks-Cole.

[29]Wright, G. (1980). *Total Rehabilitation.* Boston, MA: Little, Brown and Company.

[30]Wright, G. (1984). Professional perspectives and planning. *Journal of Applied Rehabilitation Counseling, 15*(3), 5-8.

15

PSYCHOLOGICAL ASSESSMENT AND VOCATIONAL EVALUATION

JOSEPH F. STANO
SPRINGFIELD COLLEGE

KATHERINE E. STANO
ARGOSY UNIVERSITY

STEVEN DIAMOND
SPRINGFIELD COLLEGE

CHAPTER TOPICS

- Introduction
- Role and Nature of Assessment
- Scores, Norms, Reliability, and Validity
- Assessment of Cognitive and Psychological Constructs
- Vocational Evaluation
- Evaluation Settings and Challenges
- Case Study
- Discussion Questions

INTRODUCTION

According to Gregory,[4] assessment is defined as measuring the presence or strength of one or more personal attributes. This definition can be expanded to include not only the attribute(s) of the person in question but also a person's evaluation of others and of the psychological and physical environments in which they function. Human beings are born assessing their environment, including persons and the physical environment. We assess the environment to determine the type of clothing we will wear on that day. We assess the food that we eat by using our sight, smell, and taste. We try to assess the mood of others by evaluating their facial features and nonverbal behavior. We assess the weather, the music we hear, the television that we watch—the list is endless.

When one considers the definition of assessment through a wide lens one realizes that assessment is the foundation upon which rehabilitation rests. As rehabilitation professionals, we are constantly involved in a spectrum of assessment procedures. We often work with other health care providers to perform assessment of physical functioning as it relates to living independently. We assess clients for readiness in educational and vocational programs. We assess clients regarding the functional aspects of their disabling conditions. Finally, we assess clients across various cognitive and psychological domains to assist them in plan development. This list is not exhaustive. It is used to provide examples of what we do, as rehabilitation professionals, in the assessment process.

The assessment process has, as its foundation, the referral question(s) provided by the referral source. In many Rehabilitation settings, the Rehabilitation Counselor may refer the consumer to a Psychologist or Psychometrician for the administration of the assessment device(s). It is crucial that the referring counselor frame the questions so as to provide working material for the assessment provider and consumer to use in developing an individual plan. This plan can concern vocational services, educational services, or treatment. When the questions are used in this manner process of Rehabilitation is greatly enhanced.

There are four components to this chapter. In the first section, the role and nature of assessment in the rehabilitation process is discussed. Included in this section will also be a non-technical discussion of the scientific basis of assessment: scores, norms, reliability, and validity. In the second, and largest, section of this chapter, there will be a discussion of the use of assessment to understand various cognitive and psychological components of personal functioning. The areas investigated in this section include aptitude testing, achievement testing, intelligence testing, interest and values testing, assessment of personality and psychopathology, and neuropsychological assessment. In the third section in this chapter, the settings in which assessment is conducted are briefly examined as well as challenges to assessment. In the final section of the chapter, two case studies revolving around assessment issues are provided, along with discussion questions.

ROLE AND NATURE OF ASSESSMENT

THE NATURE OF ASSESSMENT IN REHABILITATION

Anastasi[1] defined a test as an "objective" and "standardized" measure of a sample of behavior. It is important to look at each of the key terms in this definition to understand the nature of assessment. "Objective" refers to the facts that assessment instruments need to be as free of bias as they can scientifically be made. Bias refers to the ability to make a correct decision. One does not want to use a test where a person is found to have a psychological condition when the person does not; this is called a "false positive." Likewise, we do not want to use a test to predict that a client does not have a psychological condition when they indeed do; this is referred to as a "false negative."

The second key word in Anastasi's definition is "standardized." This is a reference to the fact that an instrument needs to be administered in the same exact way during each administration. This literally extends to the words that the examiner speaks. The last component of this definition to consider is "sample of behavior." Assessment instruments are used to measure a person's performance in one narrow segment of time. This segment of time or "sample of behavior" may be an accurate representation of how the person performs in everyday life or it may be quite different from how the person normally functions. In other words, the assessor must use caution in determining whether the sample of behavior measured is an accurate representation of the person's typical performance or whether the assessment results are an indication of maximum performance. Another way to think of a "sample of behavior" is to conceptualize the difference between snapshots from a camera versus a digital movie. An assessment administered by a qualified individual is akin to a snapshot, that is, a moment frozen in time. On the other hand, a digital movie documents the totality of an individual's behavior. Essentially, assessment functions as a snapshot and is therefore limited in its conclusions.

Beyond a basic definition of assessment, it is important to distinguish some of the fundamental uses of assessment in various rehabilitation settings. A first distinction can be made between individually administered tests versus group-administered tests. When examiners use an individually administered test, they can make substantial behavior observations in addition to calculating specific scores. In this context, the assessment process shares much with the interview process. When examiners use group-administered tests, they gain the results of several, or many, persons in a relatively brief period.

Several uses of testing must be described in greater detail. Each of these uses has applications to the discipline of rehabilitation. The first use of assessment is to diagnose individuals and to assist in rehabilitation planning. Rehabilitation professionals cannot truly help the individual with a disability until they know the nature of the client's life difficulties. The term "diagnosis" does not only refer to a standard label of a medical or psychological condition from an established classification system. "Diagnosis" is used by Rehabilitation professionals to refer to how persons with disabilities are able to function in their various capacities in society. In this context, "diagnosis" is much more than a sterile label. Once functioning levels are ascertained, the rehabilitation professional can then mutually work with the client to develop an appropriate and comprehensive rehabilitation or treatment plan.

A second use of testing is that of classification. In this context, the rehabilitation professional can use assessment results to aid in the classification of the person with a disability into the appropriate vocational or educational training program. Appropriate classification not only results in a greater likelihood of success, but it also results in numerable positive psychological effects for the client. A third use of assessment results is self-knowledge. An aphorism from the Greek philosophers 3000 years ago was that "knowledge is strength." This statement is just as true today as it was then. A person with a disability can use assessment results to understand self and reasons behind personal modes of thinking, feeling, and behaving. A fourth use of assessment results is program evaluation. As rehabilitation professionals, we must insure not only accurate placement of our clients into appropriate vocational, educational, and treatment programs, but we must insure that the staff of these programs are providing quality services to their clientele. We can use assessment procedures to determine program effectiveness through the measurement of the alleviation of their clients' life issues. The final use of assessment results is research. Any field of endeavor needs to have a scientific research component to be considered a viable discipline. In this context, assessment results are used to expand the boundaries of the discipline in order to determine ways of providing treatment to clients that are more effective.

Rehabilitation professionals must be deemed qualified to administer and interpret assessment instruments. Test publishers indicate the amount of education and training required of the individual who wishes to purchase any instrument. In addition, the publisher will review the qualifications of the potential buyer before selling that person the instrument. According to Gregory (2000), there are three reasons why access to tests is restricted:

- In the hands of unqualified persons, psychological tests can result in harm done to the person taking them.
- The selection process becomes invalid for persons who preview test questions.
- Leakage of item content to the public completely destroys the efficacy of a test.

In addition, rehabilitation professionals must adhere to ethical standards in all parts of their practice including standards for educational and psychological tests. Rehabilitation professionals should adhere to the Certified Rehabilitation Counselor Code of Ethics. Specific ethical standards also apply to assessment devices. The rehabilitation practitioner must be aware of the Standards for Educational and Psychological Testing that were jointly developed by the American Educational Research Association, the American Psychological Association, and the National Council on Measurement in Education.

SCORES, NORMS, RELIABILITY, AND VALIDITY

SCORES

A concept with which many people grapple is that the number of items answered correctly on an assessment device does not automatically translate into a score. The rationale behind this mode of thinking is most likely based on our experiences in the educational system. When we answered 85 multiple-choice items correctly on a final examination, we received a "score" of 85. In the case of assessment devices, when individuals take tests the scores they receive are their "obtained" scores. They obtained the score on the day of the testing. If they were to take the same test for a second time on another day, assuming memory of the prior testing experience did not have an effect upon the second set of results, they would receive an obtained score for that day.

The question becomes what is the person's "true" score. The true score is actually a theoretical concept. The mathematical and statistical bases behind these concepts are beyond the scope of the present chapter. An obtained score can also be conceptualized as a "raw" score. To understand this concept, let us use a metaphor from the area of food. There are many foods that a person may enjoy; but not in their raw form. For instance, a person may love eggs but would never think of eating one in its raw state. If that egg is prepared or "cooked" in one of many ways, it becomes part of an enjoyable meal. Likewise, a raw score received from an assessment experience may not result in any tangible information to the assessor. "Cook" the score, that is, transform it into some other scale, like a percentile, and the score can be used to provide information that is more useful. That is, indeed, what occurs with scores from assessment devices. These scores are transformed into a type of score, many times called a standard score, so that scores can be compared. The comparison can be of two or more scores of the same person on different parts of a device, or it may be the comparison of one person's score versus another person's score.

NORMS

When the evaluator wishes to compare one person's score(s) against another's, a norm group is used. This norm group is actually a compilation of results for a group of people. Norm groups can range from small and focused to large and diverse. When this comparison is made, the evaluator needs to be certain that the norm group being used is representative of the current client. For instance, the assessor would want to compare the present individual, who is in the ninth grade, versus a norm group made up of other ninth graders. It would be inappropriate, and of little or no value, to compare that ninth grade student against fourth grade students. The norm group may also be referred to as a standardization sample. The person being compared must be a representative member of the standardization sample.

This concept may also be referred to as norm-referenced testing. As indicated above, the person being evaluated is compared to, or referenced against, the norm group. Another comparison of scores involves the comparison of the score versus a standard of performance. This is called criterion-referenced testing. An example of the comparison to a standard is currently seen in the Massachusetts system of public education. For students to be considered high school graduates, in addition to passing all of the classes required for graduation, they must also successfully complete a standardized test at or above a certain level of performance. Advocates of this approach maintain that college and employers can be assured that a certain level of performance has been attained.

RELIABILITY

Imagine the situation in which the assessor has evaluated the client on a standardized device. Is there any assurance that the device is a reliable measure of the trait being assessed? The concept of reliability rests upon this scenario. In the context of assessment, reliability can be defined as stability or consistency. Whatever a test measures, its instrument should be consistent in its measurement. Consider the scenario in which the same person is measured on four different occasions with an individually administered test of intelligence. Let us agree that there are sixty days between each administration so that memory of prior responses will be minimized. On the first administration, the person receives an overall score of "bright normal," an above average score. On the second administration, the person receives an overall score of superior, which is considerably above average. On the third administration, the person receives an overall score that results in placement in the mentally impaired category. Finally, in the fourth administration the person's score is in the "very superior" range. Obviously, whatever is being measured is not being measured consistently.

Test scores need to be based upon the concept of reliability for the scores to have any meaning. The concept of reliability is based on mathematical and statistical factors that are beyond the scope of the present chapter. Test developers are able to develop and compute different indices of reliability. These indices are used to indicate the degree of reliability in a specific assessment device. There is no such practical thing as perfect reliability. Test users must realize that there will always be some degree of error in the test score.

VALIDITY

Can a test be used to measure what the test developer says that it measures? This is both the definition of validity and the question upon which validity rests. Any test developer can title an assessment device anything that they want, but is the device a measure of the construct in question? This is the question that validity can be used to answer. Validity, like reliability, is based upon established mathematical and statistical principles. These principles are beyond the scope of this chapter. Validity can be demonstrated by way of several statistical indices. The test developer must demonstrate the validity of his device by computing at least one of the validity indices. For instance, imagine that a test developer is attempting to develop a device that will measure the knowledge achieved by high school students in a World History course. This test will have to demonstrate that the content of the test items match the content of what is taught in the World History course. Without verification that there is a match of content, the test may have no validity. One would not want to use an instrument in which the validity has not been demonstrated.

ASSESSMENT OF COGNITIVE AND PSYCHOLOGICAL CONSTRUCTS

Virtually every aspect of human cognitive and psychological functioning can be assessed through various instruments and procedures. The following constructs will be reviewed in this section: aptitude, achievement, intelligence, interests and values, personality and psychopathology, independent functioning, and neuropsychological functioning. Before addressing these constructs, it needs to be emphasized that the environment in which the assessment procedures take place may have a crucial effect upon the results. The environment may include factors such as the physical locale in which the assessment takes place, the time of day and environmental conditions, and the evaluator herself/himself. Under the issue of physical locale, factors such as the size of the testing room, its comfort, and the ability of the consumer to maneuver in the physical space are factors. The second issue includes lighting, temperature, noise, and time of day. Each individual consumer may have stamina issues and these must be taken into account to maximize the likelihood of accurate performance. Finally, characteristics of the evaluator, including age, gender, and ethnicity may influence a particular consumer.

APTITUDE TESTING

The concern of aptitude testing is the ability to predict future performance for material not yet mastered. One can see immediately the importance of aptitude testing to the discipline of rehabilitation. Since the material is not yet learned or mastered, the intent of aptitude testing is to predict what the person can learn when placed into a vocational or educational training situation. The rehabilitation professional frequently needs to assist the client or student in making choices about future options. For example, what is the likelihood that the client will find success in the automotive technology-training program to which the client has been accepted? Or, into what educational track should the student be recommended at this point in time?

To understand aptitude testing, one must make the distinction between single aptitude tests and multiple aptitude batteries. To understand the component of the construct in a single aptitude test (e.g., mechanical reasoning), only the one aptitude is measured. In multiple aptitude batteries, eight or more aptitudes are measured by using a battery of tests. A single aptitude test may have the advantage of depth of analysis in that specific aptitude. Since many vocational and educational situations involve multiple capabilities, clients or students being projected into these situations would benefit from the administration of a multiple aptitude battery. Multiple aptitude batteries have the added advantage of requiring less time than a series of single aptitude tests administered individually.

The Differential Aptitude Test (DAT) is an example of a well constructed multiple aptitude battery that is frequently used in educational systems and programming. It consists of eight independent tests: verbal reasoning, numerical reasoning, abstract reasoning, perceptual speed and accuracy, mechanical reasoning, space relations, spelling, and language usage. The general aptitude test battery (GATB) has been used by the US Department of Labor since before the Second World War. It has been successfully linked to job performance in hundreds of jobs. The GATB is comprised of twelve tests that result in nine factor scores. These factor scores are general learning ability, verbal aptitude, numerical aptitude, spatial aptitude, form perception, clerical perception, motor coordination, finger dexterity, and manual dexterity. The third multiple aptitude test to be discussed is the most widely used test in existence. Every potential recruit for military service in this country takes the armed services vocational aptitude battery (ASVAB). The present test has evolved from prior versions that were first in existence at the beginning of the First World War. The subtests of the ASVAB are arithmetic reasoning, mathematics knowledge, paragraph comprehension, work knowledge, coding speed, general science, numerical operations, electronics information, mechanical comprehension, and auto and shop information.

Additionally, aptitude tests like the Scholastic Assessment Test (SAT), The American College Test (ACT), the Graduate Record Examination (GRE), the Medical College Admission Test (MCAT), and the Law School Admissions

Test (LSAT) are used to predict either college performance or postgraduate selection.

ACHIEVEMENT TESTING

Achievement tests are measures of what a person has previously learned and retained. There are two essential categories of achievement tests. Group achievement tests, also known as educational achievement tests, are administered to high school students at the same time throughout a school system. They are an indicator of educational progress for each student, for a school, and for a school system. Individual achievement tests are administered to students one at a time. They play a crucial role in diagnosing individual learning disabilities.

Over the last several years, group achievement tests have become even more prominent. A majority of states have initiated "high stakes testing" in their school systems. Although these tests are separate from the standardized group achievement tests that are commonly used by many school systems, they are achievement tests nonetheless. School system administrators may also use standardized group achievement tests as a method of assessing the progress of students in their school system. Three examples of educational achievement tests are the Iowa Tests of Basic Skills, the Stanford Achievement Series, and the Metropolitan Achievement Test.

The Tests of General Educational Development, commonly referred to as the GED, is both a goal and an attainment for many rehabilitation clients in the vocational rehabilitation system. Because of a variety of factors, many individuals may leave the school system before the attainment of their high school diploma. The rehabilitation professional works with the client to attain the GED, which is considered equivalent to the attainment of a high school diploma. This certificate may be a prerequisite for both higher education and post-secondary proprietary vocational programs. Employers also want the high school diploma, or its equivalent, as a basic condition of employment.

Rehabilitation professionals use individual achievement tests to assist in the diagnosis of learning disabilities. Historically, the diagnostic process was conducted on children and adolescents who were enrolled in the school system. The testing was conducted to help develop an individualized education program for the student. Federal and state special education laws were the impetus for these evaluations. These laws have been considerably strengthened and expanded over the last two decades. Rehabilitation professionals increasingly conduct individual achievement testing on adults who are seeking services from rehabilitation providers. For instance, a 40-year-old client seeking services from a rehabilitation agency may have been socially promoted through the grades with no concern for the student's academic underachievement. This client may require education or vocational training as part of their rehabilitation plan. Other segments of the plan may be predicated on the client completing the educational program or vocational training program. The client's success in the program is frequently based on the counselor having a thorough understanding of the client's learning style and problems. For the rehabilitation plan to be successful, individual achievement testing will need to be the foundation of the process. Examples of individual achievement tests include: the Wide Range Achievement Test-III (WRAT-III), the Peabody Individual Achievement Test-Revised (PIAT-R), and the Wechsler Individual Achievement Test-III (WIAT-III).

INTELLIGENCE TESTING

The assessment of intelligence is integral to the rehabilitation of many individuals. Many clients are participants in either educational or vocational programs. The general ability to learn is crucial in virtually all training programs in which clients engage. Before going any further, we must attempt to define the construct of intelligence. From a non-technical perspective, intelligence can be defined as the general ability to learn. This definition is sufficient in many regards. This construct is operationally defined as the ability to complete academically related tasks.

As with many other types of assessment devices, intelligence tests can be administered in either a group or individual format. The major advantage of group-administered intelligence tests is the efficient assessment of many people simultaneously. They also serve a function for use as screening procedures. These instruments may not be accurate indicators of a subject's true ability due to the lack of an individual testing relationship. Some examples of group tests of intelligence include Culture Fair Intelligence Test; the Shipley Institute of Living Scale, and the Multidimensional Aptitude Battery.

The strength of intelligence testing lies in the administration of the individual test of intelligence. In many ways, the wellspring of scientific measurement of a client's psychological construct is in the area of testing of ability. At the beginning of the twentieth century, the French government asked Alfred Binet to construct an instrument that would be used to distinguish children by ability level. The domain of ability testing has developed from these humble beginnings.

The Wechsler Intelligence Scales are the most widely administered tests in the world. David Wechsler, long associated with Bellevue Hospital in New York City, introduced the first adult version of his test in 1939. He later went on to develop intelligence scales for children and for the preschool and primary grades. All of these instruments continue to be revised and offered in relevant forms.

The Wechsler Scales are based on the presumption that overall or full-scale intelligence is a combination of both diverse verbal and performance abilities. Both the verbal and performance scales are each combinations of various subtests. The actual names of the various Wechsler scales are The Wechsler Adult Scale of Intelligence–Fourth Edition; the Wechsler Scale of Intelligence for Children–Fourth Edition; and the Wechsler Preschool and Primary Scale of

Intelligence-III. Other examples of individual ability devices include the Stanford-Binet Intelligence Scale, and the Slosson Intelligence Test.

A recent advance in intelligence testing was the development of the Wechsler Preschool and Primary Scale of Intelligence. This brief measure of intelligence can be administered using either two or four of the specific Wechsler adult subtests. The reliability and validity data associated with using two scales, versus administration of the complete scale, is quite favorable. The instrument can be used as a screening tool and the subtests can be incorporated into the full Wechsler version if that is eventually desired or indicated. The major function of this tool can be conceptualized as a screening tool.

It is crucial to emphasize that the importance of individual intelligence scales lies in the fact thousands of scientific investigations have been performed in which the relationship between intelligence and performance has been demonstrated. In other words, the assessor can use these instruments to predict probable success in either an academic or a vocational training endeavor. The ability to predict these life events is the crux of rehabilitation.

INTEREST AND VALUES TESTING

Many individuals have been exposed to vocational interest testing through the process of formal education. In high school, many students are administered an interest test either in a classroom setting or individually with a guidance counselor. The origins of interest tests date back to the 1920s, and they have been constantly refined since that time. The interest instruments are very sophisticated and based on quite involved statistical methodologies. Interest assessment must be viewed with a good deal of caution. Since interests are based to a high degree on a person's attitudes and, since attitudes are not stable, the measurement of this construct is not as exact as the measurement of ability. In addition, experts do not agree on the definition of "attitude." Finally, since interest inventories are used to measure attitudes, not abilities, a person can have high tested interests in a given vocational area, but not have high tested abilities in the same area. This last fact is the cause of much potential distress among interest assessment examinees.

Several interest tests are based on John Holland's theoretical framework. Essentially, Holland stated that there are six basic types of vocational environments: realistic, investigative, artistic, social, enterprising, and conventional. In addition, there are six types of work personalities; the same terms are used as above. A given work environment is usually a combination of two or three environments. Likewise, the work personalities of individuals are combinations of two or three of these areas. A person may be highest in the social area but also be prominent in the artistic and investigative areas. Job satisfaction occurs when there is a melding of the attributes of the work environment with the individual's personal characteristics.

The Strong Interest Inventory (SII) was first developed in the 1920s. The instrument has gone through several revisions since that time, and it may be considered the "Gold Standard" of interest inventories. This is particularly true when the client and the evaluator are considering higher education options. This instrument can be taken at the computer terminal with clients getting an extensive report of their results immediately upon the completion of the testing. The report is composed in non-technical language so that the client can assimilate the information easily. The self-directed search (SDS) is another instrument based upon Holland's typology. This instrument has the advantage of the client completing the instrument in a paper-and-pencil format. In addition, the client scores the instrument, and using support material, develops a list of educational and vocational opportunities.

The assessment of values is also crucial. In light of the fact that values are abstract concepts, they become difficult to measure. The study of values is essentially the purview of philosophers. There must be agreement as to what class of values one wants to measure. Is the goal the assessment of social values, personal values, or vocational values? The assessment of any of these classes of values may be of importance to the rehabilitation professional. In the general area, the Rokeach Value Survey (RVS) is widely used.

The area of vocational values is very important to many rehabilitation professionals. The Minnesota Importance Questionnaire (MIQ) is used to measure the vocational values and needs of individuals. The instrument is based on twenty needs with six underlying values. These values are related to work satisfaction. The instrument has been further normed using over 200 occupations utilizing occupational reinforcer patterns. An Occupational Reinforcer Pattern (ORP) is used to describe the relationship between reinforcers and the needs and values for a given occupation. They are an important index that is used by the vocational rehabilitation counselor in helping the consumer determine an occupation with which she/he has a "goodness of fit." The rehabilitation professional can best assist the client to develop their life plan by incorporating vocational values into the assessment equation.

PERSONALITY AND PSYCHOPATHOLOGY ASSESSMENT

Personality evaluation is the area of assessment that intrigues the public. Many folk tales have developed concerning this area of assessment. In addition, many individuals believe that these instruments can be used for nefarious purposes. There is no basis for these claims, but they persist in some quarters. The point of departure for the discussion of personality assessment begins with a definition. In a non-technical way, personality can be defined as "the way a person ordinarily behaves." Although this definition may be adequate in many venues, and may be accurate, it is insufficient for scientific purposes. It may be best to understand personality as a group of traits. These traits are long standing, and they are not easily modified. The Five-Factor Model of Personality is a well-regarded conceptualization of personality at this time. According to Goldberg,[3] the five factors are neuroticism, extraversion, openness to experience, agreeableness, and conscientiousness. The acronym for this system is known as OCEAN. Trait theories have a long, positively regarded, history in psychological assessment.

Personality assessment devices can be used to provide two different types of information. In the first instance, personality assessment devices can be used to provide a description of a person's response to life. This may also be called descriptive personality assessment. Three instruments that are commonly used in this manner are the Myers-Briggs Type Indicator (MBTI), the Sixteen Personality Factor (16PF) questionnaire and the Fundamental Interpersonal Relations Orientation-Behavior (FIRO-B). The MBTI is based upon Carl Jung's Theory of Types. The test taker's responses are developed into one of Jung's sixteen "types." The results are used to provide a good deal of information to the client. The MBTI has the additional advantage of having extensive validity in organizational and consulting psychology scenarios. For instance, a group of co-workers can take the MBTI, and the assessment consultant can use the results to help co-workers better understand each other and strategize ways that the work group may be able to work more efficiently.

The 16PF is based upon the work of Raymond Cattell. In this instrument, specific factor scores are used to develop five global factor scores—the "big five." The test taker is provided with a great deal of information as to how they normally function. The test taker is often personally empowered by this wealth of information. Examples of the specific factor scales include warmth, impulsivity, conformity, sensitivity, imagination, and insecurity.

The FIRO-B is a self-report device that is used to measure behavior that has its wellsprings in interpersonal needs. The instrument can be used to measure a variety of issues including relationships, the culture of the workplace and similar situations, teamwork potential, and career development issues. As with many devices of this type, a goal is for the person being assessed to become more aware of themselves and their own behavior. Personal needs and leadership behaviors can be identified.

In the second instance, personality assessment is used to determine whether any mental health problems or psychopathology exists in a given individual. There are two different ways to assess psychopathology. The first method is called projective personality assessment. Many of the instruments have a prominent place in the history of assessment. Perhaps the best-known device in this area is the Rorschach Inkblot Technique. Other projective devices include the Thematic Apperception Test, sentence completion methods, and projective drawings. The term "projective" is derived from the fact that the client "projects" his or her personality out through the instrument. For instance, the subject is shown one of the Rorschach inkblots and the examiner is told what she sees. The examiner then notes what the client stated. After the ten inkblots are administered, the examiner uses a scoring system to translate what the client stated into the client's psychological functioning.

The other major way to assess psychopathology is using structured or self-report inventories. In this type of personality assessment device the client answers items using a forced-choice format. This forced-choice can be either true-false items or a multiple-choice. The best-known test of this type is the Minnesota Multiphasic Personality Inventory-2 (MMPI-2). This instrument is one of the three most widely used in the world. The instrument is scored with four validity scales, ten standard clinical scales, and dozens of supplementary scales. The subject's score on a given scale is viewed vis-à-vis comparison groups. These comparison groups are a well-defined criterion group and an appropriate control group. This instrument is used to yield information that can be extremely useful for both the client and the rehabilitation professional in life plan development.

NEUROPSYCHOLOGICAL ASSESSMENT

Neuropsychological assessment is perhaps the most crucial area of assessment that the rehabilitation practitioner uses. The concept behind this area of assessment is the relationship between the state of the brain's functioning and its relationship to the behavior of the individual. In many types of disabilities, the functioning of the client's brain and central nervous system is impaired. Through the techniques of neuropsychological assessment, the evaluator is able to determine the state of the client's brain. One may wonder why this is necessary with the development of body scanning technology. Physicians use computerized tomography (CT) scans and magnetic resonance imaging (MRI) technology to "see" the entire body or, in part, in three dimensions. Even though these devices can be used to pinpoint the exact areas of damage, the physician cannot state what the effects upon behavior will be for that specific individual. Neuropsychological assessment devices can then be used to pinpoint the neurological and behavioral deficits because of the injury or disease process.

Bennett[2] has put forth a model of brain-behavior relationships that includes the following functions: sensory input; attention and concentration; learning and memory; language; spatial and manipulatory ability; executive functions including logical analysis, concept formation, reasoning, planning, and flexibility of thinking; and motor output. The evaluator must decide to assess each of the areas listed above or only some of these areas. Both the medical record of the individual and the referral questions guide the evaluator.

The evaluator can gather neuropsychological information using assessment devices in two major ways. The first approach is to administer an intact neuropsychological assessment battery to a client. The two most prominent batteries are the Halstead-Reitan Neuropsychological Test Battery and Luria-Nebraska Neuropsychological Battery. Ralph Reitan was a student of Ward Halstead in the 1940s and developed Halstead's original devices, and he continues to do so today. For some time, he has collaborated with Deborah Wolfson to continue his investigation of this area. These are prodigious authors and scientists.

The other approach to neuropsychological assessment is the Boston Process Approach. Under this approach, the evaluator decides which instruments to use as well as parts or subtests of other established instruments. For instance, the evaluator may use specific subtests of the Wechsler Adult Intelligence Scale in constructing a group of devices to answer specific referral questions. In addition to neuropsychological batteries, many tests instruments are used to measure a specific function. The Wechsler Memory Scale-Revised is an example of a memory test that is actually a battery itself, and the Wisconsin Card Sorting Test is used to measure some components of executive functioning.

VOCATIONAL EVALUATION

Vocational Evaluation (VE) is the foundation of the vocational rehabilitation process. Vocational evaluation is itself, a process. The importance of VE is linked with Freud's contention that the two major tasks of adulthood are to work and to love. Rehabilitation professionals cannot do anything about the love issues of their clients—the profession of rehabilitation counseling is all about the work component of our client's lives. The career development of each individual is a process. This is also connected with the contention of the Humanistic School of Psychology that all individuals are in the process of "becoming." As rehabilitation professionals, we help our clients navigate through the rapids that constitute every person's life. Vocational evaluation and assessment are used by the rehabilitation professional to facilitate that process.

There have been specific systems of vocational evaluation devices that have been developed. The common element of evaluation devices (commonly called work samples) is that they are designed to duplicate the key components of an actual job. Through the use of job analysis, the key components of the job are identified. A work sample is then constructed within the evaluation setting that requires the client to perform the key tasks associated with that particular job. As with any evaluation instrument, the development and use of appropriate norms is critical when attempting to predict the success of a client on a particular job.

Perhaps the most prominent and extensive evaluation system was developed by the VALPAR Corporation. Not only are specific vocational capabilities assessed, but work habits and attitudes are also examined. Specific vocational assessment devices that are used by the rehabilitation professional to address specific referral questions supplement these vocational evaluation systems. Let us use two different case scenarios to examine the different referral questions that may be posed to the examiner.

The first case involves a seventeen-year-old college senior who has recently been diagnosed with learning disabilities. This client wishes to achieve a bachelor's degree and a postgraduate degree in terms of formal education. Historically, the client has struggled in the classroom. A diagnosis of learning disabilities has been established. There are specific referral questions regarding the learning disabilities, and the compensation strategies that could be developed to facilitate the client's progress through future academic environments. The second case involves another seventeen-year-old. This student sustained a head trauma after being struck by a field hockey stick during a game. This student also plans to attend college. There is evidence, in the preliminary evaluation, of problems with some aspects of memory and some aspects of executive functioning. As one can see, even though the immediate goal, college education, is the same for both individuals, the referral questions are much different, and the process of vocational evaluation must be structured accordingly.

Vocational evaluation is crucially important to successful completion of the rehabilitation process for many individuals. As indicated, work is a critical component of all of our lives. Work is a life task in which we may engage for a half-century or more.

EVALUATION SETTINGS AND CHALLENGES

Evaluations can be performed in any setting in which rehabilitation and psychology professionals function. Most individuals are familiar with the role of assessment in schools because of testing in the classroom to assess academic progress. As has been shown in this chapter, assessment in the schools may involve group achievement and other types of evaluation. Children and adolescents with various disabilities may need to be evaluated for intellectual capability, neuropsychological function, and for specific learning disabilities. The list of applications of evaluation in kindergarten through twelfth grade is seemingly endless.

Evaluations are completed in a variety of occupational settings and for many occupational purposes. Evaluation may be part of the hiring process for many positions. Assessment is valuable for job evaluation and in determining good internal candidates for career enhancement. There are a myriad of military applications of evaluation. Screening and placement via assessment are universally used in military settings.

Assessment is an integral component of all rehabilitation programs. Evaluation procedures are used for screening, placement, and diagnostic purposes as well as a way to assess program effectiveness. Rehabilitation professionals can use various assessment devices to determine health status of individuals, especially concerning mental health issues. Finally, rehabilitation professionals can provide evaluations to determine the fitness of the client to participate in legal proceedings.

As can be seen by this brief list, the role of assessment in rehabilitation involves every aspect of the process. The applications of assessment in the rehabilitation process will continue to expand as the need arises.

The challenges to assessment and evaluation are rife with perils and possibilities. The perils of assessment may revolve around the issue of faking the results and/or cheating. Clients can fake or exaggerate symptoms for their personal gains. For instance, clients can exaggerate their back injury and depression in order to continue receiving workers compensation benefits.

While successful attainment of a criterion is necessary to receive one's high school diploma, some individuals may resort to cheating to insure their successful performance. In the domain of higher education, high scores on the Scholastic Achievement Test or the American College Testing instrument are necessary for entrance into the most competitive colleges. There have been increased efforts to deter cheating on these instruments over the last several years.

Evaluators who use computers in the assessment and evaluation process are presented with several challenges in the future. The issues revolve around both the access to technology and the security of information. Assessment responses are confidential information and this information must be safeguarded at all costs. As technology continues to develop, these issues will remain at the fore.

CASE STUDIES IN EVALUATION

In the case study presented below, first read the case scenario in detail, take notes, and identify issues. Then answer each of the discussion questions to the best of your ability.

CASE STUDY

THE CASE OF DOROTHY KWIATKOWSKI

Dorothy (Somolenski) Kwiatkowski is a 45-year-old female who is referred to you through the State Department of Employment and Training. Until recently, Mrs. Kwiatkowski worked as a baker for Roman Cebula Bakery in Ludlow, Massachusetts. Mrs. Kwiatkowski has worked there for over seventeen years. She started at the family owned company as a clerk in the store and gradually assumed several positions; she has been a baker for ten years.

Ten months ago, Mrs. Kwiatkowski was in a serious traffic accident. She and three of her friends were returning from a "girls night out" at the Casino in Ledyard, Connecticut. At approximately 3:00 a.m. they were approaching the intersection of Route 395 and the Massachusetts Turnpike when Mrs. Rodriques, who was the driver, fell asleep at the wheel, and the car left the road and tumbled down an embankment, eventually landing on its roof and hitting a tree. Because Mrs. Kwiatkowski was not wearing a seat belt, she was thrown from the vehicle. Another driver saw the accident occur and the state police and EMS units were summoned.

Mrs. Kwiatkowski was taken to the University of Massachusetts Medical Center in Worcester by LifeFlight helicopter. Her serious trauma was a spinal cord injury, at the fifth thoracic vertebra, a broken right (dominant) arm, and multiple lacerations and contusions. Following several weeks of recovery, Mrs. Kwiatkowski was transferred to the Weldon Rehabilitation Center in Springfield, Massachusetts. This allowed her to be closer to her family. She remained an inpatient at the Weldon Center for an additional three months.

The vehicle burst into flames and all three of the other passengers were trapped inside. The two passengers on the rear seat, Mrs. La Couer and Mrs. Keitel, were taken to the same Medical Center with extensive burns over most of their bodies. They were transferred, via LifeFlight helicopter, to the Burn Unit at Massachusetts General Hospital (MGH) in Boston after they were initially stabilized. Both survived and spent several months at MGH and they were eventually transferred to the Spaulding Rehabilitation Hospital in Boston. Both will be released within the next sixty days.

Mrs. Rodriques, in the front passenger seat of the car, was trapped inside, and pronounced dead at the scene. It was determined upon autopsy that her death was instantaneous and not a result of the subsequent fire.

Mrs. Kwiatkowski was pregnant at the age of sixteen; she kept the child, lived with her parents, and dropped out of high school. At the time of her leaving high school, she was a solid 'B' student who thought about a career as an elementary school teacher. She and the father of the child were married two weeks after Mrs. Kwiatkowski's nineteenth birthday. By that time, she had earned her certificate of General Educational Development (GED). She worked in the fast food and retail industries before commencing work for Cebula's Bakery. Today, she and her husband Zbigniew have four children, three daughters and one son. Daughter, Sofia, is 29 and married. She is a college graduate working as a high school mathematics teacher. She and her husband, Bradley, live in Isle of Palms, South Carolina. Son, Josef, is 25 and in the last year of law school at the University of Oklahoma. Daughter, Francine, is 24 and works as a corporate communication consultant in Chicago, Illinois. Daughter, Crystal, is 21 and a senior at Smith College at Northampton, Massachusetts. She plans on a career in medicine. Mr. Kwiatkowski is employed by the town of Ludlow, Massachusetts as a laborer in the Sanitation Department. He has worked in that capacity for 27 years.

DISCUSSION QUESTIONS

- Assuming that you have received Mrs. Kwiatkowski's medical records, after she signed a release, indicate what her functional physical limitations are at this point in time.
- Develop a list of vocational issues that need to be explored as part of Mrs. Kwiatkowski's rehabilitation.
- Develop a list of psychological adjustment issues that you would like to explore with Mrs. Kwiatkowski.
- What other areas do you think justify assessment?
- Speculate on both the short-term and long-term prognosis for Mrs. Kwiatkowski.

REFERENCES

[1]Anastasi, A. (1988). *Psychological Testing* (6th ed.). New York, New York: Macmillan.

[2]Bennett, T. (1988). Use of the Halstead-Reitan Neuropsychological Test Battery in the assessment of head injury. *Cognitive Rehabilitation*, *6*, 18-25.

[3]Goldberg, L. R. (1981). Language and individual differences: The search for universals in personality lexicons. In L. Wheeler (ed.). *Review of personality and social psychology*. Beverly Hills, California: Sage Publishers.

[4]Gregory, R. J. (2000). *Psychological testing* (3rd ed.). Boston: Allyn and Bacon.

WORKERS' DISABILITY BENEFITS PROGRAMS

DEANNA HENDERSON
ALABAMA STATE UNIVERSITY

MONA ROBINSON
OHIO UNIVERSITY

CARL SABO
WRIGHT STATE UNIVERSITY

JENNIFER HERTZFELD
THE OHIO STATE UNIVERSITY

CHAPTER TOPICS

- Introduction
- Workers' Compensation
- Case Study 1
- Social Security Benefits
- Case Study 2
- Short-Term & Long-Term Disability Benefits
- Transitional Work
- Case Study 3
- Conclusion

INTRODUCTION

There are approximately 50 million individuals in the United States with a disability.[29] It should come as no surprise that a percentage of those individuals are employed in some capacity. In fact, 55.8 percent of individuals age 16-64 with a disability are working. Some of those individuals acquire injuries, chronic illnesses, or disabilities while on the job. Those individuals who are unable to work due to an injury, illness, or disability may be eligible for benefits. For that reason, employers and the government, both state and federal, offer benefit programs to assist such persons. This chapter will provide an overview of workers' compensation, social security disability, short and long-term disability, and transitional work. Each benefit program will be detailed, outlining the eligibility requirements, compensation, and benefits. It is hoped that this chapter will offer rehabilitation professionals resources to identify appropriate benefit programs for workers with disabilities.

WORKER'S COMPENSATION

OVERVIEW

The various systems of workers' compensation throughout the United States are an important component of assisting workers who are injured while engaged in their employment. Workers' compensation is a term given for many insurance systems throughout the United States and other countries that provide various services and/or financial assistance when an employee sustains a physical or mental injury because of a workplace accident or chronic occupational illness.[9,20]

The first workers' compensation laws can be found in the Code of Hammurbi in Babylon in 1800 B.C.[24] Many variations of modern workers' compensation laws were developed throughout Western Europe in the 19th century, first in Germany and later adopted and modified in England.[34]

The Industrial Revolution brought many changes in the workplace and one such change was the establishment of workers' compensation systems throughout the United States.[20] Workers' compensation was the first social insurance to arise extensively in the United States.[11] Workers' compensation systems expanded throughout the United States in an effort to address the increasing numbers of injuries and illnesses associated with the Industrial Revolution era.[11]

In 1908, the first workers' compensation program (Federal Workers' Compensation and Railroad Workers' Act) was enacted.[11,24] Similar laws throughout the United States were enacted beginning in Wisconsin in 1911. The last of the original 48 states to pass workers' compensation legislation was Mississippi and it occurred in 1948.[11,25,24] All 50 states, the District of Columbia, Guam, Puerto Rico, and the U.S. Virgin Islands, along with long shore, harbor, and other maritime workers, federal employees, and coalminers have workers' compensation laws.[11]

Before the establishment of the various workers' compensation systems throughout the United States, workers and their families encountered financial disaster, as they had no means of support while attempting to traverse the adversarial legal system.[11,24] Prior to the enactment of workers' compensation systems, workers only recourse was to sue employers. Unfortunately, most workers did not have the financial wherewithal to hire attorneys, while many companies had the financial resources to work within the legal system.

The purpose of workers' compensation is twofold:

- to offer recourse to injured workers as reparation; and
- to offer a more economical way to contain cost for employers compensating workers for workplace related injuries and illnesses.

"Workers' compensation is a compromise between the needs of employees and the needs of employers."[10, p. 36] When workers' compensation laws were first being formulated in the United States, many thought it a victory for workers. Nevertheless, workers, employers, and insurance companies all tended to support the framework of workers' compensation laws, with any disagreements being over the details of the law.[9] While the workers' compensation systems lessen the need to take issues related to injuries and illnesses through the legal system, it has not completely eliminated legal actions.[11,10]

Although each state may have variations to workers' compensation laws, the major objectives associated with workers' compensation are widely accepted.[10] These objectives are:

- replacement of income,
- rehabilitation of the injured employee,
- prevention of accidents, and
- cost allocation.

Workers' compensation laws within the United States can generally be classified into two areas: Federal Workers' Compensation Programs and State Workers' Compensation Programs.

FEDERAL WORKERS' COMPENSATION

There are four major federal workers' compensation programs. All of the programs are administered by The Office of Workers' Compensation Programs (OWCP) within the United States Department of Labor.

The *Federal Employees' Compensation Act (FECA)* [5 U.S.C. § 8101-8193][7] set up a workers' compensation program for federal employees who were injured during the course of their employment. Compensation is provided for employees who, in the course of their employment duties, may be injured or die. The only exception to this is when the injury or death is caused by willful misconduct of the employee.

Those deemed disabled and covered under FECA receive two-thirds of their salary during the period they are considered an individual with a disability. If the individual deemed disabled has dependents then their disability payments may be augmented an additional 8.33%. If the individual with a disability incurs medical expenses because of the disability, those expenses may be covered under the FECA. The individual with a disability may be directed to engage in vocational rehabilitation in order to determine whether the individual can return to their previous employment or some other type of employment. If death results from an employment-related injury, survivors may receive compensation under the FECA.

In fiscal year 2010, 127,526 new cases were created. The program provided $2.86 billion dollars in benefits to approximately 251,000 workers and survivors for work-related injuries or illnesses. Over $1.8 billion was paid for wage-loss compensation, $913 million for medical and rehabilitation services, and $138 million for death benefit payments to surviving dependents.[30]

The *Longshore and Harbor Workers' Compensation Act (LHWCA)* [33 U.S.C. § 901-950][17] set up a workers' compensation program for maritime workers who work on the navigable waters of the United States, along with those working on piers, docks, and terminals. The LHWCA also covers a variety of workers including, overseas employees of defense contractors, employees at military post exchanges, workers engaged in the extraction of natural resources on the outer continental shelf, and other classes of private industry workers that are entitled to compensation benefits. The LHWCA does not cover workers if they are covered under state worker's compensation laws.

For those employees injured at their place of employment and deemed eligible under The LHWCA the following benefits may be provided:

- monetary compensation for lost wages,
- medical benefits,
- vocational Rehabilitation Services, and
- death benefits to dependents if the injury causes the employee's death.

The Act provides over $747 million in monetary, medical, and vocational rehabilitation benefits in more than 27,000 cases annually for maritime workers and various other special classes of private industry employees disabled or killed by employment injuries or occupational diseases. In addition, the compensation program maintains over $2.8 billion in securities to ensure the continuing provision of benefits for these injured workers in cases of employer inability to pay. Claimants depend on these benefits to provide food, housing, etc. for themselves and their families.[30]

The *Black Lung Benefits Act (BLBA)* [30 U.S.C. § 901-945] set up a program that requires monthly payments and medical expenses to be covered for workers who incurred pneumoconiosis, better known as "black lung disease." The mine operator is responsible for covering the expenses for affected workers under the BLBA. The BLCA also established a fund to provide payments to affected miners in situations when the mine operator is unknown or unable to pay. In addition to regular compensation benefits, if a worker dies, their surviving dependents are eligible to receive benefits. In fiscal year 2010, there were 62,524 total beneficiaries receiving a total of $238,422,875 in benefits covered under the BLBA.[31]

The *Energy Employees Occupational Illness Compensation Program (EEOICP)* provides lump-sum compensation and health benefits to eligible Department of Energy nuclear weapons workers, including employees, former employees, contractors and subcontractors, and lump-sum compensation to certain survivors if the worker is deceased. The EEOICP is authorized by the Energy Employees' Occupational Illness Compensation Program Act (EEOICPA).

Individuals may be eligible for benefits under EEOICP if they had radiation-induced cancers, beryllium diseases, or silicosis and they were exposed to radiation, beryllium, or silica while working in the nuclear weapons industry for the Department of Energy or its contractors or subcontractors. Uranium miners, millers, and ore transporters may also be eligible for benefits associated with EEOICP if they have received an award of benefits under Section 5 of the Radiation Exposure Compensation Act for the Department of Justice. In fiscal year 2010, there were 166,323 covered applicants receiving compensation benefits of $6,435,828,900 and medical payments of $865,929,865, totaling $7,301,758,765 for those covered under the EEOICP.[32] .

The *Federal Employment Liability Act (FELA)* [45 U.S.C. § 51-60],[8] while technically not considered a workers' compensation statute, does provide railroad workers injured on their job the right to compensation. However, under FELA the worker must establish that the injury is a result of the railroad company's negligence. If the worker proves their injury was a result of company negligence, under FELA they may recover lost wages, medical expenses, pain and suffering, and compensation for partial or permanent disability. If, because of company negligence, the worker dies on the job, their survivors are entitled under FELA to recover damages related to the workers death.

The *Merchant Marine Act (MMA)* [46 U.S.C. § 688],[19] which is also known as " The Jones Act," grants seamen the same defense from employer negligence as FELA grants railroad workers. Any worker who spends more than thirty percent of their time in the service of a craft on navigable waters qualifies as a seaman within the MMA. Under The MMA, an injured seaman may recover lost wages, medical expenses and treatment, and pain and suffering.

STATE WORKERS' COMPENSATION

Along with the aforementioned federal workers' compensation programs within the United States, each state has its own unique laws governing issues related to workers' compensation. The United States does not have one set of workers' compensation laws. Since there are many differences between these laws, it is difficult to make generalizations regarding these laws. Workers' compensation laws at the state level are regularly amended, revised, and rewritten which adds to the inability to generalize among state workers' compensation systems.[24,10]

Most states have adopted compulsory workers' compensation laws mandating that employers must maintain workers' compensation coverage for their employees. A few states have elective workers' compensation laws. Under this environment, an employer may choose to accept or reject coverage. However, an employer that does not accept workers' compensation coverage loses the customary common law defenses.[12,11] This leaves the employer open to more risk of injured workers suing the employer for damages associated with their work incurred injury.

Depending on the laws of the state, employers may obtain workers' compensation coverage from a State Insurance Fund, an authorized private insurance company, or an employer may choose to be self-insured. A vast majority of states allow employers to be self-insured. Employers that choose this option must set up a reserve fund to pay benefits to their injured workers. In order to be self-insured, employers generally must receive approval by the appropriate State Workers' Compensation Board.[12,11]

Eligibility and Benefits. In 1995 there were 3.6 million disabling injuries in the United States.[16] Most of the United States labor force is covered by either a Federal or State workers' compensation law although there are exceptions. Many programs exempt employees of nonprofit, charitable, or religious institutions as well as a person in domestic service, agricultural employment, and casual labor.[11,10] While workers' compensation laws vary from state-to-state, most workers' compensation claims fall into one of three categories:

- injury claims
- occupational disease claims, (including occupational hearing loss), and
- death claims.[12,11]

Injury claims are the most common claim within the workers' compensation system. In some states, the law does not separate injury and occupational claims, and is only concerned with whether or not the employee's disability is work-related.

There are certain circumstances in which an injured employee may not be covered under applicable workers' compensation statutes. Coverage within workers' compensation may be denied in the following:

- self-inflicted injuries, or injuries sustained while attempting to injure another,
- injuries sustained while committing a crime,
- injuries sustained when the employee was not on the job, and

- injuries sustained when the employee's conduct violated company policy.[12,11]

There could be a dispute as to whether an injured worker will be covered under workers compensation in several other areas.

- Place of Employment – did the injury occur at a recognized place where the work of the business is conducted?
- Off-Site Injuries – is the employee engaged in acceptable work related activities at an off-site location?
- Personal Activities during work time – is this a typically accepted practice by the employer?
- Lunch and Break Time – workers' compensation laws differ on whether an employee is covered for injuries during lunch and break times.
- Travel Time – travel time associated with the work function may be covered. Workers' compensation laws may differ and should be reviewed to determine the law in a specific jurisdiction.[12,11]

Within the workers' compensation system, injuries that are compensable mostly fall within one of the following four categories.

Temporary partial disability—injured workers are able to continue to work in light duty or part-time duty until they recover to the point of returning to their pre-injury work.

Temporary total disability—injured workers are unable to engage in any work but are expected to return to their pre-injury work level in the future. During this time, the injured worker receives workers' compensation financial assistance. This assistance is generally 66-2/3% of weekly wages up to the statutory maximum. This compensation continues until the employee returns to work. In several states, benefits are payable up to a maximum number of weeks, a maximum monetary amount, or both.[12,11] Most workers' compensation cases involve temporary total disability claims.

Permanent partial disability—injured workers are not expected to return to their pre-injury level of vocational abilities. The injured worker is expected to have the ability to return to work. Many times the worker is functioning with diminished capacity. The financial payment to the injured worker is for the injury and ensuing suffering and disability. It is also in part compensation for a potential reduction in the workers wage once they return to work. The benefit is generally calculated as the difference between pre-injury earnings and post-injury earnings.

Permanent total disability—an injured worker is determined to be disabled and unable to return to any type of substantial gainful employment. The injured worker with PTD will generally receive a weekly benefit based on a percentage of their gross salary. The compensation continues until one of the following is satisfied:

- the employee returns to substantial gainful employment,
- the employee dies, or
- the employee reaches the maximum allowable benefit. The maximum may be reached by total cost of benefit paid or reaching the maximum time period.[11]

Other workers' compensation benefits that the eligible injured worker may be able to receive are:

Death benefits are provided to survivors of workers who die because of a work-related injury. The spouse is generally entitled to death benefits for life or until remarriage. Children are eligible for benefits until age 18 or later if they have a disability or are a student.[11]

Medical benefits are covered for the injured worker in order to assist the worker in addressing all medical issues related to their work-related injury. Medical care may be required and provided in situations when there is no lost time from work and no cash benefits paid to the injured worker.[11]

Rehabilitation benefits can generally be classified in two areas, medical rehabilitation, and vocational rehabilitation. Medical rehabilitation many times will involve physical therapy under the supervision of a physician. Programs can include exercise and muscle conditioning to restore the injured worker to maximum capability.[11] Vocational rehabilitation within workers' compensation systems can include provisions for retraining, education, and job placement and guidance services. All of the vocational rehabilitation services are geared to assist the injured worker in securing appropriate employment.

Not only can the injured worker access vocational rehabilitation services through the workers' compensation laws, but they may also be eligible to receive vocational rehabilitation services through the state-federal vocational rehabilitation system. This program is administered at the state level in every state within the United States. The state-federal vocational rehabilitation system assists individuals with disabilities to become employed whether or not the disability is related to a previous work injury. The services provided can include assessment, vocational guidance and counseling, restoration, training, and job placement.

Subsequent injury funds provide employers with some financial peace of mind with respect to hiring individuals with disabilities. If an individual with a disability is hired and the person incurs an injury, the current employer is only liable for the last injury and the remainder of the award is covered from the second injury fund.[11]

SUMMARY

Workers' compensation laws were first enacted in the United States over one hundred years ago. Most workers in the United States are covered by some type of workers' compensation law. While workers' compensation laws are amended from time-to-time, the objectives associated with workers' compensation generally remain the same. These objectives generally prove beneficial to both workers and employers. The objectives are:

- replacement of income,
- rehabilitation of the injured employer,
- prevention of accidents, and
- cost allocation.[10]

CASE STUDY

Sam is a 45-year-old male who was employed as a delivery driver for Abbey Road Beverage Company for the past 15 years. Sam's job duties entailed driving to make deliveries over a route within Boston. Sam was injured approximately 12 months ago while unloading goods from his truck at a delivery site. Sam was taking cases of beverages from his truck and placing them on a hand truck to transport into the business. During this process the hand truck proved unsteady, the load of beverages began to shift and as they began to fall, Sam attempted to stop the load from falling. In the process, he fell with the load of beverages and landed hard on his right side. Sam injured his right wrist, right elbow, and right shoulder. Immediately after the accident, Sam was in severe pain and had significant lack of range of motion involving his dominate right arm. Sam reported to the nearest emergency room for medical attention.

After being examined at the emergency room, Sam was diagnosed with a bruised shoulder, a dislocated elbow and severely strained ligaments in his wrist. Sam was unable to engage in his employment because of these work-related injuries. He applied and became eligible for workers' compensation benefits. In this instance, Sam was classified as an injured worker who was temporarily totally disabled. He received wage-loss benefits during the time he was unable to engage in his work duties.

After a time of rest and recovery, Sam was re-evaluated by his doctor and was determined to be ready to begin physical restoration services. Sam was referred to physical therapy to assist him in regaining strength and range of motion. Physical therapy session to reduce the pain in his right wrist, elbow, and shoulder were also introduced. After several weeks of physical therapy, Sam progressed to the point where he had regained use of his wrist, elbow, and shoulder at pre-injury levels. Given Sam's progress, his doctor released Sam to return to work without restrictions. Sam is back at work and is doing well.

Sam received workers' compensation benefits of wage-loss assistance (2/3 of his wage) for a period of 63 days, which was from the time of his injury until the time he was able to return to work.

Additionally, his medical expenses and physical therapy were covered under his workers' compensation claim.

SOCIAL SECURITY BENEFITS

While the Social Security Act of 1935 was initially enacted to help retired workers and their dependents, it also provides income support for persons with severe disabilities who are unable to work. The Social Security Administration (SSA)[27] is the federal agency that provides financial support, cash benefits, and medical insurance to eligible individuals with disabilities. Social Security benefits are provided to older, retired Americans as well as adults with disabilities and the families in which a spouse or parent dies. Approximately 155 million people currently work and pay Social Security taxes while approximately 54 million people receive monthly Social Security benefits. Social security taxes that are being paid by employed persons fund persons who are currently receiving benefits.

There are two types of income support programs available for persons with disabilities who are unable to work due to mental or physical impairments: *Supplemental Security Income (SSI)* and *Social Security Disability Insurance (SSDI)*. Individuals with a severe disability who are unable to engage in substantial gainful activity (SGA) would be eligible. SGA is determined by the amount of income a person earns in a month. As of 2011, SGA for persons with disabilities, other than blindness, is $1000 per month. Individuals who are blind can earn up to $1640. These levels are generally adjusted annually.

SUPPLEMENTAL SECURITY INCOME (SSI)

SSI is a type of public assistance provided to persons with disabilities who meet the eligibility criteria, but who has either not worked or did not earn enough income to qualify for SSDI. Persons receiving SSI are normally age 65 or older, blind, or disabled and have limited financial resources. The amount of income the person receives is based upon household income and consideration is given to income from others living in the home. In most cases, the individual's car and home are not considered as resources or assets. Consideration in determining benefit amounts is also given if the person lives alone or in a special care facility. Most SSI recipients receive Medicaid benefits through their respective states in addition to their cash benefit. Recipients do not necessarily pay for benefits. SSI is financed from general revenues, not Social Security taxes.

SOCIAL SECURITY DISABILITY INSURANCE

SSDI is an insurance or cash payment for those who become disabled. Individuals are found disabled if they have a medically determinable physical or mental impairment; or any combination of impairments lasting for at least 12 months; or the impairment is expected to result in death; and they are unable to work prior to retirement age. Workers earn credits for work, and the credits are calculated through taxes taken from their paychecks. Normally, persons must work five out of the last 10 working years in order to earn enough credits. Beneficiaries receive pay based upon the quarters earned and paid into the system. The date last insured refers to the date in which workers have earned enough quarters of coverage to insure coverage long enough to draw benefits.

Eligibility. Individuals who work and pay taxes, earn Social Security credits. In 2011, individuals earned one credit for each $1,120 in earnings—up to a maximum of four credits per year. The amount of money needed to earn one credit usually increases every year. Most people need 40 credits (10 years of work) to qualify for benefits. Younger people need fewer credits to be eligible for disability benefits or for family members to be eligible for survivors' benefits when the worker dies.

Age, education, work experience (exertion level and skill level), severity of impairments, and substantial and gainful activity are taken into consideration when determining eligibility for benefits. Work done for pay or profit, including self-employment, is also used as a determining factor whether or not there are earnings. Working at SGA at the time of application for benefits results in a determination of *not disabled* regardless of the severity of the physical or mental impairments, age, education, or past work experience.

THE FIVE-STEP SEQUENTIAL EVALUATION PROCESS

A five-step sequential process is followed in processing disability claims appeals. Vocational experts (VEs) assist the Administrative Law Judge (ALJ) in determining the claimant's age, education, and past work background and how these factors affect the claimant's ability to perform work-related activities. The VE will provide information about how many jobs exist in the regional and national economy that can be performed by the claimant, taking into account the person's residual functional capacity (RFC).

Step 1: Is the claimant engaging in substantial gainful activity (SGA)?
SGA involves performing work for pay or profit. A claimant found engaging in SGA is found not disabled.

Step 2: Does the claimant have a severe impairment?
The claimant is found not disabled if no impairment exists that significantly restricts the ability to perform basic work activities. This is a medical question and VE opinion is not necessary at this step.

Step 3: Does the claimant have an impairment that meets or equals the Listing of Impairments guidelines for the SSA?
VE testimony is not necessary at this step. If a claimant meets or equals the listing, they are found disabled without further review of the evidence. VE opinion is not necessary at this step.

Step 4: Can the claimant do past work?

If the claimant is not engaging in SGA and has a severe impairment that does not meet or equal a listing, the ALJ determines the claimant's residual functional capacity (RFC). The RFC is a description of the work functions the claimant can perform. For example, how much the person can lift, carry, push, pull, sit, stand, and walk in terms of sedentary, light, medium, heavy, and very heavy exertion levels as defined in the Dictionary of Occupational Titles (DOT). Other considerations are given to the claimant's ability or inability to climb, balance, stoop, crouch, crawl, kneel, handle objects, see, hear, talk, and understand and carry out instructions.

Step 5: Can the claimant do other work?

If the ALJ finds the claimant cannot perform the requirements of his past relevant work, the ALJ must consider whether the claimant can adjust to other work in the national economy. In doing so, the ALJ must consider the claimant's RFC, age, education, and past relevant work. The VE will be asked to testify in cases where the RFC falls between two exertion levels or where there are non-exertion limitations.

COMPENSATION

SSI benefits are paid monthly and adjusted annually. Currently, monthly SSI payment rates are $674 for an individual and $1,011 for a couple. In 2011, the average monthly Social Security benefits were as follows:

- Retired worker: $1,174
- Retired couple: $1,907
- Disabled worker: $1,067
- Disabled worker with a spouse and child: $1,813
- Widow or widower: $1,133
- Young widow or widower with two children: $2,409

MEDICARE

There is often confusion determining the differences between Medicare and Medicaid. Medicare is the country's basic health insurance program for people age 65 or older and many people with disabilities. Medicaid is a health care program for people with low income and limited resources. It is usually run by state welfare or social services agencies. Some people qualify for one or the other, while some people qualify for both Medicare and Medicaid. The four parts of Medicare are:

- Hospital insurance (Part A) helps pay for inpatient hospital care and certain follow-up services.
- Medical insurance (Part B) helps pay for doctors' services, outpatient hospital care, and other medical services.

- Medicare Advantage plans (Part C) are available in many areas. People with Medicare Parts A and B can choose to receive all of their health care services through a provider organization under Part C.
- Prescription drug coverage (Part D) helps pay for medications doctors prescribe for medical treatment.

DETERMINING CONTINUING DISABILITY

SSA is required by law to review periodically all cases of individuals who were previously found disabled. In addition to continuing disability review (CDR), other situations may trigger review:

- voluntary reports from beneficiaries of medical improvement and return to work,
- earnings posted to the claimant's SS record,
- all medical reexamination diaries,
- reports of unsuccessful rehabilitation, or
- random spot checks.

WORK INCENTIVES

Workers engaged in substantial gainful activity are paying taxes that benefit all recipients and beneficiaries. There are several incentives to assist workers with disabilities in engaging in work. Two such incentives are summarized below:

Impairment-Related Work Expenses (IRWE) (SSDI and SSI eligible). The cost of certain impairment-related items and services that are necessary for individuals to work is deducted from gross earnings once a determination is made regarding "countable earnings" that demonstrate performance of SGA. These items and services can be used for non-work activities. For example, individuals can deduct expenses for the costs of structural or operational modifications made to their vehicle. The vehicle can be used as transportation to work and to participate in non-work activities.

The *Ticket to Work Program* is an innovative program for persons with disabilities who want to work and participate in planning their employment. A Ticket increases available choices for individuals when obtaining employment services, vocational rehabilitation services, and other support services necessary to get or keep a job. There is no cost to individuals and it is a voluntary service. Persons can use the Ticket if they choose, but they are not penalized for not using it. Individuals may be subject to a continuing disability review while using the Ticket.

The program is available in all 50 states and 10 United States Territories. Many SSDI beneficiaries and SSI disability recipients will receive a Ticket they can use to obtain services from a state vocational rehabilitation (VR) agency or another approved provider of their choice. Approved providers are called Employment Networks. Employment Networks (ENs) are private organizations or government agencies that have agreed to work with Social Security to provide employment services to beneficiaries with disabilities. The EN chosen helps individuals activate their Ticket.

CASE STUDY

Paul is a fifty-four year old man with an 8th grade education but reading below the 3rd grade level and arithmetic skills at the 5th grade level. The claimant's medically determinable impairments are uncontrolled diabetes, osteoarthritis, and right leg radiculopathy. The claimant is also being treated for depression and anxiety. Paul's limitations are as follows: occasional fine and gross bi-lateral manual dexterity, inability to grasp with his left dominant hand, unable to bend, stoop, crouch, or crawl more than occasionally.

The claimant worked as an unskilled, general laborer for the past 25 years. He is unable to return to work due to difficulty lifting and carrying 50 pounds on a frequent basis and 100 pounds on an occasional basis (heavy exertional level). He recently applied for social security benefits after a worsening of his symptoms that prevented him from being able to attend work on a regular and consistent basis. Claimant's residual functional capacity (RFC) consists of being able to lift up to 10 pounds frequently (sedentary exertional level). His mental residual functional capacity (MRFC) consists of being capable of interacting with co-workers, supervisors, and public on a less than occasional basis, unable to sustain stressors of day to day work on a regular and consistent basis, must work in a setting with duties that have simple, repetitive tasks, in an environment without fast pace, strict production quotas, and time pressures.

Paul is a person closely approaching advanced age with a limited education and, therefore, may have difficulty adapting to a new work setting at a lower exertional level since he has no transferable skills. The claimant was precluded from returning to his past work and from other work in the national economy. Thus, after a review of the medical evidence and considering vocational expert testimony, the claimant was found disabled based upon his medically determinable condition of osteoarthritis, diabetes, and mental impairments. As such, the fully favorable decision allowed the claimant to be awarded SSDI and Medicare benefits.

Short-term and Long-term Disability Benefits

Unexpected illness, injury, or disability can happen to anyone. During this time, individuals have numerous questions and often experience a myriad of emotions. If there is an inability to work because of the illness, injury, or disability, economic hardships can result. Financial woes compound the stress and strain that people may experience. Employers offer two specific benefits that can assist workers should this occur: short-term and long-term disability insurance. Short-term disability insurance (STDI) and long-term disability insurance (LTDI) benefit programs are designed to provide income replacement to employees when they are unable to work due to illness, disability, or injury. In order to work effectively with consumers with disabilities, rehabilitation professionals must be keenly aware of the various benefit programs designed to assist workers.

Overview. Short-term disability insurance is an employee elected and paid benefit designed to provide time limited financial assistance to workers who are unable to work due to a disability. Typically, to be eligible for short-term disability benefits, the employee must select this benefit upon hire and pay a monthly premium, which may vary according to the company.

Similar to STDI, Long-term disability insurance provides income replacement for individuals who are unable to work due to illness, injury, or disability. With LTDI, the disability is expected to last six months or longer. This type of benefit is for workers whose disability prevents them from working in their specific job or occupation. Unlike STDI, LTDI benefits are usually 100% employer paid and have longer elimination period (time before benefits can be activated).

Eligibility. Although the employee pays for STDI, there are still eligibility guidelines that must be met. To be eligible to draw STDI, individuals must have a qualifying event that can range from pregnancy, hospitalization, to outpatient surgery. Activation of STDI benefits generally requires the employee to work full-time and have worked for the company for a certain time. Short-term disability benefits typically are awarded for up to six months (26 weeks) provided the employee has a documented illness or disability that does not permit the employee to work in one's job or occupation. Some plans may require a 7 to 30 day waiting period prior to the disbursement of payment.

Long-term disability insurance eligibility requirements will vary from company to company and state to state. Many policies use an occupational test of disability, which means the employee has an inability to perform the duties of one's own occupation. This definition is used for the first two years. After that, the definition moves to the inability to do any occupation.[18]

Compensation. Individuals receive monetary payments that may range from about 50-70 percent of the employees weekly wage or monthly salary.[21] These payments are typically paid weekly but can be paid bi-weekly or even monthly. Workers will continue to receive compensation as long as documentation, from a qualified professional, states that the individual is unable to work due to the illness, injury, or disability. The typical timeframe for compensation under a short-term disability insurance plan is six months or less. Comparably, LTDI benefits, as the name suggests, are longer in duration and according to the Council for Disability Awareness (CDA),[3] last on average 31.2 months.

Summary. With more than 18 million people in the United States with a disability working,[22] and a record number of those individuals receiving long-term disability insurance payments,[4] the need for benefit programs such as the ones discussed here is critical. Furthermore, it underscores how valuable STDI and LTDI benefits are in lessening the financial burden on an acquired or episodic disability for workers. Rehabilitation professionals agree that early intervention is critical for reintegration into the workforce. Short-term disability and long-term disability benefits can reduce the reliance on more long-term benefits such as Social Security[18] and help workers return to work.

TRANSITIONAL WORK

According to the National Institute for Safety and Health (NIOSH), the annual direct and indirect costs of injuries, illnesses, and fatalities have been estimated to range from $136 billion to over $200 billion. That cost is expected to rise as the US workforce continues to age. The financial cost to employers in terms of benefit payments and lost productivity continues to rise each day an employee misses work. Meanwhile, the physical, emotional, and financial losses to the employee also mount while they are off work. Yet, getting people with injuries and illnesses back to work is often very difficult. Employers have relied upon progressive return-to-work strategies like transitional work as a cornerstone of their disability management programs.

Transitional work, sometimes referred to as light duty or modified duty, allows employees with temporary physical and/or psychological restrictions to work throughout their recovery. Transitional work programs aim to return injured and ill employees back to work as soon as their medical condition(s) allow.

Most transitional work programs are limited to 90 days to ensure that people are physically and mentally ready to return to work when they re-enter the workforce. When employees return to work too soon, they risk re-injury and additional time off work. Restricting the amount of time in transitional work also ensures that employees are not permanently assigned to alternative jobs.

In transitional work, employees are given tasks based on their physical capabilities and skills. As the employee recovers and restrictions change or decrease, job duties are gradually increased until the person is able to perform all of the duties of their regular job. This approach is especially effective when the person has a physically demanding job.

Other strategies often used in transitional work include ergonomic assessments to ensure proper body mechanics, purchasing tools and equipment like lifts to perform some of the physical labor, reduced, or modified work schedule to allow for sufficient recovery time outside of work, and extended or additional breaks to allow rest during the workday.

Eligibility. In order to be eligible for transitional work, the employee must have restrictions that preclude being able to perform all or some of the essential functions of the job. It has to be reasonable to assume, based on medical information from the employee's treating physician, that the person will ultimately be able to resume the job duties of their regular position. The restrictions must be temporary in nature and not expected to exceed a predetermined period unless the employee is making satisfactory progress and the physician has determined that a short extension of transitional work is sufficient to allow the person to return to his regular job.

Perhaps most importantly, the employer must be supportive of and knowledgeable in transitional work. Without someone at the job site willing and capable of finding alternative productive work or putting accommodations and modifications in place, the employee cannot return to work until he is able to do his regular job.

Compensation. Although there is no specific monetary payment amount for individuals who participate in transitional work, most employers pay 100% of the worker's normal salary once the employee returns to work. In order to entice people to participate in transitional work, the salary earned for working must be greater than what the individual was getting in disability wages. Typically, once the employee earns a paycheck, deductions for items such as medical benefits, parking, and retirement are garnished. As a result, earning partial pay would not make transitional work financially appealing to employees.

Benefits to employees. On average, employees who participate in transitional work decrease their lost workdays by 50%, which means they are earning their full salary and benefits in half the time of employees who do not participate in transitional work. By returning to work, employees reengage their social networks, which are extremely helpful when dealing with pain and recovery from illness and injury. Work has also been shown to accelerate the recovery process, reduce the chance of permanent disability, and decrease the chance of re-injury. By working, employees can regain strength and endurance while improving activity tolerances. All of the above makes employees more likely to gain a sense of well-being and self-efficacy.

Benefits to employers. Research has shown that offering a transitional work program doubles the chances that the employee will be able to return to work. When employees come back to work, costly disability payments are reduced or eliminated and associated medical costs are reduced. Conversely, the longer the person is off work, the less likely they are to return to work at all, which increases the cost of the claim for the employer and reduces the employee's earnings.

Indirect cost savings of transitional work programs include less money spent on hiring and training new employees or paying temporary employees to fill in while employees are out on disability leave. Companies that have transitional work programs have also noted improved employee morale, quality improvements, and production improvements.

CASE STUDY

Sheila is a line cook at a busy restaurant. Line Cooks are responsible for preparing meals that are eaten by restaurant patrons. They typically work on a line of grills and stoves. They use fryers with baskets that can weigh up to 20 pounds when empty. Commercial sized ovens and freezers with large heavy doors are also accessed by people in this position. In this particular restaurant, the line cook position requires the employee is able to lift up to 35 pounds frequently.

While at work, Sheila was injured when a large oven door fell open on her left shoulder. She worked full duty with the injury while participating in chiropractic care for a year. Eventually, Sheila went off work for surgical correction of the shoulder. Following surgery, four months of physical therapy was ordered. Following the structured therapy, a month-long home exercise program was also prescribed.

After five months of therapies, she gained approximately 75% of her pre-injury strength and 80% of her pre-injury range of motion in her shoulder. She was released to return to work with lifting restrictions of nothing greater than 15 pounds. She was also given repetitive motion restrictions for her affected arm. Her physician estimated that she would be able to perform her regular job duties within eight to ten weeks of her initial return to work. The physician indicated that he would follow up with Sheila four weeks after she returned to work to assess the progress of her recovery. The employer had a robust transitional work program and quickly outlined a transitional return to work plan for her.

Sheila's restrictions precluded her from opening the freezer door to get ingredients, lifting and using large fry baskets, lifting large casserole pans filled with product, and repetitively flipping items on the grill. After meeting with the employee and management, it was determined that she could remain in the kitchen where her culinary skills and knowledge of the dining facility could be used, but she needed to be assigned tasks away from the line.

Since kitchen preparatory tasks involve handling food items that are much smaller in portion, this work did not exceed her lifting restrictions. So, Sheila was assigned to kitchen prep work, which included cutting and traying desserts and making sandwiches. She could also help prepare food items like Jello and berries that were found on the salad bar. All of the food items were brought to her workstation so that she could avoid using the freezer door or carrying large crates of produce.

Four weeks into her return to work, her restrictions were amended to no lifting over 25 pounds for four weeks. She was still restricted in her performance of tasks that required repetitive motion. She was then assigned to work on the line, so more of her regular job tasks were added. She was specifically assigned to preparing food items that did not require frying in the large baskets or frequently turning items on the grill.

After four weeks on these restrictions, Sheila met with her physician who indicated that she had regained nearly all of her pre-injury strength and range of motion in her shoulder. After eight weeks on restrictions, she was released to resume her regular job duties.

Both the employee and employer spoke very highly of their experience with transitional work. Prior to her return to work, Sheila voiced concerns that she was not going to be able to resume her regular job duties after such an extended absence. She quickly learned, however, that work allowed her to continue to build her strength and range of motion while earning a full paycheck and increasing her work tolerances. She felt happier than she had since injuring her shoulder as her pain had subsided and she was contributing to her family. The employer was glad to benefit from her extensive culinary knowledge sooner than expected and not paying a temporary employee and expensive disability benefit costs.

TABLE 1

SUMMARY OF WORKER DISABILITY PROGRAMS

Benefit	Description	Eligibility	Compensation
Workers' Compensation	A form of insurance that may provide income replacement, medical benefits, and vocational rehabilitation services for individuals injured in the course of their employment.	For workers covered by a worker's compensation law they are eligible for worker's compensation benefits when an injury or illness is determined to be a result of their employment.	Can vary depending on the classification of the work related injury or illness. Temporary Total Disability – Generally 66-2/3% of weekly wages until the worker returns to work or a statutory maximum is reached. Permanent Partial Disability – Benefit is generally calculated as the difference between earnings before the injury/illness and earnings after the injury/illness. Permanent Total Disability – A statutory determined weekly benefit based on a percentage

			of their gross salary. Other Potential Compensation -Death Benefits -Medical Benefits -Rehabilitation Benefits
STDI	Income replacement for workers with a documented illness, injury, or disability lasting less than 6 months.	Enroll in program at hire Met the elimination period Pay premium Documented illness, injury or disability Inability to do one's job or occupation due to the documented illness, injury or disability	Typically pays 50-70% of regular wage/salary
LTDI	Income replacement for workers with a documented illness, injury, or disability lasting 6 months or longer.	Enroll in program at hire (often automatic) Documented illness, injury or disability Inability to do one's job or occupation due to the documented illness, injury or disability for 6 months or longer	Typically pays 50-70% of regular wage/salary
SSI Title 16	Income and health care provided for documented disability for persons with low income expected to last 12 months or longer	Set benefits adjusted annually, financial need	$674 per month
SSDI Title 2	Income and health care provided for documented disability for disabled workers lasting 12 months or longer	Benefits based upon worker's salary up to maximum monthly amount	Up to $2250 per month
Transitional Work	Modified work duties that allow employees with temporary physical and/or psychological restrictions to work throughout their recovery	Employees with temporary restrictions that are expected to fully resolve within 12 weeks	Typically 100% of wages are paid unless the employee is working less than full time hours

PROGRAM SIMILARITIES AND DIFFERENCES

Workers with disabilities often encounter difficulty accessing the array of services that were designed to assist them when faced with life-altering situations that prevent them from working. Worker disability programs were designed to help workers access services with ease. However, often time the eligibility requirements seem to be contradictory between programs. As such, workers need to be aware of the similarities and differences between the programs as well as the myriad of worker incentives available to assist them in transitioning back to work if applicable. Below is a summary of a few of the inconsistencies as well as incentives that exist between programs.

Workers' Compensation guidelines generally prefer injured workers work full-time. Workers accepting a position that pays below their pre-injury wages are eligible for living maintenance wage loss for a pre-determined time to assist them in transitioning back to work. Workers' Compensation programs include a full range of transitional work options from light work to full duty. Transitional work programs are usually accessed at this juncture if available.

If a worker is unable to work, they may be deemed temporarily disabled for a period of time. Later, a determination is made as to whether or not the person is permanently disabled at which time a settlement may be pursued to expedite closing of the claim. Injured workers may be referred for vocational rehabilitation services during the process once physical restoration has occurred.

Vocational Rehabilitation eligibility guidelines provide services to individuals with disabilities. However, a determination is made as to whether the person is feasible for services. If a person is found too disabled to benefit from work, the case could be closed. The same rules apply for Workers Compensation; a person may be eligible for services, but too disabled to work. In this case, the individual may want to apply for short-term, long-term disability or social security benefits. Short-term and long-term disability programs generally offer a variety of return-to-work incentives that vary from part-time to full-time options.

Social Security guidelines provide benefits if the person is deemed totally disabled and unable to work due to a condition that is expected to last for at least 12 months. Individuals receiving other types of compensation may not receive social security benefits depending on the amount of compensation received. Another consideration is unemployment compensation, since workers receiving this benefit have agreed that they are ready and willing to search for jobs in order to receive financial assistance. Workers applying for social security benefits typically find themselves in a conundrum when they agree to the job search requirements solely for the financial assistance of unemployment compensation. Many are unable to follow through with a job if found, but agree to look for work due to their reliance on unemployment compensation that may be the only source of income.

Another inconsistency is that social security rules do not consider part-time work or employer accommodations in making their decision to award benefits to individuals who are found disabled. Individuals who work part-time after receiving benefits will trigger a disability review. Working under SGA levels will not prevent a disability review. Workers' compensation, LTDI, STDI and

VR services encourage full or part-time work options with a disabling condition.

CONCLUSION

This chapter provided an overview of four programs designed to assist workers that have an injury or disability. These programs are offered by the government (federal and state) as well as by employers. It is important for rehabilitation professionals to know what services are available for workers with disabilities, the nuances of each service, and how to access these services. Armed with this knowledge, practitioners in the field of rehabilitation will help injured workers access benefits intended to return to daily functioning or work.

REFERENCES AND BIBLIOGRAPHY

[1]Abriola, J. J. (2009). Transitional Duty Programs Help Firms Boost Morale, Cut Workers'

[2]Comp Costs; Risk Managers Urged to Set Well-Defined Policies and Procedures to Assure Success [Electronic Version]. *National Underwriter* 25-27.

[3]Council for Disability Awareness. Retrieved August 6, 2011 from http://www.disabilitycanhappen.org/chances_disability/

[4]Council for Disability Awareness Annual Survey. Retrieved August 6, 2011 from http://www.disabilitycanhappen.org/research/CDA_ LTD_Claims_Survey_2010.asp

[5]Disability Status: 2000. Retrieved September 10, 2011 from http://www.census.gov/prod/2003pubs/c2kbr-17.pdf

[6]Dunning, K.K., Davis, K.G., Kotowski, S.E., Elliot, T., Jewell, G., & Lockey, J. (2008). Can a Transitional Work Grant Program in a Workers' Compensation System Reduce Cost and Facilitate Return to Work? *Journal of Occupational and Environmental Hygiene*, *5*, 547-555.

[7]Federal Employees' Compensation Act, 5 U.S.C. § 8101 *et seq*. Retrieved August 7, 2011 from http;//www.dol.gov/owcp/dfec/regs/statutes/feca.htm

[8]Federal Employees' Liability Act, 45 U.S.C. § 51 *et seq*. Retrieved August 7, 2011, from http://www.law.cornell.edu/uscode/45/usc_sec_45_ 00000051----000-html

[9]Fishback, Price, V., and Kantor, & Shawn Everett. (2000). A Prelude to the Welfare State: the Origins of Workers' *Compensation.* The University of Chicago Press. Chicago.

[10]Goetsch, David L. (2000). The Safety and Health Handbook. Prentice Hall. Upper Saddle River, New Jersey.

[11]Jasper, Margaret C. (2008). *Workers' Compensation Law.* Oceana. New York.

[12]Jasper, Margaret C. (2005). Injured on the Job: Employee Rights, Workers' Compensation & Disability. Oceana Publications. New York.

[13]Job Accommodations for Return-to-Work. [Online] Retrieved August 4, 2011 from http://askjan.org/index.html

[14]Kranz, G. (2003). Transitional Duty Pay Off for Employers, Charities, and Injured Workers. *The* Insider: Absence Management 12, 75-77.

[15]Krause, N., Dasinger, L.K., & Neuhauser, F. (1998). Modified Work and Return to Work: A Review of the Literature. *Journal of Occupational Rehabilitation 8* (2):113-139.

[16]Lencsis, Peter, M. (1998). Workers' Compensation: A Reference *And Guide.* Quorum Books. Westport, Connecticut.

[17]Longshore and Harbor Workers' Compensation Act, 33 U.S.C. § 901 *et seq.* Retrieved from http://www.dol.gov/owcp/dlhwc/lhwca.htm

[18]Mashaw, J., &Reno, V. (1996). Balancing Security and Opportunity: The challenge of disability insurance policy. National Academy of Social Insurance. Retrieved on September 10, 2011 from http://www.nasi.org/usr_doc/Balancing_Security_and_Opportunity.pdf

[19]Merchant Marine Act of 1920, 46 U.S.C. § 861. Retrieved August 7, 2011 from http://www.law.cornell.edu/uscode/html/uscode46a/usc_sup_05_46-10_24.html

[20]Nackley, Jeffrey D. (1987). *Primer On Workers' Compensation.* The Bureau of National Affairs, Inc. Washington, D.C.

[21]National Academy of Social Insurance. Retrieved August 2, 2011 from http://www.nasi.org/learn/workerscomp/disability-insurance

[22]Office of Disability Employment Policy. Retrieved August 6, 2011 from http://www.dol.gov/odep/faqs/working.htm

[23]Parker, M. Szymanski, E. & Patterson, J. (2005) Rehabilitation Counseling: Basics and beyond. (4th ed.). Pro-ed: Austin, TX.

[24]Power, Robert D. & Fung, Frederick, Y. (1994). *Workers'* Compensation Handbook. KW Publications. San Diego

[25]Priz, Edward J. (2005). *Entrepreneur Magazine's* Ultimate Guide To Workers' Compensation Insurance. Entrepreneur Media, Inc. Madison, WI.

[26]Shaw, W., Hong, Q., Pranksy, G., & Loisel, P. (2008). A Literature Review Describing the Role of Return-to-Work Coordinators in Trial Programs and Interventions Designed to Prevent Workplace Disability. Journal of Occupational Rehabilitation: 18, 2-15.

[27]Social Security Administration (SSA). Available: www.ssa.gov

[28]Strasser, P. (2004). Managing Transitional Work- Program Foundation. *AAOHN Journal, 52* (8) 323-326.

[29]United States Department of Commerce Economics and Statistics Administration (2003).

[30]United States Department of Labor. (2011a). Retrieved August 11, 2011 from http://www.dol.gov/owcp/dfec/about.htm

[31]United States Department of Labor. (2011b). Retrieved August 11, 2011 from http://www.dol.gov/owcp/dcmwc.statistics/PartsBandC Beneficiaries.htm

[32]United States Department of Labor. (2011c). Retrieved August 11, 2011 from http://www.dol.gov/owcp/energy/regs/compliance/progbenefits.htm

[33]Vander Kolk, Charles, J. (1993). Litigated Disability Cases: A guide for utilizing the vocational *expert*. Elliott & Fitzpatrick, Inc,

[34]Wickert, Gary L. (2009). Workers' Compensation Subrogation In All 50 States (4th ed.). Juris Publishing, Inc. Huntington, NY.

THE REHABILITATION FACILITIES MOVEMENT

LORI A. BRUCH
UNIVERSITY OF SCRANTON

STANLEY M. IRZINSKI
UNITED REHABILITATION SERVICES, INC.
RETIRED ADMINISTRATOR

CHAPTER TOPICS

- Overview
- Historical Perspective
- Early Initiatives
- Legislation
- Advocacy
- Growth
- Recent History
- The Modern Era
- Role and Value
- Professional Orientation
- Summary: Conflicting Values and Shared Outcomes

OVERVIEW

Historically and today, work has been an integral part of our society. Since the beginning of the Industrial Revolution, the American culture has emphasized the ability to work. Think about your reason for reading this chapter. More than likely it is a part of a course requirement in your rehabilitation education program. Then, stop and think for a minute about your work experiences, about your hopes and dreams, about what work means to you. Hershenson and Szymanski[7] found that work means more than an avenue to economic self-sufficiency. An occupation also defines a person's social status, as well as self-concept. So, what is work like for people with disabilities? Harris[6] stated that, "not working is perhaps the truest definition of what it means to be disabled."[p. 4] This statement was as true in 18th century colonial America as it is today. The struggle for employment has been a common experience for people with disabilities and is important to understanding the Rehabilitation Facility Movement. Before moving on, let us take a few minutes to understand the terminology that preceded the term rehabilitation facility, the purpose of a rehabilitation facility, and the legislation that defined it.

Early words to describe the places where people with disabilities found work included the European concepts of almshouses and workhouses. Phrases common to Colonial America encompassed the terms work rooms, work activities centers, opportunity centers, and workshops. In reviewing the literature in the United States post 1900's, the most frequent descriptor used was workshop.

The term *rehabilitation facility* was formally introduced in the Vocational Rehabilitation Act Amendments of 1968. It replaced the word *workshop* that was commonly used to describe places where people with disabilities found work. The purpose of the rehabilitation facility was "to provide vocational rehabilitation services to or gainful employment for, handicapped individuals, or for providing evaluation and work adjustment services for the disadvantaged individual."[18] Jones and Brabham[8] described the goal of the rehabilitation facility movement as "the complete integration of persons with disabilities, which facilities seek to do by helping them improve their daily lives and to function as independent as possible."[p.11] A common thread of the movement is based on the role of work in the lives of people with disabilities including gainful employment, relief to society, alleviation of financial and social burdens, and the creation of economic benefit and well-being. Throughout history, this movement has been greatly influenced by legislation, predominant social philosophy, population trends, unmet needs of the community, technology, and the importance of productivity in finding meaning in life. Throughout the nineties and today, the rehabilitation facility is often referred to as a Community Rehabilitation Program (CRP).

Let us take you on a journey to explore the past, understand the present, and attempt to project the future of rehabilitation facilities in the United States. Living life with a disability has never been an easy road. It is only in modern times, with the passage of the 1990 Americans with Disabilities Act, that people with disabilities were guaranteed civil rights, including the right to nondiscrimination in employment. The 21st century offered great promise to persons with disabilities, but also presented great challenges to CRP's.

HISTORICAL PERSPECTIVE

So what was life like in Colonial America and where and when did the rehabilitation facility movement begin? Imagine if you will a life much different from what we know today in the United States. Imagine...no hospitals, medicines, physicians, and specialists. Strip away our modern conveniences; forget the Internet and e-mail; gone are all of the technological and medical advances. The phrase "survival of the fittest" takes on new meaning. In many cases, the persons who did survive their disabilities were persons with minimal impairments and higher levels of functional ability. Yet, these individuals still did not have the opportunities to access mainstream society.

Several excellent books present a thorough history of disability in early America and a number of salient items can be gleaned from these works to understand the beginnings of the rehabilitation facility movement.[18, 15, 23] For instance, the legislation dominating early America was patterned after the Poor Laws of England. Poor Laws for the indigent did little to "encourage the restoration of disadvantaged persons to productivity."[18, p.76] Many of the colonists also brought with them from Europe the belief system that incorporated ideas involving superstition, sorcery, alchemy, and astrology. These views did not help the plight of persons with disabilities. Disability was often perceived as a moral question. It was given little attention unless presented as a community problem or petitions asking for assistance of the town council. Since disability was often considered to be a disgrace and resources ranged from scarce to non-existent, people with disabilities were typically kept hidden by their families with needs unmet or subject to conditions which included being publicly housed in tiny cells with no heat and little food. Opportunities for work usually consisted of being auctioned off as servants, if you were fortunate enough to have the physical ability to be useful.[18]

EARLY INITIATIVES

During the period of mid 1700s to mid 1800s, several independent, small-scale efforts were initiated that had an impact on the importance of work in the lives of people with disabilities and formed the beginnings of vocational rehabilitation. These efforts originated from several sources including church and moral societies, hospitals, educational initiatives, and social welfare organizations.[15]

The Quakers initiated early reform in the treatment of people with disabilities. One of their efforts included the establishment of the first general hospital in the colonies in 1752.[18] This hospital not only offered care of the sick but also emphasized the importance of work and humane treatment. The hospital also served a secondary purpose. It provided a meeting place for physicians, social reformers, philanthropists, educators, and legislators to plan for the needs of the community. The early hospitals that were initiated during this time not only rescued persons with disabilities from the Poor Laws, but also established a hopeful change in the direction of philosophy and treatment of persons with disabilities.

Following the efforts and examples set in early Europe, schools began to emerge. Schools for the Deaf were started in Baltimore in 1812 and in Hartford in 1817. In 1838, the Perkins School for the Blind was established in Boston. In 1845, physicians in New York were beginning to discuss the potential of persons with mental retardation as exemplified by Dr. Amarich Brigham, who wrote that their condition "may be so improved as to engage in useful employment and to support themselves; and also to participate in the enjoyments of society."[15, p. 81]

Special educational efforts continued to expand in Massachusetts, Ohio, Kentucky, Connecticut, and Illinois. In Pennsylvania in 1853, the PA Training School for Feeble Minded Children was formed and later located in Elwyn, PA, where it eventually evolved into Elwyn, a comprehensive rehabilitation facility that offered residential, educational, and employment programs.[15]

The mid 1800s witnessed many family service societies being founded to meet pressing community needs. The more progressive philosophy of these organizations stood in stark contrast to the prevailing attitude that the poor and disadvantaged were to be banished and feared. This changing philosophy created a social work-rehabilitation emphasis that was often referred to as a rehabilitation attitude.[18]

Similarly, the establishment of workshops was initially reliant on a small group of dedicated, private individuals who typically were interested in either specific disabilities or the salvation of the disadvantaged and disabled. For instance, the first workshop for the blind that was independent of a school was founded in Pennsylvania in 1874 and focused on producing brooms, mattresses, and rugs.[15] At almost the same time, work opportunities were emerging from several religious and social organizations. In 1891, the Salvation Army was organized in New York City providing work in salvage operations and often helping persons with alcohol and other personal problems. In 1895, Goodwill Industries was being formed in Boston, also incorporating salvage work as a means to provide an income for the impoverished. A year later in Connecticut, another salvage organization was established called Volunteers of America.

This group emphasized developing skills such as cabinet making, upholstery, and radio repair. The early 1900s saw the Society of St. Vincent de Paul reaching out to the poor and disadvantaged by establishing a salvage operation as well. Workshops were also beginning to emerge to meet specific community and population needs. For example, in Boston in 1877, the Cooperative Society of Visitors among the Poor started a workroom program where women did hand sewing that later merged with the Community Workshop, Inc. in 1939.[15]

As the 20th century approached, "America changed from a primarily rural/agrarian to an urban/industrial society."[21, p.14] Educational opportunities were beginning to be viewed as the right of every citizen. These earlier initiatives continued to grow and develop but pessimism and alarm also continued. A growing debate emerged. Should services be developmental or custodial in nature?

LEGISLATION

Several pieces of legislation were passed that had a direct impact on the development of work programs for people with disabilities. Worker's Compensation laws were enacted by states to protect the rights of the injured worker. The passing of the 1913 Federal Income Tax paved the road for government funding of vocational rehabilitation.[21] These events marked the beginning of the economic basis for rehabilitation justified by the rehabilitated person's improved capacity to contribute to the economy and tax base of the country. The 1917 Smith-Hughes Act established a formal federal Board of Vocational Education followed by the 1918 Smith-Sears Act, also known as the Soldier's Act, which established the first program for vocational rehabilitation of veterans with disabilities. At this time, it was becoming clear that there was a disparity between what vocational education could offer (classroom) and what rehabilitation required (highly personalized services).[27] With limited government support, vocational education programs were typically unable to accommodate the needs of students with disabilities, leaving it up to workshops to fill the gap in services. By 1920, rehabilitation services were extended to civilians with disabilities under the Smith-Fess Act. Once again, funds and services were not sufficient to meet the growing needs of people with disabilities. As a result, early rehabilitation programs were initially able to serve a relatively limited population with the typical client being an adult male with physical disabilities.[18]

During this time, a number of non-profit organizations arose to expand services to other populations. The Altro Workshop was established in New York in 1915 to meet the needs of Tuberculosis patients in transition from sanitarium to work by emphasizing the concept of work hardening.[18] The Red Cross was instrumental in the development of the Institute for Crippled and Disabled Men (ICD) in New York that initiated an experimental effort for the vocational rehabilitation of veterans.[15] Philanthropist, Jerimiah Millbank donated a building to this effort hoping to demonstrate to the federal government that vocational benefits should be available to civilians as well.[8] The 1920's also witnessed the further development of Curative Workshops for persons with orthopedic disabilities.[15] In 1933, Bell Greve showed "the difficult problems of people with chronic conditions were best approached through comprehensive medical, social, psychological, and vocational programs."[27, p. 44] As the Director of the Cleveland Rehabilitation Center, she patterned her efforts after the ICD and was a trailblazer for workshops and facilities. Unfortunately, a distinct difference in the types of programs that provided custodial care in institutions versus the sincere desire to improve the condition of people with disabilities as emphasized by Bell Greve and others continued.

For most of the 20s and 30s, people were struggling with the aftermath of war and wide spread economic depression. Eleanor Roosevelt was seen as a rehabilitationist and a beacon of hope to many poor families.[27] A key piece of legislation that was passed during this time was the 1935 Social Security Act. This act provided permanent and increased federal financial support for vocational rehabilitation and established the State-Federal Vocational Rehabilitation Program as a permanent entity that could only be discontinued by an Act of Congress.[18] While the act enabled the federal government to use workshop programs, it did not formally define them. The first definition of a workshop was not found until the 1938 passage of the Fair Labor Act. The regulations defined workshops as follows:

> *A charitable organization or institution conducted not for profit, but for the purpose of carrying out a recognized program of rehabilitation for individuals whose earning capacity is impaired by age or physical or mental deficiency or injury, and to provide such individuals remunerative employment or other occupational rehabilitation activity of an educational or therapeutic nature.*[15, p. 134]

Another prevailing belief during this time was that people who were blind had little potential for community employment.[21] Although the accepted standard for employment was sheltered work, two significant pieces of legislation began to increase other opportunities. The 1936 Randolph-Sheppard Act provided opportunities for persons who were blind to operate vending stands on federal property. This act was quickly followed by the enactment of the 1938 Wagner-O'Day Act that granted preference to workshops for the blind on certain government contracts. These two acts helped to highlight the abilities of persons who were blind[20] and resulted in the creation of the National Industries for the Blind to help coordinate government orders and contracts.[15]

In direct contrast to the 1930s, World War II resulted in significant growth in the state-federal rehabilitation programs as exemplified by the passage of the Bardon-La Follette Act of 1943. This act extended rehabilitation services to persons with mental retardation, mental illness, and blindness and established the model for comprehensive rehabilitation services.[21] This was also a time marked by significant medical advancement, improved treatment, and the development of physical medicine as a specialty. For the first time, people with disabilities found themselves to be valued members of the work force because of the labor shortages during the war. Just as quickly as people with disabilities were accepted into the work force, unfortunately, many discovered their newfound employment to be a fleeting interlude with the return of veterans. Workshops continued to offer a viable alternative to not working at all.

ADVOCACY

The authors would be remiss if they did not note the important role played by parents and other family members of persons with disabilities. The 1950s was a time of organization by the parents of children with mental retardation, cerebral palsy, and other developmental disabilities. Their struggles to resist the recommendation to institutionalize their children resulted in the formation of parent organizations that have grown into the present day United Cerebral Palsy Organization and The ARC.[25] These parents established and advocated for programs that included education, recreation, day care, counseling, diagnostic services, workshop services, employment, and community integration. They also stressed the psychosocial factors that are important in the workplace.[15] Their strenuous efforts have had and continue to have a strong influence on federal, state, and local policy and the types of services offered by rehabilitation facilities.

GROWTH

The period from 1954 to 1965 has often been described as the "Golden Era of Rehabilitation."[22] With the passage of the 1954 Public Law 565, services to persons with mental retardation and mental illness were expanding. This landmark act authorized funds for the establishment and development of rehabilitation facilities, including remodeling and expanding buildings. Funds were also available for equipment and staff. This historic legislation led to an increased number of facilities, an emphasis on quality of services, and an increase in the use of facilities. It authorized funds for vocational evaluation and work adjustment services.[15] Instrumental in the development and passage of Public Law 565 was Mary Switzer, who became the first Director of the Office of Vocational Rehabilitation in 1950 and was undoubtedly the most significant and effective leader of the modern rehabilitation movement.

During the Kennedy-Johnson era, services to people with mental retardation and mental illness increased rapidly.[2] The 1963 Mental Health Act paved the way for the deinstitutionalization movement that encompassed thousands of persons leaving state facilities and institutions and entering the community; subsequently creating a significant need for increased capacity and types of services available from rehabilitation facilities.

In 1964, the Laird Amendments allowed private funds to be matched by federal funds for the establishment and construction of rehabilitation facilities and were followed by the landmark 1965 Amendments that expanded services to persons with behavioral disorders such as drug and alcohol problems, juvenile and adult offenders, as well as to persons who were socially disadvantaged. The 1965 amendments brought the advent of extended evaluation services and the establishment of state service delivery systems and were especially significant because of the impetus they provided to the growth of workshops. The development of the state-federal and vocational rehabilitation facility partnership further expanded services by relying heavily on facilities to meet the increasing needs of persons with severe disabilities. The 1968 Amendments gave these workshops a new name: rehabilitation facility. The rehabilitation facility was defined as having three purposes: "...the provision of rehabilitation services to handicapped individuals, the provision of employment to handicapped individuals, and the provision of evaluation and work adjustment services to disadvantaged individuals."[15, p. 137]

In 1971, the Javits Amendments to the Wagner-O'Day Act (JWOD), now referred to as Ability One[16], expanded the purchase of services and products from rehabilitation facilities serving persons who are blind or have other significant disabilities. Today, through the JWOD, people with disabilities manufacture over 2000 different products and perform in over 400 job titles. The availability of contracts and services under JWOD extends to over 600 nonprofit agencies and provides employment opportunities to over 47,000 Americans who have significant disabilities. Both the National Industries for the Blind and the National Industries for the Severely Handicapped (NISH),[17] two non-profit agencies, provide technical assistance to community rehabilitation programs across the country to provide services through Ability One contracts.

RECENT HISTORY

The end of the "fabulous sixties" marked the conclusion of the growth era for rehabilitation facilities. The 1970s are distinguished by a tightening of federal funds, but a greater commitment to people with disabilities as witnessed by the Rehabilitation Act of 1973 and the 1975 Right to Education for all Handicapped Children's Act. During this time, many rehabilitation facilities were beginning to develop increased opportunities in community employment in an effort to augment their traditional workshop programs. The initiation of Projects with Industry (PWI) federal grants in 1970 encouraged rehabilitation facilities to forge valuable partnerships with the business and industry community and provided increased federal and state funds to support innovative job placement programs. At the same time, facilities were feeling the impact of deinstitutionalization and were facing the dilemma of providing the necessary supports for increasing numbers of persons with significant disabilities transitioning into CRPs. Many of these individuals required significant vocational and behavioral supports.

During the 1980s, rehabilitation facilities continued to expand programming into the community, while also maintaining workshop services for a portion of their clientele. School to work, job club, transitional employment programs, enclaves, and mobile work forces were offering increased opportunities for community employment. The 1986 Rehabilitation Act amendments included a provision for supported employment services. Despite a continuing shift to community employment initiatives, rehabilitation facilities were beginning to face sharp criticism from a growing number of persons committed to fully integrated community employment experiences for persons with all disabilities.[10, 28]

THE MODERN ERA

The nineties were marked by a strong commitment to the civil rights of people with disabilities. The Americans with Disabilities Act, the 1992 and 1998 Rehabilitation Act Amendments, and the 2004 reauthorization of the Individuals with Disabilities Act (IDEA) clearly emphasized the full involvement of people with disabilities and integration in all areas of community life. More specifically, the federal government has focused on streamlining the range of employment programs. "With the passage of the Workforce Investment Act of 1998 (WIA) and the resultant establishment of the One-Stop Career System, a less complex and more customer-focused employment and training system has become the ideal."[9, p. 33] Contained in WIA are the Rehabilitation Act amendments of 1998 along with requirements that provide for greater coordination, collaboration, and linkage among a wide variety of employment and training programs. While some of the requirements focus on state and local governance issues, there is also a stipulation that vocational rehabilitation (VR) be a required partner in the one-stop system in order to enhance services to people with disabilities.[26]

In addition, the 1999 Ticket to Work Incentives Improvement Act represents a significant effort to reduce or eliminate key employment barriers by providing options for states supporting persons with disabilities through extended health coverage, should they return to work. Key aspects of this program are the placing of vocational resources in the hands of the individual and allowing these resources to be used over an extended period of time.[9]

The sum and substance of these recent initiatives for rehabilitation facilities is the continuation of the trend to provide more and more services in community integrated environments and fewer programs within the walls of the facility itself. This trend was given even more impetus by Department of

Education Regulations (October 1, 2001) governing the State Vocational Rehabilitation Services Program (VR). These regulations now redefine successful "employment outcome" to mean outcome in which an individual with a disability works in an integrated setting as opposed to a sheltered workshop. Campbell[3] proposes that the "ultimate outcome of any good rehabilitation service should be the empowerment of its clients."[p. 67] The 21st century is a time of great promise for people with disabilities, but also a time that will require the leadership of rehabilitation facilities to continue to move beyond segregated services in responding to the hopes and dreams of the people it serves.

ROLE AND VALUE

Now that we have completed our journey through the maze of history and legislation, we will examine the rather significant role that rehabilitation facilities have played in the lives of people with disabilities, and the value of these facilities.

When all is said and done, rehabilitation facilities in this country represent a system that is almost continuously evolving and changing—it is never "static." It is often difficult to determine whether rehabilitation facilities arose as result of local needs, or whether early rehabilitation "pioneers" inspired society to change its view of people with disabilities and how they were treated.

In any event, one thing is clear, people with disabilities needed to be somewhere and that somewhere was usually some form of a rehabilitation facility. In the 1800's, the most prevalent view was that people with disabilities required custodial care. Both state and private facilities reflected the view that persons with disabilities needed to be segregated from the rest of society. Consequently, people received treatment in large residential programs separate from the community at large.

Much of this view began to change in the 1900s, first slowly, then more rapidly. Following two world wars, industrialization that produced more injured people, and rising numbers of individuals with developmental disabilities, it became abundantly clear that some community program alternatives needed to be identified. This combination of factors began to coalesce into the forerunner of today's rehabilitation facility. During the 1920s to 1930s, federal and state support for community programs was almost nonexistent. Consequently, many of the facilities began with little or no financial planning or foresight. They evolved in response to identified human need, with initiative and action coming from volunteers and charitable organizations. Most rehabilitation facilities were "non-profit" organizations that survived on a shoestring via a hodgepodge of funding sources. These non-profit organizations were guided by a volunteer board of directors. Some of the agencies engaged in salvage work, some sold products they made, and others performed jobs for the business community. They came to be known as workshops because that is what they primarily did. They provided work for people with disabilities who wanted employment, but did not fit or would not be accepted in the "real" world of work. Hence, the word "sheltered" was usually attached to workshop. The distinguishing feature of the vocational rehabilitation facility that remains to this day is that it is a unique blend of human service and business enterprise.

Work has historically been the common denominator among facilities, but it has been primarily used as a tool as opposed to a source of revenue. As this nation continued its period of industrial growth, the work performed in rehabilitation facilities also became more industrial in nature, as more and more of it was acquired from the business community through sub-contract relationships. In fact, many rehabilitation facilities resembled small industrial plants and performed a variety of assembly, packaging, and collating operations. These programs were certified by the Wage and Hour Division of the Department of Labor to pay sub-minimum wages (piece rate) because it was determined that individuals with disabilities were not functioning at a minimal level. The basic premise of the programs was that partial productivity was better than none, and that with training some people might eventually be able to achieve full employment. The role that rehabilitation facilities have played as an employer of people with disabilities has been significant, and its value to society in that capacity cannot be over estimated.

During the 1960s, the influx of federal and state dollars into the rehabilitation facilities produced substantial changes. Rehabilitation facilities not only proliferated, but many organizations constructed new buildings and became comprehensive rehabilitation facilities with an expanded scope of services. By 1992, it was estimated that there were approximately 7000 rehabilitation facilities providing service throughout the United States.[12]

The major peculiarity of the rehabilitation facility movement in this country is that it is difficult to define. It is non-profit but business related that receives some federal and state support. Yet, it could not survive without private charity, fees for service contracts, and public donations for support. In fact, it is such a diverse movement that it virtually defies one clear definition.

PROFESSIONAL ORIENTATION

In 1949, representing in part a search for identity, the National Committee on Sheltered Workshops and Homebound Programs was established. In 1952, OVR Director Mary Switzer and the National Easter Seals Society established the Conference of Rehabilitation Centers and Facilities (CRCF) for the administration and development of facilities. In 1958, over two hundred rehabilitation related personnel met in Pennsylvania to discuss definitions and other concerns of the workshop movement.[15] In 1966, the Association of Rehabilitation Centers (ARC)[25] and the National Association of Sheltered Workshops and Homebound Programs (NASWHP) incorporated the

Commission on Accreditation of Rehabilitation Facilities (CARF).[4] CARF was developed to accredit and promote quality outcomes in rehabilitation facilities. It went on to develop standards for the provision of services to persons with disabilities and for the operation of rehabilitation facilities. These standards became a part of a nationally recognized accreditation process for the facilities movement. In 1969, ARC and NASWHP merged to form the National Association of Rehabilitation Facilities (NARF) whose purpose was to advocate for facilities on important legislative issues.[15] Almost simultaneously, many states formed chapters of the Association of Rehabilitation Facilities that loosely fell under NARF's umbrella. Over the years, interest and support for national associations began to wane and eventually led to the demise of NARF.

The diminished interest in a national trade association for rehabilitation facilities may represent the diversifying nature of the facility movement during the past twenty years. Some agencies, reacting to criticism from advocates and funding sources, have closed their workshop program in order to concentrate solely on job placement activities. Recent trends toward self-determination, customized services, and individual voucher systems have produced a multitude of changes in community rehabilitation programs. Perhaps what we call the Rehabilitation Facility Movement is no longer a movement after all...perhaps it is an era that has passed.

But then again, change is nothing new for rehabilitation facilities. In fact, the capacity to change has been the key to their survival. Throughout history, rehabilitation facilities have re-invented themselves many times. It is inherent in their nature. They originally developed not by plan, but spontaneously in response to community needs. Facilities continue to reshape because they are continuing to respond to ever changing human needs and environments. In July, 2007, in an effort to unite, the American Congress of Community Support and Employment Services (ACCSES)[1] merged with the Disability Service Providers of America (DSPA). ACCSES currently represents more than 80 partner organizations in an effort to be a voice for CRPs and other disability service providers.

SUMMARY: CONFLICTING VALUES AND SHARED OUTCOMES

People with disabilities have long struggled to gain access to the mainstream of community life through the disabilities rights movement, Centers for Independent Living groups, and advocacy organizations. In early America, several voices spoke to the goals of community life for persons with disabilities. In 1840, Howe championed the rights of the blind by establishing a workshop so that they "could eventually work in their home communities."[15, p. 27] These sentiments were echoed for the deaf, injured workers, veterans with disabilities, persons with chronic health conditions, and persons with mental retardation. These pioneering spirits recognized that rehabilitation was all about community integration. Today, the goal of community integration is a mandate for people with disabilities and the most successful outcome of a positive disability rights movement.

Daugherty[5] looks at the rehabilitation facilities movement as being one of the "most significant factors in the integration of people with severe disabilities into our communities having a rich history of innovation, change, and leadership."[p. 20] So why does strong opposition exist to contemporary Community Rehabilitation Programs (CRP)? Shaw[24] discussed the negative implications that came with being a workshop and rehabilitation facility and the belief that by changing the term to community rehabilitation program it "represented a single, specific, cohesive, well-defined industry."[p. 20] Nevertheless, Shaw reminds us that it is not the case. Rehabilitation facilities and CRP's, have "broad and divergent philosophies regarding how organizations will provide services."[p. 20]

The first recognized voice of dissent came from Jacobus ten Broek in the 1950's who criticized workshops and concluded "there is no place for the 'sheltered workshop' in vocational rehabilitation."[15, p. 205] While ten Broek's ideals were easily dismissed in 1971, over the last three decades his views have gained strong support. For example, an entire book, *Closing the Workshop,* is devoted to the conversion from sheltered to integrated work.[13]

Most recently, the National Disability Rights Network (NDRN),[14] a non-profit advocacy agency, established to protect the rights of people with disabilities and their families, issued a strong position paper suggesting that workshops are nothing more than community institutions that segregate and exploit people with disabilities. The "Call to Action" further recommends that federal and state money be restricted to these programs and the elimination of the ability of CRPs to pay sub-minimum wage.

ACCSES and other representatives of CRPs responded strongly to this report while acknowledging that there may be some weaknesses with the programs, the group argues that the elimination of the sub-minimum wage would relegate people with significant disabilities to day habilitation programs where they would earn no money at all. ACCSES, also emphasized that center-based employment (workshops) offer a stepping stone to competitive employment in the community.

As noted earlier in the chapter, this is not a new debate. Moreover, as is true with most debates, there is some validity to both points of view. Certainly, there are instances where CRPs have not been vigorous enough in their efforts to pursue competitive community employment opportunities for the people they serve. There are also instances where individuals have been underpaid for center-based employment. At the same time, rehabilitation facilities have also faced enormous challenges. While attempting to expand community integrated options and competitive employment opportunities, many of these organizations are simultaneously trying to provide program services to individuals with significant disability and significant behavioral issues. All of these challenges are occurring in an environment of almost record high unemployment rates and ever-shrinking state and federal resources.

The authors propose that the value of services offered in any program serving people with disabilities is dependent upon the mission of the provider and the vision, creativity, and resourcefulness of the leadership and all involved in supporting and achieving the desired goals. There is no inherent good or bad in rehabilitation facilities, community rehabilitation programs, and/or totally integrated community services. The true value of a program is in its ability to respond to and facilitate the hopes and dreams of each individual person through self-determination, family, staff, and community resources.

As students exploring careers in rehabilitation, there is no substitute for knowing the services that exist in one's community and discovering for one's self the complexities and values of the services available or needed.

REFERENCES

[1]ACCSES. (2011). ACCSES response to NDRN paper, Segregated and Exploited-The failure of the disability service system to provide quality work. Retrieved July 15,2011 from http://www.accses.org/vendorimages/accses/HarkinLetterandAnalysisofNDRNReport012511.pdf

[2]Campbell, J. F. (1984). *An industrially integrated model versus the sheltered workshop in the vocational rehabilitation of mentally disabled persons.* Ann Arbor: University Microfilms International.

[3]Campbell, J. F. (1991). The consumer movement and implications for vocational rehabilitation services. *Journal of Vocational Rehabilitation, 1,* 3, 67-75.

[4]CARF (2001). *About CARF.* Retrieved December 17, 2001, from http://www.carf.org.

[5]Daugherty, D. V. (1992). Excerpts of Reviews and Comments. In L. G. Perlman & C. E. Hansen (Eds.), *Rehabilitation Facilities: Preparing for the 21st Century: A Report on the 16th Mary E. Switzer Memorial Seminar,* (p. 20). National Rehabilitation Association.

[6]Harris, L. (1986). *The ICD Survey of Disabled Americans: Bringing Disabled Americans into the Mainstream.* New York: Lou Harris and Associates.

[7]Hershenson, D. B., & Szymanski, E. (1992). Career Development of People with Disabilities. In R. M. Parker & E. M. Szymanski (Eds.), *Rehabilitation Counseling and Beyond,* (pp. 273 - 304). Austin, Texas: PRO-ED, Inc.

[8]Jones, C. T., & Brabham, R. E. (1992). An overview of the rehabilitation facilities movement. In L. G. Perlman & C. E. Hansen (Eds.), *Rehabilitation Facilities: Preparing for the 21st Century: A Report on the 16th Mary E. Switzer Memorial Seminar.* (pp. 66-73). National Rehabilitation Association.

[9]Kiernan, W. E. (2001). Special issues and trends in integrated employment. In L. R. McConnell (Ed.), *Emerging Workforce Issues: W.I.A., Ticket to Work, Partnerships: A Report to the 22nd Mary E. Switzer Memorial Seminar.*

[10]Kiernan, W. E., & Stark, J. A. (1986). *Pathways to Employment for Adults with Developmental Disabilities.* Baltimore: Paul H. Brookes Publishing Co.

[11]McConnell, L. R. (2001). *Emerging Workforce Issues: W.I.A., Ticket to Work, and Partnerships: A Report to the 22nd Mary E. Switzer Memorial Seminar.* National Rehabilitation Association.

[12]Menz, F. (1992). Resource development and rehabilitation capabilities. In L. G. Perlman & C. E. Hansen (EDS.), *Rehabilitation Facilities: Preparing for the 21st Century: A Report on the 16th Mary E. Switzer Memorial Seminar, (pp. 45-65).* National Rehabilitation Association.

[13]Murphy, S. T., & Rogan, P. M. (1995). *Closing the Shop: Conversion from Sheltered to Integrated Work.* Baltimore: Paul H. Brookes Publishing Co.

[14]National Disability Rights Network. (2011). *A Call to Action: The failure of the disability service system to provide quality work.* Retrieved July 15, 2011 from http://www.ndrn.org/en/component/content/article/24-hompagestories/261-report-finds-exploitation-at-work.html

[15]Nelson, N. (1971). *Workshops for the Handicapped in the United States.* Springfield, Illinois: Charles C. Thomas Publisher.

[16]NISH. (2001). *About JWOD.* Retrieved December 20, 2001, from http://www.nish.org.

[17]NISH. (2011) About NISH. Retrieved July 15, 2011, from http://www.nish.org.

[18]Obermann, C. E. (1965). *A History of Vocational Rehabilitation in America.* Minneapolis, Minnesota: T. S. Denison & Company, Inc.

[19]Public Law 90-31, *Vocational Rehabilitation Amendments of 1968,* Section 10 [b].

[20]Risley, B., & Hoehne, C. (1970). The vocational rehabilitation act related to the blind. *Journal of Rehabilitation, 36,* 5, 26-31.

[21]Rubin, S. E., & Roessler, R. T. (1987). *Foundations of the Vocational Rehabilitation Process (3rd edition).* Austin, Texas: PRO-ED, Inc.

[22]Rusalem, H. (1976). A personalized social history of Vocational Rehabilitation in America. In H. Rusalem & D. Malikin (Eds.), *Contemporary Vocational Rehabilitation.* New York: New York University Press.

[23]Scheerenberger, R. C. (1983). *A History of Mental Retardation.* Baltimore, Maryland: Paul H. Brookes Publishing Co.

[24]Shaw, K. (1998). Community rehabilitation organizations: Transition to what? *American Rehabilitation, 24,* 1, 19-25.

[25]The ARC. (2001). *History of the ARC.* Retrieved December 20, 2001, from http://www.thearc.org.

[26]VanErden, J. D. (2001). One-Stops and Partnerships. In L. R. McConnell (2001). *Emerging Workforce Issues: W.I.A., Ticket to Work, and Partnerships: A Report to the 22nd Mary E. Switzer Memorial Seminar.* National Rehabilitation Association

[27]Walker, M. L., & Wiegmann, S. M. (1997). History and Systems: Mostly Mavericks. In D. Maki & T. Riggar (Eds.), *Rehabilitation Counseling: Profession and Practice,* (pp. 39-54). New York: Springer Publishing Company.

[28]Wehman, P., & Moon, M. S. (1988). *Vocational Rehabilitation and Supported Employment.* Baltimore: Paul H. Brookes Publishing Co.

INDEPENDENT LIVING: A PHILOSOPHY IN REHABILITATION

ALO DUTTA

MADAN M. KUNDU

SOUTHERN UNIVERSITY

CHAPTER TOPICS

- Overview
- History of the Independent Living Movement
- Legal Mandates Related to Independent Living
- Centers for Independent Living
- Evaluation of Independent Living
- National Council on Independent Living
- International Perspective

Jeff Gunderson's voice is choked with worry. He is about to reenter the place he called "A concentration camp." It is a nursing home, one of two where Gunderson, who has cerebral palsy, was sent from the time he was eighteen until he turned twenty-seven.

Shapiro, 1994, p. 237

OVERVIEW

Independent living can be defined as the ability of a person with a disability to perform self-care activities and participate in the process of self-determination in the least restrictive environment.[57] The term most commonly refers to living in the community and not in an institution. In addition, independent living is an attitude, an ideology, a way of life, and a socio-political movement of global dimensions. The philosophy of independent living is based on honoring the rights of people with disabilities to equal opportunities, self-determination, empowerment, and self-respect. This is in absolute congruence with the fact that people with disabilities are experts on their own lives and that they have the right to assume full control over their lives. The true motto is to ensure that people with disabilities have the same rights, choice, control, and freedom as their counterparts without disabilities.[34,40,52]

The Constitution of the United States established certain inalienable and self-evident rights such as the right to life, justice, liberty, and the pursuit of happiness. In spite of these guarantees, many Americans have historically had to prove their worth to attain these rights, particularly if they were disabled, women, poor, or members of a disempowered minority. People with disabilities are certainly no exception in the sense that they had to purchase social equity with the lives of many.[5,52]

Freedom is always an expensive commodity.[24] In economics, commodity is a term used to mean any marketable product created to satisfy needs. Necessity is an important reason for infringement of human liberty or freedom.[15] At the turn of the Twentieth century, sexual segregation of people with mental and physical disabilities was commonplace. Currently recognized as a crime against humanity, forced sterilization was conducted to prevent the reproduction of defective genetic traits.[25] Forced sterilization of those suffering from mental illness and epilepsy became popular in 1910. Forced sterilization was legalized in 1937 by 28 states. Later, legislation was passed in some states banning the public appearance of "defective" people. People with deafness were barred from becoming witnesses in a trial or serving on a jury. Effects of these practices were overly pronounced among persons of racial and ethnic minority backgrounds, women, and other marginalized groups.[9]

The cost of enabling persons with disabilities to live freely has traditionally been considered too high. By their very nature, institutions such as nursing homes are built on the medical model. Many are restrictive, paternalistic, and suppressive of the pursuit of happiness.[5,9] This underprivileged and "dependent caste" status has promoted low education, high unemployment, underemployment, dependence on social services, and challenging living conditions, which collectively result in a low quality of life among persons with disabilities.[47] However, the cost of exclusion and discrimination is prohibitive in terms of lost opportunities and reduced quality of life for individuals with disabilities and their families.[56]

At the beginning of the Twentieth century, this legalized dependency and ostracism had been challenged unsuccessfully by legislation and uncoordinated efforts of well meaning people. By the mid 1900s, people with disabilities felt a strong urgency to unify and organize a movement to dismantle institutionalization and promote integration in the mainstream of society.[9,40] Gradually, disability rights and advocacy efforts initiated the independent living movement that became a significant political force thriving on the notion that regardless of the type, people with disabilities share a common history of struggle and once united can make a difference in social structure. In this context, Ratzka[40] states that:

> *We are the last minority to fight for our rights and we will not go away. Even with the most sophisticated prevention, early detection, and rehabilitation services, there will always be people with disabilities and we have to build our societies in such a way that everybody can live in them with dignity and self-respect. And we have to start now.* [p. 1]

HISTORY OF THE INDEPENDENT LIVING MOVEMENT

Deinstitutionalization, the driving force behind the independent living movement, is an attitude that focuses on independence, citizenship, mobility, individuality, self-determination, empowerment, and integration into the mainstream of society.[42,49] The term denotes the process of keeping individuals with disabilities in the community and reducing dependence by creating programs to address their overall developmental needs. It strives to establish appropriate community-based living infrastructures so that consumers, especially those with significant disabilities, can receive services in the least restrictive environment.[58]

The seed for the independent living movement was sown in the early 1960s when a student with respiratory quadriplegia secondary to polio enrolled at the University of California, Berkeley. Ed Roberts, who used an iron lung, became the first student with a significant disability to be admitted to an American university. To publicize this important milestone, a local newspaper printed an article entitled *Helpless Cripple Goes to School.* By 1965-66, due in large part to the active involvement of Ed Roberts and a few service providers in the community, the enrollment of students with disabilities increased considerably. By 1969, the Cowell Residence Program, supported by the California Department of Rehabilitation, grew to 12 disabled students. This program, housed at the Student Health Center, provided sheltered living and resembled the supervised conditions of an institution. The students' movements were confined to a largely inaccessible campus. The total effect of the situation resulted in the students becoming increasingly aware of the lack of control that they had over their own lives. This increased their need for self-determination.[5,60]

In the fall of 1969, the students organized a "Strategies for Independent Living" class under the university's group study program. The primary aim was to develop a proposal for establishing a facility similar to the Cowell Resident Program but under the direct control of residents. The program was open to non-residents as well. Upon investigation, Ed Roberts learned that the U.S. Office of Education assisted disadvantaged students and was interested in allocating 10% of its funds to services for students with disabilities. The students wrote a proposal to secure funding for a Physically Disabled Students' Program (PDSP) that adopted a holistic and integrated approach to service provision. The three main philosophical traits of the program are listed bolow.

- People with disabilities are the experts in identifying their needs and the ways to address them.
- The needs of those with disabilities can be addressed via comprehensive programs providing a wide array of services.
- People with disabilities should be fully integrated into society.[47,60]

Due to the encouragement of PDSP, a group of disabled individuals met in 1971 to discuss the establishment of a community-based service program. They called it the Center for Independent Living (CIL). The CIL was designed as a coalition of people with all types of disabilities working toward a common goal. Once the conceptual framework for the center was in place, a source of funding became the main concern. Three months after its incorporation in 1972, the CIL was awarded a one-year $50,000 grant by the Rehabilitation Services Administration, U.S. Office of Education, to develop a comprehensive service program.[5,9,60] This center currently provides peer counseling, advocacy, independent living skills training, attendant referral, transportation, health maintenance counseling, housing referral, and wheelchair repair services.[34]

Concurrently with the University of California at Berkeley, students with disabilities at the University of Illinois at Urbana-Champaign started working toward the establishment of community living facilities. This resulted in the transfer of four students with disabilities from a nursing home to a modified house near campus. This student activitism helped the university to become one of the most accessible campuses in the country.[34]

LEGAL MANDATES RELATED TO INDEPENDENT LIVING

The concept of independence—the goal of the total rehabilitation process—is considered the key to growth and maturity, and a required stepping-stone to adult life. It focuses on the right to be an active part of the community, to have choice, to receive high-quality service, and to refuse service.[27] Vocational rehabilitation is designed to be a means of freeing oneself from both unwanted dependence and the restrictions imposed by social and environmental forces. As per Martinez,[28] independent living philosophy professes that each person has the right to independence through maximum control over his or her life by making choices in performing everyday activities. These activities may include managing one's personal life, participating in community life, fulfilling social roles, enhancing self-determination, and minimizing physical/psychological dependence. Despite the desirable qualities of self-determination, the positive aspects of dependency in the lives of humans as social beings cannot be completely overlooked. The proper balance of dependence, independence, and interdependence is required to satisfy our physical and psychosocial needs. However, excessive dependency, defiance, or over independence can result in under or non-achievement of one's rehabilitation goals.[58,57]

Since the early 1960s, it was believed that the independent living movement had the potential to emancipate not only persons with disabilities but also millions of other disadvantaged Americans. During the past few decades, the movement has become a powerful force devoted to promoting the philosophy of consumer control, equal access, and self-reliance as the building blocks of independent living for those with disabilities, thereby reducing oppressive marginalization of persons with disabilities.[24] The focus was bi-directional, i.e., to empower persons with disabilities to take control of their own lives; and to influence social policies and practices to promote community integration.[12] Since disability is a restriction of activity caused by contemporary social organization, a significant factor that contributed to the development of the independent living movement was the formation of social organizations. Social organization can be described as patterns of social interaction—a combination of the prevailing modes of doing things (how things ought to be done), the social structure (normative order), and the existing concepts of right, normal, or wrong behavior. Social organizations are reflections of both prevailing wisdom and prejudices.[16] Clubs and sports groups, as parts of social organizations, provide excellent networking opportunities and tend to increase the sense of unity and commonality for people with disabilities. The current cross-disability social change groups and independent living centers grew out of associations for athletes with disabilities.[17]

The independent living movement gained strength with the passage of the Rehabilitation Act of 1973. The major thrust of this Act was integration, mainstreaming, and holistic participation of persons with disabilities at all levels in society. The legislation mandated services to persons with severe disabilities, post-employment services, protection of client rights, promotion of consumer involvement, protection of the civil rights of persons with disabilities, and support for research. The word "vocational" was deleted from the Act in order to meet the needs of those individuals with significant disabilities.[48] Section 130 of the Act mandated a Comprehensive Needs Study to assist individuals with significant disabilities who "cannot reasonably be expected to be rehabilitated for employment but for whom a program of rehabilitation could improve their ability to live independently or function normally within their family and community."[38, p. 374] The Nixon administration authorized the implementation of a comprehensive needs study to determine the rehabilitation needs of those with significant disabilities.

Five independent living rehabilitation projects were established (Seattle, New York, Salt Lake City, San Antonio, and Berkley) that adequately demonstrated the need for such programs.[43] Research conducted under the 1973 Act suggested that independent living does not have to be a separate system. Independent living programs can function as a complementary component of the vocational rehabilitation service delivery system.

The Rehabilitation Comprehensive Services and Developmental Disabilities Amendments of 1978[39] amended the 1973 Act. The amendments further strengthened the independent living movement. Title VII, Part A of the Act mandated that State Rehabilitation Agencies administer the federal rehabilitation program and authorized them to contract with other agencies to provide comprehensive services. Independent living services were defined to include any of the following:

- counseling services including psychological, psychotherapeutic and related services,
- accessible and modified housing,
- appropriate job placement services,
- transportation,
- attendant care,
- physical rehabilitation,
- therapeutic treatment,
- needed prosthesis and other appliances and devices,
- health maintenance,
- recreational activities,
- services for children of preschool age; including physical therapy, development of language and communication skills, and child development services.

Title VII, Part B authorized the Commissioner of the Rehabilitation Services Administration to make grants to state agencies having approved independent living plans and to establish and operate independent living centers offering services such as:

- intake counseling and peer counseling,
- referral, attendant care, programs for the blind and deaf,
- advocacy regarding legal and economic rights and benefits,
- housing and transportation referral and assistance,
- community group living arrangements,
- independent living skills, training on maintenance of equipment,
- individual/group social and recreational activities,
- job seeking skills and placement counseling, and
- assistance of substantial benefit in promoting independence, productivity, and equality of life of persons with disabilities.

Title VII, Part B also states that persons with disabilities have significant involvement in policy, direction, and management of such centers. In order to be eligible to receive financial assistance, a state must submit a state plan to the Commissioner of the Rehabilitation Services and establish a Statewide Independent Living Council (SILC). The plan must be modified every three years and has to be jointly designed by the designated state unit (or state vocational rehabilitation agency—general and/or blind) and the chairperson of SILC. The Council members, who are appointed by the governor for a maximum of three years, represent the special interests of state agencies, local agencies, and persons with disabilities, parents, and guardians of individuals with disabilities, directors of CILs, private businesses, and other appropriate individuals or organizations. The majority of the Council membership, i.e., at least 51%, must be individuals with disabilities, or their parents or guardians.[23]

Title VII, Part C authorized state agencies to provide independent living services to older blind individuals (55 years and older) whose visual impairment is so severe as to make gainful employment extremely difficult, but for whom independent living goals are feasible. Services include:

- outreach,
- visual screening,
- surgical and therapeutic treatment to prevent, correct, or modify disabling eye condition,
- eye glasses and visual aids,
- braille instruction and reader services, and
- mobility training, guide services, and transportation.

Independent living provisions realistically addressed the long ignored needs of individuals with significant disabilities. The movement legitimized "non-vocational" objectives and became a viable alternative to "employability" for those with significant disabilities in the rehabilitative process.[23]

The Rehabilitation Act was further amended in 1984. These amendments mandated that SILCs provide guidance for the development and expansion of independent living programs. The act emphasized a comprehensive evaluation of CILs to identify areas of improvement and recommend continuation of the federal grant supporting the center.[21] These newly incorporated policies of inclusion acted as a catalyst to the formulation of federal and state laws impacting access to voting and air travel, independence in education and housing, and culminating with passage of the Americans with Disabilities Act (ADA) in 1990.[44]

The Rehabilitation Act Amendments of 1992 expanded the CILs' role and responsibilities. The CIL became an equal partner with each state's vocational rehabilitation agency in the independent living process. The SILCs were given added responsibility to assist in the development of the state independent living plan for the state vocational rehabilitation agencies and to oversee its implementation.[41]

The effectiveness of the legislation discussed above was later strengthened by the passage of the Americans with Disabilities Act (ADA) of 1990. This civil rights act rekindled the hope of people with disabilities to have the opportunity to participate in their communities and become fully functioning members of society. Advocates of independent living used the ADA as a platform to translate the act's empowering mandates into integration, independence, and productivity for those with disabilities.[22,23]

The concept of independence and self-advocacy were reinforced by the Workforce Investment Act of 1998. Title I, Vocational Rehabilitation Program, of the act included the following descriptors of independent living, e.g., consumer control, peer support, self-help, self-determination, equal access, and individual and system advocacy. The importance of the philosophy of independent living was re-emphasized for the purpose of maximizing leadership potential, empowerment, independence, and productivity of those with disabilities.[54]

CENTERS FOR INDEPENDENT LIVING

The independent living movement, which grew out of the recognized needs of persons with disabilities to rise above the boundaries of the traditional professional dominated model of service delivery, rallied around the slogan "nothing about us without us." The prevailing medical model of disability-related service delivery, that reduces a person with a disability to a descriptor of impairment level and assumes a bio-medical state of normalcy as an appropriate outcome of services, gradually gave way to a social-contextual model. Under the new model, disability is accepted as a part of human diversity and/or the result of discrimination in policies, practices, research, training, and education. Individuals with disabilities, as authority figures, are able to discharge a wide array of responsibilities in pursuance of full expression, independence, and community integration.[1,2] This transition enables disability rights advocates and consumers to demand respect from well qualified service providers who often make decisions without client involvement.[3,50] By the mid-1990s, the consumer driven approaches permeated all strata of the traditional rehabilitation service delivery system. The CILs are another direct outcome of the disability rights activism. The CILs release the full potential of those with disabilities by promoting greater choice and autonomy.[36] The consensus was on the involvement of persons with disabilities in decision-making related to all aspects of life because disability was not the concern of a special group but an experience of day-to-day living.[28]

Two of the driving forces of the CILs are the concepts of independence and dependence. Dependence is not always degrading and undesirable. Some dependency needs, whether one has a disability or not, apply through the life span. However, it is important to learn how and when to ask for help or exhibit dependence. Similarly, people with disabilities need to know when independence is appropriate. Since human beings do not function in a vacuum, learning to value dependency that serves important social and economic purposes promotes healthy social interaction. For example, a person should be able to rely on others, to ask for and accept assistance, and to delegate responsibility. "Dependence as a value ought to be held in the same high regard as independence."[57,p. 409] Yet, the role of over-accommodation, in the name of addressing dependency needs, must always be controlled as it can downplay formidable thoughts, feelings, beliefs, and ideas expressed by persons with disabilities and result in promoting learned helplessness.[33]

A Center for Independent Living is neither a residential nor a transitional facility. These CILs are consumer-controlled, community-based, cross-disability, nonresidential, private, nonprofit agencies designed and operated within a local community by individuals with disabilities and provide an array of independent living services. A CIL is usually a facility that coordinates the efforts of professionals, persons with disabilities, families, volunteers, and interested entities to enable those with significant disabilities to achieve independent living and maximum potential within their own families and communities. The initial cornerstone of a CIL was service and advocacy.[20,58] Because the initial focus of the CIL was on people with blindness or orthopedic impairment, the constituents were relatively young and resided in university settings. Gradually, the efficacy of the independent living philosophy spread among people with other disabilities and the heterogeneity of the clientele increased tremendously.[34] Additionally, CILs became a strong advocacy voice on diverse national, state, and local issues. Services provided by these centers are often devoted to ensuring physical and programmatic access to housing, education, employment, transportation, communities, recreational facilities, and health care and services. Over the past three decades, 336 consumer-controlled CILs were established nationwide with approximately 253 satellite locations.[45] Currently, there are about 779 CILs in the country providing services to a diverse array of individuals with disabilities.[20]

The CILs offer a comfortable atmosphere for people with disabilities to determine their goals, to choose the types of services and the provider of needed services. The representatives on CILs governing boards are primarily people with disabilities in an attempt to turn the managerial power over to the consumers. The independent living concept is accomplished utilizing three factors:

- community option development,
- consumer services, and
- management.

First, *community option development* can be promoted via public awareness, technical assistance, and advocacy. It can assist the consumer in becoming more self-sufficient and less dependent on the CIL.[6] These CILs have been successful in replacing expensive medical and vocational services with low cost consumer services.

Second, *consumer services* include peer counseling, independent living skills training, attendant care, advocacy, and information and referral.[6,20] Counseling services provided by a nonprofessional, or peer counselor, especially one who is facing the same challenges as the consumer, increases understanding and provides a wellness model.[7] Attendant care or Personal Assistance Services (PAS) provide the support and assistance a person may need to attain the optimal level of independence at home, school, work, and in society. Such services may include sign language interpretation, housing assistance, transportation, personal care management, employment assistance, help with activities of daily living, and non-medical assistance such as changing a urinary catheter. The key concept behind PAS is consumer control and prevention. It is strongly believed that persons with disabilities can safely deliver attendant care with some training from the consumer requiring those services.[20,50] As per ILRU,[19] since PAS facilitates independent living for society (e.g., elderly, children, those with chronic conditions), it should be considered a right rather than a special privilege granted for the benefit of persons with disabilities.

Advocacy is a necessary skill to help oneself achieve independence. It includes the actions taken by individuals on behalf of one or more persons to ensure their rights and interests. Advocacy can be provided in the areas of employment, transportation, disability policy, housing, public access, health care, education, insurance issues, telecommunication, and vocational rehabilitation.[55,58] Information and referral services are geared toward educating individuals on all aspects of a disability, their civil rights, and available community resources. Systems advocacy focuses on protecting civil rights, supporting positive change in disability related legislation, and empowering Consumers to become self-advocates. Certain advocacy tools and techniques used by CILs are listed below:

- Use of a phone tree (2-3 people calling a few others and continue the process) to share important and time-barred information.
- Phone campaign (selected people from all over the state call lawmakers on a single issue) is an effective mode of attracting attention for lawmakers and state/federal officials.
- Letters to legislators is an excellent way to voice concerns about policy issues.[19]

The third component behind the success of a CIL is sound *management* with substantial consumer control and direction in the planning, implementation, and evaluation stages. The centers typically hire administrators and staff with disabilities. The consumer driven approach acts as a catalyst in promoting a community environment that provides support and encouragement for those with disabilities.[6]

Proponents of independent living trusted the idea that differences in disability outcomes can be largely attributed to environmental factors. They used this idea as a determinant in providing reasonable accommodations to people with diverse functional abilities. This gradual shift in support for the ecological perspective of disability siphoned a part of the available resources and services into addressing community living needs of persons with disabilities and their families.[46]

In spite of obvious differences between CILs and state-federal vocational rehabilitation programs, the partnership of these two complementary faces of Rehabilitation Services Administration funded activities, have proven to be extremely beneficial to both clients and service providers. Formal agreements have usually acted as the basis for these collaborations but informal working agreements between local CILs and vocational rehabilitation agencies have existed as well. This team effort continues to provide a plethora of independent living and employment-related services to clients training in basic skills, literacy, and language skills; job referral and information, work motivation and self-esteem building, clerical/computer/ other specific skills training, transportation services, job coaching, etc.[13]

Though the numbers of CILs have increased substantially, rural residents in 40% of the nation's counties do not have access to independent living resources and services, including transportation, accessible and affordable housing, PAS, appropriate nursing home and medical care facilities, telecommunication links, opportunities for economic participation, etc.[46] Annually, the existing CILs provide direct services to 212,000 individuals living in 1,896 (60%) of American counties. The median budget of a CIL is $328,000 and the average is $530,000, with a lower limit of $55,000. Typically, $200,000 is required to operate an entire CIL. It has been determined that an additional $71.5 million is required to establish 218 more CILs to address the independent living services needed by Americans with disabilities.[51] The ecological model of disability adds to the justification for infrastructure redevelopment in rural locations with emphasis on enhanced participation and decision making authority of persons with disabilities.[46]

In spite of having a higher prevalence of disability than the general US population, minority communities have been sporadically outreached by the existing disability and health-related service delivery systems. The needs of people from diverse cultural backgrounds continue to remain largely unmet. The challenges facing Independent Living Centers in meeting these needs are as follows: language barriers, lack of cultural competency among service providers, under representation of ethnic minorities on CIL staff, inadequate outreach efforts directed at potential consumers, housing instability of clients generating geographic mobility, prevailing belief that families should take care of persons with disabilities, family conflict resulting from inadequate adjustment to disability, and regrets or fears originating from lessons learned by the consumer in negotiating the social support system. Additionally, the fact that about 14% of the US population is foreign born may require CIL staff to have knowledge of disability status, individualized needs, sources of natural support, employment status, and Citizenship and Immigration Service rules and regulations. Even though proportionately more foreign-born persons with disabilities (40%) are employed compared to those born in the US (35%), effects of various disability-related, contextual, linguistic, and cultural factors are more pronounced in this population.[59] Hiring of staff with diverse ethnic and linguistic backgrounds will facilitate modification of the independent living philosophy to make it more inclusive and universal.[4,11]

EVALUATION OF INDEPENDENT LIVING

Individuals with disabilities, like everyone in society, desire life satisfaction and opportunities to participate in their respective communities. In spite of society's desire to mainstream them as active, independent, and contributing members, people with disabilities continue to be marginalized and in certain instances are not even considered good candidates for community integration.[14] The moral responsibility of society is to provide individuals with disabilities the support needed to access housing, transportation, health care, educational systems, and the opportunity to participate in the labor force. The implementation of independence requires considerable effort and finances, and the financial return may not be encouraging for those who measure improvement in terms of dollars. Nevertheless, when does the value of equity and justice outweigh efficiency and utilitarianism? The success of the movement will largely depend on the extent to which society is willing to sacrifice overall efficiency and assist those with disabilities to work and live an autonomous life.[36]

Radical individualism, the cornerstone of a modern market economy, thrives on the assumption that a person maximizes his/her ability by choosing the best available alternatives and by operating as an autonomous unit. The concept works best when an individual does not encounter any hindrance in the decision making process. In the context of the prevailing socio-political climate, disability and its effects cannot be considered solely as individual issues,[2] rather they are functions of body structure and functions, activity, and participation. The *International Classification of Functioning, Disability and Health* (ICF) states that changes in body function and structure impact a person's capacity to engage in activities as a function of environment as well as one's actual level of performance in his/her usual environment.[56]

Consumer sovereignty is often assumed in interpreting rational economic behavior i.e., it is the power of consumers to determine the types of goods and services that must be produced. Theoretically, consumers, not producers, are the best judge of the products that benefit them the most. Since economic choice has always been limited for those with disabilities, equalization of resources, access, and opportunities may not be the appropriate solution to the question of modes in providing adequate financial support for this population. Likewise, equalization of choices will necessitate prudent allocation of resources to alleviate the effects of the prior disadvantaged status. The efficacy of CILs should be judged on their ability to respond to the diverse capabilities of people with disabilities requiring accommodations to reach their full potential.[36]

Increased government spending on independent living programs over the past several years has resulted in the necessity to evaluate their efficacy on a continuous basis. The need to formulate and revise appropriate independent living goals and ascertain effective ways of determining their progress in meeting these goals demands increased accountability.[18,34] Progress was measured initially in terms of client-specific gains as a function of services delivered. Later, the concept of more comprehensive consumer gain regardless of services received was incorporated into the accountability process.[8,31] According to ILRU,[18] outcomes measurement should include:

- developing a logic model of an ILC consisting of input, output (e.g., activities and participation), and outcomes or impacts (short-, medium-, and long-term),
- identifying the outcomes measurement goals and linking them to the data collection process, and
- creating measurable indicators of each outcome.

In congruence with the above framework, ILRU[18] designed a list of desired outcomes divided into three broad categories and a set of 12 measurable outcome indicators.

Desired Outcomes	Measurable Outcome Indicators
IL services:	
1. Clients will have the skills, knowledge, and resources to support their choices.	1. Number and percentage of consumers served by the center within the first nine months of the past federal fiscal year who can list at least two skills, types of knowledge, and/or resources they have now that they did not have before receiving service from CIL.
2. Clients become more independent.	2. Number and percentage of consumers served by the center within the same time frame as #1 who can list at least one specific way in which he/she is more independent now than before receiving IL services. 3. Number and percentage of open IL program goals achieved within the past federal fiscal year by consumers served by the center CIL within the first nine months of the past federal fiscal year.
Information and Referral:	
1. Clients get the required information.	1. Number and percentage of clients contacting the center during the past federal fiscal year who report that they received the requested from the CIL. 2. Number and percentage of clients contacting the program during the first nine months of the past federal fiscal year who can name at least one resource he/she used as a referral from the IL program.
2. Clients advocate for increased community support.	3. Number and percentage of clients served by the program within the first nine months of the past federal fiscal year who can list at least one specific personal advocacy activity he/she has performed. 4. Number and percentage of clients served by the program within the same time frame as #3 above who can list at least one systems advocacy activity he/she has performed.
Systems Advocacy:	
1. Identification of barriers and problems.	1. Number of activities conducted during the past federal fiscal year to identify or confirm the primary barriers/problems in the community that prevent clients from leading more independent lives.
2. Formulation of a consumer agenda for change.	2. Presence within the center's annual plan of a section containing an explicit systems advocacy work plan.
3. Decision makers respect and abide by the consumer agenda.	3. Number of positive changes achieved or negative changes prevented during the past federal fiscal year in legislation, policies, practices, or services at the local, state, or federal level that address the barriers/problems identified by consumers of the center.
4. Methods and practices promote independence.	4. Number and percentage of consumers served by

the center within the past federal fiscal year who moved out of an institution and are living in a self-directed community-based setting.

5. Number and percentage of consumers served by the center within the past federal fiscal year who continue to reside in a self-directed community-based setting despite having the risk of moving into an institution

Environmental and life status indicators play an important role in independent living. In a study of 111 adults with spinal cord injury, marital status, transportation barriers, and the degree of medical supervision required proved to be significant predictors of attainment of independence. The last two factors negatively impacted independent living.[10]

McAweeney, Forchhmeimer, and Tate[29] reported that consumers with unmet needs were either those with the least or the most functional limitations. Peer recreation and peer support groups were the two most needed services. This finding was contrary to the opinion that CIL services such as transportation, personal assistance, housing, and advocacy need to be improved. Nosek[35] studied 67 persons with orthopedic impairment to assess the effects of personality factors and functional abilities on the achievement of independent living goals. It was concluded that participants with more psychological independence had less restrictive living arrangements, spent less time in rehabilitation facilities, and encountered fewer communication problems. A high level of social independence was directly proportional to self-sufficiency, assertiveness, education, earning power, and marital status. Functional abilities did not seem to have any effect on the level of independence.

According to Gooden-Ledbetter et al[14] possession of skills required to promote interdependence and enhance level of self-efficacy are predictors of life satisfaction and independent living for persons with disabilities. This interdependence approach enables clients to demonstrate that they are able to accomplish tasks either by themselves or by instructing another individual how to complete the task to the client's satisfaction. Interdependence emphasizes the idea that people need people and difficult activities can be performed well by teaming up with others (resulting in increased self-efficacy belief). Therefore, CILs need to ramp up self-efficacy and interdependence training of clients with disabilities.

A society that offers fewer choices fosters greater inequity. Economists may argue that an equitable distribution of resources to informed individuals making selections from an equal number of choices is too expensive. Society has a responsibility to persons with disabilities to prevent relegating them to second-class citizen status. As optimal independence cannot be accomplished without non-discriminative practices; comprehensiveness, appropriateness, and efficiency of services; and equity in participation, it is important that independent living programs be established, operated, and evaluated in a sensitive manner.[13,26]

NATIONAL COUNCIL ON INDEPENDENT LIVING

This national membership organization was established in 1982 to represent CILs and individuals with disabilities. The founders were a small group of renowned disability rights activists, e.g., Mr. Max Starkloff, Ms. Marca Bristo, Mr. Charlie Carr, and Dr. Judy Heumann. The efforts of NCIL, a non-profit entity, have been commendable in standardizing requirements for consumer control in management and delivery of services provided CILs. Largely supported by an extensive network of committed and dedicated volunteers from CILs and related organizations, in 1992 NCIL opened its national office in Arlington, VA. Later the office moved to 1710 Rhode Island Ave, NW, Fifth Floor, Washington D.C. 22036. The establishment of an official domicile facilitated its efforts to eliminate disability-related discrimination and unequal treatment. The organization is run by a disability majority governing board comprised of 22 members that meets four times a year. A seven member executive committee is entrusted with making policy-related decisions. Ten regional representatives to the governing board act as liaisons between NCIL board, staff, committees, and stakeholders in their respective regions. Member supports and services include information and referral, training on disability-related issues, and assistance geared to help accomplish systems change within local communities. The organization is considered a strong voice for independent living and consumer-driven advocacy for people with disabilities around the country. NCIL offers internships to policy-oriented individuals to assist the Director of Advocacy and Public Policy in monitoring laws, policies, and regulations related to the organization's priorities. This unpaid internship also offers opportunities such as legislative relations with Capitol Hill, writing action alerts and parts of advocacy newsletters, and regularly tracking key issues.[32]

INTERNATIONAL PERSPECTIVE

On a global scale, independent living is a social movement geared to promoting self-organization, civil rights, self-help, and the enhancement of quality of life for millions of people with disabilities. It continues to be one of the central themes in the development of self-organization and self-determination of persons with disabilities throughout the world. A primary ingredient of the movement is the sense of commonality among its constituents. Providing benefits and services is considered a prelude to the establishment of independent living in the industrialized world. Services can be categorized as economic support, vocational rehabilitation, education, and formulation of government organizations to address disability related issues.[37] The importance of providing these basic services was first recognized in the 1960s in Latin American, Spanish, and Portuguese speaking Europe, Africa, and Asia. Due to financial and infrastructural constraints, the benefits of disability awareness and rehabilitation services could reach only a very small number of people in these countries.[17]

In 1962, French students, who wanted more control in obtaining the services they needed to become self-sufficient, formed the Group for Integration of Physically Disabled Persons (GIHP). France ultimately became the leader in providing peer support, one of the core concepts of independent living services. Between 1970 and 1980, self-help organizations were established in South Africa and Latin America. In the following decade, the United Kingdom, Canada, Germany, Ireland, Austria, The Netherlands, and Uganda followed suit.[17]

A study conducted to evaluate the INCARE personal assistance program in Ireland found that Irish people with disabilities have little input in setting the public policy that impacts their lives. It was found that the primary reason was that they have little or no representation in the decision making process. Services are planned, delivered, and evaluated without any consumer involvement. To achieve self-direction and obtain adequate services to meet their needs, individuals with disabilities are forced to employ a personal assistant.[30]

The civil rights movement among African Americans led world leaders to recognize the importance of legislative action to promote equal opportunities for those with disabilities. In 1969, Rehabilitation International created the universal symbol of accessibility. The principal purpose in creating the symbol was to emphasize the need for promoting architectural accessibility in all facets of society. In 1981, the International Year for Disabled Persons provided an impetus to the disability rights and independent living movements and emphasized the need for self-determination among those with disabilities. National organizations were established in Sri Lanka, Uganda, Jamaica, China, the United Kingdom, South Africa, Brazil, Fiji, Thailand, and the Philippines.[17]

In 1980, white South Africans participated in the Rehabilitation International Congress. Upon their return home as newly indoctrinated members of the independent living community, they found that their black counterparts had been practicing the philosophy for years as part of the anti-apartheid campaign. The European Network on Independent Living (ENIL) was established in 1990 to lobby for personal assistance services and to educate politicians about the independent living philosophy.

In 1992, the first CIL was founded in Ireland to implement the INCARE program for developing a consumer controlled personal assistance service.[36] Gradually, the movement gained support in Asia, especially in Japan, with the active support of European and US disability rights leaders.

The scope and breadth of the concept of independent living and related services vary widely in different parts of the world. Persons with disabilities in the developed world define independence as a reflection of maximization of choice and minimization of segregation. Independence in the developing world means survival more than equity. For example, independent living services in Brazil, unlike those in North American and Europe, includes employment support more often than systems advocacy.[37]

Additionally, the United Nations Convention on the Rights of Persons with Disabilities (UNCRPD) and its Optional Protocol were adopted on December 13, 2006 during the sixty-first session of the General Assembly. It was opened for signature on March 30, 2007. There were 82 signatories to the Convention, 44 signatories to the Optional Protocol, and one ratification of the Convention (as of March 2012, UNCRPD has 153 signatories and 111 parties). This continues to be the highest number of signatories in history to a UN Convention on its opening day. The UNCRPD, the first comprehensive human rights treaty of this century, was implemented starting May 3, 2008. The Convention was meant to be a human rights instrument with a focus on social development. It was designed to spell out in detail the rights and fundamental freedoms of persons with disabilities and establish a code of implementation. This was the result of the realization that a change of perception was necessary to improve integration and the advancement of persons with disabilities in their communities by combating stereotypes/prejudices and promoting public awareness of the capabilities of the target population. The importance of freedom of choice and right to independent decision making was also emphasized. The general principles of UNCRPD are as follows:

- importance of inherent human dignity, autonomy, freedom of choice, and right to life,
- non-discrimination,
- full integration and community participation,
- respect for human differences as natural part of diversity,
- equality and equity,
- accessibility,
- equality of gender, and
- rights and evolving capabilities of children with disabilities.[53]

The international movement has had many positive outcomes. It has increased the incomes of people with disabilities, facilitated the use of assistive devices and personal care assistance, promoted the accountability of the funds allocated for services, and integrated people with disabilities into their communities. This success has not been without its detractors. The concept of independence has been widely criticized by several developing countries as a culturally loaded term. A direct result of this criticism brought about the coining of a new term "inter-dependence" to express the meaning of independent living more comprehensively. This new term cannot dislodge the deep-rooted belief in the doctrine of independent living that has kept the dream of self-organization, self-determination, empowerment, and self-direction alive for many with disabilities around the world.[17]

REFERENCES

[1]Albrecht, G. L., Seelman, K. D., & Bury, M. (Eds.). (2001). *Handbook of Disability Studies.* Thousand Oaks, California: SAGE Publications.

[2]Barnes, C., & Mercer, G. (2003). *Disability.* Cambridge, UK: Polity Press.

[3]Basnett, I. (2001). Health Care Professionals and Their Attitudes toward Decisions Affecting Disabled People. In G. L. Albrecht, K. D. Seelman & M. Bury (Eds.), *Handbook of disability studies* (pp. 450-467). Thousand Oaks, CA: Sage Publications.

[4]Bradley, C. (2000). *A commitment to inclusion: Outreach to unserved/underserved populations.* Houston, TX: Independent Living Research Utilization.

[5]Brown, S. (2001). *Freedom of movement: IL history and philosophy.* Retrieved October 14, 2001, from http://www.ilru.org/ilnet/files/ bookshelf/ freedom/freedom14.html

[6]Budde, J., & Bachelder, J. (1986). Independent living: The concept, model, and methodology. *The Journal of the Association for Persons with Severe Handicaps, 11*(4), 240-245.

[7]Carter, T. D. (2000). *Peer counseling: Roles, functions, boundaries.* Houston, TX: Independent Living Research Utilization.

[8]Clowers, M., Haley, D., Unti, W., & Feiss, C. (1979). *Independent living project: Final report.* Seattle, WA: division of Vocational Rehabilitation and University of Washington.

[9]Curtis, B. (2001). *The need for independent living programs: An historical context and summary of progressive independent living services.* Unpublished manuscript, Technical Assistance Project, Center for Independent Living, Berkeley, CA.

[10]DeJong, G., Branch, L. G., & Corcoran, P. J. (1984). Independent living outcomes in spinal cord injury: Multi-variate analyses. *Archives of Physical Medicine and Rehabilitation, 65*, 66-73.

[11]Eglehart, A. P., & Becerra, R. M. (2002). Hispanic and African American youth: Life after foster care emancipation. *Journal of Ethnic and Cultural Diversity in Social Work, 11*(1-2), 79.107.

[12]Ells, C. (2001). Lessons about autonomy from the experience of disability. *Social Theory and Practice, 27*(4), 599-615.

[13]Gooden-Ledbetter, M. J., Cole, M.T., Maher, J. K., & Condeluci, A. (2007) Self-efficacy and interdependence as predictors of life satisfaction for people with disabilities: Implications for independent living programs. *Journal of Vocational Rehabilitation, 27*(3), 153-161.

[14]Gorton, G., Hayashi, F., & Rouwenhorst, G. (2008). *The Fundamentals of Commodity Futures Returns, Working Paper*. Philadelphia: Wharton School.

[15]Hanson, S., & Temkin, T., (1999). *Collaboration between publicly-funded rehabilitation programs and community-based Independent Living Centers*. Retrieved March 29, 2012 from http://www.wid.org/publications/rrtc-ildp-issue-brief-collaboration-between-publicly-funded-rehabilitation-programs-and-community-based-independent-living-centers/

[16]Henslin, J. M. (2008). *Essentials of Sociology: A Down-To-Earth Approach*, (7th Ed) Boston: Allyn and Bacon.

[17]Independent Living Research Utilization (ILRU). (2009). *Performance measurement plan for 12 outcome indicators for the CIL Program*. Houston, TX: Author.

[18]Independent Living Research Utilization (ILRU). (1999). Global perspective on independent living for the next millennium. *Symposium on An International Summit conference on Independent Living*. Houston, TX: Author.

[19]Independent Living Research Utilization (ILRU). (2001). *System advocacy: Using your power to effect change*. Houston, TX: Author.

[20]Independent Living Research Utilization. (2011). *Directory of independent living centers and SILCs*. Houston, TX: Author.

[21]Jones, A. (1986). *Detailed Survey of the Rehabilitation Amendments of 1986, Public Law 97-506*. Dunbar, WV: West Virginia Research and Training Center.

[22]Kennedy, D. M. (1992). Symposium: Compliance and quality in residential life. Foreword. *Mental Retardation, 30*(3), V-VI.

[23]Kundu, M., & Schiro-Geist, C. (2006). Legislative aspects of rehabilitation. In P. Leung, C. Flowers, W. Talley, & P. Sanderson, (Eds.), *Multicultural issues in rehabilitation and allied health* (pp.17-43). Osage Beach, MO: Aspen Professional Services.

[24]Lachat, M. A. (1988). *The independent living service model: Historical roots, core elements, and current practice*. Hampton, NH: The Center for Resource Management, Inc.

[25]Largent, M. A. (2008). *Breeding contempt: The history of coerced sterilization in the United States*. New Brunswick, NJ: Rutgers University Press.

[26]Le Grand, J. (1991). *Equity and choice*. London, UK: Harper Collins Academic.

[27]Longmore, P. K. (2003). *Why I burned my book and other essays on disability*. Philadelphia: Temple University Press.

[28]Martinez, K. (2003). The road to independent living in the USA: An historical perspective and contemporary challenges. *Disability World, 20*, Retrieved April 8, 2007, from http://www.disabilityworld.org/09-10_03/il/ilhistory.shtml

[29]McAweeney, M. J., Forchheimer, M., & Tate, D. G. (1996). Identifying the unmet independent living needs of persons with spinal cord injury. *Journal of Rehabilitation, 61*(3), 29-34.

[30]McGettrick, G. (1994). *Nothing about us without us. Evaluation at the INCARE Personal Assistance Programme*. Dublin, Ireland: Center for Independent Living.

[31]Muzzio, T. (1980). *Independent living programs and evaluation, basic principles for developing a useful system: Issues in independent living.* Houston, TX: Independent Living research Utilization.

[32]National Council on Independent Living. (2012). *History*. Retrieved March 28, 2012 from http://www.ncil.org/about.html

[33]Nelson, T. D. (2005). Ageism: Prejudice against our feared future self. *Journal of Social Issues, 61*(2), 207-221.

[34]Nosek, M. A. (1997). Independent living. In E. M. Szymanski & R. M. Parker (Eds.), *Rehabilitation counseling: Basics and beyond* (pp. 191-223). Austin, TX: Pro-ed.

[35]Nosek, M. A. (1984). *Relationship among measures of social independence, psychological independence, and functional abilities in adults with severe orthopedic impairments*. Unpublished doctoral dissertation. University of Texas at Austin.

[36]O'Shea, E., & Kennelly, B. (1996). The economics of independent living: Efficiency, equity and ethics. *International Journal of Rehabilitation Research, 19*(1), 13-26.

[37]Priestley, M. (Ed.) (2001) *Disability and the Life Course: global perspectives.* Cambridge, U.K.: Cambridge University Press.

[38]Public Law 93-112 (1973). *Rehabilitation Act of 1973*. Washington, D.C.: Government Printing Office.

[39]Public Law 95-602 (1978). *Rehabilitation Comprehensive Services and Developmental Disabilities Act Amendments of 1978*. Washington, D.C.: Government Printing Office.

[40]Ratzka, A. D. (1997, September). *Independent living and our organizations.* Paper presented at the meeting of the conference of the Disability Rights Advocates Hungary, Siofok, Hungary.

[41]Richard, L. (2000). *Composition of Statewide Independent Living Councils.* Houston, TX: Independent Living Research Utilization.

[42]Rioux, M. H. (2002). Disability, citizenship and rights in a changing world. In C. Barnes, M. Oliver & L. Barton (Eds.), *Disability studies today* (pp. 210). Cambridge, UK: Polity Press in association with Blackwell Publishers.

[43]Rubin, S. E., & Roessler, R. T. (1995). *Foundations of the vocational rehabilitation process* (pp. 333-347). Austin, TX: Pro-ed.

[44]Schmeling, J., Schartz, H. A., & Blanck, P. (2004). The new disability law and policy framework: Implications for case managers. In F. Chan., M. Leahy & J. Saunders (Eds.), *Case management for rehabilitation health professionals* (pp. 88-121). Osage Beach, MO: Aspen Professional Services.

[45]Seekins, T., Enders, A., & Innes, B. (1999). *Centers for independent living, rural, and urban distribution.* Missoula, MT: The University of Montana, The Rehabilitation Research and Training Center on Rural Rehabilitation Services.

[46]Seekins, T., Ravesloot, C., Rigles, B., Enders, A., Arnold, N., Ipsen, C., Boehm, T., & Asp, C. (2011). *The future of disability and rehabilitation in rural communities*. Missoula, MT: The University of Montana, The Rehabilitation Research and Training Center on Rural Rehabilitation Services.

[47]Shapiro, J. (1994). *No pity: People with disabilities forging a new civil rights movement*: New York, NY: Times Books.

[48]Schiro-Geist, C., & Kundu, M. M. (2001). *Placement Handbook for Counseling Persons with Disabilities*. Unpublished manuscript.

[49]Shoenfeld, E. (1975). Deinstitutionalization/community alternatives. In K. Mallick, S. Yuspeh, & J. Mueller (Eds.), *Comprehensive vocational rehabilitation for severely disabled persons*. Washington, D.C.: George Washington University Medical Center, Job Development Laboratory.

[50]Smith, Q., Smith, L. W., King, K., Frieden, L., & Richards, L. (1993). *Health Care Reform, Independent Living, and People With Disabilities. Issues in Independent Living No. 11*. Houston, TX: Independent Living research Utilization.

[51]The Rehabilitation Research and Training Center on Rural Rehabilitation Services. (1999). *Estimating the cost for achieving universal access to Centers for Independent Living*. Missoula, MT: The University of Montana.

[52]United Nations. (2010). *Monitoring the convention of rights of persons with disabilities*. Retrieved March 15, 2012 from http://www.ohchr.org/Documents/Publications/Disabilities_training_17EN.pdf

[53]United Nations. (2012). *The convention on the rights of persons with disabilities*. Retrieved March 29, 2012 from http://www.un.org/disabilities/default.asp? navid=14&pid=150

[54]West, L. L., Corby, S., Boyer-Stephens, A., Jones, B., Miller, R., Sarkees-Wircenski, M. (1999). (2nd Ed.). Integration transition planning into the IEP process. Arlington, VA: Council for Exceptional Children.

[55]White, G. W., Nary, D. E., & Froelich, A. K. (2001). Consumers as collaborators in research and action. *Journal of Prevention and Intervention in the Community, 21*, 15-34.

[56]World Health Organization. (2001). *International classification of functioning, disability and health.* Geneva: Author.

[57]Wright, B. A. (1983). (2nd Ed.). *Physical disability - A psychosocial approach.* New York, NY: Harper & Row.

[58]Wright, G. N. (1980). *Total Rehabilitation* (pp. 733-789). Boston, MA: Little Brown and Company.

[59]Xiang, H., Shi, J., Wheeler, K., & Wilkins, J. R., (2010). Disability and employment among U.S. working-age immigrants. *American Journal of Industrial Medicine, 53*(4), 425-434.

[60]Zukas, H. (1975). *CIL history: Report of the state of the at conference, Center for Independent Living.* [RSA Grant 45-p-45484/9-01.] Berkeley, CA: Center for independent Living.

19

EMBRACING CULTURAL SENSITIVITY FROM A SOCIAL JUSTICE PERSPECTIVE

VIVIAN M. LARKIN
MORGAN STATE UNIVERSITY
DOTHEL W. EDWARDS JR.
ALABAMA STATE UNIVERSITY
KEITH B. WILSON
SOUTHERN ILLINOIS UNIVERSITY
YOLANDA V. EDWARDS
WINSTON SALEM STATE UNIVERSITY

Chapter Topics

- Overview
- Objective
- Introduction
- Key Concepts and Definitions
- Working With Diverse Groups and Disabilities
- Legislation, Professional and cultural Issues Impacting Services
- Multicultural Competencies and Possible Barriers
- Summary
- Case Studies
- Discussion Questions

OVERVIEW

The foundation guiding modern-day provisions of rehabilitation services is embedded in the Rehabilitation Philosophy offered by Dowd and Emener.[12] This philosophy, referred to simply as the "Rehabilitation Philosophy," holds that all people should be treated without prejudice. Although theoretical in nature, the social justice perspective is premised on a belief that all people, with or without disabilities, should be treated with dignity, valued as worthy citizens, and free to make their own choices. While it is not clear if the framers of the Rehabilitation Philosophy intended to include factors such as race, ethnicity, religion, sexual orientation, et cetera, over time, many professionals in the field have encouraged movement toward embracing a more culturally competent approach to service delivery. In this new era, where developing a culturally competent rehabilitation professional is the expectation, it is paramount that an expanded and more inclusive philosophy be adopted. We offer the following *New Era Rehabilitation Philosophy*:

> *All people, irrespective of physical ability, race, ethnicity, place of origin, gender, religion, sexual orientation, age, or migration status, will be treated with "unconditional positive regard." In the delivery of rehabilitation services, professionals must deliver fair and equitable culturally appropriate services, while maintaining client dignity and valuing clients as worthy citizens. These services must emphasize self-determination, social responsibility, and interdependence.*

This philosophy is a concept whose time has come. It gives rise to a renaissance for the delivery of services to clients from diverse backgrounds. The New Era Rehabilitation Philosophy also lays the foundation for this chapter and provides a blueprint for rehabilitation professionals, systems, and advocates.

Social Justice Work can be conceptualized as scholarship and professional action designed to change societal values, structures, policies, and practices, so that underserved/disadvantaged groups gain increased access to these tools of self-determination.[18] Over the last 20 years, rapidly changing demographics of individuals seeking services through vocational rehabilitation programs across the country have drawn considerable attention to the need to address cultural competence in professional service delivery. Many differences separate clients with diverse backgrounds from European Americans. These differences include privilege, access, communications and style, body language, beliefs, and expectations. For many individuals with disabilities in underserved/under-represented populations, cultural differences are experienced as a fundamental component of everyday life.

More recently, rehabilitation professionals have begun to question the appropriateness of using a single standard of service delivery to meet the needs of diverse groups of people who have many different world views and life experiences.[8] It is thus imperative for service providers to not only have awareness of and sensitivity to the impact of the disability, but also to the many diverse backgrounds of consumers (e.g. race, gender, religion, sexual orientation, age, immigration status, ethnicity). This chapter will focus on the following four topics/issues relevant to cultural sensitivity, professional competencies, and standards for rehabilitation practices:

- The significance of valuing and respecting differences/diversity.
- Acknowledging one's own biases/stereotypes.
- Recognizing the socio-political influences of poverty, racism, ageism, sexism, immigrate status.
- Managing the dynamics of differences/diversity.

OBJECTIVE

Readers will:

- develop an awareness of and sensitivity to one's own cultural heritage,
- demonstrate an understanding of how one's own biases, attitudes, and belief systems influence the provision of rehabilitation services,
- demonstrate a working knowledge of various cultures and the ability to gather facts/information about these diverse groups,
- learn to value and respect cultural differences,
- demonstrate an awareness of sociopolitical influences such as racism and discrimination,
- begin to develop a philosophy and method for providing culturally competent services, and
- demonstrate an understanding that the development of cultural competences is an ongoing process.

INTRODUCTION

> *In rehabilitation... judgments or estimates regarding client potential may determine the educational and career opportunities that are made available to clients, dramatically affecting future direction and quality of life.*[6]

The most recent Commission on Rehabilitation Counselor Certification's *Code of Professional Ethics for Rehabilitation Counselors*[11] provides guidance for the practice of professional conduct and in ethical decision-making when working with individuals from culturally diverse groups and backgrounds. The updated code advances the notion that all rehabilitation counselors will develop cultural competencies leading to appropriate interventions and services that are in harmony with the client's values and cultural perspective. The focus on curriculum development in preparing rehabilitation counselors continues to receive considerable attention.

The discussion related to culturally relevant competencies for vocational rehabilitation professionals is a comparatively new arena for the field. These conversations were driven by recent legislation, resulting from the overwhelming outcries by advocates, people with disabilities, and clients from diverse backgrounds demanding equal access, opportunity, and inclusion, and removal of individual and systemic barriers to appropriate services. Throughout the history of vocational rehabilitation, social justice has been a key underlying concern of the vocational rehabilitation movement; everyone deserves equal access to appropriate services, health care, and other economic and political opportunities. The shift in the demographics of the United States and the populations served by social service organizations beginning in the late 1970s and early 1980s dictated the need to incorporate a more relevant educational curriculum—one that embodied a social justice orientation.

The 1980s ushered in an era of professionals who resurrected the concept of social justice and introduced it as a key component of the counseling educational curriculum. Sue and others[37] were among the first to introduce and incorporate multicultural counseling competencies in the educational curriculum for counselors. Their model is widely endorsed by experts in the field of cross-cultural counseling. The following three domains identify the characteristics of a culturally competent counselor:

- counselor awareness of their own cultural values and biases,
- counselor awareness of client's worldviews, and
- culturally appropriate intervention strategies.

Three competency areas characterize each domain:

- the counselor's beliefs and attitudes about their own cultural and racial heritage, and the counselor's beliefs about other people's cultural and racial backgrounds,
- the counselor's understanding of cultural diversity, and
- skills gained from experience working with diverse populations and cultural sensitivity trainings.

Ponterotto[27] offers the "stage model" which is used to describe the "racial identify" and consciousness development process of white counselor trainees involved in a multicultural learning environment. He theorized that white counselor trainees/students follow a similar pattern of progression on their journey to valuing and accepting differences. Based on his classroom experiences, he observed trainees passing through four stages of development.

In the early stages of training, white counselors were often in denial or totally unaware that cultural differences exist. Most had not considered the impact of projecting one's own cultural values onto clients that held different worldviews; and they, more often than not, consider their values superior to those of the client. Ponterotto[27] noted that by the end of the course he could observe a notable shift in perspective in his students. His model advances the idea that racial consciousness development among white counselor trainees is not only valuable but also paramount to any discussion in developing culturally competent counselors. Ponterotto's[27] model consists of four stages:

- The pre-exposure stage is that stage in which the student has given little thought to multicultural issues or their role in a society where racism and oppression remain a dominant factor.
- The exposure stage is where students are led to examine their own cultural values and to see how their values have become "encapsulated" and taken for granted—in this stage, many students begin to feel both angry and guilty.
- In the Zealot-Defensiveness stage, students respond to their newfound feelings in one of two ways, either by taking on the "minority plight" or by retreating from multicultural issues.
- In the final stages, Integration, the strong dichotomous feelings emergent in the Zealot-Defensive stage subsides. The zealousness exhibited by some students' decreases and these students become more balanced. Those students who had withdrawn from active class participation have been led to process their feelings and now are more open, acquiring a new interest, respect, and appreciation for cultural differences.[p.151]

Ponterotto[27] notes that not all students reach the integrated stage and those who do reach it do so at varying times during the training.

Influenced by the work of Sue and others,[37] Middleton et al,[24] in "A call to Action" paper proposed specific multicultural rehabilitation competencies and standards that characterized a professional culturally competent rehabilitation counselor. Like Sue et al,[37,35] Middleton[24] organized each of the cultural competencies based on three characteristics:

- rehabilitation counselors' awareness of their own assumptions, values, and biases;
- understanding the worldview of the culturally different client; and
- developing appropriate rehabilitation intervention strategies.

Consistent with the framers of this cultural competencies model each characteristic has three dimensions:

- beliefs and attitudes,
- knowledge, and
- skills.

The model consists of nine competency areas that rehabilitation counselors should develop and 35 specific competencies. To assist new learners and professionals in developing these skills, explanatory statements based on the work of Arredondo et al.[2] are offered. A more detailed dialogue on how to acquire cultural competencies for working with individuals with disabilities from diverse backgrounds will be discussed later in the chapter.

KEY CONCEPTS AND DEFINITIONS

The following concepts and definitions are offered to help the reader move through the chapter with an enlightened understanding of terminology. A number of different definitions can be found throughout written literature for the term diversity. For the purpose of this chapter, the authors define diversity in the following manner:

Diversity represents a community of individuals bringing together a wide-range of demographic, cultural, ethnic, physical abilities, and many other differences to help create a climate that values and respects differences in a safe and supportive environment.

The U.S. Administration on Aging[40] developed the following toolkit of definitions for professionals seeking to enhance their skills when serving diverse communities:

Acculturation
The degree to which an individual adjusts, fits into, or adopts another culture as his/her own.

Assimilation
Adopting another cultural group's values, beliefs, behaviors, and attitudes.

Cross-Cultural Communication
Interaction between diverse individuals or groups.

Culture
A group with shared values, religion, language, and/or heritage. (Culture refers to more than just race and ethnicity; it also applies to groups, their members, and affiliations.)

Cultural Awareness
Being mindful, attentive, and conscious of similarities and differences between cultural groups.

Cultural Barrier
A difference in cultural values and perceptions about treatment, care, and services that limit a person's ability to access services.

Cultural Brokering

Bridging, linking, or mediating between groups or persons from different cultures to reduce conflict and/or produce change.

Cultural Competency

The capacity to function effectively as an individual or organization within the context of the cultural beliefs, behaviors, and needs of consumers and their communities.

Cultural Misalignment of Services

When services do not fit or are not valued in a community.

Cultural Proficiency

Policies and practices of an organization, or values and behaviors of an individual, that enables the agency or person to interact effectively in a culturally diverse environment. Cultural proficiency is reflected in the way an organization treats its employees, clients, and community.

Cultural Sensitivity

Understanding the needs and emotions of one's own culture and the culture of others, and understanding how the two may differ.

Diversity

Ethnic, socioeconomic, religious, and gender variety in a group, society, or institution.

Ethnic Group

Individuals who share values, traditions, and social norms.

Intercultural Differences

Differences within cultures; for example, differences between Vietnamese, Chinese, Korean, Japanese, or Filipino populations within the Asian culture.

Linguistic Competency

The ability of an organization to communicate effectively and convey information in a manner that is easily understood by diverse audiences.

Operational Knowledge of Serving Diverse Populations

A demonstration of how to serve diverse populations.

Race
A division of humankind possessing traits that are transmissible by descent and sufficient to characterize it as a distinctive human type.

Structural Barrier
Technical or logistical factors that limit a person's ability to access services.

Technical Knowledge of Serving Diverse Populations
Knowledge of how to serve diverse populations.

Worldview
The sum of a person or group's perspectives including opinions, judgments, and beliefs based on culture, values, and life experiences.

WORKING WITH DIVERSE GROUPS AND DISABILITIES

As the ethnic and racial diversity of populations in the United States increases, so have the number of individuals with disabilities from diverse backgrounds.[17] The increase in diversity has produced disparities and inequities, leaving poor and underserved communities with limited access to quality employment. This section will address major racial and ethnic groups as well as special populations dealing with disabilities.

AMERICAN NATIVES AND ALASKAN NATIVES

Among racial and ethnic groups, American Natives have the highest rate of disability (21.9%) when compared to other groups (African Americans 20 %, Caucasians 19.7%, Hispanic origin 15.3 % and Asian/Pacific Islanders 9.9 %).[23,41]

American Natives and Alaskan Natives are highly heterogeneous groups composed of over 450 distinct tribes (technically, Alaskan Natives belong to corporations, not tribes). There are large within-group and between-group differences among the different tribes in family structure, customs, and language. According to Sue & Sue,[38] over 60 percent of American Natives are of mixed heritage, having black, white, and Hispanic backgrounds. American Natives also differ in their degree of acculturation. History has revealed discrimination toward various ethnic and racial minorities, but the experience of American Indians has been a unique one. American Native populations have decreased to 10 percent of their original size. Their dialects are disappearing due to outsiders' attempts to "civilize" them. As a result, families and culture have been dismantled. Many of their children were separated from their tribes during their childhood and placed in schools intended to reshape their ideals and they were forced to adopt the western culture, customs, practices, and beliefs of the European people. The result created a population of American Natives who are very suspicious of the motives of White Americans, and most American Natives do not expect to be treated fairly by non-Indian agencies.

American natives and Alaska natives represent the highest rate of disability of any ethnic groups within the U.S. at approximately 22%.[26, p.5] Added to the disability rate is a high rate of unemployment. According to the 2000 United States Census,[41] American Natives and Alaska Natives had the highest rate of unemployment at 7.6% compared to 3.7% overall. The percentages increase based on tribe. Balcazar, et al,[4] indicated five factors that contribute to unemployment:

- location of tribal lands,
- inability to use land as an economic resource,
- lack of educational opportunities on tribal lands,
- tribal mistrust of government programs, and
- the struggle to maintain tribal sovereignty.

Although there have been several laws and programs put in place to focus on removing environmental barriers, limiting discrimination, and addressing unemployment, American natives and Alaska natives are still underserved by human service programs.

ASIAN AMERICANS

The Asian American population is growing rapidly and is currently over 11 million. The increase is due to changes in the immigration laws. With the exception of Japanese Americans, the majority of Asian Americans are foreign born. There are at least 40 distinct groups of Asian Americans that differ in language, religion, and values.[33] Individuals of Chinese decent represent the largest group of Asian Americans. Of the 11.9 million Asians in the United States, Chinese Asians comprise approximately 20% of the Asian American Population. Chinese in the United States are a heterogeneous group including people from mainland China, Taiwan, Hong Kong, and other Southeastern Asian countries.

There is a belief that Asian Americans represent a "model" minority. This term "model" minority associated primarily with Asian Americans (e.g. Chinese, Japanese, Indian, Filipino, and Korean) refers to their status as high achievers in education, and jobs. They are often found working in "white collar" professions such as investment banking, medicine, and engineering.

The 1997 Census figures support this notion, documenting as many as 42 percent of Asians/Pacific Islanders over the age of 25 possess at least a bachelor's degree versus 26 percent of their white counterparts. Asian Americans are adequately represented at Ivy League schools such as Harvard, MIT, and UC-Berkeley. Despite having high levels of academic achievement, Asian Americans fear academic failure compared to their Caucasian peers. Rates of intermarriage are high. However, a bimodal distribution exists, with some groups of Asian Americans having a higher rate of poverty and lower educational levels than are found in the general population.

The Chinese term for disability is *canfei*, meaning "handicap" and "useless" and *canjii* meaning "handicap" and "illness." Disability is associated with imperfection of the self. The concept of disability is viewed as punishment for a dead relative with a disability or sins of the person's parents. Korean culture believes that supernatural agents can cause disability. An example of this could be punishment from God or a curse of the devil for their sins or those of their parents or ancestors. The Vietnamese concept of disability is a belief in reincarnation that holds that from birth to death to after-life a person assumes the same identity in physical or spiritual form. Therefore, persons who committed evil deeds will not only be punished by being reincarnated as a less significant life form, but their descendants will suffer the same consequences. Many individuals from religious backgrounds and rural areas with limited medical resources will visit temples to pray, worship, or perform rituals in order to identify the cause of their health problems and seek a solution.

Mental health is believed to be achieved through self-discipline, exercise of willpower, and the avoidance of morbid thoughts. Underutilization of mental health services may be due to cultural factors such as shame and the practice of handling of problems within the family. The misunderstanding or lack of knowledge about a disability can cause a tremendous amount of fear, hostility, alienation, and blame. For example, the findings of Wang, et al,[43] showed Chinese students were more positive toward people with physical disabilities than toward developmental disabilities and mental disorders. They are also more accepting and sympathetic toward an acquired injury that causes physical limitations than toward congenital, physical, or mental disorders.

AFRICAN AMERICAN

The African American population accounts for approximately 12.3 percent of the U.S. population.[41] The poverty rate for African Americans remains nearly 3 times as high as that of white Americans (33.1% versus 12.2%) and the unemployment rate is twice as high (11% versus 5%).[41] African Americans' disadvantaged status, coupled with racism and poverty, contributes to such statistics. When a disability is added, the statistics show that African Americans are the most marginalized group in the United States. According to the U.S. Census Bureau,[42] individuals with disabilities, especially those with significant disabilities, remain the most marginalized in terms of employment and economic opportunities, with employment rates of only 26% and earnings less than 50% of their nondisabled counterparts. Couple minority status with disability and the employment picture is even worse.

Bellini[5] contended that African American persons have both higher rates of work disability and higher rates of severe disabilities. Wilson, et al.[47] confirm that the increase of minorities and women in the workplace will result in a more diverse approach to work readiness. Therefore, more African American consumers are likely to seek vocational rehabilitation services. Recent statistics indicate that race appears to be a major factor in the incidence of disability. African-Americans, among other underserved groups, appear to have disproportionately higher rates of disability.[29, Section 21] The rate of severe disability within the 55-64 year old age group was 20% for whites, 28% for Hispanics and 35% for African Americans.[10] Within the working population (age 16-64), African Americans had the highest rate of disability, 12.75% compared to 11.7% for Native Americans, 9.1% for Hispanics and 7.4% for white Americans.

For many African American adolescents, life is complicated by problems of poverty, illiteracy, and racism. Even with transitional vocational services, African American youth with disabilities, demonstrated significant differences in types of services.[14] The results indicated that Caucasian transition clients were more likely to receive vocational services, especially diagnostics and treatment, job search assistance, and job placement services. African American clients were more likely to receive job readiness training than were Caucasian and Native American clients.

*Research has suggested that **commonly held stereotypes** regarding some people of color can influence clinical perception and judgment.*[32]

LATINO AMERICANS

There is a wide variation of physical characteristics within the Hispanic population. Many have some resemblance to North American Indians, blacks, Asians, and Europeans, depending on their country of origin. While Mexicans are of mostly Mestizo ancestry, Cuban Americans and Puerto Ricans are mostly of Spanish descent, and Latin America contains a mixture of African and Asian influences. According to the U.S. Census,[42] Latino Americans constitute a population of over 35 million and are currently the largest minority group in the United States. Latino Americans are a highly heterogeneous population representing individuals from more than 26 countries, with large between-group and within-group differences. Some individuals are oriented toward their ethnic group; others are quite acculturated to mainstream values/white America. Some have lived for generations within the United States, while a large proportion are recent immigrants.[25] As a group, the average age of Latino Americans is almost 9 years younger than that of white Americans. The majority of Latino Americans are situated in metropolitan areas of the United

States. Latinos are overrepresented among the poor, high-unemployment groups, and those who live in substandard housing.

According to Wilson, Senices and others [49,30] the words "race" and "ethnicity" are defined in two separate ways. Race is defined as one's outward physical appearance while ethnicity deals with shared culture, values, beliefs, language, and spirituality. Carter,[9] and Wilson and Senices[49] stated that one's phenotype (i.e. skin color) is the principal characteristic in determining the intensity of discrimination in the United States. Researchers have shown that it is more difficult for Blacks and Black Latinos than for White Americans and White Latinos to access vocational rehabilitation services.[47,49,19] This body of research suggests that there is preferential treatment for European Americans or people with white skin color. Dziekan and Okocha[13] found that Latinos with disabilities are less likely to be accepted for services while whites were accepted for services more than any other racial or ethnic group. While skin color may be a factor in accessing services, several variables such as education, socioeconomic status, and English proficiency can also contribute to accessing services.[50]

LEGISLATION, PROFESSIONAL, & CULTURAL ISSUES IMPACTING SERVICES

LEGISLATION

The foundational principles—Life, Liberty, and the Pursuit of Happiness are constitutional rights that United States citizens embrace. In theory, these rights exemplify what individuals strive for and expect. Invariably, achievement of these rights requires the use of resources that are often limited. As a result, segments of the population such as individuals with disabilities, particularly individuals with severe disabilities, require disability policy to aid in the achievement of these fundamental human rights. According to Sales,[32] these rights mandate the U.S. government to impart adequate services to ensure equal access to all citizens.

Much can be said about the origin of the disability rights movement. Like other civil rights movements of the 1960s and 1970s, the disability rights movement effectively implemented nonviolent strategies to move disability policy to the national and international arena. Although there are several federal/state disability policies, the passage of Section 21 of the 1992 Rehabilitation Act[29] directly addresses the need for providing "culturally competent" vocational rehabilitation services to an increasingly diverse population of individuals with disabilities. Section 21 of the act was established based on three factors:

- higher rates of disability among culturally diverse populations,
- under-representation in the public vocational rehabilitation system, and

- limited vocational rehabilitation outcomes among culturally diverse populations as compared to the mainstream cultural group.[21]

Since the 1980s, others have documented that consumers who are a part of traditionally underserved groups tend to experience poor vocational rehabilitation outcomes compared to their white/European American peers.[3,19,16,48,49,1] Despite the implementation of Section 21, there still exists an ethnic and racial disparity within the vocational rehabilitation process. Research suggests that the cause of poor vocational rehabilitation outcomes among these groups consist of:

- stereotyping,
- high rates of poverty among underserved racial and cultural groups,
- lower educational attainment,
- lack of knowledge of vocational rehabilitation services, and
- low expectation of racially/culturally diverse clients among vocational rehabilitation counselors.[3,16,39,30,45]

Although rehabilitation counselors are well trained to assist individuals with disabilities, factors such as personal barriers, if not realized, can negatively impact consumers in receiving appropriate and meaningful vocational rehabilitation services. Social science literature, specifically the rehabilitation counseling literature, suggests that the theoretical underpinnings of the Social Ecological Model (SEM) provide effective strategies and interventions to address disparities among individuals with disabilities. This is particularly true among individuals with disabilities from minority or underserved groups and assists in improving cultural competency among rehabilitation counselors.

SOCIAL ECOLOGICAL MODEL (SEM)

Established by Bronfrenbrenner,[7] the SEM is a construct that explores the interconnectedness of social elements in an environment. Since Bronfrebrenner's introduction of this social construct, several interpretations of the model have been reported in the literature. Figure 1, developed by McLeroy et al.[22] defined the model based on five distinct interconnected domains:

- individual,
- interpersonal,
- organizational/institutional,
- community, and
- public policy.

Noted researchers in the vocational rehabilitation (VR) field utilized this model to discuss disability disparities among individuals with disabilities who are from underserved groups, in relation to access and outcomes within the state VR program.[20] For the purposes of this chapter, domains 3, 4, & 5 provide strategies and interventions that promote increased cultural competency among rehabilitation counselors. Table 1 provides strategies to promote successful vocational rehabilitation outcomes among underserved groups.

TABLE 1

STRATEGIES/INTERVENTIONS FOR REDUCING DISABILITY DISPARITIES AND INCREASING CULTURAL COMPETENCY

Domain 1 (Individual)	• Self advocacy • Peer Support • Leadership development • Micro aggression	• Directive counseling, role plays • Observations • Peer counseling • Higher commitment to self advocacy/partnering with provider
Domain 2 (Interpersonal)	• Respect cultural differences • Understand communication differences • Peer Support • Leadership development • Micro aggressions	• Peer networks & support groups • Increase self-awareness of biases & evaluation readiness • Establish a systematic tool to evaluate three factors (e.g. cultural identity & adj. to disability)
Domain 3 (Organizational/ Institutional)	• Respect cultural differences • Understand communication differences • Peer support • Leadership development • Integrate cultural compentency into organization using 4 steps.	• Agency personnel diversity • Evidence based cultural competency practices • Debiasing techniques • Cultural competency asset assessment • Evaluation organizational readiness
Domain 4 (Community)	• Respect cultural differences • Understand communication differences • Leadership development • Partnerships with community organizations	• Micro aggression • religious Involve organizations • Cultural brokering

Domain 5 (Public Policy)	• Diverse pre-service training for Rehabilitation Counselors • Leadership development • Partnerships with community organizations	• Micro aggressions • More cultural competent language in legislation • Educates policy makers/hold accountability

McLeroy K.R., Bibeau D., Steckler A., Glanz K. *"An ecological perspective on health promotion programs"* Health Education Quarterly 15:351-377, 1988.

FIGURE 1

SOCIAL – ECOLOGICAL MODEL

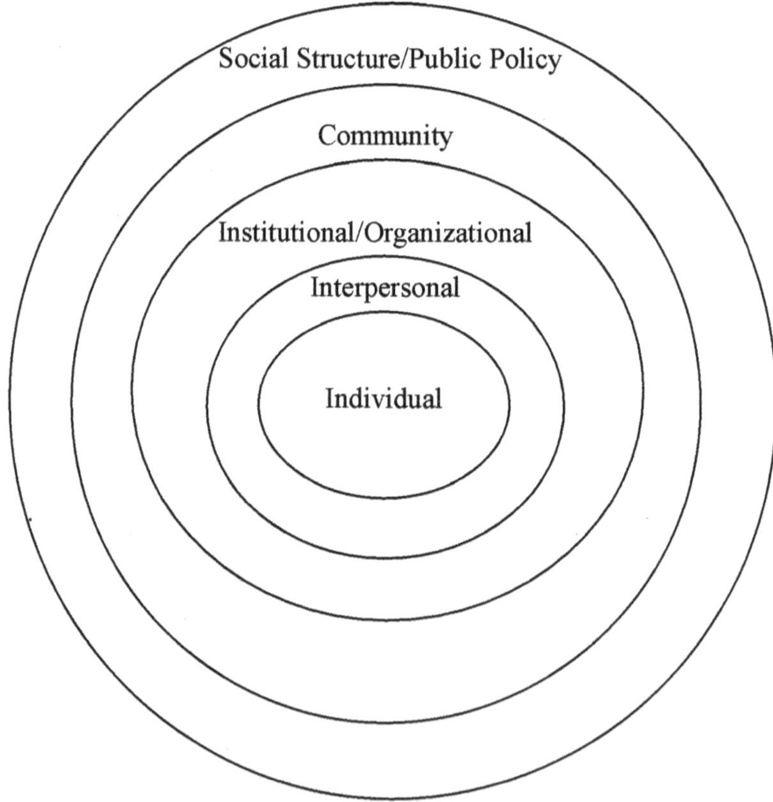

McLeroy K.R., Bibeau D., Steckler A., Glanz K. *"An ecological perspective on health promotion programs"* Health Education Quarterly 15:351-377, 1988.

Pluralism** is the cultural, social, and structural ways in which ethnic groups are maintained as distinct groups within a single political state—**Peaceful Coexistence.

MULTICULTURAL COMPETENCIES AND POSSIBLE BARRIERS

There is a common belief that we are all considered multicultural individuals and we are multicultural beings.[2] As mentioned previously in the chapter, the increased numbers of diverse populations in the United States will necessitate a change in the way human service personnel conduct business. While there undoubtedly are several models to address cultural competencies, the framework proposed in 1992 by Sue, et al,[35] is most relevant to our discussion on cultural sensitivity and competencies in human service fields. We assert that the multicultural competency (MC) model proposed by Sue, et al,[35] was one of the first of its kind in human service fields to acknowledge the connection between how one is perceived and treated, the outcomes related to the counseling process, and how the counseling process may be perceived by clients from diverse backgrounds. Although implementing training surrounding cultural sensitivity is viewed as a value added activity in many organizations, there are still barriers that must be overcome when looking to transport such training to many organizations in human service fields. Three general levels of Multicultural Competencies have been discussed in the literature:

- awareness,
- knowledge, and
- skills.

AWARENESS

The first level of MC is that of being aware. Awareness, or being cognizant, can take many forms and may be behaviorally manifested several ways. Simply put, the awareness of an individual can be, for the first time, understanding that men and women have different contextual experiences.[35] For example, it has been reported for some time that men are paid significant more money for the same job than women who have the same educational level and experience. Being aware of such a fact can come from several sources such as watching television, attending a workshop, or reading a newspaper. Because of this lack of awareness and not understanding that women and men have different contextual experiences, men may be lead to invalidate women. By extension, in the context of human services, many women may feel isolated, frustrated, and not appreciated by some men. They cannot communicate the realities of sexism in the United States. Awareness is a critical level of MC because it may place issues and concerns of groups who may be under represented on the cognitive radar of the person who is in the dominate group (e.g., European American).

KNOWLEDGE

The second level of MC is that of acquiring knowledge. Of course, knowledge acquisition can take many forms.[35] Once a male discovers that women and men have different contextual experiences in the workplace, a male may seek more information about fields where women are paid less than men. The male's pursuit of this kind of knowledge may lead him to prescribe to certain newsletters about women's issues. He may also use some of his time to research salary inequities in the workplace by attending seminars and going to the library and reading more about wage inequities and women who are African American.

Another part of knowledge acquisition could also be the male being retrospective about how he might have contributed to wage discrimination when he was in a supervisory position during his lifetime. As pointed out in the aforementioned example, gaining knowledge can be about "others" and the "self." Being aware that sexism exists, and then gaining information about why and in what context, are the first two levels of MC.

We cannot emphasize enough the vital role of self-understanding before seeking understanding about other groups. If you have ever flown in a commercial airline, you may recall the flight attendant mentioning what passengers should do in the event of an emergency. The message might sound something like this:

> *In the event of an emergency and the cabin looses pressure; put the mask over your face before attempting to place the mask over the face of your infant.*

The simple take-away message—you first have to help yourself before attempting to help others. In the context of underrepresented populations, you first have to understand yourself (e.g., understanding what it means to be a white male in the United Sates), before you can accurately have empathy to validate others who may not look or have similar values as yourself. Self-knowledge and knowledge of other peoples' perceptions of you and your group are a necessary cognitive advancement that is critical before connecting to people who are different! Knowledge alone will not lead to appropriate services and advocacy for underrepresented groups. In fact, Wilson[49] believes that outcomes in vocational rehabilitation service and other human service programs for underrepresented populations are not much different now from when the proliferation of multicultural and cross-cultural curriculum was added, over 20 years ago.

SKILLS

The third level of MC is that of acquiring specific skills to assist individuals you are serving. More specifically, skills may involve applying the awareness (e.g. being cognizant that certain groups may have different experiences in the

United State when compared to European Americans), knowledge, (e.g. information that might be collected through various resources about other groups or one's self), and skills (e.g. the specific application of knowledge to a certain population) to facilitate rapport, understanding, and validation.[35] There are times when we have both the awareness and knowledge of certain cultural groups but fail to implement these skills to increase rapport and to validate underrepresented populations. It cannot be assumed that human service providers implement actions and behavior in a contextual fashion to validate the client. This is simply not the case in most situations. It is clear that many rehabilitation counselors may possess the awareness and knowledge to facilitate and validate the experiences of groups that are different than they are, but it is unrealistic and not the status quo to expect validation and implementation of affective skills to groups that may be different.

TRUST: A BARRIER TO CULTURAL COMMUNICATION

There are several possible variables (e.g., trust, worldview, sociopolitical realities) to intercultural communication between those who may be in the majority group and those in the minority group. We think the link between many of the possible barriers to intercultural communication is trust. Trust is the thread that might run through many of these barriers. Trust will be succinctly highlighted as that essential fiber needed for positive outcomes of underrepresented groups in the U.S. who may seek services from the human service systems.

Trust. While there has been a lot written about trust and the reason why people and groups distrust one another, it is undeniable that trust is considered the bedrock of any relationship. Although trust is usually viewed on an individual level, groups can be suspicious of other groups. This can present problems with intercultural communication and relationships on both the micro (individual level) and macro (group level). In the interpersonal relationships literature, Smith,[34] in a national sample, reported that African Americans and European Americans tend to have the largest gap in their perceptions of race relations and tend to distrust one another more than other racial/ethnic groups in the United States.

Mistrust is both historical and contextual in nature. This may be because of stereotypes and biases put forth by the media and other institutions. It is common for European Americans who may be open to interacting with and developing a more than superficial relationship with groups who are underrepresented, to maintain rigid perceptions of these groups. The resulting manifestation—distrust—will yield stressful and isolated feelings for groups who may not be part of the European American group. Though it is beyond this chapter to delineate all of the attributes of trust, we believe trust is the substance that will enable both human service professionals and the clients they serve to produce outcomes that are more positive for clients who are underrepresented within the various U.S. vocational systems.

In the medical research literature, Rajakumar, et al,[28] investigated racial differences in parents' distrust of medicine and research and found some alarming results. In the study, African American parents were significantly more distrustful toward medical research than European Americans. Rajakumar, et al,[28] reported that the less education and the more children in the household were greater predictors of distrust among many African American parents compared to European American parents.

The Tuskegee Syphilis Experiment was conducted from 1932 to 1972 on African American men in the late stages of syphilis. Physicians informed African American men that they were being treated for "bad blood." The physicians did not intend to treat the men for syphilis. By the end of the experiment, many of the men died because they did not receive treatment for the disease. Many may argue that African Americans have a right to distrust not only the medical establishment, but also many of the Caucasians who carried out and benefited from the study in the name of science. While the results of the Rajakumar, et al,[28] study were not drawn from a national sample, it suggests that African Americans tend to be distrustful of European Americans because of past historical incidents. For more on past and contemporary injustices committed on African Americans, please see *Medical Apartheid* by Harriet A. Washington.[47] Distrust is a major variable in intercultural communication and relationship between European Americans and people who are underrepresented in the United States.

SUMMARY

As the ethnic diversity of populations in the United States increase, so have the number of individuals from diverse backgrounds with disabilities.[17] This increase has produced disparities and inequities among the nation's poorest and underserved communities, creating limited access to quality health care, employment, and other services important to their well-being. In an effort to improve rehabilitation outcomes for clients from diverse backgrounds, counselor trainees and professionals are seeking to enhance their cultural competencies, skills, and knowledge. The Multicultural Competency (MC) Model proposed by Sue, et al,[35] was one of the first in the human services arena to acknowledge the connection between how one is perceived and treated, the outcomes related to the counseling process, and how clients from diverse backgrounds perceive the counseling process.

As Berven[6] notes, clinical judgment is basic to the entire rehabilitation counseling process. Rehabilitation outcomes are also influenced by client characteristics, the socio-political influences of poverty, racism, ageism, sexism, immigration status, and the counselor's ability to provide culturally appropriate services and manage the dynamics of differences/diversity. It is imperative that culturally competent counselors be aware of their own assumptions about human dynamics, values, and biases and how their assumptions might impact client outcomes. Counselors must also acquire awareness, knowledge, skills, and develop an understanding of their clients' worldview. Trust is also essential to the development of any counseling relationship. Trust allows the counselor to develop appropriate interventions to serve their clients.

CASE STUDY

CASE STUDY OF JANE

Jane's (African American) Employee Assistance Program (EAP) representative referred her for counseling because of her continuing depressed mood and panic attacks. She is a 37-year-old part-time graduate student who lives with her husband of 10 years. She states that her husband has been extremely supportive; however, recently he is becoming less supportive. Jane and her husband have no children due to the level (L-4) of the spinal cord injury (SCI) that she sustained at age 25. Despite her inability to conceive, she and her husband strongly desire to have children. Six years ago, she completed course work for a Ph.D. in sociology, but Jane has not begun the dissertation process due to episodes of depression and anxiety. She describes herself as being unhappy through much of her life, post injury, with no long periods of feeling happy.

Since the SCI, Jane's academic and vocational histories have been erratic. She has a master's degree in psychology and worked for two years as an intake counselor at an addictions treatment facility, but she found this work too upsetting. Because of this, she began a Ph.D. program in sociology and completed her course work, but her recurring episodes of depression and panic attacks has placed the dissertation process on hold indefinitely. Recently, her dissertation chairperson indicated that she needs to continue to make progress or she will be asked to take a leave of absence from the program. Although Jane's diagnosis is chronic depression and anxiety, when she is asked about "low" periods, she describes many episodes of having abnormal mood swings that have lasted for days. During these times, she would stay at home in her bedroom.

DISCUSSION QUESTIONS

1. What are the key variables/ characteristics of Jane that are active in this case study?

2. Which variables/characteristics of Jane could present difficulties in Jane's life?

3. Are there any variables that are identified in question #1 that could cause you to feel unprepared or uncomfortable as a counselor?

4. As a counselor, what additional questions would you ask to better assess her situation?

5. How would you demonstrate "*empathy*" in this case?

6. Identify possible resources or strategies that could improve her situation. You may use credible research articles, Internet websites, etc. to support your response.

CASE STUDY OF ROSETTA

Rosetta is a 35 year old Vietnamese American woman with two young children (from a previous relationship) and a partner whom she has shared a monogamous relationship with for 5 years. She was diagnosed recently with severe post-traumatic stress disorder (PTSD) and major depressive disorder, severe, chronic type with psychotic features, from serving five tours in the Iraq and Afghanistan wars.

She was being treated by a family medicine doctor for depression and PTSD. Rosetta's fear about using medicine and her heavy cannabis use had kept her from making the progress that might have been expected given the nature of her disorders. Her pattern had been to take her medication long enough to begin to experience improved function and then stop taking it.

At the prompting of her partner, she eventually agreed to therapy. With consistent therapy, Rosetta's mood improved dramatically. She was able to stay on her medication and make lifestyle changes that began to improve her quality of her life.

Rosetta's vocational history is very inconsistent. Her most recent employment stints were in the retail sector. However, her time in these jobs has been short and ended in termination due to Rosetta's explosiveness around the public, supervisors, and coworkers. It appears that these explosive tendencies may have been related to her drug use and her refusal to take her antidepressant medication.

Her present stability has allowed her to begin envisioning herself as a productive employee. She is motivated to acquire a "real job," to bring "honor" back to her family, and to gain acceptance from her long-term partner. She is concerned that she will relapse if she is exposed to a stressful environment.

DISCUSSION QUESTIONS

1. What are the key variables/characteristics of Rosetta that are active in this case study?

2. Which variables/characteristics of Rosetta could present difficulties in Rosetta's life?

3. Are there any variables that are identified in question #1 that could cause you to feel unprepared or uncomfortable as a counselor?

4. As a counselor, what additional questions would you ask to better assess her situation?

5. How would you demonstrate "*empathy*" in this case?

6. Identify possible resources or strategies that could improve her situation. You may use credible research articles, Internet websites, etc. to support your response.

REFERENCES

[1]Alston, R. J., & Rucker, R. (2009). Minority clients in rehabilitation: Reactions to race by rehabilitation counselors. *Rehabilitation Counselors and Educators Journal, 3(1),* 17-29.
[2]Arrendondo, P., Toporek, R., Brown, S. P., Jones, J., Locke, D. C., Sanchez, K., & Stadler, H. (1996). Operationalization of the multicultural counseling competencies. *Journal of Multicultural Counseling and Development, 24,* 42-78.
[3]Atkins, B. J., & Wright, G. N. (1980). The statement- Three views of the vocational rehabilitation of Blacks. *Journal of Rehabilitation, 46*(2), 42-46.
[4]Balcazar, F., Suarez-Balcazar, Y., Taylor- Ritzler, T., Keys, C. B. (2010). Race, Culture, and Disability: Rehabilitation Science and Practice. Sudbury, MA: Jones and Bartlett Publishers.
[5]Bellini, J. (2002). Correlates of Multicultural Counseling Competencies of Vocational Rehabilitation Counselors. Rehabilitation Counseling Bulletin January 2002 vol. 45 no. 2 66-75.

[6]Berven, N. L. (1997). Professional practice: Assessment. In D. R. Maki & T. F. Riggar (Eds.), *Rehabilitation counseling: Profession and practice* (pp. 151–169). New York: Springer.

[7]Bronfrenbrenner, U. (1979). *The Ecology of HumanDevelopment*. Cambridge: Harvard University Press.

[8]Bryan, W. V. (1999). Multicultural aspects of disability: A guide to understanding and assisting minorities in the rehabilitation process. Springfield Illinois: Charles C. Thomas Publisher.

[9]Carter, R. T. (1995). The influence of race and racial identity in psychotherapy: Toward a racially inclusive model. New York: John Wiley.

[10] Census Bureau (1997). U. S. Department of Commerce. Economics and Statistics Administration Bureau of The Census. CENBR/97-5 Issued December 1997 (http://www.census.gov/prod/3/97pubs/cenbr975.pdf).

[11]Code of Professional Ethics for Rehabilitation Counselors http://www.crccertification.com/pages/crc_ccrc_code_of_ethics/10.php

[12]Dowd, E. T., & Emener, W. G. (1978). Lifeboat counseling: The issues of survival decisions. *Journal of Rehabilitation*, 9, (2), 34-36.

[13]Dziekan, K. I., & Okocha, A. A. G. (1993). Accessibility of rehabilitation services: Comparison by racial-ethnic status. Rehabilitation Counseling Bulletin, 36, 183-189.

[14]Edwards, Y. V., Betters, C., Caldwell, T., Chamberlain, Fowler. D, Rogers, R, & Worthy, K. (2011). Racial/Ethnic Differences in Transitional Vocational Rehabilitation. Rehabilitation Counselors and Educators Journal. *5*(1) 40-48.

[15]Emener, W. G. (1991). An empowerment philosophy for rehabilitation in the 20th century. *Journal of Rehabilitation*, 57, (4), 7-12.

[16]Fiest-Price, S. (1995). African Americans with disabilities and equity in vocational rehabilitation services: One state's review. *Rehabilitation Counseling Bulletin, 39*, 119-129.

[17]Fujiura, G., & Yamaki, K. (2000). Trends in Demography of Childhood Poverty and Disability. Exceptional Children, *66*, 187-199.

[18]Goodman, L. A., Liang, B., Helms, J. E. Latta, R. E., Sparks, E., & Weintraub, S. R. (2004). Training Counseling Psychologists as Social Justice Agents: Feminist and Multicultural Principles in Action. The Counseling Psychologist, *32*, 793-837

[19]Herbert, J. T., & Martinez, M. Y. (1992). Client ethnicity and vocational rehabilitation case services outcome. *Journal of Job Placement, 8*(1), 10-16.

[20]Lewis, A., Alston, R. Imparato, A. J., Rumrill, P. D. & Wilson, K. B. (2009). Strategies to Address Disability Disparities (webcast) Retrieved July 14, 2011from: http://www.worksupport.com/training/webcastDetails.cfm/155

[21]Lewis, A. N., Shamburger, A., Head, C., Armstrong, A. J., & West, S. L. (2007). Section 21 of the 1992 Rehabilitation Act Amendments and diversity article Journal *of Vocational Rehabilitation* 26 89-96.

[22]McLeroy, K. R., Bibeau, D., Steckler, A., & Glanz, K. (1988). An ecological perspective on health promotion programs. Health *Education Quarterly.* 15, 351-377.

[23]McNeil, J. M., Americans With Disabilities: 1991-92, U.S. Bureau of the Census, Current Population P79-33, U.S. Government Printing Office, Washingtn, D.C., 1993.

[24]Middleton, R., Rollins, C., Sanderson, P. L., Leung, P., Harley, D. A., Ebener, D., Leal-Idrogo, A. (2000). Endorsement of Professional Multicultural Rehabilitation Competencies and Standards: A Call to Action. Rehabilitation Counseling Bulletin, July 2000 vol. 43 no. 4, 219-245

[25]Moore, C. L. (2001). Racial and ethnic members of under-represented groups with hearing loss and VR services: Explaining the disparity in closure success rates. Journal of Applied Rehabilitation Counseling, 32(1), 15-20.

[26]National Council on Disability (2003, August 1). People with disabilities on tribal lands: Education, health care, vocational rehabilitation, and independent living. Retrieved may 25, 2007, fromhttp://www.ncd.gov/newsroom/publications/2003/tribal_lands.htm

[27]Ponterotto, J. G. (1988). Racial consciousness development among White counselor trainees: A stage model. Journal of Multicultural Counseling and Development, 16(4), Oct 1988, 146-156.

[28]Rajakumar, K, Thomas, S. B., Musa, D., Almario, D., and Garza, M. A. (2009). Racial difference in parents' distrust of medicine and research. *ARCH Pediatr Adolsc Med,* 2, 108-114.

[29]Rehabilitation Service Administration. (1973). Rehabilitaton Act of 1973 as amended 29 U.S.C. 701 et seq. (1993) (amended 1992)

[30]Rehabilitation Service Administration (2008). Reporting manual for the case service reporting (RSA 911) Washington. Dc: Author

[31]Rosenthal, D. A (2004). Effects of Client Race on Clinical Judgment of Practicing European American Vocational Rehabilitation Counselors. *Rehabilitation Counseling Bulletin 47*(3) pp. 131–141.

[32]Sales, A. P., (2008) Chapter One, History of Rehabilitation Movement: Paternalism to Empowerment, chapter revisions for new edition in J. Andrew and C. W. Fabian (Eds.). Rehabilitation services: An introduction for the human services professional (2nd ed.). Linn Creek, MO: Aspen Professional Services.

[33]Sandhu, D. S. (1997). Psychocultural profiles of Asian and Pacific Islander Americans: implications for counseling and psychotherapy. *Journal of Multicultural Counseling and Development, 25*, 7-22.

[34]Smith, T. (2006). Taking america's pulse III: Intergroup relations in contemporary america. The National Conference for Community and Justice: New York, N.Y.

[35]Sue, D., Arredondo, P., &McDavis, R. (1992). Multicultural counseling competencies and standards: A call to the profession. *Journal of Multicultural Counseling and Development*, 20, 64-88.

[36]Sue, D. W. (2001). Multidimensional facets of cultural competence. *The Counseling Psychologist, 29, 790-821.*

[37]Sue, D. W., Bernier, J. E., Durran, A., Feinberg, L., Pedersen, P., Smith, E. J., (1982). Position paper: Cross-cultural counseling competencies. *The Counseling Psychologist, 10*, 45-52.

[38]Sue, D. W. & Sue, D. (2003). Counseling the culturally diverse: theory and practice. Wiley Publishing

[39]Thomas, K. R., & Wienrach, S. G. (2002). Racial bias in rehabilitation: Multiple interpretations of the same data. *Rehabilitation Education, 16*(1), 81–90.

[40]U.S. Administration on Aging. "A toolkit for Serving Diverse Communities. http://www.aoa.gov/AoARoot/AoA_Programs/Tools_Resources/DOCS/AoA_DiversityToolkit_full.pdf (Retrieved June 23, 2011.)

[41]U.S. Census Bureau (2000). Data highlights. Available at www.census.gov.

[42]U.S. Census Bureau (2002). Population profile of the United States. Washington, DC: U.S. Government Printing.

[43]Wang, M. H., Chan, F., Thomas, K. R., Lin, S. H., and Larson, P. (1997). Coping style and personal responsibility as factors in perception of individuals with physical disabilities by Chinese international students. Rehabilitation Psychology, *42*(4), 302-316.

[44]Washington, H (2008). Medical Apartheid: The Dark History of Medical Experimentation on Black Americans from Colonial Times to the Present. Publisher Harlem Moon New York

[45]Wheaton, J. E. (1995). Vocational rehabilitation acceptance rates for European Americans and African Americans: Another look. *Rehabilitation Counseling Bulletin, 38,* 224–231.

[46]Wilson, K. B. (2010), what does it mean to be a culturally-competent counselor? Paper presented at the meeting of the American Counseling Association, Multicultural Social Justice Leadership Academy, Pittsburg, PA.

[47]Wilson, K. B., Harley, D. A., McCormick, K., Jolivette, K., & Jackson, R. L. (2001). A literature review of vocational rehabilitation acceptance and rationales for bias in the rehabilitation process. *Journal of Applied Rehabilitation Counseling, 32*(1), 24-35.

[48]Wilson, K. B., Jackson, R., & Doughty, J. (1999). What a difference a race makes: Reason for unsuccessful closures within the vocational rehabilitation system. *American Rehabilitation, 25*, 16-24.

[49]Wilson, K. B., & Senices, J. (2005). Exploring the vocational rehabilitation acceptance rates of Hispanics and non-Hispanics in the United States. *Journal of Counseling and Development 83*(1), 86-96.

[50]Wilson, K. B. & Senices, J. (2010). Access to vocational Rehabilitation services for black latinos with disabilities: Colorism in the 21st century. In F. B. Balcazar, Y. Suarez-Blcazar, T. Taylor-Ritzler, & C. B. Keys, (Eds.) *Culture, Race and Disability: Issues in Rehabilitation Research and Practice* (pp. 81-96). Sudbury, MA: Jones and Bartlett.